The Croati

The Croatian Adriatic

Features of cultural and natural interest

Tourist Guide

Published by
(c) Naklada LJEVAK Zagreb,
Palmotićeva 30.

For the publisher
Petra Ljevak

ISBN 978-953-178-856-4

Edited by
Radovan Radovinović

Design
Igor Masnjak

Chapters written by
Ivo Babić (Trogir);
Joško Belamarić (Korčula, Lastovo, Vis); Josip Bratulić (Istria); Tomislav Đurić (Brač); Srećko Ljubljanović (Dalmatian Wines); Ivan Jindra (Rijeka); Radoslav Tomić (Split); Nikola Petrak (Dubrovnik) and Radovan Radovinović

Translated by
Janet Tuškan and Graham McMaster

Sub-editing and proofreading by
Graham McMaster

Maps by
Naklada LJEVAK

Typesetting by
Studio Ljevak, Zagreb,
Palmotićeva ul. 30.

Photographs by
(p. 391)

Printed and bound by
"Zrinski", Čakovec

TOURIST GUIDE

THE CROATIAN ADRIATIC

NAKLADA LJEVAK

Zagreb, June 2007.

Contents

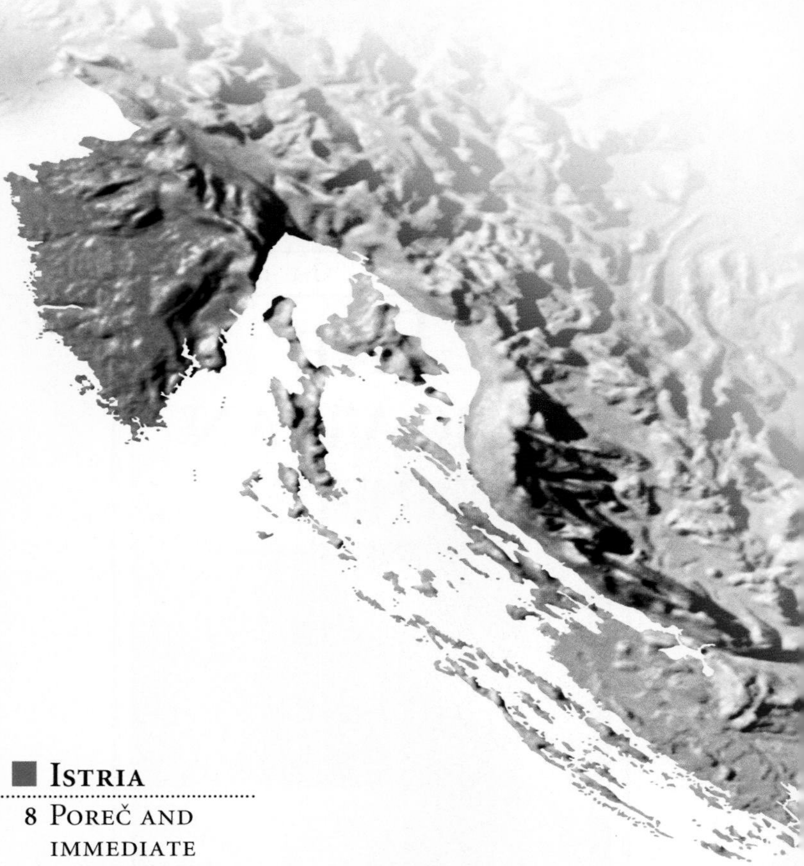

North Dalmatia

Central Dalmatia

South Dalmatia

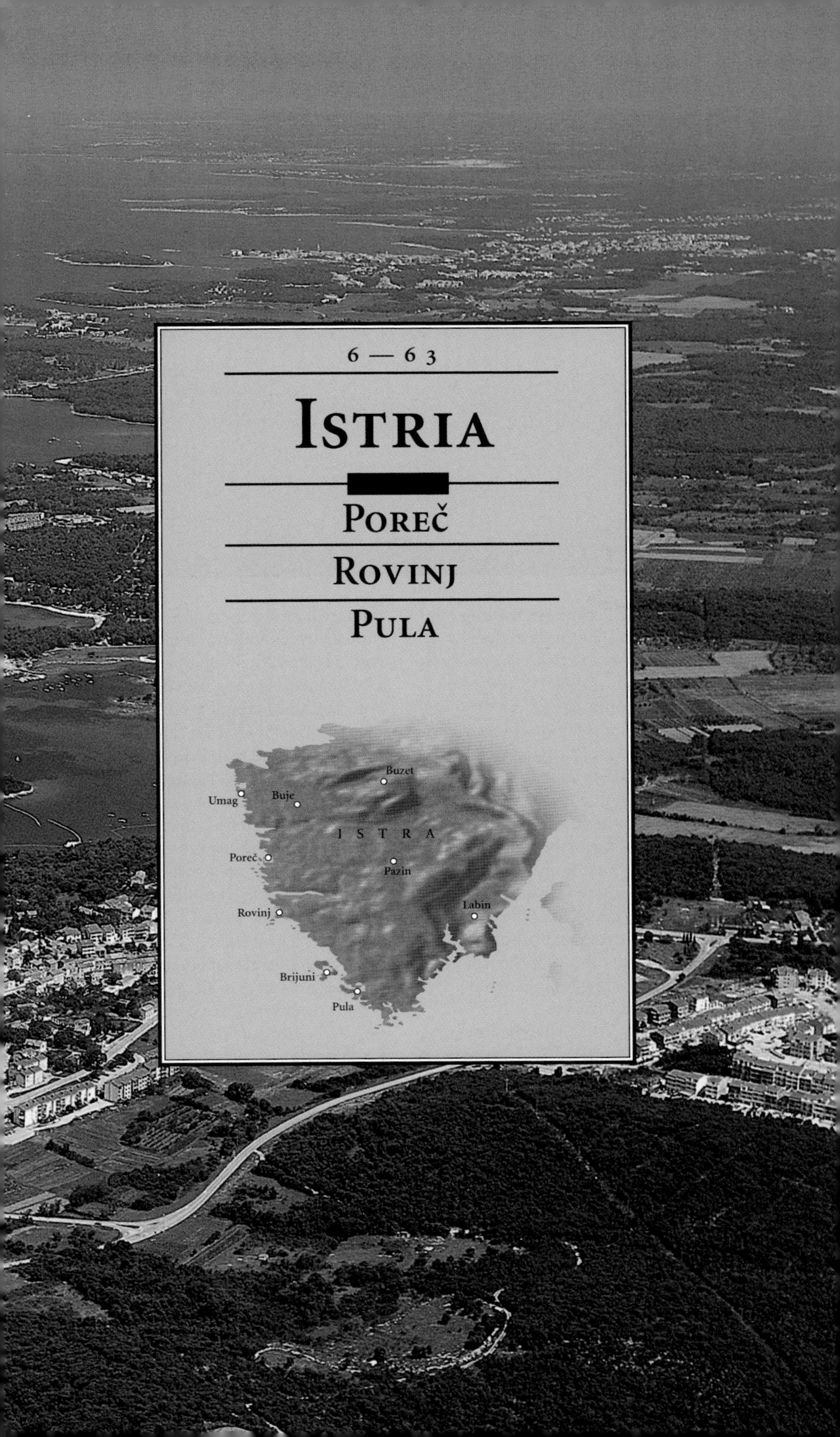

6 — 63

ISTRIA

POREČ

ROVINJ

PULA

Poreč

POREČ IS SITUATED 45° 14' N, 13° 36' E. IT HAS A POPULATION OF 10 448, THE POPULATION OF THE MUNICIPAL ADMINISTRATIVE REGION BEING 14 705. MEAN TEMPERATURES FOR JANUARY: AIR, 4.1 °C; SEA, 10 °C. MEAN TEMPERATURES FOR JULY: AIR, 22.6 °C; SEA, 23.2 °C.

The Prehistoric Period. Archaeological finds from the Pical site confirm the existence of Poreč as a settlement as early as the Neolithic era (from 4000 to 1800 BC). Finds from the Bronze Age (about 2000 BC) are plentiful. The most famous prehistoric site in the Poreč area is Picugi, which was the home of an Illyrian tribe known as the Histri in about 800 BC. This tribe gave their name to the region known today as Istria. Even in prehistoric times there was a protected harbour built in the Poreč area which provided shelter for fishing boats and merchant vessels sailing along the Istrian coast. Finds of Etruscan and painted pottery from Apulia (6th to the 5th century BC) witness to lively trading links between Southern Italy and Istria.

The Roman Era. In 177 BC the Roman Consul Claudius Pulcher captured and razed the capital of the Histri, Nesactium, to the ground as part of his Istrian campaign, but he did not succeed in breaking the resistance of the Illyrian tribe. Istria was finally conquered and subdued in 129 BC. From that time Parentium (Poreč), which is situated on the road from Aquileia to Pula, began to play an important role in the Roman colonisation of Istria. Parentium was an important military base; on the peninsula a fortified Roman army camp was built up together with a walled city (Oppidum, see Decumanus). During the reign of Caesar, Poreč became a municipality and in Tiberius' time it attained the status of a colony - Colonia Julia Parentium. A large part of Istria was used as agricultural land by the Poreč colony and was crossed by good roads, which have to a large degree remained intact to the present day. Christianity soon reached the well-populated area of Poreč, and as early as the middle of the 3rd century there was a Christian community with its own bishop. The community had its own secret church, or oratium (Domus Ecclesiae), which was a hall equipped for meetings of the Christian community, and a baptistery (now in the complex of the Maurus baptistery).

Detail of the mosaic of the Euphrasian Basilica

The Migrations of the Nations. From ancient times right through to the Middle Ages, Poreč came under influences from the East, the North and the West, and in the early Middle Ages, its ethnic make-up changed radically. Towards the end of the 6th century the Slavs and Avars invaded Istria, but Poreč resisted their attacks. As the Slavs (Croatians) began to populate the deserted land around Poreč and other Istrian coastal settlements, and finally settled permanently around the middle of the 7th century, they began to work the fields and to use the grazing land and forests of the townspeople. At this time Poreč was ruled by the Goths, led by Odoacer and Theodoric.

Under Various Rulers. With the collapse of the Roman Empire and its division, Poreč came under the jurisdiction of the Eastern Empire. When Justinian effected a reunification, Poreč was allotted to the Byzantine Empire in 539 and came under the Franks in 788. Charles the Great ceded Poreč to Mark Friaul. There is an important historical document still in existence from this time - The Placitum of Rižan (804): the cities accused the Rector John of bringing in the Slavs who had grown in strength and were working the cities' fields without paying tithes or any other dues. John, whom the Slavs served as border guards, was naturally unwilling to break up his army in favour of the townsfolk, as they held the border with the Byzantine Empire on the one side and the coast on the other. As the hold of the Frankish rulers on Istria weakened, the Bishops of Poreč became stronger and emerged as strong feudal lords who took over the city and extended and confirmed their rule in some other areas of Istria (for example, Pazin). The Patriarch of Aquileia made good use of the conflicts and disagreements between the Poreč city elders and the bishops and brought the city under his own authority in 1232. Conflict between the rich citizens and bishops continued until Poreč was conquered by Venice and brought under its control in 1267.

Under the Venetians. Poreč was the first Istrian town to fall under Venetian rule. Other towns were conquered in the period up to 1420, by which time Venice had finally rounded off its Istrian possessions, occupying all the port towns from Koper to Plomin. During the war between Genoa and Venice, the Genoans sacked the city and carried away the relics of St. Maurus, the Patron Saint of Poreč (1354). As well as by wars (with the Genoans, the Uskoks of Senj, the Turks and various pirates) Poreč was frequently decimated by the plague in the 15th, 16th and 17th centuries, so that its population fell from 3000 at the time of the Venetian occupation to 100 in the 17th century. For this reason the Venetians brought in people from Dalmatia, Bosnia, Montenegro and Albania to populate the desolate city and its surroun-

Poreč, 16th century engraving

dings, especially during the 18th century.

Under Austrian Rule. After the fall of Venice (1797) Poreč came under Austrian rule, along with the rest of Venetian Istria. Following a short-lived period of French rule, it returned to Austria under whose rule it recovered economically, which is reflected in the restoration of city buildings and monuments. The burghers and several feudal lords mercilessly abused the peasant (Croatian) population; for example in Poreč itself a specific form of usury developed by which peasants borrowed a sum of money at 365% interest (as many days as there are in a year). This caused the ruin of many peasant small-holders in the area around Poreč. Many were forced to become serfs on the very property which they had had to give up as a result of their debt. In the mid 19th century, Poreč was the seat of the Istrian Regional Parliament (from 1861). The parliament met in the Parliament Building (now a gallery); the Austrian authorities favoured the minority Italian community, and no one was allowed to speak Croatian in the Parliament. Because of the chauvinistic attitude towards the Croatian representatives, the Austrian central government was finally forced to disband this Parliament.

Old street

From 1918 to the Present Day. Following the fall of Austria, Poreč once again came under Italian rule, along with the rest of Istria. During World War II, especially in 1944, Poreč suffered heavily from bombing. Allied planes emptied their lethal loads as many as 34 times on the city, damaging numerous monuments and destroying 75% of the houses in the city. After World War II, the Allies divided the area of Trieste and Istria into three zones: the Free Territory of Trieste (Zone A), the Slovene coast (Zone B) and the rest of Istria as far as the Rijekan suburb of Kantrida (Zone C). In 1947 Zone C was assigned to (Yugoslavia) Croatia; by the London Treaty of October 5, 1954 Trieste went to Italy, and Zone B to Yugoslavia (partly to Croatia, partly to Slovenia).

Poreč was liberated in 1945, and rebuilding began immediately. Rubble was removed, and the old heart of the city was approached with special care. The renovation of this war-ruined city was done with particular care. Today, many of the architectural treasures have been restored, while Poreč is also the city with the biggest tourist industry in the whole of the Adriatic coast. In 1989 the city recorded a total of 4,759,000 tourist bed-nights (the area of the commune had 92,400 beds for holiday-makers in 1992). ■

SIGHTS

The Basilica of Euphrasius*** (▶▶▶ p. 12)

The Decumanus*** (NUMBER ❼ ON THE PLAN), the main street in Poreč, has been preserved as the main east-west route right from prehistoric times when Poreč was already a port. It became the main street in the Roman army camp, stretching from the tip of the peninsula and continuing to the temples at the end. When the Roman settlement Oppidum was built, this route became its main street (Decumanus Maximus) and was intersected (north-south) by the Cardo. The Decumanus ended in a forum (in fact 2 forums).

Facade of the Euphrasian Basilica

Marafor Square** (NUMBER ❶ ON THE PLAN). This is on the site of the ancient forum. It covers the area of an insula (45x45m). Some of the original paving of the forum is still intact today, and some houses on the square have no foundations as they have been built directly onto the stones of the forum.

••••••••••••

The **Parliament Buildings*** (to the north of Marafor Square, NUMBER

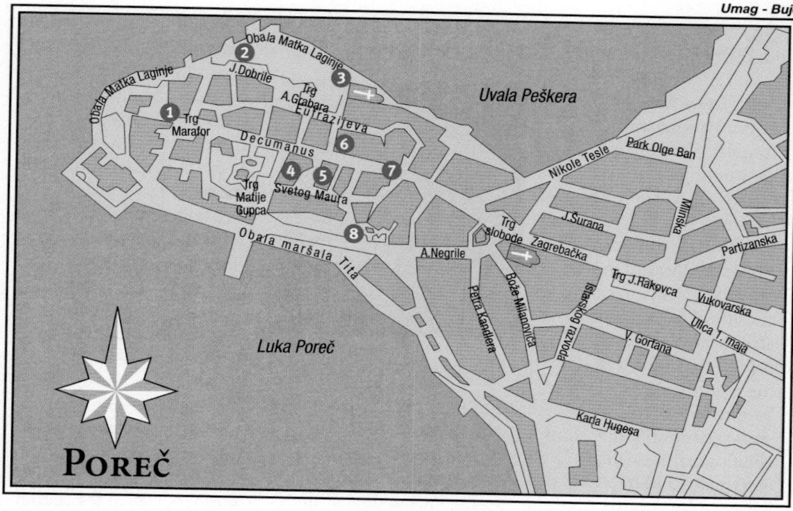

❷ON THE PLAN). The seat of the Istrian regional parliament is a converted Franciscan church built between the 13th and 14th centuries (the bell tower of the church was built in 1731). A floor was built inside the church in the second half of the 19th century, so the lower half acted as a cellar and the upper half was the parliament chamber. The stucco work in the upper half dates from 1751. These premises are now used as a museum.

•••••••••••

Other Important Buildings. The period from the Romanesque to the Gothic era, following the architectural stagnation between the 7th and the 11th centuries, was a period of intense building within the framework of the established parameters of the ancient city. Several excellent examples of Romanesque architecture still remain; the **Canon's House**** (Kanonička kuća, 1251, NUMBER ❻ON THE PLAN), the **House of the Two Saints**, (Kuća dvaju svetaca, NUMBER ❹ON THE PLAN), the Romanesque **commoner's house** ** with its balcony just in front of the entrance to Marafor Square. (Examples of Gothic architecture are especially apparent on the Decumanus and the Cardo, and most particularly at the crossroads of these two streets.) Towards the end of the 15th century, because of the threat from the Turks, several fortified buildings were built. These are: the **Round Tower** on the sea front (Okrugla kula, from 1474, NUMBER ❽ON THE PLAN), and the tower at the eastern city gate (1473). The most prominent 16th century buildings are the **Polezini Palace** and the **Sinčić Palace**, which now houses the Poreština folk museum.

•••••••••••

The **Poreština Folk Museum**** (Zavičajni muzej Poreštine in Sinčić Palace, 9a, Decumanus, NUMBER ❺ON THE PLAN). The building which houses this museum is a fine example of 17th century architecture; it used to belong to the aristocratic Sinčić family. The museum was founded in 1884, and was previously housed in a large building on Marafor Square. It has been in Sinčić Palace since 1950. The museum has a collection of stone monuments, a prehistoric collection, a collection from classical times, one from the Middle Ages, an ethnological collection and a permanent exhibition of the Second World War in Poreština. The **collection of stone monuments** is in the atrium of the palace. It includes some massive pedestals of ancient sculptures and capitals from the Temple of Neptune. Especially significant is the Greek gravestone of Hermes, with a relief showing the grape and olive harvest, the altar of Titus Abudius Verus and a votive tablet of Minerva Flanatica. The **prehistoric**

►►► p. 13

The Basilica of Euphrasius ***

(NUMBER ❸ ON THE PLAN). This is actually a complex of buildings constituting a rare example of early Christian (early Byzantine) architecture. The building was consecrated by Bishop Euphrasius in the 6th century and now consists of a four sided atrium, an octagonal baptistery (to the west of the atrium), a triple-naved basilica, joined to a trefoil-shaped memorial chapel, an elliptical narthex (to the east) and the Bishop's Palace (to the north). The **atrium** was built after the basilica and is covered on all four sides by a portico which houses a rich collection of stone monuments. On the upper parts of the facade to the west and east, some traces of old mosaics still remain. The present ones were restored in the 19th century. The **baptistery** was built in

Bishop Euphrasius, detail of the mosaic

the 5th century together with the pre-Euphrasian basilica, and underwent considerable alterations during the building of the Euphrasian basilica in the 6th century. It is an octagonal building, in the centre of which is the font, also octagonal, a hollow which was used by Christian converts who were baptised by total immersion. It appears that the baptistery was in use in this way right up the middle of the 15th century. After the walls of the baptistery in Zadar were destroyed in the Second World War, this became the only remaining remnant of early Christianity of its kind still intact in Croatia. Alongside the baptistery a bell tower was built in the 16th century and from the top of it there is a splendid view over Poreč, the surrounding countryside and the sea.

The **Euphrasian basilica** has for the most part retained its original shape but accidents, fires and earthquakes have altered a few details. Following the earthquake in 1440 the southern wall of the central nave of the basilica was restored, so that in place of the windows, which were destroyed, windows were built in the Gothic style. The ciborium in the sanctuary was built in 1277 and the stone altar rail has been reconstructed from fragments of the original. In the course of its long history the Euphrasian

basilica has seen many changes. Since it is the third church to be built on the same site, it conceals previous buildings, for example the great floor mosaic of the previous basilica from the 5th century. A novelty of the Euphrasian basilica is that rather than being enclosed by a straight wall, as all sacred buildings were up to that time, it makes use of the breadth and length of the apse of the central nave, built in the shape of a polygon from the outside, whilst the two aisles end in smaller semicircular apses, hollowed into the wall. Thus the Euphrasian basilica

The Euphrasian Basilica

is the earliest example of a triple apsed church in Western Europe. The capitals in the basilica and atrium are typical examples of Byzantine architecture, as are the columns and tiles on the altar rail and the abundant mosaics. The best preserved mosaics are in the central apse, and they are also the most significant remains of the monumental art of the 6th century. Most impressive of all is the representation of Christ

Detail of the mosaic of the Euphrasian Basilica

with the Apostles, and beneath it a frieze of 13 medallions with a picture of Christ as the Lamb in the centre, surrounded by 12 medallions depicting various martyrs. The mosaics at the foot of the apse and the rich encrustations were brought from the Temple of Neptune, whilst the stucco and plastic work are from the time of Euphrasius. In the half dome of the apse there is a beautiful composition showing the Madonna on a throne, surrounded by the martyrs and the builder of the basilica, Bishop Euphrasius. In the centre of the apse there are representations of scenes from Mary's life, the *Annunciation* and the *Visitation.* The **Bishop's Palace** was also built in the 6th century, but very little remains of the original building. The side chapels of the basilica were built later, in the 17th and 19th centuries. Near the Basilica is the **Poreč parish collection,** with forty-odd exhibits, some of which are important fragments of mosaic (the oldest coming from the 3rd century), crosses (13th century), choir stalls and some altar pieces (15th to 17th centuries). Because of its great value as a monument, the Basilica has been placed by UNESCO on its list of sites of the World's cultural heritage. ■

collection includes items from the early Stone Age right up to the arrival of the Romans in Istria. It has some very important items from the Illyrian necropoles Picugi and St. Martin of Tar (Sveti Martin Tarski). Particularly significant is a Bronze Age chalice which was found in Poreč harbour. The classical collection has a very beautiful and valuable collection of Roman cultural remains (Terra Histria, Bacchus, Diana) as well as a floor mosaic from a Roman villa on Cape Bossalo, near Poreč. There are also some beautiful glass, iron, bronze and pottery fragments from classical times in the area around Poreč. The **medieval collection** includes several fragments of early Christian sarcophagi, pieces from stone church furniture from the 6th to the 8th centuries, and some woven decorations from Poreč. There are some important remains from a 13th century Slavic necropolis. Especially interesting are the 15th century Poreč coat of arms and a large Glagolitic headstone from 1589. The collection of paintings by old masters includes a portrait of the famous Carli family from Koper and a beautiful portrait of Antonio Facchinetti. There is a valuable collection of hunting rifles and an 18th century English chest carved with war scenes. The ethnological collection shows national costumes from Poreština, household tools and weapons.

Excursions

Sveti Lovreč**

17 km from Poreč, on the road to Pula, population 1400

Although the present settle-

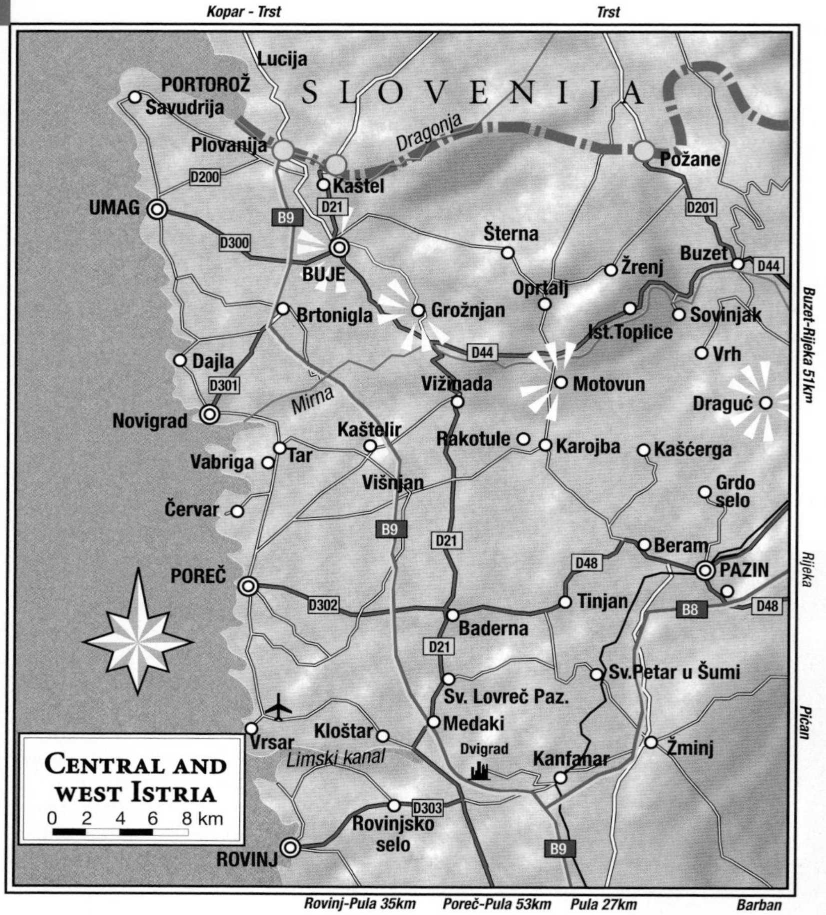

ment of Sveti Lovreč probably dates from the 9th or 10th century, the layout of the town and remains of old walls witness to the fact that Lovreč was in fact inhabited in prehistoric times. At the beginning of the 14th century, it was the centre of the Venetian military command in Istria, and then the seat of military leaders for the area of Istria south of the river Mirna (hence the old name Sveti Lovreč Pazenatički, from paize — Venetian for province). The **Parish Church of St. Martin** (Sveti Martin) with nave and two aisles dominates the wide town square. The church, which dates from the mid-11th century, has three semi-circular apses at its eastern end. The simple outer walls are in keeping with the tradition of early Christian Istrian churches. Some individual elements, such as the raised rear wall, show the influence of Ravenna, while the apses and the architectural decorative carvings demonstrate the strong influence of the early Romanesque. The church was given a new facade in 1838. The remains of frescoes in the centre of the northern and southern apses date from the 11th century and they are in a mixture of Ottoman and Byzantine styles. A later layer of frescoes, from the 14th century, covers an older layer in the northern apse, and is influenced by the Italian school. In the 15th century side **loggia** there is a **stone monument collection** with examples of ancient, pre-Romanesque and Romanesque fragments and monuments. Inside the church there is a 17th century coloured and engraved polyptych and a Gothic statue of the Madonna. The simple and solid bell tower is decorated with Romanesque double windows. Beside the church there is the town loggia which was built in the 15th century. Opposite it on the town square there is a post once used for the punishment of offenders. Beside the town gates is the **Church of St. Blaise** (Sveti Blaž) which was built in 1460, in popular Gothic style with rustic frescoes inside.

••••••••••••

Motovun***

24 KM INLAND FROM POREČ, POPULATION 983.

The town grew up on the site of an ancient city (Kastelijer) 277 m above sea level. In the 10th and 11th centuries it belonged to the Bishop of Poreč. From 1278 it was taken over by Venice and surrounded by solid walls which are still intact today, and are now used as a walkway with unique views over the four corners of Istria. Below the old buildings in the centre of the town, suburbs grew up on the south west with Gothic gates. The suburbs retain both Romanesque and Gothic elements in their architecture. All three parts of the town are connected by a system of internal and external fortifications with towers and city gates, built between the 14th and 17th centuries, and containing elements of Romanesque, Gothic and Renaissance styles. The **main square** **, which is reached by crossing the outer square and is situated between two towers with a city gate is dominated by a huge bell tower, separate from the church, which was used as a watchtower and contains some old breastplates. It was built in the 13th century. On the broad square itself is the **Parish Church of St. Stephen** (Sveti Stjepan) built right at the beginning of the 17th century according to sketches by the well-known Venetian architect Andrea Palladio (1508-1580). A Renaissance loggia built in the 17th century hangs from the eastern city wall. Most of the remaining buildings were built during the 16th and 17th centuries. In the entrance hall of the Renaissance city keep built in the 16th century is a **collection of stone monuments** showing finds from Roman times (grave stones and cippi), fragments of medieval inscriptions and the arms of various Motovun families. The coats of arms on the inside and outside of the keep belong to Venetian families, who were leading citizens when the tower was built. In Motovun in 1475, Andrea Antico was born (Antiquus, de Antiquis, Andrija Motovunjanin, presumed Croatian surname Starić). Antico is famous as the inventor of the first movable wooden types for printing musical scores and was in general the first publisher of scores. He started publishing in Rome in 1510, and after obtaining a patent from Pope Leo X he published polyphonic music and music for the organ. He published his last collection in Venice in 1539. He was also a composer.

••••••••••••

Istrian landscape

Motovun

Veli Jože and Motovun. Motovun is known among today's population of Istria as the city of Veli Jože, the good, gentle giant who represents the Croatian people of Istria. The story written by Vladimir Nazor, one of the most important of Croatian writers of the 20th century, was a response to the national struggles of the Croats for equality (1900-1914). The tale is known today throughout Croatia, while the character of Veli Jože (Big Joe) is quite correctly linked with the city of Motovun. Motovun was the battlefield where the poor and the rich minority fought. And the character of Veli Jože and his creator Vladimir Nazor became symbols of national resistance, the fight for freedom and the brotherhood of all the inhabitants of Istria, Croats and Italians, during the national struggle against fascism.

Veli Jože

••••••••••••

The **Forest of Motovun.** An area of about 10 square kilometres in the valley of the River Mirna, below the town of Motovun, of which about 280 hectares (2.8 km^2) is specially protected. This area differs completely not only from the nearby forests but also from those of the entire surrounding karst region because of its wild life and its moist soil. The most common tree in the forest is the English or brown oak (Quercus robur) and it is thus comparable to the Slavonian oak forests. In order to preserve natural conditions for the development of the Motovun forest, the protected area is occasionally flooded, even though the River Mirna is controlled and its entire valley protected from flooding. The Forest of Motovun is well known for the rare and expensive fungus truffle (Tuber magnatum) which grows successfully there. Since this fungus grows underground, it is gathered with the aid of specially trained dogs.

••••••••••••

On the road to Motovun, 13 km from Poreč, lies the compact town of **Višnjan***. It has a wide square, and a loggia with a view over the sea. It has been inhabited since ancient times. In the parish

church there are three paintings on canvas which date from the 16th century, in the style of Palma the Younger, and a painting of the Madonna, which is the work of the Zadar master, Zorzo Ventura (1598). The **Chapel of St. Anthony** (Sveti Antun) at the entrance to the town, is a simple Gothic building with 16th century frescoes and a wooden carving of St. Anthony, the Abbot, from the same period. The road from Višnjan to the south leads to the village of **Bačva***, where there is a Gothic portal to the Church of the **Mother of God** (Majka Božja od Karmela) which was restored in the 17th and 18th centuries. Inside the church is the grave stone of the Glagolitic priest Stipan Deković with a chiselled relief and inscription in Glagolitic script. In the Fraternity **Church of St. James** (Sveti Jakov), in the semi-circular apse and nave there are frescoes from the 16th century, and on the altar there is a wooden multi-coloured triptych, which is the work of the Istrian master Alvisa Orso from Motovun.

To the north of Višnjan, on the road which leads to Motovun through the Mirna valley (8.5 km from Višnjan) is **Vižinada****. In the centre of this small town stands the 19th century, neo-classical **Church of St. Jerome** (Sveti Jeronim) which was built on the site of an 11th century Romanesque church. A communal Baroque cistern has also been preserved. Beside the road, above the town, there is a war memorial to those who fell in the 2nd World War, which is the work of Nenad Krivić.

To the south of Motovun, on the Pazin road, to the north of the village of Karojba is the village of **Rakotule****. In a field off the road lies the cemetery **Chapel of St. Nicholas** (Sveti Nikola), a single-naved building in the Romanesque style. It was built in the 14th century, by the Venetian Barbo family who settled in Motovun. In the 15th century the chapel was extended at the front. On the walls of the older part there are frescoes by two Italian masters from the mid 14th century who were inspired by Giotto. One painted *Maiestas Domini* in the apse and the chapel's patron saint St. Nicholas. The other artist depicted scenes from the life of the same saint on the side walls of the chapel. Both artists show a special sense of space, plasticity and figure characterisation.

•••••••••••

Novigrad*

14 KM TO THE NORTH OF POREČ, POPULATION 4 000.

There was an ancient city in the broad area of what is now Novigrad (Aemona). In the 5th-6th centuries it was called Neapolis. From the early Middle Ages and right up until 1828 it was the seat of the Bishopric, from 1270 it was under the Venetians until their fall, and it suffered a good deal of damage from the Turks in 1687. The old city centre is situated on a peninsula. The triple-naved basilica of St. Pelagius dates from the 8th century, and the present **church**** was built on the foundations of the old basilica in the 15th and 16th centuries. Beneath the presbytery there is a late Romanesque crypt. In the sacristy of the present parish church, the former basilica, 15th century antiphonaries are kept with their simple and beautiful initials.

Novigrad

Novigrad has retained its medieval structure and layout, with narrow, winding streets and small shops. The fortifications belong to the medieval era: the town wall still stands with its battlements and two round towers. There are examples of secular architecture from the time of the Venetian empire, such as the town loggia and several houses built in Venetian Gothic style. The collection **of stone monuments*** was founded in 1897 beside the cathedral. Since 1964 it has been housed in the Rigo Palace, which belongs to the Urizio family. On the first floor there is a collection of ancient gravestones and secular monuments from Novigrad and the surrounding area. There is a valuable collection of Byzantine and medieval fragments and woven ornamentation, as well as the remains of stone church furniture and decorative carvings. Particularly important are the remains of a stone pyx engraved with the name of Bishop Mauricia (about 780) and pictures of mythological animals. In the courtyard of the palace there is a private collection of stone monuments, from various sources, which belonged to the Urizio family.

••••••••••••

Vrsar*

9 KM TO THE SOUTH OF POREČ, POPULATION 1 872

Vrsar has been inhabited since prehistoric times. In the immediate surroundings, on the peaks of nearby hills, there are the remains of Illyrian settlements (fortresses). In ancient times it was called Ursaria (ursus means bear) from which derived the present name Vrsar. It was a good harbour from where the ancient people exported, amongst other things, Istrian stone. On the sea front there are the remains of a Roman country villa (villa rustica). In the early Middle Ages Vrsar came under the Poreč Bishopric, and was the bishop's summer residence, which is why the town was fortified relatively early. The old town centre developed around the bishop's castle (later Kastel Vergotini). The western **town gates** are still standing, and beside them an 18th century chapel, with a characteristic upper room. From the Romanesque era, when Vrsar was a town settlement on top of a hill, the Parish Church of **St. Mary**** (Sveta Marija) remains. It has a nave and two aisles, with three apses, of which the central one is longer than the other two. It dates from the 12th century and is one of the most significant Romanesque buildings in Istria. **The Dušan Džamonja Gallery**, Valkanela 5 (a street in the direction of Poreč). Gallery, Workshop and Sculpture Park of Dušan Džamonja (born 1928), renowned Croatian sculptor with a highly personal style, very well regarded in the world at large. Džamonja's works are exhibited in many of the world's major cities, for example in the Museum of Modern Art in New York, the Tate Gallery in London and the Musée National d'Art Moderne in Paris.

Vrsar

••••••••••••

The **Lim fjord*****(Limski zaljev, 4.5 km to the south of Sveti Lovreč). This is in fact a flooded limestone valley (9 km long, average width 600 m), which

The Lim Fjord

runs from the centre of Istria, from Pazin to the south, to Kanfanar where it turns sharply to the west. Owing to its geological history, this fjord is one of the most instructive examples of limestone hydrological development. The Lim stream used to flow through the valley but dried up regularly, and was really only present after heavy rain. The Lim fjord has the appearance of a canyon. The sides rise to 150 m, sinking to 20 m when they reach the sea; they are overgrown with maquis and have some special characteristics. The southern bank, facing the north, is covered with deciduous trees (oak and ash), while the north bank, facing the sun, has more evergreen flora. The vegetation has recently suffered a great deal from fires. The fjord is rich in fish, and high quality oysters and mussels. Because of the special conditions of the sea water in the channel (less salt content, a higher concentration of dissolved oxygen and well-researched temperature gradients) sea flora and fauna are particularly well developed. The channel is a natural breeding ground and wintering place for many breeds of fish. For this reason it is a special reserve and is protected by a conservation order. At the end of the fjord there is a hotel.

••••••••••••

In the past, the Lim fjord separated the Poreč and the Pula agricultural areas, which is how it came to be called Lim (from the Latin "limes" meaning threshold). The area around the fjord was settled very early on. Along the banks of the bay there are many caves where traces of human life from the New Stone Age on have been discovered.

According to legend, in the 11th century St. Romualdo lived in one of these caves (Sveti Romualdo's cave). He was the founder of the Benedictine Monastery of St. Michael (Sveti Mihovil), the ruins of which remain on the northern side of the bay, near the village which is still called *Klostar* today. (Klostar means monastery). On the site of the monastery, which was built in the 11th century, even earlier (6th century) there was an Early Christian Chapel of St. Michael. The Benedictines added a large abbey in the 11th century. In the apse of the older chapel there are some small fragments of frescoes from about 1100 still preserved. On the triumphal arch of the newer church there are fragments of frescoes by Benedictine masters of the Ottoman era (11th century).

••••••••••••

Buje

34 KM FROM POREČ, 17 KM FROM RIJEKA, 19 KM FROM KOPER, VIA KAŠTEL, 13 KM FROM THE SEA AT UMAG, POPULATION 3 001.

The oldest part of the town, which is circular in shape, was built on the top of an isolated hill, which shows its prehistoric origins. It was linked to the ancient settlement of Bullea. During the Middle Ages it belonged to the Istrian counts, from the 12th century it came under the Patriarchs of Aquileia and in 1412 it was taken over by the Venetians, who partially demolished the defensive walls. The walls were later restored.

Buje has retained its

Buje

medieval structure, with a central square, walls and towers. The houses are built in Venetian provincial style: under one roof, on the ground floor a stable, store, and cellars, and upstairs the living quarters. The Venetian influence is particularly obvious in the town loggia and several patrician palaces. A palace in the Venetian Gothic style dominates the main square, with a painted 15th century facade. On the square there is also a column with measures of length from the 16th century.

SIGHTS

The **Parish Church of St. Servulus*** (Sveti Servul) was built on the foundations of a Roman temple and dates from the 16th century. In the 18th century the triple-naved church became a single-naved one. A septum was included in the earlier church. The facade of the church has remained unfinished. Some Roman stelae are built into the foundations of the church, along with some gravestones and medieval fragments. Along the top of the facade there is a Romanesque relief of angels.

••••••••••••

The **Church of St. Mary*** (Sveta Marija) is a single-naved building from the 15th century, with a later classical facade. The bell tower dates from the 16th century, and is separate from the church. It bears the coats of arms of the Venetian Rectors and the Venetian lion of St. Mark. In the sacristy are several Gothic

sculptures and Baroque paintings with 18th century views of Buje.

••••••••••••

The **Buje ethnographic collection*** is in the People's University (Narodno Sveučilište) and includes ethnographic material from Buje and Bujština. Particularly worth seeing are the forge from Zrenj (18th-19th century) and the display of looms and woven articles, also from Zrenj.

EXCURSIONS

Grožnjan**

7 KM TO THE EAST OF BUJE, POPULATION 193

Grožnjan is a fortified medieval town, on a raised area of land over the right bank of the River Mirna. It was mentioned for the first time in 1103. It was ruled by the Patriarchs of Aquileia until 1358 when it came under Venice. In the second half of the 14th century Grožnjan was the administrative centre for the western part of Venetian Istria. At that time the town walls and watch towers were repaired. Of these, only the main town gates remain, which at one

Grožnjan

time had a drawbridge. Beside the gates there is a Renaissance loggia and above it was the grain store (fondaco) at the time when the Mirna was still navigable as far as Bastija, which lies below Grožnjan. In the town centre is the **Parish Church of St. Mary, St. Vitus and Modestus*** (Sveta Marija, Sveti Vid i Modest) from the second half of the 18th century. It was built on the site of an older church which was mentioned in the 14th century. The church contains valuable late Baroque altars, beautiful pilasters with richly modelled capitals. The church also has valuable wooden Renaissance choir stalls in the presbytery, which also show signs of the influence of folk art. Since 1969, Grožnjan has been the venue for the **Young Musicians**, (Međunarodni kulturni centar Hrvatske glazbene mladeži), or the International Centre for the Young Musicians of Croatia, which has summer schools in the town every year. Young musicians from all over the world meet here. There is also in the town an **Artists' Colony**, with many artists having their studios and galleries here. These activities are the dominant ones in the city today. The Young Musicians' Centre has renovated and taken over 14 buildings which were previously just bare walls, so that now there are a concert hall and 15 studios for the work of the summer school, a summer stage and so on.

A man from Banjol at his prayers

Oprtalj**

16 KM TO THE EAST OF BUJE, OVER THE STERNA OR 24 KM ALONG THE MIRNA VALLEY. 380 M ABOVE SEA LEVEL, POPULATION 118

The town is situated on the site of a pre-historic fortress. It was settled in ancient times, and in the Middle Ages it was the property of various feudal lords. In 1209 it was ruled by the Patriarchs of Aquileia and in 1490 it was taken over by Venice. The medieval walls which surround the town are well preserved because houses built much later use them for support. In front of the entrance to the town there is the town loggia which dates from the 17th century. It now contains a **collection of stone monuments.** The medieval arrangement of narrow winding streets, small squares and covered alleys has remained more or less the same right up to the present day. The entrance to the town is through the old town gates. Most of the houses are on two floors. In the centre of the town there is a square with the **Church of St. George**** (Sveti Juraj), with a separate four-sided bell tower. A presbytery with a polygonal end wall was built in the 15th century inside the old church which is divided into three parts by columns with pointed arches. At that time a Gothic net vaulted ceiling was added to the original building. In the 17th century the church was extended and given a new stone facade. It has a valuable altar and paintings from the 16th, 17th and 18th centuries. It also possesses a valuable painting of the Carpaccio school. The painting *The Madonna of the Rosary* is the work of the Italian 18th century master M. Furlanetto.

Some beautiful medieval frescoes have been preserved in churches outside the town. In the fraternity **Church of St. Mary**** (Sveta Marija) below Oprtalj, which was built in the 15th century and extended in the 17th-18th centuries, the master Clerigin from Koper painted scenes from Mary's life on the

triumphal arches and on the south wall in Renaissance style in 1471. Three other Istrian early Gothic masters painted similar scenes. In the **Church of St. Leonard**** (Sveti Leonardo) there is a 17th century

Buzet

altarpiece by Zorzo Ventura from Zadar. In the **Church of St. Rochus** (Sveti Rok) there is a fresco by the prominent Istrian master Anton of Padova (an Istrian village) from 1535 with a series of pictures of saints. In the single-naved Romanesque **Church of St. Helen** (Sveta Jelena) which is about 1 km to the south of Oprtalj, on the road for Motovun, there is a fresco by the Istrian master Clerigin of Koper. About 4.5 km from Oprtalj is the village of **Zrenj** which some think was the ancient town Stridon where St. Jerome (Sveti Jeronim, Hieronymus Sophronius Eusebius, c. 340-420) was born. He was an author of sacred writings and the first translator of the Old Testament from the original into Latin. Some writers believe that Stridon lay 12 km to the south of Postojna, somewhere near Pivka, whereas earlier tradition places St. Jerome's Stridon in Štrigova near Čakovec or even in Dalmatia.

Buzet

54 KM FROM POREČ, 48 KM FROM RIJEKA, POPULATION 1721.

This small town is situated on a lonely hill in the northern part of central Istria in the middle of a wide valley where the River Mirna flows. The location has been inhabited since pre-historic times. Beneath Buzet was the cross-roads of the main routes from the north to the south (at the foot of the limestone massif Ćićarija) and from the west to the east (from the karst to the sea along the Mirna valley). The present settlement is spread out at the foot of the hill, in the Funtana area. In Roman times the hill town was known as Pinguentum, from which came the Old Slavonic Plzet, or Blzet and then today's form, Buzet. Many archaeological finds date from the time of the great migrations: below the town a food store from the Langobard-Avarian-Slavic migrations has been found (Brežac about AD 600), an old Slavonic burial ground (Mala Vrata 9th-10th centuries), and an ethnically mixed settlement, Byzantine (soldiers) and Slavic (peasants and their families), in the area of Mejica. After all these movements, the town became a Slavic community with a local chieftain at its head. In the Middle Ages it was the property of the Patriarchs of Aquileia, and then various feudal families, until it was taken over by the Venetians in 1421. After 1511 the military leadership of Venetian Istria had its headquarters in Buzet. It remained under Venetian control until their empire fell in 1797. During the 15th century the town was frequently subjected to attack by the Turks, so it had to be protected by high walls. The present appearance of the town also dates from this time. Once the danger from the Turks had passed, homes were built along the walls. Two gates remain intact, the main one from 1547 (Vela vrata) and the northern gate (Mala vrata) from 1592.

SIGHTS

In the centre of the town there is a large Baroque **communal cistern** with Baroque architectural decorations. On the main square, on top of the hill and on a terrace which has been cut out of natural rock, stands the Parish **Church of the Assumption**** (Uznesenja Marijina) which was restored in 1784. The church has many valuable silver items amongst its treasures, which are the work of local masters. In the fraternal Church of **St. George** (Sveti Juraj), on the northern side of the town, which was built at the beginning of the 17th century (1611), there is a large altarpiece showing the *Miracles of St. Anthony (Sveti Antun of Padua)*. It is of the Tiepolo school. The wooden choir stalls are the work of a local master of the second half of the 18th century. The **cemetery church** which was built in 1651, has some Roman carved reliefs built into its stonework. The Folk Museum of the **Buzet Region**** (Muzej Buzeštine) was founded in 1963 and consists of a collection of stone monuments, archaeological, ethnographic, cultural and historic collections, as well as an exhibition of more recent history in the Buzet area. The museum also houses several old craftsmen's workshops which have been preserved, both in the museum itself and in the town (a baker's, a potter's, a combmaker's and a blacksmith's). The stone collection includes examples of cult carvings (sacrificial altars) gravestones (stelae, cippi, tituli); special prominence is given to representations of the god Silvanus and the goddesses Diana and Ceres. The archaeological collection includes finds from the area around Buzet, from pre-historic times, the Roman era and more important finds from the time of the great migrations. There are some very significant finds from the old Slavic burial ground below Buzet. The ethnographic, cultural and historic collection has objects relating to the spiritual and material life of an Istrian village: national costumes, town and village furniture, as well as documents relating to the period of the National Revival in the second half of the 19th century, and of the period of Fascism and the national resistance during World War II, and contains original documents and items that round off the historical presentation of the Buzet area from pre-historical times until the present day.

Stipan Konzul Istrian was born in Buzet. He was a Croatian Protestant writer from the second part of the 16th century, who printed the first book in the Glagolitic, Cyrillic and Latin alphabets in Urach in Germany, as well as several books in Italian. Important editions in Croatian include the New Testament and other religious and religious propaganda books.

Excursions

Draguć***

14 KM TO THE SOUTH EAST OF BUZET ON THE ROAD TO CEROVLJE; POPULATION 79

This is a medieval settlement in the hilly part of central Istria. It is situated on a hillside over a deep valley and the houses are arranged to the left and right of the only street. The facades of the houses, both one-storey and those on two floors, are linked together in a picturesque whole. The street, the only thoroughfare, leads to a broad square where stand the parish church and bell tower. The outer walls of the inner town centre used to serve for defence, while the houses along the street acted as reinforcement. The Venetians fortified the town against the Turks, but also from the attacks of the Uskoks of Senj who had advanced as far as Draguć, for this town played a significant role in the defence of Venetian Istria.

••••••••••••

Before the entrance to the town, by the road side, on what is now a graveyard, stands the **Church of St. Elisaus*** (Sveti Elizej). This is a Romanesque single-naved building with a coved apse. Inside the church there are some Romanesque frescoes by a local artist from the end of the 13th or the beginning of the 14th century. Outside the town, above the Draga valley, stands the votive **Church of St. Rocco***** (Sveti Rok), which is a single-naved church, in the shape of a parallelogram, with lancet vaulting. It was built in the 16th century and the portico in front of the church was built in 1565. Inside the church there are some frescoes by the local Istrian master, Anton of Padova

Draguć

(who was born in the village of Kašćerg, near Padova, in central Istria). In 1529 he painted all the walls and the ceiling, using Renaissance forms and transforming them into folk motifs. In 1537 he subsequently painted the altarpiece. His name is to be found in a Glagolitic inscription over the church doors, but he signed his altar piece in the Latin script and language. Especially impressive amongst his paintings are

Imago Pietatis, The Flight into Egypt, and The Adoration of the Magi.

●●●●●●●●●●●●

Istarske toplice*

THE ISTRIAN SPA; 10 KM FROM BUZET ON THE ROAD TO POREČ

This has been a spa-town since Roman times. The sulphur and radio-active

Pieta, detail from a fresco of the Church of St. Rocco

baths are the best known in central Europe, but they must be used under supervision. The temperature of the water in the pools is between 30 and 35 degrees centigrade. These baths are especially beneficial in the treatment of the following ailments: chronic rheumatism, vertebral injuries, sciatica, lumbago, chronic respiratory infections, postaccident or post-operative treatment, dandruff, eczema, acne, gynaecological problems, sterility and hormonal imbalance.

●●●●●●●●●●●●

Roč**

10 KM FROM BUZET ON THE ROAD TO RIJEKA, POP. 146

Roč was first inhabited in pre-historic times. In classical times another settlement grew up in the fertile valley on the site of the present day village of Rim. Around the military base a town developed which has left no visible traces. In the 6th century AD there was a church there, the **Church of St. Maurus** (Sveti Mouro), and an inscription, which has been lost, mentioned the Bishop of Trieste Frugiferus. Some old Slavic graves have been found in Roč from a slightly later date. In the Middle Ages Roč was fortified with walls and towers (in about 1420), parts of which remain. The Romanesque **Church of St. Rocco**** (Sveti Rok) shaped like a parallelogram and with a covered-in apse, has two layers of frescoes. The older layer shows the work of 16th century Italian masters. In the **Church of St. Anthony**** (Sveti Antun), a Gothic structure from the 12th century, there is a votive cross engraved with the Glagolitic alphabet of Roč (from about 1200). The triple-naved **Church of St. Bartholomew*** (Sveti Bartol) has a presbytery in Gothic style; on the right-hand side altar there is a painting by an unknown Venetian master. In the Middle Ages Roč was the centre of Glagolitic writing. The town had several significant Glagolitic codices, missals, breviaries and a collection of various writings, which are today in Vienna, Copenhagen and Zagreb. Not far from Roč in the village of Nugla the famous Novak Missal was found, now in Vienna, which served as a basis for the first printed books in Croatia and Yugoslavia. It is a Croatian-Glagolitic missal dating from 1483. In honour of the Glagolitic tradition in Istria and Croatia, a **Glagolitic Avenue** (Aleja glagoljaša) has been set up between Roč and Hum and is a unique form of museum.

●●●●●●●●●●●●

Glagolitic was the first Slavic alphabet which was devised by Constantine Cyril before leaving on his mission to the Moravian Slavs. The first Slavic books were written in this alphabet: selections from the Old and New Testaments and later the basic liturgical repertoire of the Slavic Church. The Glagolitic script is the work of a highly philosophically and artistically cultured man. It is stylised, and formed in a specific manner. It does not

Glagolitic script

correspond to any European or Asian script. In its original form it consisted of 38 letters which were totally in keeping with the Slavic phonetic system; it was also a numerical system, each symbol also represented a number, as was the case with the Greek alphabet (and also the Cyrillic one).

Glagolitic came to Croatia very early on,

maybe as early as the time when Cyril was on his mission to Moravia. In Croatia the original rounded Glagolitic soon began to acquire a more angular form, and thus a specific type developed, Croatian Angular Glagolitic. Most medieval Croatian inscriptions are written in this form. It was reserved for liturgical monuments until printing appeared, when it also appeared in books, but in everyday use a cursive and simpler form developed for handwriting. Most Croatian medieval literature and writings were written and preserved in the Glagolitic script, and this script is therefore considered to be Croatia's national script. In the centuries when Glagolitic was threatened by prohibition and persecution, its scholars began to regard the great church teacher Jerome as its creator, and so from that time Glagolitic came to be known as the Jerome script. This is why there is such a lot of interest amongst Croatian humanists in Glagolitic as a specific script and in texts written in this script. The first book printed in Croatian, a Missal, was printed in Glagolitic in 1483.

••••••••••••

This Glagolitic Avenue** stretches over an area of 7 km and was instituted in 1977, dedicated to scholars of Glagolitic, pupils and leaders in the literary, educational and cultural advancement of the activities of the Holy Brothers, Constantine Cyril and Method, the Slav apostles and educators. It consists of 11 monuments which show the development and historical roots of Glagolitic in Croatia and especially in Istria.

The Cyril and Method Table

••••••••••••

1. The **Column of the Čakav Assembly** is a 2 meter high stone column in the shape of the Glagolitic letter "S". This is the letter in the old Slavonic term "slovo" which means: the word, understanding, Logos, Verbum.

••••••••••••

2. The **Cyril and Method Table** is a round stone table on three legs. There are inscriptions in three alphabets on its edge: Glagolitic, Cyrillic and Latin script. It says "The Table of Constantine Cyril and Method" (Stol Konstantina Kirila and Metodija).

••••••••••••

3. The **Collection of Kliment of Ohrid** is set up beneath an oak tree and consists of a stone lectern and stone seats arranged around it. It is in memory of the first Slav University which was founded by Kliment, a pupil of the Holy Brothers, after he had been expelled from Moravia, and gone to Macedonia.

••••••••••••

4. A **collection of stone monuments** is set up in the village of Brnobići near the church and within the small square in front of the church. On the wall which encloses the square, there are copies of the most significant Glagolitic stone monuments: the Baška Tablet (a reconstruction of the

The Rise of the Istrian Law book

original text), the inscription from Plomin, the Tablet of Valun, the Inscription from Krk and so on.

••••••••••••

5. The **refuge of the Croatian Lucidar** is a memorial to the Glagolitic scholars who in the Middle Ages were responsible for advances in literature and knowledge. The famous medieval Encyclopaedia, the Lucidar, was probably revised here in Istria. The Istrian mountain Učka was, for the Croatian reviser, his Olympus whose peak rose high above the clouds.

••••••••••••

6. The **Grgur Ninski look-out point** was set up in memory of the Croatian Bishop Grgur who fought in the 10th century (during the time of the Croatian dynasty) for the rights of his national church organisation. In the 19th century he became a symbol of resistance against domination by Rome and Vienna. His memorial is a stone block in the shape of a book with carvings in three alphabets: Glagolitic, Cyrillic and Latin.

••••••••••••

7. The **Rise of the Istrian Law Book** (Istarski razvod) is the most impressive monument in the Avenue. A path leads through stone gates in the shape of the Glagolitic letter "L" up past Glagolitic letters which spell the words "ISTARSKI RAZVOD", (an important cultural and historical legal document) to the regional round table and a spring at the far end. The letters by their shapes remind us of original objects the artist (the sculptor Želimir Janeš) has included in his monument (chapels, baskets, kilns).

••••••••••••

8. The **Wall of the Croatian Protestants and Heretics** is above the monument to the "Istarski Razvod". Set in the wall, which is in the form of an Istrian dry stone wall, is the Glagolitic letter S in the form of a water or sand clock; beside it are the names of Croatian Protestants, Heretics and those who fought for truth. In the wall, on tablets, fragments of sentences from the introductions to Protestant books are engraved. These books were published in Germany in all three alphabets, for the use of the South Slavs.

The Column of the Čakav Assembly

••••••••••••

9. The **Žakan Juraj resting place** is reached through a short cut across the ravine or by road. It is situated beside the road and consists of huge stone blocks symbolising a book. The inscription is a quotation by Juraj Žakan from Roč who, with these words, announced the publication of the first Croatian and Yugoslav printed book, a Glagolitic missal dating from 1483. Around the block there are 7 stones in the shapes of Glagolitic letters used for printing, which spell the words ŽAKN JURI.

••••••••••••

10. The **Memorial to Resistance and Freedom** stands in front of the entrance to Hum, the smallest city in the world. It is a stone column, made out of three stone blocks placed one on top of the other, which represent three historical eras: Ancient times, the Middle Ages and the Modern era. The inscriptions on the three blocks are from ancient (Latin), and medieval (Glagolitic-Croatian) sources and songs of the Istrian Partisans in the Second World War. The memorial commemorates the struggle for freedom and justice from ancient times to the present day.

••••••••••••

11. The **town gates of Hum** are solid double gates, covered with copper plates and decorated with 12 medallions representing the 12 months of the year according to old calendars, showing life and work in the fields, houses and village courtyards. There is an invitation to enter the town engraved on the knocker, but also a warning to anyone who comes with evil intentions.

The Glagolitic avenue was created by the sculptor Želimir Janeš aided by Josip Bratulić. The idea and name for the whole thing came from the writer Zvane Črnja. It takes about one hour to see the entire avenue on foot.

••••••••••••

Hum*** is a medieval settlement which rises above a beautiful valley. On its western side it is enclosed by town walls and on the remaining sides houses are built into the defensive walls. It was mentioned for the first time in documents dating from 1102, at which time it was called Cholm which comes from the old Croatian Hum, and from which comes the Italian name Colmo. A bell and watch tower was built in 1552 as part of the town's defences beside the town loggia. The present **Parish Church of St. Jerome*** (Sveti Jeronim) with its classical facade was built in 1802 on the site of an earlier church which was built by the local master Juraj Gržinić. The painting over the main altar is the work of the Venetian artist Baltazar D'Anna (16th century) from Flanders. The painting of the Abbot St. Anthony over the side altar is the work of the Istrian artist of the 19th century, Ivan Baštijan. The church houses a rich collection of late Gothic chalices, monstrances and pyxes. In the graveyard there is a single-naved Romanesque church, of **St. Jerome***** (Sveti Jeronim), with a semi-circular apse hollowed out of the otherwise straight front wall. Inside the church there are frescoes from the second half of the 12th century of high artistic quality, with signs of strong influence from Byzantine artists. As well as fragments of the *Annunciation* on the triumphal arch and the *Visitation* on the south wall, the *depiction of Christ's sufferings* on the northern wall is especially noteworthy. The frescoes were commissioned by the Patriarchs of Aquileia, or rather their lawyers, when Hum was under their authority as the residence of one of the richest servants of the Patriarchs. The "Hum Glagolitic wall writings" are preserved in the church, written in the formative period of Glagolitic (the second half of the 12th century) and they are one of the oldest examples of Croatian Glagolitic writing in Istria. Hum, like Roč, was a centre of Glagolitic literary culture in the Middle Ages. Two Glagolitic breviaries have been preserved from Hum, but they are now kept in Zagreb.

Pazin, to the left the Castle above the Pazin abyss

••••••••••••

Pazin

32 km from Poreč, 55 km from Rijeka, 54 km from Pula, population 4 986. It is The County town of the Istrian County

Pazin was mentioned for the first time in documents of Emperor Otto II in 983, where he confirms the fortress Pazin (Castrum Pisinum) as the property of the Bishop of Poreč. The fortress of Pazin, later the castle, was built in the 9th century in the centre of Istria, hence the German name for Pazin, **Mitterburg.** It stands at the crossing of roads from hilly eastern Istria leading to Poreč, along the Draga valley to Lim and Rovinj and the centre of the peninsula towards Pula. In the 12th century it was held by Majnard Schwarzenburg (in Latin documents he is known as "Cernogradus") who founded the Pazin County (earldom). Pazin - and the County of Pazin - then had several changes of feudal master. Coats of arms record these changes on the facade of the castle; they were mainly German families: Eppenstein, Wermar, Moorsburg, Sponheim, Andechs, Wittelsbach and finally the Counts of Gorz. In 1374 it was inherited by the Habsburgs who gave it out in fief to various families, the last of which was the Montecuccoli family in 1766. The castle was also the residence of the governor of the county, who had the title of Captain (kapetan).

Pazin played a central role in the establishment of boundaries in Istria, as can be seen in the important medieval Croatian document, the **Istarski Razvod** (the Istrian law book). In the 16th century Pazin county included 25 village and town communities or

Battle of the Angels, fresco from the Church of St. Nicholas in Pazin

communes (parishes). During Napoleon's reign, it was part of his Illyrian Provinces, and once the French had withdrawn, following a decisive battle fought near Pazin in the Beram valley, it became part of the newly formed Rijeka region until 1822. Pazin then became the capital of the Istrian region (1825-1861) an area which included the entire Istrian peninsula. While political life subsequently mainly centred around the Istrian Regional Assembly in Poreč, Pazin remained, even after 1861, the centre of cultural and political life for Croatians in Istria. In 1899 a Croatian grammar school was founded there and then a second, and political, cultural, and educational societies. The arrival of the Italians in 1918 in Istria and also Pazin meant the end of the flourishing political and cultural life of the town. Many Croatians had to move to Yugoslavia, or go overseas, to America. Even before the Italian surrender in 1943, the provisional leadership of the people's struggle for liberation was founded in the Pazin area. Pazin was liberated for the first time on 19th September 1943. The People's Liberation Council (NOO) made the historic decision three days later to join Istria to Croatia. On the 25th September 1943 there was a session of the regional NOO for Istria in Pazin, when earlier decisions were confirmed, concerning the secession of Istria from Italy, and the unification of Croatia with Yugoslavia. German units which then occupied Istria avenged themselves savagely on the Istrian people. Pazin was liberated again on 6th May 1945. Pazin was rebuilt, industrialised and built up into the political, cultural and educational centre of central Istria.

••••••••••••

Sights

The **Parish Church of St. Nicholas**** (Sveti Nikola) on the southern edge of the town, was mentioned in 1266. The late Gothic polygonal sanctuary has ribbed and stellar vaulting which was added in 1441. This kind of vault was to become the pattern for a whole series of Istrian village churches during the 15th and 16th centuries. The church was extended and redecorated in Baroque style in the 18th century. Beside the central nave two side naves were added. The walls and Gothic vaulting were covered in high quality Gothic frescoes from the 15th century, which were the work of a talented South Tyrolean master. The frescoes show scenes from the Bible, as well as the life of St. Nicholas. With the frescoes in Beram and Hrastovlje, they represent the peak of Istrian medieval art. The solid bell tower, which is separate from the church, was built in 1705.

••••••••••••

The **Franciscan church**** has a late Gothic presbytery from 1481. The Franciscan monastery, which goes with the church, was built between 1463 and 1477, and the late Gothic presbytery is from 1481. It is of the same type as the one in the parish church. There used to be a polyptych by Girolamo da Santacroce on the main altar dating from 1536.

••••••••••••

In the centre of the town in **Park Velikana** (Park of Great Men) there are about 15 busts of well-known and deserving Istrian warriors (Dobrila, Laginja, Gortan etc) as well as an early sculpture by Džamonja "The Awakening of Istria" (Buđenje Istre). In front of the building of the College, in 1993, a bust of Herman Dalmatinac was put up (Hermanus Dalmata, H. Slavus, H. de Carinthia and H. Secundus, assumed to have been born about 1110 in the northern part of Istria). Dalmatinac was a translator from Arabic into Latin, and was most at work in Paris and Cordoba; he is considered a pioneer of European and Croatian science. Below his name is carved: XII SAEC. PARS PRIOR/ CROATA HISTRIANUS/ PHILOSOPHUS / MATHEMATICUS / PRIMUS IN ARABICIS.

••••••••••••

The **Castle**** (Kaštel), situated over the gulf through which flows a stream called the Fojba, was probably built in the 9th century, but it received its present appearance in the 13th and 14th centuries. The four wings of the building are arranged around a central courtyard with a large wall. Most of the surrounding perimeter walls date from the 15th century. The north western side is from the 16th century. The castle is entered over a drawbridge. Below the castle houses belonging to noble families were built in the 15th, 16th and 17th centuries, and houses of the ordinary people and artisans were built along the roads leading up to the castle on open land, on the site of an old annual fair and along roads leading from the East and West.

••••••••••••

The **Ethnographic Museum of Istria**** is housed in the castle. It was opened in 1955 as the People's Museum and has served as the Istrian Ethnographic Museum since 1961. It has a collection of old bells from Istrian churches dating from the 14th to the 20th century. The museum is both a place for exhibitions and for research with special displays of agricultural, cattle breeding, hunting and fishing equipment. There are also displays of old crafts and a valuable collection of national costumes and jewellery. There is furniture from a town house, town and country chests and valuable examples of majolica. Since 1983 there has been a permanent archaeological exhibition called "The Pazin area from prehistory to the Middle Ages".

••••••••••••

Excursions

Beram***

5 KM TO THE NORTHWEST OF PAZIN, ON A HILL ABOVE FERTILE FIELDS

Beram developed as a fortified settlement on the site of a prehistoric town. In the Middle Ages Beram had walls and a high square-shaped tower. The Parish Church of St. Martin** (Sveti Martin) was built in 1431 according to a Glagolitic inscription, and at the beginning of the 19th century it was extended with a new nave. Some frescoes by an unknown Furlanian master of the 15th century line the walls of the old church, the walls and groined vault of the late-Gothic presbytery, as well as the triumphal archway. The old altar in the old sanctuary remains from the Gothic church, and beside it there is a stone font with an engraved Glagolitic inscription with the date, 1493. There is also a stone tablet with Glagolitic writing which tells of the building of the old church in 1431. The late Gothic stone relief with a depiction of St. Martin on horseback is the work of a local 14th or 15th century master. The Croatian artist Celestin Medović (1857-1920) made the altarpiece for the restored church, with a picture of the equestrian saint. In the sacristy there is an ecclesiastical robe with figures of saints embroidered in silk, which dates from the 15th to 16th century. There is also a beautiful collection of Church treasures (chalices, crucifixes etc). Some Glagolitic illuminated codices, missals and

Beram, the interior of the Church of St. Mary

breviaries from the 14th and 15th centuries are now housed in the National and University Library in Ljubljana. In Beram there is also the house where Vladimir Gortan was born (1904-1929). He was a fighter against Fascism, who was shot by the Italian Fascists in 1929. The house now contains a memorial exhibition with documents relating to his life and death. In a field, on a small hill, on the other side of Beram, not far from the Pazin-Poreč road, there is a memorial to him erected in 1951, designed by Zdenko

Sila and Zdenko Kolacio.

Dance of Death, a detail of the fresco of the Church of St. Mary

About one kilometre to the north-east of Beram, in a quiet wood, there is the cemetery chapel of **St. Mary of the Stone Tablet***** (Sveta Marija na Škrilinama)

which contains some very famous frescoes. It is a 15th century Gothic building, constructed after the pattern of the old Parish Church of Beram. The nave, which is in the shape of a parallelogram, and the sanctuary are equally wide. During renovation work in the 18th century, the Gothic vault in the sanctuary was demolished with its Gothic ribbing and this was replaced by a straight ceiling. Windows were built into the side walls of the sanctuary and an entrance hall was built onto the front of the church. At that time the nave was also given a painted wooden ceiling. Some frescoes were destroyed, some damaged but despite this the Beram Cycle is one of the most completely preserved sets of medieval frescoes. They were the work of Master Vincent from Kastav and his assistants about 1474. The late-Gothic frescoes in Beram show, on about 46 painted areas, the lives of the Madonna and Christ as well as various local Saints. On the western wall are *Adam and Eve, The Wheel of Fortune*, and *The Dance of Death*. On the northern wall is the *Adoration of the Magi* which is 8 metres long.

Gračišće**

8 KM TO THE SOUTHEAST OF PAZIN, ON THE PAZIN-KRŠAN ROAD; POP. 467

Gračišće is a village situated on the side of a hill over a deep valley. It was organised as a medieval fortress early on, the home of free peasant-gentry who were mentioned in the 15th century by the Urbarium of the County of Pazin. At that time Gračišće was self-governing and had its own seal as a free community. The citizens of Gračišće, as free peasant-gentry, had Croatian surnames. The town was surrounded by walls with Romanesque town gates and a keep which date from 1500. There is a 1549 loggia by the main entrance to the town. On the main square are several noteworthy buildings: The **Palace of the Salamun family**** from the 15th century with its biphorium in the Venetian Gothic style; the **Gothic Bishop's Chapel**** from the 15th century, which shows signs of strong central European influence: it has a rib vault in the nave, the apses are polygonal and the windows have rosettes. The votive **Church of St. Mary**** (Sveta Marija), the Madonna as helper of those who are barren, is in a quadrangle with a barrel vault, dating from 1425. 15th century frescoes have been discovered in the apse. The church was built by Petar Beračić, a local man. The triple-naved **Church of St. Euphemia** (Sveta Eufemia) with its three enclosed apses, dates from 1383. The church contains a

Romanesque Crucifix from the 13th century. The parish church of St. Vitus (Sveti Vid), outside the town centre, is a triple-naved Baroque building with a striking facade; it was built in 1769. It also contains carved choir stalls ecclesiastical robes and liturgical equipment from the 18th century.

••••••••••••

Lindar**

6 KM TO THE EAST OF PAZIN

This is a small town to the east of Pazin on a high hill which rises over a fertile valley, and its walls are still standing. On its eastern side it can be reached by way of a plateau. It was probably inhabited as early as pre-historic times (the name Lindar is probably of Illyrian origin). The oldest remaining houses, low single-storey buildings, which were until recently covered by stone slabs, date from the 15th and 16th centuries. Lindar has retained the structure of a medieval settlement. The streets serve as communication with the far side of the hill, and are built up on both sides with low houses. The **loggia** was built in the 17th century. The **Chapel of St. Fabian and Sebastian** (Sveti Fabijan i Sebastijan) was built from donations by a local man and contains Glagolitic inscriptions from 1531. In front of the town stands the single-naved **Church of St. Catherine***** (Sveta Katarina) which was built towards the end of the 14th century or the beginning of the 15th century. It has a Gothic crossed rib vault divided into two parts, which is supported by consoles. On the northern wall a local artist painted a medieval allegorical representation of "The Living Cross" in 1409, a late-Gothic iconographic schematic presentation on the theme of Redemption.

••••••••••••

Pićan*

12.5 KM TO THE SOUTHEAST OF PAZIN; POPULATION 315

In Roman times this settlement was a military base and was known as Petina. From this evolved the Italian name Pedena, and the Croatian name derives directly from the Latin. It was already inhabited in pre-historic times and kept the character of a fortified town. From the 5th to the 18th centuries Pićan was the seat of a bishop. In the Pićan Bishopric, Mass was said in Old Slavonic. According to legend, the Bishopric was founded by the Emperor Constantine. In the Dark Ages it was a Glagolitic Bishopric, and later, until the 17th century, most of the Priests were Glagolitic scholars. This was discontinued in 1788. It is no legend that the Bishopric really existed in AD 539 when Emperor Justinian, having broken the power of the Goths, founded it in the centre of Istria. According to tradition the first bishop was St. Nicephorus (Sveti Nicefor) whose rule is recorded very early in Pićan. Throughout the Middle Ages the town was organised along the lines of a Slavic (Croatian) commune with a local chieftain and captains. Remains of the medieval walls have been partially preserved. In some places homes are built into the wall, making use of the ancient brickwork. The town gates are still standing, dating from the 14th to the 15th century. A cathedral with a nave and two aisles was built in the 18th century on the site of the old cathedral, and today it is the **Parish Church of the Annunciation**** (Navještanja Bl. Djevice Marije). On the main altar there is a painting by Valentin Metzinger (1699-1759) who came from France and worked in Slovenia and Croatia. Outside the town, on the hill where the cemetery is now, there is a single-naved

Gračišće

Romanesque church with a semi-circular convex apse, which is dedicated to **St. Michael** (Sveti Mihovil). Inside there are Gothic frescoes from the first half of the 15th century.

••••••••••••

Sveti Petar u Šumi*

(ST. PETER IN THE FOREST) 11 KM SOUTHWEST OF PAZIN, 27 KM TO THE EAST OF POREČ; POPULATION 1 011

A Benedictine monastery was built in this settlement, on the top of a hill, as early as the 13th century. When the monastery fell into disuse and ruins, it was taken over by Paulites from the monastery on the lake i.e. from Čepić, in 1459. At that time, new **cloisters**** were built from materials which had been preserved: on the ground floor there are wide Renaissance arcades, which are not just decorative, but also functional. The monastery expanded right up to the second half of the 18th century. Its chapel, now the **Parish Church of St. Peter and St. Paul**** (Sveti Petar i Pavao) was renovated in Baroque style and received

Pićan

symbols typical of the Paulites: the facade was divided up by columns and niches with stone figures of the Saints in a definite geometric pattern. The bell tower belongs to an earlier age. A Renaissance top was built on Romanesque foundations. Now it is in keeping with the whole of the Baroque church. The church is single-naved, with a long wide sanctuary. The nave extends into side chapels which are separated by solid columns bearing the weight of the heavy Baroque groin vault. The altars in the side chapels date from the second half of the 18th century, as do the organ, pulpit, and the carved choir stalls. The last two side chapels are fitted with leather wall coverings. The renovation of the earlier Romanesque and Gothic buildings was carried out in Rococo style at its peak, as was also the case in the Croatian hinterland (Hrvatsko Zagorje).

••••••••••••

Umag

32 KM NORTH OF POREČ, ABOUT 7 769 INHABITANTS.

The older part of the town is situated on a peninsula, and the new part spreads over the mainland alongside earlier settlements on the north side of the town. On the southern side of the peninsula, where Umag lies, there is a shallow harbour. As early as ancient times there was a settlement on the low-lying peninsula known as Umacus. Umag was inhabited in Roman times. In the Middle Ages it came under the Bishop of Trieste until the town was handed over to the Venetians in 1248, and then, at the fall of Venice, to the Austrians until 1918. The Italians held it until 1943. From 1945 it was part of "Zone B" and finally became part of Yugoslavia in 1953. It has retained a structure typical of a medieval town. The defensive walls from the Middle Ages and the fortifying towers from the 14th century have not been well preserved. The **parish church** is built in Baroque style and houses part of a Gothic church polyptych dating from the 15th century.

••••••••••••

SIGHTS

A **collection of stone monuments** is housed in the town keep. On the ground floor there are Roman gravestones (stelae), and a tablet dating from the Dark Ages, decorated with braided engravings. There are also valuable medieval stone fragments several of which are engraved with heraldic symbols.

••••••••••••

A spa town and health centre. Very recently a **Centre for Throat and Facial Therapy** was opened. The following ailments may be treated in Umag: chronic inflammations and allergies of the respiratory organs; chronic rheumatic diseases; diseases of the throat and nose, voice disorders; neuralgia; paralysis; and cosmetic surgery of the face and throat.

••••••••••••

Umag as a sports centre. In the last decades the tourist development of Umag has been directed towards sports, especially tennis. Umag, alongside Bol, on Brač, is the best known centre on

The Church of St. Peter in the Woods

the Adriatic for the organisation of tennis events. Since 1990, at the end of July, Umag has been the organiser of the International Croatian Championships, the Croatian Open ATP Tournament. Some of the best-known names in world tennis meet at this tournament, which gives social life in Umag a particular attraction while the tournament is on. But it is not only the world's best tennis players who come to Umag; the town has a total of 64 courts available to holiday-makers and other visitors.

Excursions

Savudrija
6.5 km from Umag; population 241

This town was inhabited in ancient times. According

Umag

to tradition, the Venetian navy defeated the navy of Frederick Barbarossa and Pope Alexander III near Savudrija in 1117. This scene has been immortalised in the Doge's palace by Domenico Tintoretto (1518-1594).

To the south of Savudrija, where the nudist beach is nowadays, there are the remains of the ancient and medieval settlements known as **Sipar**, which were probably destroyed by pirates in the 11th century. On a point near Savudrija there is a lighthouse, 36 m high. ■

Umag-Tennis centre

Rovinj

ROVINJ IS SITUATED 45° 06' N, 13° 40' E. IT HAS A POPULATION OF 13 461. JANUARY MEAN TEMPERATURES: AIR, 4.9 °C; SEA, 9.2 °C. JULY MEAN TEMPERATURES: AIR, 22.6 °C; SEA, 23.1 °C.

The Prehistoric Period. Archaeological finds show that Rovinj and its surrounding area (Rovinjština) were inhabited in prehistoric times. Like the rest of Istria, Rovinjština was settled by the Illyrians, the Histri. The topographic features of the settlement (Rovinj was an island right down to the 18th century, with a natural wall of rock to the west) made it easily defensible from the sea, and allowed access to the nearby mainland. Even before Roman times, Rovinj was a fortified town.

The Roman Era. The Romans finally conquered Istria in 177 BC. On the foundations of the old Illyrian settlement, they built their own Ruginium but it remained an insignificant place throughout the entire Roman era. When the Empire was divided, Rovinj, along with the whole of Istria, came under the Eastern Empire.

Under Various Rulers. Under Byzantine rule, Rovinj was part of the Exarchate of Ravenna (from the 6th century) and from 788 part of the Frankish state. Anonymous of Ravenna mentioned the town in the 8th century as Ruginio, or Rugino. The Slavs, who settled in Istria from the 7th century, called the settlement Rovinj. Being on the coast, it was the target of frequent attacks. For this reason in the Middle Ages it had to be protected by walls. In the 9th century the Neretvans threatened the town many times in their campaigns along the western coast of Istria, and in 876 they pillaged it and set it alight. From the 10th to the 12th centuries the citizens of Rovinj developed their own self-governing communal system: an assembly of townspeople (arenga) and a Great Council. Various noble families ruled the town for three centuries, and in 1209 it came under the authority of the Patriarchs of Aquileia.

One of the historical coats of arms of Rovinj

Under the Venetians. Rovinj was one of the first Istrian towns to fall under the

Venetians, in 1283. Venice restricted and then abolished the town's self-government, and brought in a "podesta" who was always a Venetian nobleman. During the wars between Genoa and Venice, the Genoans sacked the town, and after the fierce battle of 1379 the town strengthened its surrounding walls. In 1559 and 1599 Rovinj was attacked by the Uskoks of Senj and they subsequently sacked and burnt the town as belonging to their Venetian enemies. Rovinj also suffered from frequent outbreaks of plague, which often struck Istria, but these plagues also contributed to urban development. Many families fled to Rovinj from various other towns in Istria in the 17th century to escape infectious diseases. Thus Rovinj developed within the city walls, and later also extended beyond them. Once the danger from the pirates and the Turks had passed (end of the 17th century) Rovinj spread further beyond the old town centre. At the beginning of the 17th century, the neighbouring hill on the mainland was also built up and in 1710 a church and monastery dedicated to St. Francis (Sveti Franjo) were built. In 1763 the channel between island and mainland was filled in.

Venetian lion

The last two hundred years. After the fall of Venice in 1797 the townspeople of Rovinj chose 18 representatives from an assembly of all the male heads of families (of whom there were 1,016), who took on the administration of the town. They remained in power, with a few alterations, until 1813 when the Illyrian provinces were abolished. Up to the second half of the 19th century, Rovinj was the biggest town and harbour on the western Istrian coast. Once Trieste and Pula began to grow and become more important, Rovinj stagnated, that is, it had the same number of inhabitants as in the 18th century. The opening of the tobacco factory in 1872 brought a little life and economic growth to the town, and a year later it gained a railway link to the Divača-Pula line. Between the two wars Rovinj stagnated once more, and again the population failed to increase, but after World War II it once again knew a period of prosperity. ■

Rovinj, aerial photograph

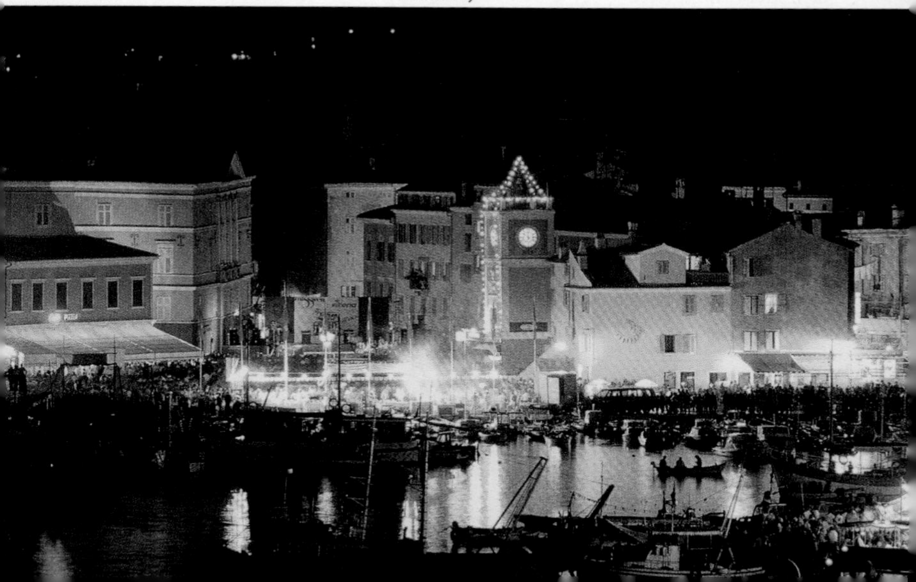

Summer night in Rovinj

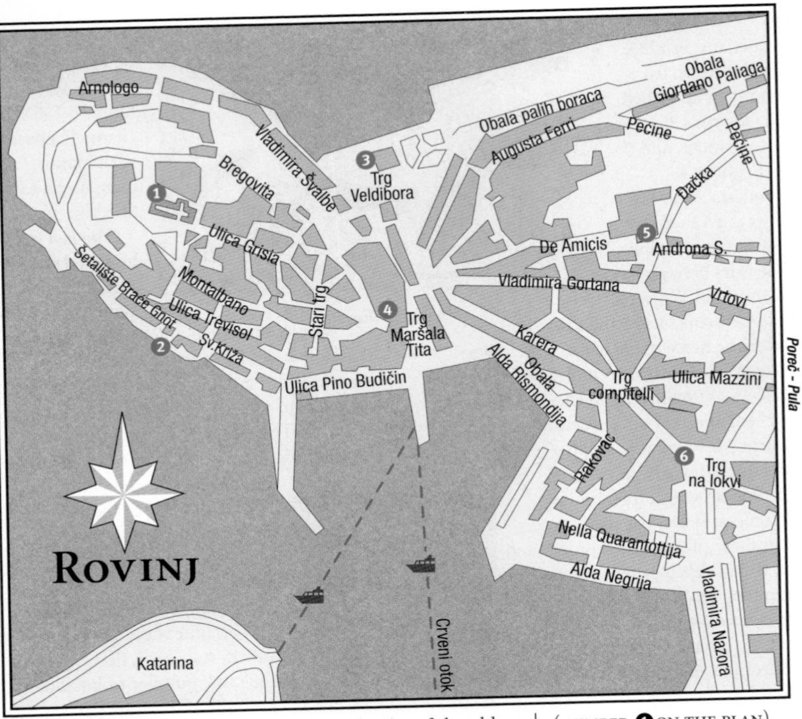

SIGHTS

The **Old Town Centre.** The inner town is packed onto a small island (actually a limestone rock) which dictated its shape. Its steep, narrow and winding main street with covered passageways and small squares, reveals, more than other Istrian towns, the peasant character of a medieval settlement. The closely-packed agglomeration of houses, high and narrow, ascends stepwise to the hilltop, where the Church of St. Euphemia (Sveta Eufemija) stands. The town centre has been surrounded by a wall since the Dark Ages and is entered through seven gateways, of which three have retained their original appearance. **The Balbi Arch,** (Luk Balbi, NUMBER ❹ ON THE PLAN) - today's **city gate** - is a Venetian construction built in 1680 on the site of the old town gates. From it leads **Bregovita Street**** (Bregovita ulica), picturesque and interesting, built in the 18th century with covered passageways and frescoes below the eaves. There is an open-air art exhibition every year in Grizia Street (Grizia ulica).

•••••••••••••

The **Church of St. Euphemia**, Crkva Svete Eufemije or Svete Fume (NUMBER ❶ ON THE PLAN) stands on the hilltop. It was built on the foundations of an early Christian church, St. George (Sveti Juraj), whose first phase dates from the 5th and 6th centuries, and second phase from the 9th and 10th centuries. The present parish church is Baroque, (nave and two aisles), built according to the plans of the Venetian architect Giovanni Dizzi during the second and third decades of the 18th century. It was consecrated in 1756. It is a church of pilgrimage, especially on its Saint's day (16th September) when believers and travellers from all over Istria gather there. The **bell tower** is a copy of the one at St. Mark's in Venice, built about 70 years before the church. It took 26 years to build, is 60 m high and is the tallest in Istria. In 1758

Grizia - open-air exhibition

a large statue of St. Euphemia was placed on its spire. The statue is fixed on bearings so that it turns according to the direction of the wind. Inside the church, the most interesting item is the sarcophagus with the body of St. Euphemia. It is a stone sarcophagus in late Classical style, according to 4th and 5th century models. It contains the preserved body of the Saint. According to legend, she was tortured in Chalcedon (near Constantinople) during the reign of Diocletian (304) in various ways, and finally on a wheel with knives, after which she was thrown to the lions, who would not touch her. When Chalcedon was conquered by the Turks her body was brought to Constantinople. During the Iconoclastic Controversy (800), according to Church tradition, her body disappeared from Constantinople and was washed up on the beach near Rovinj on 13th July, 800.

St. Euphemia, Gothic relief

The story is illustrated on the wall near the sarcophagus. The church also has other valuable treasures: *The Last Supper* by Titian's successor, Giovanni Contarini (1574) and the paintings *Christ in the Garden of Gethsemane* and *The Sleeping Apostles*, both of which originate from Venice. The sculptures in the church are the work of the Venetian sculptor Gerolamo Laureato. The church also has a rich silver collection. These are the remains of a rich inventory which was confiscated by the Fraternities during the rule of the French (1805). In the sanctuary, which dates from 1803, there are several valuable paintings by E. Zanfurnari.

●●●●●●●●●●●

The Baptistery** stands on Freedom Square (Trg Slobode, NUMBER ❻ ON THE PLAN) near the bus station in the southern part of the town. It is a heptagonal Romanesque chapel of the Church of the Holy Trinity (Crkva Presvetog Trojstva) built towards the end of the 12th century. It has all the characteristics of Romanesque architecture: from the outside it is heptagonal, on the inside it is circular with seven niches and a dome. Light enters through three openings on the outside which lend a special harmony to this small structure. Inside the baptistery there is a stone screen with scenes of Golgotha, the Madonna, St. Peter, and John the Baptist.

●●●●●●

Rovinj fiesta

The Franciscan Monastery** (on the eastern side of the town, 36 De Amicis Street, NUMBER ❺ ON THE PLAN). This stands on the top of the hill which faces the old town-centre of Rovinj. Both the monastery and the church were built at the beginning of the 18th century in the Baroque style. The monastery was started in 1702. In the monastery there is a museum which was founded in 1979 and houses a beautiful collection of ecclesiastical robes, icons, paintings and sculptures from the 18th to the 19th centuries. There is a valuable collection of illuminated manuscripts and liturgical equipment. The monastery also possesses a rich collection of old books.

••••••••••••

Holy Cross Church* (Sv. Križa) stands right next to the old town gates, and was built in the 14th century. A vestibule was added in 1492.

••••••••••••

The **Folk Museum*** (Zavičajni muzej, NUMBER ❹ ON THE PLAN). It was founded in 1954 and houses the following collections: an archaeological collection; a collection of documents relating to modern history; an ethnographic collection and a gallery of old masters from the 16th to the 19th centuries, with over 250 works of art. The museum also has a rich library, including the library of the Istrian historian Petar Stanković (from the turn of the 18th and 19th centuries). There are also occasional art exhibitions in the museum, and there is a collection of paintings by the contemporary Croatian painter Vilko Šeferov.

From a collection of pictures

••••••••••••

The **Aquarium*** of the Ruđer Bošković Centre for Marine Research is housed in a building which has served this purpose for more than 100 years. There are examples of flora and fauna from the sea around Rovinj, the Northern Adriatic and the western coast of Istria.

••••••••••••

To the south of Rovinj, in the suburb called **Zlatni Rt** (Punta Corrente, the Golden Point) there is now a park which was set up in 1890, with exotic trees. This was the site of an ancient stone quarry right up until the 18th century. Stone from here was used to build the Doge's palace in Venice and the famous Church of Santa Maria della Salute.

The Aquarium

••••••••••••

Crveni Otok*** (Red Island) lies to the south of the Muntrav point and actually consists of two islands - St. Andrew (sv. Andrija) and Maskin - which are joined by a harbour wall. They lie 1.5 nautical miles by boat from Rovinj town harbour. The island has an exceptionally mild climate, and is completely covered with evergreen vegetation, especially myrtle and bay. It was inhabited in prehistoric times. There are visible remains of the Roman era in the sea and on the beach.

Zlatni rt (Golden Point)

Crveni otok

In the 6th or 7th century a church was built on the island in the shape of a Greek cross with a semi-circular apse. There used to be a monastery there too, or at least a hospice, as early as the 6th century, at a time of very strong links between Istria and Ravenna, during the time of Justinian's reconquests. The monastery was founded by Archbishop Maximilian, who was born in Veštar, not far from Rovinj, and who later donated his family estates to the monastery. It was held by the Benedictines until the 13th century, then in the middle of the 15th century the Franciscans renovated it once it had become deserted. Its first guardian following this restoration was St. John of Capistrano (1386-1456) who defended Belgrade in 1456, when the Turks suffered a heavy defeat. In memory of this Christian victory, the custom of ringing the church bell in the afternoon was introduced, at the time when the news reached Rome. The Franciscans held the monastery until 1809 when their leaders removed them from the island. In 1820 the island was privately owned. The monastery and church suffered severe damage in 1852 when the whole complex was converted into an oil mill, and then an even worse fate when it was turned into a cement factory - the church bell tower serving as a chimney. In 1890 the island was sold to Baron Ivan Georg Hütterodt, who turned it into a park and restored the monastery buildings.

In the chapel and the castle on the island there is an exhibition of paintings by Aleksandar Kirchner showing the development of the Austrian merchant fleet and navy. There is also a display on the development of seafaring and fishing in Rovinj. In the chapel there is a collection of Istrian frescoes.

••••••••••••

The Rovinj Coast***
Western Istria as a whole is considered to have special natural characteristics (Red Istria), but the area around Rovinj has unusual features which set it apart as an area of natural interest, and it is therefore protected. The jagged coastline is backed by extraordinarily rich natural forests of pubescent oak (Quercus pubescens) and holm oak (Quercus ilex) as well as plantations of pine forests. The most valuable of Rovinj's natural beauty spots are the parks on Zlatni Rt (Punta Corrente, Golden Point) and by the hospital. Both were planted at the beginning of this century. On Zlatni Rt particularly significant are: the avenue of cypresses (Cupressus sempervirens), the Italian stone pines (Pinus pinea), the cedars (Cedrus sp.) and copses of Aleppo pines (Pinus halepensis), silver firs (Abies alba), holm oak and other exotic trees.

Excursions

Bale*
14 km to the Southeast of Rovinj; on the road Pula - Trieste - Rovinj

Bale, a small town to the southeast of Rovinj, on the cross-roads of the Pula-Trieste-Rovinj highroads.

By road it is about 14 km to Bale from Rovinj. Bale is situated on a small hill above a limestone plateau. This shows that it grew up on the site of a pre-historic settlement, which was transformed into a military base in ancient times. It was part of the Pula agricultural area (ager) and is on the Roman road which went from Pula, through Fažana, near Peroj to Cape Betika. At Bale it turned to the left of the Lim valley and went down to Dvigrad, continued on to Lovreč and from there to Trieste. In the Middle Ages Bale was held by the Patriarchs of Aquileia, and from 1332 it was under the Venetians. It has retained the structure of a town of the Dark Ages, with the remains of the town walls, tower and gates.

••••••••••••

The **castle** is a prominent feature. It belonged to the Soardo family, and from 1618 to the Bembo family. Originally it consisted of two four-sided towers which were linked by a drawbridge. The following buildings are also medieval: the town loggia, a grain store (fondacco), and the Praetorian's palace. The **parish church** was built in 1880 on the site of an old triple-naved basilica from the 9th century, some fragments of which are kept in the crypt. There is also a collection of fragments of stonework in designs of braiding and early-Romanesque carvings. Inside the church itself there is a wooden Romanesque crucifix (13th century). The wooden Romanesque polyptych on the side altar and the liturgical robes and other items are from the 15th to the 18th century. Beside the early medieval **Church of St. Elijah** (Sveti Ilija) there is a bell tower standing apart which has elements of Romanesque architecture.

Brachiosaurus, one-time resident of Istria, after a drawing by Renzo Zanetti.

The **Church of the Holy Spirit** (Duh Sveti) was built in popular Gothic style in the 15th century. In the **Church of St. Anthony** (Sveti Antun), there are some late Gothic wooden carvings, and the partial remains of Gothic frescoes. There is a rich museum collection in Bale consisting of: archaeological, cultural and historic, ethnographic and modern history collections.

Dinosaurus Histriae. In the surrounds of Bale (Porto Colone Bay) there is a protected area, the Palaeontological Park. This is a new find, pronounced by world palaeologists the discovery of the century. At the time of the Mesozoic, Istria was a part of the mainland, and the presence of these giant creatures shows that it was covered by luxuriant vegetation. On the mainland and in the shallows of Porto Colone Bay a great many fossilized dinosaur bones have been found. The reptiles inhabited this area a hundred million years ago. The great amount of bones found leads to the supposition that this area was a dinosaur graveyard, or a place in which, on account of some natural event, they died in great numbers. Palaeontologists have determined that the bones found belonged to two species of these giant prehistoric creatures. One of them is Brachiosaurus, a four legged herbivore with a neck about 10 metres long, weighing about 30 tons. These were the biggest dinosaurs ever to have existed. In addition to this find, the wider surroundings are full of dinosaur traces. Footprints can be seen in Brijuni (Punta Barbana), in Pula (Punta Verudela), in Cervar near Porec, on the Fanoliga islets near Premantura and Levan. More details about this matter can be found in the book of Flavia Forlania, *Dinosaurus Histriae* (Bale-Rijeka, 1995).

••••••••••••

Dvigrad**, the ruins of a medieval town in the valley of the Draga, 3 km by road from Kanfanar. Dvigrad (Dvagrada, two towns or Duecastelli) as its name suggests consists of two fortresses, or two settlements. Both places, which are in a strategically good location overlooking a stream flowing from Beram to the Lim fjord, date from pre-historic times and were important in the Roman era. In the early Middle Ages the northwestern fortress was known as Castel Parentin, and the one on the southwest as Moncastello. Castel Parentin became deserted early on, but Moncastello, with its new name Duecastelli, or Dvigrad, Dvagrada as it is called in the **Istarski razvod** (the Istrian law book) continued to flourish (right up until 1631), despite being emptied and destroyed several times, by plague, epidemics and an unhealthy climate, as an important strategic point in Venetian Istria. In that year

Dvigrad

Dvigrad was finally deserted because of its unhealthy climate and the plague which was sweeping across Istria, and the inhabitants moved to local villages and especially to Kan-fanar. What are now ruins formed the defensive walls and towers and within the town there are many medieval architectural remains. The oldest is the early medieval **Basilica of St. Sophia**** (Sveta Sofija) whose walls contain fragments of carved braiding from an early Gothic church.

••••••••••••

Not far from Dvigrad, by the Kanfanar-Margani road, there is a cemetery with a single-naved Romanesque church, **St. Mary of Lakuć**** (Sveta Marija od Lakuća), which has an enclosed apse. Inside the church are frescoes by a late-Gothic Istrian master (end of the 15th century). The same artist also painted a Madonna on the facade of the church, below the semi-circular canopy, as protector of the people, but this picture has been washed away by rain. He also painted pictures in the **Church of St. Anthony** on a hill opposite Dvigrad. He is known in literature as the "colourful master".

Detail of a fresco from the Church of St. Vincent

••••••••••••

Kanfanar*

3 KM SOUTH EAST OF DVIGRAD

A settlement at the crossroads of the routes for Pula and Rovinj, Trieste and Pazin, and the railway station for Rovinj. This settlement originates from the time when people moved here from Dvigrad, especially after the plague which swept across Istria in 1630. A pulpit from Dvigrad with a painting of St. Sophia (Sveta Sofija) holding a town in each hand was moved into the new church, **St. Silvester's** in 1696, along with painted doors from the 16th century, two wooden statues and an illuminated 15th century Year Book (Liber Anniversariorum). The **Church of St. Agatha** is two kilometres from Kanfanar towards Barat. It is a pre-Romanesque single-naved church with a semi-circular apse, which is three-sided from the outside. The church contains early 11th and 12th century Romanesque frescoes, which show Byzantine influence.

••••••••••••

Svetvinčenat*

(SAVIČENTA) SVETI VINČENAT, 5.5 KM SOUTHEAST OF KANFANAR

A town on the Pula-Pazin road was the possession of the Patriarchs of Aquileia who gave it to a Pula family, the Sergijas (Castropola). In 1330, in a battle between the Patriarch Pagan and Count Ivan Henrik, the patriarchal army sacked Svetvinčenat. After that the town passed into the hands of the Poreč Bishop who, in 1389, handed it over to the Venetian Morossini family. In the war between Venice and the Emperor Charles V the Venetians held Svetvinčenat and it remained the

Žminj, the Parish Church of St. Michael

possession of the Morossinis. Later there were conflicts between Venice, the Morossinis and the Bishops of Poreč. Svetvinčenat shared the fate of other Istrian towns under the Venetians, until the fall of their empire.

•••••••••••

The **Church of St. Vincent**** (Sveti Vinčenat), which stands in the cemetery, was once an abbey. It is a single-naved Romanesque church with three enclosed apses. The walls are decorated with three layers of frescoes: all that remains of the oldest layer are faded traces of pigment; the second layer was painted over all the church's walls by Ognobenus from Treviso at the end of the 13th century. In terms of its encyclopaedic, hagiographic and theological plan, the Romanesque cycle of 13th century frescoes in this church is the most comprehensive in Istria. Ognobenus was greatly influenced by Byzantine art and theology. The third, newest layer of frescoes belongs to a period of Italian influence in the second half of the 14th and the first half of the 15th century. These are part of the renovated church.

•••••••••••

The **Church of St. Catherine** (Sveta Katarina) at the entrance to the town is a simple 15th century Gothic building with a lancet vault in the apse; its vestibule was added in the 18th century. The church is built of dressed stone and it contains 15th century frescoes. The **Gothic Church of St. Anthony** (Sveti Antun) is a rectangular shaped building. The **Parish Church of the Annunciation** (Navještenje Marijino) dates from the 16th century. It has a coffered ceiling and a beautiful altar from 1555. Particularly noteworthy amongst the church treasures is a carved 16th century wooden door near the sacristy and two paintings on canvas, an altarpiece in the style of Palma the Younger: *The Madonna and the Saints* and G. Porte, known as Salvijati *The Annunciation.* The interior was restored in the 19th century. The most beautiful example of secular architecture in Svetvinčenat is the fortified seat of the Counts, the so-called **Palazzo Grimani****, which previously belonged to the Morossini family (from 1331 to the middle of the 17th century), and was rebuilt in 1589. It is a four-sided tower with a strong base, corner towers and a simple facade. The **town loggia**** dates from the 18th century. The town also has some Renaissance private homes.

•••••••••••

Žminj

6 KM NORTH OF SVETI VINČENAT; POPULATION 722

Žminj is a small town on a limestone hill in the central part of Istria, on the road from Pula towards Pazin. There are signs of human life dating from the Palaeolithic age in the area around Žminj, also a large number of finds from the Bronze Age. Not far from the town, near the church of St. Foška, the remains of a late Classical to early Medieval settlement have been found, and in Žminj itself an early medieval Slavic burial ground (9th - 11th centuries). In the Middle Ages, Žminj was in the border area between Venetian and Austrian Istria. As part of Pazin County it was fortified by walls which are still standing on the north western side. Of the four towers which used to make up the castle, only one remains. The town suffered from German bombing during the Second World War (1943).

•••••••••••

On the wide town square stands the Baroque **Parish Church of St. Michael** (Sveti Mihovil) which has a rich collection of treasures: a Baroque pulpit and a marble altar with paintings of the Venetian school (17th and 18th centuries). In the southern side chapel is a carved wooden altarpiece, the work of a local Istrian workshop from the beginning of the 17th century, with a carving of the shepherds worshipping. A Gothic crucifix is also artistically interesting. In the sacristy are outstanding ecclesiastical robes (16-18 c.). Beside the parish church, on its northern side, there is a small Gothic chapel, of the **Holy Trinity**** (Sveto Trojstvo), which is a single-naved building, with a lancet vault in the nave, and a four-sided apse. The chapel contains high quality frescoes from 1471, with scenes from the life of Christ. These are in the so-called "soft style" characteristic of artwork from Alpine regions at that time. At the south west entrance to the town stands the early Gothic Fraternity Chapel of **St. Anthony**** (Sveti Antun) which was built by the master Armigirius in 1381. The chapel is single-naved with a four-cornered apse and barrel and lancet vaults. The window on the eastern wall has a stone transenna and the one on the south wall has stone bars. The interior of the chapel is painted with high quality late 14th century frescoes by an unknown artist clearly from one of the Venetian workshops of the Trecento. ■

The Wines of Istria.

The Istrian region has about 10,000 hectares given over to the grape vine. The most important wine centres are Buje, Poreč, Motovun, Pazin with Vodnjan, Novigrad, Buzet, Rovinj and Labin. The best known red wines are Merlot, Teran, Bourgogne, Cabernet Sauvignon and Barbera, while of whites there are Malvasia, White Pinot and Muscat otonel. **Merlot,** dry wine of a ruby red colour, is a premium wine or an appelation contrôlée wine. The best known come from Buje and Poreč. That from Buje has an alcohol content of from 12.5 - 14% and 5-8 g/l total acids. Merlot is drunk at its best after ageing.

Cabernet Sauvignon, is a premium red wine; that from Poreč can stand comparison with the best in the world. Alcohol content 12-13%, 5.5 - 7 g/l total acids. **Teran** is a quality red wine with a dark ruby colour, the colour of hare's blood, as it is said; along with Malvasia, this is the most widely distributed wine in Istria. Teran produced by the Agropazin winery has 11% alcohol content and 8.10 g/l total acids. This wine matures early and is drunk while quite young. **Malvasia** is a quality white (yellow) dry wine with greenish gleams. The alcohol content of Malvasia from Buje is 12.5 to 14%, with 5-7 g/l total acids. An aperitif wine and a dessert wine are also produced which have an alcohol content of 15%. The Rovinj winery offers a white table wine in which Malvasia is dominant.

The alcohol content of this wine is 11%, and there are 5-6 g/l total acids. The Istrian rosé is called **Hrvatica.** This is a quality appellation contrôlée wine from the Buje wine growing region. It is produced from a grape of the same name to which 15% of Verduzzo Trevigiano is added. It has the colour of unripe cherries. It has 10.5% alcohol and 5.6 g/l of total acids. ■

Pula

PULA IS SITUATED 44° 52' N, 13° 51' E. IT HAS A POPULATION OF 58 594. JANUARY MEAN TEMPERATURES: AIR, 5.8 °C; SEA, 10.3 °C. JULY MEAN TEMPERATURES: AIR, 23.2 °C; SEA, 21.9 °C.

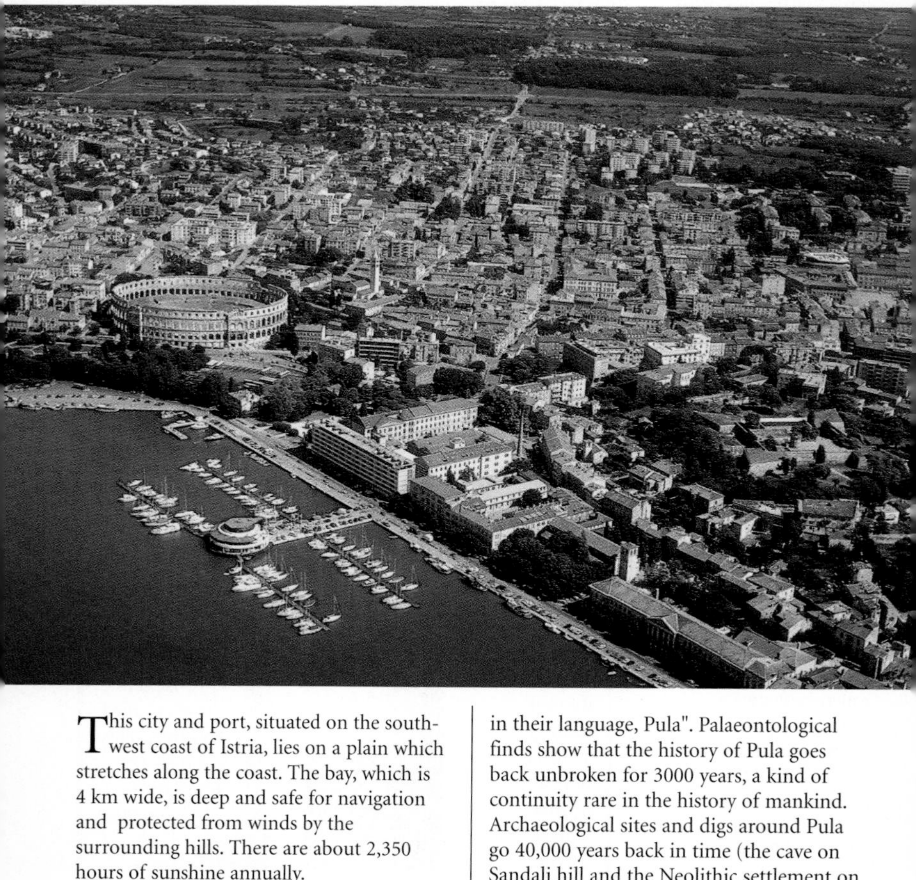

This city and port, situated on the south-west coast of Istria, lies on a plain which stretches along the coast. The bay, which is 4 km wide, is deep and safe for navigation and protected from winds by the surrounding hills. There are about 2,350 hours of sunshine annually.

Prehistory. Pula is the oldest town on the Eastern Adriatic coast. It was first mentioned by the Greek writers Callimachos and Lychophron in the third century BC, and they link the foundation of the town with the legend about the Argonauts. According to Lychophron, when Jason and Medea had taken the golden fleece, they fled up the Danube (Danube-Hister) to the west and "by the gravestone of the blond haired Harmony, snakes founded the city of the Fugitives, which they called in their language, Pula". Palaeontological finds show that the history of Pula goes back unbroken for 3000 years, a kind of continuity rare in the history of mankind. Archaeological sites and digs around Pula go 40,000 years back in time (the cave on Sandalj hill and the Neolithic settlement on Briuni). In Pula itself the remains of gigantic city walls were discovered near the Kaštel. In the 11th century BC Pula was a settlement of the Illyrian tribe, the Histri. Their settlement was situated on the hill in the centre of the town (Kaštel) and was built according to the standards of Illyrian architecture, i.e. the layout of the houses followed the configuration of the terrain and went in ever decreasing circles towards the centre, the peak of the hill. The name "Pola" is of pre-Roman origin

Roman alabaster urn, 1st century

Fragment from a sarcophagus, 2nd century

and means town or a spring of fresh water. Before the Roman occupation of Istria, Pola or Polae was of secondary importance to the main Illyrian town of Nezakcij, the centre of political and religious life in Istria, which was far richer and more significant. Pula's importance grew in the second half of the 2nd century BC when the Roman army conquered Istria in 177 BC and fortified the Eastern Adriatic coast.

The Roman Era. As a rule the Romans moved former inhabitants to other places and moved soldiers and Roman citizens into their own newly-founded towns. Only in strategically important settlements did the natives continue to live as Roman citizens. About 40 BC Pula became a Roman colony. Its agricultural area stretched to the Lim fjord in the west and to the River Raša in the east. The original settlement included an important military base on what is today the Kaštel - the second centre of Pula grew up around the Kaštel and below it, on the flat land along the sea front. This was the trading, naval and craft centre of the town. From the very beginning of the Roman occupation, Pula was a military town. During the civil wars it suffered damage but was rebuilt during the reign of Caesar Augustus (27 BC -AD 14). At that time Pula became urbanised, adapting itself to the geographic characteristics of the landscape and around buildings which already existed. Pula received the rights of a municipality and a new name: Pietas Iulia. As it was a strong administrative centre a number of important buildings were constructed: two theatres, a monumental amphitheatre (the Arena), a forum, temples dedicated to Romulus and Augustus. Pula was surrounded by walls. It became such an important town not only because of its strategic significance for Rome, but also because of the lively economic life of the surrounding area, which was rich in both crops and livestock, and, along the coast, in olives and vineyards. There was also well-developed fishing and trade, especially in wood. Despite the Roman presence, the native population continued to worship their own Illyrian and Illyrian-Celtic gods, and thus Illyrian religious traditions continued alongside the official Roman religion until the appearance of Christianity. This mixture of ethnic backgrounds, religious traditions and strong trading links with the East and neighbouring Aquileia opened the doors for an early conversion to Christianity. When in AD 425, under Theodosius II, Christianity became the one and only acceptable religion, Pula became a Bishopric. As early as the first half of the 4th century there was a small church in Pula (on the site of the present-day Cathedral), to the north of which a similar larger church was built. In the second half of the 5th century a large triple-naved basilica was built with a rectangular ground plan. The sanctuary is separated from the naves by three arches and a small semi-circular wall behind the seating for the priests. Fragments of floor mosaics have been preserved. The old arrangement in the church has remained more or less intact. When the Roman Empire divided in 395, Pula came under the Eastern Empire of Byzantine.

The Migrations of the Nations. Terrified by the threat from the Western Goths, the inhabitants of Pula restored and strengthened their city walls. This is why bits of staircases from the ancient theatre and amphitheatre, gravestones from the Roman burial grounds and parts of demolished buildings are to be found built into the walls. Pula also took in many fugitives from Panonia and Noricum at this time. The well-organised local church took on the responsibility of caring for fugitives. From this same period many

Triton, 1st century relief

graves with skeletons and funerary treasures have been discovered. At this time Roman and Greek cultures mingled together.

Under Various Rulers. The Eastern Goths occupied Pula, and ruled from 493 until 538 AD Following the Byzantine-Gothic wars (538-555) Pula once again came under Byzantine rule, and this mainly took the form of strong domination by the Church.

Sacrificial altar, 2nd century

A new wave of fugitives came to Pula some time before and during the migration of the Slavs (599-611). The proximity of the Byzantine capital (i.e. Ravenna) was felt and this contributed to the development of Pula as well as to the defence of the Byzantine Empire. Following Ravenna's example, a huge basilica of Mary was built on the site of the old Temple of Minerva, with a Benedictine Abbey (at the same time as the Euphrasian basilica was being built in Poreč). The building was commissioned by the Archbishop of Ravenna, Maximilian, who was born in Veštar, to the south of Rovinj. The triple-naved basilica was 32 m long, 19 m wide and elaborately decorated. The Venetians demolished it in 1243, but the huge marble columns which were brought to Pula from Asia Minor were moved to Venice in 1549 on the orders of the Venetian senate by the well-known Renaissance architect Jacobo Sansovino. They now stand on St. Mark's Square, or more precisely in the Marciana Library, and in the church Santa Maria della Salute.

Colonisation by the Slavs and Frankish rule. The migration of the Slavs, aided by the Avars, was very powerful; traces of destruction from the very beginning of the 7th century in the Pula area are visible. Because of the general stagnation and the smallness of the population, after the waves of migration calmed down, the Slavs (the Croats) colonised the abandoned estates around Pula. In about 788 the Franks became the new political masters of Istria; in that year, Pula and Istria came under Frankish rule. Pula once again became the biggest and most important Istrian city, but it was distracted between its sea and land orientations, that is, between the desire to become a sea power and the wish to occupy the rich agricultural hinterland. At that time, Venice was still paying a tribute to the Croatian princes for the right of unhindered passage through the Adriatic. During the 11th century, Venice began ruthlessly occupying the neighbouring cities. Pula finally lost its position of a strong, fortified city in the 12th century. In 1145 it took the first oath of fealty, while in 1195 the Venetians looted the town deplorably. In 1331 Pula gave up the struggle and placed itself under the protection of the Serenissima.

Under the Venetians 1331-1797. When the Venetians took over Pula, the city had 6,000 inhabitants. The Slavic (Croatian) and Roman ethnic groups had come to the fore in city life. During the 13th and the 14th centuries enterprising craftsmen and traders from Dalmatia and some Italian towns and villages began to arrive in the city. After the plague and more destruction suffered during wars (1347, 1350, 1354, 1379, 1421, 1517) Pula began to decline rapidly. In the 15th century it still had 5,000 inhabitants but in the following century only 1,000. The Venetians carried away everything they could from the city: marble columns, tiles, sarcophagi, mosaics and well heads. Of all Venetian possessions, Pula suffered the most tragic fate. It came to be known as the "city of corpses" or the "city of the dead" (città cadavero). It was probably while it was in this state that Dante Alighieri came to know it and mentioned it in his "Divine Comedy". For 3 centuries the death rate overtook the birth rate. In 1631 Pula had only 300 inhabitants and when Venice fell it only had twice that.

Under the Austrians. The change of rulers in 1797 did not change Pula's status to any great degree. It was not until after 1848

Archaeological Museum

Best wishes from Pula, postcards from the beginning of the 20th century

that Pula came to be included in the strategic and economic plans of the Habsburg empire. From 1850 onwards warehouses were built and in 1853 Pula was proclaimed the chief port of the Empire. Experts from Vienna, Graz, Bohemia and Sweden began to arrive and recruit a workforce from the local Croatian villages. Whilst in 1842 Pula had 1 126 inhabitants, 15 years later the population had increased 7 times and towards the end of the century it had reached 40 000, a quarter being soldiers. This rise in the population was not accompanied by advances in social and cultural life. Pula came to be known as a "cultural Siberia". The official language was German, and Italian was the everyday language. The Croatian population was systematically assimilated, with the Germans and the Italians competing for their allegiance. It was not until the end of the century that the Croats (and the other Slavs) began to develop their own national awareness. The work of the Socialist. party was also evident in the city as they gathered adherents from the workers in the shipyards. The Croatian Reading Room was founded in 1869 and the Cyril and Method Society in 1893. The building of the railway brought Pula nearer to Central Europe.

The Italian Occupation. When the Austro-Hungarian Empire collapsed, Pula was occupied by Italians on the basis of the secret Treaty of London of 26th April 1915. Despite promises to protect the rights of the non-Italian population, the rights of the Croats were not respected. Croatian schools were closed down, the Croatian Educational Society was disbanded and the National Cultural Centre was burnt down. The working classes were already becoming organised in 1920 in the fight for better economic conditions at work and free political activity. A general strike by shipyard workers and May Day demonstrations were put down with much bloodshed. The position of Croats and Slovenes worsened still further in 1926 when Italy was taken over by a Fascist dictatorship. Other workers also suffered as machines were taken away and workers made redundant. This situation continued until Italy surrendered in 1943.

Liberation from Fascism. The Yugoslav Army liberated Pula in 1945, but was forced to retreat as Anglo-American units marched into the city and remained there until 1947. It was not until 1947 that Pula finally became part of its mother country, Croatia, in the new Yugoslavia. It then began to develop rapidly as the industrial and tourist centre of Istria. ■

Marble torso of Roman emperor

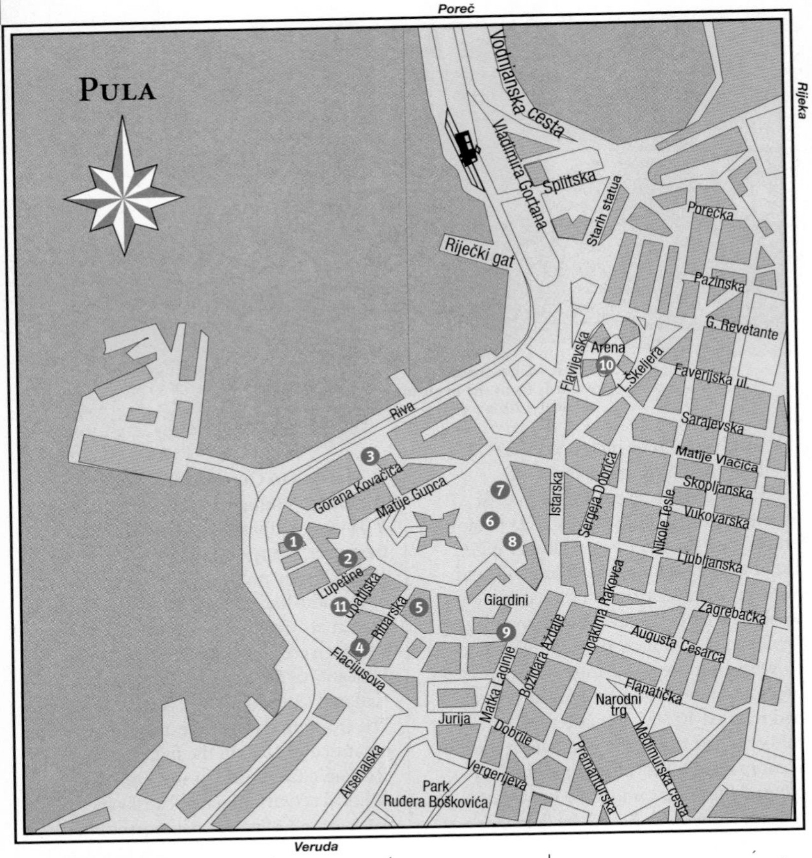

SIGHTS

The **Arena***** ►►►p. 50
The **Triumphal Arch of the Sergii***** (NUMBER ❾ ON THE PLAN) was built between 29 and 27 BC in honour of the three Sergii: Sergius Lepidus, Gaius Lucius Sergius and Gneius Sergius who held high military and civil offices in the Empire. The arch was placed at the entrance to the main street, alongside the city gates, and it has three covered archways. When the city gates were demolished in 1826 and 1829 the arch remained standing alone. It is decorated only on the city side. Beside the pilasters there are slender columns with Corinthian capitals; the archways the arch are decorated with winged Victories (the goddess of victory), adorned with wreaths. The frieze is decorated with putti bigae and Roman and barbarian weapons. The arch was built at the expense of Salvia Postum in memory of her close family. On the corners and in the centre there used to be statues of the three Sergii. This triumphal arch is a unique honorary and memorial structure from ancient Istria and as such has always attracted a great deal of attention from scholars and artists: sculptors, architects and painters. Sketches of the monument have been found amongst the works of Michelangelo, Sangallo and Piranesi, Cassas Adma and many others painted it.

The Temple of Augustus** (NUMBER ❶ ON THE PLAN) stands on what is now the Republic Square. It is a well-balanced rectangular building, standing above a wide staircase. A huge entrance hall opens onto the square, with four columns across the front and one on each side. The walls are built of large, regularly shaped stone blocks. Over the capitals in the entrance hall there is an architrave, and above it a particularly beautiful frieze. The words of the inscription on the frieze were cast in bronze. Judging by the inscription, or rather the dedication to Emperor Augustus (Pater Patriae, the father of the fatherland), the temple was built between the year 2 BC and the death of Augustus in AD 14 Beside the Temple of Augustus, there was also a temple to Diana, but all that remains of it is the front wall, which was built into a Romanesque and Gothic palace in 1296, and was damaged in a fire in 1379. It was repaired in 1697. The palace has a wide pillared loggia, and Baroque windows.

The **Chastisement of Dirca. Mosaic**** (NUMBER ⓫ ON THE PLAN) on the courtyard side; a large floor mosaic was discovered in 1959, dating from the 2nd century AD. It is divided into 40 decorated areas. In the central area of the eastern side of the mosaics, a figural composition of the mythological cycle "the Chastisement of Dirca" is dominant. The remaining areas are decorated with rosettes, fish, dolphins and birds.

The **Maria Formosa Basilica (del Canetto)**** (NUMBER ❹ ON THE PLAN). Only the southern burial chapel remains of this magnificent 6th century basilica, along with the northern wall and part of the northern rotunda. The burial chapel is in the shape of a Grecian cross and has a highly decorated polygonal exterior, with blind archways on the outer walls. Three original stone window bars still exist, the most beautiful of which is on the eastern side of the square-shaped base. The shell of the apse was decorated with a mosaic, part of which has been preserved (some fragments are in the Archaeological museum). Beneath the stucco cornice in the side chapels there are the remains of 14th century frescoes. The entire church was demolished and the pillars and mosaics were taken to Venice.

The Chastisement of Dirca, central panel of the mosaic

The Hercules Gate* (NUMBER ❽ ON THE PLAN) is the oldest remaining Roman monument in Pula. It dates from the first century BC

The Twin Gates* (PORTA GEMINA; NUMBER ❼ ON THE PLAN) date from the 2nd century AD Their solid pilasters are decorated with smooth columns, above which an architrave joins together the two archways which make up the gate. The Archaeological Museum is reached through this gate. Beyond the museum, on the slopes of the hill where the Kaštel (castle) is situated, there is a theatre, dating from the 2nd century AD. Its foundations are intact, as are its semi-circular orchestra and the semi-circular auditorium. The building, which was 62 m long, was entered through three huge gateways. The podium could be reached from various angles and the orchestra was reached from two sides. The auditorium was divided into two levels by an aisle.

In the **Cathedral**** (NUMBER ❸ ON THE PLAN) in its present form there are elements preserved of all the

▶▶▶ p. 52

Forum

The Arena***

(NUMBER ❿ ON THE PLAN) a three storey high Roman amphitheatre. In terms of architectural conception, size and preservation, this is the most outstanding monument remaining from ancient Pula. It is the sixth largest remaining amphitheatre in the world. The four-storied Coliseum in Rome and the amphitheatres in

Capua Verona, Arles and Catania are larger. Since the amphitheatre in Pula is in better condition than the one in Verona, and higher than those in Capua, Arles and Catania, it could be said that, after the Coliseum in Rome, it is the most magnificent structure of its kind in the world. The Arena (the word comes from the Latin "arena" meaning sand) is circular, 132.45 m x 105 m and 32.45 m in height. It is built of Istrian stone. The central part of the Arena measures 67.90 x 41.60 m. The outer wall consists of foundation stones, then two storeys of arcades of 72 arches. The upper storey has 67 square windows and on top there is a cornice made of blocks of stone. At its peak it held 23,000 spectators. It was not only the scene of staged fights for the entertainment of the masses, but also a place for business, social life and entertainment. It is thought that the

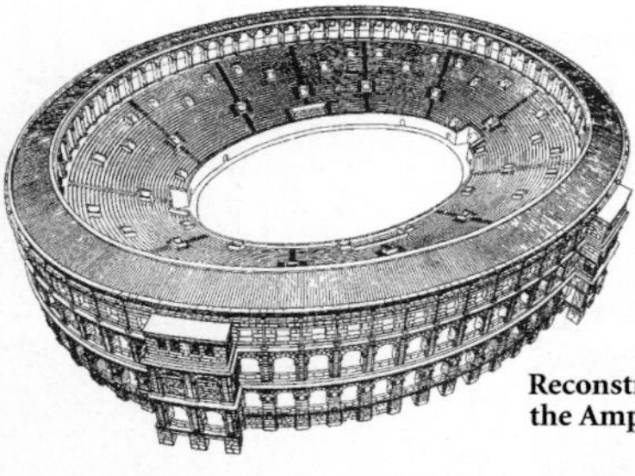

Reconstruction of the Amphitheatre

The southwest tower

Memorial tablet to Senator Gabrielle Emo**

foundations of the first, smaller amphitheatre were laid by Emperor Augustus at the beginning of his reign. They were extended by Emperor Claudius, and the final version dates from the reign of Flavius (AD 69-81). Old legends have it that the Arena was finished and decorated by Emperor Vespasian to fulfil the wishes of his lover in Pula, Antonia Cenida. Croatian folk legends tell how the Arena was built by fairies (hence the old name "Divič-grad", the town of the fairies) during the night, and when they heard the cock crow they left it unfinished, which is why the Arena has no roof. Some special features of the Arena are the four stone towers, and on the northwest side, a reservoir with water to supply the fountains. In AD 404 gladiator fights were banned and the arena became a cattle market. In the Middle Ages it was a source of building materials for medieval Pula and the surrounding villages. In 1583 the Great Venetian

The main entrance today

Senate decided to demolish the amphitheatre, take the stones to Venice and reconstruct it there. The demolition was prevented by the Venetian Senator Gabriele Emo, to whom a plaque was placed on the north western tower as a sign of gratitude.

significant phases of its construction: the rear wall dates from the 4th century; the sanctuary with its pillars and capitals, the floor mosaic, the arched apse and the raised wall with seats for the priests date from the 5th century; the gable of the central southern entrance is 9th century; the sacristy is 13th century; the internal layout, with its huge columns is 15th century; the facade was begun in the 16th century, and the bell tower at the end of the 17th. The Renaissance portal dates from 1457 and was part of the original church of St. Michael (Sveti Mihovil) on the hill, which used to be a Benedictine Abbey.

••••••••••••

The Orthodox **Church of St. Nicholas** (Sveti Nikola, NUMBER ❺ ON THE PLAN) is on the northern side of the Kaštel. It is a single-naved building with a polygonal apse, built around the year 600. The surface of the outer walls is broken up by lesenes (projecting vertical strips); the arch of the apse is similar to the triumphal archway in a cathedral. The columns bearing this arch have crosses carved on the capitals. The church was given over to the Orthodox immigrants from Cyprus and Naples in 1583. The wooden iconostasis is from the beginning of the 18th century and is the work of the Greek master Tomios Batas.

••••••••••••

The **Franciscan church and monastery**** (NUMBER ❷ ON THE PLAN). The church is triple-apsed and was built on the western slope of the Kaštel in 1314. The architect paid a great deal of attention to making the interior magnificent in a simple way, but did decorate the surfaces of the outer walls. The church has a blind arcade on the cornice beneath the roof, a chevron motif on the bell-tower, a magnificent Romanesque portal and a beautiful rose window on the facade. In the central apse there is a wooden polyptych from the 15th century which is one of the best examples of medieval Istrian carving. By the northern wall there is a wooden Gothic statue of the Madonna. The monastery was built in the 14th and restored in the 15th century. The Romanesque Chapel of St. John (Sveti Ivan) in the centre of the west wing of the monastery, with its Gothic portal, also contains a mosaic from the beginning of the 14th century which is in its original location.

••••••••••••

Dante and Pula. Dante Alighieri mentioned Pula when he described the entrance into the sixth circle of Hell, Dis, where heretics burn in stone graves resembling sarcophagi. In Pula the graveyard, with ancient and early-Christian sarcophagi stretched from the city right to the Arena, and then on towards the agricultural area. These sarcophagi were later taken to Venice. Dante wrote: "For as at Arles, where soft the slow Rhone slides,/ Or as at Pola, near Quarnaro's bay,/ That fences Italy with its washing tides,/ The ground is all uneven with the array,/ On every hand, of countless sepulchres," (Hell IX, lines 112-116; trans. Dorothy L. Sayers).

Dante Alighieri

••••••••••••

James Joyce in Pula. Joyce came to Pula from Trieste on 28th or 29th October 1904 as a twenty-two year old. He came with his common-law wife, Nora Joseph Barnacle, and found work as a teacher of English in the Berlitz school in Pula, a branch of the one in Trieste. His first flat was in what is today Laginjina Street (no. 2/II), and he moved to his second home (7 Medulinska street) in December, because the first flat had no heating. At that time Nora gave birth to their child. In letters sent from Pula he wrote that he was working hard: teaching English, learning German, translating and writing. He felt that Pula was "a God-forsaken place" and called it the "sailors' Siberia". Five months later he was forced to leave Pula, following a spy scandal uncovered by Austrian counter-espionage agents. His major crime was associating with Italians. In his novel "Portrait of the Artist as a Young Man" there is a notable sentence; "a day of multi-coloured clouds, born from the sea", which critics have attributed to Pula.

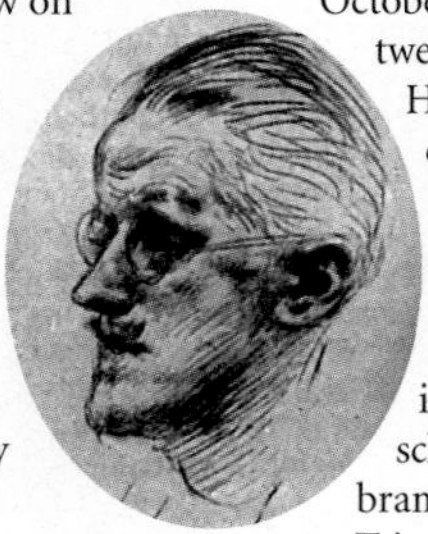
James Joyce

Museums and Collections

The Istrian **Archaeological Museum***** (NUMBER ❻ ON THE PLAN) was founded in

1901/2 as the City Museum and in 1925 became the Istrian Regional Museum. In 1930 it became the Istrian Archaeological Museum. On the ground floor, in the corridors, there is a display of **stone monuments** from ancient times (i.e. from the 1st to the 4th centuries), then from the Roman era to the early Middle Ages (4th-9th centuries). On the first floor there is a prehistoric collection including finds from the Romuald grotto and the Šandalj caves and stone monuments from Nezakcij. On the second floor is an ancient (Roman) collection, where abundant finds from Istria, and

Archaeological Museum

especially from Pula, are arranged chronologically. There are decorative carvings, Roman building materials, ceramic lamps, bronze and iron objects, items connected with arts and crafts, pharmaceutical and cosmetic utensils, and a particularly beautiful collection of glass objects. The later Roman and early

Detail of the »Viniculture and Olive Growing in Istria« collection

Ancient mill

medieval exhibition on the second floor is dedicated to the later classical period and the time of the migration of the nations (the 5th and 6th centuries). These are mostly new finds. There is an important collection of items from graves from the 7th to the 12th centuries from sites near Motovun, Buzet and Žminj (these were graves of Slavs).

••••••••••••

Ancient sculpture ** (The Temple of Augustus, Forum). This collection of stone monuments from the Pula area was founded in 1802. In 1815 when the temple was restored, the collection was extended. The present exhibition dates from 1968 and includes the most beautiful examples of Roman sculpture, especially portraits. Apart from stone sculptures, there are also examples of bronze work. Especially impressive are: a large stone torso which was part of a statue of the Emperor and was discovered on the site of the great Roman theatre; a statue of the Emperor with a kneeling slave; the head of Atis from Pula, etc.

••••••••••••

Wine and Olive Production in Istria in Ancient Times (the Arena, in the underground gallery). This collection was founded in 1880 and was expanded up to 1925 as a collection of stone monuments, but from 1969 it has been an exhibition of wine and olive production in the Roman era. There is a display of the development of wine and olive production in Istria using tables and maps, and also a typological overview of seals and amphorae, copies of old maps, a reconstructed wine-press and an original olive mill.

••••••••••••

The **Medieval Collection of Stone Monuments** and the **Exhibition of Copies of Frescoes** in Istria (the Franciscan Monastery, 5, Uspon Balda Lupetine street). This exhibition hall was arranged for stone monuments in 1963. In the atrium and in the eastern wing of the monastery there are some stone fragments from the Middle Ages which are also chronologically related. The Chapel of St. John (Sveti Ivan) is particularly worth seeing, especially because of its mosaics *in situ*. The **exhibition of copies of Istrian frescoes** shows frescoes from the 9th to the 17th century, and includes the following sections: the Romanesque era, Gothic frescoes, and the Renaissance.

••••••••••••

The **Historical Museum of Istria** (Povijesni muzej Istre, Uspon Muzeja 14). This museum is in a Venetian fortress which was built between 1629 and 1638 using plans drawn up by A. Devill, in the shape of a star with four bastions and two entrances. The museum shows the development of the labour movement in the 19th century, the Italian occupation of Istria and the Fascist dictatorship, and the resistance of the Istrian people. Most exhibits relate to the People's War of Liberation in Istria (the Second World War); some show the

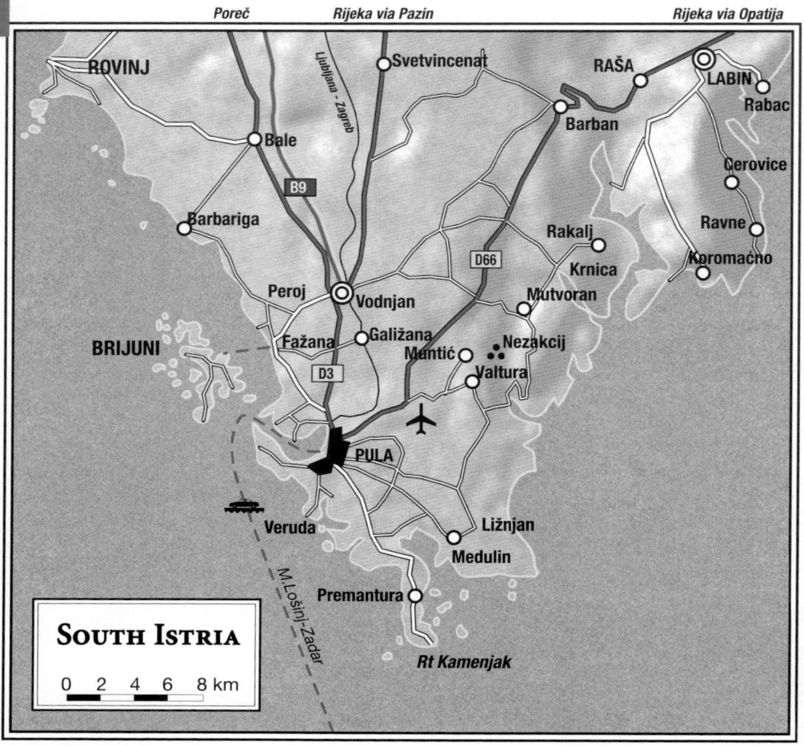

riots that occurred during the Anglo-American occupation of Pula and the diplomatic struggle to unite Istria and Pula with Croatia.

••••••••••••

Excursions

Medulin*

10 km from Pula; pop. 2 580

To the south-west of Medulin lies the Kaseja peninsula with its 2 km of sandy beaches and line of forests. There are also the remains of a pre-historic settlement. In the Bijeca Bay there are the ruins of a pre-Romanesque chapel. On the northern part of the Vizula peninsula are the remains of a Roman villa rustica (a country mansion).

••••••••••••

Nesactium*

Nezakcij, 1 km from Pula, 2 km north of Valtura.

The most famous and most important archaeological site in Istria. Here there are archaeological remains from prehistoric, classical and early medieval times, all of them enclosed within late-Roman city walls. Thus the history of the settlement may be traced from the Bronze Age up to the beginning of the 7th century AD when Nezakcij was burnt down and completely destroyed

Medulin

Premantura

during the advances of the Avars and the Slavs into Istria. The Nezakcij archaeological site is well-arranged and includes the remains of Roman thermal springs and a forum. The foundations of two Roman temples have been uncovered as well as the ruins of a late-Roman single-storey house and the remains of an early-Christian basilica. The remains of the pre-historic entrance into the city have been preserved, along with parts of the walls. Finds from Nezakcij (Vizace) are kept in the Archaeological Museum in Pula. Titus Livius tells of an Illyrian king, Epulon, who in 177 BC took his own life and the lives of his close family, rather than become a slave of the Roman conquerors. The Roman writer sought in this way to praise the courage of the barbarian citizens, for whom freedom was more precious than life.

Premantura*

12 KM FROM PULA

Premantura is the southernmost settlement in Istria. It was built on the site of an early Illyrian and Roman settlement. The well-arranged beaches are protected from south-westerly winds. From Premantura a white road leads out to the furthest point in Istria, Kamenjak. On a rock in the sea, on the small island of Porer there is a 31 m high lighthouse.

Vodnjan*

10 KM FROM PULA, ON THE ROAD FOR TRIESTE; POP 3 406

This small town has retained the character of a medieval walled settlement. Within the ring of houses which once formed the town's defensive wall, narrow and irregular streets along the main thoroughfare link together the town's tightly packed neighbourhoods. It was mentioned for the first time in 1150 as Vicus Atinianus. In about 1300 a castle was built on the western side of the town but was demolished at the beginning of the 19th century. The settlement spread to the north-west and the south-east, along the main street which crosses through the centre of the town. A cistern in the St. Laurentius (Sv. Lovro) quarter of the town dates from the Roman era. Graves containing urns and bones have been found on the road leading to Pula and Bale, also classical inscriptions near the Church of St. Lucia (Sv. Lucija). In the immediate vicinity of Vodnjan there are three prehistoric castles: Madona di Traversa, Montemolino and Castellier. On the main square stands the Baroque Parish Church of **St. Blaise***** (Sv. Blaž). On the site of the present church there was a Pre-Romanesque church until 1760. Some remains were built into the walls of the present church: broken stones with examples of braiding ornamentation and three Romanesque reliefs. In the Baroque church there is a Renaissance custodia dating from 1451, an altarpiece from 1321, and *The Last Supper* by G. Contarini from 1598. More medieval works of art were brought from St. Lorenzo church in Venice in 1818, including the outstanding picture (tempera on wood) of St. Leone Bembo. There is also a beautiful painting of the Madonna (also tempera on wood) which is an example of late Byzantine art; the Madonna with two Saints is the work of the early Venetian Quattrocento artist Jacobello del Fiore. A reliquary of silver gilt and some of the church's ecclesiastical robes date from the 14th century. The church possesses a **Collection of Sacred Art**** with a rich collection of works of art: paintings, icons, sculptures, church vessels and robes. The community of Vodnjan has set up its own **Museum Collection**** in the Betika Palace, including a rich ethnographic collection gathered mainly from Vodnjan and its surrounding area. In August the **Bumbarske svečanosti** (the Bumbar festival) is held in Vodnjan. Bumbar is a local word for an inhabitant of Vodnjan. To the east of the road leading to Bale, amongst the vineyards, stand the ruins of a single-naved Romanesque church with an enclosed apse, dedicated to **St. Margaret** (Sveta Margarita), which houses frescoes from the 15th century (*Maiestas Domini, the Apostles and the Annunciation*). On the road to Juršići stands **St. Quirinus Church** (Sveti Kvirin), which was originally a triple-naved basilica with three semicircular apses, stone furniture and architectural decorative carvings from the 6th, 7th and 8th centuries.

•••••••••••

Several Roman burial grounds have been unearthed in the area around **Peroj*** (4 km to the south of Vodnjan). Following a series of plague epidemics which totally wiped out the original population, in 1648 the Venetian government moved 15 orthodox families there from Montenegro. Most of the present population of Peroj are descendants of those immigrants, and they have preserved their customs, religion and language. There are two churches in the village. The Church of St. Stephen* (Sveti Stjepan) is an early Romanesque building with Romanesque frescoes from the 13th century. The church dedicated to **St. Spiridon*** (Sveti Spiridon) houses icons from the 11th to the 18th centuries. About 3 km to the northwest, between Peroj and Mandriol stands **St. Foška's Church**** (Sveta Foška) which is an early medieval triple-naved basilica. Across the entire width of the wall of the central apse there is a composition showing the Ascension, which probably dates from the 12th century. ■

Vodnjan

Brijuni***

THIS IS A GROUP OF 14 ISLANDS OFF THE SOUTHWEST COAST OF ISTRIA, DIVIDED FROM THE MAINLAND BY THE TWO KILOMETRE WIDE FAŽANA CHANNEL. THE BIGGEST ISLAND IS VELI BRIJUN (5.6 KM²). THE OTHERS ARE MALI BRIJUN, SVETI MARKO, GAZ, OBLJAK, VANGA (KRASNICA), PUSTI (MADONA), VRSAR AND OTHERS. THE CLIMATE OF THE ISLANDS IS VERY MILD, THE MEAN AIR TEMPERATURE IN JANUARY BEING 5.8 °C AND IN JULY 22.8 °C

Finds of stone and metal objects, the graves and castles of prehistoric man show that the Brijuni islands were settled before they were colonised by the Romans. They were ruled by the Romans from 177 BC. The Romans called them the Pullariae. In the first century several examples of the Roman villa rustica were built on Veli and Mali Brijun and on the eastern part of Krasnica. As early on as this, the islands were summer resorts, for rich citizens of Rome. After the fall of the Roman empire, the islands shared the historical fate of Istria. First of all they were ruled by the Goths, then by

Veliki Brijun,
Verige Bay to the left

Byzantium (up to 778), then by the Franks and the Patriarchs of Aquileia, being taken over by Venice in 1331. The Venetians ransacked Brijuni just as they did Pula. In 1893 the islands were bought by an Austrian industrial magnate, Paul Kupelwieser, who turned them into a resort for wealthy tourists. Hotels, bathing places, horse racing tracks, golf links and tennis courts were all built. Eighty kilometres of roads were made, and an aqueduct was constructed, the water being brought in a pipeline across the Fažana Channel. The famed German bacteriologist, Nobel Prize winner Robert Koch (1843 - 1910) helped in the reconstruction of the islands.

Lighthouse on Cape Peneda

•••••••••••

After World War I, the management of the islands was plagued by crises. As private property, they were subject to great taxes. After the death of the owner, Herr Kupelweiser, the situation deteriorated still further. In 1920 there was a freak accident, a thunderbolt striking a byre and fifty horses dying. Fires raged the following year. The government shut down the casino, and the whole property was mortgaged. The islands were annexed by Italy in 1936 and remained part of Italy until the capitulation in 1943. At the end of the war, the Brijuni were subjected to Allied bombing. Highly destructive bombs were dropped on the built-up part of the island and many of the hotels were destroyed. At the end of World War II the Brijuni were joined to Croatia, and in 1948 the reconstruction of the damaged and abandoned buildings began. When the White Villa was built, the Brijuni islands became the residence of Josip Broz Tito, and were closed to the general public. In 1983 the islands were proclaimed a national park, and in 1984 were opened to the public.

Byzantine castrum

Sights

The remains of Roman **villae rusticae** ** (number ❼ on the plan). This is a complex that stretches all along a bay and includes a group of luxurious buildings meant for various uses, and a quay. In the centre were three temples, one to Venus, one to Neptune, and one to some unknown deity. The temples contained apartments for the priests, farm buildings, thermae and various halls. The buildings were linked by corridors with an open peristyle loggia looking on to the sea. The walls of the rooms were painted red, yellow and green.

•••••••••••

On the western coast of Veliki Brijun, in Dobrika Bay, a large defensive building called the Byzantine castle *** (number ❹ on the plan) has been preserved. These remains show that the settlement was used continuously all the way down to the 16th century. The complex consisted of residential apartments and farm buildings. In the centre of the island there are several buildings: a square tower from the 12th (or very early 13th) century is the most important monument of medieval architecture (number ❺ on the plan).

The **Church of St Germain** ** (Sv. German) is a Gothic construction from 1481. It was built on the foundations of a still earlier building. This little church has a permanent exhibition of copies of frescoes and **Glagolitic writing** from the region of Istria and the Kvarner islands. **Kaštel** (❻ on the plan) is a 16th century building that was renovated in 1721. Today there is an archaeological collection in it. The **White Villa** (number ❸ on the plan) was the residence of Tito; in it, on July 19, 1956, the Brijuni Declaration was signed, the founding document of the Non-Aligned Movement.

Apart from the collections, there are several valuable sculptures in the open air. In the old Roman quarry is Engelhardt's memorial stone to Robert Koch. On a well near the collection is a sculpture called *Woman of the Coast* by Fran Kršinić (1897 - 1981).

•••••••••••

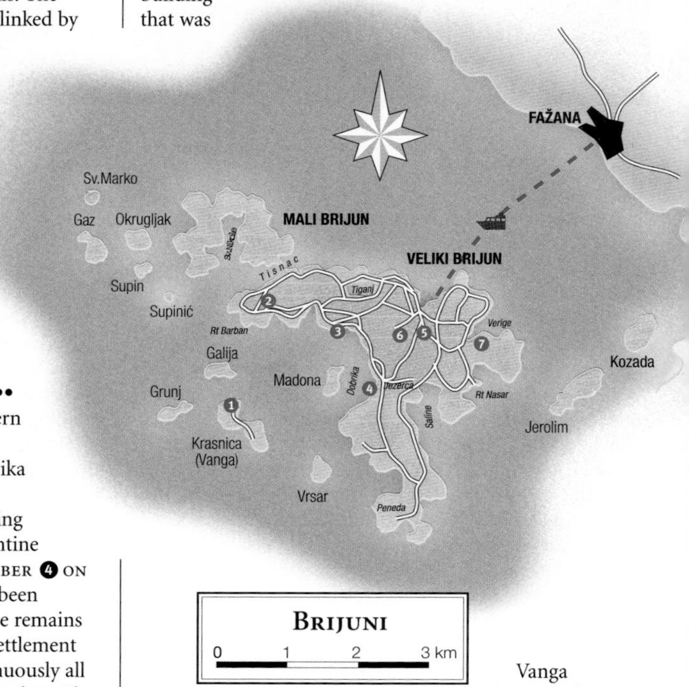

Vanga (Krasnica) (number ❶ on the plan) is closed to the public.

•••••••••••

The Flora and Fauna of Brijuni.

The Brijuni are distinguished by their luxuriant vegetation, and

safari park (NUMBER ❷ ON THE PLAN). The sea fauna is also quite abundant. As well as an abundance of fish, crustaceans and molluscs, sponges will also grow in this clear and protected sea. Here the biggest Adriatic molluscs grow, pen shells, reaching up to 70 cm in length, in the soft interiors of which pearls can occasionally be found. ■

Remains of a Roman villa rustica

the parks are first rate works of the art of horticulture. On Veli Brijun there are about 600 indigenous plant species, most of them of a Mediterranean kind. Here cedars, bamboos, and the pyramidal yew have become acclimatised, while on Vanga the dwarf spruce grows. There is also much exotic vegetation that Tito received from foreign statesmen. Particularly worthwhile are the forests of holm oak and laurel which are very characteristic of the region. The most valuable part of the island from the point of view of vegetation stretches from the Villa Brijunka in the south, and the most lovely forest is found east of the White Villa. The fauna is less well researched. There are ideal conditions for birds to winter here, and there are colonies of the white wagtail, the robin, the great tit and the jackdaw. Birds of prey also come to the island, including buzzards, hawks, sparrow hawks, and ravens. The stocking of the islands with animal species has gone on since the end of the 19th century, and has been particularly vigorous in the last three decades. There are numerous herds of fallow deer and moufflons, both moving at will with the zebras, ostriches, llamas and giraffes in the

Tegetthof Fortress on the Vela Straža hill

Remains of the Basilica of St. Mary

Labin

42 KM FROM PULA, 60 KM FROM RIJEKA, POPULATION 7 904

Labin stands on a hill which rises over a limestone plain, at 320 m above sea level. The land falls rapidly towards the sea, in the direction of Rabac stream and the tourist complex of the same name, which is 5 km from Labin. Labin nowadays consists of two separate settlements: the old medieval city on the hill, which is Labin in the strict sense, and a new settlement which has developed at the foot of the hill and is known as Polabin. On the site of present day Labin there was a prehistoric walled settlement, and during the Roman era a town called Albona. Several architectural and epigraphic fragments dating from the Roman era have been discovered in the town. With Buzet, Labin is one of the earliest Croatian towns in Istria. It was owned by the Patriarchs of Aquileia until 1420 when it was taken over by Venice. At that time the population began to separate into two class groups, the Patricians and the Commoners. It shares the history of other towns in Venetian Istria. When Venice fell, it came under Austria until 1918 when it was taken over by Italy. The Italians ruthlessly oppressed the local population, especially the workers in the local coal mine. On 2nd March 1921 the Labin mineworkers occupied the mine, organised a watch and took authority into their own hands to support their demands for better working conditions, and by way of response to the provocations of the Italian authorities and the ever stronger influence of Fascism in Istria. This was the era of the Labin Republic, which lasted until 8th of April 1921, when the rule of the workers was broken by the police and the army.

Labin and Rabac (left)

Sights

Labin is the best preserved example of an acropolis style settlement in Istria. In the Middle Ages only the peak of the hill was surrounded by walls, the part now known as Gorica, where the present parish church stands. Once they had occupied the town, the Venetians fortified it with new walls in 1587, and thus the second town quarter Dolica came into being. The same year the town gates of **St. Flora*** (Sv. Flor) were built, in the style of the Renaissance. Outside the town walls, on Črčak Square, is the town loggia dating from 1662, which was restored first in 1777 and subsequently more recently. Inside the loggia there is a **collection of stone monuments****. The town is irregularly shaped, with streets leading up a large number of steps to the top of the hill. Architecturally outstanding are: the **Praetorian's Palace*** (Pretorska palača) with its Renaissance double windows; patrician palaces of the Renaissance type, with their spacious inner courtyards, such as the Scampicchio Palace from the 16th century; and Baroque palaces with their strongly emphasised symmetrical facades such as the Franković-Vlačić, Manzin and Negri palaces (17 c.) and the Battiala-

Parish Church of the Nativity of the Madonna

Lazzarini palace (18 c.). This last today houses the Folk Museum. The **Parish Church of the Nativity of the Madonna** (Porođenje Blažene Djevice Marije) was built in 1420 in Gothic style. It has a large Gothic rose window on its facade. Inside are several 17th century paintings by Venetian artists, which is also the case in other churches in Labin.

••••••••••••

The **Folk Museum**** (Narodni muzej) is located in the Battiala-Lazzarini palace. The archaeological collection consists of stone monuments from the 1st and 2nd centuries. The stelae show the merging of Illyrian and Roman traditions; local Illyrian cults are heavily emphasised on the stelae and altars. There are several collections. The mining collection shows a working pit, there is a small ethnographic collection relating to the Labin area, a memorial collection of the advanced Istrian education expert Giusepina Martinuzzi (1844-1924), and a library formed from bequests by Giusepina Martinuzzi and Herman Stemberger.

••••••••••••

The **Matija Vlačić Illyrian Memorial Exhibition**** (Memorijalne zbirke Matije Vlačića Ilirika) founded in 1975, is located in the house where this Istrian Protestant writer was born (1520-1575). He was professor of theology at many European universities, one of Luther's most important collaborators, a great philosopher and historian, and a fighter for the ideological purity of the Protestant movement. Vlačić was the founder of an irreconcilable stream within

Interior of the Parish Church

the German Protestant movement (Flacionism) which fought against concessions being made with Rome, the Emperor

Plomin Bay

and the princes in Germany.

••••••••••••

Not far from Labin, on the road to Plomin, is the **Dubrova sculpture park***. The works on exhibition were created at the Mediterranean Sculpture Symposium which is held every year in August. Many sculptors have carved their works here, mainly in Istrian stone, and left their works to the sculpture park.

Excursions

Barban**

14 KM TO THE SOUTH OF LABIN; POPULATION 250

A fortified town in the Middle Ages, was part of the Pazin County and the Croatian commune. Austria lost Barban in 1474 when it came under Venice, which sold it in 1535 as an inheritable estate to the Venetian Loredan family. The town has preserved its medieval defence system: the town, or rather the town square, is reached through the **Vela Vrata*** (the Great Gate) which was built in 1718. The square extends into the main street, with rows of terraced houses on either side. The town loggia was built in 1555, and formed part of this terrace. Its upper storey used to serve as a grain store (fondacco). It has a tower with a clock on its front wall. By the town square stands the large single-naved Parish **Church of St. Nicholas**** (Sveti Nikola) one wall of which forms part of the defensive wall, and the bell tower was built on the foundations of a medieval defensive tower. The church has a straight ceiling with raised choir stalls and was built in 1700. It has five marble Baroque altars; the paintings are the work of Venetian artists of

Plomin in early spring

the 16th, 17th and 18th centuries. The painting over the central altar has been attributed to a Paduan (Alessandro Varotari 1588-1648). The church also houses a late Gothic 15th century custodia, Baroque wooden decorative elements from the 18th century, silver chalices, candlesticks and icon lamps from the 16th, 17th and 18th centuries. In the eastern part of the castle stands **Loredan Palace*** dating from 1606, whose covered portico on the first floor opens onto the enclosed inner courtyard. The **fraternity Church of St. Anthony**** (Sveti Antun) **the Abbot**, a parallelogram shaped building, is an outstanding example of popular Gothic architecture. It was built in front of the Vela Vrata and has some excellent frescoes from the beginning of the 15th century, which used to cover the walls, and lancet vaulting. They show the influence of the Italian school of the 15th century. Inside the church there are also several Glagolitic graffiti, the oldest dating from 1420. In **St. Jacob's Church**** (Sveti Jakov) there are Gothic frescoes from the middle of the 15th century in the northern "soft" style. The Istrian scholar from the turn of the 18th and 19th centuries, Petar Stanković, who was born in Barban, had a house built there in Classical style, using fragments from older buildings. Every third Sunday in August, there is an exhibition of tilting at the ring in Barban; this old chivalric sport, renewed in 1976, is similar to, but older than, the Sinj Alka. Men galloping on horseback seek to take a ring suspended above the track on the tip of their spear.

Plomin**

11.5 KM NORTH OF LABIN

This village is situated over Plomin bay, on a cliff which falls steeply (180 m) to the sea. The settlement was built over Plominska Draga which cuts deeply inland and, having been flooded, became Plomin bay. From the lookout point over Mašnjak point there is a beautiful view of the bay with its steep

Crurch of St. George in Plomin

cliffs and crystal clear water. There is also a magnificent view to the east, towards Cres. The village grew up on the site of the Illyrian settlement Flanon, which was mentioned by Ptolemy. It had the same name in Roman times. In the Middle Ages it was the property of the Patriarchs of Aquileia, and in 1420 was taken over by Venice. The walls dating from the 13th to the 14th centuries have been partially preserved, as has the fortification system from the 16th to the 17th centuries. On the south wall of the Romanesque **Church of St. George the Elder**** (Sveti Juraj Stari) there is a Glagolitic inscription from the 11th - 12th centuries, which is one of the oldest examples of Croatian Glagolitic. The Parish **Church of St. George**** (Sv. Juraj) from 1474 has a wooden Renaissance altar and carved choir stalls.

On the way from Labin to Plomin (7 km from Vozilić) on the edge of the now dry Lake Čepić is Čepić village, in whose graveyard stands the early medieval **Church of St. Justus** (Sveti Just) (Croatian monuments call it Žust). It is a rectangular building. On the outer walls there are corner lesenes and, beneath the opening for the bells, the wall is built in the herring bone pattern (opus spicatum). The church has a large supporting arch over the portal. On the small island which used to rise out of the lake, the Paulites built a **church and monastery**** in the 15th century dedicated to **St. Mary** (Sv. Marija). Once the monastery was dissolved the buildings were converted for farm use. The rustic Baroque altar and pews from the old church were moved to the new church, which was built in 1882. ■

64—127

Kvarner

Rijeka

Islands

Rijeka

RIJEKA IS SITUATED 45° 20′ N, 14° 26′ E. IT IS THE COUNTY TOWN OF THE COASTAL AND MOUNTAIN (PRIMORSKO-GORANSKA) COUNTY, WHICH HAS AN AREA OF 3 578 KM² AND A POPULATION OF 315 761. THE CITY ITSELF HAS A POPULATION OF 143 800, AND IT IS THE BIGGEST PORT IN CROATIA. MEAN TEMPERATURES FOR JANUARY: AIR, 5.5 °C; SEA, 10.7 °C. MEAN TEMPERATURES FOR JULY: AIR, 23.8 °C; SEA, 23 °C.

The prehistoric period. The area where Rijeka now stands was settled by Illyrian tribes as early as the Iron Age. It is thought that this area formed the border between two tribes: on the Trsat and Kastav hills lived the cattle-rearing Japodians, while the Liburnians settled closer to the sea. They were skilled seafarers who protected their settlement with their own fleet of galleys and sailing ships (the so-called liburne).

The Roman Era. Roman expansion on the Eastern Adriatic coast went across Istria, so that the Liburnians and the near-by Histri were conquered as early as the 2nd century BC. The defeated Liburnians became allies of the Romans against the rebellious Japodians and the more distant Dalmatians. In the writings of the geographers Claudius Ptolemy and Pliny the Elder, and also on Peutinger's chart (a copy of a Roman map), the Roman settlement at the mouth of the river Rječina was called "Tarsatica". It was a cross-roads on the main route linking Senj with Tergestum (Trieste) and still more distant Aquileia. Tarsatica was also a key base and command post in the Roman defence system. At the end of the 4th century, under threat from the barbarians, it was enclosed by defensive walls and there was an organised military border, the Liburnian limes as it was called. Even today, the visible remains of the ancient defensive walls behind the city reach a height of 2.8 m, and archaeological remains in the centre of the city (today's Korzo) bear witness that city walls were also built. At the end of the 5th and in the first half of the 6th century, the region from the Raša River in Istria to the Krka River in Dalmatia was called Liburnia Tarsaticensis, which suggests that Tarsatica was the capital of Liburnia in that period.

The Migrations of the Nations. On their

Remains of the city ramparts

arrival in this part of the Balkans, in the 7th century, the Slavs found it ruled by Byzantium. In the conflicts between Byzantium and the Avars, with whom the Slavs had come, the Croats changed sides to support the former. However, in the conflict between Byzantium and the Franks, the Slavs allied themselves to the Franks, from whom, once they had secured victory, they gained their autonomy. But even this alliance did not last long. History records that in 799 the inhabitants of Tarsatica killed the Friulian Count, Eric, the favourite of Charles the Great, in battle. Although some suppose that the Frankish king avenged himself for the death of his friend by sacking and burning the town, it was still mentioned by its Roman name in 996, when the German emperor, Otto III, granted the patriarch of Aquileia the right to the see of Tarsatica, which proves that it had by that date not lost its importance as an at least local centre. The city existed, then, with now only a Croat population, until the Germans, some hundred years later, realised their aspirations and extended their rule to the Rječina. Then Tarsatica lost the advantages it had enjoyed as a border town, and disappeared from the historical sources. It can be assumed that the population mainly migrated to the left bank, and gave their new home the name of Trsat, the Croat version of Tarsatica in which the memory of the Roman city lives on.

Under Various Rulers. We can pick up the written history of the city once again in the 13th century under its new name of Rika/Rijeka/Reka of St Vitus. That this was an important enough place on the trade routes can be concluded from the fact that in 1281the Great Council of Venice announced that "the men of Rijeka are our enemies". The excellent position and the abundance of water had an essential effect on the development of medieval Rijeka, while economic changes also had a stimulating effect. At the beginning of written sources, the city and the estate of Quarner as it was called (from Rijeka via Kastav, Veprinac, Lovran and Mošćenice to Brseč, which borders with Plomin) was held by the lords of Duino, whose heirs at the end of the 14th century were the German Wallsee family. Because of the German suzerainty, the estate was politically and administratively linked with Carniola, but this did not have much effect on the links with Croatia and the Croatian ethnic composition. Nearby Trsat had a completely different history: in 1223, the Hungarian-Croatian king, Andrija, gave it to the princes of Frankopan together with Vinodol (see below).

Under the Habsburgs. The Wallsees kept the Quarner estate until 1466,

Rijeka, engraving from the 17th cent.

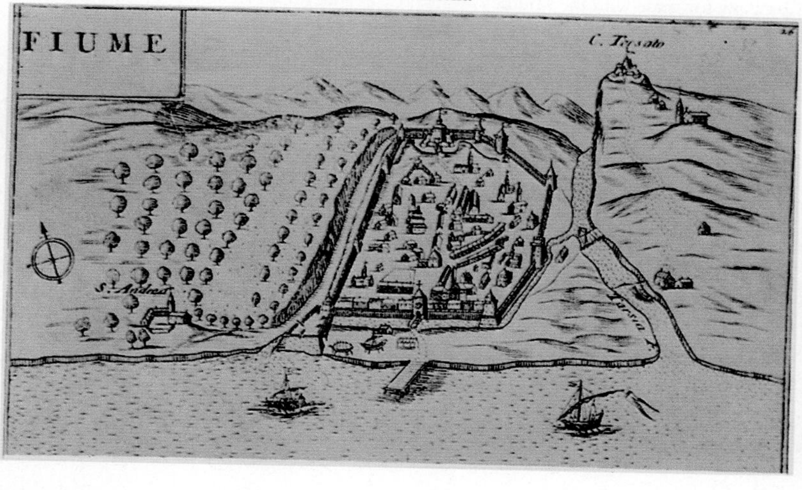

when it was taken over by the Habsburgs, who had been holding Trieste since 1382. Thus Rijeka, by purchase, a half a century before central Croatia, came under the most powerful dynasty in Europe, the Habsburgs, and from them received the status of a free city in 1530. The town's geographical location and status threatened Venice's monopoly of the Adriatic so at the same time as there were openings for independent growth, a time of conflicts with the Venetian republic also began. In the first decades of the 16th century Rijeka was a battleground of the wars with the Venetians; the greatest devastation overtook the town in 1509. For some time, Rijeka's fate was dictated by the proximity of the Turks; in the organisation of the Military Frontier, Rijeka played the role of a supply centre, but when forced to make a choice between Rijeka and Trieste for further development, the Habsburgs favoured Trieste, as the roads between Trieste and Vienna were safer. It was only when the Spanish inheritance was divided (1714) and the Habsburgs received Sardinia, Naples and the Netherlands, that their interest in the Adriatic began to grow. Thus in 1719 Rijeka became a free port and in 1721 a branch of the Eastern Trade Company for trade with the Middle and Far East was established. In 1726, a new road was built, called the Karolina, linking Rijeka and central Croatia. Foreign capital and experts from all over Europe (Dutch, Belgian, Italian, French and English) were drawn by the possibilities of profitable investments and came to Rijeka, gradually giving the city's upper classes a cosmopolitan character. Beyond the old, typically Mediterranean city centre, magnificent buildings grew up characteristic of Central European architecture. Building outside the city walls began in 1780, according to a new urban plan.

High school at Sušak, and Rijeka port, at the beginning of the century

Under the Hungarians. Following the short lived annexation to Croatia during the reign of Maria Theresa (1740-1780), in 1779 Rijeka was separated from the Severin county, and as a "corpus separatum" was ceded to Hungary. The Hungarians' interest in having an outlet to the sea was the driving force behind the city's development and towards the end of the 18th century, making use of the area in its rear, it became a huge building site. Above all, the port at the mouth of the Rječina was no longer suitable, so they began to reclaim land from the sea

Rijeka and Trsat, 1728

The shipyard in Rijeka
1854

and build a new quay for a new harbour. From 1787 onwards, along the site of the demolished south wall of the city, buildings in Baroque or classical style were built. Even today they still bound Rijeka's main street, the Korzo. The short period of French administration interrupted commercial activity so despite the fact that at that time the Lujzinska cesta (road), which even today links Rijeka with Karlovac, was completed, this was a time of stagnation for Rijeka. The entry of the Croatian army led by the Ban Jelačić in the turbulent year of 1848 broke the 20 year period of Hungarian domination, but Hungarian interests were still tied up with capital investments in Rijeka and so in 1868, on the basis of the falsification of a paragraph of the Croatian-Hungarian Compromise, it once again fell to Hungary. The intensive development of the city, which already had strong shipbuilding and chemical industries, and paper and machine factories (the first torpedo was invented and produced in Rijeka in 1866), reached a peak at the turn of the 19th and 20th centuries. At this time the most magnificent buildings were also erected: the Governor's palace, the theatre, the Jadran (Adriatic) and Modello palaces. New city quarters were also built and in 1873 Rijeka obtained a railway link with Karlovac, Zagreb and Central Europe and a year later with Ljubljana. Thus, the previously leading Croatian ports of Senj and Bakar became provincial. Croatians in Rijeka at this time had no political rights, although they had many representatives in the Croatian Assembly. Many famous people lived or started their career in Rijeka: the politicians Marijan Derenčin, Erazmo Barčić, Ante Starčević, Frano Supilo, the linguist Fran Kurelac, the writer Eugen Kumičić, the composer Ivan Zajc.

The twentieth century. The social climate enabled Frano Supilo to make the local paper Novi List into a paper that had a crucial effect on Croatian politics. Promoting a new approach to Croatian politics, the Rijeka Resolution aimed against German interests and seeking unification with Serbia was formulated here in 1905. The Croatian-Serbian coalition was formed with Frano Supilo at its head; he left it in 1909 in disappointment.

In the First World War, for joining the Allies, Italy sought territorial expansion, and was promised part of Croatia under the Treaty of London, but not including Rijeka. However, the Italian army occupied the city for 17 days after 1st December 1918, when the Hungarian Governor left. Although it seemed that the Allies would not allow this to happen so easily, the poet, dramatist and wartime lieutenant-colonel Gabriele D'Annunzio became involved, gathered his followers together, and in September 1919 entered Rijeka with 200 soldiers and 35 officers. In the general confusion, made worse by deserters and Italian sympathisers, he crowned his little adventure by proclaiming Rijeka to be Italian and his own state. In November 1920 the Yugoslav and Italian governments signed the Treaty of Rapallo on the position of frontiers, according to which Rijeka was to become an independent free state. Under pressure from the regular Italian army, D'Annunzio and his legionaries withdrew but the Italian autonomists led by Dr Riccardo Zanella, a supporter of the State of Rijeka, started to carry out their intentions in 1921, but only for a short time. On March 1922, Rijekan fascists managed to pull off a coup, and Zanella fled to Yugoslavia. Since Mussolini's fascists took power in Rome in the same year, fascist Italy annexed Rijeka (the Treaty of Rome) and fixed the border along the Rječina, or the Mrtvi Kanal (the Dead Canal). The town of Sušak, which at this time had already taken over Trsat's role as administrative centre, became Yugoslavia's port and began to develop in terms of trade and tourism. Under the Italians Rijeka began to stagnate without its natural hinterland. This era will be remembered for the ruthless policy of Italianisation. In 1941 the Italian army crossed the border at the Rječina and occupied Sušak and the hinterland as far as Ogulin, but after their surrender in 1943 both towns fell under German occupation until May 3, 1945 (Sušak until April 21, 1945). In 1947 the formal resolution was made to annexe Rijeka to the rest of Croatia, and in 1948 Sušak and Rijeka were joined into a single city. Since then, Rijeka has known powerful development as a Mediterranean port and Central European city.

City centre, to the left the Modern Gallery and the Science Library

Together with Sušak and the environs, Rijeka is today a city with more than 200,000 inhabitants, the largest port and the travel (mainly in transit) centre of a strong tourist region. Road and rail links (above all the motor-way to Zagreb, now nearing completion), shipping and air lines (the airport on the island of Krk, now linked by Krk Bridge to the mainland) make it possible for many guests to come into this country and open up Istria and the interior, now through the Učka tunnel as well, to the Kvarner islands, towards Dalmatia and the ski resorts on Platak and Snježnik. With nearby Gorski Kotar (24 km by road) and its favourable climate, Rijeka offers the rare experience of swimming in the sea and skiing in the mountains on the same day. Because of the development of Rijeka and Opatija, this, the oldest resort in Croatia, is now a suburb of Rijeka. ■

Sights

The remains of the **Liburnian Limes*** (NUMBER ⓬ ON THE PLAN). The remains of Roman fortifications built and added to from the 2nd century BC until the fourth century AD. They are an important archaeological monument and significant in the history of Europe. In the city itself the best preserved limes (perimeter wall) is on the Uspon Buonarotti (Buonarotti Rise) by the steps which lead up to the top of the hill known since the 18th century as "Kalvarija". On the more distant Katarina hill the limes is easier to follow and here it reaches its greatest height (2.8 m); from the path it takes, there is a magnificent view over the Kvarner bay, Trsat hill and on the other side, Mt. Učka and the fortress on Pulac. According to sources from the 17th century the wall was known as "The Chain of the World" (Catena mundi). The path of the Liburnian limes in Rijeka is easily visible in graphics by Trost which were published in 1689 by J.W. Valvasor and which show its continuity, which is probably why it received the title mentioned above.

Roman gate (arch)

•••••••••••

Roman Arch* (Stara vrata, gateway, NUMBER ⓫ ON THE PLAN). The oldest archaeological monument in Rijeka dates from the 4th century. The gate is

Interior of the Church of the Assumption

only decorated on the side facing the sea: the arch rests on two Tuscan pilasters without capitals, it is surrounded by a multi-layered decorative band. Since 1700 it has attracted attention and been interpreted in various ways: it is said that this gate is "a miraculous arch for it has been standing upright for 13 centuries, with no iron or mortar"; it has been linked with the victory of Emperor Claudius II over the Goths in the 70s of the 3rd century AD and with the celebration of Tiberius' victory over the Pannonians and the Illyrians, while some sources claim it was built as a triumphal arch in the 1st century. Latest opinions are divided over the question of whether this was the city gate, the gateway to the Castrum or the gate to the Praetorium, the so-called Alpine clausura, which, together with other archaeological finds, would confirm that this was the site of the original Tarsatica fortress and the starting point of the Liburnian limes.

••••••••••••

The **Cathedral of the Assumption of the Blessed Virgin Mary**** (Uzašašće Blažene Djevice Marije) and the **Leaning Tower** (Kosi toranj, NUMBER 15 ON THE PLAN). The church's present Baroque appearance dates from the 18th century, but there are signs that there was a church on this site as early as the 5th century, destroyed during the migrations of the nations. It was rebuilt and destroyed again in the year 800 when Charles the Great took his revenge on the inhabitants of Trsat for the death of Count Eric. Evidence of age can be seen in the 10th century figure of Christ on the southern wall of the church and in the bell-tower, which is known as the "leaning tower". It is 33 m high and leans over about 40 cm. It was built in Romanesque and Gothic styles. The date 1337 is engraved over the entrance to the tower. It is thought that this was the year it was restored. The present main altar and presbytery, with their rich Baroque stucco work and triumphal arch of black marble, were built in the 18th century. In the right-hand aisle is the oldest altar, which was built in 1601; on it there is a beautiful painting of St. Peter receiving the keys, the work of the Rijeka artist Ivan Franjo Gladić, from 1640. The Rijeka painter Ivan Simonetti (1817-1880) is the artist of a copy of the *Assumption of Mary* on the main altar in the central nave and *John the Baptist* in the left-hand aisle (the middle of the 19th century). On the altar of St. Phillip Neri, to whom the people of Rijeka turned as their protector from earthquakes, there is a beautiful depiction of old Rijeka by Metzinger dating from 1750.

••••••••••••

The **Church of St. Jerome**** (Sveti Jeronim) and the old **Augustinian monastery** (NUMBER 7 ON THE PLAN). The Church of St. Jerome was built by the Princes of Duino from 1315, and their descendants completed it and built the Augustinian monastery in 1408. The original Gothic church was restored after earthquakes which hit the city in the 18th century (1750 and 1768) and at that time it also gained its Baroque facade. Still visible from the outside are the Gothic windows on the presbytery, the oldest part of the church. The Gothic style is also

The Church of St. Jerome

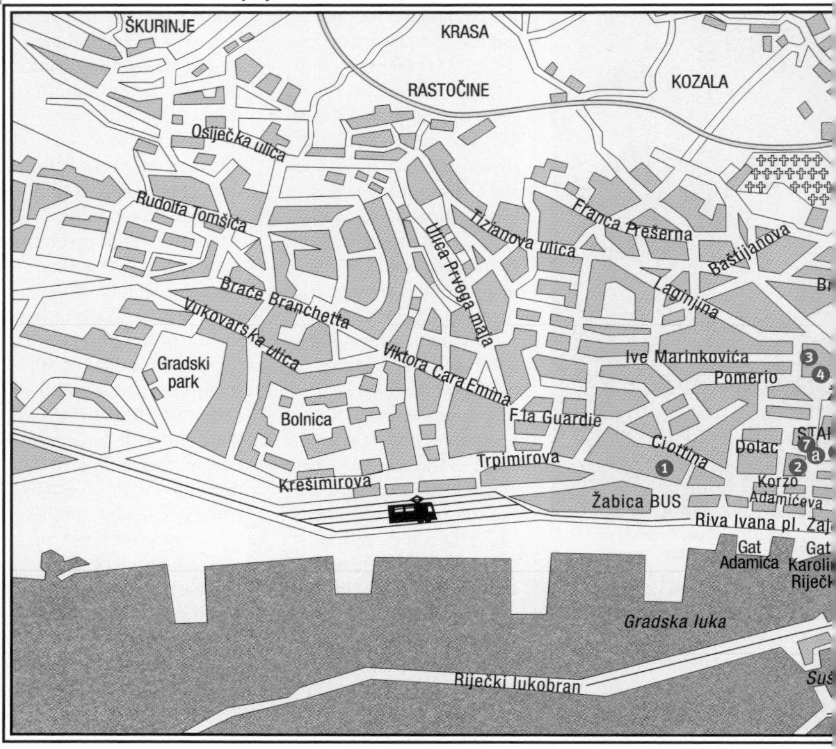

preserved in two chapels built in the 15th century. One of them serves as a sacristy today, and in the other divine service is held on occasions. The painting over the altar in it is the work of the Rijekan painter Ivan Simonetti (1850), and the remains of the original frescoes on the vaults have been partially restored, although they are still partially covered with decorations by the Senj painter Ludvig. The cloisters date from the 14th century and there are gravestones of 29 Rijekan families transferred from the church at the end of the last and the beginning of this century. The monastery was the spiritual and cultural focal point of the city. The world famous cartographer Ivan Klobučarić (1550-1605) from Dubašnica was once prior of it. The Venetians burnt the monastery down while they were sacking the city and from then on it was deserted. From 1786 it served as a hospital for a short time, and from 1833, when it was renovated in neo-classical style it was the town hall (Municipium). Today the Dominicans used part of the monastery, while in the other part are archives and the rectorate of the university.

"Handing over the keys" in the Church of the Assumption

••••••••••••

The **remains of the city walls** (NUMBER ⓰ ON THE PLAN). These walls surrounded the city until 1780 when Joseph II gave permission for the demolition of the keep and walls, as the city's development demanded their removal, and they were no longer necessary for defensive purposes. Only some ruins remain, most clearly visible near the cathedral, between the school playing fields and the raised area of the small park. While foundations

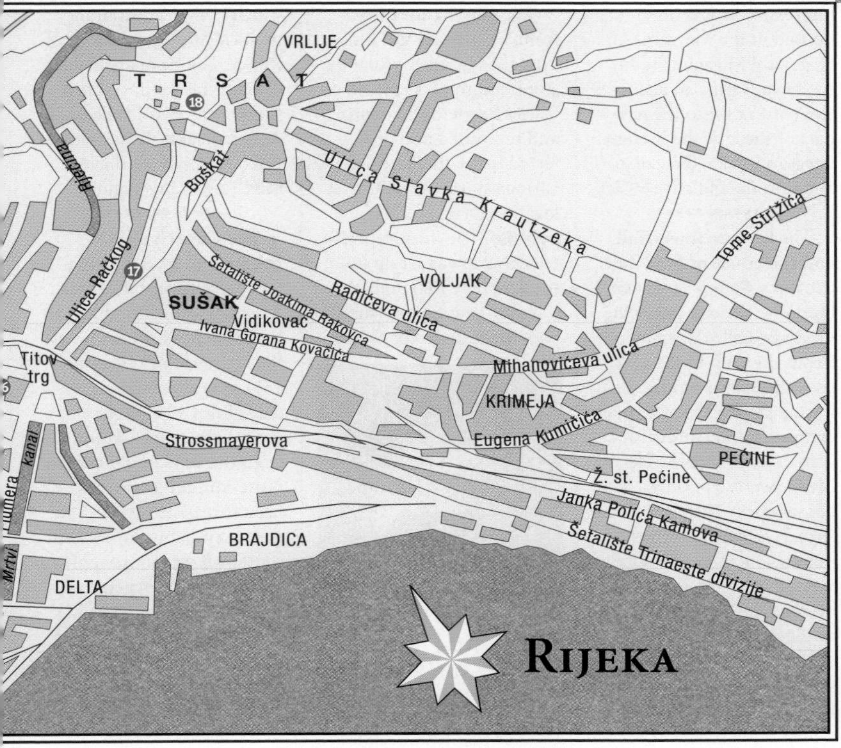

were being dug for new buildings on the Corso (Korzo) and in Ante Starčević street, some walls were discovered dating from the 4th century which show that the medieval structure was built immediately on to the ancient walls. Part of the ancient walls has been preserved in the "Dva Lava" (two lions) café.

••••••••••••

The **City Tower*** (Gradski toranj, NUMBER ❾ ON THE PLAN). The tower with four clocks is the symbol of Rijeka and was renovated in 1983. This outstanding structure, on the border between the old and the new parts of the city, received its present Baroque appearance towards the end of the 18th century. Its main decorative

City Tower

elements are: a relief of the two-headed Habsburg eagle over the entrance archway dating from the 17th century and the relief busts of Leopold I and Charles VI, emperors who gave the city its coat of arms, and the status of a free port, dating from the first half of the 18th century. The Rijeka sculptor and builder Antonio Micchelazzi surrounded them with a trapezium frame of white stone. He created other pieces of architectural work in the second half of the 18th century (after the earthquake). During the restoration work of 1890, the architect Filiberto Bazarig (Bacarić) introduced Renaissance elements to the building. The tower was part of the city's medieval fortifications and served as the entrance on the seaward side of the city. In the 16th century it was still the same height as the surrounding walls. At one time a moat ran alongside those walls, and by the gate into the tower there was a drawbridge which was removed in 1775. Its impressive lock is now housed in the Maritime and Historical Museum. Today the tower forms an attractive entrance into the new part of the city, the liveliest street in Rijeka, the Corso, and into the old city.

••••••••••••

The **former Town Hall and the house of Ivan Zajc** (NUMBER ⓫A ON THE PLAN). Opposite the city tower the old town hall still stands (from the 16th to the 19th centuries), also significant for the fact that the Croatian composer and conductor Ivan Zajc lived there. He composed the popular heroic opera *Nikola Šubić Zrinski.* This, the former house of an imperial captain, was adapted in 1532 to become the Town Hall. The original single-storey building, with a Renaissance atrium on the ground floor, was redecorated in the Baroque style and extended by one floor in 1740. In the second half of the 18th century, as the city developed, it took on new functions and became too small. In the third decade of the 19th century the town hall was moved to the building of the former Augustinian monastery, and this house passed into private ownership. So Ivan Zajc came to spend his childhood here. On the square, formerly a market place and the centre of the city, which has been recently revitalised, a fountain was built on the occasion of the 150th anniversary of the paper factory (1821). The architect Igor Emili made use of elements of the old factory mill in this many faceted monument.

••••••••••••

The **City Banner Column*** (NUMBER ❼A ON THE PLAN). This circular stone column was placed on Rijeka Revolution Square, and renovated and protected in 1970. There are various stories as to its first location, origins and purpose. The most probable tells how it was set up by the Emperor Maximilian as a sign of gratitude to the people of Rijeka for their loyalty in the war against the Venetians in 1508. Apart from this date, the Rijeka coat of arms is also engraved in high relief, along with St. Vitus (Sveti Vid) the patron saint of the city, with a model of the city in his hand and the text of the Emperor's guarantee which is significant in the political and legal history of Rijeka. The circular shield, which is now empty, once showed the two-headed Austrian eagle. It was removed by the French during their rule in this region.

St. Vitus, patron saint of Rijeka, detail on the pole of the city flag

••••••••••••

The **Church of St. Fabian and St. Sebastian** (NUMBER ⓳ON THE PLAN). A small Gothic building with two bells, which bears the engraved inscription 1562 over the entrance. It dates from 1291, however, according to the account from the time of a diocesan visitation. It has twice been threatened with destruction, but in the 19th century it was thoroughly repaired at the expense of Rijeka fishermen who considered it to be a votive church. Between 1970 and 1975 it was preserved as a cultural monument.

••••••••••••

The **Church of St. Vitus**** (Sveti Vid, NUMBER ❽ON THE PLAN). The present church, a magnificent octagonal structure, in the typical Jesuit Baroque style, was built in the first half of the 17th century on the site of the old church or chapel of St. Vitus, the city's patron saint, which had existed from the 9th century. Towards the end of 1627,

St. Vitus' Church

Miraculous crucifix in the Cathedral

the Jesuits came to Rijeka and this very old church was given to them for their use. With financial contributions from Baroness Ursula Tannhausen, they very soon began to build a new church, using the basilica Santa Maria della Salute in Venice as their model. The building works lasted for more than 100 years; however, part of the main altar was finished in 1659, and the building was consecrated on May 6, 1742. Nowadays, it is a metropolitan church, not complete, work that was supposed to start in 1912 being prevented by the war. The facade is incomplete and two bell towers are missing. The altar *The Mourning Madonna* is the work of Venetian artists: the columns are by Leonardo Picassi and the statue is by Augusto Benvenuti. This altar belongs to one of the oldest fraternities in the world. Antun Michelazzi of Grado created the altar of St. Joseph and the pulpit out of African marble. The statues of St. Barbara and Catherine are from the old church. There is also a copy of Titian's painting of *The Assumption* by the Rijekan artist Ivan Simonetti. At the beginning of the 18th century Pasquale Lazzarini from Gorica made a new marble altar on which stands a miraculous crucifix brought from the ruined Chapel of St. Rocco (Sveti Rok). Beside it there is a large stone. A story from 1296 tells of one Petar Lončarić who, dissatisfied with his luck at cards, cursed the crucifix and threw a stone at it. The earth opened up beneath him and swallowed him up, and the crucifix started to bleed. Since then it has been considered miraculous.

It was recorded that in 1296 a certain Petar Lončarić, dissatisfied with his bad luck at cards, cursed the crucifix and threw a stone at it. The earth opened up and swallowed him, and the crucifix began to bleed, since when it has been held to be miraculous. The stone is still standing at the left hand side of the crucifix with an inscription in Latin saying "With this stone the crucifix was struck in 1296". The new stained glass, from designs by the artists Kokot, Šiško, Bužanović and Milić, was made in the Žaja workshop in Zagreb. Since 1995 a collection of the Jesuit heritage in Rijeka has been displayed in the church´s gallery.

In 1993 on the 360th anniversary of higher education, Rijeka University put a plaque on the arch that goes over the pavement by the church recalling this part of the Jesuits´ work. "In this place alongside the northern gate was the Jesuit College in which a high school was established, the study of theology begun, and philosophy taught from 1725. King and Emperor Ferdinand II issued a charter on July 31, 1633 making the rights and privileges of people who had been to this school equivalent to those of the students of European universities." Since Croatia has been independent, the ceremonies relating to St. Vitus have been reestablished; they are held every year from June 12 to June 15, and are accompanied by entertainments and religious and artistic events.

The **Church of St. Nicholas** (Sveti Nikola, NUMBER ⑩ ON THE PLAN). This church was built on

St. Nicholas' Church (Orthodox)

the model of the Orthodox church in Karlovac which was finished in 1790. It is a fine example of Baroque Neo-Classicism by the Rijeka architects Ignatius Henck and Giuseppe Capovillo. The valuable icons were bought in Vojvodina. Serbs living in Rijeka traded with this area. Particularly outstanding is the painting of the *Coronation of the Madonna* by Janko Halkozović and the drawing of *St. Sava and St. Simeon* (Sveti Sava i Sveti Simeon) by Zakarije Orfelin.

••••••••••••

The **Market** (NUMBER ⓭ ON THE PLAN). The covered market halls were built in the second half of the 19th century, when similar buildings were also built in other great European cities (Trieste, Graz and Vienna). Two halls were completed in 1881 using metal and glass constructions designed by the architect Izidor Vauchning. At that time this was a novelty, and they still serve their purpose today. The third hall in the series (the fish market) was built on the site of an old building which served the same purpose. Because of the war, building work

City market place

continued until 1918. The Rijeka architect Carlo Pergoli combined Viennese Secession and Neo-Romanesque styles in this beautiful building. The Venetian sculptor Urbano Bottasso was also involved in its design. On a base of red brick he created decorations in grey Istrian stone, continuing the pattern on the inside of the building.

••••••••••••

The **Ivan Zajc National Theatre** (Hrvatsko narodno kazalište "Ivan pl. Zajc", NUMBER ⓮ ON THE PLAN) was built on land reclaimed from the sea in 1885 and designed by the Viennese architects Fellner and Helmer (who came together in 1873 and specialised in theatre design). They designed 53 European theatres. It was completely renovated in 1981 and is now once again the home of 4 companies: the Croatian drama, Italian drama, Opera and Ballet. The facade of the building is in Neo-Renaissance style with decorated pediment following Palladio's model, and this sets the pattern for the entire outer wall. The groups of figures of the cornice of the facade by the Venetian sculptor Augusto Benvenuti are considered to be his most important work. They represent Drama and Music. Over the pediments, angels hold the coat of arms of Rijeka. Artists belonging to the Viennese sculptors' society, Kauffungen and Fritsch, created the figurative reliefs on the tympanum (Apollo with nymphs) and the remaining ornamental work. The interior of the theatre is in Neo-Baroque style, with three rows of boxes, a balcony, and a beautiful Rococo ceiling. The allegorical paintings of operetta, dance, love, concert and religious and military music are the work of Franz Matsch and the brothers Gustav and Ernst Klimt. The exquisite lamps were, when the theatre was opened, the first electric lights in Rijeka. All this is a sign of the city's ambition that the theatre should demonstrate its culture and wealth. Rijeka actually had its first theatre in 1765: the prominent merchant Ljudevit Adamić opened a new theatre in 1805 and this stood on the site of the present Modello Palace until 1883, when it was demolished. Stones from Adamić's theatre were used in the foundations of the present theatre.

Modello Palace

The tradition of carefully selected guest appearances, mainly operatic, was conti-

The Ivan Zajc Theatre

nued in the new building of the Commune Theatre (the Verdi Theatre from 1913), which still did not have its own ensemble: the opening with Medea Borelli in the role of Aida, the presence of Puccini at a performance of *Manon Lescaut* (1895), a guest performance by Enrico Caruso, who is considered to have started his brilliant career in the Rijeka theatre (1898), Mascagni's conducting, the appearance of Gigli in *Aida* (1941)... Of the leading Italian dramatic troupes that continued to appear here, the appearances by the Rijekan actress Irma Gramatica (1897 and 1898) were particularly noted, and the greatest attraction must have been the performance of the French Sarah Bernhardt ensemble in 1899. Croatian artists did not have access to the theatre, nor to Adamić's theatre, and no other Croatian name than that of Ivan Zajc, the composer and conductor, who succeeded his father and worked here from 1855 to 1862 is recorded. Nevertheless, Croatian cultural societies, of which the National Reading Room in Rijeka is the most important, organised almost continuous guest appearances by Croatian artists, among whom the most important were Andrija Fijan, Marija Ružička-Strozzi, Ljerka Šram, Nina Vavra, Milica Mihičić, Mila Dimitrijević, Dragutin Freudenreich and Ivo Raić. Even so, Croatian was not spoken on the stage of this theatre until 10th May 1945 and in 1946 the first regular season began, and the National Theatre Ensemble was founded. Since 1953 it has been called the Ivan Zajc Theatre after the famous Croatian composer Ivan Zajc, the "Croatian Verdi", a native of Rijeka. Since 1990, the adjective "Croatian" being added to it, the theatre in Rijeka has been counted as the fourth national theatre, alongside those in Zagreb, Osijek and Split. In 1982 a statue was placed in the park in front of the theatre in his memory.

Ivan Edler Zajc

The **Palace of Justice** (NUMBER 6 ON THE PLAN).

This palace was built in Secession style at the beginning of the 20th century on the site of the old Captain's Castle. In it the Hungarian architect F. Stigler together with Rijeka engineer G. Grassi succeeded in creating a magnificent and architecturally harmonious building which is also functional. The palace is entered up a central double staircase, leading to a monumental portal decorated on both sides with an allegorical relief of a female head with its eyes blindfolded. This great Secession building also houses the prison and dominates the architecture of the old city.

The **Capuchin Church*** (NUMBER 1 ON THE PLAN).

Capuchin Church

On the 50th anniversary of the miracle at Lourdes, building work began on this monumental Gothic church. From 1904 to 1908 the crypt was built and dedicated to Mary the Comforter of Souls in Purgatory, and the upper church was opened for services in 1923. In front of the church there is a broad level area with two stairways in the shape of the letter "V". The church was designed by C. Budinis and is characterised on the outside by rich Venetian elements, and on the inside by monolithic granite pillars.

••••••••••••

Trsat** (NUMBER ⑱ ON THE PLAN). Trsat is a steep hill, 138 m high, rising over the gorge of the Rječina

Cellar of the Trsat fortress (exhibition space)

river, about a kilometre away from the sea. It was strategically significant from the earliest times right up to the 17th century. In the time before the Illyrians there was a fortified settlement, and then the Illyrian (Japodian) fortress Tarsatica. Following this there was a Roman look-out point and from the 13th century it was the property of the Counts of Krk. Later it belonged to the Frankopans. Together with Vinodol, the Croatian-Hungarian King Andrija II presented Trsat to Vid II of Krk. Towards the end of the 15th century the Habsburgs ruled Trsat and, even though it belonged to Croatia and the Frankopans, would not give it up because of its excellent position for the protection of Rijeka. The inhabitants of Trsat and Rijeka waged their fiercest battles with the Venetians in 1508, while in 1527 the Turks made inroads into the city for a short time. In the 16th century, Trsat was more often in Habsburg than Frankopan hands, and was mainly ruled by the Captains of Rijeka or Senj or leaseholds. After the execution of Fran Krsto Frankopan in 1671 following the Zrinski and Frankopan conspiracy, the Habsburgs took Trsat over completely. It was attached for a short time to the state of Severin, and in 1778 Maria Theresa placed it under the municipality of Bakar, where it remained, with a short break during the Napoleonic wars, until 1874 when the community of Trsat was founded.

Trsat was an extremely patriotic Croatian town, and, together with Sušak, demonstrated its attachment to its mother country at every opportunity, and its independence from Rijeka, which was part of Hungary.

Trsat, above the canyon of the Rječina

The centre of political and cultural life in Trsat was the Croatian Reading Room, founded in 1877, with many cultural, educational and sports societies. Many memorial inscriptions and monuments bear witness to the resistance by the people of Trsat and Sušak to Italian and German occupation, a mortuary made according to plans by the architect Zdenko Sila and Zdenko Kolacio being outstanding.

••••••••••••

Trsat Castle*** (NUMBER ⑱ ON THE PLAN), stands on the site of an old Roman fortress and was built in the first half of the 13th century by the Frankopan Counts of Krk. From the beginning of the 15th century it had a succession of lords, but was most often owned by the Habsburgs. In 1528 the Senj Captain Gašpar Raab bought the castle and adapted and greatly strengthened it. Once the danger from the Turks had passed at the end of the 17th century, and firearms had come into use, Trsat fortress was less important and was left allowed to fall into ruins, a process which was completed by an earthquake in 1750. Count Laval Nugent, Marshal and military commander of the Austrian coastal area, bought the ruins off the city, for an annual payment of one forint. He engaged the Venetian builder Paronuzzio and repaired the towers, decorated the interior and even built himself a mausoleum in the style of a Doric temple with four marble pillars supporting the facade. After his death his

Mausoleum of Laval Nugent

impoverished descendants deserted the castle and it once again fell into ruin until 1960. Since then it has been restored and enriched by the presence of art exhibitions, summer concerts and theatrical performances. Thus, this cultural and historic monument and look-out point with its views over Učka, the Bay of Kvarner and the islands of Cres and Krk, as far as the Velebit mountains, has become one of the most interesting tourist attractions in Rijeka. Below the Castle lies the Parish Church of St. George (sv. Juraj), built in the 13th century.

•••••••••••

The **Shrine of Our Lady of Trsat**** (Gospa Trsatska). This church on the flat area at the top of Trsat hill is the subject of a legend dating from the 13th century. In 1291 Mary's house in Nazareth is said to have appeared here, then mysteriously disappeared later, to be discovered in Italy, in Loreto, where it still stands today as a shrine. Historian Vjekoslav Klaić wrote that the Franciscan monastery, together with the pilgrimage shrine of the Church of the B.V.M. at Trsat was the "most worthy foundation" of the princes of Frankopan. Tradition ascribes the building of the first church here to Count Nikola I (1307-1343) in 1291; it was extended and added to by his descendants. At the request of the princes Ivan and Stjepan, Pope Urban V gave pilgrims to Loreto from the Croatian coastal area a miraculous painting of the Madonna in 1367; this triptych, the work of an unknown artist, is attributed by tradition to St. Luke the Evangelist, and is today on the main altar. In 1453 Martin Frankopan added on a nave, and built a monastery alongside the church, occupied since 1468 by the Franciscans who are the guardians of the cult, which attracts many of the faithful. A new artistic contribution to the church was made by Vladimir Kirin (1894-1963), with five pictures on the greenish marble slabs with which the shrine is lined, and another by Ivo Režek (1898-1979) who portrayed the 14 stations of the cross in fresco technique. One of the guardians of the Trsat monastery was the outstanding Glagolitic expert and writer of books in Croatian, Latin and Italian, Franjo Glavinić (1585-1652).

Votive Church of Our Lady of Trsat

•••••••••••

Entrance porch to the Trsat steps

The **Trsat stairway*** (Trsatske stube, NUMBER ⓱ ON THE PLAN) begins on the banks of the Rječina, beside a bank building, and leads up to the plateau at 138 m above sea level. There are 561 steps in all and they were built for pilgrims on their way to the votive church. Work was started on them in 1531 by Petar Kružić, hero of battles against the Turks. The Baroque entrance hall in the form of a triumphal arch was built in the first half of the 18th century, and the votive chapels on level ground near the church by the steps, between the 15th and the 18th centuries, one chapel each century.

MUSEUMS AND COLLECTIONS

The **Maritime and Historical Museum of the Croatian Coast**** (Pomorski i povijesni muzej Hrvatskog primorja, Ulica žrtava fašizma 18; NUMBER ❹ ON THE PLAN). This museum is housed in the former

Maritime and Historical Museum (part of the exhibition)

Governor's palace, which was completed in 1896 according to the plans of a leading Hungarian architect, Alajoš Hausmann. The museum houses objects from the cultural and political history of Rijeka and the Croatian coast (Hrvatsko primorje), with the emphasis on seafaring. There are old weapons and furniture, jewellery from the 10th century found in the area around Vinodol and Crikvenica, national costumes and ethnographic finds. There are many pictures and old engravings bearing on the history of Rijeka, especially its maritime history. There is also a large collection of model sailing

Permanent Glagolitic exhibition in the Science Library

ships and a rich collection of stone monuments.

••••••••••••

The **Natural History Museum**** (Šetalište Vladimira Nazora, NUMBER ❺ ON THE PLAN). The permanent collection includes examples of marine and land life in the Rijeka area, medicinal herbs, and geological and palaeontological finds. There is a particularly interesting collection of snails and shellfish from the oceans of the world.

••••••••••••

The **Modern Gallery**** (Moderna galerija, NUMBER ❷ ON THE PLAN). From the Rijekan Salon, as it was called, two art exhibitions developed; now they alternate every summer, from June 15 to September 15, enjoying an international reputation. In even years the International Biennial of Drawings is held, and in odd years the Youth Biennial. The gallery also

Exhibits in the Modern Gallery

has a stock of its own, and organises exhibitions all the year round. In the building of the Modern Gallery, and part of the University Library, is the permanent exhibition of Glagolitic* (number 2). This exhibition includes the first Glagolitic inscriptions, for instance, a cast of the tablet of Baška (1100) which was found in the Church of St. Lucy (Sveta Lucija) in Jurandvor on the island of Krk. In glass cases there are handwritten missals and breviaries from the time when the artistry of Croatian writers, miniaturists and illuminators was at its height (14th and 15th centuries), inscriptions on frescoes and examples of the first printed books in Croatia, including a missal from 1483, printed just 30 years after printing was invented. The first books printed in Rijeka are also on display, these date from 1530 and 1531, the time when Bishop Šimun Kožičić founded the first Glagolitic press there.

••••••••••••

The **Rijeka Carnival.** Rijeka and its surroundings have been famed since the Middle Ages for their carnival celebrations. The tradition has never been abandoned, but has at times been forced out of the city into the environs (Opatija, Kastav, Crikvenica) to form a tourist attraction (the so-called Summer Carnival) or shifted into the closed quarters of hotel ball-rooms. But in the last few years carnivals have been increasingly held in the streets and squares, particularly in the Corso. The biggest fiesta is organised for the last Sunday before Lent; this is

Carnival procession

an international carnival parade, with a procession of maskers and carnivalesque customs from the Croatian coast, from inland Croatia, and abroad as well. The International Rijeka Carnival is becoming the biggest in Europe, with several thousand masks, seen by a hundred thousand spectators.

••••••••••••

Wine in Rijeka is mainly related to the firm Istravino export of Rijeka. This is a firm that has an old tradition in the making of specialised wines such as **Prošek Istra** (a dessert wine produced by a special process from over-ripe grapes of the finest varieties of Istrian grapes), **Istra Vermouth** (aromatised wine) and **Bakarska vodica** (a semi-dry sparkling wine that for a long time was the synonym for sparkling wine in the whole of the country). Leading IVEX wines are those from coastal Croatia: **Vrbnička Žlahtina** (a quality appellation controlée dry white wine from the island of Krk), **Pazinska Malvazija** and **Motovunski Teran** (quality appelation contrôlée wines from the wine regions of central Istria) and **Plavac Ston**, a typical southern style red wine, with appelation contrôlée, from the Pelješac peninsula.

••••••••••••

Excursions

Bakar*

14 KM SOUTHEAST OF RIJEKA, POPULATION 1 566.

There is no evidence of settlement in Bakar in pre-Roman times, but the favourable position of the bay where the most protected parts of the village are situated suggest the possibility. One theory is that this was the northerly entrepot centre in the expanding amber trade in about 2,000 BC; another is that Phoenicians sailed into this bay in the third century BC. The original names Bolcera, Volcera and Velcaera derive from the old Celtic Vel-kier which means "stone bay". Roman graves from the 1st and 2nd centuries AD indicate that the Romans ruled here at the beginning of Christian era. In the first half of the 7th century the Croats settled in the region between Vinodol and Bakar with the permission of the Byzantine emperor, Heraclius. There is no evidence of any conflict, thus it is thought that the numerical superiority of the Slavs led to the gradual assimilation of the Liburnians, the Romans and the Celts.

From the middle of the 9th century the Croatian coast was part of the administrative district of Krbava which means that Bakar was part of the Croatian state from the time of the Croatian Prince Trpimir. But in those turbulent times, territory passed from Byzantine rule to the Avars, the Franks and the Croatians in turn. The two most powerful Croatian noble families ruled Bakar: from 1223 to 1544, the Frankopans; until 1670 the Zrinskis. Despite the fact that there was little peace during that whole period the town developed and prospered. Enemies frequently skirted it or attacked it without success. The most difficult time for the people of Bakar was in the 16th and the beginning of the 17th century when the Uskoks defended it from the Turks, but became the cause of bloody sieges by the Venetians. However the trade which had begun so well in the 15th century never really died out and in the 17th century it developed so successfully that Bakar began to threaten Rijeka. The rivalry between the two towns led to real trade wars which went on until the fall of the Zrinskis and the Frankopans in 1671, when Austria snatched Bakar for itself. As part of the so-called Austrian coastlands, following several decades of crisis, Bakar once again regained its position and in the middle of the 18th century it exceeded Rijeka and even Zagreb in terms of number of inhabitants (it had 7,800, Rijeka 3,000 and Zagreb 2,000). Maria Theresa gave it the status of a free port in 1778 and the following year it became a Free Royal City with the rights of a municipality. During Napoleon's rule commercial life died out, but the real decline of the town was caused by the disappearance of sailing ships and the move to steam transport and especially the railway link between the Danube valley and Rijeka which bypassed Bakar (1873). From 1882 it became part of Croatia and gradually developed as a fishing and tourist centre. Its maritime tradition was maintained by the famed Nautical Academy which was opened in 1849. The development of Bakar as a tourist town was halted by the building of a refinery in nearby Urinj, and even more so by the construction of a coking plant, which was closed in 1994, but is still hinted at by the giant conveyor and a 252 m high chimney. Today Bakar is a port for bulk cargoes (the sea is deep) and the city is looking forward to a revitalisation programme which will emphasise ecological values.

Bakar

SIGHTS

The **City Museum*** (Gradski muzej) is located in the family house of the founder, Dr Ivo Marochini, in Ulica Koguli. It is still not institutionalised, and can be visited with prior notice to the city services. The museum looks after documents which give a survey of Bakar's rich history and contains more than 400 items, a rich library and valuable archives, and is divided into various collections.

•••••••••••

The **Castle*** (Kaštel) was built in 1530 on an area of level ground in Bakar upper town, about 50 m above sea level. It began to fall into ruins following the collapse of the Croatian feudal lords Frankopan and Zrinski, but its death blow came with the earthquake in 1750. The town council met here until the end of the 18th century, and later it became a military base. Through the centuries the entrance tower and other raised parts were levelled off and covered over with a single roof. The premises are now used by the St Andrew cultural and artistic association. Not far from the castle is the Roman House, a Renaissance building which is at least 300 years old. The **Church of St. Andrew** (Sveti Andrija), the parish church and the largest church in the town was built on the site of an older, 12th century, church which was totally destroyed in an earthquake and rebuilt in the middle of the 19th century. Of the old church, only the bell tower remains, which dates from the 18th century, as well as some medallions and Baroque marble statues of St. Anne and St. Joachim. The oldest painting - the **Holy Trinity** from the 15th century - is attributed to Girolamo da Santa Croce. In the treasury of the church, a Romanesque cross, a 16th century reliquary of St. Ursula, a Baroque chalice

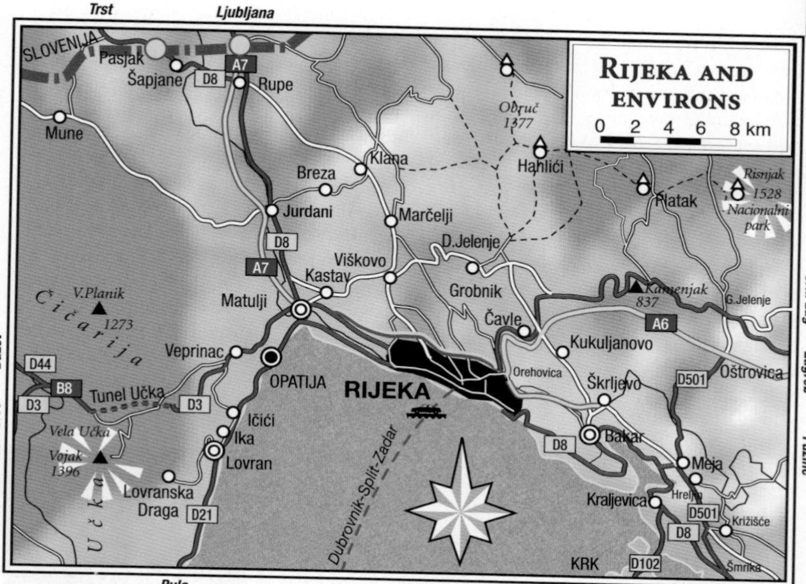

and other things are kept. There are also catacombs in the church.

•••••••••••

St. Margaret's Church (Sveta Margareta) was built in 1658 and houses beautiful paintings of St. Margaret, St. Barbara and St. Katherine by the Slovene artist Valentino Metzinger (1702-1759). The Church of the Madonna of the Port, built in the 16th century and renovated in 1753 is located in the graveyard. There are paintings by anonymous Venetian painters in the church. The **Turkish house**, located below St. Andrew's Church, has a lower wall in the shape of a regular rectangle, while the upper wall is an irregular pentagon. This unusual building dates from the 15th or the 16th century. The Town Hall, known as the Magistrat (Primorje 38) dates from 1564 and has been restored to house the local tourist office.

•••••••••••

The **vineyards of Bakar**, planted in so-called "anthropomorphic" soil, i.e. soil which man has brought from elsewhere and surrounded with dry stone walls in order to plant vines, were once the source of a local "champagne" ("Bakarska Vodica", Bakar water) made from the grape called Žlahtina. The roads and railway lines built in the first half of the 19th century destroyed the best vineyards, and because of the difficulty in maintaining them and the scarcity of labour were abandoned. In 1972 the dividing walls, from Bakar to Bakarac, were declared to be a zone of ethnographic interest and a cultural monument. Today Bakarska Vodica is made of selected wines by Istra Vino in Rijeka.

•••••••••••

Kastav**

11 KM FROM RIJEKA, 378 M ABOVE SEA LEVEL, POPULATION 2118.

Present day Kastav stands on the foundations of what was probably a fortress of the Japodian tribe. In the Mišinci valley close to the town, there is a prehistoric necropolis with urns and Hallstatt jewellery. In the Middle Ages Kastav was the centre of a feudal estate which, besides Kastav, also included Mošćenice and Veprinac. From that time Kastav developed from a rural settlement into a town with municipal status. It received its charters at the beginning of the 16th century. They were written in

Ruins of St. Mary's Church

Croatian, in Glagolitic. In 1866 the first public Croatian reading room was founded in Kastav. The medieval Istrian artists Vincent and Ivan of Kastav (15th century) were born in the town as well as a member of the Istrian Revival movement, Dr. Matko Laginja, the "father of Istria". There was a Teacher Training School in Kastav where the Croatian poet Vladimir Nazor worked as a lecturer.

Sights

Present day Kastav has retained the features of a medieval town: it is situated on a hilltop and parts of the walls with which it was at one time surrounded are still standing. The fortified **town gate** stands at the southern entrance to the town and there is a square with a bastion (Forticum) to the south of it, in front of the town. On the square there is a town loggia which was built in 1571 and restored in 1825. Opposite it stands a Baroque chapel. The town's main thoroughfare crosses through the centre of the town, from the town gates to the parish church. A network of narrow and winding streets branch off on either side. Public life at one time centred on the **Lokvine Square** (or Kapetanova lokva) in the old part of the town. In the centre of the square there is a cistern with an inscription engraved into its stone wall, which mentions that the townsfolk drowned Captain Morelli for abusing his power and taking illegal taxes. On the square there is also a 15th century Gothic church and the Captain's residence. The Baroque Parish Church of St. Helen (Sveta Jelena Križarica) was built in 1709 and the bell tower dates from 1724. The church has rich Baroque furnishings while the best view is considered to be obtained from in front of the church. The famous Dragutin Hirc in his book called *The Croatian Coast*, wrote: "That's the Kastav view for you, gorgeous, indescribable, divine, because you can see the whole of the Kastav region, the whole of the coastal area, the majestic peaks, the valleys, the azure sea, and above it all the sapphire sky, and the brilliant sun that turns it all into a heaven on earth."

Kastav, a view of Opatija and Učka; Risnjak

The **Kastav Area Museum Collection** (Spinčićeva ul. 47) is located in the building of the old commune of Kastav. The museum is a branch of the Maritime and Historical Museum of the Croatian Coast in Rijeka. The exhibits present the cultural, historical and material development of the Kastav area. At the very end

The Risnjak National Park**

is an area that has been set aside in the most beautiful part of Gorski Kotar. It is 15 km from Rijeka (as the crow flies). The most recent law of 1997 expanded the area of the park, which encompasses the mountain massifs of Risnjak and Snježnik and the source region of the Kupa as well as the drainage basin of the Krašićevac brook: all told an area of 64 km². Risnjak itself is part of the Dinaric mountain range, but it also forms the border area and is a natural link between the Alps and the Balkan mountains. The highest mountain is Risnjak, 1528 m above sea level. In terms of geology it is an area of high mountainous karst. The vegetation is very diverse. Thirty different plant communities have been recorded of which the most common are beech and fir forests (Fagetum illyricum abietotosum) which go up to

Lynx, a rare carnivore of the mountains

1240 m and then are replaced by sub-alpine beeches (Fagetum croaticum subalpinum). The highest vegetation (not only on Risnjak but in all of the Croatian mountains) is a belt of mountain pine (Pinetum mughi croaticum). The fauna is also diverse, but has been less well researched. There are particularly many species of birds and mammals, including several types of chamois, while since 1974 the area has once again been inhabited by the lis (lynx). The best way of getting to know Risnjak is by making use of the hostel on the mountain itself. It is open from 1st May until 31st October and sleeps 29. It is 31 km from Rijeka by road via Gornje Jelenje (24 km) and then another 7 km on second class roads in the direction of Lazac. There is another hour and a half climb on marked mountain paths from the car park in Vilje. ■

Risnjak

The view from Risnjak

Peak	m	km	0°
Sv. Gera	1178	66	50
Sljeme	1033	125	56
Dragomalj	1154	14	88
Skradski Vrh	1043	23	93
Klek	1102	45	115
Bjelolasica	1534	32	124
Viševica	1428	24	144
Mali Rajinac	1699	76	155
Osoršćica (Lošinj)	588	87	194
Učka	1401	37	244
Planik	1273	35	257
Slovenski Snežnik	1796	22	322
Triglav	2863	121	330
Snježnik	1506	3	290
Ojstrica	2349	104	1
Kum	1219	81	26

of Kastav stand the ruins of an unfinished 18th century Jesuit church, known as the "crkvina".

Many folk customs have been preserved in Kastav and its surrounding area, particularly those relating to carnival and grave vintage. Especially popular are the **Kastavski zvončari** (youths dressed in furs and hung about with little bells) who appear during carnival time, but not only then. There is a special local festival to do with the vintage held on the first Sunday in October known as "Na belu nedelju" (White Sunday); this festival is little known outside Kastav, but is really worth seeing.

••••••••••••

Platak*, is a recreation centre and a popular place for outings from Rijeka (1100 m above sea level). It is 26 km from Rijeka, 17 km on the Zagreb road to a left hand fork and then another 9 km. On Saturdays there is a special bus service. On the southern slopes of Mt Snježnik there is a broad meadow and a recreation centre at 1111m. In winter months Platak is a good ski centre. This resort is an example of the effective combination of Adriatic and mountain tourism. Platak is a base for hill-walking expeditions: the peak of Snježnik (1506 m), considered to be one of the most beautiful look-out points in the whole of Croatia, is about 2 hour's walk; to the peak of Obruč, it takes 4 hours 30 minutes; to Risnjak, 3 hours. By road to Slovenski Snežnik it is about 40 km, to Trstenik 15.5 km and to Klana (towards Trieste or Opatija) 31.5 km.

••••••••••••

Opatija

15 KM WEST OF RIJEKA, POPULATION 8 360.

Opatija is the centre of a 43 km long riviera which begins at the most northerly point of the Kvarner Bay, and comes to an end near Brseč. Situated at the foot of Mount Učka, the Opatija riviera is protected by the mountain and therefore has a mild climate. Fresh air from Učka alleviates the summer heat and due to the mild winter climate, the tourist season here lasts throughout the year.

Present day Opatija developed alongside the former

View of Opatija

"opatija" Sanctus Jacobus ad Palum (The Abbey of St. James). It was mentioned for the first time in 1453, but only after the French occupation in 1813 did a small settlement begin to develop around the Abbey. The development of modern Opatija began in 1844, when the Villa Angiolina was built. Opatija was Austrian until the end of the First World War (from 1867 Austro-Hungarian), and following the Rapallo Peace Treaty in 1921 it came under Italy. From 1945 it was governed by the military and in 1946 was ceded to Croatia in the Yugoslavia of the time. Opatija is now one of the major tourist resorts in not only Croatia but the whole of the Mediterranean.

The history of tourism. Thanks to its favourable geographic location and abundant vegetation, Opatija developed rapidly after 1844. The building of the southern branch of the Vienna-Trieste railway line, that is, the Rijeka branch, gave it a special boost, and the Matulji railway station became Opatija's station. In the same year Rijeka was linked by rail with Zagreb and Budapest, and the rapid growth of Opatija as a tourist resort began. The following hotels were built: Kvarner (1884), Imperial (1885), and then the present hotels Atlantik, Slavija, Bellevue and Amalija, parks, walkways and a harbour. The whole urban and architectural concept of Opatija is dictated by the line of the coast and the town's function as a resort. The architecture bears hallmarks of the Austrian builders: a variety of styles, but harmonised, and linked together in a whole which gives an impression of respectability. This quality was taken up by post-war local architects in their designs. Opatija got electric lighting in 1895, mains water in 1897 and had its first encounter with the film just three years later than Paris, in 1898. At the end of the century it was called "the Austrian Nice" and became a meeting place for the aristocracy from all over Europe. Between the two wars, during the Italian occupation, Opatija stagnated, but it received a

Centre of Opatija

breath of new life after 1945 when it became the tourist centre for the northern part of the Adriatic coast. Together with Lovran, Opatija has more than 10,000 beds for tourists.

Opatija as a climatic health resort. Because of the very suitable climate that characterises the town all the year round, Opatija has become a very well known climatic health resort. This development was helped greatly because Đuro Matija Šporer (1794-1884), physician and writer, and Antun Feliks-Jačić (1813-1898), member of the Medical Academy of Marseilles, lived here. A special role was played by the renowned German surgeon Theodor Billroth (1829-1898). He arrived in Opatija in 1894 after he had already achieved fame for the first resection of the stomach (1881) and the introduction of the anaesthetic ether-chloroform. Officially, Opatija became a health resort on March 4, 1889 and in 1908 the 4th Thalassotherapy Congress was held here. The climate and the health care establishments of Opatija help in the treatment of chronic rheumatic ailments, sciatica, lumbago, bronchitis and bronchial asthma, chronic inflammations of the respiratory tract, cardiac and dermatological illnesses and post-traumatic states.

Sights

The **Church of St. James*** (Sveti Jakov) stands to the west of the Kvarner Hotel. It was built on the site of the Benedictine abbey which stood there from the 12th century, and was the focal point of what was to become modern Opatija. The present church was built in 1937 by a reconstruction of a building from 1793 which had belonged to Kastav Parish. The church has fragments of an older church from 1506 built into its walls. A plaque over the door mentions this in Latin elegiac verse, along with the year the church was built.

••••••••••••

The **Parish Church of the Annunciation of the Blessed Virgin Mary** (Navještenje Blažene Djevice Marije) was built in this century (1906) according to plans of the German architect Gabriel Seidl, the designer of the Deutsche Museum in Munich. Notable as an example of eclecticism, this building was designed in the Florentine Quattrocento style.

••••••••••••

The **Villa Angiolina** is in the Perivoj Prvog Maja (May Day Park) and was the first building in the modern development of Opatija. It was constructed in 1844 in Neo-Classic style by the Rijekan citizen Iginio Scarpa. His family were hospitable people, and enjoyed having guests so the villa was always very busy. The guests repaid their hosts with exotic plants, and so a botanical garden grew up around the villa. The French composer, and

Villa Angiolina

guest in Opatija, Jean Charles de Pauer composed the "Villa Angiolina" polka in 1858. In 1873 the villa was bought by Count Chorinsom, and then by the Viennese firm Southern Railways which invested large sums of money in Opatija. Nowadays the building houses the Tourist Association and a library and reading room named after Viktor Car Emin (1870-1963), the Croatian writer.

••••••••••••

Opatija Park. The park was started by Iginio Scarpa. At the same time as building the Villa Angiolina, between 1845 and 1882, he planted plants that sea captains brought him from China, Japan, South America, Australia and other parts of the world. After Scarpa's Park, there has been constant work on the horticulture of Opatija. The **Zora** (Aurora) **Walkway** stretches longitudinally above Opatija, from 50 to 180 m a.s.l. It was laid out in 1890 and expanded in 1901. Margerita Park (3.5 ha in area, still having many of the plants originally placed here, such as planes, oaks and the Judas tree) was laid out after 1900. The coastal way from Volosko to Lovran (the Matko Laginja Walkway in its central part) is particularly attractive. It is a unique promenade that extends for 11 km, with beautiful specimens of cypresses, oaks and palms.

The **Đuro Matija Šporer Arts' Pavilion** is situated to the west of the Church of St. Jacob. A former ice-cream parlour has been transformed into an art gallery with exhibitions by local and Croatian artists. On a rock in the sea not far from the pavilion there is a bronze sculpture entitled "Greeting

to the Sea" which is the work of Zvonko Car and was placed there in 1956.

••••••••••••

Volosko** This old fishing settlement is linked with Opatija today by the coastal walkway (Lungomare). It developed as the port of Kastav, but is mentioned in documents as early as 1543. The Baroque church in Volosko was built in 1708.

••••••••••••

Excursions

Lovran**

6 km south of Opatija, population 3 400.

The town centre is situated above a cove, but the newer part of the town has grown up on the sides of Gorica hill. Lovran has an especially mild climate, and its abundant Mediterranean vegetation is typical of this area. The Lovran sweet chestnut is particularly well-known. Over the past century Lovran has been developed as a winter tourist resort. Present-day Lovran was mentioned as Lauriana for the first time in the 7th century; the nephew of Charles the Great, Henrik of Strasburg, was killed not far from here. Lovran was part of the Croatian State during the rule of the national dynasty, and later fell under the Patriarchs of Aquileia. From 1275 on it was part of the Pazin County, and therefore shares the history of that part of Istria. Lovran was burnt down several times during the period of fierce conflicts and merciless battles between the Uskoks and the Venetians (1599-1612 and 1614).

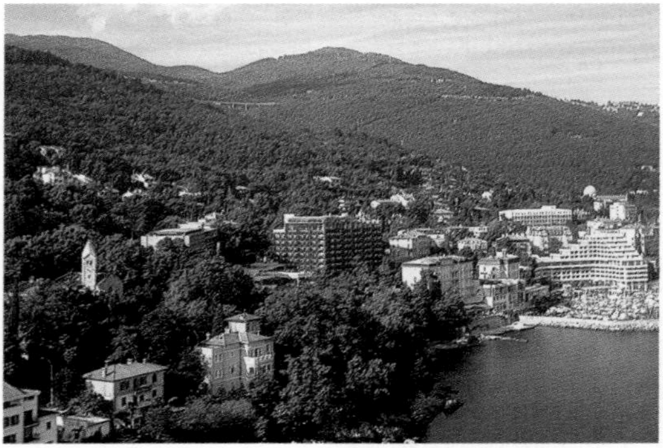

Lovran at the foot of Učka

On the town square there is a medieval town tower and the **Parish Church of St. George**** (Sveti Juraj), a Gothic building dating from the 14th century. The church has a rectangular sanctuary which was given a late Gothic net vault in 1470 on the model of the vaulting in the sanctuary of the cathedral in Pazin. The church also contains late Gothic frescoes by Istrian masters, covering the new ceiling, the walls of the sanctuary and the triumphal arch. They date from around 1470 to 1479. These frescoes form the highest quality and most complete collection of Gothic frescoes in eastern Istria. The church was extended in the 17th and 18th centuries. On the main square there is also a house with an engraved image of St. George. On the sea front there is a Romanesque chapel, restored in the Gothic era, which has a portal decorated with braiding ornamentation, and a doorway characteristic of this region (lopica), with a covered porch in front of the entrance to the church. The church also has some later Gothic frescoes (from the 15th century) and a 16th century Glagolitic gravestone.

Mošćenička Draga

13 km from Opatija, population 472.

Is a village which developed in a dry gorge, cut deep into the Učka massif. Due to its mild climate and its 2 km of white pebble beach, as well as its lush vegetation, this former fishing village has developed into a tourist resort with bathing areas, newly built hotels and a camp site called Draga.

Mošćenice** is a small town in eastern Istria, on the hill above Mošćenička Draga, at 173 m above sea level. It has about 330 inhabitants. It is a favourite spot for outings because of its dominating position over the Kvarner Bay and its picturesque Mediterranean architecture. It is one of the oldest settlements on the eastern coast of Istria. It was mentioned for the first time under its present name in 1384. Mošćenice has retained the character of a medieval fortified town. The outer walls of the houses on the periphery served as defensive walls, and encircled the closely packed town centre. On the only remaining town gate are carved the Habsburg coat of arms and the year 1634 when the gates were probably repaired. The loggia in front of the gate dates from the 17th century. On top of the hill, where all the winding streets eventually lead, a triple-naved church stands out. It has Baroque vaulting and a huge bell tower. On the main altar there are five stone statues by I.

Mošćenice

Contieri (from the beginning of the 18th century). The church has a collection of stone monuments including: choir stalls and naive stone relief work from the 17th century. In Mošćenice it is also worth going to see the ancient "toš", an oil press which is still in use today.

••••••••••••

Učka**. Mount Učka rises behind the Opatija riviera. It forms a single morphological unit together with the Ćićarija range which stretches from the bay of Trieste to Rijeka. Učka is a limestone massif with numerous areas of karst, stretching for 20 km from the Poklon Pass (920 m) to Plomin Bay, and is between 4 and 9 km wide. Učka differs from all the other coastal mountains in Croatia because of its abundant vegetation on the seaward side. Best known are the forests of sweet chestnuts in the area around Lovran. Učka's highest peaks are considered nature reserves and memorial areas. The highest peak is Vojak (1401m above sea level), from which there is a magnificent view over the whole of Istria, the Bay of Trieste, the Julian Alps and the Adriatic islands, right down to Dugi Otok.

The view from Vojak

Peak	m	km	0°
Slovenski Snežnik	1796	39	29
Obruč	1376	25	43
Risnjak	1528	36	62
Bjelolasica	1534	49	91
Viševica	1428	47	94
Mali Rajinac	1699	84	131
Televrin (Lošinj)	588	71	169
Sisol (Cres)	833	13	182
Slavnik	1029	33	328
Triglav	2863	125	348
Nanos	1313	65	347
Planik	1273	8	354
Grintovec	2558	121	13

••••••••••••

There are several marked trails for walkers up Učka. By road the peak can be reached via Veprinac (12 km from Opatija via Ičići, or by bus from the city).

••••••••••••

Veprinac*

12 KM FROM OPATIJA, POPULATION 843.

Veprinac grew up on the site of a pre-historic settlement (earthworks) on the slopes of Ćićarija and was mentioned for the first time in 1374 in the will of Hugo Devin (Duino). It remained in the possession of the Devin family until 1399 when it passed to the Wallsees. From 1466 it belonged to the Habsburgs and thus shared the fate of Kastav. In 1500 it obtained a charter in the Croatian language. There are still some old registry documents in existence written in Glagolitic script. The town is in two parts: the older part which grew up around the church and the castle, and the newer, lower part which lies on the road to Učka. Some parts of the town wall remain from the fortress, with a gate built into the structure of the old town hall ("Komuna"). Beside the entrance into the upper, older part of the town there is a medieval castle. In front of the town gate is the town loggia and opposite it **St. Anne's Chapel** (sv. Ana), which has been redecorated in Baroque style. The highest point of the town is reached through the gate, by a wide paved path and steps. Here we find the **Parish Church of St. Mark** (Sv. Marko), a medieval church with Baroque decorations. The church and the bell tower are separated from the town by a high wall. The parish church contains beautiful old carved choir stalls.

From Veprinac it is 14 km to the top of Učka via the Poklon Pass. It is two and half hours' walk by mountain paths, also via Poklon. The top of Učka may also be reached by marked mountain paths from Lovran (4 hours' uphill walking via the villages of Dindići and Ivulići, and to the left of Kaluže plateau), also from Medveja and Mošćenička Draga (5 hours' uphill via the deserted village Mala Učka).

The **Učka tunnel** is on the road between Matulji, Veprinac and Lupoglav and links the Kvarner area with the interior. It is 5,062 m long and is therefore consi-

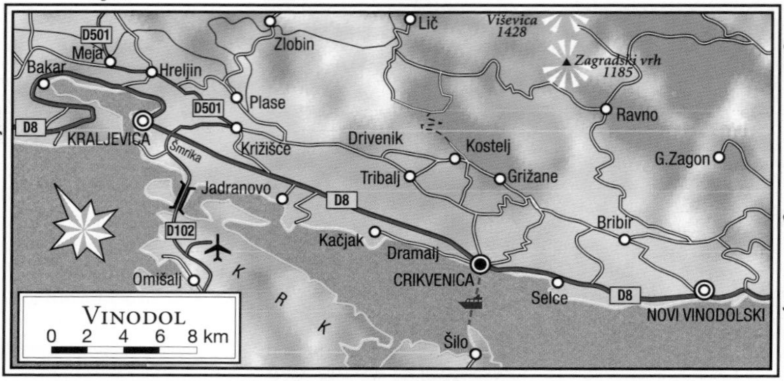

dered a "long" tunnel. It is the longest in Croatia. Preparations began for its construction in 1971, boring began on 27th August 1976 and was completed on 5th May 1978. It was opened for traffic in 1981. Before the tunnel was built, traffic had to travel by the road through the Poklon Pass (at 920 m), but because of the steep gradients and climatic conditions, this was a barrier to the speedy development of the Rijekan hinterland. This tunnel shortens the journey from Rijeka to Rovinj, Poreč and Koper by about 20-37 km.

••••••••••••

Paz*

10 KM FROM UČKA TUNNEL, TO THE WEST, 17 KM FROM PAZIN.

This is a medieval settlement, including the ruins of a medieval castle which was once the property of the Walderstein family. In the **Parish Church of the Assumption** (Uznesenje Marijino), which has been decorated in the Baroque style, there is a late Gothic stone custodia, dating from 1496. The **Church of St. Vitus** (Sveti Vid), in the graveyard, outside the town, is a single-naved building, with two originally enclosed apses and a barrel vault ceiling. In the 17th century the church was extended to the front and the apses were broken. The frescoes, influenced by Venetian Gothic, are the work of Master Albert, who painted them in 1461. They have been preserved on some parts of the apses that remained intact following the thoroughgoing reconstruction of the church in the 17th century.

••••••••••••

Vinodol

Vinodol is a 2-3 km wide valley which stretches 24 km from Bakar Bay to Novi Vinodolski, and is separated from the sea by a ridge 2 km wide and up to 300m high. In the valley are the towns of Tribalj, Drivenik, Grižane and Bribir, and the villages of Belgrad and Kotor. At the entrance to the valley, on the sea, lies Novi Vinodolski. This was the scene of many important events in Croatian history. In history Vinodol is actually a wider concept: the Vinodol Law from the 13th century mentions that apart from the above mentioned places the towns of Grobnik, Trsat, Hreljin and Bakar to the north-west and Ledenice to the south-east also belonged to the Vinodol feudal lords. It was first mentioned as "Vallis vinaria" in the Chronicle of Diocles the Priest in the 12th century. In the Roman era a road passed through the valley which linked Aquileia with Senj (Senia) and there are traces of settlements from that time. The Croatians moved into Vallis vinaria (Wine valley) in the 7th century. In 1225 the Croatian-Hungarian King Andrija II ceded the valley to the Counts of Krk (later the Frankopans) who owned nine communes. The Frankopan Counts ruled for more than 4 centuries and

Vinodol valley

from here spread all over Croatia. Venetian occupation, Turkish expansion and Austrian pressure all had an adverse effect on Northern Croatia which was known as "the remains of the remains of a once powerful kingdom". The Frankopan Counts no longer had the strength to defend Vinodol and so the area fell to the Zrinski family in 1544. Together with Senj, Vinodol remained Croatia's gateway to the world, and good use was made of it. Thanks to trade with the hinterland, agriculture, vineyards, olives and cattle, as well as ship building, and later tourism, Vinodol developed into a region with a strong economy.

Crikvenica

37.5 southeast of Rijeka, population 7 329 Mean temperatures in January: air 5.8 °C, sea 10.8 °C. Mean temperatures in July: air 23.4 °C, sea 21 °C.

This is the largest settlement on the coast of the Vinodol coastal area,

Crikvenica, the Castle to the right

and grew up on an area which was a settlement in the Roman era (a military base) called Ad Turres. Its name comes from the word crkva (church - in dialect crikva) because of the church which was built towards the end of the 14th century at the mouth of the River Dubračina. In 1412 Nikola Frankopan also had a Paulite monastery built in the same place. Beside the church and the monastery at the mouth of the Dubračina, the nearby port of Grižane grew up. In 1760 the castellan moved from Bribir to Crikvenica and thus it became the centre of the whole of Vinodol. But Crikvenica's development was not because of Grižane, but because of the proximity of Rijeka: first of all it developed as a fishing village, then as a seaside resort and tourist centre for the entire Vinodol riviera. In 1877 a harbour was built in Crikvenica, in 1888 a bathing beach and as early as 1891 Frischauf published a book in Graz entitled *Curort und Seebad Crikvenica* (The Cure and Bathing Town of Crikvenica) which was the first town guide. In 1895 the Hotel Therapia was opened with 120 beds and a Hydrotherapy Institute. In 1902 the Hotel Crikvenica was built, in 1903 the Bellevue and in 1905 the Miramare. Due to its favourable climate, in the space of just 16 years Crikvenica became the most important resort on the riviera.

Sights

The **Frankopan Castle**** (Frankopanski Kaštel) was built in 1412 by Count Nikola Frankopan of Krk (1393-1432) as a foundation. He is known for the fact that, having proved his supposed relationship to the Roman noble family Frangipani, he received permission from the Pope to use the surname (1430). His sons shared the family's extensive wealth and founded 8 branches of the Frankopan family in 1449. Nikola Frankopan gave money to the Paulites, which was a very large order at that time in Croatia (they had 207 monasteries all together in Europe, 127 of which were in the Croatian-Hungarian Kingdom). The Paulites had schools in their monasteries, which was also the case in Crikvenica, and it is therefore thought that Julije Klović (see the monument in Drivenik) learnt to write here. The monastery was dissolved in 1786. The castle was a two storey building, fortified by a cylindrical tower which, together with the church

Crikvenica, the quayside

(later reconstructed in the Baroque style), form an enclosed unit. Once the monastery had been dissolved it was bought by the Crikvenica community and given to Archduke Joseph who had it converted into a home for sick soldiers. It has also been a children's home. While it was called "Ladislavov dječji dom" (The Ladislav Children's Home) its Governor was the Croatian poet Vladimir Nazor. The castle has been turned into a hotel today.

••••••••••••

Convalescent and health centre. Because of its climate, Crikvenica is suitable for the treatment of chronic rheumatic illness, discopathy, sciatica and lumbago; bronchitis and bronchial asthma; chronic inflammations and allergies of the respiratory tract and other organs. Treatment is carried out by the Thalasotherapia.

••••••••••••

The **Aquarium** (Vinodolska ul. 8) Occupying an area of about 200 m², with more than twenty pools, the aquarium has, apart from Adriatic fish, fifty or so species from Indonesia, Sri Lanka, Hawaii and other tropical waters. Particularly interesting are the bloodthirsty piranha that live on the bottoms of calm rivers and swamps in Africa and South America. There is also a shop selling shells.

••••••••••••

The **Crikvenica Swimming Marathon** is held every year on the City Day (August 15, day of the Assumption). The race is between the island of Krk (Šilo) and Crikvenica, a distance of 3.8 km. In 1996 the 86th marathon attracted 27 participants, from Germany, Slovenia, the Czech Republic and Croatia, the winner covering the distance in 46 minutes 25 seconds.

Excursions

Grižane**

5 km to the northeast of Crikvenica, at the foot of the Velika Kapela massif, population 368.

This town was first mentioned in 1275. The ruins of a medieval castle rise up on

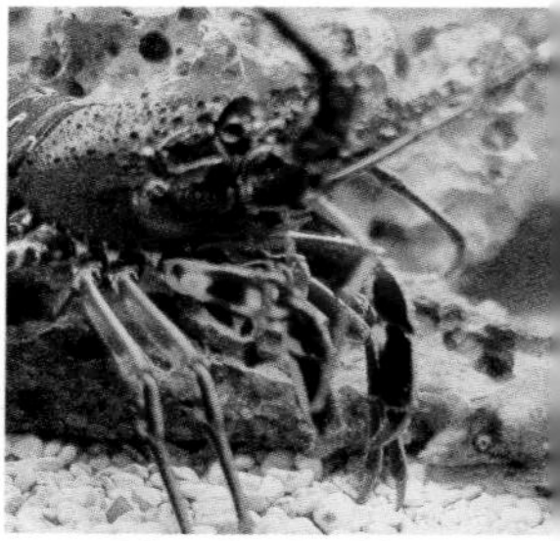

Crikvenica, detail from the Aquarium

the rock. It used to belong to the Frankopans and then to the Zrinskis. In the middle of the town stands the Church of St. Martin and a memorial to the suffering woman of Grižane. There is also a memorial to Julije Klović (see Drivenik) and to those who fell in the anti-fascist struggle.

••••••••••••

Drivenik

8 km from Crikvenica on the road to Hreljin.

From 1225 this was in the possession of the Frankopans, and from 1576 of the Zrinskis. On top of a solitary hill are the ruins of a medieval castle belonging to the Frankopans and the Zrinskis. In the town itself stands the **Parish Church of St. Dominic** (Sveti Dujam) which was reconstructed in 1821, and the Church of St. Stephen (Sveti Stjepan) which has a Gothic sanctuary. In the cemetery chapel there are Baroque frescoes from the 18th century. **Julije Klović Memorial***. In the centre of Drivenik in the courtyard of the primary school there is a memorial to Julije Klović, a fine Croatian Renaissance miniature artist, known to his contemporaries as "the Michelangelo of miniatures". He was born in Grižane in 1498, but not much is known of his childhood. When he was 18 he went to Venice where he worked as a medal maker. He learned to paint from Giulio Romano in Mantua, where he also began to paint miniatures. Then he found work at the court of the Croatian-Hungarian King Ludovik II until the King's death in battle at Mohacs in 1526. When he was 29 he became a monk, but left the monastery with permission from the Pope. He painted for the Pope in Rome and for Cosimo de Medici in Florence. He was a friend of Michelangelo, Vasari and Brueghel and he introduced El Greco (1570) to the circle of patrons in Rome. His works are included in all important collections. His most famous piece, **Horae Beatae Mariae Virginis**, is in the collection of the Pierpont Morgan Library in New York. El Greco painted him with Michelangelo, Titian and Raphael (in his painting **Christ driving the traders from the Temple**, which is part of a private collection in London). Klović died in 1578 in Rome and was buried in the Church of San Pietro in Vincoli. This memorial was set up in 1978 and is the work of the sculptor Zvonko Car.

Julije Klović, detail from the painting of El Greco

Selce*

3 KM TO THE SOUTHEAST OF CRIKVENICA, LINKED BY A FOOTPATH.

This village developed on land belonging to the Zrinskis, and formed the harbour for Bribir, which is 5 km away. As well as having interesting and original rural coastal architecture, the village is also the site of a reconstructed storehouse belonging to the Zrinskis. The Parish Church of St. Catherine was built in 1888.

Bribir*

5 KM TO THE EAST OF SELCE, ON THE ROAD FROM HRELJIN TO NOVI VINODOLSKI, POPULATION 1756.

Bribir was in the possession of the Frankopans from 1225 and in the 15th century it belonged to the Counts of Celje. It was then taken over by the Croatian-Hungarian King Matthew Corvin and from the 16th century it belonged to the Zrinskis. Until 1809 it was still surrounded by walls and defensive towers. Only on the northern side are there the remains of the castle which was built in 1302. There is also a Baroque church, St. Peter and St. Paul (Sveti Petar i Pavao) which was built on the foundations of an older church mentioned in the Glagolitic inscription from 1524. This church at one time had the richest furnishings in the coastal area. Today it still houses numerous paintings, including the painting *The washing of the feet* by the Venetian artist Palma the Younger, and in the treasury there is a Romanesque cross from the 13th century, which is the work of the master Milonić. Ugrini, near Bribir, is the birthplace of the botanist Josip Pančić (1814-1888); there is a memorial bust of Pančić by the Frankopan tower. The family of the writer and historian Mihovil Kombol (1883-1955) also comes from Bribir, and there is a bust erected in his honour in the park. Bribir is also the starting point for hill-walking expeditions in the area around the coastal edge of the Mountain High Plains* (**Zagradski vrh*** 1185 m) or to the peak of Kapela (Viševica 1428 m). It is 20 km from Bribir to Mokro (car park by the Poli Vagabundi restaurant). The climb to Zagradski vrh takes one hour and begins behind the restaurant, goes across the meadows Stankove lazi and Zagradi, but becomes quite steep and there is no path towards the peak. There is a beautiful view over Gorski Kotar and the Bay of Rijeka. The climb up **Viševica*** takes 2 hours on foot. There is a marked

Selce

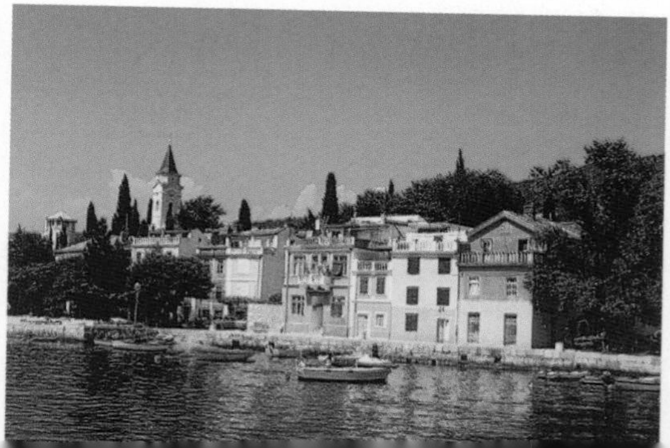

footpath leading up from the restaurant, which goes along the road for 15 minutes and then into the woods and uphill to the right, then via the peak at 1207 m. The path goes round **Viševica** peak to the east and leads to the Plavuš voda spring. From the spring there is another half hour's steep climb up the southern ridge. There is a particularly beautiful view over Risnjak and Rijeka Bay.

Kraljevica

26 KM FROM RIJEKA, POPULATION 2 965.

The name of this town is connected with the legend that during the Tartar invasion (1242) the Croatian-Hungarian King Bela IV hid here (Kralj in Croatian means King). Four centuries later Petar Zrinski built a castle in the small fishing village in the natural harbour of Hreljina, and subsequently a port. After the Zrinski and Frankopan conspiracy that failed in 1671, Kraljevica came to share the fate of all Zrinski or Frankopan property. The castles were sacked and the town fell to the Austrian Empire. In 1728 the Austrian Emperor Charles VI (the father of Maria Theresa and the Croatian-Hungarian King Charles III) began to build a considerable port at the end of a road which went from Karlovac to the sea. Once the road between Karlovac and Bakar had been completed, Kraljevica became a ship-building centre. While other nearby towns developed during the 19th century thanks to tourism, Kraljevica grew due to ship-building. The first steam-ship, the Marie Anne, was built in this yard in 1836. At the beginning of the 20th century, the ship-yards specialised in iron ships and repair work.

Kraljevica, Scott Bay

SIGHTS

The **Old Zrinski Castle*** stands in the centre of the town. It is a triangular early Baroque building, with two inner courtyards, which together with a church encloses a small square. On a cistern in one of the courtyards there is the inscription CPAZ 1651 (comes Petrus a Zrinio), but the date refers to the time the well was built and not the building. The castle was built in the first half of the 17th century. The Church of St. Nicholas (Sveti Nikola) with its Baroque bell tower dating from 1790 was at one time a storehouse for salt.

The **New Zrinski Castle*** (also known as Frankopan) stands on a peninsula on the way to Bakar and was built by Petar Zrinski in 1651. It was modelled on late Renaissance castles in Italy. It is rectangular in shape (44 x 36m) with a cylindrical tower on each corner. The original building had only one storey but after 1883 the Jesuits added another floor. The castle is empty today.

Novi Vinodolski

47 KM SOUTHEAST OF RIJEKA, 9 KM SOUTHEAST OF CRIKVENICA, POPULATION 4 046.

This picturesque coastal town is built on a hill called Osap, at the point where Vinodol opens out to the sea. It developed around the Frankopan castle which was built in the 13th century. The word "Novi" (new) is as opposed to the old, Roman settlement which existed in the nearby bay. It was built on the spot which protects the entrance to Vinodol. The town was completely dependent on the interior and had no connection with the coast until the harbour was built

Novi Vinodolski

in 1868. It was mentioned in 1288 as a seat of the Vinodol Counts. After the Frankopans were given Vinodol in 1225 by the Croatian-Hungarian King Andrija II, and the inhabitants of Ledenice, Bribir, Grižane, Drivenik, Hreljin, Bakar, Trsat, Grobnik and Novi Vinodolski had become their serfs, a law was instituted (**Vinodol Codex**) on 6th of January 1288 by which the new feudal lord (Leonard Frankopan) regulated the lords' relationship with the serfs. This law was formulated in the Croatian language in the Čakavski dialect and written in Glagolitic, and includes regulations for criminal and civil law and the legal processes by which Vinodol was run right up until 1850. This historic legal document has much greater than just local significance. It was the first true legal codex amongst the Slavs, and its contents make it an important document of Croatian culture.

●●●●●●●●●●●●

Over the centuries Novi Vinodolski was the target of attacks by both the Turks and the Venetians. In 1527 the Turks burnt the town down and the people were killed or taken away as slaves. The Venetians sacked the town in 1598, 1613 and 1615 because it offered refuge to the Uskoks of Senj (see Senj). When the Zrinski-Frankopan conspiracy had been crushed in 1671, the Habsburgs plundered and destroyed the castle. In 1754 Vinodol became part of the Austrian coastal area and Novi Vinodolski became the most important town in the area. In 1788 a school was opened there and in 1845 the National Reading Room was founded. In 1868 the harbour was built, and in 1878 a bathing beach set up.

Novi Vinodolski is the birthplace of several prominent personalities from the Mažuranić family. The philologist Antun (1805-1888) was born here, as were his brother Ivan (1814-1890) the Croatian Ban and poet, and the creator of the heroic epic *Smrt Smail-age Čengića* (The Death of Smail-aga Čengić), the writer Fran (1856-1928), and the travel writer Matija (1817-1881). The legal writer Vladimir Mažuranić was also a member of the same family, as was the well-loved children's writer Ivana Brlić-Mažuranić.

●●●●●●●●●●●●

Sights

The **Old Castle of Novi Vinodolski****. This is the castle which was built by descendants of Count Dujam of Krk (1118-1163) once they had increased their domain on the mainland by the gift of the Croatian-Hungarian King Andrija II (1205-1235). The Counts of Krk (see Krk), were local nobility, vassals of the Croatian-Hungarian kings and Venice. In the 15th century they took the surname Frankopan, and right up to 1671 together

Vinodol Codex

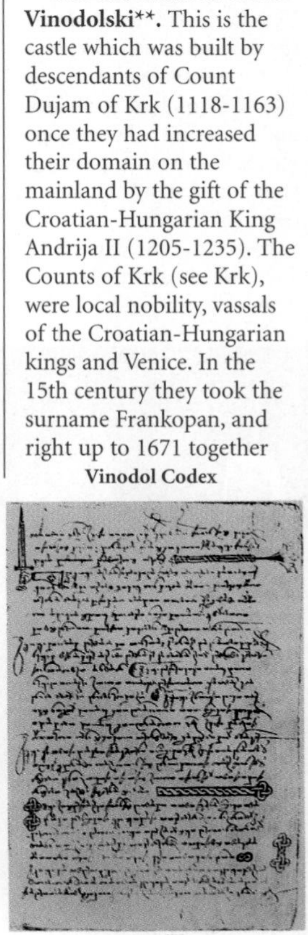

with the Zrinskis were the most influential Croatian nobles. The original ground plan of the Frankopan castle, dating from the 13th century, was rectangular and fortified with towers; on the south-eastern side there is still one square tower standing known as Kvadrac and on the south-western side there is a circular tower. The oldest remaining parts are Gothic, and are still visible despite reconstruction work in the Renaissance. The present day entrance to the castle leads from a square, where a new gate has been built on the site of the former "great palace", where, according to legend, the Vinodolski zakon (the Vinodol Codex) was drawn up and signed in 1288.

••••••••••••

The **Church of St. Philip and St. James*** (Sveti Filip i Sveti Jakov) is the parish church and stands in the centre of the town. According to the date, 1520, which is carved in Arabic, Roman and

Interior of the Church of St. Philip and St. James

Glagolitic numerals on the western side of the sanctuary, this church's late Gothic polygonal sanctuary dates from the 16th century. The year 1520 is probably in memory of the church's renovation. In the 18th century the church was reconstructed in Baroque style. In front of the main altar there is a gravestone with the picture of Bishop Christopher of Modruš, who fled to Novi Vinodolski from the Turks and died in 1499. From that time the church became the seat of the diocese. There is a wooden Madonna from the 15th century on one of the side altars.

••••••••••••

In the Gothic **Church of the Holy Trinity** (Sveto Trojstvo) there are some frescoes from the 15th century. Canon Antun Mažuranić had the Baroque altar made. A sacred collection has been established in the little church.

••••••••••••

The traditional **Novljansko kolo** (a chain dance from Novi Vinodolski) is performed every year during the Carnival (on Sundays, Mondays, and Tuesdays from the afternoon right into the night). This dance is older than the Vinodol code and it is still danced today in the same manner as it was danced when the code was written. Hundreds of dancers take part, everyone who is up to it, both young and old. The dance has an eight bar rhythm which is given by 3 or 4 pairs of singers. They sing in praise of the Zrinskis and Frankopans, the Uskoks of Senj (see Senj) who frequently found refuge in Novi Vinodolski; extracts of Mažuranić's epic *The Death of Smail-aga Čengić* are also sung. ■

Chain dance from Novi Vinodolski

The Kvarner Islands

Cres and Lošinj

The island of Cres (405.78 km²), after Krk, is the largest island in the Adriatic. Together with Lošinj (74.68 km²) and the neighbouring inhabited islands Unije (17 km²), Ilovik (6 km²), Susak (3.75 km²), Vele and Male Srakane (1 km²) and 25 smaller uninhabited islands, the Cres-Lošinj group is the largest island complex in the Adriatic, with a total surface area of 513 km², 16% of the total surface area of all the Adriatic islands.

Landscape

The islands of Cres and Lošinj are separated at Osor by an 11 m wide channel, but since ancient times they have a shared history, firstly under the Greek name Apsyrtides and then as the Osor islands; today, part of the Coastal and Mountain County, they are linked by a common administrative and economic policy.

From the north to the south of these islands it is 83 km by road (the total length of the islands is 99 km) so the climatic characteristics also depend on geographical location: the average temperature in January in the northern parts of the island is 5 °C with 900-1000 mm precipitation annually, whereas in the south, the average temperature is 7 °C and there are 800-900 mm of precipitation annually. The average January temperature in Mali Lošinj is higher than in many places further south.

In the northern part of Cres, there are large forests of hop hornbeam (Ostrya carpinifolia), pubescent oak (Quercus pubescens), European hornbeam (Carpinus betulus) and holm oak (Quercus ilex). The central area is occupied by pastures, olive groves and vineyards, but in the southern part, because of the well-developed animal husbandry, there was only very poor vegetation until the intensive planting of coniferous forests during the 19th century. In terms of fauna, the islands abound in small and feathered wild life, birds of prey, song birds, and sea gulls. One especially interesting feature is that there are no poisonous snakes on the islands. The

most common domestic animals are sheep, so Cres is famous for lamb and good quality cheese. Lošinj is rich in fish and has the best-known sports fishing centre on the Adriatic.

Cres and Lošinj were settled in prehistoric times. Before the Roman invasion (2nd century BC), the islands on the eastern coast of the Adriatic were inhabited by the Illyrian tribe the Liburni. There were 66 registered Liburnian settlements on these islands. However, during the Roman era, there was a break in the continuity of settlement on Lošinj. Osor (Apsorus) was an important Roman and Byzantine town, and Cres (Crepsa) and Beli (Caput insula) have been known as settlements since the Roman age, but Lošinj was settled as late as 1280. The Croats came to Cres in the 10th century (see Valunska ploča, the Valun Tablet) when the island was part of the Croatian state. From 1000 to 1358 it was under the Venetians. It belonged to the Croatian-Hungarian kingdom for some 60 years, and then came under the Venetians again until 1797. The Venetians were replaced by the Austrians (1814-1918) and they by the Italian occupation until 1943. AVNOJ and ZAVNOH (The Anti-Fascist Council of the National Liberation of Yugoslavia), created the legal basis for the islands, together with Istria, to become part of Croatia within ex-Yugoslavia (Croatia). Nowadays Cres and Lošinj are amongst the most important tourist resorts in Yugoslavia. In 1962 there were fewer than 7,000 beds available for tourists, but that number has risen in the subsequent period to over 32,000. ■

Cres, harbour and square

Cres (Town)

Located 44° 58' N, 14° 25' E.
Population: 2 382.

The town has developed in the Bay of Cres, on the western, most fertile part of the island. It is 26 km from the ferry port of Porozina, 5 km from the ferry at Merag, and 53 km from Mali Lošinj.

The origins of the town are still not clearly known. The exact site of Roman Cres has not been established but it is thought that it was in the area near Lovreški (Palacine) on the coast beneath St. Bartholomew's hill (Sveti Bartolomej) where there are the remains of a Roman villa rustica and a necropolis. It is known that Roman Crepsa was granted the rights of a town during the reign of one of the first Emperors (Augustus or Tiberius). After the fall of the Western Roman Empire (AD 476) the area was inhabited by Goths for a short period. It then came under the Byzantine Empire and was joined to the Croatian state in the 10th century. Because of its proximity to Venice, of all the Adriatic islands it remained the longest under Venetian rule. During the entire period from the first campaign of Pietros II (1000) to the fall of the Venetian Empire (1797) Cres was only ruled by the Croatian-Hungarian kings between 1358-1409. In the time when the official language of the Venetian administration and church was Latin, or rather Italian, in Cres and its surroundings Glagolitic was used for legal documents, registers, books of the religious fraternities, the community roll and public announcements, as well as private correspondence. After the fall of Venice (apart from a short period of French occupation) the town came under Austrian rule, and on 4th November 1918 it was occupied by the Italian army. This occupation was confirmed in 1920 in the Treaty of Rapallo, and Cres was not liberated until 1943.

SIGHTS

The **Town Walls*.** In the Middle Ages Cres was surrounded by walls. The town centre was at that time on the eastern side of the town. In the 16th century (1509-1610), the Venetians built new walls and a system of corner defensive towers, so that the whole town became one rectangular entity. The walls were demolished in the last and in this century, but the round tower on the north western corner remains, with 200 m of wall and two town gates built in the high Renaissance style.

The **Parish Church of St. Mary of the Snow**** (Sveta Marija Snježna) stands in the town square. It is a triple-naved building, dating from the 15th century, with a separate bell tower from the 16th century. The portal is basically Gothic, but the facade and the sculptured decorations on the semi-circular arcade are Renaissance. Inside the church there is a 15th century Gothic sculptured Pieta and the parish offices house a **collection of pictures** dating from the period between the 15th and the 17th centuries. The most valuable is a polyptych by Alviseo Vivarini, entitled *St. Sebastian with the Saints.*

The **Church of St. Isidore**** (Sveti Sidar) was originally the parish church and stands behind the Petris Palace. It is the oldest church in the town, partially built in Romanesque style but with a Gothic facade. Amongst its valuable treasures the church possesses a 15th century wooden statue of St. Isidore and fragments of a Gothic polyptych.

Monument to Franjo Petrić

The **Monastery and Church of St. Francis**** (Sveti Franjo; in the eastern part of the town). The church belonged to one of the mendicant orders. It was built in the 14th century and has beautiful carved choir stalls. The monastery is constructed around two cloisters; from the capitals in the smaller cloister it can be dated to the 15th century. The monastery houses a collection of Gothic sculptures, incunabula and codices from the 15th century, and a collection of furniture from the 16th and 17th centuries. There is also a copy of a Glagolitic missal, which was printed in Senj in 1494.

Municipal Museum (Gothic biforium)

The **Town Museum****, is housed in the Arsan Palace. It has exhibitions of collections from prehistoric and Roman times including an impressive collection of Roman amphorae, which were found in the sea off Pernat point and date from the 2nd century BC. There are also examples of stone braiding, ethnographic items, icons, wooden sculptures and a collection of coins.

In the Arsan Palace in 1529 one of the most important philosophers of his time, **Franjo Petrić**, was born (Petrišević, Franciscus Petricius). He was a member of the family of the town judge, Stjepan. The Petrić family claimed to be of aristocratic Bosnian lineage, and Franjo was expelled from Cres because of his anti-Venetian attitude and leanings towards Protestantism. After his expulsion he first of all studied alone, later started schooling in Venice, and then as Vlačić's (s. Labin) protégé continued his studies in Ingolstadt and finished in Padua. He knew Greek, and studied philosophy and literature. He translated from Greek and possessed a valuable collection of Greek texts (which is partially housed in the Escorial near Madrid). He had 13 books published, in which he expounded an original view concerning the essence of the world, and demonstrated a lively interest in natural sciences, sensing their approaching revival. He wrote about geometry, history, poetry and military matters. He translated Zoroaster's prophecy (Zarathustra) from Greek into Latin, and also Hermes Trismegistus. He was a patriot: in Rome he published manuscripts by authors from his home area and works by Kotrljić (v: Dubrovnik). He died in Rome in 1597 and was buried in the monastery at San Onofrio.

Beli

•••••••••••

St. Peter's Monastery** (Sveti Petar) is a Benedictine monastery. It houses a collection of icons and codices from the 15th century.

•••••••••••

Holy Cross Chapel* (Sveti Križ) is outside of the town. The Way of the Cross leads up to it; this is composed of wooden reliefs, which are the work of an unknown local master.

Excursions

Beli**

18 KM FROM POROZINA, 20 KM FROM CRES, ON THE EASTERN COAST OF THE ISLAND, POPULATION 38.

Beli is a picturesque little town, situated on an isolated hill, accessible with difficulty. It is one of the oldest walled settlements on the island, and was inhabited in prehistoric times. In the Roman era it was known as Caput insulae (the head of the island). Thanks to its strategic position, it was one of the largest settlements at that time. Since the early middle ages Beli has been a Croatian town, and has shared the fate of all the other settlements on the island. It is situated on the edge of the island, and has now been transformed into a museum town. The Town Square on the top of the hill is enclosed on one side by the 18th century parish church, which was built on the foundations of a **Romanesque**

Flock of griffon vultures

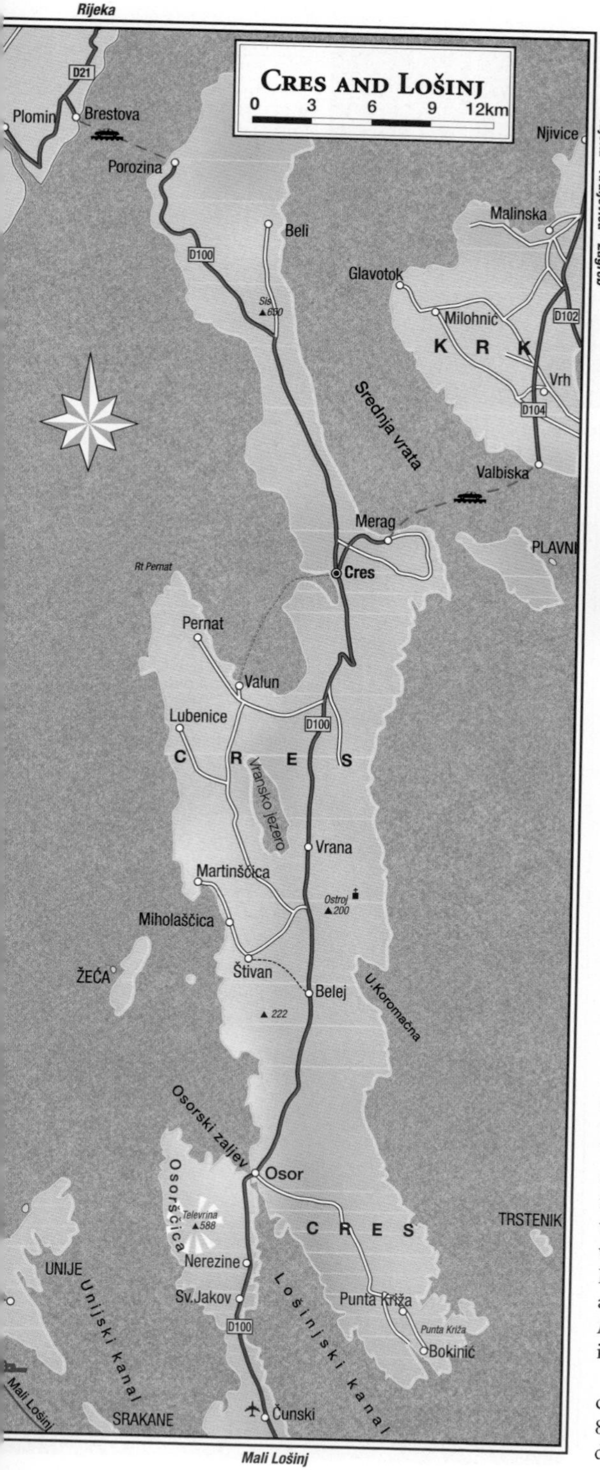

church, St. Mary's. In the sacristy there are some crosses of copper from the 13th to the 14th centuries. In the loggia which runs along the south wall of the church, there is a fragment of stone braiding on a stone bench. In the cemetery there is a Gothic church, St. Anthony's (Sveti Antun) which dates from the 15th century.

The old school building houses the **International**

Ornithological Reserve, instructions to visitors

Educational and Research Ecocentre, which takes care of the conservation of the natural, historical and cultural heritage of the island of Cres, and particularly of the **Kruna Special Ornithological Reserve**. Here nest golden eagles, peregrine falcons, snake eagles and swifts. The best known of the birds that nest here is the griffon vulture (Gyps fulvus). The Ecocentre building is the starting point for the **ecological trail called "Stoz Tramuntana I"**. A three and a half a walk will take you round some twenty points, which are marked with works by the sculptor Ljubo De Karina on which verses and thoughts of the poet Andre Vid Mihičić are inscribed.

Near Beli there is a complete **Roman bridge**, 8 m long, spanning a 12 m deep gorge. It was repaired

Valun

in 1878 and has that date engraved on its side. Near Beli there are five Romanesque medieval churches which are all in ruins. In the valley there is the deserted Church of St. Lawrence (Sveti Lovreč).

••••••••••••

On the road from Porozina to Cres, which passes through Beli, 5 km before Cres, the 45th parallel is marked to the east of the road. This line is equidistant from the equator and the north pole.

••••••••••••

Valun**

BY ROAD 15 KM FROM CRES, BY BOAT 4 NAUTICAL MILES, POPULATION 68.

A picturesque farming-fishing village, once compared to Saint Tropez. In the sacristy of the parish church the **Valun Tablet** is built into the wall. This is an inscription dating from the 11th century and is the oldest Glagolitic inscription in Croatia (s. Glagolitic). Only the first line is written in Glagolitic, the second and third lines are in Latin script (Caroline). Three names are mentioned on the tablet and their relationship to one another: Teha-grandmother (baka), Juna-son (sin) and Bratohna-grandson (unuk). From the text it is not clear whether this was a gravestone or whether these were donors to the church, but it has great significance for the national culture. As far as is known at the moment, this marks the beginning of the history of Glagolitic in Croatia. The Croatian and Latin scripts bear witness to the coexistence of the Croatian people with the older Roman inhabitants, and demonstrate that in the 11th century they still had not begun to name themselves after saints and martyrs.

••••••••••••

Lubenice***

7 KM SOUTHWEST OF VALUN, ONE OF THE OLDEST SETTLEMENTS, THE "PEASANT TOWN" OF THE CRES-LOŠINJ ARCHIPELAGO IS ALMOST ABANDONED TODAY, WITH 28 INHABITANTS.

Together with Osor, Cres and Beli, it is a prehistoric and then Roman settlement (Hibernicia, from hibernus — wintry). It occupies a natural defensive position that was almost impossible to take; located on a cliff 378 m above sea level, it is enclosed by walls on the east. Creating a very impressive view, it was described by a travel writer as "Sleeping Beauty's sleeping castle". It is also possible to get to it from the sea, from a sandy beach, by a goat path, the ascent taking an hour. The churches of Lubenice show that it was once an important place. In front of the city is the Gothic Church of St. Anthony the Hermit from the 15th century, and the ruins of the Romanesque Sv. Nedjelja, while in the city is the three-naved Church of the Presentation of the Virgin Mary, restored in the 18th century and expanded in 1907. In the sacristy of the church

Lubenice

Osor, engraving from the 16th century

is the old artistic inventory, and a wooden sculpture of St. Nicholas from the 15th century which once adorned the altar in the church belonging to the saint on the southern rim of the town.

••••••••••••

Vrana lake** (Vransko jezero), in the centre of Cres (the village of Vrana above the lake is 15 km from Cres) is a fresh water lake, 1.5 km wide and about 7 km long. The town of Cres has been supplied with drinking water from the lake since 1953, and the towns of Mali and Veli Lošinj received their supplies ten years later. It was thought at one time that the water in the lake was linked to some mainland source by underground streams, but it has since been established that it in fact originates from the atmosphere. This lake is a crypto-depression, i.e. its bottom lies 74 m below the surface of the sea, but its surface lies about 13 m above it (the level oscillates by about half a metre). The lake contains pike, tench and carp. There are also eel, whose origin is unclear.

••••••••••••

Osor**

32 km from Cres, 21 km from Mali Lošinj, population 73:

This town is situated on the isthmus which joins the islands of Cres and Lošinj. Present day Osor has 100 inhabitants, but in the Roman era it was the capital of Cres and Lošinj. According to some sources, at one time it had as many as 20,000 inhabitants, and the entire Cres-Lošinj group of islands was named the Apsyrtides - "the Osor islands". So what is now a small town has had a rich and turbulent history.

In prehistoric times it was inhabited by members of the Illyrian tribe of the Liburni. Liburnian Osor was known as an important base on the amber trade route which ran from the Baltic to Greece, and so it had well-developed sea links. The Liburni built massive walls (by the present cemetery) and there were earthworks and towns in the surrounding area. The latest research shows that they probably dug the channel between Cres and Lošinj. In the Roman era Osor (Apsorus) was at one time the largest Roman town on the Eastern Adriatic coast, after Pula. It had the status of a municipality, was surrounded by walls, and in the town there were a forum, hot springs and mains water. It is certain that there was a channel in Roman times and that Osor was a maritime centre and the centre of the Ravenna navy. It is also certain that during the Avar and Slavic invasions, Osor survived, that is, it was not destroyed. Once the Roman Empire had fallen, Osor became part of the Byzantine Dalmatian province. It became the seat of a Bishop in 530, but was burnt down in 841 by the Saracens (Arabs). From the 10th century it admitted the authority of the Croatian rulers, but in the 11th century it came into Venice's field of interest. The Croatian kings gave the town certain privileges, which were confirmed by the Byzantine rulers and the Croatian-Hungarian Kings. With the appearance of larger ships (15th and 16th centuries), the shallow port was no longer functional, and the town lost its former importance. The centre of the island's government shifted to Cres. From 1409 to 1797 Osor was under the Venetians, but it was already far from the centre of events. It experienced a further decline during the French occupation (1805-1814), while it was under the Austrians (1797-1805 and 1814-1918), and during the Italian occupation (1920-1943). Renovation work began in Osor at the end of the 60s, and nowadays during the tourist season Osor is the venue for a series of summer happenings and has a permanent exhibition entitled "Sculpture and Music".

SIGHTS

The Roman walls* run along the isthmus to Bijar Bay (to the north of the town) and also partially through the present cemetery. In Bijar (Vier) Bay there are the remains of an early Christian cathedral complex built some time after AD 530, as well as the remains of the 15th century St. Mary's Church.

•••••••••••

Osor

The **Cathedral of the Assumption**** (Marijina Uznesenja), built in the second half of the 15th century (1463-1497) and restored in 1969, is famous for its Renaissance portal (of the Lombard type) and its early Renaissance decorations. The sanctuary and the bell tower were built in the 17th century. The main altar is Baroque (17th century) and amongst its valuable paintings are *The Annunciation* by Palma the Younger, a polyptych entitled *The Madonna and Saints* dating from 1570 which is the work of Zucato Armini and a large altarpiece by Andreo Michielli (1542-1617). During the summer season the Cathedral is the venue for the Osor Musical Evenings.

•••••••••••

The **Church of St. Gaudentius**** (Sveti Gaudencije), immediately to the southwest of the Cathedral, was built in the 15th century. It has Gothic lancet vaulting and the remains of wall paintings and wooden Gothic sculptures from the 15th century. St. Gaudentius of Osor was born here, was Bishop of Osor from 1018 to 1042, and is the patron of Osor and the sub-patron of the diocese of Krk. His feast day is June 1.

Osor, the Center

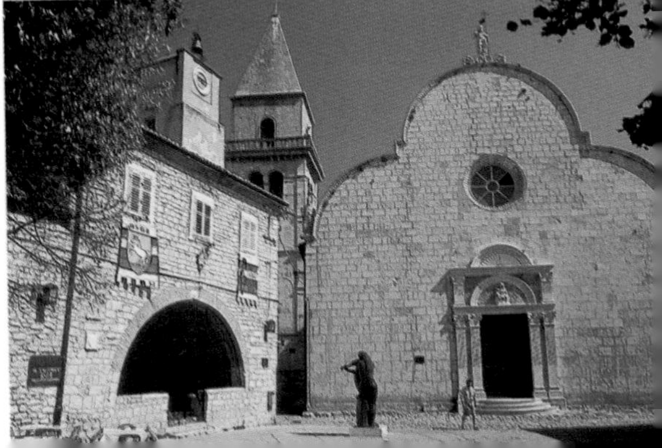

Snakes are crawling on the ground in the paintings that depict him. The meaning of the snakes is not certain; some say that it refers to his period as a hermit on the mountain of Osorčica, others claim that the snakes represent his enemies in Osor, while others again link his ministry with the fact that there are no snakes on the islands. From this legend derived the local mariners' custom of keeping a stone from the island in their pocket or wallet (a Saint Gaudentius stone) as an amulet to protect them against snake bites in foreign countries.

••••••••••••

The **Bishop's Palace**** was built on the site of an older building in the 15th century. The attractive building is decorated with braiding motifs. In the capitulary hall there is a collection of sacred art (ecclesiastical robes, and gold and silver liturgical equipment and other items from the Cathedral treasury).

••••••••••••

The **City Museum*** (the former city hall) has an archaeological exhibition which mainly consists of items of Roman glass. Amongst its sculptures there is the head of Octavian, the oldest representation of a Roman ruler on the Eastern Adriatic coast. The coin collection is an indication of the flourishing trade in this area. In the atrium there is a collection of stone monuments, including two outstanding stone inscriptions with Roman religious symbols, which date from the 5th century AD when Christianity became stronger and it was possible to express publicly thoughts relating to the new faith.

••••••••••••

EXCURSIONS

Nerezine*

5 KM FROM OSOR IN THE DIRECTION OF MALI LOŠINJ, POPULATION 379.

This is the largest village on the island of Lošinj and is situated beneath the Osoršćica mountain (588 m at the peak, Televrin). It was mentioned for the first time in the 14th century, but according to legend is the site of the ruins of the temple of Artemis where Medea killed her brother, Apsyrtos, the son of the Colchian King (in ancient times Lošinj was known as Apsyrtides). Apollonios Rhodios wrote about this (in about 250 BC) and later Alberto Fortis in his work *Saggio d'osservazioni Sopra l'isola di Cherso et Ossero* (Essay concerning observations on the islands of Cres and Lošinj) 1771.

••••••••••••

In the village there is a **Franciscan monastery**** which was the votive offering of a Venetian family of the 16th century, with cloisters and a chapel which date from 1510. The chapel contains an altarpiece by Girolamo da Santacroce and the painting *The Madonna and Child* by an unknown Venetian master of the 15th century. The monastery had a fine library and archives that have been moved to Rovinj. The Parish Church of Our Lady of Health was built in 1877. The parish church reveres St. Margaret (July 22) and the Church of St. Francis, St. Anthony and St. Francis (on August 1 and 2).

Osoršćica* is one of the most beautiful island mountains and the first to draw the attention of walkers. The Austrian Tourist Club had the path to the Church of St. Nicholas (Sveti Mikul or Sveti Nikola) constructed in 1887. It is an hour and half's ascent from Nerezine to the church, and two hours to "Televrin" peak. From the peak there is a fine view over Istria, the Velebit mountains and the Croatian coastal area. ■

Osoršćica

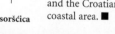

Mali Lošinj

SITUATED 44° 31' N, 14° 25' E.
POPULATION 6 422.

This is today the largest town of the Cres-Lošinj island group and is the seat of certain common administrative services. It was mentioned for the first time in 1398 as Malo Selo and as part of the property of the Osor feudal lords (Veli Lošinj, which was inhabited earlier, was at that time known as Velo Selo). At first the town grew slowly: in the 15th century the Venetians raised a fortress on the highest point, and this is partially still standing today. In the 17th century, Mali Lošinj developed at the expense of Osor, and the inhabitants took up fishing, seafaring and boat building as opposed to farming and cattle rearing, so that in the 18th century Lošinj was already beginning to develop as a maritime and shipbuilding town. The first large ship was built in Mali Lošinj in 1799, and by the mid-19th century it already had 6 shipyards employing more than 650 workers and building ships with up to 2,500 tonnes capacity. The ship owners of Lošinj (in 1869 they owned 127 ships with 73,000 tonnes capacity) transported cheap grain from the Black Sea ports to Europe, making clever use of the wars being waged at the time (between the Russians and the Turks, and the Greeks and the Turks) thus becoming extremely rich. As a result of this wealth, homes and business premises were built and Mali Lošinj flourished. In the age of sailing ships, up until the introduction of steam transport, only Trieste was a stronger maritime and ship building centre in the Northern Adriatic. In 1880 Mali Lošinj had 5,500 inhabitants. In 1780 a private Maritime College was opened in Mali Lošinj and a state college in 1855. Its maritime prosperity, beautiful countryside, and above all its favourable climate all contributed to the development of tourism. It has around 2,580 hours of sunshine a year and very little cloud, and is therefore one of the sunniest places in Europe. Mali Lošinj is also a climatic cure town, and in 1893, 415 tourists registered there. The following year there were as many as 893. During the Italian occupation, development was held back, but after the war the region of Cres and Lošinj experienced a tourist boom. In 1949 there were 6,939 tourists, and in 1984, 265,782, for these are islands that are very attractive to tourists.

Lošinj, 1842

Mali Lošinj

The **Church of St. Martin**** (Sveti Martin) stands in the cemetery on the eastern side of the island and is the oldest building in Mali Lošinj. It was built between 1450 and 1490 and has been rebuilt several times. It has valuable stone sculptures of a rustic nature.

The Baroque **Parish Church of the Nativity of the Virgin**** (Rođenje Marijino) was built between 1696 and 1757. On the altar, apart from pictures of the Virgin by A. Vivarini, there are reliquaries of St. Romulus. On the

Harbour at Čikat

first altar on the left hand side, or northern wall, in a composition containing St. Nicholas, St. Rocco and St. Anthony of Padua a view of Mali Lošinj in the 17th century is included. On the second altar the patron saints of the Kvarner islands, and St. Gaudentius, St. Kvirin and St. Christopher are depicted. On the right hand wall, the first altar is dedicated to the Holy Cross, and the marble crucifix is the work of Bartolomeo Ferrari. Much of the fine inventory of the church is made up of gifts by sea captains of Mali Lošinj. Valuable archives from the beginning of the 15th century are kept in the church.

••••••••••••

Mali Lošinj harbour*** (Valle d'Augusto) is the best and one of the most beautiful natural harbours on the Adriatic. Only Boka Kotorska and Šibenik harbours can be compared with it. Some sources mention that this harbour provided protection for the fleet of Emperor Augustus when it sailed into battle against Mark Anthony under the orders of his admiral Agrippa, in the year 31 BC.

••••••••••••

In front of the Chapel of St. Anthony on the Quay (Riva) is a **bust of the Lošinj man Josip Kašman** (born 1847 or 1850), world-famed opera singer, called king of the baritones in his time. The first Croat to appear the Metropolitan Opera, Kašman was a pupil of Ivan Zajc (s. Rijeka). In

order to avoid having to serve in the Austrian army he deserted to Italy, and subsequently appeared under the name of Giuseppe Kaschmann, of whom one encyclopaedia writes as follows: "an outstanding interpreter of the characters of the Italian bel-canto repertoire, subsequently one of the leading Wagnerians". He returned to Zagreb in 1909 when a military amnesty was proclaimed. He died in Rome on February 7, 1925.

••••••••••••

Piperata*** (the artistic collection of the Open University; Ul. Vladimira Gortana 35). This contains dozens of works by artists purchased in the post-war years. It includes mainly works of the Venetian masters of the 17th century, of various schools and techniques, as well as items with artistic value which at one time belonged to seafarers from Lošinj.

••••••••••••

Čikat***, a peninsula, 1.5 km from the town covered in thick pine forests, which together with the forests towards Veli Lošinj, and the forests around the bay of Krivica, Plijeski and Vinikova, is the trade mark and symbol of Lošinj. All these forests were planted at the initiative of the botanist **Ambroz Haračić** (1855-1916) from Lošinj, who was a teacher at the Maritime College. In the most beautiful part of the bay there is a monument to him, the work of the sculptor Ante Starčević. In the park there is also the Chapel of the Annunciation from the 19th century, with votive paintings (ex voto) of seafarers. The numerous hotels on the peninsula have not destroyed the harmony of forest and sea, on the contrary, the successful combination of gardens and architecture has created an attractive unity.

••••••••••••

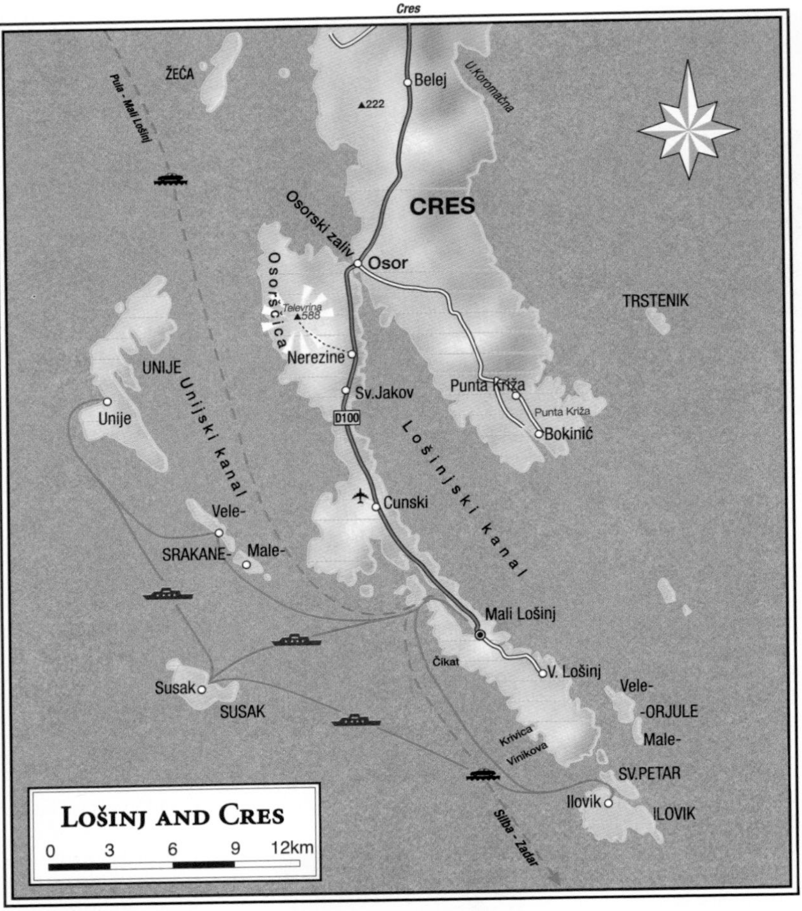

EXCURSIONS

Veli Lošinj**

4 KM SOUTHEAST OF MALI LOŠINJ. **POPULATION 983.**

The town dates from 1280 (it is the oldest settlement on the islands of Lošinj) when 12 Croatian families settled in the area of present day Veli Lošinj, led from the coastal area by Obrad Harnović. In the 15th century, along with Cres, Lošinj came under the Venetians who fortified Velo Selo (Large Village) against attacks by Uskoks (see Senj). Once this danger had passed, Veli Lošinj took up seafaring. It was a town of famous sea captains and in the Rovenska Bay a shipyard was built. But neighbouring Mali Lošinj had a more favourable location as well as the ability to expand, so the centre of the island's life moved from Veli to Mali Lošinj.

••••••••••••

The **Church of St. Anthony** (Sveti Antun) **the Hermit** was built in the 18th century on the foundations of a church dating from the 15th century, and extended in 1774. The church houses several paintings by Italian masters, of which the better known are *The Madonna and Child* by B. Vivarini from 1475, *St. Francis* by B. Strozzi, *St. John the Baptist* by L. Quereno, *The Adoration of the Magi* by F. Hajez, *St. Gregory* by L. del Cossa and *Souls in Purgatory* by F. Potenza. The rich artistic inventory of the church derives from the golden period of seafaring in Lošinj. The seven Baroque altars and the paintings were donated by the master mariners of the town, and bought most often in Venice. Thus, according to some authors, the church has the biggest collection of paintings in the Kvarner islands.

Veli Lošinj

•••••••••••

The **Church of St. Nicholas*** (Sveti Nikola) is the oldest church in Veli Lošinj, built in Gothic style. It is interesting for its secular paintings, portraits of seafarers in national costume.

•••••••••••

Lošinj Park** was planted by Karl von Habsburg. It contains about 200 species of trees from all over the world. It is interesting that of about 1100 plant species which grow successfully on Lošinj, about 80 were brought by Lošinj sailors from far corners of the world. Thus Lošinj is now covered with exceptional vegetation and is the most interesting area in this respect in the entire Adriatic.

In the waters off Lošinj a group of **bottle-nosed dolphins** (*Tursiops truncatus*) have taken up permanent residence. Research has been done into these marine mammals since 1987, and they constitute one of the best-researched populations in the whole of the Mediterranean. The population has been estimated to contain some 140 individuals, 120 of which have been identified and named. Dolphin lovers can help in their protection and research into them, adopting a dolphin or taking part in the well-established Dolphin Day, celebrated in Veli Lošinj the first Saturday in August. (Contact: *Plavi svijet*, Zad bone 11, Veli Lošinj, Croatia; adp@hpm.hr).

•••••••••••

Veli Lošinj as a climatic cure town. Its climatic characteristics (above all the stable humidity of the air) ensured Veli Lošinj the reputation of being a climatic cure town as early as 1885. The following ailments can be treated there: bronchitis and bronchial asthma; chronic infections of the respiratory organs; allergies of the respiratory and other organs; psoriasis, eczema, acne; general weakness and physical exhaustion. Treatment is given for allergic illnesses in the children's hospital which has a department for adults, temporarily closed.

•••••••••••

Ilovik*, an island of flowers, 9 nautical miles from Mali Lošinj harbour, one mile to the south of Lošinj, population 145. It was settled as early as prehistoric times. On top of Straža hill there are the remains of prehistoric earthworks. There are the ruins of a "villa rustica" on the neighbouring island of St. Peter (Sveti Petar), which bear witness to life during the Roman era. Today the municipal graveyard is here, boats being used for the funerals. In the 11th century Benedictines built a monastery known as "Sancti Petris de Nemois". The remaining wall of the monastery now forms part of the wall around the local cemetery. The present-day Parish Church of St. Peter was built on the

Dolphins

foundations of the monastery's chapel which was demolished in the 19th century. In a field near Sićardija there are the ruins of an early medieval chapel dedicated to St. Andrew (Sveti Andrija). During the rule of the Venetians a defensive tower was built on the neighbouring island in 1597, as protection against the Uskoks (see Senj). It is now in ruins. The local people are fishermen or tend vineyards.

Croatian Apoxiomen

••••••••••••

In 1996 an authentic antique statue called '**Croatian Apoxiomen**' was found south-east of the island of Lošinj, near Vele Orjule, on the sea route from Greece to Italy. According to historians, the statue is called 'An Athlete After Exercise'. It is believed that this bronze statue was cast at the end of the 1st century B. C. and that it somehow found its way into the sea between 50 and 70 A. D. Restoration of the work took seven years. Experts now agree that this piece of art belongs in the very top echelon of world sculpture: It can be compared to 'The Athlete from Ephesus' in Vienna or to marble statuary in the Museum of Uffizi in Florenze. The statue is now in the collection of the Archaeological Museum in Zagreb.

••••••••••••

Susak***, an island in the immediate vicinity of Mali Lošinj, is a natural and social phenomenon of both the Adriatic and the Mediterranean. It lies 6 nautical miles to the west of Lošinj (i.e. from the jetty on Čikat) and covers an area of 3.75 km², with a total circumference of 11.25 km. Its appearance and geological characteristics give the impression that it is part of some far away world: it is covered with a thick layer of sand deposits which create a unique landscape. This sand island is 98 m in height and is covered with two kinds of plant life: vineyards and reeds. If there had been no reeds the island would never have existed at all, it would have been swept away by the wind over the centuries. Despite the fact that it is not far from Mali Lošinj, the island remained isolated for a thousand years, and this can still be seen in its national costume, speech and even in the appearance of its inhabitants. Some of the interesting things on Susak are the simple dwellings built with dry stone walls, based on plans which date from prehistoric times. As regards works of art, the most valuable items include a large **Romanesque carved wooden crucifix***** which is known as "Veli Buoh", to be found in the Parish Church of St. Nicholas, dating from 1770.

Susak

Women's traditional costume from Susak

••••••••••••

Unije*, an island 15 nautical miles from Mali Lošinj harbour, population 81. The island covers an area of 16.7 km² and is 10 km long. There is evidence of life on this island during the Roman era (a villa rustica on the site of the present day village). The Church of St. Andrew (Sveti Andrija) dates from the 15th century, but has been rebuilt since. In the village itself there is a stone oil storage basin which is particularly interesting because of its Glagolitic inscription (s. Glagolitic) dating from 1654. It stands in the wine cellar belonging to the Nikolić-Agatić family. The villagers are fishermen and viticulturists.

••••••

The Island of Krk

Krk is the largest island in the Adriatic (405.78 km²). It is 38 km long and, at its widest, 18 km in breadth. There are a total of 68 settlements (14 of them having populations of over 200) with 16 402 inhabitants.

Old Croatian coat of arms, on the portal of St. Lucy's Church

Prehistory. Archaeological finds show that the island has been inhabited without a break since the Neolithic age. According to Greek and Latin sources, Curicta (Krk) is one of the Apsyrtidian or Electridian islands held by the Liburnians. There are the remains of prehistoric settlements near Baščanska Draga and Bronze and Iron Age earthworks near Malinska, Dobrinj, Vrbnik, and Baška.

The Roman Era. Krk came under the Romans once they had defeated the Liburnians. The town of Krk (Curicum) became a town with Italic law whose status evolved to give it the rights of a municipality. Nothing is known about the internal organisation of the town of Krk from this time. Near the present day Franciscan monastery the remains of thermal baths have been found. The defensive walls of Roman Curicum were amongst the most secure of all the towns on the Eastern Adriatic fortified by the Romans. Work began on their construction during the Civil War in Rome (50 BC) and they were further strengthened in the 60s of the 2nd century AD, to enable them to withstand attacks by the Quadi and the Marcomanni who were at that time threatening the Adriatic. Not far from Krk in 49 BC there was a decisive sea battle between Caesar and Pompey, which was described impressively by the Roman writer Lucan (AD 39-65) in his work *Pharsalia.* When the Empire was divided, Krk came under the Eastern Roman Empire.

The Migrations of the Nations. The walls of the town Krk could not withstand attacks by the Avars (7th century), but in contrast to Salona, Scardona and Aenona, life in Krk quickly returned to normal. The Slavs penetrated into the town on several occasions. They retained many of the Roman names they found there and so it is said that Krk has a "mosaic dialect". Following the Treaty of Aachen (812) the entire island was ceded to Byzantium and was governed according to the norms of that Empire. During the reign of Emperor Constantine Porphyrogenitus (the 10th century), Krk was known as Vekla, of which the Romanized variant, also used by the Venetians, was Veglia.

The Time of the Croatian Counts and Kings. There are no extant documents showing when Krk became part of the Croatian state. It is known that from around 875 the Byzantine town paid the Croatian rulers 110 gold pieces a year to be able peacefully to keep their hold there. It is also indisputable that Krk was under the Croatian kings during the reign of King Zvonimir (see the Baška Tablet). While the Croatian state was being established, Krk found itself on the Venetians' route to the Mediterranean. The Venetians conquered the town for the first time in 1001, and from then Krk's history was closely linked with the history of the Serenessima for 7 centuries. During the reign of Petar Krešimir IV the Croatian rulers regained their power, but the Venetians took Krk for the second time in 1118.

The **Reign of the Krk Counts** (from 1430 the Frankopan family). When the Venetians conquered Krk for the second time in 1118, the local noble family, the unknown Dujams, received Krk as part of a pact with Venice, and they became Counts. When Dujam died (in 1163) Venice allowed his sons to make their position hereditary, after a payment of 350 Byzantine gold pieces as tax. In a short time the Krk Counts became so strong that at one time (from 1244 to 1260) Venice rescinded

Sopila players from Dobrinj

their authority. This failed to impede their rise however. They increased economic exploitation, but they also endeavoured to strengthen old traditions and rights with various statutes (the Vinodol Code 1288 and the Vrbnik Statute, 1388). Dujam's youngest son, who died in 1209, succeeded in extending his authority to the mainland, began to serve the Croatian-Hungarian King and received the district of Modruš. Due to his economic strength and social standing, his opponents fought each other for his favour. The Counts became so strong that no power could threaten them (until the Turks). Members of this family were leaders in Split, Trogir and Senj, and from 1392 one of them became a Croatian-Dalmatian Ban. In 1430 they took the surname Frankopan, claiming to have Roman origins. That year they adopted a coat of arms showing two lions breaking a piece of bread (Latin: frangere pane, break bread). From 1449, the descendants of Nikola V founded eight branches of this family, and together with the Zrinski Counts were the ruling feudal family in the whole of Croatia right up to 1671. The Frankopans produced seven Croatian Bans, and many of them were patrons of Croatian artists.

Coat of arms of the Frankopan family

Under the Venetians (1480-1797). Krk was the last Adriatic island to become part of the Venetian Empire. Due to its location, closest to the Uskoks of Senj (s. Senj) it served as a lookout point and the first line of defence against the Uskoks. From that time the ruler was a Venetian noble, but the Small and the Large Councils both had a certain autonomy. The Doge controlled the clergy but public documents were written in Glagolitic which was adopted here more than anywhere else. At the beginning of the 16th century the inhabitants of inland Croatia began to settle on Krk in their flight from the Turks, but Krk suffered a decline like all other Venetian property. In 1527 the town had 10,461 inhabitants and in 1571 it had 8,000.

Under the Austrians. This began with the fall of Venice in 1797 and was briefly (1806-1813) interrupted by Napoleon's Illyrian Provinces. In 1822 the Austrians separated the island from Dalmatia and linked it to Istria, so that Krk, Cres and Lošinj came under direct rule from Vienna. This link contributed to the Croatian National Revival and together with Kastav, the town of Krk played a leading role in the spread of Croatian education and culture.

20th Century. The Italian Occupation (1918-1920) was brief, and Krk was handed over to Croatia, then in Yugoslavia, by the Treaty of Rapallo. Italy took Krk again in the Second World War (1941-1943), and German occupation followed from 1943-1945. It was liberated on 17th April 1945. The post-war development of Krk was led by tourism. The largest tourist resort on the island is Haludovo near Malinska. The building of an airport and then a bridge over to the mainland ensures the future of the development of tourism on this island. In Omišalj there has also been industrial development.

View of Krk

Krk (Town)

LOCATED 45° 5' N, 14° 35' E.
CITY AND PORT ON THE WESTERN COAST OF THE ISLAND OF KRK.
POPULATION 3 411.

Krk, harbour

SIGHTS

The **Cathedral***** (The **Assumption of the Virgin Mary**) is an extremely interesting piece of architecture. It is a Romanesque building which has been added to several times. Its present appearance dates from the 12th century. As early as the 5th or 6th centuries there was a Christian temple built on the foundations of Roman baths. The columns in the interior (both Roman and Romanesque) clearly show the variety of styles present in this building. In the left-hand nave of the cathedral there is a Frankopan chapel from the 15th century with a Gothic vault. There are also gravestones in the cathedral of the Krk Bishops from the 14th to the 16th centuries, as well as a Gothic crucifix and a Gothic sculpture of the *Madonna in Glory.* The Frankopan silver altarpiece is the work of P. Koler from 1477. Particularly impressive are two Renaissance lecterns and a wooden pulpit from the 17th century. The altar piece *The burial in the grave* is the work of G.A. Pordenone (G.A. de Sacchi, 1483-1539). In a chapel in the right-hand nave there are four paintings by C. Tosca from 1709. In the Bishop's Palace there is a **collection of paintings** by Italian masters of the 16th and 17th centuries. It is thought that the most valuable painting is a *polyptych of St. Lucy* (Sveta Lucija) by Paolo Veneziano (?-1362), the most significant figure in Venetian art in the first half of the 14th century. This painting was once in the Glagolitic Abbey of St. Lucy (Sveta Lucija) in Jurandvor (where the Baška Tablet was also housed).

•••••••••••

St. Quirinus*** (Sveti Kvirin; adjoining the cathedral). This Romanesque basilica is a most unusual church. It is a double-naved building from the 10th or 11th century. A street now runs through what was its aisle. The entrance to the church is through the bell tower which was built from the 16th to the 18th centuries. Inside the church there are fragments of Romanesque frescoes.

•••••••••••

The **city towers and walls** also belong to various eras. The square shaped tower (Kamplin) dates from 1191, from the time of the Krk Counts Bartol and Vid. The walls and bastions on the sea front are from the time of Nikola Frankopan (1407). The cylindrical tower and the town gates are Venetian, from the 15th or 16th century.

•••••••••••

Other items of interest. In P. Franolić street (number 11) there is the **Canon's House** (Kotter House) with a Glagolitic text from the 11th century. The early-Romanesque basilica **Our Lady of Good Health** (Gospa od Zdravlja) which dates from the 12th century, is not far from the **Church of St. Francis*** (Sveti

Church of St. Quirin

Frane). Together with its monastery this Franciscan church dates from the 13th century and is situated near the northern entrance into the town. Outside the town there are the ruins of a pre-Romanesque church, St. Lawrence's (Sveti Lovro).

Baška

Excursions

Baška***

Nova Baška, 18 km from Krk, population 959.

Baška was the largest town on the island until 1910. In 1900 Baška had 2000 inhabitants and Krk 1600. Prehistoric earthworks around Baška and archaeological remains bear witness to settlements here in early times. During the Roman era the settlement was situated on the sea front (there are the remains of a villa rustica) and in the Middle Ages the settlement developed to the north of the present town on St. John's Hill (Sveti Ivan) where there is now a graveyard. In 1380 the Venetians sacked and burnt this settlement, and since then the town has grown up again on the sea front. Baška is considered to be one of the most beautiful towns on the Adriatic because of its picturesque maze of streets, squares and passageways. **St. John's Church** (Sveti Ivan) stands on the hill by the graveyard. The original church was early Romanesque but was burnt down in 1380 by the Venetians. It was later rebuilt and has remained standing ever since. Not far from the church there are the ruins of a Medieval castle known as Bosar, but called "Korint" by local people. This was probably the site of the old settlement known as Karintija. The **Church of the Holy Trinity*** (Sveto Trojstvo) is situated in front of the entrance to the town and was built in the 18th century. The church houses paintings such as *The Last Supper* by Palma the Younger and *The Coronation of the Madonna* by Franjo Juričić, as well as a collection of wooden and stone sculptures from the 15th to the 16th centuries.

Jurandvor**

1 km from Baška on the road to Krk.

In Jurandvor is the **Church of St. Lucy** (Sveta Lucija), which was built in about 1100 on the ruins of a villa rustica and an early Christian church from the 6th-7th centuries. Inside the church was the **Baška Tablet** (Baščanska ploča) (197 x 99cm in size), the oldest dated written example of the Croatian language. It is written in Glagolitic and was discovered by scholars in 1851. The original is now kept in the Croatian Academy of Sciences and Arts; in the church is a copy. The tablet records how the Croatian King Dmitar Zvonimir (who died in 1089) gave Abbot Držiha a piece of wasteland and names the witnesses. The second half of the inscription tells how

St. Lucy's Church

Baška Tablet

Abbot Dobrovit built the church along with 9 monks. In the meantime the screen, whose left side used to be formed by the Baška Tablet, has been reconstructed.

Dobrinj***

20 km from Krk, population 122

Dobrinj is in the north-eastern, agriculturally rich part of the island. It is the oldest Croatian settlement on the island, and in the Frankopan era it formed one of four centres of communes on the island of Krk. It was mentioned under its present name in 1100. Although it is close to a natural harbour, the settlement grew up in a more strategic location, on a 200 m high hill. It has no defensive wall, as the walls of a ring of village houses served this purpose. It was an important centre of Glagolitic culture, and registers were kept here from the 16th century, the first in Croatia. During the economic crisis in the 19th century, many inhabitants emigrated to

Dobrinj

America, and thus Dobrinj lost its former importance on the island. The **Parish Church of St. Stephen*** (Sveti Stjepan) in the centre of the settlement has been rebuilt on several occasions, and therefore contains elements of both late Gothic and Baroque styles. The church was mentioned in 1100. The rectangular pres-

Dancers from Dobrinj

bytery was built in 1602, and the original single-naved building was converted into a triple-naved church by the addition of side chapels in the 18th century. On the main altar there is a multicoloured wooden relief dating from 1602, with the figure of St. Stephen in the centre and members of the Dobrinj fraternities Not far from the parish church, above the square of Dobrinj, is the **Church of the Holy Trinity** (also called St. Anthony's by the local people), dating from the 16th century with a bell-tower of 1725. In its park, the former graveyard, a look out point called Zemljina has been arranged, which has a fine view over Kvarner. Here is a rectory which has a very valuable collection of ecclesiastical art. Among the exhibits the following stand out: a Gothic reliquary of St. Ursula which is the work of a local goldsmith, gold-plated crucifixes from the 15th century, a pyx from the 16th century, and an embroidery in gold thread on red silk depicting the coronation of the Madonna and the figures of St. Stephen and St. James from the 14th century. South east of the rectory, in a traditional four storey house, is the Dobrinj Ethnographic Museum, with 1,200 exhibits. In nearby Soline the Counts of Frankopan had saltworks. In the nearby village of Sveti Vid, 1 km to the east of Dobrinj, there is an early Romanesque chapel, which was an endowment of the "famous Dobroslav" from 1100. There is also a Romanesque church, St. Philip and St. James* (Sveti Filip i Jakov), in Soline, dating from the 13th century.

During festivals or at weddings the sound of the sopila can be heard; this is a traditional instrument like

Soline Bay; medicinal mud

an oboe. This ancient instrument, with its piercing sound, is played in pairs, one of the players having a large and the other a small instrument. Sopila music and Glagolitic writing are part of the identity of Dobrinj, and in recent times schools have been opened for learning both the sopila and Glagolitic.

Biserujka Cave** (6 km northeast of Dobrinj, in the village of Rudine, above Slivanjska Bay). In the middle of a bare karst landscape, an undistinguished stone house hides the entrance to a lovely cave 12 m under the

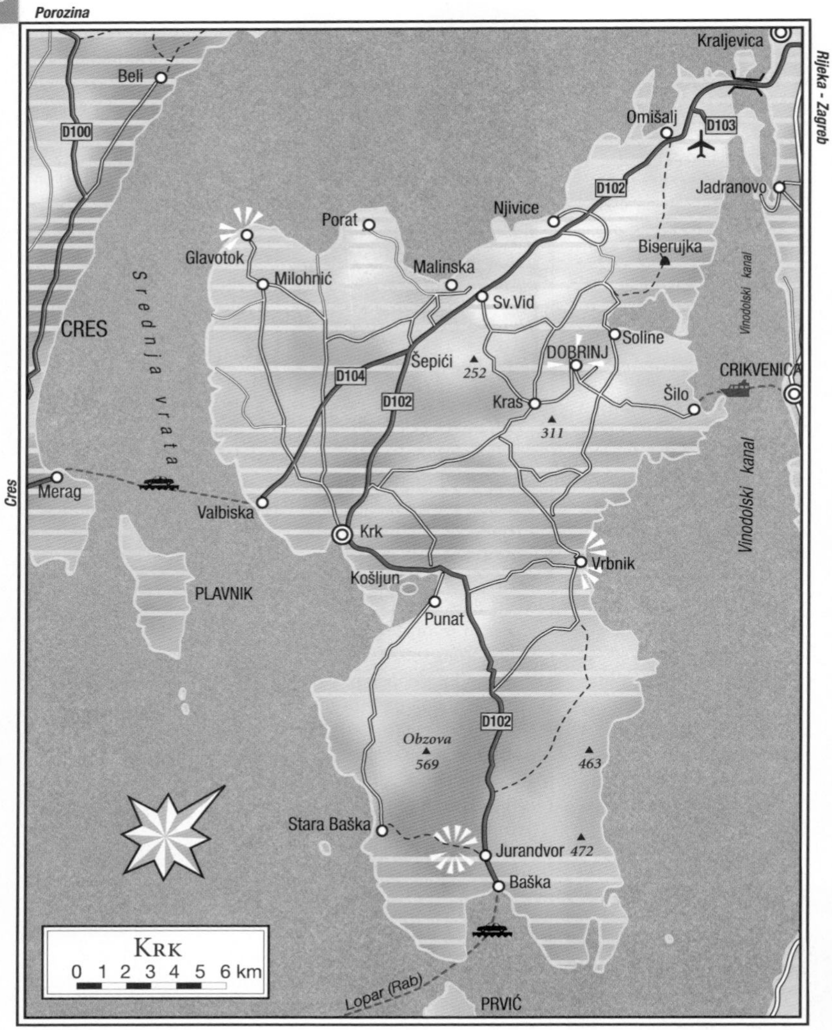

surface. Although it is not very long, only 110 m, this cave has everything that is characteristic of karst phenomena. It has lots of typical features such as stalactites and stalagmites and a lovely gallery or hall, which is suitable for the holding of concerts. However, because of the low temperature (13 °C), people cannot stand being there for very long, and only short musical appearances take place. Since 1997 the cave has

Biserujka Cave

been arranged for sightseeing, and the hosts can take groups of 25 at a time.

•••••••••••

Glavotok**

15 KM NORTHWEST OF KRK.

Glavotok is the westernmost point of the island facing the island Cres. At one time it belonged to the Frankopans, but in 1473 they gave it to the Third Order Franciscans, who were Glagolitic scholars. The church was built in around 1507 in a style typical of the "men-

Malinska, a fishing village

dicant orders". The choir was extended in the 17th century, and the facade renovated in 1879. The main altarpiece *The Madonna and Child* is the work of an unknown Venetian master of the 17th century. *St. Francis and St. Bonaventura* is the work of G. da Santacroce. The monastery was built on land given by the Frankopans. It includes archives and a library with Glagolitic texts, gravestones and a well with folk art carvings and Glagolitic inscriptions.

Malinska*

8 KM NORTH OF KRK, POPULATION 607.

Malinska was first mentioned in the 15th century, and since the 19th century has developed as a port (Dubašnica) for the export of wood. The Parish Church of St. Apollinare in Bogovići was built in 1857 on the foundations of an older church. **Porat*** is a village on the northwest coast of the island, 3 km south of Malinska. There is a Franciscan Third Order monastery and the Church of St. Mary Magdalene dating from 1500 in the village. On the altar of the church there is a polyptych by Girolamo da Santacroce. The refectory houses paintings by local artists from the 17th century. The monastery also contains a beautiful **museum and library**. West of the village, in St. Martin's Bay, the ruins of a Benedictine monastery and church from the 11th and 12th centuries can be seen.

Omišalj**

23 KM TO THE NORTH OF KRK, POPULATION 1 790.

Omišalj is built in the form of an acropolis on a hill 82 m high and, with the town of Krk, is the oldest settlement on the island. Its name is of Roman origin (from Castrum Musculum). Near present-day Omišalj (in Sepen Bay) was the Roman town of Fulfinium (Fertinates or Foretani) which was a community of pilgrims who obtained Italic rights. In the Middle Ages Omišalj was one of four Franciscan towns on Krk. The castle, belonging to the Frankopan Counts, stood by the main entrance into the town. It was built in 1420, and demolished this century. In the last hundred years Omišalj has been developing as a tourist resort, and in the last decade chemical plants have been built. The Parish Church of the Assumption (Stomarina) is a triple-naved Romanesque basilica and was mentioned in 1213. In the 16th century a dome was added and a rectangular choir, then a bell-tower in 1536. The church contains some beautiful stonework with braiding ornamentation from the 9th century and several Glagolitic inscriptions. The most valuable painting is a polyptych by Jacobello del Fiore. There is a collection of stone monuments in the sacristy, including the particularly significant gravestone of the last Benedictine Abbot, with a Glagolitic inscription from 1471. On the south side of the bell-tower a loggia was built in the 16th century. The Romanesque Church of St. Anthony of Padua (Sveti Antun), the Church of St. Helen (Sveta Jelena) dating from 1470, on the eastern side of the broad square, and St. John's Church (Sveti Ivan) from 1442 are also worth mentioning here. There are also the ruins of the Prince's Palace, which was built in the 14th to the 15th centuries, and a 15th century "Poncirov" house, with Gothic details. At the

Omišalj

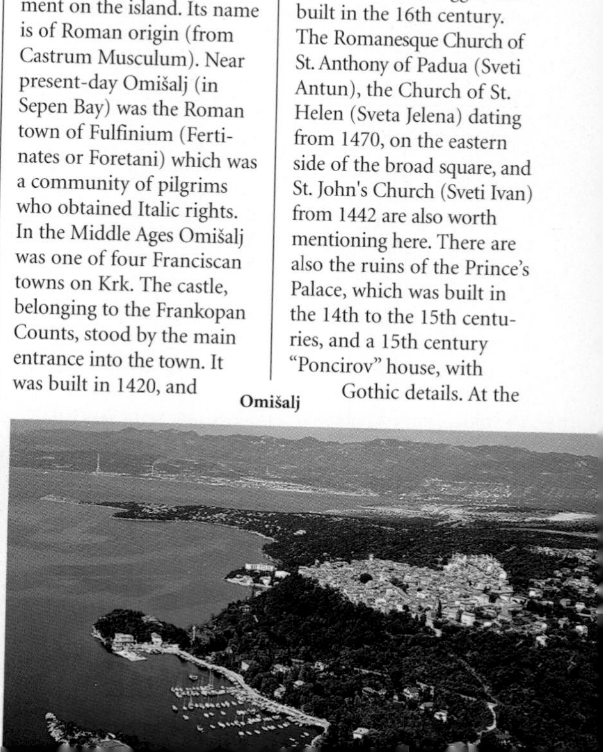

Košljun, Punat in the background

far end of the harbour stands Gradec fortress. In Sepen-Fulfinium Bay are the ruins of an early Christian church from the 5th century, which is linked by local tradition to the Glagolitic Benedictine Abbey of St. Nicholas (Sveti Nikola). Every year on 15th August the festival of the first fruits, "Stomorina", takes place. **Njivice*** (7 km south of Omišalj, population 1 169) lies on the Beli Kamik coast; it is a new development and one of the most attractive holiday-making complexes on the island.

••••••••••••

Punat**

7 KM TO THE EAST OF KRK, POPULATION 1 784.

Punat is the largest settlement on the island of Krk. It grew up near the straits known as Usta and received its name from a bridge ("ponte" in Italian). As "Villa di Ponte" it was mentioned in 1480, but it was not until the 18th century that the town centre was formed. The old, common people's houses date from that time, with their sturdy open-air staircases and balconies built along their facades. One of the oldest buildings is an olive mill from the 18th century. The **Parish Church of the Holy Trinity** (Sveto Trojstvo) was built in 1773 and rebuilt in 1934. The main altar with its *wooden carvings and painting of Christ's baptism* is the work of Domenico F. Maggiotta from the 18th century. In 1787 it was brought from the Paulist St. Nicholas' Church (Sveti Nikola) in Senj. The church also contains a late Gothic *wooden polychrome sculpture of St. Anne with a Madonna and Child* from the 15th century.

••••••••••••

Facing Punat, in the bay Puntarska Draga, lies the small island of **Košljun*****, which is rich in vegetation. It covers an area of 6.5 hectares. In Roman times there was a villa rustica here belonging to a landowner from Krk, and in the 11th century a Benedictine monastery was built on its foundations. This was abandoned in 1447, and the Frankopans moved in Franciscans in their place. The present church was built by the Franciscans in 1480. By the jetty there is a **statue of St. Francis** with a wolf, a frequent iconographic motif for this saint. As well as the statue there is also a text written in Glagolitic over the main entrance to the monastery, "Mir i Dobro" (peace and well-being) which is also dedicated to St. Francis. In the monastery there is an **ethnographic collection** including articles used by farmers and fishermen on Krk from the end of the 19th century and the beginning of the 20th century.

Cloister of the Monastery on Košljun

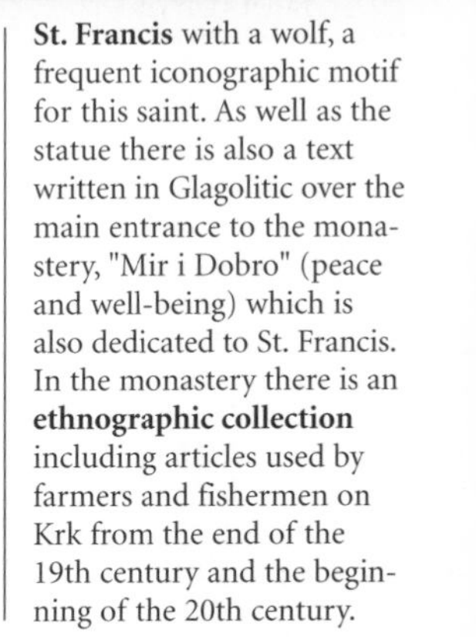

From the collection of the Museum

There is also a **permanent exhibition of church artefacts** housed in the old Benedictine church from the 12th century. As well as old masters (G. da Santacroce, F. Ughetto, Medulić and F. Jurić) the collection also includes works by more recent Croatian artists and sculptors such as: Dulčić, Bulić, Lacković Croata, Radauš, Orlić and Kršinić. The monastery also owns a rich library of some 15,000 books which contains the Missal of Hrvoje of 1404, a Jewish

Bible from the 11th century, Glagolitic sermons and Ptolemy's Atlas, printed in Venice in 1511. The **Church of the Assumption** was built in 1523, and also has fine furnishings.

●●●●●●●●●●●●

At the end of the bay on the road to the town of Krk, stands the pre-Romanesque **Chapel of St. Dunat**** (Sveti Dunat), which is a fine example of old Croatian architecture. It dates from the 9th century and is one of the most significant buildings in Croatia. It is similar to St. Donat's Church in

Vrbnik

Zadar, Holy Cross (Sveti Križ) in Nin and St. Peter's (Sveti Petar) in Omiš.

●●●●●●●●●●●●

Vrbnik***

11 KM TO THE EAST OF KRK, POPULATION 944.

Vrbnik stands on a cliff 48 m above the sea, so picturesque it is celebrated in traditional song. It grew up on the site of a prehistoric settlement and in the Middle Ages it was a Frankopan castle. It was mentioned for the first time in 1100, and in 1388 it received a charter written in Glagolitic. In the past century it has spread beyond the old town centre and is now one of the commune centres. The old town walls are still visible only towards the south-west. The **Parish Church of St. Mary****, on raised ground in the centre of the town, was built in the 15th and 16th centuries. The Renaissance bell-tower was built in 1527. The main altar piece, *The Assumption* is the work of an anonymous Venetian painter of the 16th century. A particularly valuable painting is the *Last Supper* by Marin Cvitović of Kotor, which dates from 1599. The St. Mary Chapel and the Gothic polyptych of St. Anne are the work of local masters of the 15th century. **St. John's Chapel** (Sveti Ivan) in the graveyard is a Gothic building, constructed in the 15th century, for the Fraternity of St. John, which still exists today. In the bay of Sveti Juraj there is a medieval church with the remains of Romanesque wall decorations.

●●●●●●●●●●●●

The **Vitezić Brothers Library** (Placa Vrbničkog statuta 4). Ivan Vitezić, Bishop of Krk (1806-1877) and his brother Dr Dinko Vitezić, a member of Parliament, left Vrbnik a fine library of more than 10,000 books and manuscripts. One of the most valuable is a Kochler "Atlas of the World". Some of the books have been moved to the National and University Library in Zagreb). The library is not open all the time, but can be viewed on prior arrangement.

●●●●●●●●●●●●

The **Bačin Dvor Gallery** (Ulica Glavača) exhibits works produced during the work of the Vrbnik Graphic Academy (run by Zdravko Tišljar and Frano Paro). The gallery is open in the tourist season.

●●●●●●●●●●●●

Krk Bridge links the island of Krk to the mainland. This original and bold approach has won world acclaim. It was built in two stages, one support being on the island of St. Mark (Sveti Marko). The bridge is 1,309.5 m long in total, the arch between the mainland and St. Mark's island being 390 m long , exceeding the then (1981) longest span (in Sydney) by 85 m. The bridge was built by local engineers (Šram) and construction workers.

●●●●●●●●●●●●

The best known wine from the island of Krk is **Vrbnička Žlahtina**, a high-quality appelation contrôlée wine. It is made from a grape known as "žlahtina". It is light yellow to straw-yellow in colour, has a fine, subtle aroma and is dry. Three co-ops produce the wine in Vrbnik today: the General Agricultural Co-op, the Katunar Bros Co-op, and the Gospoja Co-op of Ivan Toljanić. ■

Krk Bridge

The Island of Rab

This island belongs to the Kvarner group. It is the ninth largest in the Adriatic, with a total area of 90.84 km² and is 21.5 km long, 7.2 km wide. A population of 9 600 lives in eight settlements. The island is dominated by three ridges, the largest of which is Kamenjak (the peak is known as Straža, 408 m) which sweeps steeply into the sea of the Velebit channel, making the island unapproachable from that side. The coastline is jagged, the north-western side being the most rugged. The climate of the island differs from that of the mainland and also other nearby islands. In terms of hours of sunshine (2,499 annually) Rab is one of the sunniest places in Europe. The average winter temperature is 6.7 °C and in summer 23.2 °C. Rab is also one of the greenest islands in the Adriatic. Woods cover more that 40% of its surface.

Prehistory and the Greek period. On the site of present day Rab, there was a settlement of the Illyrian tribe of the Liburnians. From the time when the Greeks attacked the east coast of the Adriatic from Magna Graecia (Syracuse), Rab came into their area of interest. It is thought that archaeological finds on Kaštelin Point (s. Kampor) and Zidine Point (s. Lopar) are the remains of Greek settlements. The defeat of the Liburnians in a sea battle in 365 BC also took place somewhere between Krk and Rab. Once Rome had defeated the Illyrian Queen Teuta (229 BC) and the Histri (177 BC), Rab came under their control.

The Roman Era. Under the Romans Rab became a naval port and a politically organised town called "Arba". It is known that the Roman town was surrounded by a wall, had aqueducts, thermal baths, temples and probably theatres, but there are very few archaeological remains to help reconstruct its urban structure. According to inscriptions on some stones it seems that the town prospered most during the reign of Emperor Antonius Pius (138-161). During the reigns of the later Emperors, Rab (Arba) was the seat of Bishops.

The Migrations of the Nations. As only well-protected towns could fend off the attacks of the Avars and Slavs, and Rab's walls were not secure, during the 7th century Arba was razed to the ground. However while Byzantine authority was being established over the Adriatic area (in about 750), the town was rebuilt. Once the border between Charles the Great and Byzantium had been established by the Treaty of Aachen in 812, Arba once again came under Byzantine rule, along with other towns such as Osor, Krk, Trogir, Split and Venice. It is thought that the Croats completed their settlement of the Eastern Adriatic coast by the end of the 7th century, and that by the end of the following century, the former inhabitants had been assimilated into the Slavic people.

St. Christopher; patron saint of Rab

The Time of the Croatian Counts and Kings. When the Byzantine Emperor Basileios I the Macedonian (867-886) was forced to issue a decree by which Dalmatian towns had to pay taxes to the Croatian Counts in 878, Rab (Arba) became a Croatian town. Not long after that Byzantium ceded the jurisdiction of the church to Rome in order to secure a treaty with Tomislav against the Bulgarians. On that occasion the Patriarch of Constantinople presented Rab with the bones of St. Christopher, as it was an important Slavic town. But Croatian Rab became a barrier to Venetian plans for political and economic expansion down to the Mediterranean. The Doge Pietro Orseolo initiated a war in 1000 and received from Rab its assurance of "loyalty". This period lasted while the Croatian Kings were weaker. In 1070 King Petar Krešimir IV presented the island with the Monastery of St. Petar in Draga and thus demonstrated that he was in fact the true ruler of the island and the town. Furthermore, he established the authority of the Bishop of Rab over Primorje, Lika and Pag. This brought great prosperity to Rab, but it was also the cause of conflict with the Bishop of Zadar. When Croatia accepted the Hungarian Koloman as its King, he too confirmed the privileges given to Rab by Petar Krešimir (1107). Until 1409, the continuity of rule was broken from time to time, depending on relationships between

Byzantium and Venice, but also on who gave the town the choice of ruler.

Under the Venetians (1409-1797). The first 60 years of Venetian rule on the island were backed up by a military regime, for Rab was the closest of all Venetian possessions to the Uskoks of Senj. In the middle of the century (1449 and 1456) Rab suffered its first disaster, the plague. The epidemic wiped out a large part of the population and Rab was left with no real work force. Refugees moving from the mainland could not compensate for the consequences of the plague. The second blow to Venice was the discovery of America and the transfer of the main trade routes to the West. The glory of the Serenissima began to fade. Not even the gain of new territories in Dalmatia at the expense of Crete could achieve any greater security and in 1797 Napoleon finally broke its 400-year reign over the Mediterranean.

Under Austria (1815-1918). For the first time in 2,000 years Rab was no longer on a major trade route and its importance dwindled until it became a province. In 1828 the Bishopric was dissolved. The Austrians supported the predominance of the Latin population so that it was not until 1897 that Croatian was introduced as the official language. Towards the end of the last century (23rd May 1889) the town was declared to be a bathing resort and a cure town. Since then it has mainly been a tourist resort.

The Twentieth Century. Rab became part of Croatia in the Kingdom of the Serbs, Croats and Slovenes Yugoslavia by the Treaty of Rapallo in 1920. The humble beginnings of the tourist trade could not compensate for all the town lost as its inhabitants emigrated inland into mainland Croatia and to countries outside Europe. During 1941-1945 it was occupied but in the past half century Rab has made good use of all its advantages and developed as one of the strongest tourist centres on the Adriatic. In 1984 the island had as many as 5,820 beds for tourists, and over a ten month period received 63,817 visitors. ■

View of the Rab

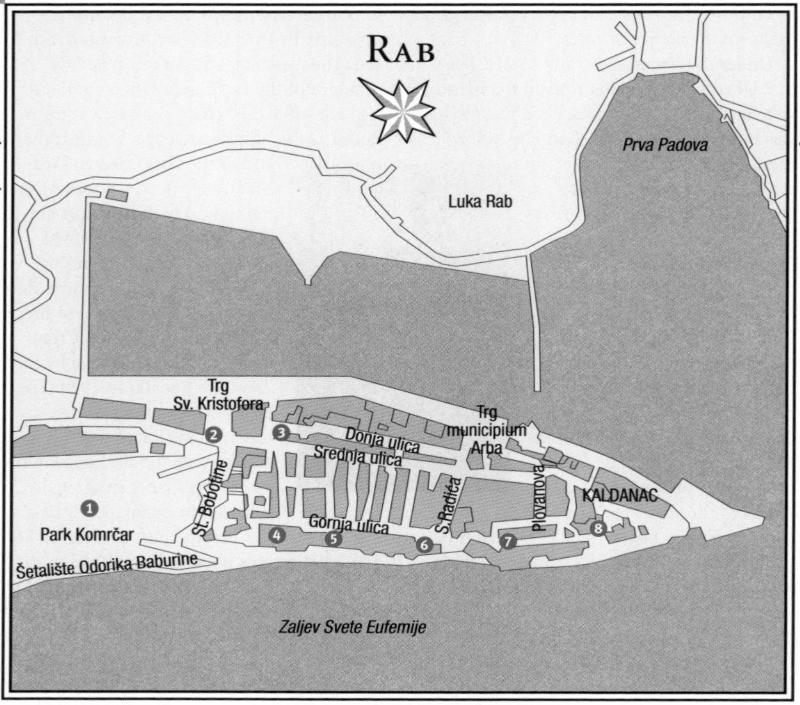

Rab (Town)

LOCATED 44° 45' N AND 14° 45' E; POPULATION 563; MEAN JANUARY TEMPERATURES: AIR 7.1 °C, SEA 10.7 °C; MEAN JULY TEMPERATURES: AIR 23.6 °, SEA 23 °C.

SIGHTS

St. Mary's Church*** (Svete Marije Velike, NUMBER 8 ON THE PLAN), is a triple-naved basilica and one of the most significant Romanesque buildings on the Eastern Adriatic coast. It was built in the 11th century and was consecrated (by Pope Alexander III in person) in 1177. When the Bishopric was established it became the Cathedral. It was built on the site of Roman ruins where there had also been another church dating from the 7th

Facade of St. Mary's Church

or 8th century, which had been demolished. Some materials from the earlier building were used in the construction of this church. The relief on the left-hand wall with the figure of Christ also dates from that time. The church was renovated in the 15th century and at that time a *Pieta* by Petar of Trogir was placed over the main altar. Inside the church there is a particularly beautiful relief made up of braided ornamentation and early Christian eucharistic symbols (at the back of the canopy), wooden choir stalls dating from 1445 and a gravestone with a representation of Bishop Ivan Scaffa which is the work of Andrija Aleši, a pupil of Juraj Dalmatinac (s. Šibenik, the memorial to Juraj Dalmatinac). There is also a painting of *The Madonna and Child* probably by Marco di Martino and dating from the 15th century. The octagonal font (in the St. Peter chapel) was made by Petar Trogiranin in 1497. He was a prominent local master at the transition from Gothic to Renaissance who, ten years earlier had been working at

Church of St. Justine

the court of King Matthew Corvin in Buda. The Cathedral has a very valuable organ built by the famous master, Petar Nakić, (Nachini, Nanchini; 1694-1760 or 1770). The reliquary with the bones of St. Christopher is in the church treasury. It was given to Rab by the Patriarch of Constantinople when the Bishopric came under the jurisdiction of Rome in around 923. When, in 1075, Rab succeeded in withstanding the Norman siege (the only Dalmatian town to do so) this victory was attributed to the Saint and so from that time he became the town's Patron Saint. There is a gilded cross here, with miniatures, which was presented to Rab in 1111 by Koloman as a sign of his recognition of a charter which Petar Krešimir IV had earlier granted to Rab. There is also a bell-tower, 25 m high, which was built at the same time as the church. The only other building like it in the Mediterranean, with its monoforium, biforium, triforium and tetraforium, is the bell-tower in Pomposa near Ferrara.

Church of St. Andreas

••••••••••••

The **Church of St. Andrew** with the **Benedictine Convent*** (Sveti Andrije, NUMBER ❼ ON THE PLAN). This is an 11th century basilica which received its final form during the Renaissance. One of the five altars, built in 1765, is in the Baroque style. On the left-hand side altar there is a copy of a polyptych of the Vivarini school. The original was taken to Boston in 1876. The church's bell tower was built in the Romanesque style in 1181.

••••••••••••

St. Justine's Church** (NUMBER ❻ ON THE PLAN) was built in 1574 on the site of the earlier church of St. Thomas (Sveti Toma). The Romanesque capitals (beneath the gallery) are remnants of the older building. The church has a beautiful wooden Renaissance altar, and above it on the northern side there is a painting entitled *The Death of St. Joseph* which is the work of the Venetian school of the 17th century. The bell tower with its Romanesque windows was built in the 17th century. The church has been turned into a Museum of Sacred Art in which there are artworks from the Cathedral treasury, and the gilded cross with miniatures given by Koloman to the town in 1111.

Belfry of St. John's

••••••••••••

The **Church of St. John the Evangelist*** (Sveti Ivan Evanđelist; NUMBER ❹ ON THE PLAN) is a pre-Romanesque basilica from the 6th or the beginning of the 7th century. It was almost in ruins but was restored after the 2nd World War. The floor of the apse behind the main altar is one piece of evidence that this is an

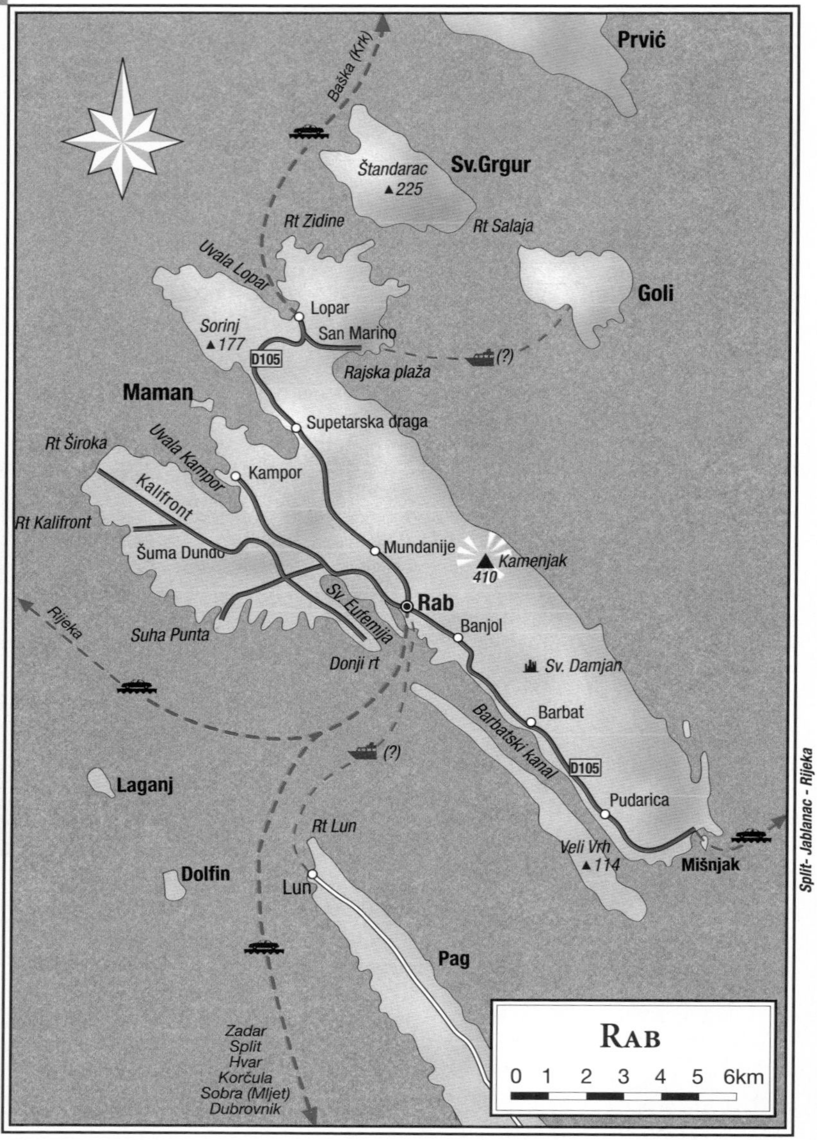

early-Christian building. It is covered by a mosaic with braided ornamentation, and shows the influence of Roman architecture. The bell-tower is still in good condition. Part of the complex of buildings are the ruins of a monastery dating from the 11th century. It was originally held by Benedictines, and then from 1298 to 1783 it was the possession of Franciscans. From 1786 it was the Bishop's palace, but was abandoned in 1833 because it was in bad condition.

••••••••••••

The **Chapel of St. Anthony the Little*** (Sveti Antun Mali; NUMBER ❸ ON THE PLAN) is a small, easily-overlooked Baroque building, standing between two palaces in the Srednja Street. It was built in 1675. There is an exquisite antependium with marble inserts from the 17th century.

••••••••••••

Holy Cross Chapel* (Sveti Križ; NUMBER ❺ ON THE PLAN) was once the Chapel of St. Anthony (Sveti Antun). There is a legend in connection with this chapel from the 16th century, which tells how the Christ on the chapel's crucifix wept because of the immoral lifestyle of the local people. From that time on it has been known as the Weeping Holy Cross (Santa Croce Lacrimosa). In the 18th century the ceiling of the chapel was decorated with Baroque stucco work by the Sommazi brothers from Switzerland.

••••••••••••

Komrčar Park* (NUMBER ❶ ON THE PLAN) spreads over an area of 16 hectares. Towards the end of the 19th century it was laid out by the head forester Pravdoje Bella whose bust has been placed here. The park is the pride of Rab and is considered to be one of the most beautiful parks on the Eastern Adriatic coast. There are many examples of Mediterranean flora represented here.

••••••••••••

Mark Antun Gospodnetić (Marcus Antonius de Dominis) was one of the most important personalities of his time. He was born in Rab in 1560 into the family of the lawyer Jeronim. He taught mathematics in Padua and Rome and philosophy, rhetoric and logic in Brescia. In 1600 he became the Bishop of Senj and in 1602 the Archbishop of Split. Because of his undogmatic nature, he came into conflict with the church leaders in Split, and this became so intense that he was forced to flee, first of all to Venice (1606) and then to Protestant England (1616) where he became Dean of Windsor. In London he had his greatest work published, *On the Ecclesiastical State*. He did not maintain his position to the end, but returned to Rome. He did not receive pardon for his sins however. Death saved him from the Inquisition, but he was condemned posthumously and his body was burned in Rome on 21st December 1624. Even though his work in the field of the natural sciences is also significant, the greatness of de Dominis lies in his rebellion against authority and dogmatism, against the suppression of a man's freedom of thought.

Rab archers

Mark Antun Gospodnetić

14th century Madonna and Child in the parish church

••••••••••••

Kamenjak Hill** (408 m above sea level) is one hour's walk from the town, first along the road leading to Lopar (Mundanijsko polje) and then beside the Sunga stream, to the right, up the hill. As a guide you can make use of the Vela Draga channel, telegraph poles and the cable car which supplies the radio transmitter. At 325m (15 minutes below the peak) there are the remains of a mountain look-out point. There are few 400 m high hills which offer such a splendid view.

••••••••••••

Kalifront Forest** (called "Panjača" and "Dundo") 4 km west of Rab. The name "Panjača" was given because all the young trees grew up from stumps (panj means stump). In the last war almost all the two-hundred year old trees were cut down. They were up to 20 m high and 1 m in diameter. Up until that time this had been the most beautiful forest of holm oaks (Quercus ilex) in the entire Mediterranean. Now it is the largest forest complex on Rab, which is protected because of its rich vegetation and its unique beauty.

EXCURSIONS

Kampor**

6 KM NORTHWEST OF RAB BY ROAD.

In St. Euphemia Bay on a small area of raised ground by the sea, there is a **Franciscan monastery** with a Romanesque church dedicated to St. Euphemia, which was mentioned in 1237, with cloisters and a Chapel of St. Bernard (Sveti Bernardin). The monastery was built in 1458 by the Rab patrician Petar Car (de Zaro). The building work was carried out by Juraj Dimitrov Zadranin, who had a workshop in Rab in 1445. In the papers relating to the foundation of the monastery, the Croatian name Rab is mentioned for the first time alongside the Roman name Arba. Juraj Dimitrov also built the Gothic chapel of St. Bernard, which was renovated in the 17th century in Baroque style. Of particular interest are the church altar rail with its braided decorative patterns, which dates from the 9th century (it was brought here from Rab), a late-Gothic wooden crucifix and the polyptych *The Madonna, St. Bernard of Siena and the Saints*, which dates from the time when the prominent Venetian artists, the brothers Antonio (1415-1476 or 1487) and Bartolomeo (1432-1499) Vivarini, were working together. Unfortunately the church's cassetted ceiling has been damaged, so only 23 pictures are visible on wood showing the life of St. Francis of Assisi. In the monastery there is a **collection of stone monuments** with Roman inscriptions and fragments of early medieval carving (crux gemmata from the 7th century) and a sarcophagus with figured relief from the end of the 15th century which contains the body of the founder of the monastery, Manda Budrišić. Apart from its library, the monastery also houses a museum collection (the Gallery of Brother Ambroz Tesen) which consists of archaeological finds, sacramental items, votive gifts to the monastery, a collection of coins, coral items with beautifully worked initials, ancient books, and objects of ethnological interest.

Lopar

Kampor

On **Kaštelina point** are the ruins of a former Greek acropolis. In the village there is a graveyard as a memorial to the infamous concentration camp which was set up here in 1942 by the army of the Fascist Italian occupation.
The camp held 13,000 prisoners, Jews, anti-Fascists and their children from Slovenia and Gorski Kotar. Of these, more than 4,500 died. The graveyard was designed by Edo Ravnikar and the mosaic composition is the work of Marij Pregelj.

••••••••••••

Lopar*

14 KM FROM RAB, 1 200 INHABITANTS.

On Zidine point the remains of a Greek fortress are still visible. In the village is the Church of St. Mary (Sveta Marija) from the 14th century which has been rebuilt several times, and is therefore not protected as a particularly valuable

One time penal colony, Goli Otok

monument. The legend of the origins of the State of San Marino is connected with Lopar. It tells how in the middle of the 3rd century the mason Marin (Marinus) from Lopar worked on the fortress in what is now Rimini. As a Christian, he fled from Diocletian's army and hid in the Monte Titano hills, led the life of a hermit and built a chapel and monastery. Marinus was canonised and later, the State of San Marino grew up from the centre created by the monastery. The tradition of this legend has been preserved right up to the present day, and there is a strong bond of friendship between the inhabitants of Rab and San Marino.

Supetarska Draga

••••••••••••

Goli otok (island "Goli", 4.73 km²). This now abandoned, one-time prison in communist Yugoslavia, has been compared with Devil's Island in French Guiana. It is occasionally visited by groups of tourists and former inmates. On the whole it is accessible from Lopar, but in the season day and half-day trips are put on from Rab. The camp was established in 1949 after Tito broke with the Soviets, and the island was prepared for the reception of followers of Stalin, the so-called Cominformists. As far as is currently known, 17,000 people came through it. The first inmates were supporters of Stalin, and then the island became a place of internment for all people who came into conflict with the ruling ideology, or those who had had some private disagreement with the officials. It was known for special kinds of torture, the purpose of which was to destroy people's self-respect. When a new convict arrived, he had to run a gauntlet of several hundred people, all of whom had to beat him with a stick or kick him at least once. After the Cominformists, it received political prisoners, criminals, and finally was a juvenile detention centre (1988). The sadistic treatment of prisoners has been described in numbers of books. There was a prison camp on the neighbouring island of Sv. Grgur as well. ■

128 — 155

The Velebit Coastal Area

Senj

Velebit

The Island of Pag

THE VELEBIT COASTAL AREA

SENJ AND THE SEAWARD SIDE OF THE VELEBIT MOUNTAINS BELONG TO A SPECIFIC HISTORICAL REGION WHICH IS KNOWN AS "THE CROATIAN COASTAL AREA". THE SOUTHERN PART OF VELEBIT BELONGS TO DALMATIA, BUT IT IS TAKEN HERE AS ONE ENTITY. AS THE ISLAND OF PAG IS MOST COMMONLY REACHED FROM THE VELEBIT COASTAL AREA, IT IS ALSO INCLUDED HERE.

Senj

SENJ IS SITUATED 45° N, 14° 55' E. 69 KM FROM RIJEKA, 155 KM FROM ZADAR, POPULATION 5 470

This city has a unique position on the eastern Adriatic, which accounts for its rich past. Immediately behind it (14 km to the east) is Vratnik (698 m above sea level), the lowest mountain pass between the sea and the interior. The road to Senj is the shortest route to the coast from Zagreb, also linking the Sava and Danube valleys to the east. For these reasons, Senj's first development was as the port serving a large part of the hinterland. Senj's position has been influenced by its special climatic conditions: frequent gusts of cold air from the continent over "low-lying" Vratnik mean that Senj is the coldest town on the Adriatic in the winter. ■

Senj, with Prvić behind

Prehistory. Senj (Senia) was known to Greek historians as a town of the Illyrian Liburnian tribe. It was mentioned for the first time by Pseudoscilax in the 4th century BC. The Liburnians' northern neighbours were the Histri, about 60 km away, and to the south were the Delmati, about 120 km away. The Japodi were to the east, only about 20 km beyond the mountains, but their culture and farming methods were completely different. Some consider Senj to be a Japodian town, as Senj was from the earliest times a centre for the exchange of goods between the Japodi and the Liburnians.

The Roman Era. Senj came under the Romans at the same time as the rest of the Liburnian territory in the 2nd century BC and it was a strategically important town, a merchant port and the point of entry into the interior. According to the Greek historian Appian (the author of 24 books of Roman history) Senia was Octavian's (later

Gaius Julius Caesar Octavius, 63-14 BC) starting point for his campaign against the Japodi. In 31 BC Octavian conquered Sisak, 200 km away, and it is thought that his march on that town began in Senj. Later, a Roman road was built from Senj into the interior. Roman Senia was surrounded by defensive walls, it had municipal administration, public buildings and temples. On the one hand it was situated on an important route from Aquileia and Tergeste (Trieste) via Burnum (s. Šibenik, Krka) to Salona (s. Split, Solino) and on the other hand it was an important centre of trade with the hinterland. Thus Senia also had a customs post. When the Avars and the Slavs invaded in the 7th century it was razed to the ground, and in the 8th century it came under the Franks.

Coat of arms of the city of Senj

The Time of the Croatian Counts and Kings. Senj was rebuilt as a trade centre in the 8th and 9th centuries thanks to its geographic location. During the period of the consolidation of the Croatian state Senj had both a municipal administration and a bishop (from 1154), but it remained on the periphery of historical events. The most important events took place in the region between Nin and Split. It was only after Croatia entered an alliance with Hungary in 1102 that the northern coastal area became politically significant once again, and thus in later centuries Senj became one of the most important Croatian towns. In 1271 the Frankopans came to Senj from the island of Krk (s. Krk). They were the leading feudal family in Croatia and were vassals of the Croatian-Hungarian kings and Venice. From 1271 on, the Frankopans were in power in Senj, and from 1302 they were its Counts. During the Frankopans' rule the town lived principally from trade, and the people of Senj were some of the richest townsfolk in the Kingdom. Ships were built in Senj, and from the port, wood, grain, meat and leather were exported. Cloth, salt and craft articles were imported. Many foreigners, from Venice, Ancona, Dubrovnik and Genoa, lived in the town. With connections like these the rulers of the town were able to exert political influence on the statesmen who passed through Senj on their way to Rome, Jerusalem, Prague or Budapest. Thus the seat of the Frankopans in Senj contributed considerably to the reputation and spread of the power of that family in Croatia. The city has retained the form it received during this period right up to the present day. The invasion by the Turks into country very close to Senj (in 1463 the Turks conquered Bosnia) brought changes to the commercial and political life of the city. In 1453 Matthew Corvin was elected Hungarian (and Croatian) King. He sought to do away with the anarchy that existed amongst the powerful Patricians, in order to be able to confront the

Senj port in the 19th century

Turks with a strong state. This powerful ruler succeeded in holding up their advance, and went on to create the first centralised state in Central Europe. As regards Senj and the Frankopan family, Corvin did not allow them to have independent talks with Venice, and in the end he took the town from their control in 1469 and set up an army captaincy there, the germ of the later "Vojna krajina" (military border area), which was a unique military and political institution defending Europe against the Turks. The Frankopans' loss of Senj, was certainly contributed to by the fact that after the death of Nikola IV (1432) the sons feuded and the family split into eight branches. Four of these continued to play a significant role for two more centuries, until the last Frankopan was executed in Wiener Neustadt after a rebellion against the Habsburgs in 1671.

In 1537 Senj became the home of the **uskoks**. Uskoks were refugees from the regions which had been conquered by the Turks, and thus, as experienced warriors and a strong military force, they were considered by Austria as defenders of the "vojna krajina" (military border area) and were based in Senj. The city and the military units were ruled directly by the Archduke in Graz. In 1559 there were 253 Uskoks in Senj, in 1573, 352 and in 1602 there were between 500 and 600. In larger battles when they were joined by the border guards the total rose as high as 2,000. They also had their own navy, consisting of ships with 35 to 50 oarsmen, which could be carried over land. If they became surrounded they would take their light-weight boats over the hills and disappear.

When they no longer received money from Austria, they became pirates. The military skill of the Uskoks in battle against the Turks at first astounded Austria and Venice, but once Venice had signed a truce with the Turks in 1574, attacks by the Uskoks on Venetian ships trading with Turkey caused an irreconcilable conflict. When Austria failed to disband them at Venice's request they became the cause of many conflicts between Austria and Venice, and even Pope Clement VIII became involved in attempts to solve the situation. Venice and the Turks signed a treaty against the Uskoks in 1613. Senj was besieged by 85 armed ships and 6 galleys with 12,000 soldiers on the seaward side, and landwards by 4,000 Turkish horsemen. However, the town's heart remained intact. In 1615 open war flared up between Venice and Austria because of the Uskoks, and the issue was discussed in European diplomatic centres. On 26th October 1617 peace was declared from Madrid by the mediation of the German Emperor Matthias and the Spanish King Philip III. Out of fear of the European coalition, as this treaty was signed, Austria finally agreed to disband the Uskoks and thereby hand the Adriatic over to Venice. More than 130 Uskok families were moved out of Senj 140 km to Žumberak. Once the immediate danger from the Turks had passed, the people of Senj sought to be joined to the Croatian Ban (Viceroy of Croatia). However all attempts to bring Senj out of the Austrian military organisation and put it under the Croatian Ban failed. Thus, from 1752 to 1776, Senj was part of the "Austrian coastal area" whose centre was in Trieste. It did not become part of Croatia until 1871. In the middle of the 18th century, the Austrians once again began to show an interest in the Adriatic. Charles V had the first road built between Bakar and Rijeka in 1726, and then his grandson Joseph II built a road from Karlovac to Senj in 1779 (the road which led from Vienna). It became known as "Joseph's Road". Although Senj

An Uskok from Senj

was still under military control (the "vojna krajina" was not abolished until 1871) the building of this road advanced the development of the port in Senj and the renewal of flourishing trade links. However this period was very brief. In 1873 the Zagreb-Rijeka railway link was opened and thus Rijeka, which had previously been known as "Senj's Rijeka" because of its lessening importance, took over the role of main coastal port and Senj sank slowly into the background. ■

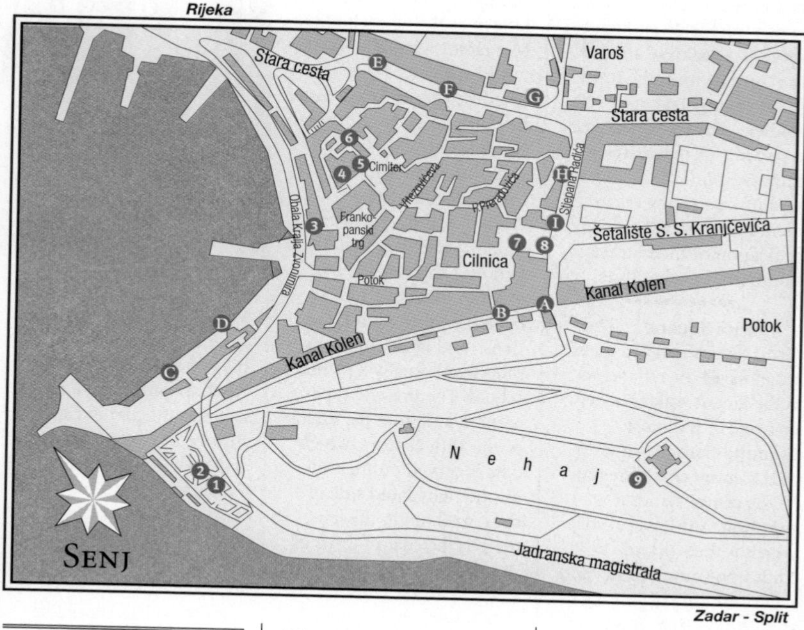

SIGHTS

The **Fortress, the City Walls**.** Apart from the exemplary courage of its inhabitants, Senj has also its defence systems to thank for its survival and continuing independence. Its fortresses, walls and Towers were not all built at the same time; Senj was fortified in Roman times, but the present defences date from the 13th to the 15th century. According to sketches from the 17th century, the town had a circumference of 1,100 m and 13 Towers: Castle Tower (**A**) was part of Senj castle on Cilnica (see below); Radomerić Tower, demolished when the Great Gate was built (**I**); the Gulden Tower (**H**), which also served as a prison at one time and was demolished in 1902; Lipica or Salapan Tower (**G**) which was built on old foundations in the 17th century; Rondel or Trebinac (**F**) which is circular and was badly damaged in an earthquake in 1913; Leo's or the Pope's Tower (**E**) which is the best preserved (the popes after Alexander VI contributed to the building of Senj's defences, and this tower was built by Pope Leo X in the period between 1513 and 1521). A garrison consisting of 25 infantrymen was housed in the tower. On the western side of the town there were three Towers: St. Prossy Tower, Turina and the Boatman's Tower, which were demolished at the end of the last century (in about 1874) when a road was built linking Rijeka and Split. Šabac (**D**) was built in the 13th century and formed part of the coastal defences. It was renovated in 1954 and now houses the harbour office and the tourist association, which gives out information relating to fishing, rowing boats and diving. Naša Tower (**C**) is now fitted out as a coastal wine cellar. Mera Tower is interesting in that until 1785 a stream flowed through it to the sea. Philip's Tower (**B**) also formed part of Senj castle up to 1779 and was the main landward entrance into the town. The gate has now been bricked up. During the era of the Uskoks the towers were 3 to 5 metres higher than the level of the present road. They have sunk due to streams flooding down from the mountains. The towers were connected together by walls which were wide enough to serve as a walkway around the town. Within the walls there was a garrison of 900 soldiers. The walls were last repaired (for defensive purposes) in 1747. Vienna sent its best engineers to work on them, which is an indication of their strategic importance at that time.

•••••••••••

Cilnica Square** (The Great Square - Velika placa, NUMBER 7 ON THE PLAN) is the largest square in Senj and one of the most beautiful Baroque squares in the entire coastal region. In the centre stands a **fountain*** in Classical style which is the work of Engineer Konrad Zettel and dates from the beginning of the 19th century. It was renovated in 1845 by Kajetan Knežić, the famous builder of the first modern roads in Croatia (see Majorija). On the eastern side of the square there is a **castle*** (Kaštel) which was the former residence of the Frankopan Counts. The castle was built in about 1340 as a solid defensive rectangular structure with three corner, and one central tower. Apart from the state apartments it also had loopholes and openings for cannon, a chapel which was known as the Church of St. Margaret (Sveta Margareta) until 1469, and dungeons. Over the centuries the castle has served various purposes: from 1469 it was the seat of the Senj captains founded by Matthew Corvin, and the seat of a military garrison, then the famous Ožegovićianum, a boarding school attended by many prominent Croatians, and later a grammar school and finally a primary school. The present appearance dates from the middle of the 18th century, which date is carved on the wall on the right-hand side of the corridor. On the left there is the coat of arms of the Croatian-Hungarian King, Matthew Corvin (1443-1490) surrounded by six smaller coats of arms of the countries which made up the Kingdom. On the facade of the building there is a memorial plaque which says "In memory of Pavao Ritter Vitezović, the Croatian poet and historian. Senj 7th January 1652, Vienna 1713". His surname is a Croatian form of Ritter, his father being from an Alsatian family. He was a significant figure in Croatian history, as a writer, historian, politician (a Member of Parliament), director of the national printing house and a librarian. In his work *Croatia rediviva* (1700) he expressed the desire that all Southern Slavs should be united and called Croats. He was the first to distinguish the Southern Slavs from the Slavic peoples as a whole, as a distinct ethnic entity. Many events have taken place in the castle. One of the most significant and historically characteristic was at the beginning of the 17th century, when the adviser to the Austrian Archduke and his Commissioner in Rome and Venice, Josip Rabatta, was given the task of removing the "disobedient" Uskoks to nearby Otočac. Rabatta began a campaign of terror against the Uskoks and was deaf to the pleas and protests of the Croatian Ban, but when he attempted to murder the much-loved Uskok leader Jurica Sučić,

Uskočka street

Marker of the 45th parallel

the Uskoks killed him (on 31st December 1601) and cut off his head. This event has been described by the writer August Šenoa in his short story *Beware the Hand of Senj* (Čuvaj se senjske ruke). The **northern side** of the square comprises two buildings which today house the city council. In the Uskok era the right-hand building was a hospice and hospital for old people, and until the beginning of the 19th century the **right hand building** was the Church of the Holy Spirit (Sveti Duh). The building was damaged in 1810 and restored in 1816 to be used as a seminary. In 1845 this was declared an Institute of Philosophy. It received its present appearance in 1896. The square is closed on the western side by three buildings which made up a salt warehouse in the 18th century.

•••••••••••

The **Cathedral of St. Mary***** (Sveta Marija; NUMBER ❺ ON THE PLAN) stands on a slightly raised area and was built on the foundations of a pagan temple. It is the oldest building in Senj. The cathedral was built basically in Romanesque style, with a particularly beautiful facade of fine bricks. In the first half of the 18th century it received side aisles, and it is now a triple-naved basilica. All the altars and other works of art also date from that time. The most valuable monument in the cathedral is the grave of the Bishop of Senj, Ivan Cardinalibus, which is located over the entrance to the sacristy and is in the style of Gothic wall graves of the early Trecento. It is worth pointing out that on the lower part of the relief depicting the *Holy Trinity*, there is the rectangular coat of arms of the Petrović family from 1491, which is the oldest known example of a variant of the Croatian state arms, which were in official use from 1527.

•••••••••••

During the war the cathedral was badly damaged but was restored in 1950 and 1985. Since 1248, when the Bishop of Senj received permission from the Pope to use Glagolitic, the Cathedral of St. Mary has faithfully preserved the memory and teachings of the brothers Cyril and Method. For this reason on the occasion of the 1100th anniversary of the death of Method a memorial was placed in front of the church written in Glagolitic (to the left) and Latin script with the following text: "To mark the 1100th anniversary of the death of Method, who, with his brother Cyril, was the originator of Slavic literacy and the Slavic liturgy, this monument was raised by the people of Senj, in the town of Senj, the cradle of the Croatian Glagolitic heritage, in the year 1985".

It is particularly interesting to note that it was from this church that Glagolitic spread to other Slavic countries. A Moravian Count, on a journey to Aquileia, stayed in Senj in 1337. He later became the Czech King, Karlo, founder of the first German University in Europe (in 1347), and he was so impressed by Glagolitic that he introduced it for use in the Prague monastery of Emmaus, with the Pope's permission.

•••••••••••

The Permanent Exhibition of the **Sacred Heritage**** (Cimetar 7, to the right of the entrance into St. Mary's Cathedral). Although since 1969 the seat of the Rijeka and Senj archdiocese has been in Rijeka, the treasure of this ecclesiastical centre (seat of a diocese in the 5th century, renovated in the 12th century after destruction in the migrations of the peoples) remained in Senj. In the collection there is a crosier of the Bishops of Krbava

Cathedral of St. Mary

from the 15th century, a chalice of the Senj goldsmith Martin Živković from the 15th century, portraits of the bishops from 1617 to 1969, liturgical robes and vessels, the remains of the monumental heritage of earlier Senj churches and other things.

•••••••••••

The **City Museum**** (NUMBER ❹ ON THE PLAN) is housed in the Vukasović palace, a Gothic and Renaissance building which dates from the end of the 15th century. On the ground floor of the building there is an archaeological collection and a collection of stone monuments with exhibits from the prehistoric and Roman eras. On the first floor there is a collection from modern times (1914-1945) and on the second floor a collection showing the development of Glagolitic and Glagolitic printing, as well as "Senj in literature and culture". In the east wing there is a natural history collection, with rare examples of Velebit flora and fauna. On the third floor there is a maritime collection, and collections relating to trade and transport, and the Bunjevci ethnographic collection. These were inhabitants of the area around Senj in the 19th and 20th centuries. Due to the high reputation of the Vukasović family at the Venetian court, this building was known as "Maria Theresa's house".

Exhibit of the collection of the Monumental Heritage

•••••••••••

Senj's medieval printing works (NUMBER ❻ ON THE PLAN). In the suburb of Gorica, in a part of the town which has not changed at all for centuries, over the door of house number 24, leading to the courtyard, there is a stone inscription with a coat of arms and a Glagolitic inscription from 1477 recording that this was the home of Martin, Canon of Senj. There are many reasons to believe that this house was the site of the Senj printing works between 1494 and 1508 (before it was moved to Rijeka) and that in 1494, only 39 years later than the Gutenberg Bible, the second edition of a Glagolitic missal was printed here. The Canon was related to the printer Silvester Bedričić. Printing came to Senj from Venice. The first edition of a Glagolitic missal was printed by the famous Venetian printer Andrea Torresani (1451-1529) who first printed the works of Aristotle and Plato, and who was mentioned by Erasmus of Rotterdam in his *Colloquies*. The Senj Canon Blaž Baromić and the priest and arch-deacon Silvester Bedričić assisted in the printing of that work. Although the site of the printing of the first Croatian book is still a moot point (it is supposed by some that printers existed before this in Draga near Senj as well as in Kosinj), these printing works are an indication of the special role of Senj in the cultural life of the Croats.

•••••••••••

The **Great Gate*** (Velika vrata, NUMBER ❽ ON THE PLAN) was built in 1779, but its present appearance dates from 1843. It stands on the site of the Radomerić tower, which was demolished. The gate also marks the end of "Joseph's Road" the shortest and most convenient route from the interior to the northern Adriatic. The road was built in 1776-1779 and its significance for upper Croatia could be compared with importance that the Via Appia Antica had for Italy. The inscription *Josephinae finis* ("the end of Joseph's Road") is engraved on this classical portal, and to the left of the gate the distances from Senj in German miles are indicated; to Vratnik (1,25 mile, 9.5 km),

Great gate, beginning of the Joseph's road

Modruš (5.25 miles, 40 km) Karlovac (13.5 miles, 102.5 km), Zagreb (21 miles, 153.2 km) and Vienna (63 miles, 478 km).

•••••••••••

St. Mary's Church** (Sveta Marija od Arta; NUMBER ❷ ON THE PLAN).

It is known as the "sailors' church" and was built on the coastal fortifications in the 15th century, but its present appearance dates from the 18th century. The majority of the church's treasures are gifts given by sailors "ex voto". Especially attractive are models of merchant and war ships.

The **Writers' Park*** (NUMBER ❶ ON THE PLAN). In this park there are busts of famous Croatian writers who were born in Senj. On the stand of each bust there is a passage from one of the writer's works relating to his native town.

Vjenceslav Novak (1859-1905): "My Senj/ what my mother is to me/ in the circle of my dear loved ones/ what a sweet secret is in my heart/ what my eye is/ over all my senses/ this you are, O Senj/ lovely dwelling place, of my Croatian home/ Hold on, my Senj:/ you will live/ you will be young/ you will rejoice".

Milutin Cihlar Nehajev (1880-1931): "You are our Siena and our Ghent/ This Senj of Krsto Frankopan and Silvije Kranjčević/ worthy not only of filial love/ but also the attention of all those/ who love and seek deep/ signs of the nobility of their people".

Silvije Strahimir Kranjčević

Silvije Strahimir Kranjčević (1865-1908): Verses to The City of Senj: "As steel, you noble dragon, when black flocks are hunted, you defending lion, standing firm, enduring, you giant of the Croats, your brow clear, you speak boldly, image of Uskoks, Through the ages, old, new, for freedom, for the downtrodden".

Nehaj Fortress

On the bust of the dramatist **Milan Ogrizović,** the author of the drama *Hasanaginica* (s. Makarska, Imotski) the following dates are written: "11th February 1877 - 8th December 1932".

Nehaj*** (NUMBER ❾ ON THE PLAN), 10 minutes from the "Great Gate" or the car park in the southern part of the town, towards Zadar. The Nehaj fortress, built on a 62 m high hill known as "Trbušnjak" was an important part of the defences of the town of Senj.

The builder of the tower, the Senj Captain, Ivan Lenković, reckoned that Senj could only be defended if a fortress was built on the nearby hill which could act as a look-out point over the approach to the city and prevent enemies remaining for any length of time beneath the city walls. For this reason, while the fortress was being built (1551-1554), the land between the hill and the city walls was cleared, which involved the demolition of all old buildings (churches and monasteries) which were in the way. The fortress was completed in 1558, built in the shape of a crown, with a rectangular floor plan, each side being 23.5 m long and the total height being 18m. It has three floors, which narrow towards the top. On the corners there are four towers, pointing to the four cardinal points. The fortress could house up to 100 people, and from its watch towers, guards could receive visual (most often secret) signals relating to the movement of the enemy.

In the period from 1964 to 1976 the fortress was restored and fitted out as a museum with exhibits relating to the history of the Uskoks and the "Captains of Senj" in the wars against the Turks and Venetians. It now houses part of the inventory of the former mausoleum of the "Uskoks of Senj", which was damaged in the war. To the left and right of the path leading to the fortress, there are the remains of a graveyard, where urns containing the ashes of the people of ancient Senj were buried.

•••••••••••

The **Senj International Summer Carnival** arose from the tradition of the winter (carnival) masquers. Since 1967 the carnival has been shifted to the tourist season, being held in the second week in August. Because of the high level and good organisation, Senj has become a member of the Association of Carnival Cities of Europe, and the carnival brings together numbers of teams from home and abroad.

EXCURSIONS

Summer carnival in Senj

Along the *Josephina* towards Karlovac and Zagreb, 5 km from Senj, in Senjska Draga, lies the **hamlet of Holly Cross** (Sv. Križ). As early as the 14th century there was a Benedictine monastery, of Holy Cross. It is assumed that the first Croatian Glagolitic printing house was in it, and that the Missal, the first Croatian printed book, was produced in 1483.

According to A. Glavičić, **Senjska Draga** is the place of origin of the famed Senj Bura, a cold anticyclonic wind that starts blowing after rain in Lika, when dwarf cumulus clouds appear above Vratnik.

Vratnik** is 14 km from Senj on the road to Zagreb and the Plitvice Lakes. It has an excellent look-out point. Apart from being one of the most important road links between the Adriatic and the interior, Vratnik also forms a natural border between Kapela (to the left) and Velebit (to the right). Below Vratnik, 2 km lower, lies the village of **Majorija.** Here a Classical chapel to **St. Michael** (Sveti Mihovil) was built in recognition of the importance of this road, and a spring was also dug; it is known as "the Emperor's spring". Below the rock behind the chapel there is the **grave of Major Josip Kajetan Knežić** (1786-1848), a famous builder of roads in the karst, who reconstructed this road.

•••••••••••

Sv. Juraj* (9 km to the south of Senj, population 691) Via Oltari (15 km

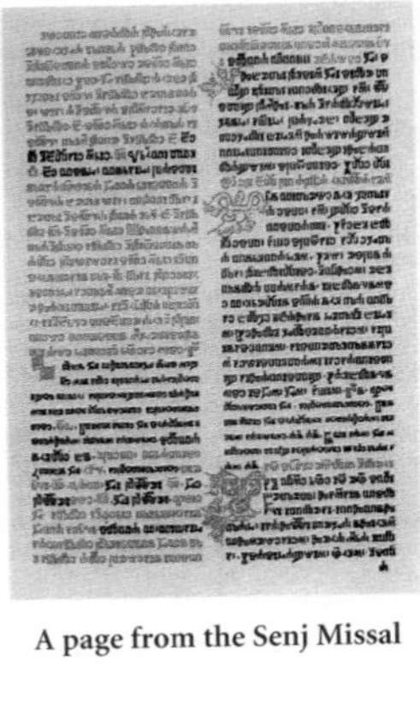

A page from the Senj Missal

Plitvice National Park (Plitvička jezera)***

From Vratnik (via Otočac) the road leads to the **Plitvice National Park*****, which is located in the wooded hills between the mountains Mala Kapela and Plješivica.

The Plitvice lakes consist of 16 lakes, joined together like a series of steps. The first lake is at 636 m above sea level, and the last is 133 m lower. They are linked by waterfalls and cascades. The lakes mainly lie in a south-north direction, are 8 km long and cover an area of 1.92 km². The deepest lake is 46 m deep. They are divided into two groups: the Upper (12 lakes), formed of dolomite rock, which are broad and surrounded by a peaceful landscape; and the Lower (4 lakes) formed from limestone. These are smaller and lie beneath 70 m high rock cliffs. The clarity of the water in the lakes is also a phenomenon. This depends on the density of the plankton, and in the largest lake, Kozjak, one can see up to 8.2 m. The Plitvice lakes have been registered by UNESCO as part of the world's natural heritage. ■

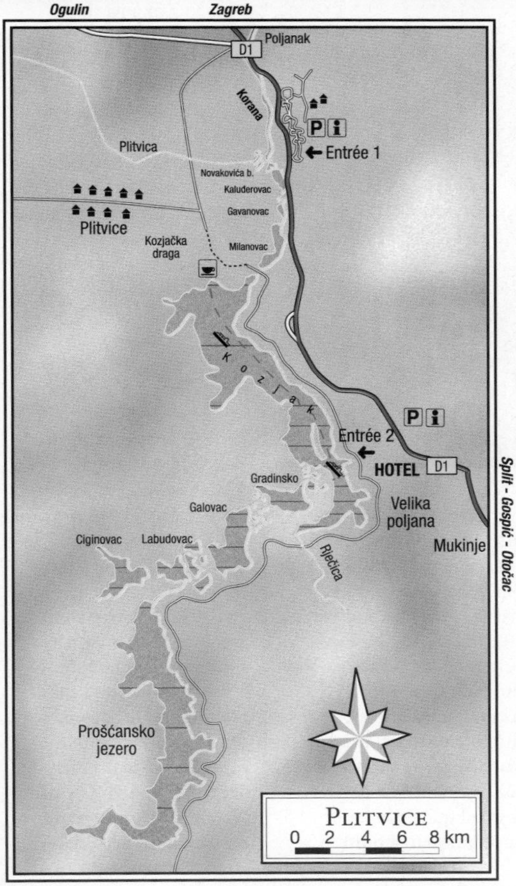

from Senj, 1002 m a.s.l.) the route leads through the centre of the Northern Velebit mountains (s. Zavižan). The history of this picturesque coastal town reaches back into prehistoric times. On the nearby hill of **Gradina** (where there is a lookout point, to the south of the town, 10 minutes walk away) remains of a larger and more important settlement known as Alopsoi have been found. It was mentioned as the home of the Lopsa tribe in the 4th century BC. To the north-west of Gradina, along the bay, a Roman settlement known as Lopsica has been discovered, dating from the end of the first century BC. It was an important administrative and trading centre for the Romans and had municipal rights. Lopsica was destroyed during the migrations of the nations. Croats built a small fishing and farming community on the ruins of the Roman settlement. In 1242 a Benedictine monastery and the Church of **St. George** (Sveti Juraj) were built. The town took its name from the Saint's name. During attacks by Tatar invaders the church and the monastery were destroyed, and a new church, **St. James and St. Philip*** (Sveti Jakov i Filip), was built on the ruins of the monastery. It was deserted in the middle of the 19th century. The ruins of this church stand on the old local graveyard and are now one of the most significant examples of Gothic architecture below the Velebit mountains. Nowadays, the Parish Church of **St. George** (Sveti Juraj) is used for services. It was built in 1852. The Chapel of **St. John** (Sveti Ivan) was built in

1807. The area around Sv. Juraj was covered in thick forests until the end of the 17th century, but they were cut down over the centuries by the Venetians and the local authorities, leaving the western side of the mountains completely bare. A road was built in 1765 to facilitate the exploitation of the forest, passing through Oltari to Krasno, and wood was exported from Jurjevo harbour to all parts of the Mediterranean. The coastline immediately around Jurjevo is very jagged with many small bays and beautiful sandy beaches, such as: Rača, Žrnovnica, Ažić Lokva, Lukovo, Klada Donja and Starigrad Donji. In this part of the Adriatic, below Velebit, there are many underground streams which flow out into the sea influencing its salt content and creating significant changes in water temperature.

•••••••••••

Jablanac*, 40 km to the south of Senj on the Adriatic high road, 27 km north of Karlobag. The starting point for trips into Velebit and a ferry port for Rab and Pag. A village and port on the coast of the Velebit channel. On the peak of Klaćenica (above the mountain hostel) there are the remains of some large Illyrian earthworks from the Bronze Age. Jablanac was settled in Roman times, but was mentioned for the first time in 1179 as a Croatian parish. In the 16th century, it was burnt down by the Turks and the inhabitants fled to the island of Rab. In the middle of the 17th century it was settled once again. Close to the village (1 km to the south) is **Zavratnica Bay***** which resembles a fjord and is one of the major tourist attractions of the northern coastal area. It is 1 km long, 50-150 m wide, with a narrow entrance and very steep sides. The geological origin of Zavratnica is very different from the formation of fjords. A mountain stream became flooded as the surface of the sea rose, and so a bay was formed quite similar in appearance to a fjord.

•••••••••••

Zavratnica Bay

Velebit

The Velebit range is the largest in Croatia and the longest in the Dinara massif. Although these mountains do not initially impress by their height, by the power of their appearance and length, they have made a deep impression on the physical and psychological culture of our people: their history, literature, trade and sciences. This is certainly true. What Olympus is to the Greeks, Lovćen to the Montenegrins, Triglav to the Slovenes, so Velebit is to the Croats. From Vratnik, above Senj, to Zrmanja three regions, Primorje, Lika and Dalmatia, stretch from the north-west to the south-east for a distance of 145 km. The important characteristics of Velebit are its simple, solid form (it is not broken up), steep cliffs, the nakedness of the seaward side and the wood-covered slopes of the Lika side. The basic geological characteristic of the mountains is karst; flora and fauna are abundant, the flora being particularly well known. The best time to visit Velebit is in July, August or September (the average day for the last snow of winter is 3rd June). There are large differences between day and night air temperatures. There are on average 158 days a year with a minimum temperature below freezing, and the mountains are covered with snow for 132 days in the year. The snow is at its deepest in the middle of March (112 cm), but due to the Mediterranean nature of the climate, it is unstable

Rožanski kukovi

over most of the range and is therefore not suitable for winter sports. On the seaward side, winds can reach hurricane force, not only making it unsafe for mountaineers, but sometimes forcing traffic to halt. The most popular spots on Velebit are: the peak of Vučjak, above Zavižan, the botanical gardens on Zavižan, Rožanski kukovi, Štirovača and the Paklenica National Park (Since 1999, Northern Velebit has been a national park).

In older European literature Velebit was known as Montagna della Morlacca. The Venetians called it Morlachia, which derives from the fact that there used to be Morlaks, black (mauros) Latins or black "Vlasi" (Wallachians) shepherds of Romanic origin, living in the Velebit area down to Lake Skadar after the Slavic colonisation. These same shepherds fled from the Turks from Velebit to Krk or into Istria.

••••••••••••

The **Velebit Botanical Gardens****, are situated in Modrić doca at the foot of Zavižan cliff. They are 15 minutes' walk on the Zavižan road from the hostel to the south-west, and then 100 m along the fence. These botanical gardens were opened in 1966 and are situated at 1,480 m above sea level and spread over an area of 30 hectares of mixed terrain, forests, meadows and bare stone. As well as plants that are indigenous to other parts of Velebit but rarities in this region there is a sub-alpine forest with spruce (Picea excelsa), beech (Fagus silvatica) and mountain pine (Pinus mugo). There are also rock plants: mountain yarrow (Achillea clavenae), edelweiss (Leontopodium alpinum) and mountain daphne (Daphne alpina). Some plants are not found anywhere but on the Velebit mountains: Velebit degenie (Degenis velebitica), and the Croatian siberia (Sibirea croatica) have only been recorded on Čvrsnica and Čabulja in Hercegovina, apart from on Velebit. The gardens have a circular path and individual plants are indicated by their name and species. The flora of Velebit has been the subject of research for nearly 200 years by foreign and local scholars. Particularly noteworthy is the Hungarian botanist Arpad Degen (1866-1934) who recorded 2,200 types of wild plants on Velebit. His work *Flora velebitica* was published in four volumes between 1936 and 1938.

••••••••••••

Velebit degenie

Vučjak** **above Zavižan,** 8 minutes' (50 m) climb from the hostel on Zavižan. The hostel can be reached from Sv. Juraj by road to Oltari (15 km) and then (200 m beyond the village to the right) another 16 km on the forest road. If you take the bus which goes to Krasno between Jurjevo (Sv. Juraj) and Oltari, it is a 2 hour 45 minute walk to the hostel from Oltari. From Gornja Klada or Starigrad Gornji, the hostel on Zavižan may be reached by the marked mountain path on foot in about 5 to 5 and a half hours. Vučjak is at

Mountain lodge on Zavižan

1,645 m above sea level. It is a stony peak which affords a splendid view across to the Slovene Alps, the Žumberak mountains, Medvednica and (some say) to the

The view from Vučjak

Peak	m	km	0'
Snježnik	1610	2,5	25
Veliki Kozjak	1620	10	153
Plješivica	1653	1,9	45
Lubenovačka v.	1470	5,7	155
Zalovačko bilo	1630	1,0	86
Vratarski kuk	1650	5,9	160
Buljevac	1550	1,5	104
Rivino	1638	1,9	170
Mali Rajinac	1699	3,7	128
Gromovača	1675	4,9	172
Pivčevac	1676	1,8	131
Veliki Zavižan	1677	1,5	189
Hajdučki kukovi	650	6,7	147
Zavižanska kosa	1620	0,5	213

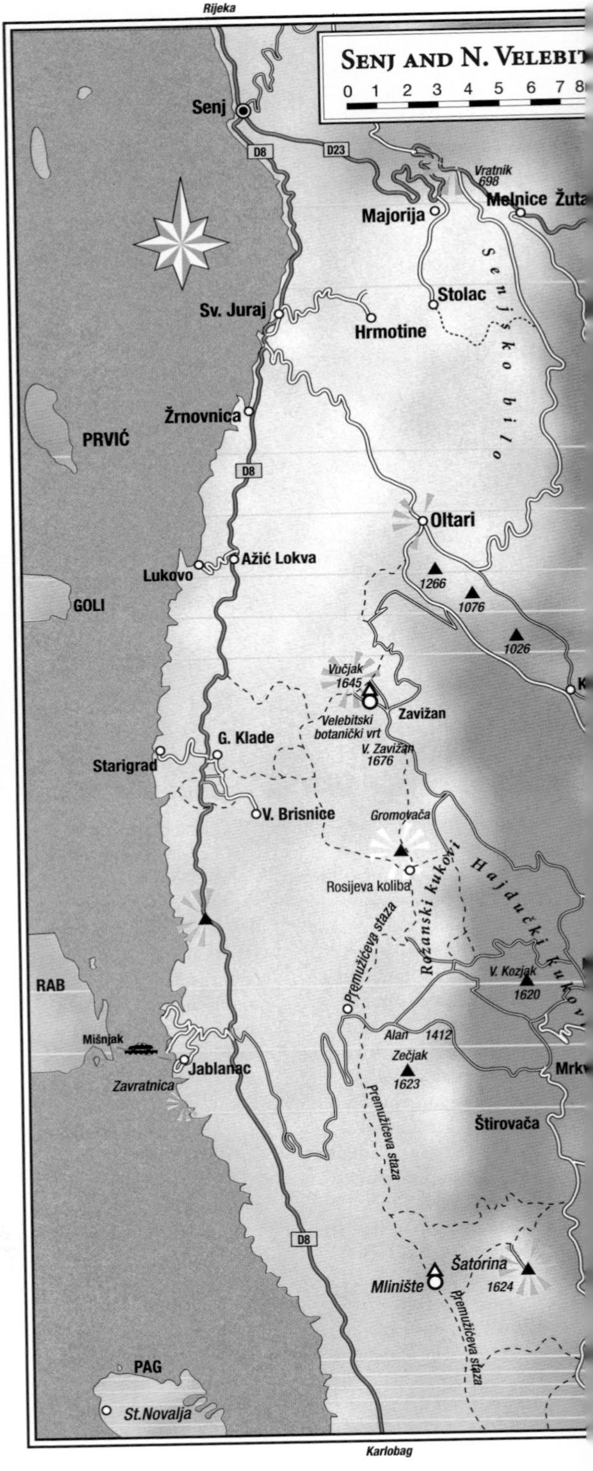

Apennine peninsula. Otherwise the best view is of Istria, the sea with the islands of Krk, Prvić, Rab, Cres and Lošinj. Before any expedition in the northern Velebit mountains one should take a note of the view from Vučjak, which gives the best idea of the mountain.

••••••••••••

Rožanski kukovi***. The setting off point is the hostel on Zavižan. Then take the Premužić path (the tourist path) which begins at the botanical gardens and goes via Veliki Alan to Oštarije above Karlobag. The route may be covered in 17 hours, the section from Zavižan to Veliki Alan in 6 hours. The "kukovi" (Hips) is a folk name given to large stone masses which rise up over the surrounding countryside. Two and a half hours' walk from the hostel on Zavižan lies the first "kuk" Gromovača (1 675 m). The centre of the rocks begins immediately behind Rossijeva Koliba (a mountain hut) which is also 2.5 hours' walk from the hostel. The most interesting part of this rocky region is on the path from Rossijeva koliba to Crikvena (1,641 m), half an hour's walk from the hut. In an area of about 18 km^2 there are more than fifty stony peaks (all over 1,600 m) some with bizarre shapes: in the shape of towers, spires or obelisks. Here all the phenomena of karst rock meet - chasms, dizzying heights, crevices, caves, natural gateways and passes. Because of the abundant variety of this area of the Velebit range and its authenticity, Rožanski kukovi have been declared a nature reserve. The most well-known and

Lilyum cattaniae

the most popular are Novotnijev kuk, Rossijev kuk and Premužićev kuk.

••••••••••••

About two and a half km to the east of the Rožanski kukovi there are the **Hajdučki kukovi*****. The terrain is much wilder, and there are parts even today where no human foot has trod. An expedition to these rocks should only be undertaken by the most skilled of mountaineers. In recent times, 1995, in the area of Hajdučki kukovi, **Lukina jama** was discovered, which, with a depth so far established of 1,392 m (1996) is one of the deepest caves in the world, and the deepest in southeast Europe. What makes it very particular is that it is completely vertical. At the bottom of the pothole is a water course with branches that are still unexplored. A kind of leech was discovered in the pothole, which has been ascertained to represent a new species, genus and family; it has been named "Croatobranchus mestrovi".

••••••••••••

Štirovača**, (from Jablanac by forest road via Veliki Alan and Mrkvište, 25 km; from the Premužić path, from the Alan shelter, 2 hours' walk; from Karlobag by road via Sušanj 42 km). In contrast to most of the rest of Velebit, Štirovača is a huge valley enclosed on all sides by slopes up to 1 500 m high. It is 8 km long and 1 km wide. On the flat bottom of this karst area there is a thick coniferous forest, very attractive in its beauty. This forest, full of wild romantic landscapes, was declared a National Park in 1929, although this was later forgotten. The valley consists of five main parts and it was named after its most northerly part. Each part has springs

Velebit landscape

of fresh water (the temperature being about 5 °C) which become streams in rainy seasons. These same streams later become the source of the river Rječina, which although it is only about 10 km away from the Adriatic, is part of the Black Sea drainage area. From

Štirovača you can go on a trip up Šatorina (1,624 m), the highest peak in Central Velebit (from Štirovača it is 2.5 hours on the marked paths to Šatorina, or an hour and 40 minutes by the Premužić path, which is also marked).

Karlobag

66 KM FROM SENJ, 90 KM FROM ZADAR, POPULATION 531.

This small coastal town is situated at the foot of the Velebit mountains, beneath the lowest road pass over the mountains (929 m). It has such strong connections with the interior that its town centre is completely different from other Mediterranean settlements. Pliny and Ptolemy mentioned it as the Roman "Vegia". During the migrations of the nations Vegia collapsed, but in the 7th century the Croats built a new settlement to the west of the Roman town, called Skrisa (Opidum Scrissi) which was later known as Bag, the seat of the noble family Tugomirić, then of the Gušić and Kurjaković families. The Turkish invasion of Lika completely changed the course of this town's development. In 1525 it was completely destroyed by the Turks, leaving only a fortress with a small military presence. While Venice was considering whether to completely abandon or to rebuild the town, the people of Senj turned to the Austrian Archduke Karl (the founder of the "Vojna krajina", the military border area) and he built a new town in 1579, which, from 1580 became known as Karlobag. However, just as the town had been restored (1592) the Venetians took over the fortress and destroyed the town. Right up until 1683 Karlobag was inhabited only by military units. Another Habsburg ruler (also called Karl) was responsible for Karlobag's further development, the last male member of the family and father of Maria Theresa, Karl VI. His interest in this town was the result of his so-called "Adriatic orientation", for before him Austria had shown no interest in the Adriatic. He had a harbour built and planned a road from Gospić. His grandson Joseph II joined Karlobag to the "Vojna krajina" in 1776 and in 1786 built another road over Velebit. During Napoleon's rule, Karlobag also suffered shelling from English warships, in 1813.

The most important monument of culture in the town is the **Capuchin monastery** with St. Joseph's church (Sveti Josip) of 1713. A small exhibition of ecclesiastical art, an archive and a library is arranged in the monastery. The Baroque Parish Church of St. Karl Boromejski, 1776, built on the site of a church of 1615, is today in ruins.

Karlobag in the 19th century

EXCURSIONS

SEE MAP ON PAGE 152

Karlobag's location makes rugged hill walking expeditions and hikes on Velebit possible (s. Oštarije), as well as trips into inland Croatia (Zagreb 245 km, the Plitvice lakes 105 km, Gračac 90 km), and, by the Adriatic High Road southwards, 47 km to Starigrad-Paklenica and the Paklenica National Park. Karlobag is also a ferry port for the island of Pag.

Oštarije*

17 KM FROM KARLOBAG, ON THE ROAD FOR GOSPIĆ, POP. 31

The road itself gives an excellent view over the sea and the island of Pag. The well-known Croatian artist Zlatko Šulentić (1893-1971) when writing about the Mediterranean said: "Its most beautiful sea is at Karlobag in Croatia, the most majestic hills along the Bay of Corinth and the mildest climate on the coasts of Spain, in wonderful, hot Andalusia". Oštarije is the largest mountain settlement on Velebit, and it is ideal for a longer stay because of its healthy climate. The boundary between the Northern and Southern Velebit passes through it and it is a starting point for those who wish to get to know these mountains. The Premužić Way leads into the northern part (see Velebit, Rožanski kukovi) and for Southern Velebit, right down to

Paklenica or Prezid on the Obrovac-Gračac road. It is six hours to Šugarska duliba; to Jelova ruja two and a half hours; to the hostel on Visočica three hours; to Struge, six hours; the hostel to Velika Paklenica, 3 hours. This part of Velebit was until not long ago a favourite of hill-walkers and climbers. However the area was the scene of fighting during Serbian aggression against Croatia, and was thus mined. For this reason, visits are not yet to be recommended unless you have an experienced guide. Immediately before Oštarije (3 km), over the saddle in the mountains,(33 steps lead up from the road), there is a look-out point called **Kubus.** It is a large stone cube placed on four stone balls, set up in 1846 in memory of the completion of the third road between Gospić and Karlobag.

Ante Starčević (1823-1896)

••••••••••••

Gospić (40 km east of Karlobag, population 6 031) was mentioned for the first time when the Turks retreated from this area in 1689. From 1733 on, it developed as the centre of the Lika Regiment, part of the Military Border. From being a military headquarters, it was to develop into the economic and cultural centre of the whole of Lika. The Baroque **Parish Church of the Annunciation of the Virgin** was built in 1783. It was very seriously damaged during Serb aggression in 1991. The **Museum of Lika** (Dr. Ante Starčević st. 27) is located in a building erected at the end of the 18th century for the Lika Regiment. It is the Lika regional museum, and has archaeological (a considerable number of exhibits relate to the Japodians, or Japodi, an Illyrian people), ethnographic and art collections (Picture Gallery). From Gospić it is only 5 km via Pazariška street to the village of **Veliki Žitnik****. Here Ante Starčević (1823-1896) was born; politician, philosopher and writer, he was one of the founders of the ideology behind the movement to turn Croatia into a state of its own. A memorial house has been arranged in the village; apart from documents about the life and work of Dr Ante Starčević, it also has a cultural, historical and ethnographic collection. Also 5 km from Gospić, but to the west, is the village of **Smiljan***, where the world-renowned physicist Nikola Tesla (1856-1943) was born. The house where he was born and a museum are open to visitors. The **'Memorial Center Nikola Tesla'** was opened to honor the 150th anniversary of Tesla's birth. It is organized thematically and uses a multimedia approach for the scientific and popular presentation of Tesla's work. The Center includes a reconstruction of **Tesla's laboratory** in Colorado Springs (1899/1900); it was here that Tesla produced artificial lightning and experimented with wireless power transmission and high-voltage electricity. The exhibit includes a prototype of Tesla's **radio controlled boat** (1898) and a model of his **disk turbine**. There is also a hi-tech children's playground. In front of Tesla's home there is a statute of Tesla by the sculptor Mile Blazevic. ■

Reconstruction of Tesla's laboratory in Colorado Springs

Tesla's home and a statute

The Paklenica National Park***

Paklenica has the greatest variety of karst formations and is therefore the most impressive phenomenon of the Velebit mountains. The park lies on the seaward side of the southern part of Velebit. Since it would not be possible to make the entire Velebit area a national park in the relatively small Republic of Croatia (the total area of Velebit is about 2000 km^2, and of Croatia, 56,538 km^2) only its outstanding areas have been protected in this way. Along with Rožanski kukovi and Hajdučki kukovi in the north, the Paklenica area is the most attractive part of Velebit. Here there are canyons and valleys cutting through the mountains and driving deep beneath the highest peaks of the area. The National Park covers an area of 3,617 hectares and is made up of Velika and Mala Paklenica (Great and Small Paklenica). In terms of geology, like the entire massif, Paklenica is formed from layers of young Palaeozoic, Mesozoic, young Palaeocene and Quaternary, and that mostly of limestone and dolomite. Only in the higher regions of Paklenica is there a constant water supply, water only reaching the lower areas and flowing to the sea after heavy rain. Thus the canyons are in fact dried up river beds.

The vegetation of Paklenica is also very interesting. Half the surface area (1,840 hectares) is covered with forests of black pine (Pinus nigra) and beech (Fagus silvatica). The largest area is covered with coastal beeches (Fagetum croaticum seslerietosum). The most beautiful forests are near Ivine vodice. Some rocks are overgrown with small bushes such as hawthorn (Crataegus), Christ's thorn (Paliurus spina christi), terebinth (Pistacia terebinthus) and heather (Satureia montana). The mountain meadows are full of a variety of flowers. Of special interest are the white narcissus (Narcissus augustifolius), the blue primrose (Primula kitaibelina), the Velebit bells (Campanula velebitica), gentian (Gentiana), white or red carnations (Dianthus) and yellow flax (Linum capitatum). It is worth mentioning some rare species such as the Velebit saxifrage (Saxifraga velebitica), the blue flowered aubretia (Aubrietia croatica), and the Velebit colombine (aquilegia kitaibelii). Owing to huge ecological variations the fauna of Paklenica is not only rich but also extremely diverse, depending on whether it lives on the naked seaward side or in the wooded land-

Great Paklenica

Griffon vulture in the nest

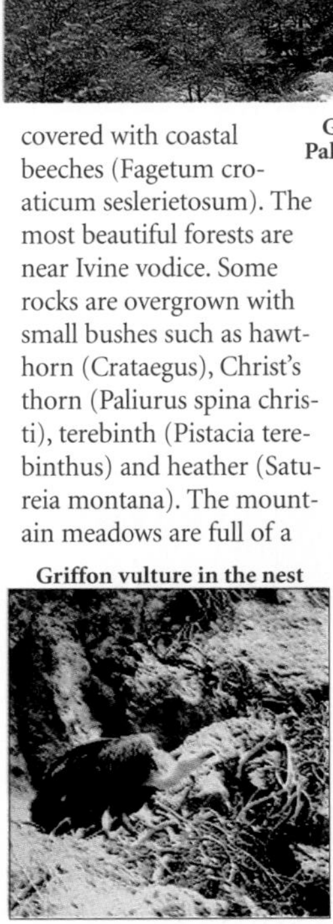

Mountain lily

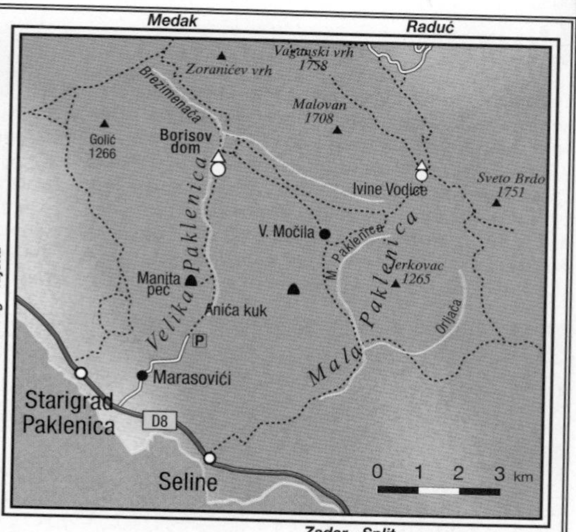

scape of the interior side. On the seaward side the bird life is particularly interesting. There are various kinds of falcon (Falconiformes) and owls (Strigiformes), the majestic griffon vulture (Gyps fulvus), the grey eagle (Aquila chrysaetos) and the eagle owl (Bubo bubo). The best-known butterfly is the red Velebit Apollo (Parnassius apolo velebiticus). In the areas which are less accessible it is also possible to find the most famous poisonous snakes: the viper (Vipera ammodytes) and the common viper (Vipera berus). Apart from these poisonous snakes, you may also find the harmless ring snake (Natrix natrix) and slowworm (anguis fragilis). Deeper inside Paklenica, the most important inhabitant is the bear (Ursus arctos). There are also foxes here (Vulpes vulpes), roe deer (Capreolus capreolus), rabbit (Lepus europaeus), red deer (Cervus elaphus) and wild boar (Sus scrofa).

••••••••••••

Velika (Great) Paklenica can be reached from the southern end of the village of Starigrad-Paklenica and behind the village of Marasovići. At the entrance to the gorge there is a car park (3.5 km from Starigrad). It is two hours' walk from the car park to the mountain hostel in the base of the canyon. The first half an hour takes you through a narrow gorge, squeezed between gigantic rocks reaching up to 400 m in height. This is the most impressive part. From the gorge we enter a meadow, and the path leading to Manita cave goes off to the left. Expeditions from the mountain hostel are only for those who are properly equipped for mountains. It is six hours' walk to the most attractive peak, Sveto brdo (Holy Hill, at 1 753 m), and five hours to Vaganski vrh.

••••••••••••

Mala (Small) Paklenica is 3 km from Velika Paklenica. It is reached from the village of Seline, 2.5 km to the east (30 min. walk). There is no real path, but the way is marked with mountaineering symbols. After 3 km (at 470 m a.s.l.) a path leads off to the left to the mountain hostel in Velika Paklenica, and to the right (through the Orljače canyon) the path climbs up to Sveto brdo. The time needed for the climb depends on the skill of the individual. Mountain guides state 3-4 hours to the mountain hostel and 10 hours for Sveto brdo (from Seline). ■

Beach at Starigrad--Paklenica

Pag

THE ISLAND OF PAG BELONGS TO THE NORTHERN DALMATIAN GROUP OF ISLANDS (TOGETHER WITH THE ZADAR ISLANDS). IT COVERS AN AREA OF 284.6 KM², AND FROM NORTH-WEST TO SOUTH-EAST IS 63 KM LONG (AFTER CRES IT IS THE LONGEST ADRIATIC ISLAND). THE WIDTH VARIES FROM 1.5 KM TO 10 KM IN THE NORTH. THE SIDE FACING THE VELEBIT MOUNTAINS IS STEEP AND INACCESSIBLE, WHILE THE OUTER SIDE IS EXTREMELY VARIABLE. IT HAS MORE THAN 250 KM OF JAGGED COASTLINE, MAKING PAG ONE OF THE MOST INDENTED ISLANDS. THE ISLAND HAS 24 SETTLEMENTS WITH 8 000 INHABITANTS (10 SETTLEMENTS WITH MORE THAN 300 INHABITANTS). ADMINISTRATIVELY, THE NORTHERN PART OF THE ISLAND BELONGS TO THE SENJ AND LIKA COUNTY, AND THE SOUTHERN PART TO THE ZADAR COUNTY.

View of the town of Pag, saltworks to the right

Prehistory. Like other Adriatic islands (from Cres and Rab to Mljet) Pag was inhabited in the early Stone Age. Apart from a few rare traces of Neolithic culture, this fact is demonstrated by the results of linguistic research. Cissa, the old name for the island of Pag, and what was once the largest settlement on it, the present day Caska, is a relic of pre-Illyrian toponomastics. In the middle of the second millennium BC, the island was settled by members of the Illyrian tribe, the Liburnians. There are Illyrian necropoles near Šimuni, Kolan and in the area around Novalja.

The Roman Era. The Romans subdued the Illyrian tribes in the middle of the first century BC. They did not build any significant settlements on the island, but the land was given to people not only from Rab (Arba) and Zadar (Iadera), but also from Rome. The well-known Roman family of Calpurnius Piso, had possessions around Caska and Novalja. Remains are to be seen around Caska, in Kolan and Novalja. The name of the island and the biggest village derives from Roman times: pagus means village in Latin.

The Migrations of the Nations. The Slavs, together with the Avars, settled in this region at the end of the 6th and the beginning of the 7th centuries. Immigrants soon arrived on Pag too, whilst the old population had partly died out or fled to safer areas (s. Velebit). As the island had no large settlements it did not come into the Byzantine province of Dalmatia.

The Time of the Croatian Counts and Kings. From the time when the Croatian Bishopric was founded in Nin (867), Pag came under the jurisdiction of the church there (and later under Zadar). Two centuries later (1070) the Croatian King Petar Krešimir gave the Rab church "...Kissa with all its belongings...". Thus the divided island (the northern part under the jurisdiction of Rab, and the southern under Zadar) was for a long time a battlefield in conflicts between the two Bishops. From the 13th century, Pag fought a long battle to be freed from the influence of Zadar. The interest in Pag arose from the fact that from ancient times salt had been extracted from large, shallow pools, by evaporating sea water. In these frequent battles, Pag often came off badly, and periods of independence and freedom were brief. In 1244 King Bela IV gave Pag the title of "Royal Free City" in gratitude for help given in various battles. But not long after that, wars began again with Zadar, and the island did not regain its own administration until 1380 when Ludovic reconfirmed the privileges given to the island by Bela IV. One of the conflicts between Zadar and Pag was settled at the Nin Assembly in 1396, and after 26 days of debate it was decided to remove Pag from Zadar's area of jurisdiction. Thus for the third time, Pag received the title of "Free City".

Under the Venetians (1409-1797). When Dalmatia came under Venetian rule, the centuries long wars between Pag and Zadar finally came to an end. Pag was under Venice economically speaking, but its status was similar to the status of other Dalmatian towns. The most important event of this period in Pag's history was the change in the location of the main settlement on the island. During previous conflicts the former "capital" Cissa had been completely destroyed, and the new rulers were forced to build their own town. The settlement moved in the middle of the 15th century from Stari Grad, about half a kilometre to the west, to the location which it now occupies.

Under the Austrians (1806-1813 interrupted by the French occupation). During Austrian rule the island experienced an economic and cultural revival. In 1808 a school was founded in Pag and a regular court was instituted. Laws providing for the local language to be used in schools and the courts were passed in 1872. The investment of a million crowns in the production of salt not only considerably improved its quality, but also increased the overall production levels. Communications between Rijeka and Zadar were also improved and many roads were built.

Traditional costume from Pag

The twentieth century. At the end of the First World War (1918) Pag became part of the new state. The sharp social conflicts frequent in pre-war Yugoslavia also affected Pag. Strikes in the saltworks broke out in 1924, 1927 and 1937. In April 1941 Fascist Italy occupied the city and began to implement its brutal laws. Under the occupation forces an infamous concentration camp was set up in Slano Bay on Pag, where thousands of Jews, Serbs and Croats died. The Germans followed the Italians, and the town was finally liberated on 5th April 1945. In the last decades, the island has seen many of its possibilities for tourism realised, assisted by the bridge which has linked the island with the mainland since 1970. ■

Pag (Town)

46 km from Maslenica Bridge on the Adriatic highway; Located 44° 27' N, 15° 1' E, population 2 701.

Sights

The **city as a whole****. The foundation stone of the city was laid on 18th May 1443, and it was built according to plans by the famous Renaissance builder Juraj Dalmatinac (s. Šibenik). As the city was planned as a fortified settlement, it was surrounded by walls, which were demolished after the fall of Venice. The remains of these walls can be seen in various parts of the city (an outer wall by what is now Varoš, restored wall foundations in Uhlinac, a section of a stone wall near the local community building, and a tower by the Benedictine monastery). Pag has retained the distinct coherence of its original layout: it has a large paved square which is intersected by two streets, Glavna (Main street) or Vela ulica which begins immediately beyond the bridge on the site of the former Lančana vrata (Chain Gate, Porta Catena), then, running south-west to north-east, ends near the Church of St. George (Sveti

Juraj) on the site of the former Kopnena vrata (Land Gate, Porta Terraferma). The other street intersects Vela ulica at right angles, and it is slightly narrower. It begins at the former St. Anthony Gate (Sveti Antun) on the south-eastern side of the city and runs to the north-western gate, Uhlinac. This strict cruciform plan divides the city into quarters known as: Sveta Marija, Sveti Jakov, Sveti Antun and Sveti Juraj. Within each quarter there is a multitude of smaller streets running between the buildings.

Nucleus of the city

The **Parish Church of the Assumption**** (Uznesenje Blažene Djevice Marije) stands in the centre of the main square and dates from the 15th century. It was started at the time when the foundations of the new city of Pag were laid in 1443. It is in the shape of a basilica, in Gothic style, but with many Renaissance elements. Of particular interest is the original facade which forms the main entrance, with a lunette and relief depicting the Madonna with her arms reaching out as a symbol of her protection of the people.

The Parish Church of St. Mary

Level with the lunette there are two windows typical of Gothic architecture. In the centre of the facade, to the right, there is a statue of St. George and to the left a statue of St. Michael. St. George and St. Michael were the patron saints of the city as early as the time when the Croats on the island were converted to Christianity. Just below the top of the facade there is the most beautiful decorative object in the church - a large and highly ornate stone rose window, which reminds us of the rosette motifs (*roželica*) on the famous Pag lace. To the left of the rose window there is a statue of the Madonna, and to the right, a figure representing the Archangel Gabriel. High up on the gable there is the figure of an angel looking onto the city square. The side walls of the church, facing Vela street, consist of a row of blind arcades,

Traditional dance from Pag

Stone rose window

including two doors with Renaissance portals. The left-hand wall of the church ends in the bell-tower which was built around the year 1562. The interior of the church is triple-naved. The central aisle is separated from the

Sacred painting "Madonna and Child"

side aisles by colonnades of seven pillars.

The **Juraj Dalmatinac Monument** (s. Šibenik) is the work of the renowned artist Ivan Mirković, who was born in Pag.

••••••••••••

The **Rector's Palace*** (Knežev dvor) also stands on the main square. This is an impressive building, built of large stone blocks, from the second half of the 15th century. Its portal forming the entrance to the courtyard from the main street (Vela ulica) is particularly interesting as it is presumed to be the work of Juraj Dalmatinac. The palace once included the tower with the sun dial, although the sun dial is from a later date, and the ground floor of the tower once served as the city prison.

••••••••••••

The **Bishop's Palace*** stands next to the Rector's and has never been completed. It was conceived as a balance to the Rector's residence, both buildings being in the form of the letter "L", symmetrically enclosing the square.

••••••••••••

St. George's Church* (Sveti Juraj) stands at the end of Vela ulica. St. George is the oldest patron saint of the city. This church was built in the middle of the 15th century and is a longitudinal basilica which was once linked to the city's defensive walls by its northern facade and bell-tower. The simple Renaissance facade was built somewhat later than the church itself.

••••••••••••

The **Church of St. Francis** (Sveti Franjo) is in the same quarter of the city and has a distinctive Renaissance portal. The Franciscan monastery linked with the church is today only partially preserved.

••••••••••••

The **Church of St. Margaret**** (Sveta Margarita) rises up on the other (western) side of the city. It is a triple-naved basilica in the shape of a Latin cross, whose central aisle ends in a rectangular apse. The facade is simple and broken only by the main portal, a rose window and biforium in a vertical line in the centre. The facade is crowned by an arrangement of bells with three openings. Beside the church there is a **Benedictine monastery**, which was founded, like the church, in the eighties of the 15th century. The **monastery's treasury** houses many valuable works of art: two pieces by the Venetian artist of Flemish origins, Baldassare D'Anno (1560-1639), two altarpieces with the figures of St. Anthony of Padua and Our Lady of Carmel; *The Assumption of the Madonna* (at one time adorning the

Remains of old Pag

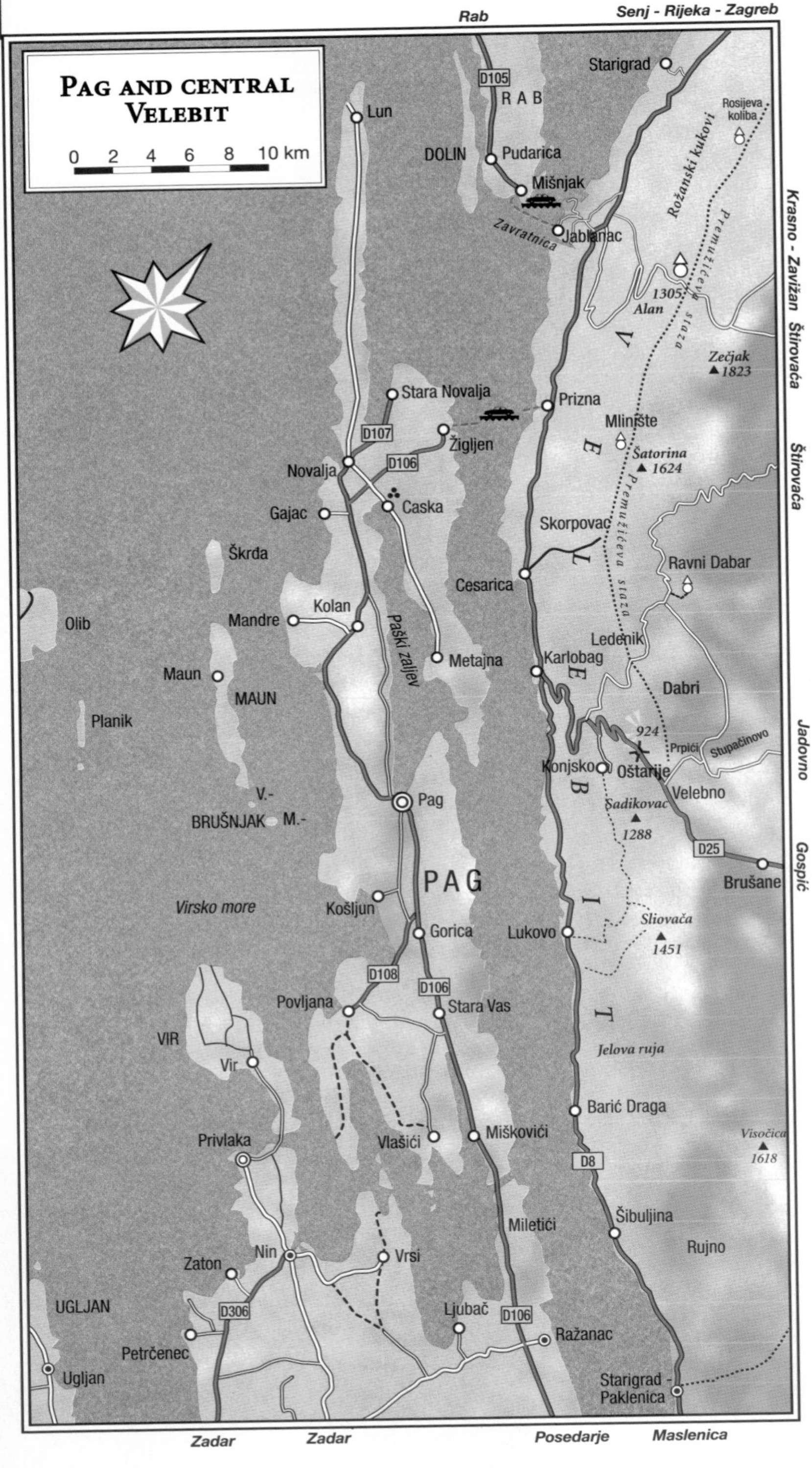
Pag and central Velebit
0 2 4 6 8 10 km
Rab
Senj - Rijeka - Zagreb
Starigrad
D105
RAB
Lun
DOLIN
Pudarica
Mišnjak
Zavratnica
Jablanac
Rosijeva koliba
Rožanski kukovi
Premužićeva staza
Krasno - Zavižan
1305
Alan
Štirovača
Zečjak
1823
V
Stara Novalja
Prizna
D107
Žigljen
Mliniště
Šatorina
1624
E
D106
Novalja
Caska
Gajac
Skorpovac
Škrda
L
Cesarica
Ravni Dabar
Kolan
Mandre
Olib
Paški zaljev
Ledenik
Metajna
Karlobag
Maun
MAUN
Dabri
E
Planik
924
Prpići
Stupačinovo
Jadovno
Konjsko
Oštarije
V.-
Velebno
Pag
B
BRUŠNJAK
M.-
Šadikovac
1288
D25
PAG
Brušane
Gospić
Virsko more
Košljun
I
Sliovača
Gorica
Lukovo
1451
D108
D106
Povljana
Stara Vas
VIR
T
Jelova ruja
Vir
Barić Draga
Privlaka
Vlašići
Miškovići
Visočica
1618
D8
Šibuljina
Miletići
Rujno
Nin
Vrsi
Zaton
UGLJAN
D306
Ljubač
D106
Ražanac
Petrčenec
Ugljan
Starigrad - Paklenica
Zadar
Zadar
Posedarje
Maslenica

main altar in the Cathedral) which has been ascribed to Tintoretto; a 15th century Madonna (in tempera on wood) by an unknown artist. The monastery also houses other valuable ecclesiastical art.

•••••••••••

Pag Old Town* (Stari grad; to the south-west of the present town). Only the parish church and the ruins of a later Franciscan monastery remain. This church is a triple-naved basilica with three apses. It is dedicated to the Assumption of Mary, who later became the city's patron. Structural elements of the interior point to the Romanesque era: the main aisle is separated from the side aisles by massive columns. The facade of the church in Stari grad shows the custom typical of the Renaissance of dividing it into three parts with cornices. The lowest part includes a portal with the figure of the Madonna in the lunette, which corresponds to the motif in the lunette on the parish church on the main square. In the central section there are sculptures of the saints (St. Peter, St. George, and St. Martin), and under the gable the central place is taken by a rose window, protected on both sides by the figures of angels.

Excursions

Caska

2 KM EAST OF NOVALJA.

This is a deserted settlement and also the name of a bay in the north-western corner of the Bay of Pag. As late as 1961 about 20 people still lived here (in 1921, 48 inhabitants), but now Caska is just an archaeological site, although once the capital and main settlement on the island. There was probably a Roman fortress here known as Cissa (or Kissa, Quessa, Gissa etc.). The Croats named this fortified town Kesa (or Kisa) and for this reason the Byzantine Emperor Constantine Porphyrogenitus (in the 10th century) named the entire island Kissa. The settlement was still full of life in the Middle Ages right up until the time when (at the end of the 14th century) it suffered damage in the rebellions of the people of Pag against Zadar. There are many ruins which are remains of the Roman era. Some walls and houses from Roman times are now under water due to the subsidence of the Eastern Adriatic coast. On a small hill there are the ruins of a Romanesque church, St. George's (Sveti Juraj), which was probably built in the 11th century on the foundations of an even older church.

•••••••••••

Novalja*

21 KM NORTHWEST OF PAG, POPULATION 2 117.

The necropolis and burial mounds in the area around the town date from the Iron Age and show the continuity of life here from prehistoric times up to the present day.

View of Novalja

The town received its name from the time of Roman rule here when Novalja was a Roman port ("novalia" in Latin means port, or wharf). At that time Novalja was a larger settlement connected by aqueduct to Kolan, situated deep in the island's interior, and by a tunnel to Stara Novalja (Old Novalja; known as Talijanova buža). Nowadays, Novalja is the most important tourist centre on the island of Pag.

Pag lace

Pag is world famous for its lace and decorative items made from linen thread. It can be compared with lace from Brussels or Venice. Most often it is in the form of four-pointed star or rose motifs. At first this lace was made as a decoration for shirts and scarves, but later for furniture, curtains, table cloths, ecclesiastical robes and coverings for church furnishings. Pag lace is made "micano" (the decorative effect "toledo" is obtained by drawing threads from the linen and forming loops) or "rizano" (double ravelling to supplement white embroidery in a geometric succession). "Paški teg" is a technique by which some threads remain in the cloth as others

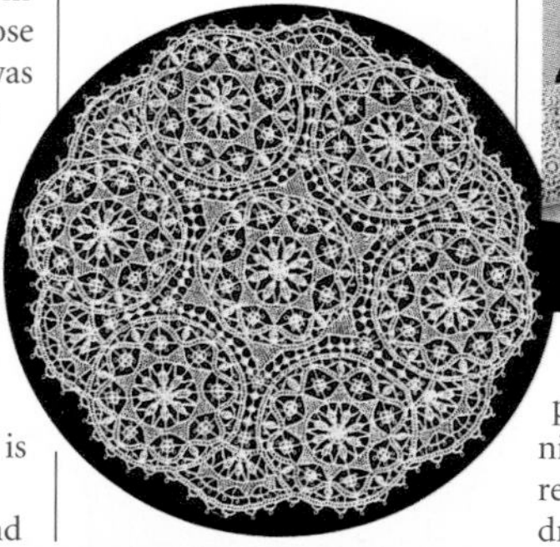

are pulled through, thus producing square openings, through which the remaining threads may be drawn as necessary. Geometric ornamentation is thus worked on the resulting network. The reputation of Pag lace was so great that, during the Austrian rule of the island, two women from Pag lived permanently at the Viennese court, making Pag lace for the Emperor and his entourage. ■

In the present day graveyard, the remains of an early Christian graveyard basilica have been found, and in the centre of the town there is the **Church of the Mother of God of the Rosary*** (Majka Božja) which was built in the 17th century on the foundations of two earlier churches. Thus there are three sacred buildings one on top of the other. The first and oldest was an early Christian basilica from the 4th or 5th century which was as least twice as large as the present church. On that are the remains of a medieval building. Inside the church in the right-hand corner of the rectangular apse, one metre below the level of the present floor there are the remains of the apse of the medieval church and a fragment of a Roman mosaic from the early Christian basilica. The **Church of St. Catherine** (Sveta Katarina) was built in the last century in neo-classical style. The **Town museum** (Mjesni muzej) is next to St. Mary's Church and houses items

Cheese from Pag; a feature of Croatian cuisine

Wind rose in the city loggia

from the history of the local inhabitants. In Stara Novalja (Old Novalja), 5 km to the north, is the church of **St. Mary of Trinčel**, which was built in the 15th century, and renovated in 1988, as a votive offering for protection against abortion, divorce and AIDS.

••••••••••••

On the way from Pag to Novalja, to the west of the road, lies the fishing village of **Šimuni**. Fishing has been the traditional occupation here for many generations. This bay, cut deep into the land, is a secure refuge for many fishing boats. Four kilometres inland is **Kolan*** (with 600 inhabitants) which is the main agricultural centre on the island. In the village there is a small ethnological collection. Three kilometres from Kolan towards the sea is the small harbour of Mandrač, which was used by the people of Kolan as an outlet to the sea. The tourist complex of Gajac (4 km south of Novalja) was built on the border between the Senj and Zadar counties.

Northwest of Novalja (about 20 km) is the village of **Lun*** which is traditionally oriented towards Rab (due to its location at the far end of the island). The olive trees, which are hundreds of years old, growing out of bare rock at the entrance to the village are particularly impressive.

••••••••••••

Wines and food. A high quality wine known as "Žutica" is made in limited quantities on Pag. Apart from olives, the major gastronomic specialities are cheese and lamb. The rich Pag cheese is world famous and the lamb is considered among the highest quality meats on offer in the Croatian market. The quality of the meat and cheese derives from the aromatic plants growing on the otherwise sparse Pag pasture lands, which are grazed by the sheep. Pag sage honey is of a particularly high quality, and much in demand on the market. ■

Pag landscape

156 — 217

NORTH DALMATIA

ZADAR

ISLANDS

ŠIBENIK

Zadar

Located 44° 8' N, 15° 13' E; centre of the Zadar County, which extends over 3 643 km^2 and has a population of 165 593. Population of the city is 71 928.
Mean January temperatures: air 6.3 °C, sea 11 °C. Mean July temperatures: air 24 °C, sea 22.8 °C.

Prehistory. Archaeological finds in the area where the city now stands show that there has been a settlement here since the 9th century BC. It is certain that from the 4th century BC what was then Iadera (Iader) was a strong Liburnian maritime centre and that it had good trading links with Greece, both with the metropolises and with Greek colonies on Sicily.

The Roman Era. Of all Illyrian settlements on the Eastern Adriatic coast, Iadera was the first to be attacked by the Romans. At the beginning the Liburnians were allies of the Romans in their struggles against the southern Delmats, but in the 2nd century BC the Romans conquered the Liburnians. Iadera developed as a Roman town, settled by Romans and Romanized peoples from the very beginning of the Empire. At that time it received the basic characteristics of a city, with a regular street lay-out, which has remained the same up to the present day. The city was surrounded by walls and had three gates. It also had a forum, a capitol and an amphitheatre, thermal baths and sewers. From the reign of Emperor Trajan it also had an aqueduct 35 km long bringing water all the way from Vrana lake. Good roads linked the city with the interior and other Roman towns. Later finds witness to Roman cults and to the high artistic standard of Roman sculpture. There are few material remains of the early Christians

Statue of Augustus

in Zadar. The Roman period includes one mystery: it is absolutely certain that in the 6th century the city suffered some kind of catastrophe, for the city which the Avars and the Slavs found in the early years of the 7th century was on a level one metre higher than the Roman city.

The chest of St. Simon, detail

The Migration of the Nations. Zadar is the only place on the Adriatic which resisted the Avars and was not destroyed by them. For this reason, after the division of the Empire, it became the seat of the Emperor's representative and took on the role of the leading city on the Adriatic coast. However, because of its distance from the capital (Constantinople) Byzantine rule was formal, and the influence of the newly arrived Slavic element became stronger.

The Time of the Croatian Counts and Kings. The year 878 is taken as the beginning of the period of what one could call Croatian rule, when Emperor Basileios I the Macedonian made a proclamation by which Byzantine cities had to pay taxes to the Croatian rulers. The payment of taxes for the peaceful enjoyment of one's own territory is a sure sign that that authority has been enforced. The very fact that Zadar remained a Glagolitic diocese (with Slavic masses) and that it did not accept the decision of the Split Synod to introduce the Latin language, are an indication of the fact that relations between Zadar and the interior had become close and mutually dependent. The reason was that, in conflicts with increasingly

ambitious Venice, Zadar grew to rely on inland Croatia and found itself leading the Dalmatian cities against the Venetians. Of all cities on the Eastern Adriatic coast, Zadar offered the most fierce resistance to Venice. From the very first offensives by the Doge Peter II Orseolo (997 and 1000) right up to 1409, when King Ladislav of Naples sold Dalmatia off, Zadar was conquered and liberated seven times, and taken over six times: in 1096, 1118, 1202, 1243, 1313 and 1346. In its relations with Zadar we may plainly see all the cunning and brutality with which the Serenissima treated its neighbours; for example they raised the status of the Bishopric, but under their own authority (Grado 1154). Then there was the mercenary crime of the French Crusaders, who in 1202, when they found themselves without money, paid Venice for boats to Jerusalem by conquering and destroying Christian Zadar. Geoffroy de Villehardouin (1150-1213), the French historian and commissary for the organisation of the Crusades, who came to Venice in 1201 to make arrangements for transport, wrote that Zadar was "the strongest city in Slavic lands, and one of the strongest in the world".

Right up until 1409, Zadar was from time to time the seat of the Croatian and Croatian-Hungarian Kings, with the last coronation on Croatian soil taking place in Zadar in 1403. That restless century was also Zadar's golden era. It saw the blossoming of trade and crafts which brought about a cultural upsurge, to which buildings and works of art from the Romanesque and Gothic eras still bear witness.

Under the Venetians (1409-1797). What Venice failed to achieve by force, it achieved in 1409 by financial means. The Hungarian King Ladislav of Naples sold Zadar and part of the coast for 100,000 ducats and Zadar became the seat of the administration of Dalmatia and Albania. Its economic development however was entirely directed towards the needs of Venice. In the area around the city both agriculture and cattle breeding developed and within the city itself, various crafts. However, Zadar was only permitted to export to Venice, and had to pay double customs duty for exports to other places. When Venetian Zadar came under the threat of the Turks (from 1468 to 1478 there were eleven Turkish offences in the Zadar area) the Venetians built defensive walls in the 16th century, and Zadar became the strongest Venetian fortress on the Eastern Adriatic coast. During Venetian rule, Zadar was not only settled by Latin immigrants, but the authorities actually banned marriages with the local population. Also, because of their fear of rebellions, Venice banned the storing of food supplies for more than four days.

Detail of the pre-Romanesque altar rail

Under the Austrians (**1797-1805** and **1813-1918**). The short-lived French period brought to Zadar, as well as to the whole of Dalmatia, the spirit of a new age and advances in the economy, law and education. But in 1813 Austria, assisted by the English Navy, conquered Dalmatia and formed a special administrative region, with its centre in Zadar. Thus Austria did not fulfil the wishes of the people of Zadar to be united with Hungary (and thus with Croatia). On the contrary, Austria introduced a policy of Italianisation in the city, with the use of the Italian language, thereby making communication with the interior impossible. Nevertheless Zadar was the centre of the national revival in Dalmatia. In 1838 the Magazin of a publisher Božidar Petranović was published for the first time and in 1844 the weekly *Zora dalmatinska* (Dalmatian Dawn) whose editor was, for a time, the Croatian poet Petar Preradović. A Croatian primary school was opened in 1885 and a grammar school in 1897. The period of Austrian rule was not one of great prosperity. For instance, in 1858 the city had 7 300 inhabitants, and three centuries earlier in 1527 it had 8 000.

The twentieth century (**1918-1944**). The end of the First World War brought national liberation to most of the Eastern Adriatic coast but not to Zadar. In 1918 the city was occupied and in 1920 the Rapallo Treaty assigned the city to Italy. In this Italian enclave a policy of enforced Italianisation was introduced, especially during the Fascist regime. About half of the population (8 000) moved to other places in Yugoslavia, and the city was occupied by immigrants from

Zadar in the 19th century

Italy. Isolated as it was from its natural hinterland, the city had no chance to develop. During the Second World War, Zadar suffered terrible bombing and by the end of the war it was almost entirely in ruins. At the second sitting of AVNOJ (The Anti-Fascist Council of the National Liberation of Yugoslavia) on 29th November 1943, it was decided to unite the occupied territories with their mother country and on 31st October 1944 the National Liberation Army marched into Zadar. Since World War II Zadar has been raised from the ruins, many cultural and historic monuments have been restored and the city has developed as a strong economic and tourist centre.

After the Serb rebellion in 1991, organised after the first democratic elections in ex-Yugoslavia, Zadar found itself on the very edge of the territory occupied by the rebels. Connections with Zagreb were cut for over a year, and the only link was via the island of Pag. Zadar was severely damaged in the war. Its historical bastions were damaged (Grimani, Moro, Kopnena vrata, Kaštel and Veliki arsenal) as were sacred buildings (Church of St. Chrysogonus, the Convent of St. Mary, St. Anastasia and St. Simeon). What was in essence a siege of the city lasted until January 22, 1993, when the Croatian army liberated a good deal of the hinterland of Zadar as well as Maslenica. This meant that Zadar was once again linked with Zagreb, and then in the Oluja (Storm) in 1995. campaign the whole of the hinterland was liberated. ■

Sights

The **City Gates** and **Fortress.** Although Zadar was a fortified city in Roman times, only the towers and gates which date from the 15th and 16th centuries are still visible today. These walls protected Venetian Zadar from the Turks, who at that time held most of the Croatian interior and came right up to the gates of the city. Only two of the four city gates are still preserved and in working order.

The **Mainland Gate** (Kopnena vrata, Porta Terraferma; NUMBER 21 ON THE PLAN) is the most beautiful Renaissance monument in Zadar. It was built in 1543 by the well-known architect from Verona, Michele Sammicheli. Over the main entrance is engraved, the city coat of arms showing St. Chrysogonus (Sveti Krševan) on horseback, and the lion of St. Mark. In front of the gate there was at one time a drawbridge over the Foša canal.

The **Port Gate** (Lučka vrata, Porta Marina; NUMBER 9 ON THE PLAN) was built in 1573; on its outer side it is decorated with a sculpture of the Venetian lion and on its inner side, part of a Roman triumphal arch has been included. On the upper Renaissance part, the city's coat of arms is also engraved with a plaque in memory of the victory of the Christians over the Turkish fleet at Lepanto in 1571. Beside the Mainland Gate, a row of defensive structures on the land side have remained standing: the Great Fortress, the Five-Cornered Bastion and the Five-Sided Tower on the Five-Well Square (Trg pet bunara). The **Great Fortress** (Velika tvrđava; NUMBER 13 ON THE PLAN) was built in 1560 on the site of the old suburbs, where there had also been an amphitheatre in Roman times. It was built by Sforza Pallavicino, whose coat of arms is on the outer wall. In the years 1880-1890 a wooded park was planted around the fortress, including Mediterranean and exotic plants.

The **Five-Cornered Bastion** (Peterokutni bastion; NUMBER 24 ON THE PLAN) although built in 1574, is still suitable for modern

Porta Terraferma (Mainland Gate)

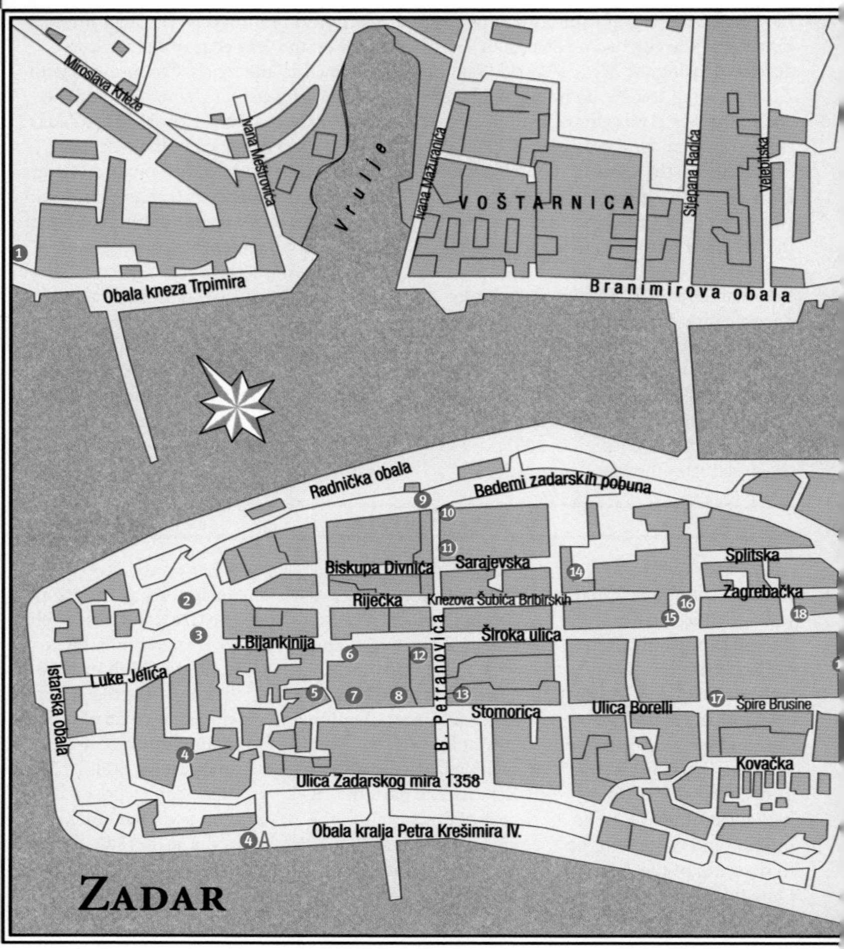

weapons because of its architecture. In 1829 a park was planted here too, including fragments of numerous decorative items which at one time adorned public buildings. The **Five-Sided Tower*** (Babja kula or Peterostrana kula; NUMBER ⓴ ON THE PLAN) is the only tower which has remained standing from the medieval defences of the city. It was built in the 13th century. Where it once had battlements, it now has a terrace, built in the 17th century. On the raised square (which now serves as a backdrop for the open-air theatre) there are five wells, dug in 1574. Considering their age, they are an incredible feat of hydro-engineering. The whole city was supplied with water from these wells right up to 1838 when new water mains were built.

••••••••••••

The **Citadel*** (Citadela; NUMBER ㉒ ON THE PLAN) is a corner bastion in the picturesque quarter of Foša. From late Roman times until the 18th century, this was also the site of an active defensive bastion, with a garrison. The Venetians built the present tower in 1548. Inside the citadel there is an open-air stage. Diagonally opposite the citadel there is a keep The **Castle** (Kaštel; NUMBER ❷ ON THE PLAN) which was the main tower guarding the entrance to Zadar harbour. From the 13th century a chain city gate also existed for this purpose. The present tower was built in 1570. Only the lower part of the eight-sided

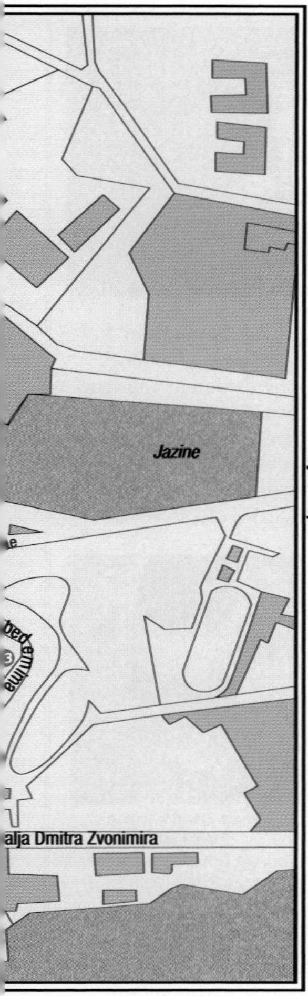

tower of the old castle remains, with a supporting wall and a smaller building, an arsenal, where gunpowder was stored. The nearby Baroque building was built as a harbour warehouse in 1752 and is known as the **Veliki Arsenal** (the Great Arsenal; NUMBER ❷ ON THE PLAN).

••••••••••••

The **Forum***** (NUMBER ❼ ON THE PLAN). The dimensions of the Roman forum were 90 m x 45 m. It was enclosed on three sides by an ornate colonnade under which there were statues. Beside the forum, raised up by about 3 m, there was a capitol on which stood a monumental temple. The paving stones of the forum remain, along with a stairway leading to the portico, the walls of a tabernacle and one of two huge columns in front of the capitol (14 m high with a Corinthian capital), which in the Middle Ages and the Venetian era served as a "pillar of shame" (for the public humiliation of offenders). It still has the remains of iron chains hanging on it. On the forum there are now archaeological fragments, gravestones and sarcophagi, and three decorative stone reliefs.

••••••••••••

St. Anastasia*** (Sveta Stošija; NUMBER ❻ ON THE PLAN). In a city which has been called "little Rome" because of its numerous churches (30), the Cathedral of St. Anastasia is considered to be the most impressive basilica. It was built in Romanesque style and consecrated in 1177 by Pope Alexander III. When the Venetians sacked Zadar in 1202, the church was

Romanesque facade of the Cathedral of St. Anastasia

looted and destroyed, but building was begun again in the 13th century. The church was finally finished in 1324. Many consider the facade of St. Anastasia to be the most beautiful in Dalmatia. Apart from Romanesque arcades with narrow pillars, the facade is decorated with masterly portals. In the centre of the Gothic ornamental moulding over the main entrance there is the figure of the Madonna sitting with the figure of St. Zoilo to her left and St. Anastasia to her right. On the left and right there are two statues

►►► p. 165

The Forum, the Church of St. Donat on the left

St. Donat***

(Sveti Donat; NUMBER ❽)

St. Donat is considered to be the finest example of Dalmatian architecture of the Old Croatian period. It was built at the beginning of the 9th century and belongs to the pre-Romanesque period. It is an original variant of the architectural form used in Byzantine buildings in the 9th century. The Zadar

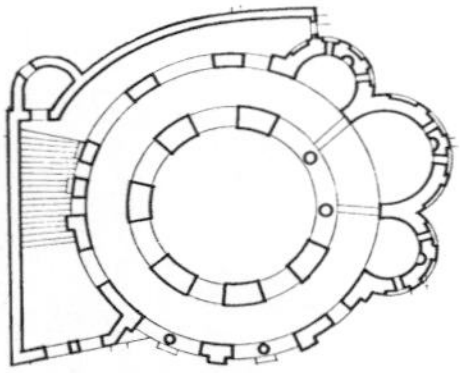

Ground plan of the church

Musical evenings

Bishop and diplomat, Donat (8th-9th centuries) is credited with the building of this church. He led the representation of the Dalmatian cities to Byzantium and Charles the Great, which is why this church is similar to Charles' court chapels, especially the one in Aachen. It was built on the Roman forum and materials from Roman buildings were used in its construction. Amongst the fragments which are built into its foundations it is still possible to distinguish the remains of a sacrificial

The interior, a worm's eye view

altar on which is written IVNONI AVGUSTE IIOVI AVGUSTO. The church is 27 m high and is characterised by simplicity and technical primitivism. Overall it gives an impression of monumental strength and thus has become the undisputed symbol of Zadar. Its use has varied during its lifetime; during the rule of the Venetians and Turks it was a warehouse, and also during the French occupation and when under the Austrians. After the liberation it was an archaeological museum for a short time and it now serves as a concert hall because of its excellent acoustics. ■

of Apostles, and the side doors have figures of the Angel Gabriel and Mary (the Annunciation) and the semi-circular mouldings bear Romanesque likenesses of the Lamb of God (Agnus Dei). The **interior** of the cathedral includes an early Gothic ciborium over the main altar. On the front side of the canopy is the date 1332 and the name of a bishop (I. Butovan) who had the main portal built. The front of the altar is decorated with pre-Romanesque braiding ornamentation. The choir stalls, in Venetian "flamboyant" Gothic, date from 1418 and are the work of the Venetian master carver Matteo A. Moronzon. In the main apse there are some Romanesque choir stalls from the 12th or 13th century. In the left-hand aisle, on the altar, there is a chest which was commissioned by Bishop Donat at the beginning of the 9th century, as a shrine for the relics of St. Anastasia. The cult of St. Anastasia began in the church after Bishop Donat had brought her bones from Constantinople. In the right-hand aisle there is a large wooden crucifix which is also the work of the master M. A. Moronzon. To the left of the door which at one time joined the cathedral to the baptistery (which was destroyed in the Second World War), there is a marble plaque in the wall mentioning the visit of Pope Alexander III to Zadar in 1117, when he was greeted with "Slavic songs". Beneath the sanctuary there is a **crypt** dating from the 12th century, which was originally intended as a place to keep and do homage to the relics. There is a Romanesque altar to St. Anastasia with an antependium showing the martyrdom of the saint, and a stone container with her relics. The cathedral's treasures and original paintings are an important part of the permanent exhibition of Church Art in St. Mary's Convent (Sveta Marija; see below). On the southern wall of the cathedral there was at one time a six-sided baptistery, which was destroyed in the Second World War. The cathedral's bell-tower was built up to its first floor in 1452, but completed according to the plans of the English architect and scholar Thomas G. Jackson as late as 1892.

•••••••••••

The **Church of St. Mary***** (Sveta Marija) and the **Benedictine Convent** (NUMBER ⓭ ON THE PLAN). The founder of the convent and church was the widow Cicca (Čika), a relative of the Croatian King Petar Krešimir IV. She succeeded in obtaining permission to found a Benedictine Convent from her "brother" in 1066, enabling not only the building of that convent but later, the Church of St. Mary. Cicca's successor, who has also left a mark on the national culture, was her youngest daughter, Večenega. The Church of St. Mary is a triple-naved basilica, built on the site of a Romanesque church. It was consecrated in 1091, and in the 16th century it was rebuilt in Renaissance style. Its facade is similar to the cathedrals in Šibenik and Hvar, as well as St. Saviour's Church (Sveti Spas) in Dubrovnik. The interior of the church has pillars which belong to its Romanesque phase, and stucco work from the late-Baroque era. The church was badly damaged in the war, and therefore now has a considerably reduced inventory. On the left-hand side, in a classical frame, is the gravestone of the Zadar noble family, the Fanfognas. Next to the church and the bell-tower stands the Romanesque **"Kapitul"**, a hall for convent gatherings. In the wall there is the gravestone of the Abbess Večenega from 1111. The sarcophagus is surrounded by Latin inscriptions: the uppermost mentions how during the reign of King Koloman, Večenega had the bell-tower and the "Kapitul"

St. Mary's Church and Benedictine Convent

built, and the other inscriptions praise the works of the late Abbess.

The inscription on the Večenega tombstone runs as follows (translated): "Shining with great glory here lies buried Vekenega, who built the bell-tower and the capitulary hall. She died in the 1111th year of Christ´s incarnation. It is the fifth year that King Koloman has ruled us, and the tenth since Gregory became bishop./ May whoever looks on this pray with the words 'Rest in peace; let the coffin cover her body, and her soul rise aloft'./ You who come here bend your gaze and when you see this tomb, say 'Give peace, Lord, to this pious soul'. Everything in the world is in constant motion, like the waves of the sea, and whatever is born decays and dies. Večenega, who, pure of heart, always followed God, did not really die but was born in death. Wishing to keep a good way of life, in her deeds she showed the nuns what she instructed them in words. She guarded the entrance into this fold well against the sleights of enemies. During her rule the house and the place prospered. She moved to the other world on the feast of SS. Cosmas and Damian to inherit eternal life in the divine mansions."

Čika's cross (Zadar Gold and Silver Collection)

The church's **bell-tower** is Romanesque. Below the cornice which divides the first floor from the ground floor, there is a marble strip, with the date 1105 and symbols relating to King Koloman, the donor of the bell-tower. On the first floor is Večenega's chapel with a groin and rib vault, the oldest of its kind in Europe.

After the liberation of the country, the convent was restored and a **permanent collection of church art** was set up. It is better known as *The Gold and Silver of Zadar* (Zlato i srebro Zadra). In eight rooms in this two-storey building there are about 150 exhibits: gold, sculptures and stone carvings, wood carvings, embroidery, paintings and crafts, dated from the 7th to the 18th century. Most of the objects are priceless in their value for the Croatian cultural heritage. The most valuable part of this exhibition are the reliquaries. In the Middle Ages the belief that the bones of saints have special powers to heal diseases, drive out evil spirits, confirm the truth or promises spread amongst the new nations of Europe and a cult of worshipping the bones of saints or martyrs developed.

Reliquary from the 15th century (Zadar Gold and Silver Collection)

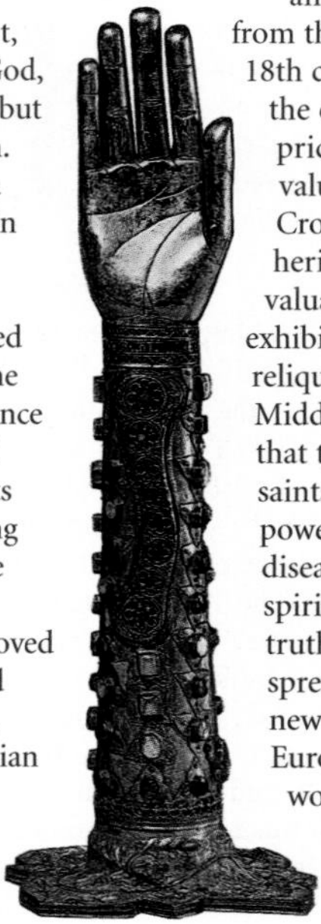

The main expression of that worship was the creation of a special container for their bones and other sacred objects, using precious metals. They might be in the form of small boxes, bags, stands, small altars, and, as the Middle Ages developed, even in the shapes of that part of the body to which the bones belonged (eg. a hand, a foot etc.). The oldest exhibit is *The Cicca cross* from the 7th or 8th century which was brought to Zadar from Palestine. Most of the other reliquaries contain the bones of the patron saints of Zadar. Although these saints are also revered in other places, these relics have special features which show their Zadar origins. In contrast to the gold exhibits, most of the paintings on display here

V. Carpaccio, "St. Martin and the Beg (Zadar Gold and Silver Collection

actually come from Venice. The painting *The Madonna and Child* (in room 3) is attributed to P. Veneziano. The most valuable item is a *polyptych* (hall 5) with pictures of St. Anastasia, St. Martin, St. Simon, St. Peter, St. Jerome, with the donor, the Canon of Zadar and notary Martin Mladošić, and St. Paul. The polyptych was painted towards the end of the 15th century by Vittore Carpaccio (1455-1526). In the next hall (6) there are two paintings by Palma the Younger (1544-1628), and in the 7th hall paintings by Riccardi, Carlo Loti, J. Gropelli, A. Corradini, G. Pitteria and Pietro Mera. Amongst the works of native artists, the best known is the painting of the Madonna and Child, known as *Our Lady of Good Health*, by Blaž Jurjev from Trogir, dated 1447. Amongst the valuable items with Croatian origins is *Liber moralium in Job*, in Beneventana script from the 12th century (hall 2). The Zadar Beneventana (written in the minuscule script which preceded Gothic) has no analogy in any other western

Madonna and Child, 15th century

Chest of St. Zoilo (Zadar Gold and Silver Collection)

European country. The finest example of a Dalmatian manuscript written in Beneventana is the *Večenega Gospel* from 1085 which is in the Bodleian Library in Oxford.

The exhibits in this national treasury were saved in the last war thanks to the Abbess Benedikta Braun, who had them walled into the base of the bell-tower. The reliquary shrine of St. Simon (Sveti Šimun, see the Church of St. Simon) was also preserved in this way.

••••••••••••

The **Church of St. Chrysogonus***** (Sveti Krševan; NUMBER ⓫). Before this church, there was a Benedictine monastery on this site, founded in 908, as the first and greatest monastery on the Eastern Adriatic coast. It is thought that the monastery was built from gifts given by Croatian rulers as early as the 10th century. A deed of gift from 1069 still exists, showing how King Petar Krešimir IV (who was responsible for the renewal of the Croatian state and reigned from 1053 to 1075), gave the monastery the island of Maun "in our Dalmatian sea" and supplied the basic materials necessary for its work. The monastery was the centre of the resistance to Venice over four and a half centuries. It opposed the archbishops appointed by Venice, and requested that the army of the Croatian Ban come to Zadar (1356-1358) etc. Elizabeta Kotromanić the wife of Ludvig I (see the shrine of St. Simon) was temporarily buried here, and the coronation of the Croatian King Ladislav of Anjou probably took place here. Above all the monastery was the focal point of the Croatian character of Zadar and for this reason the figure of St. Chrysogonus was used in the city's coat of arms. Only the Romanesque biforium on the side walls adjoining the right-hand apse still reminds us of the old monastery.

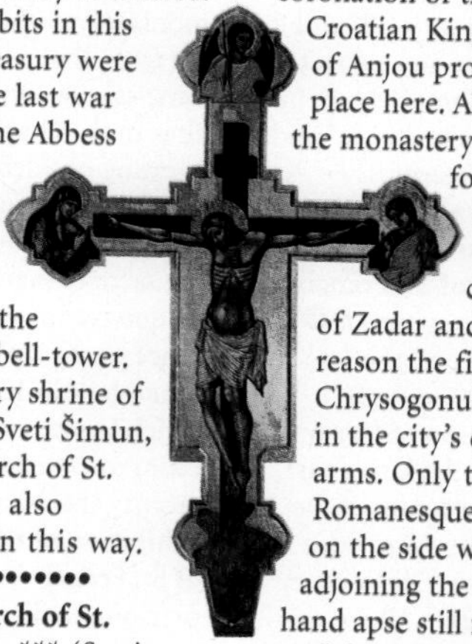

A famed wooden crucifix (Zadar Gold and Silver Collection)

The present church is a Romanesque building from the 12th century (it was consecrated in 1175), whose most attractive aspect is the outer walls of the three apses. Inside the church there are ancient columns with Corinthian capitals. There are only faint traces of frescoes dating from the 13th and 14th centuries. In front of the highly ornate altar (1701) with its marble statues of the Zadar patron saints, St. Chrysogonus, St. Simeon, St. Anastasia and Zoilus, the bones of St.

Chrysogonus from the third century are kept. The church also has a painted crucifix (353 cm x 249 cm in size) which dates from about 1380 and is attributed to a follower of Lorenzo Veneziano, Jacopo di Bonomo. The church's bell-tower, which was built alongside the front of the church in 1546, has never been completed. In front of the church there is a **statue of Petar Zoranić** (1508-some time after 1543) a citizen of Zadar and Renaissance poet, who wrote the first Croatian pastoral novel *Mountains* (Planine) in 1536. He was a patriot who sought to celebrate his "scattered inheritance" and to extol its beauty.

The **Church and Monastery of St. Francis** (Sveti Frane; NUMBER ❹). The church and the monastery (the first Franciscan monastery on the Eastern Adriatic coast and still the centre of the order in the region) was begun in the 13th century in Gothic style. The buildings have been re-built several times and therefore have elements from many different cultural eras. The choir stalls inside the church are in the Venetian Gothic style, and the chapel and the monastery cloisters are from the Renaissance. On the central altar in the chapel there is a painting entitled *St. Francis of Assisi* which is the work of Palma the Younger. In the sacristy there is a plaque commemorating the peace treaty signed in this monastery in 1358, by which Venice renounced its claim to Dalmatia. In the sacristy there is an **exhibition of the treasures of St. Francis**. As well as precious chalices and choir books, wooden Gothic sculptures and paintings (a 15th century polyptych from Ugljan with 29 sections, which has been ascribed to Dujam Vušković of Split), the most valuable of all items in the treasury is an illustrated crucifix (200 x 193 cm) which has been dated to 1180. In age it can be compared with the first crucifix from Sarzana in Tuscany, and, in terms of its exceptional style, with the mysterious crucifix number 432 in the Uffizi gallery, which is considered to be most unusual and exceptional. It is the oldest and most valuable illustrated crucifix on the Adriatic.

Polyptych of Dujam Vušković (Collection of the Monastery of St. Francis)

Madonna (13th century) from St. Simon's Church

The **Church of St. Simeon***** (Sveti Šimun; NUMBER ⓲). This Baroque building was built on the site of an early Christian church built at the end of the 5th or the beginning of the 6th century. Its present appearance is the result of several phases in its history. From the earliest phase an impressive wall remains with seven biforia on the south side, and an entire colonnade with an archivolt. From the Romanesque era there is a relief inside the church entitled *The Birth of Christ.* The northern wall with frescoes from the 14th century belongs to the Gothic phase, and there are also some traces of the Renaissance. Its Baroque appearance is a result of reconstruction in 1632, and the bell-tower was added in 1707. Over the main altar is the **shrine of St. Simeon** (**sarcophagus**), an outstanding work, considered to be one of the most interesting pieces of work in gold in Europe. The goldsmith Francis of Milan

Chest of St. Simon

(Francesco di Antonio da Sesto) made it between 1377 and 1380, assisted by Andrija Markov from Zagreb, Petar Blažev from Rača, Stjepan Pribičev and Mihovil Damjanov. It was commissioned by Elizabeta (Jelena), the wife of the Croatian-Hungarian King Ludvig I of Anjou, one of the most powerful European rulers of his time (1342-1382). It is made of cedar wood, covered in 240 kg of silver plate and a considerable quantity of gold. It is 1.92 m long, 80 cm wide and, including the lid, 1.27 m high. On the front of the lid there are 13 relief compositions, the figure of St. Simeon and two sets of the arms of Anjou on the sides. The same coat of arms in the shape of a buckle can be found in the treasury of Aachen Cathedral, for Ludvig I was the grandson of Karl Martel, the son of Karl II King of Naples. The central relief on the front, *The Presentation in the Temple* is based on a fresco by Giotto in Padua. In this way Francis of Milan introduced Giotto's work to Dalmatia. On the left-hand side is the relief *The Discovery of the Saint's Body*, which is an interpretation of the story of how the bones of St. Simeon came to Zadar. On the right is the relief *The Arrival of King Ludvig I in Zadar*. From an historical point of view this is the most interesting work as it interprets an event which occurred almost at the same time as the chest was being made. Ludvig enters the city with the shrine, returning the saint to the

city from which the Venetians had removed him. The left-hand side relief (over which is the Anjou coat of arms) shows *The Boat in the Storm.* On the right side (beneath the other coat of arms) is the scene *The Theft of the Finger.* This scene has been interpreted in various ways because of the large number of figures represented. Older writers say that it shows Elizabeta stealing St. Simeon's finger in order to have a male heir. On the back of the chest the central position is taken by an inscription in Latin "Simeon the Righteous, holding Jesus, born of a Virgin, in his arms, rests in peace in this chest, commissioned by the Queen of Hungary, mighty, glorious and majestic Elizabeta the Younger, in the year 1380. This is the work of Francis of Milan". To the left of this text is the scene *Queen Elizabeta with her daughters presenting the chest to the saint* and on the right, *The Death of Ban Kotromanić,* the Queen's father. As the Queen's father was a Bosnian Ban, and Bosnian rulers were accused of the Bogumil heresy, this scene is meant to show that the Queen's father was a good Catholic. The three scenes on the back of the lid show *The Perjurer, The Goldsmith* and the scene *The Miracle with the Foot.* The inside of the chest is also illustrated showing five miracles performed by the saint. In the background, dating from 1497, there are pictures of the patron saints of Zadar. The chest is opened every year on St. Simeon's day (8th October)

St. Peter the Elder

and only then is its interior visible, full of precious votive gifts. This beautiful gift was probably given to Zadar because the royal couple needed the support of the Zadar people. It was the period when Zadar frequently belonged alternately to the Venetian Empire and the territory of the Croatian-Hungarian king. Thus Ludvig I wanted a strong community in Zadar to form a bond between his South Italian possessions, and the Polish and Croatian-Hungarian state. For this reason St. Simeon was the best choice. He was the most popular saint in Zadar, his relics had never been given sufficient honour and Zadar considered them to be authentic, as opposed to the ones which were in Venice.

••••••••••••

The **Chapel of St. Andrew and St. Peter**** (Sveti Andrija i Sveti Petar; NUMBER ⓮) is now an art gallery. An unusual feature of this building is that it is in fact two churches joined together. The one in front was a single-naved chapel, dating back to early Christian times and is built of many Roman fragments. The apse and the southern wall formed the Chapel of St. Andrew and then in the Middle Ages the double-naved chapel, St. Peter's, was added (in the 10th century). In the left-hand apse there are Romanesque frescoes from the 12th century.

••••••••••••

The **Church of Our Lady of Good Health*** (Gospa od zdravlja; NUMBER ❸ ON THE PLAN) is a Renaissance church from 1582, and was redecorated in Baroque style in the 18th century. However the church was damaged in the war. The church contains the grave of Archbishop Vicko Zmajević, the founder of the Illyrian seminary and defender of Albanian Christian refugees who settled in Arbanasi, a suburb of Zadar.

••••••••••••

St. Elijah's Church* (Sveti Ilija; NUMBER ❺ ON THE PLAN) is a medieval church which was redecorated in Baroque style in the 18th century. It has been an Orthodox church since 1578, originally for Venetian subjects, but since the middle of the 18th century it has belonged to the Serbian Orthodox Church. Inside the church there is a valuable collection of icons dating from the 16th to the 19th centuries.

••••••••••••

St. Michael's Church* (Sveti Mihovil; NUMBER ⓱) is a Gothic building from the 14th century with an interesting facade. A relief in the lunette shows the Archangel Gabriel binding souls and there are three walled-in busts of Roman origin. In the Middle Ages these busts were given haloes. The interior is dominated by a relief crucifix from the 13th century and a stone font from the 15th century.

••••••••••••

The **Dominican Monastery** (Špire Brusine Street). The Dominicans arrived in Zadar in 1228, during the age of the mature Bogumil movement in Bosnia, which the local clergy could not prevent. They obtained a house and chapel by the Church of St. Chrysogonus, and in 1266 they started building their own monastery. This was a large building, 60 m x 40 m. The church was consecrated in 1280. It is a typical Dominican building: simple and functional. In 1396 the General School, the **first Croatian university**, was founded in the monastery. This was one of the rare institutions in the 14th century that obtained the privilege of opening its own theological faculty. In 1553 it obtained the status of a privileged school with the right to give academic degrees. This meant that it was on the same level as the universities of Paris, Rome, Bologna and Florence; there were 27 such in the Europe of the time. The Zadar college had two faculties, one of philosophy and one of theology, and it was open to local and foreign clerics and laymen. It kept up connections with foreign schools and thus had an international character. As a university, it is 273 years older than that in Zagreb, and according to the granting of its first doctorate, 325 years. The French closed it on January 8, 1807, and turned it into a barracks.

National Museum

Museums

The **Archaeological Museum**** (Šime Kožičić Street; NUMBER 12) was founded in 1830 and, after the archaeological museum in Split, is the oldest in the country. It includes finds from the entire central Dalmatian region. It has a prehistoric collection (on the 2nd floor) the most interesting part of which is exhibits of Liburnian culture, and a Roman collection (on the first floor) with a large collection of lamps, pots, decorative objects and sculptures. The early medieval collection (on the ground floor) has pre-Romanesque (old Croatian) stone monuments. The most valuable exhibits are considered parts of church furniture, pluteuses from the demolished Church of Holy Sunday (Sveta Nedeljica), from Zadar Cathedral and the Church of St. Lawrence, and a stone fragment with an inscription including the name of Prince Branimir.

••••••

The **Folk Museum**** (Narodni muzej; divided between several sites). The **Ethnographic Department** (Medulićeva 2; NUMBER 19). The collection is divided into two parts: handicrafts from the Dinar region (inland), from the coastal area and the Zadar islands. There are national costumes (mostly from Pag and Novigrad), old household objects, folk instruments and objects relating to folk arts and crafts. The **Cultural and Historical Department** (Poljana Pape Aleksandra III; NUMBER 10). The department is on the ground floor and in the courtyard. It includes two models of the city and numerous exhibits belonging to the period from the Romanesque to the Baroque and gives an insight

National Museum, cultural history collection

into residential architecture in Zadar through the centuries. On the first and second floors there are documents and objects illustrating the history of the National Revival in the second half of the 19th century, the labour movement and the antifascist struggle in the Zadar area. The **Natural History Department** (Medulićeva street 2; NUMBER ⓳ ON THE PLAN) has the task of collecting and exhibiting the fauna and flora of Dalmatia. The museum has an interesting fossil collection.

••••••••••••

The **Art Gallery*** (Medulićeva street; NUMBER ⓳) has displays of works by Dalmatian artists and sculptors from the 19th and 20th

Market in the city centre

century, including a large part of the works of the Zadar artist Franjo Salghetti-Droli (1811-1877).

••••••••••••

The **Maritime Museum*** (Pomorski muzej; in Brodarica in the building of the Institute of the Croatian Academy; NUMBER ❶) has a collection of models of Adriatic ships, from the

Art Gallery

"Sagena", an old Croatian warship, to modern ships, as well as ship's instruments and votive pictures by sailors. The museum also houses a "Ladva", the only surviving example of a boat made by hollowing out a single tree trunk, which was in use from the Neolithic age to the end of the 19th century.

••••••••••••

The **People's Square**** (Narodni trg; NUMBER ⓰ ON THE PLAN) has been the centre of public life in Zadar from the Renaissance to the present day. On its northern side is the Renaissance building of the **City Watch** (Gradska straža) which was built in 1562 (the bell-tower was added in 1768). The building now houses the ethnographic museum (see above). On the southern side is the **City loggia**, also Renaissance, but now enclosed in glass, which was built in 1565. The loggia has now been converted into an exhibition hall. It still contains a stone table from 1600. Next to this are the buildings of the Commune Assembly which were built during the Italian occupation in 1936. Between the buildings of the Assembly and the City Watch (now a cafe) there was once a pre-Romanesque chapel dedicated to St. Lawrence (Sveti Lovro). In the 18th century this chapel served as a prison.

••••••••••••

Sea Organ (Obala kralja Petra Krešimira IV, NUMBER **❹A** ON THE PLAN) is an avantgarde musical installation designed by architect Nikola Basic. It is a unique project that simulates the music of the waves and wind. ■

Sea Organ

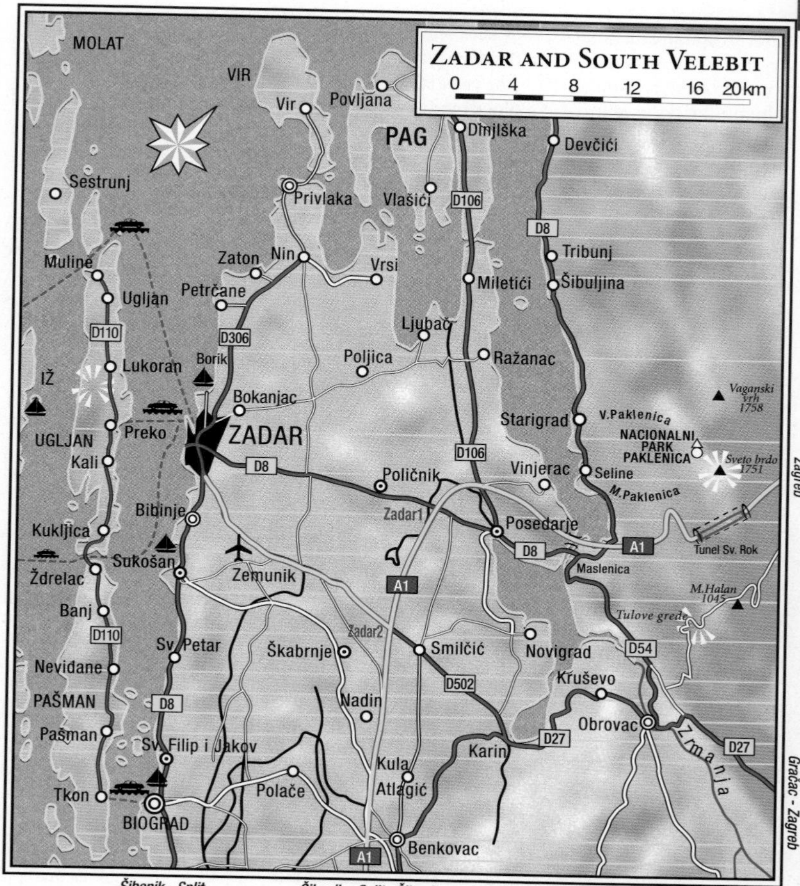

Excursions

Biograd

28 km southeast of Zadar, population 5 278; mean January temperatures: air 6.6 °C, sea 11.9 °C; mean July temperatures: air 24.2 °C, sea 22.6 °C.

The area around Biograd has been inhabited since prehistoric times, but it is thought that the town of Biograd was founded in the 9th century by Croats. There is no firm evidence that the Illyrian and Roman Blandona was situated on the site of present day Biograd. Most probably Blandona lay at the foot of the Trojan earthworks, southeast of Kakma, 7 km from Biograd. In contrast to Zadar (Iader) and Nin (Aenona) Nadin and Karin, there is no Liburnian settlement in the Biograd area which has remained inhabited until the present day, nor has any name been retained. But it is known that the area around Biograd was part of the Liburnian culture and that it had trading links with Greece, Italy and the entire Balkan peninsula. After the Liburnians, the Romans took over and further developed their maritime skills. Three Roman quays have been discovered in the Biograd area; in the present-day Pakoštane harbour, in Tukljača near Turanj and in the area around Kumenat, to the south of Biograd. There a farm has also been discovered, with

Crest of the royal city of Biograd

about 10 000 square holes carved into the stony ground, for the preparation of humus bricks used in wine and olive growing.

The Byzantine Emperor Constantine Porphyrogenitus first mentioned Biograd in the 10th century. He was a contemporary of King Tomislav, and called the town Belogradon. It is interesting to note that the Slavs frequently called their capital cities "white" (bijeli). Biograd became the capital in about 1018 during the reign of King Krešimir III. It became a Bishopric in about 1050 and Petar Krešimir IV had a Benedictine monastery built there. For a short time it was under the Normans. In historical literature it is mentioned that in 1075 the Norman King Amico took Petar Krešimir captive, and forced him to give up Nin and Biograd as ransom. However Krešimir's heir, King Zvonimir (1075-1089) also ruled Biograd, so it seems this arrangement was short-lived. At that time Biograd was one of the most important Croatian towns. When King Petar Svačić died there in 1102 in the dynastic and civil war (the last king of Croatian blood) in the same year the Hungarian King Koloman from the Arpadović dynasty was crowned there as the new ruler of the Croats. Croatian Biograd was a thorn in the flesh to Venice so they razed it to the ground in 1125. It was rebuilt but it never regained its former glory after 1125. When the Crusaders destroyed Zadar in 1202, those fleeing from Zadar took refuge in Biograd and it became known as Novi Zadar (New Zadar). Up to 1409 Biograd was in the hands of the Counts of Cetina and the Templer of Vrana, but once it fell to Venice, along with the greater part of the coast, it became the Venetians' border town against the Turks and the site of constant battles between the Christians and the Muslims.

Biograd

In 1598 it became the headquarters of the Croatian army for defence against the Turks, with about 300 border guards. They were however insufficient for its defence and it was razed to the ground by Ibrahim Pasha in 1646. When the Turks withdrew from the Dalmatian coastal area the town was rebuilt and until the end of the First World War it shared the fate of Zadar and the entire eastern coast. In 1923 the Italian occupation came to an end following the Treaty of Rapallo and it was joined to Yugoslavia. Nowadays Biograd is one of the most attractive tourist areas on the Adriatic. During the Serb aggression of 1991-1992 it suffered very considerable damage from long-range artillery.

SIGHTS

The **Parish Church of St. Anastasia*** (Sveta Stošija) was built in 1761. Inside the church there is a fine Gothic altar with a painting of the church's patroness. The painting *The Madonna of the New Moon* (on the left-hand wall) is a votive offering from the 16th or 17th century and is mentioned in literature as being of particular value.

••••••••••••

The **Folk Museum*** is part of the Zadar museum. As well as an archaeological collection presenting the few remaining monuments from the time of the Croatian rulers (decorative architectural fragments) and items of old Croatian

Ancient vase in the collection of the museum

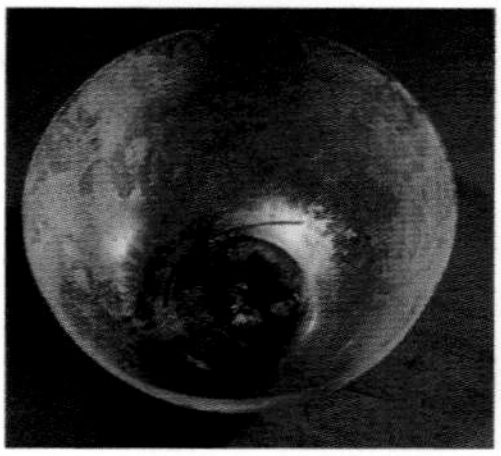

material culture, the museum also houses an interesting collection of "Treasures from the bottom of the sea", a collection of items from a wreck off Gnalić in the Pašman Channel.

•••••••••••

Historic Locations in Biograd. Biograd **Cathedral** is in the centre of the town, to the east of the parish church. It was built in the 11th century and was once an impressive triple-naved basilica with a belfry on the facade. The **Monastery Church of St. John** (Sveti Ivan), stands in ruins in the garden belonging to the Jelačić family. It was a triple-naved Romanesque basilica, 27.5 m x 12.5 m in size, and was also built in the 11th century. It was the church of the Benedictine monastery founded by King Petar Krešimir IV at the same time as the Bishopric was founded, in about 1050. In 1076 the church was consecrated by Archbishop Lovro of Split in the presence of the Pope's representative. The **Convent Church of St. Thomas** (Sveti Toma; remains of the apse are in front of the Zorica house, a few hundred metres to the east of St. John's). This church was built as a basilica and belonged to the Benedictine convent which was also founded by Petar Krešimir IV. The Hungarian King Koloman was crowned in this convent in 1102 as King of the Croats.

••••••••••••

The Pašman Channel

The Island of Pašman**

15 MINUTES BY FERRY FROM BIOGRAD

Up until 1885 the island was joined to the island of Ugljan but then a channel was dug which was later made deeper, up to 4m, and now a bridge connects the two islands. Pašman is the "twin" of the island of Ugljan: it is similar in length, surface area and location with similarly placed settlements. The one significant difference is that Pašman gravitates towards Biograd, and Ugljan towards Zadar. The island has seven settlements: Tkon, Pašman, Mrljane, Neviđane, Dobropoljana, Banj and Ždrelac. In Tkon, Pašman and Neviđane there are ruins from the Roman era. When the Biograd Bishopric was founded in 1050 the island was part of its property, but from 1126 it was the property of the Archbishop of Zadar. During the time when the Venetians destroyed Biograd and the Turkish invasion the island was inhabited by those fleeing from the mainland.

Tkon (752 inhabitants). With Neviđane, Tkon is the largest settlement on the island. The **Parish Church of St. Thomas*** and the summer residence of the D'Erco family, built in the 18th century, are some of the better known buildings. The painting of the Madonna on the main altar of the parish church has been ascribed to the Zadar artist Petar Jordanić (the end of the 15th to the beginning of the 16th centuries), who is also the artist of a painting *The Madonna and Child* in Vienna, painted in 1508. Jordanić is also known for the fact that together with the envoy I. Detrik he was sent by the people of Zadar to the Count of Krbava in 1501 to work on combined defences against the Turkish invaders. Jordanić had the job of sketching the area to assist in the planning of military operations.

The **Monastery of St. Cosmas and St. Damian***** (Sveti Kuzma i Damjan) on Ćokovac hill is a Romanesque Benedictine monastery which was built after the destruction of Biograd in 1125. The monks of the Benedictine Abbey of St. John moved here from Biograd. It has often served as a fortress because of its advantageous position and

Cloister of the Monastery of St. Cosmas and St. Damian

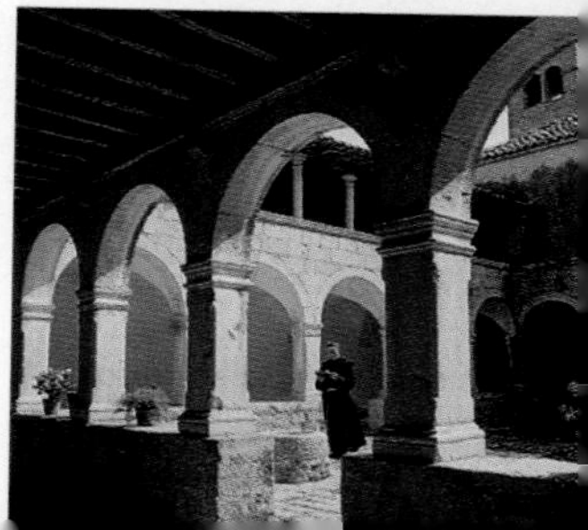

therefore has also suffered damage in various battles. The monastery was for a long time a centre of Slavic forms of worship and Croatian Glagolitic literature. It was dissolved in 1808. In the monastery there is a small Gothic chapel which was restored in 1367-1418 with three Renaissance altars and several Glagolitic inscriptions. The most interesting item in the chapel is an illustrated crucifix (195 x 164 cm), which is thought to date from 1418. Experts still cannot agree as to the artist who made it. He is anonymous but is known as "The Master of the Tkon Crucifix" (or maestro di Elsino) in a polyptych showing scenes from the life of this saint, now in the National Gallery in London.

St. Dominus Monastery* (Sveti Dujam; 3 km north of Tkon in the village of Kraj). This monastery has been here for 6 centuries. It houses a museum including the painting *The Madonna on the Throne* which is the work of the *Master of the Tkon Crucifix.*

••••••••••••

Vrgada*

CAN BE REACHED BY MOTOR BOAT FROM BIOGRAD (2 N/M) AND MURTER; 261 INHABITANTS

This is the largest and the only inhabited island amongst about 20 small islands south of Pašman, covering an area of 3.7 km². Its north-eastern part is wooded with small bays and sandy beaches. On a small hill over the graveyard there are traces of an Illyrian, Roman and early medieval tower. St. Andrew's Church (Sveti Andrej) dates from the year 900. There is also the summer residence of an Italian baron from the 17th century. This village was mentioned by Constantine Porphyrogenitus as "Lumbrikation".

Monastery on Ćokovac Hill

Vrgada

••••••••••••

Vrana*

10 KM FROM BIOGRAD, POPULATION 703

Not far from the village there are the remains of Illyrian earthworks, the Zadar aqueduct from the Roman era and the ruins of an early medieval castle (Castrum Aurannae) from the 9th century. After 1076 the Benedictine monastery of St. Gregory (Sveti Grgur) stood here, and served as a residence for the Papal legate in Croatia. This was a gift of the Croatian King Dmitar Zvonimir to Gebizon, the legate of Pope Gregory VII when he attended the king's coronation in Solin. Later it was the property of the Knights Templar, and then of the Order of St. John, until they were expelled by the Venetians in 1409. In 1538 it was taken over by the Turks. During the Turkish occupation (until 1647) the monastery was an important Turkish fortress. When the Venetians captured it again, the castle was completely destroyed.

Famous frieze in Šopot near Benkovac

In the immediate vicinity of the castle is **Maškovića han****. Built in 1644 as a caravanserai by Jusuf Mašković from Vrana, it is one of the few examples of Turkish architecture in Dalmatia. Franjo (Francesco Laurana, Delaurana) and Lucijan Vranjanin were born in Vrana and here they received their early artistic education. They worked in Italy and are better known abroad than in their native country. Franjo (1420/25 -1502) built the triumphal arch in Naples, and other works in Provence and Marseilles. His marble busts of women are in museums in Palermo, Vienna, Berlin, Paris and

Maškovića han

New York. Lucijan (about 1420/25-1479) is famous as the court architect to Federigo da Montefeltro of Urbino. He designed the Pallazo Ducale, the most important palace in Urbino.
Lake Vrana** (Vransko jezero) is the largest lake in Croatia (covering an area of 3 000 hectares. It is 13.6 km long and 2.2 km wide, with an average depth of 3.9 m). It originated as a drowned karst field, and in the north west part there are the remains of natural marshes. It is joined to the sea by a series of natural underground streams and one man-made canal, and therefore its water is brackish. The lake is the home of many species of birds and fish. The most interesting fish in the lake are the eels (s. the migrations of the eel under Neretva) grey mullet and smelt. In 1948 fresh water fish were introduced to the lake, such as carp, catfish, pike and others, upsetting the ecological balance in the lake, causing the eels and mullet to lose their habitat. Amongst the many birds which live here is the last remaining Mediterranean colony of various kinds of heron (Ardea) in Croatia.

••••••••••••

Benkovac*

21 KM FROM BIOGRAD,
34 KM FROM ZADAR,
30 KM FROM OBROVAC,
POPULATION 2 635

This town lies on the border between the regions of Ravni Kotari and Bukovica. It was at one time on the Roman road from Iader (Zadar) to Burnum, and is now at the crossing of eight roads. It was also a strategically important place on the border between the Venetian and the Turkish Empires. Above the town there are the ruins of a castle which belonged to the Benković Beys from Livno. During Serb aggression, the town was occupied, and the Parish Church of the Nativity of the B.V.M. was razed to the ground. The Orthodox Church of St. John the Baptist was built in 1885. The surrounding area is rich in historical sites.
Šopot (2 km southwest of Benkovac) was a foundation of Prince Branimir, from the 9th century, and a place where one of the most valuable

Croatian monuments was found: a decorative architectural fragment dated 888, in which the name of the Croats is first mentioned: "Branimiro comes...dux Cruatorum cogit (avit)" or "Branimir the count... prince of the Croats thinks..." **Podgrađe**, west of Benkovac, is the Roman settlement of Asseria. The area around Benkovac is well known for wine making, and in the town itself there is a wine cellar.

Nin

17 km from Zadar, population 1 250

When the well-known Italian travel writer and biologist Alberto Fortis (1741-1803) set out from Zadar for Nin in 1771 to see this town with such a glorious Roman and Croatian history, he was disappointed with what he found there. He wrote, "The ruins of Nin, which should offer abundant food for those fascinated by the ancient, have suffered so much in the destruction which has come upon that unhappy town that there remain only a few visible traces" and... "not only is there nothing left to show the greatness of the Roman age, but there are no traces of the glory of the Barbarians which would remind us of the centuries when the Croatian kings ruled here". In the meantime, archaeological research, conservation and restoration work and especially the organisation of the collection known as **The Gold and Silver of Nin** have ensured that at least partially, the town's present appearance gives some idea of its past.

Nin, City Gates and Lower Bridge entrance into the city

Prehistory. The oldest traces of life in the area of Nin date from the Neolithic era and thus can be placed at about 5,000 BC. It is however significant that Nin is the best-known and richest Illyrian (Liburnian) site in Dalmatia with hundreds of graves which have been discovered and researched. According to an anonymous Greek writer of the 4th century BC, Pseudo-Skylax, who described a voyage on the Mediterranean, Nin (Aeona) was an important administrative, economic and cultural centre of the Liburnians.

The Roman Era. Nin (Aeona) came under the Romans in the last decade of the first century BC. It soon (under Emperor Augustus) gained the status of a munici-pality, with its own city council. It had a forum, amphitheatre, aqueduct and was surrounded by city walls. The temple, decorated with statues of many Roman emperors, is the largest yet discovered in Croatia.

The Period of Croatian Rule. At the beginning of the 7th century, Nin fell to the Avar and Slavic invaders, but nevertheless avoided being completely destroyed, thanks to its location. This fact, along with the speedy disappearance of the old Roman inhabitants (s. Necropolis below) enabled the new Slavic population quickly to form one of the most important centres of political, ecclesiastical and cultural life in Croatia. In about 800, Frankish missionaries began to baptise the Slav population. One of the most significant archaeological finds in

The Mare Nostrum document, published in Nin

Nin is a six-sided stone font, known as the Višeslav-font (the original is in the Museum of Croatian Archaeological Monuments in Split and there is a copy in the collection in Nin). Fifty years later Count Domagoj (865-876) founded a Bishopric in Nin which had jurisdiction over the entire Croatian state. This was the period when a struggle broke out between Rome and Byzantium over the sovereignty of Croatia. In terms of ecclesiastical affairs, these conflicts were expressed in the issue of who was to consecrate bishops in Croatia and Dalmatia. The Bishop of Nin, Teodozije, remained neutral, but Count Branimir (879-892) at the time when the Dalmatian bishops conceded Byzantine rule, declared himself definitely on the side of the Roman Church. Another event of European importance is part of the history of Nin. In 885 the older of the "Slavic apostle" brothers, Method, died (he was born in Thessalonica sometime before 820), and Latin and German priests started to persecute the Slav priests (disciples of Cyril and Method), accusing them of teaching heresy and using forbidden forms of worship. Pope Stephen IV banned the Slav liturgy and Count Svatopluk expelled all Slav priests. Some of the 200 expelled priests and their followers took refuge with the Bishop of Nin and Count Branimir. Thus the Slav liturgy came to Croatia, and it was first used by the Bishop of Nin (see Buzet, Roč). There was no permanent capital in Croatia until the reign of Dmitar Zvonimir (1075-1089). Nin was one of the frequent temporary residences of, for instance, Branimir, who obtained independence from both the Franks and Byzantium (who from 889 were paid taxes by the Venetians to be able to cross the sea), and then Tomislav, the first king to be crowned (925), during whose reign the royal navy included 180 ships with about 15 000 oarsmen and 5 000 sailors. Sunken ships from this era have recently been discovered in Nin harbour.

Once Croatia had entered an alliance with Hungary (1102) Nin became an independent city commune with many privileges. As late as 1371 the Croatian-Hungarian King Ludvig of Anjou held an assembly of the nobility and citizens of Croatia here, as it was "the capital and royal Dalmatian city".

Under the Venetians. Before 1409, when Dalmatia was sold off to the Venetians, Nin only admitted Venetian authority between 1328 and 1358. After 1409 it shared the fate of other towns on the Eastern Adriatic coast, but due to its location, Nin was also in the border area between Venice and the Turkish Empire and was therefore fortified. From 1500 Nin was attacked by the Turks. In 1570 Venice demolished the city so that the Turks would not be able to make use of it, and in 1646 the inhabitants were moved away. The city was restored in 1699, but it was never to regain the importance it once enjoyed. ■

Sights

The **Parish Church of St. Anselm** (Sveti Anzelmo) **with Treasury***** (NUMBER ❸). According to tradition, Saint Anselm (Asel) was one of Christ's seventy disciples and the first Bishop of Nin. He set out to preach the Gospel in Gaul and from there came to Nin and converted many people to Christianity. The church was built on the site of a former Romanesque and Gothic building. The side chapel, reliefs of the saints and the northern portal are all that remain of the old church. Beside the church there is a **treasury**, which has only 28 exhibits in all (of which 23 are of gold, two wood carvings, two of

►►► p. 181

Holy Cross Church***

(Sveti Križ; NUMBER ❹)

Holy Cross Church which is built in the shape of a domed cross, is one of the finest examples of old Croatian architecture. It has been dated to about 800 but historians do not entirely agree on this. It has been preserved more or less unchanged. It was built by Godežav (Godečaj) the regional leader, and his name can be seen over the doorway. This is thought to be the oldest preserved inscription from the age of the Croatian rulers. Inside the church there is also an inscription with the name of Count Branimir from the second half of the 9th century. Since Nin became a Bishopric during the reign of Count Domagoj, and a bishop's seat is called a cathedral, it is said that this is the smallest cathedral in the world (its circumference is about 36 paces). Despite its small size, this church gives an exceptionally monumental impression. Researchers were confused by the regularity of its dimensions, despite the "incompetence" of the builders in creating straight lines. The Dubrovnik artist Mladen Pejaković found the answer. According to him, the building is built in such a way that the sun's rays have a special position in the plans of the floor and walls. The dimensions and lines of the walls, corners, shape, width and height of the doors and windows arise from calculations governed by the sun. These calculations have allowed the creation of a building which is at one and the same time a clock, calendar and place of worship (s. drawing). ■

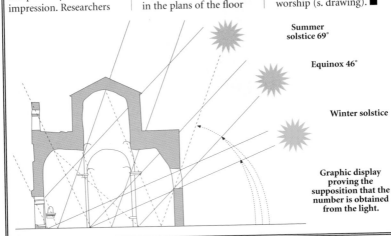

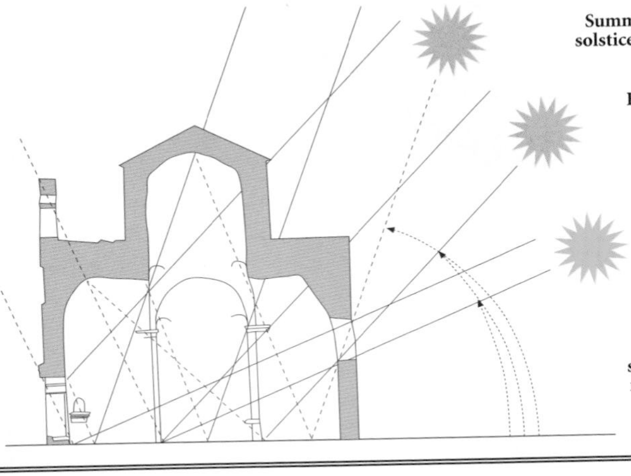

Graphic display proving the supposition that the number is obtained from the light.

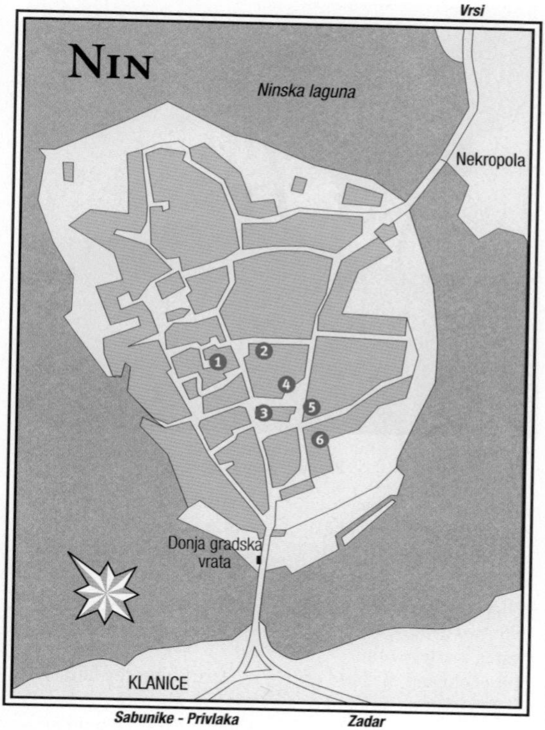

textiles, and one ornamental lock), but in terms of value these exhibits are worthy of the greatest metropolis. Apart from their artistic value, they conjure up the life and cultural level of this city throughout its history. Two gold exhibits (a reliquary with the shoulder blade of St. Anselm and a reliquary of an unknown saint) belong to the period of Caroline gold work of the 8th and 9th centuries. The remaining golden articles are examples of the local gold work of the Romanesque and Gothic eras. The reliquary *The hand of St. Anselm* was commissioned by the Croatian Ban Pavao Šubić (a well-known figure in history, the ruler of Zadar, part of Bosnia and probably of the land of Zahumlje) as an offering for the soul of his brother Juraj. The reliquary was made by the goldsmith Šimun between 1303 and 1311. There is also a ring which was given to the church by Pope Pius II (who was pontiff from 1458 to 1464). A similar ring is in the gold collection in the Museo Nationale in Florence. Some votive offerings given by ordinary people (men's and women's jewellery) from the area around Zadar and Nin demonstrate the wealth of folk art which existed until very recently.

••••••••••••

The **Archaeological Collection*** (NUMBER ❷ ON THE PLAN). This collection belongs to the archaeological museum in Zadar and is modest considering the value of archaeological finds from the area near Nin, most of which are in the archaeological museums in Zadar and Split, Vienna and Italy. Here there are items belonging to the prehistoric era (before the Liburnians and items of Liburnian material culture), remains of Roman culture and objects relating to the material culture of the Croats before their conversion to Christianity, as well as later, right up to modern times. Along with old Croatian burial treasures (jewellery, weapons and everyday objects), in terms of value, the copy of the Višeslav font is outstanding. It is a six-sided stone font, found in the area around Nin, with braided decorations including the text "In the time of Count Višeslav". It has been dated to the beginning of the 9th century, and Višeslav is thought to be the first Croatian Count known by name. There are also some fragments of two old Croatian ships from the 11th century, which were found in Nin harbour. In the courtyard there is a gravestone from the 14th century with the name of a Count of the Šubić family (of Bribir). This family figured in Croatian history from the 12th century along with the Zrinskis, right up to the end of the 17th century when Petar Zrinski was killed in a rebellion against the Habsburgs in Wiener Neustadt in 1671.

••••••••••••

The **Bishop Grgur Ninski Memorial** (NUMBER ❺ ON THE PLAN). Bishop Grgur of Nin was the most famous and most courageous Croatian bishop from the time of the establishing of the Croatian state (the end of the 9th to the beginning of the 10th century). He was brought up in the spirit of the old Slavonic religion, as a Glagolitic scholar, and, as a high ranking priest, he was advisor (and Chancellor) to the Count and King Tomislav. After the foundation of the Nin Bishopric in 867, he was the third bishop of Nin after Teodozije and Adalfredo. The Nin Bishopric was recognised as a separate Croatian Church by the Pope in 879 and its head was given the title "episcopus Chroatorum" (Dalmatian towns were at that time under the jurisdiction of the Patriarchs of Constantinople). When the Dalmatian towns returned to the jurisdiction of Rome in 923 along with the Archbishop of Split, there were conflicts between the church in Nin (under Bishop Grgur) and the Archbishop of Split (Ivan). Grgur refused to submit to the Split Archbishopric and so during the nationalist struggles of the 19th century, the idea arose of Grgur Ninski as a fighter against the attempts by the Latin clergy to suppress the Glagolitic mass. The Church Synod, which met in Split in 925 and 928, decided to abolish the Nin Bishopric and Grgur was moved to become Bishop of Skradin.

●●●●●●●●●●●●

The **Croatian Court.** The names *Kraljevac* and *Dvorine* (NUMBERS ❶ AND ❻ ON THE PLAN) show the site of the King's residences while he reigned from Nin. Both Branimir and Tomislav worked from Nin. King Petar Krešimir IV issued a well known decree entitled *Mare Nostrum* in Nin in 1067, by which he donated the St. Chrysogonus monastery in Zadar. The court of the Croatian rulers was organised along the lines of the Frankish court. The kings were surrounded by court heads, sword bearers, ostlers, a cup bearer, a valet with two deputies, a shield bearer, master of the household and the head of the Benedictine monastery.

St. Nicholas in Prahulje near Nin

Excursions

St. Nicholas' Church*** (Sveti Nikola) in Prahulje, 1 km southwest of Nin, was built on a burial mound in the 11th century. The portal is Romanesque, and during the wars between Venice and the Turks a tower was built in the centre of the church.

●●●●●●●●●●●●

Apart from the burial mound where St. Nicholas' Church has been built in Prahulje, in the area around Nin there are **several mounds** up to 2-3 m in height. They are not natural, but man-made, for the burial of the dead. They date from prehistoric times but later immigrants also honoured the old cult and buried their dead there. The burial of the dead in such mounds on the Eastern Adriatic coast continued from the Bronze Age right up to the early Middle Ages. It was the most common form of burial amongst the Illyrians in the Iron Age. In the period before their conversion to Christianity, Croatian immigrants also buried their dead in this way. Research has shown that the Croats practised the rite of burying and not burning the dead, which custom continued much

Gregory of Nin, Ivan Mestrović's monument

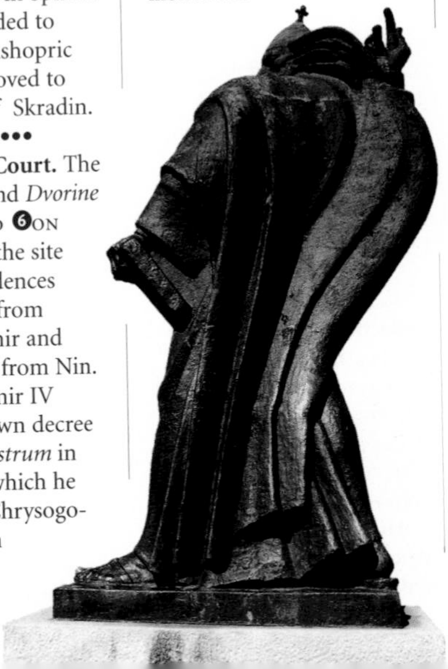

longer amongst other Slavs. Although burial customs change very little with time, the rapid change from burning to burying is one sign that the old Croatian culture was heavily influenced by the native (Romanized Illyrian) population, which also had a powerful effect on their further social and cultural development.

••••••••••••

Bokanjačko blato is a lake which appears periodically during rainy seasons and covers an area of 5 km². At its deepest it is 5 m. The lake is also fed by underground streams through which eels come. Apart from eels, in the broader area (to Novigrad and Obrovac) there are also wild tortoises (Testudo hermanni), of a type which is considered to be a natural phenomenon of Croatia, as it is the only living representative of an otherwise extinct species (from the later carbon area). Apart from similar Greek tortoises (Testudo graeca) there are no other such animals in Europe. They are protected from hunters and the export of them is banned.

••••••••••••

Novigrad*

25 KM NORTHEAST FROM ZADAR, POPULATION 542

Due to its out-of-the-way location, Novigrad has not developed or grown over the years. It was mentioned at the beginning of the 13th century as Castrum. During the dynastic wars in Croatia (1385-87) Elizabeta Kotromanić was imprisoned and murdered there (see Zadar, St. Simeon's Church). Between 1409 and 1797 Novigrad was under the Venetians, and for a short time (1646-1647) under the Turks. On the hill above the town are the **ruins of the medieval castle of the Gusić-Kurjaković family.** The early medieval church, **St. Katherine's** (Sveta Kata), with the remains of a monastery, houses fragments of a screen with braided ornamentation. The layout of Novigrad is interesting, with its characteristic dense maze of narrow streets, passageways, stairways and the low, stone houses of the ordinary people. The Parish Church of the Nativity of the B.V.M. was built in 1890 on the site of a church of 1500 destroyed by the Turks. During the Serb occupation (1991-1993), the town was looted and the Croat population driven out.

Novigrad from a Venetian engraving

••••••••••••

Novigradsko more is a bay with a surface area of 28.65 km² which was formed by erosion in the layers from the later Eocene era. At its deepest it is 37 m deep and its temperature varies by about 20 °C. On the western shore is the village of Posedarje (1 300 inhabitants) which was mentioned in the 12th century as the property of the Croatian Counts. On the small island off the harbour there is the Gothic Church of the Holy Spirit (Sveti Duh) from the 12th or 13th century and in the village there are two Baroque churches. The Parish Church of Our Lady of the Rosary (expanded and given Baroque features in 1700) was damaged by shelling in the recent war. On the coast there is a little Romanesque church, of the Assumption of Mary.

Novigrad

••••••••••••

The liqueurs produced in Zadar

Zadar is the home of **Maraschino**, a liqueur from the fruit of the Maraska sour cherry (Prunus cerasus var. Marasca). This cherry has a special character in Dalmatia, having even medicinal qualities, and the tradition of producing the liqueur is four hundred years old. It was upon this product, according to a 16th century recipe, that the Zadar liqueur works was built in 1822. This liqueur is known world-wide; Marshall Marmont wrote about it in his memoires, and Balzac mentioned it in his novel *Un debut dans la vie*. Maraska also makes other liqueurs: Cherry Brandy, Kirsch (sweet); Pelinkovac, Vlahovac and Half (bitter).

The village of **Karin** (600 inhabitants) is twelve kilometres from Novigrad at the southern end of a smallish bay called Karin Sea (Karinsko more), 54 km² in size, and 12.5 m deep in the middle, with highly salty water. Its castle Miodrag was a settlement and fortress of the Illyrians and Romans (Corinium, with the status of a municipality), Croats (the centre of the Karinja tribe), Turks and Venetians. By the sea there is a Franciscan monastery. On this site there was a Benedictine Abbey built in the 9th century, on whose ruins a Franciscan monastery was built in the 15th century. The monastery was destroyed during the wars with the Turks and restored at the beginning of the 18th century. The Church of the Immaculate Conception (Bezgrešnog začeća Blažene Djevice Marije) was built on the site of the old Benedictine church. It was restored in 1735, 1890 and 1979. In the recent war (1991-1995) the Serb rebels mined and destroyed this church.

Obrovac

44 KM FROM ZADAR, POPULATION 1 061

Obrovac is 12 km inland from the Adriatic highroad at Maslenički most. It is a cross-roads on the road for Zagreb (via Gračac and Plitvice lakes) for Šibenik (via Benkovac) and the setting out point for trips into the southeastern Velebit (the road for Lovinac). As the river Zrmanja is navigable up to Obrovac, it is possible to enter the town by boats of up to 2.5 m draught, but there are no regular passenger lines. It was built in the neighbourhood of the Roman settlement of Clambetae, and is mentioned first time under the name of Obrouez. In 1337 it was owned by the princes of Krbava, the Kurjaković family, and around 1470 Obrovac, civitas Obrowacz, had 80 tax chimneys. Above the town (13 minutes' walk from the centre) there are the ruins of an old castle which belonged to the Kurjaković family. The town came under Venice in 1409 and was the seat of the proveditore. From 1527 to 1684 Obrovac was under the Turks and was a nest for pirates who attacked not only Venetian ships but also the inhabitants of Pag, Rab and Krk. Obrovac became significant again in the history of the Croats and Yugoslavia at the time of the 1848 revolution.

The Obrovac

Obrovac

Waterfall on the Zrmanja

community called on other Dalmatian communities to protect Slavic Dalmatia and on 21st April 1848 it was the first community to join the campaign to unite Dalmatia with Croatia and Slavonia. During communist Yugoslavia it was supposed to develop into an industrial town, but the Obrovac Kombinat (plant) became a synonym for economic failure. In independent Croatia it plans to develop as a tourist town. The **Parish Church of St. Joseph** was built in the 18th century, renovated at the end of the 18th, and destroyed by Serb insurgents in the 1991-1995 period.

EXCURSIONS

The **River Zrmanja*** flows through the centre of Obrovac. Up to its mouth (10 km from Obrovac) it forms a canyon and is navigable for vessels up to 2.5 m displacement. The most beautiful landscape is above Obrovac. Here is Bilišanske luke (harbour), to which one can get from Gornje Bilišane on the road to Ervenik, while by Ogar there is a 27 m high waterfall. The lower course of the river forms the natural border between the coastal area and Dalmatia. It is 69 km long altogether and in its upper reaches it flows underground. It passes through an area of karst stone which is without vegetation, creating the impression of a stone desert.

••••••••••••

Cerovačke pećine**. These caves have been under conservation order since 1961. They are 25 km from Obrovac on the road for Gračac via Prezid and then from Gračac towards Knin (4 km) to the car park in the village of Kesići. It is 15 minutes' climb to **Donja pećina** (Lower cave) and another 10 minutes to **Gornja pećina** (Upper cave). Donja pećina has been explored up to 2 000 m in length. After 670 m of passageways there is a complex of streams and caverns where there are lakes and waterfalls. In the opening of the caves the remains of some prehistoric pottery from the Illyrian and Celtic cultures have been discovered. Gornja pećina is smaller, 1 200 m in length, but is considered to be more beautiful, especially the White Crystal cavern which contains the most beautiful stalagmites.

••••••••••••

Krupa Monastery (24 km from Obrovac by road towards Ervenik; turn left at Žegarski Kaštel). It is thought that this monastery was founded in 1642 by Bosnian monks fleeing from the Turks. It is the largest Serbian Orthodox monastery in Croatia. The **monastery's treasury** has a collection of 50 icons, of which the most valuable are the Italo-Cretan icons by Jovan Apaka from the beginning of the 17th century, and a collection of liturgical objects and pictures. In 1995 the monks abandoned the monastery and it is now (1997) closed.

••••••••••••

Tulove grede***. By the Lovinac road to Vrhprag (18 km from Obrovac) and then one hour's climb to the peak (1 127 m). This climb is only for those with mountaineering experience and equipment. Tulove grede are part of south-eastern Velebit, a distinct unit because of its location, direction and morphological characteristics. It is a stone plateau of bare karst, which without the Tulove grede and the Crnopac peak (1 404 m), would look like a stone desert.

Tulove grede

••••••••••••

The North Dalmatian Islands

These islands stretch 150 km from Silba in the northwest to the Ploče peninsula in the southeast. As well as the Zadar islands, they include the Kornati islands and the Šibenik group of islands (see Šibenik).

Ugljan

Ugljan is the first island in the Zadar archipelago (2 nautical miles from Zadar), has a surface area of 50.21 km^2 and is 22 km long. It is joined to the island of Pašman (see Biograd) by a bridge. A narrow channel (4 m deep) was dug in 1883. It has been inhabited since prehistoric times. It is one of the most densely populated islands on the Eastern Adriatic and the inhabitants work in tourism, fishing and farming and some are sailors. Its name has changed in the past: Insula de Corano, Lucorani, Cuclize but it has been known as Ugljan since 1325. Since ancient times, the people have been seafarers and fishermen, and in recent times have turned to farming and tourism. Ugljan olives, figs and vines are highly prized for their quality.

●●●●●●●●●●●●

Preko

HALF AND HOUR BY FERRY FROM ZADAR; POP. 1 376

Preko is the largest settlement on the island and a ferry port linking the island with Zadar. Before the Second World War it was the seat of the administration of all the Zadar islands. The town was settled in the Roman era. By the ferry quay is the Romanesque church, **St. John the Baptist** (Ivan Krstitelj) from the 12th century. The old parish church, Our Lady of the Rosary stands on the local cemetery. It was built in 1765. The new parish church was built in 1967. Above the town is **St. Michael's Fortress**** (265 m above sea level.) The fortress was built in the 13th century by the Venetians, and it surrounded a Benedictine monastery which had existed since the 10th century. There is a look-out point with views over Velebit, Pag, Ravni kotari and the Kornati islands. In the sea off the town there are two small islands: **Galevac***, on which there is a Franciscan monastery of the Glagolitic scholars, built in the 15th century; and **Ošljak**, which is a picturesque fishing village where everyone has the same surname (Valčić). There is also an old Croatian chapel from the 10th century on the island. **Lukoran** (5 km northwest of Preko) consists of two villages: Veli Lukoran and Mali Lukoran (in Sutomiščica Bay). In several places in the village there are remains from the Roman era. In the Middle Ages Lukoran belonged to the Benedictines from Zadar (see St. Chrysogonus in Zadar). In the village cemetery there is a chapel with characteristics of the Romanesque era, which was rebuilt in the 17th century. Beneath the hill Zmorašnji Lukoran there are the remains of a Gothic chapel which, according to legend, was built in the 15th century by Egyptian monks. The Croatian poet Petar Preradović here composed his patriotic song "Zora puca".

Preko

Sights

Kali

3 KM SOUTHEAST OF PREKO, THE MOST IMPORTANT FISHING VILLAGE ON THE CENTRAL ADRIATIC, POP. 1 790.

This town was mentioned for the first time in 1343. The **Parish Church of St. Lawrence*** (Sveti Lovro) was built in Baroque style in 1698 on the site of an older building. On the southern hill over the village stands the **Chapel of St. Peregrine*** (Sveti Pelegrin) which was built in the 14th century. A road leads from the village to the opposite side of the island and the bay of Lamjan. Confirmation of the fact that Kali is the biggest fishing village in the Adriatic can be found in the **Kali Fishermen's Night.** This festival is held every year, during the last days of July or the first days of August, on the night of the full moon (the fishermen do not go out).

•••••••••••••

Kukljica

8 KM SOUTHEAST OF PREKO, 5 KM FROM KALI, IN THE FAR EASTERN PART OF THE ISLAND, POP.673

Because of its position it is the door to the Kornati National Park and the Telaščica Nature Park. It was first mentioned in 1345. In Kostanj bay there are the ruins of the **Gothic Church of St. Jerome** (Sveti Jerolim) from the 15th century. The **Parish Church of St. Paul*** (Sveti Pavao) was built in 1666. It has several Glagolitic inscriptions (see Glagolitic). In the votive church of Our Lady of the Snows (on the coast, not far from the town) is a miraculous statue of the Virgin, which on August 5, the festival of Our Lady of the Snows, is honoured by being taken on board ship with a great retinue. The location of this town means it has two "seas": "upper" and "lower". Thus the island of Mišljak belongs to the village on the eastern side, and on the west, the islands Karantunić, Golac, Bisage and Školj Veli. The road to the island of Pašman leads out of Kukljica (see Biograd).

Kali

Kukljica

•••••••••••••

Ugljan (village)

12 KM FROM PREKO; AT THE EXTREME WESTERN PART FROM THE ISLAND; POP. 1 384

Northwest of Preko (15 km) on Kuran hill (to the southeast of the village) are the ruins of some pre-historic earthworks. On the point which closes off the harbour on its northeastern side, the **Franciscan Monastery of St. Jerome**** (Sveti Jerolim) was built. The monastery dates from 1430 and the cloisters from the 16th century. The cloisters have three decorated Romanesque capitals included in their walls, taken from a building in Zadar. Šimun Begna (Benja) Kožičić (born 1460) was buried in the monastery in 1536, according to his epitaph on a plaque on the wall. He was a canon in Zadar, Bishop of Modruš and founder of the Glagolitic press in Rijeka, editor of liturgical texts, a translator and writer. His

Veli Iž

speeches in Latin at the Lateran Council were very famous. These, which were later printed in Venice, lamented the hard conditions in Croatia and sought help for the defence against the Turks. Part of the monastery is a single-naved Gothic church of 1447. In **Gornje selo** (Upper Village), once the estate of the Califi family of Zadar, known since the 19th century as the Brčić Mansion, the family of the Austrian national Erwin Roth restored the prestigious **Ćosić Mansion**, in memory of the famed Croatian patriot and world known basketball player Krešimir Ćosić (1948-1995). The Mansion can only be viewed by prior agreement. **Muline** (2 km from Ugljan to the west) is a rich archaeological site from the Roman era. There is a Roman pier, a villa rustica, a mausoleum, a temple (martyrium), the ruins of a mill (hence the name Muline from "mlin", which is mill in Croatian) and other farm buildings. West of Muline (400 m) is the island of **Rivanj**** (pop. 30). Undiscovered by the tourist industry as yet, it has all the potentials for growth.

Pašman (s. Biograd)

Iž

This island covers 17.6 km², is 12 km long and about 9 nautical miles away from Zadar. It is surrounded by 10 smaller islands. It stands out in the Zadar island group for several reasons: it produces relatively large quantities of fruit and vegetables, and has 78 000 olive trees and 100 hectares of woodland. Iž is the only island in Dalmatia where the inhabitants work as potters. It has been inhabited since prehistoric times. The Byzantine Emperor Constantine Porphyrogenitus (in the 10th century) called the island Ez. The Croats moved here in the 11th century but the largest number of people moved here during the wars between Venice and the Turks. It belonged to noble families and citizens from Zadar.

Traditional pottery workshop on Iž

Iž Veli, in the western part of the island. On the small hill called Veli Opačac (to the east of the village) there are the remains of dry-stone walls which surrounded an Illyrian settlement. The **Parish Church of St. Peter** and **St. Paul** (Sveti Petar i Pavao) was mentioned in the 14th century and has been rebuilt many times over the years. **St. Rocco Chapel** (Sveti Rok) was built in the 17th century. The school buildings are in Romanesque style and were built in the 14th century, as the castle of the Zadar family, the Canaghiettis. Before the harbour there is a small island called Rutnjak which has been arranged as a park and bathing area. In Veli Iž there is also a **Folk Museum***. (The Memorial House, the local collection of the Zadar National Museum.)

••••••••••••

Iž Mali, 6 km east of Iž Veli, and the older of the two settlements. It has an interesting old Croatian chapel, **St. Mary's**** (Sveta Marija) which dates from the 9th or the 10th century. This is the present day baptistery, for in the 17th century a rectangular nave was added to the chapel. Not far from here there is a fortified castle and the Chapel of St. Anne (Sveta Ana). Mali Iž was for centuries a centre of Glagolitic scholarship, largely thanks to the work of the writer, translator and publisher Šimun Budinić (Budineo, Budineić, 1530-1600) who lived for a time on Iž. The War Memorial was erected in honour of those who died in the World War II. Iž was annexed by

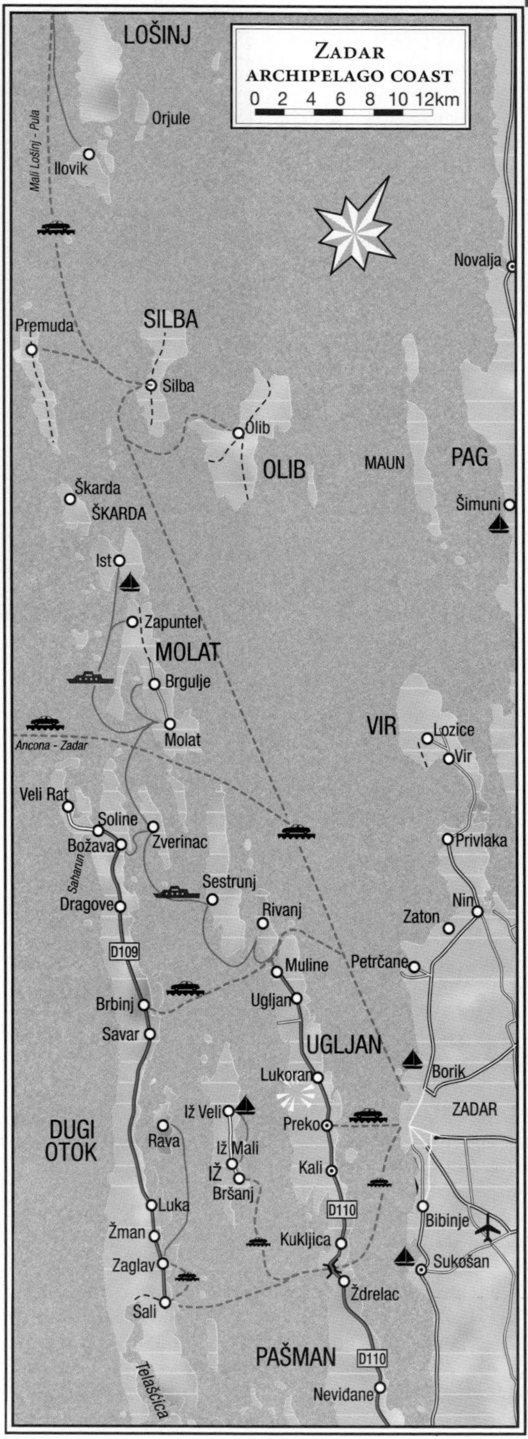

the Italian occupation forces in 1941, but the entire population resisted the occupation. The first people from Iž entered the war in 1941 and joined the Partisans (in Lika), and from September 1942 almost all the young men of Iž were in the National Liberation Army.

Dugi otok

Dugi otok (Long Island) is the biggest island in the Zadar group. In size it is the seventh largest Adriatic island, being 45 km long, and covering an area of 124 km². More than 1500 hectares are covered with vineyards, orchards and arable land, about 752 hectares are pasture land and about 300 hectares undergrowth which in some places is used as forest land. The vegetation is more pronounced in the northern and central areas of the island. The south-eastern part belongs to the Kornati National Park. The island has been inhabited since prehistoric times. The Byzantine Emperor Constantine Porphyrogenitus (in the 10th century) mentioned it under the name of Pizuh, and later it is called Insula Tilagus in documents ("pelagos" in Greek is sea), and its Latin name was Insula maior. In the 15th century it was registered as Veli Otok. The old and main (now vanished) settlement on the island was located in its southern area. It has only been inhabited significantly since the Turkish invasions (15th-16th centuries). Until then the island belonged to Zadar monasteries and citizens. Nowadays there is a total of 10 settlements on the island, and they are all on the north-eastern side. The main occupation of the people is fishing, and then farming (vine and olive growing).

Božava

Božava**

18 NAUTICAL MILES FROM ZADAR, 35 KM FROM SALI

Božava is situated in a wooded area and is one of the most beautiful settlements on the Zadar islands. As a settlement it has existed continuously since Illyrian times. On the hills Kruna and Gračina there are some signs of Illyrian settlements, and on the level ground there are remains from the Roman era. The Croats moved here in the 9th century. It was mentioned as Bosana in 1327. It frequently suffered attacks, and there are some traces of defensive walls (from the 18th century) visible by some houses with courtyards surrounded by stone walls with gun holes.

The **parish church of St. Nicholas**** dates from the 9th century and contains three Gothic processional crosses made in the 14th and 15th centuries by the Zadar master goldsmiths Pavle Petrov and Stjepan Kotoranin. The **Chapel of St. Nicholas**** (Sveti Nikola), in the graveyard, is said to have been built in the 9th or 10th century. Over the door there is a carved relief of St. Nicholas and the year 1469. Inside the chapel there is a Gothic crucifix from the 15th century, which is considered to be one of the most valuable pieces of carving in Dalmatia. There are also two pre-Romanesque tablets with braided ornamentation. It is about an hour and half's walk from Božava (via Soline) to Veli Rat, and about half and hour to Saharun Bay.

Soline (2.4 km from Božava; 70 inhabitants) was first mentioned in the 12th century and was named after the salt pans in the Soliščica Bay. The Church of St. James (Sveti Jakov) was mentioned in the 15th century, rebuilt in the 16th century and restored in the 19th century. To the south, 1 km from Soline is **Saharun**** the most beautiful bay (and beach) on Dugi Otok. The beach is surrounded by woods, but it is often completely deserted because of the small population on this part of the island.

•••••••••••

Veli Rat (87 inhabitants). This area has been inhabited since the Roman era and was mentioned as "ad Punctas" in 1327. Nowadays its people are mariners and farmers. In the village there is a Baroque church, St. Anthony's (Sveti Ante) which was rebuilt in 1866. Northwest of the village (about half an hour's walk) is one of the largest lighthouses on the Adriatic, built in 1849 and 41 m high. To the southwest of the village (about 40 minutes' walk) is the most beautiful sandy bay on the island, Saharun (s. Soline).

•••••••••••

Dragove, 4 km east of Božava, 400 m from the sea. It was mentioned in the 14th century as a Croatian settlement (the property of nobility of Zadar). The **Parish Church of St. Leonard** was built in the 12th or 13th century. On Dumbovica hill, from which there is a fine view over the surrounding area, stands the **Chapel of Our Lady of Dumbovica,** which was mentioned in the 15th century. At the foot of the hill there are the remains of some Roman buildings. In the village there is a monastery, (St. Anthony's) which was deserted in the 16th century.

•••••••••••

Savar** (9 km from Dragova, about 5 km from Sali) was first mentioned in the 13th century. The most interesting thing here is the **Church of St. Peregrine** (Sveti Pelegrin) which was mentioned for the first time in 1300 and whose presbytery (the area behind the main altar) is in fact a pre-Romanesque chapel. It is one of the more important examples of old Croatian sacred architecture. The parish church was built in the 17th century, and its treasures include a Baroque font with a Glagolitic inscription from the 16th century which at one time belonged to St. Peregrine's Church.

•••••••••••

Sali*

13 NAUTICAL MILES FROM ZADAR; THE MAIN AND LARGEST TOWN ON THE ISLAND, POPULATION 765

It was mentioned in 1105 as the property of the convent of St. Mary in Zadar. The Venetian authorities granted the people of Sali exclusive rights to the rich fishing ground of the Kornati islands. Fishing encouraged the growth of the village and at the beginning of this century the "Mardešić" fish canning factory was built. The **Gothic Parish Church of the Assumption**** (Uznesenje Marijino) was built in the 15th century on the site of the former pre-Romanesque church some of which (some braided reliefs) can be seen in the niches of the Gothic side doorways. The church has a rich treasury: a Baroque main altar, carved of wood and dating from the 17th century, paintings entitled *The Death of Christ* and *The Madonna and Child* (by Juraj Čulinović, about 1435-1505), Gothic and Renaissance chalices, candlesticks and gravestones in Glagolitic. In the village there are three Renaissance houses and the house of Petricoli in rustic Baroque style.

•••••••••••

Sali

There are some remarkable localities in the environs of Sali. The most attractive is **Telaščica****(no. ❶ on the of the Kornati map), one of the largest and most beautiful bays in the Adriatic. Until 1997, it was part of the Kornati National Park, but is today part of a nature park that includes the 146 m high **Grpaščak** Cliff (no. ❷ on the Kornati map; access is possible from the sea) and the salt water lake, **Mir**. Telaščica is about 10 km long, between 160-1800 m wide, and actually consists of three smaller bays. It has the reputation of being a good, safe harbour for all kinds of vessels. The northeastern side of the bay is completely bare, but the southwestern shore is covered in thick forests of pine, olive and fig trees. From Tripuljak bay it is five minutes' walk along a footpath to Lake Mir, which covers an area of 0.23 km² (90 m x 300 m) and is 10 m deep. The water temperature in the lake is up to 6°C higher than that of the sea in summer. An interesting phenomenon here is the change in the water level of the lake according to the variation in the level of the sea. The level of the lake also changes, but slightly later than that of the sea. On the hill called Koženjak there are the remains of Illyrian walls, and in **Mala Proversa** (no. ❸ on the Kornati map) the remains of a Roman villa. There is a superb view of the Grpašćak cliff and the open sea. **Grpaščak** (number ❷) is the longest (10 km) and highest (50-100 m) cliff on the Adriatic.
From the landward side it can be reached from Lake Mir. **Zaglav***, 4 km west of Sali; 230 inhabitants. Here there
is a Franciscan monastery with the Church of St. Michael (Sveti Mihovil) from the 15th century, housing a wooden Gothic crucifix from the 15th century. **Žman** (6 km from Sali; 270 inhabitants) is a village known as an old centre for olive oil.
Luka, 8 km west of Sali. Until the 15th century the village was called Luka Sv. Stjepan (St. Stephen), after the medieval church of the same name. Near the village is **Kozja peć**, a cave with a wealth of beautiful cave formations in a chamber 30 m in length.

Grpaščak Cliff and Mir Lake

Silba

Although it is only 4.5 nautical miles from the southernmost island in the Cres-Lošinj group, Silba belongs to the Zadar archipelago. It covers an area of 15 km² and is 8 km in length. It is mainly covered in maquis, and its coast is characterised by pebble and sandy beaches. It has been inhabited since Roman times. The Byzantine Emperor Constantine Porphyrogenitus (in the 10th century) mentioned it as Selbo. The name comes from the Latin for wood, "silva". From 1091 it was the property of the Zadar Convent of St. Mary and thus belonged to Zadar. According to Venetian documents it also was part of the

Marija Ujević Sculpture Park

Zadar community. After the fall of Venice in 1797 right up until 1918 when it became part of Yugoslavia, Silba remained under Zadar.

••••••••••••

Silba (village; pop. 265) is the only settlement on the island, situated at its southernmost tip. The village has two harbours, 700 m apart. It was once a strong maritime centre, its greatest growth occurring in the 17th and 18th centuries. As late as 1850 it still had 1435 inhabitants but once steam replaced sailing ships the people failed to keep up with the new developments and turned their attention instead to sheep rearing and fishing. Silba has three churches. The oldest is **St. Mark's*** (Sveti Marko; in the graveyard) which is an example of medieval architecture and has a fine wooden altar. The **Parish Church of the Assumption*** (Uznesenje Marijino) is a Baroque building from 1637. Inside the church there are paintings by the Italian artist Carlo Ridolfi (1594-1658) and a silver Baroque crown which was used on the occasion of the folk festival "the choosing of the king". The **Church of Our Lady of Carmel** (Gospa od Karmela) was once part of a Franciscan monastery and it houses a self-portrait by Carlo Ridolfi. The village is dominated by the **Toreta** lookout tower with its external stairway which was built in the second half of the 19th century by Captain Petar Marinić.

••••••••••••

Our Lady of Carmel in Silba

Marija Ujević Sculpture Park. In the center of the town of Silba, renowned Croatian sculptress Marija Ujević (who was born in Zagreb in 1933) presents her most dynamic sculptures and reliefs in memory of her ancestors. Her work is an important part of contemporary Croatian art.

EXCURSIONS

Olib, an island with a village of the same name, 3.2 nautical miles east of Silba. It covers an area of 25.6 km² and is about 9.5 km long. The island narrows in the middle to about 1400 m. The vegetation is lush on the western side. The village now has 147 inhabitants, and its main products are wine, oil and cheese.

The **Parish Church of St. Anastasia** (Sveta Stošija) was built in 1632 and restored in 1868. In the courtyard of the church there is a collection of old Glagolitic codices (see Glagolitic) and items connected with folklore. By the parish church there is a mortuary with an inscription telling how in 1476 people fleeing from the Turks moved here from Vrlika, led by Jure Cetinjanin. The Parish Church of the Assumption, was built in 1899. In Banve Bay lie the ruins of a triple-naved church and the Monastery of St. Paul, abandoned in about 1200.

••••••••••••

Premuda, an island with a village of the same name, 4.2 nautical miles west of Silba. The island covers an area of 9.2 km² and the village is in its northern area. Roman sources name the island Pamodos or Pirotima. As Pirotima it was included in Peutinger's maps which is an indication of its importance in that era, but otherwise there is no other particular information known about the island. During the First World War Italian gun boats sank the ship *Szent Istvan* not far from the island. ■

Olib

Šibenik

Location 43°48' N, 15°54' E. Population 37 689. County town of a county Šibenik - Knin that extends over 2 994 km², with a population of 116 159. Mean January temperatures: air 6.9°C, sea 13°C; mean July temperatures: air 24.4°C, sea 22.4°C.

Šibenik has a special position among the cities of the Adriatic. Whereas Solin, Trogir, Hvar and Vis were originally Greek, then Roman and Byzantine before they became Croatian cities, Šibenik is a "new town", built as a counter-weight to Byzantine Dalmatia. Thus Šibenik is the oldest Croatian and Slavic city on the Adriatic although there are few traces of a settlement in this area from the time of the immigration of the Croatians.

The city was mentioned for the first time in 1066 as "Castrum Sebenici" on the occasion of a visit to the city by the Croatian King Petar Krešimir IV. At this time the medieval Croatian state was at the height of its power. After that however, Šibenik remained only 50 years in an independent Croatian state for, in 1102, Croatia entered an alliance with Hungary. From that time on, Šibenik was for 243 years part of the state of Croatia-Hungary (1105-1116, 1124, 1133-1168, 1180-1322 and 1358-1412). During this time it received the rights of a municipality, and the status of city (1167), became the centre of a diocese (1298) and thus obtained the legal and political bases to become a well-developed economic, political and

cultural centre in the 14th century. It was under the Byzantine Empire from 1168 to 1180, and admitted Venetian authority, or rather submitted to their rule, for more than four hundred years: 1116-1124, 1125-1133, 1322-1357 and 1412-1797. During Venetian rule Šibenik was for a time the largest city in Dalmatia: in 1553 it had 1275 houses and 8200 inhabitants. The French occupation lasted from 1805 to 1813. At first it was part of the Kingdom of Italy and then of the Illyrian Provinces. From 1813 to 1918, together with its hinterland, Šibenik became part of the Austro-Hungarian Empire. It became part the Kingdom of the Serbs, Croats and Slovenes after the Treaty of Rapallo in 1922.

The history of Šibenik is linked with another Balkan power - Turkey. From the year when the Turks conquered Bosnia (1463) to their defeat outside Vienna (1683), the Turks were Šibenik's nearest neighbours, enemies kept out by the defensive walls, but also trading partners who had a strong influence on the city's prosperity. Šibenik's loyalty to Venice can also be explained by the proximity of the Turks. This was a logical move, to choose the lesser of two evils.

Although the city has been the subject of many enduring influences throughout its history, Šibenik has never lost its Croatian character. Thanks to the economic policy of the Venetians (especially in the 15th century), which never significantly limited its economic development, Šibenik was always a strong cultural centre and therefore its cultural heritage is also enormous. During the recent war, Šibenik was close to the edge of the territory held by the rebel Serbs, and many civilians were killed or injured from artillery and air attacks, while several buildings belonging to the cultural heritage and inside the old city centre were damaged. ■

St. Michael, patron saint of Šibenik, sculpture in the Cathedral

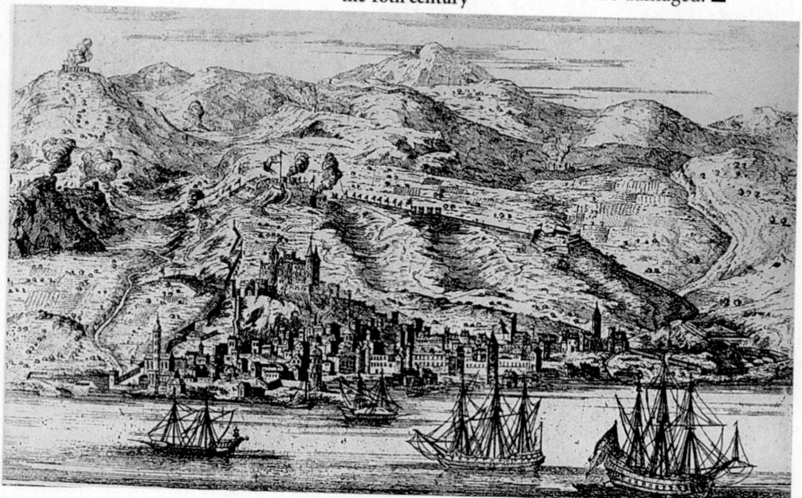

Šibenik, engraving of the 18th century

Sights

The **Cathedral of St. James***** ▸▸▸ p. 198

The **Juraj Dalmatinac Memorial***** (NUMBER ❼A). Juraj Dalmatinac, also known as Juraj Matejić, Georgius Dalmaticus and Giorgio da Sebenico, was not only the builder of Šibenik Cathedral but, in the words of Cvito Fisković, "also a powerful artistic personality, in whose fertile imagination and openness the special characteristics of the Croatian coastal region were brought to light, at the twilight of the greatest European styles." He was born in Zadar, but the year of his birth (it is thought that it was 1400) and his schooling

remain unknown to the present day. He came to Šibenik in 1441 from Venice at the urging of Bishop Juraj Šižgorić. There are many indications that in Venice he worked with the Bon brothers on the portal of the Doge's palace (Porta della Carta). As well as in Venice, he also worked in Ancona during the building of the cathedral in Šibenik, and in 1451 he designed the Merchant's Loggia (Loggia dei Mercati) and the portal of S. Francesco delle Scale church. In his native country his work includes ecclesiastical, residential and defensive buildings (Minčeta in Dubrovnik). He also worked on urban design (Pag). He realised great and harmonious architectural ideas, but he never overlooked the intricate details of fine moulded plastic work. He was a master of the Gothic style, but moved from Gothic to Renaissance, and in some of his compositions and figures he anticipated elements of the Baroque. He was a teacher. His pupils included Andrija Aleši and Andrija Budičić. He died in Šibenik in 1473 and his memorial was created by Ivan Meštrović who came from the area around Šibenik (see Drniš), and was the greatest Croatian sculptor of the first half of the 20th century.

••••••••••••

The **City Loggia***** (NUMBER ❽) was the seat of the City Council during the Venetian period. It was built between 1533 and 1542. In the Second World War it was totally destroyed by bombing, but was restored after the war. The building is stylistically characteristic of the Sanmichelli school (Verona 1484-1559) and is considered to be the finest loggia in Dalmatia, with its impressive harmony, pillars, lions' heads and balustrade.

••••••••••••

The **Church of St. Barbara**** (Sveta Barbara,

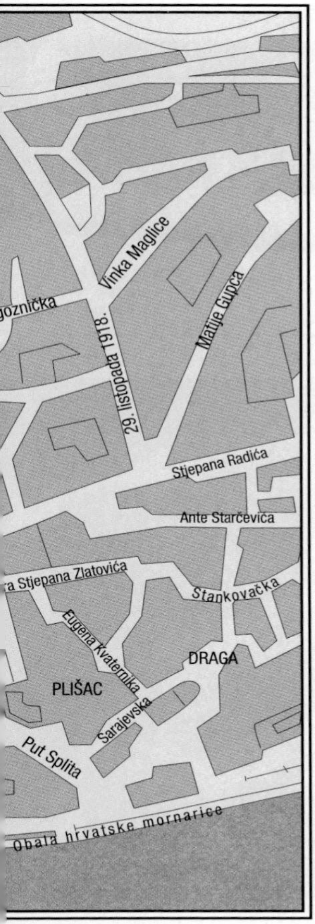

NUMBER ⑩) was built in the 15th century in Gothic style. Beside the main bell-tower a larger one was built in the 18th century in Baroque style. On the facade there is a statue of St. Nicholas (Sveti Nikola) which is the work of the sculptor and builder, Bonino of Milan, who is thought to be one of the first builders of the cathedral in Šibenik. He was also the creator of the richly decorated Gothic window on the side wall. Inside the church, two chapels, the work of the Šibenik artist Ivan Pribislavić (Magister Johannes), are considered to be particularly valuable in artistic terms. Pribislavić was a pupil and main co-worker with Juraj Dalmatinac. There is a **Museum of Ecclesiastical Art** in the church today, in which there are some very important works from the 14th to 17th centuries.

••••••••••••

The **Church of St. Nicholas***** (Sveti Nikola; NUMBER ⑪) was built in the 17th century in Baroque style and belonged to the Fraternity of Mariners and Shipbuilders. For this reason the church contains many votive offerings (ex voto) and the interior is made particularly lively by models of sailing ships. There is also a fine coffered ceiling with about 30 paintings, portraits, coats of arms and the names of prominent families of Šibenik of that time.

••••••••••••

St. John's Church** (Sveti Ivan; NUMBER ⑫), was once the Church of the Holy Trinity, built in the 15th century and restored in 1544 and 1643. The exterior stairway leading to the choir and the ornamental moulding over it, showing St. John between kneeling believers (brothers) is the work of Ivan Pribislavić. The beautifully stylised bell-tower has never been completed. The large window at the foot of the tower is the work of Nikola Firentinac. On the bell-tower there is also a "Turkish clock" which was brought from Drniš to Šibenik after the Turks had withdrawn. The church was damaged during Serb air and artillery attacks in 1991-1992.

••••••••••••

The **New Church** (Nova Crkva) (to the northwest of the Church of St. John in Ulica Nove crkve). The church was built at the beginning of the 16th century by the side of the Gothic hall of the Fraternity of St. Mary of the Castle, which was mentioned as early as the 13th century. The coffered ceiling is the oldest example of a painted ceiling in the whole area of Venetian Dalmatia; it was done by J. Mondello and associates. It was painted in unique Mannerist fresco paintings begun by Mihovil Parkić (1617) and continued by Antun Meneghin (1628). It was damaged in the recent war for Croatian independence.

••••••••••••

The **Church of the Holy Spirit*** (Sveti Duh; NUMBER ⑬) was built towards the

▸▸▸ p. 200

City loggia

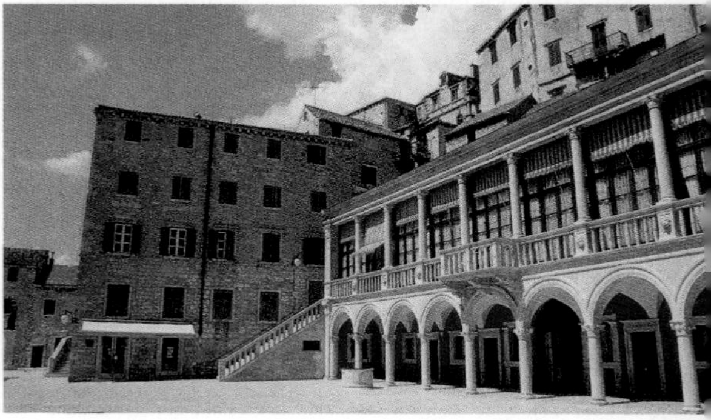

Frieze of heads on the cathedral

The Cathedral of St. James***

(SVETI JAKOV; NUMBER ❼ ON THE PLAN).

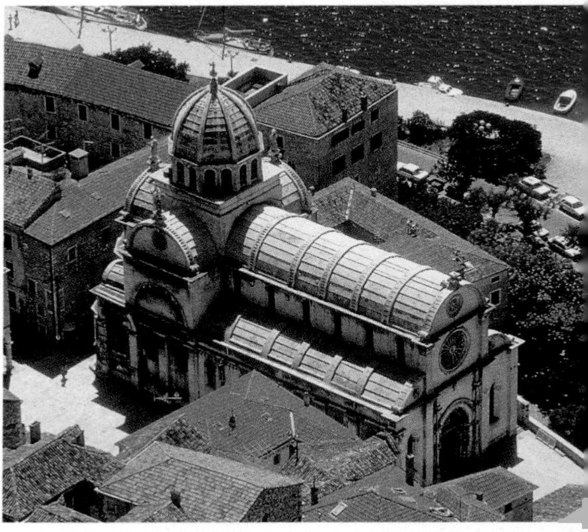

Šibenik's cathedral is the most important architectural monument of the Renaissance in Croatia. Building work was started on it in 1431 on the site of a Romanesque cathedral which had been demolished earlier and it was built in three phases: from 1433 to 1441; then up to 1473; and finally up to 1536. Most of the restoration work was done between 1850 and 1860 and subsequently between 1992 and 1997 (after being shelled by the Serb aggressor on September 18 and 19, 1991). It is built entirely of stone: limestone from a nearby stone quarry and marble from the island of Brač. It is interesting to note that this cathedral has no bell-tower. A tower on the adjoining city walls served this purpose. The first stage was the work of Italian masters and local masons: Francesco di Giaccomo, Lorenzo Puncio, Antonio di Pier Paolo, Bussato, Bonino di Jacopo da Milano and Andrija Budičić with Grubiša Slavičić. At that stage it was conceived as a simple church. The western main portal was built, the northern portal (The Lion Gate) and the first chapel. In the period between 1444 and 1477 the building work was directed by Juraj Dalmatinac, who was invited to come from Venice as the investors were not satisfied with the beginnings of the work. They considered that too little had been done for the money spent. Juraj Dalmatinac altered the original plan: he added the transept and apses so that the ground plan of the cathedral was in the shape of a cross; he built the presbytery, sanctuary and his masterpiece, the baptistery. The apses are decorated on the outside with 74 carved Renaissance portraits immortalising important contemporaries and figures who had for some reason particularly impressed the architect.

Cathedral, cross-section

Inside the cathedral there are four large, evenly matched columns on which the dome rests. The builder decorated the capitals and came to arrangements with the nobles who were to finance the building of chapels, on condition that they would be free to choose their own builders. Juraj Dalmatinac, with tremendous skill, combined architectural and decorative elements of the late Gothic and the Renaissance to create a unified entity. In 1477 the building work was taken over by Nikola Firentinac (?- Šibenik 1505), a foreigner from the Donatello school of sculpture, who developed as a sculptor and builder in Dalmatia and who is considered to be a Croatian artist. He was left with the task of completing the extensive galleries, building the vault in the central nave, placing the dome on the four completed columns and covering it with stone tiles. Master Nikola freely interpreted Juraj Dalmatinac's plans, in the style of the Tuscan Renaissance. Although the dome of Šibenik Cathedral was built after the dome in Florence, Nikola Firentinac used an octagonal drum in its construction, before Bramante and Michelangelo, in its original function as the transition from the square base to the circular dome. The execution of the cupola was one of the supreme achievements of Renaissance architecture. Around the dome he placed statues of saints, which are his own work. The cathedral was not completed even in his lifetime, but finally by Bartolomeo da Mestre and his son Giacomo in 1536.

Pulpit

Inside the cathedral, in the first chapel on the right-hand side, there is the *sarcophagus* of the bishop, humanist and writer Juraj Šižgorić (c.1420-1509) which is the work of Andrija Aleši based on a design by Juraj Dalmatinac. Aleši also created the statue of St. Elijah which stands behind the bishop's throne. On the left-hand side is the sarcophagus of Bishop Ivan Štafilić, during whose life the

Carved text about the building and builder of the cathedral

Cathedral font

cathedral was completed. Beneath the choir there are the graves of two bishops, with reliefs: on the right Bishop Calegari and on the left, Bishop Spingarola. The latter is the work of the local artist Antun Nogulović. Opposite the famous Altar of the Holy Cross (Sveti Križ) made by Juraj Petrović of Split in 1455, there is a chapel where Juraj Čulinović (Giorgio Schiavone) is buried (1433 or 1446-1505.) Čulinović is one of many "Sciavoni" (Slavs) who worked in Italy, but he is best known as a pupil of Francesco Squaracione (1397-1468) of Padua, and excelled his teacher. His works can be found in London (The National Gallery), Paris (Musée Jacquemert-André), Berlin (Kaiser-Friedrich Museum) and elsewhere. On the altar there is a painting by Felipe Zaniberti (a pupil of the Titian school). Amongst other altars, to the left of the entrance is the Altar of the Three Kings with a painting by Bernardo Rizzardi. The sides of the altar are decorated with reliefs of two angels holding the scroll of Nikola Firentinac, set into shell-shaped niches. The **Cathedral Treasury** includes works by the Renaissance master Horacije Fortezza of Šibenik (1530-1596), an exceptional goldsmith and miniaturist. He chiselled the covers of matriculae for rural fraternities. His work can be seen in London (a gold plate in the Victoria and Albert Museum) and in Venice (battle scenes and illustrations of myths in the Museo Civico Correr). ■

end of the 16th and the beginning of the 17th centuries in Renaissance style. It was designed by Antun Nogulović. The neighbouring fraternity house can be reached via the choir of the church, through a passage with heavily decorated Gothic columns.

••••••••••••

The **Church of the Assumption of the Virgin***** (Crkva Uznesenja Bogorodice, NUMBER ⓮ ON THE PLAN) is an Orthodox church. Until 1808 this was the Church of St. Saviour of a Benedictine convent (mentioned in 1390, gaining its Baroque appearance in the 17th century) It belonged to the Templars, and then to flagellants, and finally to the Benedictine sisters. In 1808 Napoleon founded a bishopric in Šibenik for the orthodox people of Istria, Dalmatia, Dubrovnik and Boka Kotorska, and called by them Crkva **Uspenije Bogomatere.** The church's bell-tower, built by the Šibenik builder Ivan Skoko, is considered to be one of the finest of its type on the Adriatic. The iconostasis is the work of Aleksej Lazović.

••••••••••••

The **Church and Monastery of St. Dominic**** (Sveti Dominik; NUMBER ❹), were built at the beginning of this century on the site of a demolished church. In the west wall there is a Renaissance portal from the old church. The most valuable painting in the church is thought to be *St. John the Evangelist*, by the most important representative of Venetian Mannerism, Palma the Younger (Palma il Giovane, Venice 1544-1628). The

The Church of St. Barbara

monastery's library owns several incunabula, and the painting *Ecce homo* of the Venetian-Byzantine school is considered to be the finest work.

•••••••••••

St. Francis' Church*** (Sveti Frane; NUMBER ⓰) was built in the 14th century in Gothic style. In accord with the concept of poverty at that time, the church is single-naved, and, in terms of architectural decorations, modest. The ceiling is of larch wood and was not decorated until 1674, with scenes of the life of St. Francis by the Venetian workshop of G.B. Volpat). On the main altar there is a painting by Matej Ponzoni (Pončun; Rab 1586 - Venice some time after 1663). Inside the church there are four more altars built according to sketches drawn by Jeronim (Girolamo) Mondelle, a builder and wood carver from Verona, who married into a Šibenik family (the Kolunić-Rotas). Over the choir is an organ built in 1726 by the well-known organ builder Petar Nakić (1694-1760 or 70) known as "the famous Dalmatian mathematician". Nakić also carved about 500 organ cabinets in Italy and 15 in Dalmatia.

The **treasury** and monastery library are extremely rich. They include the largest collection of incunabula (140) and handwritten codices (144) of which the oldest (written with musical notes) dates from the 10th century. There is also the *Šibenik prayer* (Šibenska molitva) from the 14th century, the oldest example of the Croatian language written in Latin script. During artillery attacks and aerial bombardment by the Serb forces in 1991-92 both church and monastery were damaged.

•••••••••••

Holy Cross Church* (Sveti Križ; NUMBER ❶) was built from white, cut marble at the beginning of the 17th century. The church's facade with its large window with 12 medallions showing the figures of the 12 Apostles, is the work of Antun Nogulović (Šibenik 1634). The coffered ceiling and the woodwork in the church are the work of Jeronim Mondelle, the creator of the wooden altar in St. Francis' Church.

City street

•••••••••••

St. Lawrence's Church* (Sveti Lovro; NUMBER ❺) was built towards the end of the 17th century in Baroque style. Inside the church there is a particularly valuable painting by Andreo da Murano. In the night between 6th and 7th September 1985 the church was badly damaged by fire.

•••••••••••

The **Foscolo Palace**** (NUMBER ❻) was built in the middle of the 15th century at the time when Juraj Dalmatinac was working in Šibenik. The building has Gothic windows, but the facade is decorated with Renaissance reliefs of fantasy scenes. In 1648 it was donated to the Franciscans. The monastery owns a rich library, archives and a picture gallery. The most valuable items in the monastery are thought to be the painting *Our Lady of Milk* by Juraj Čulinović (who is buried in the cathedral) and the *Kosirić codex*, written on parchment and illustrated with a wealth of miniatures.

•••••••••••

The **Bishop's Palace**** (NUMBER ❼B) was built beside the cathedral in the 15th century. The portal of the palace, in late-Gothic style, is the work of Andrija Budičić, a pupil of Juraj Dalmatinac. On the facade there is a triforium with the coats of arms of Bishop Juraj Šižgorić and the city's rector. The interior portal is stylised

View of Šibenik

in the manner of the Renaissance with a fluted threshold and ornamental doorposts. The interior arcades have simple, but stylised capitals. Over the triforium stands a statue of St. Michael, the city's patron. The palace's chapel houses two exceptional polyptychs. One is the work of the Šibenik artist Nikola Vladanov (1390-1466) and shows the Madonna covering a group of believers with her robe. This polyptych is considered to be the finest work of Dalmatian art from the first half of the 15th century. The other shows the Madonna with four Saints, and it comes from the circle of Blaž Trogiranin, an artist of the first half of the 15th century whose many works can be seen in Dubrovnik, Split, Korčula, Zadar and Trogir. His paintings are composed in the manner of a Byzantine icon, with some Gothic elements. The palace was damaged during Serb artillery fire and bombing during the war of 1991-1992.

••••••••••••

The **Castle and the City Walls**** (NUMBER ❷). The castle was built in 1000 on a hill 70 m over the sea and it was known as "castrum sancti Michaeli". The city wall descends towards the city, fortified with towers in places. It was mentioned for the first time in 1116 when it was destroyed by the Venetian Doge, Ordelafo Faliero. The wall has only been partially preserved. Of seven city gates (demolished in the 19th century) only one remains. The present appearance of the castle dates from the 18th century. The earlier fortress was destroyed after an explosion in the gunpowder house, and nothing was left standing. The oldest part of the building dates from 15th century.

••••••••••••

St. Nicholas' Fortress*** (Sveti Nikola) is located at the mouth of the canal and protects the city from the seaward side. It was built between 1540 and 1547 after two smaller fortresses had been demolished in 1505. Venice entrusted the building of this fortress to Gian Girolamo Sanmichelli, the nephew and pupil of the famous Italian architect from Verona, Michaele Sanmichelli (1484-1559). It is probable that he also assisted in the building of

Fortress of St. Nicholas

the fortress. The originality of its architectural conception is seen in the clever use of chiaroscuro, attained by the use of a rustic technique (bugato). Above all, this building succeeds in uniting military strength and aesthetic expression.

•••••••••••

St. John's Fortress** (Tanaja; NUMBER ❸ ON THE PLAN) is a star-shaped construction, built in 1646 as a defence against the Turks, on a hill 115 m above sea level. Once they had conquered Bosnia, the Turks began to be a threat to Šibenik (1463), especially in 1522 when they came as close as Skradin. The fortress was built at the last minute, and by the following year (1647) it withstood a 20-day siege by 40 000 Turkish soldiers.

Exhibit of the City Museum

•••••••••••

Šubićevac* (NUMBER ⓯ ON THE PLAN). Not far from the fortress is the memorial park *Park strijeljanih.* Here on May 22, 1942 the Italian fascists shot 26 members of the resistance movement. The monument was set up in 1960, and is the work of Kosta Angeli Radovani and Zdenko Kolacio.

A performance in the Šibenik International Children's Festival

•••••••••••

The **Šibenik City Museum**** (Gradska vrata 3, NUMBER ❾C ON THE PLAN) was founded in 1925. Its permanent collection gives an overview of the history of Šibenik and the surrounding area, from prehistory to the Middle Ages. The history of the city is shown chronologically from 1066 to the present day. There is a collection of amphorae, ancient epigraphic items, weapons, coins, paintings and sculptures of the 20th century and a small natural history collection. During shelling and bombing by Serb forces in 1991-92, the building of the museum was damaged.

Organ of Petar Nakić

•••••••••••

The **International Children's Festival.** Since 1958, every year at the end of June and beginning of July, Šibenik has hosted the International Children's Festival, composed of theatrical, cinematic, musical and pictorial exhibitions and events put on in locations all over the city. The Festival maintains a high level, top professional performers for children and some of the best children's ensembles taking part.

•••••••••••

The Summer Organ School. Since Šibenik has a number of valuable organs, every year in the second half of August the Summer Organ School is held. Teachers and course members play on the organs in the Church of Holy Cross (organ of an anonymous master of the 18th century), in Nova crkva (Master G. Giaccobbi of 1859), in St. Francis' Church (Master Petar Nakić, 1726, and a Heferer organ of 1967), in the Church of St. John (Zupan brothers, 1908), the Church of the Madonna outside the City (Master Jenko, of 1958) and in the Cathedral of St. James (Jenko, 1968).

►►► p. 205

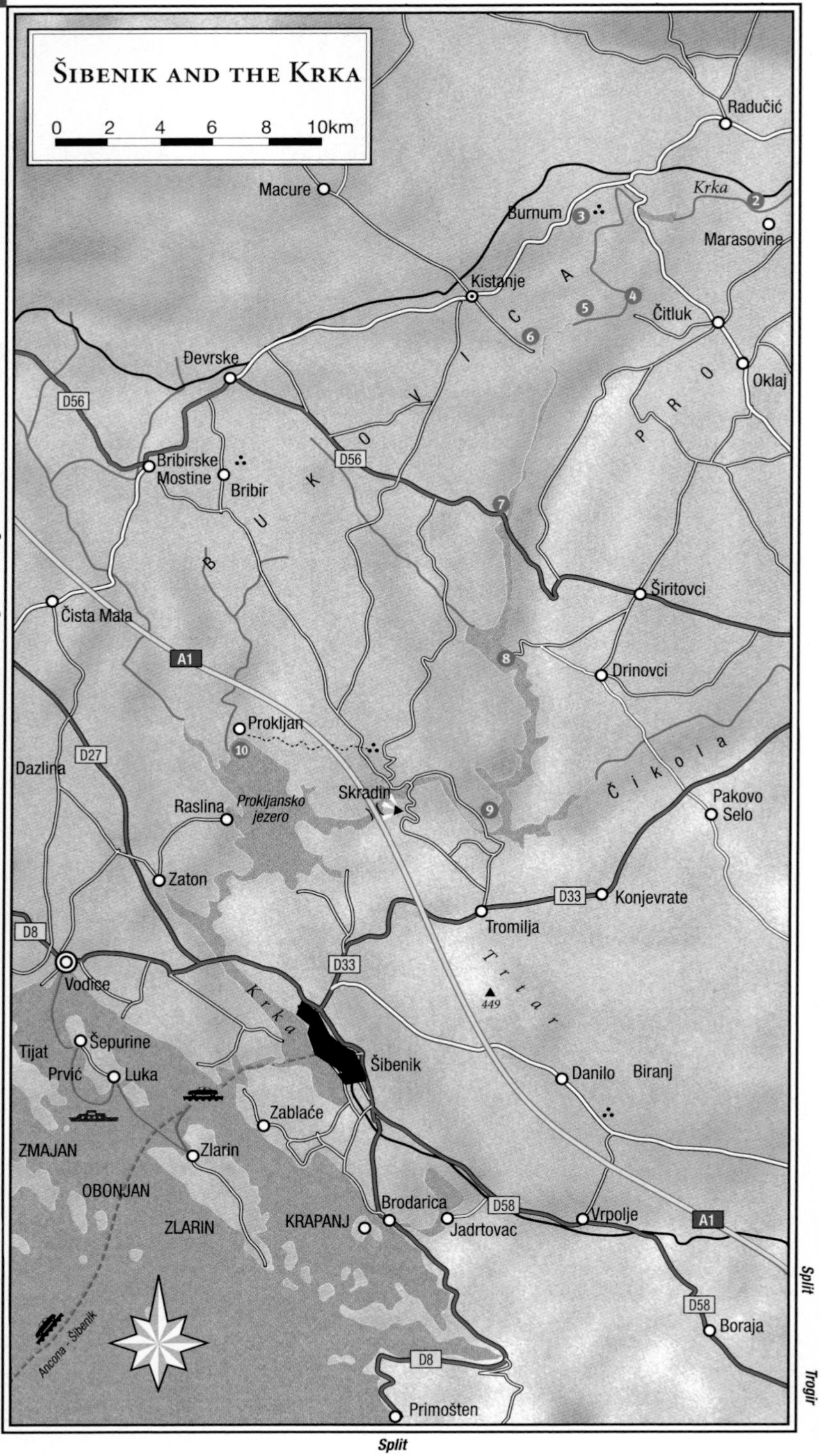
Šibenik and the Krka
0 2 4 6 8 10km
Raducić
Macure
Krka
Burnum
Marasovine
Kistanje
Čitluk
Oklaj
Đevrske
D56
Benkovac
Bribirske Mostine
Bribir
BUKOVICA
PRO
Zagreb-Zadar
Širitovci
Čista Mala
Obrovac - Gračac - Zagreb
A1
Drinovci
Prokljan
D27
Dazlina
Čikola
Skradin
Pakovo Selo
Raslina
Prokljansko jezero
Zaton
D33
Konjevrate
Tromilja
Zadar
D8
Vodice
Trtar
449
Krka
Šepurine
Tijat
Prvić
Luka
Šibenik
Danilo
Biranj
Zablaće
ZMAJAN
Zlarin
OBONJAN
D58
Brodarica
Vrpolje
ZLARIN
KRAPANJ
Jadrtovac
Split
Ancona - Šibenik
Boraja
Trogir
Primošten
Split

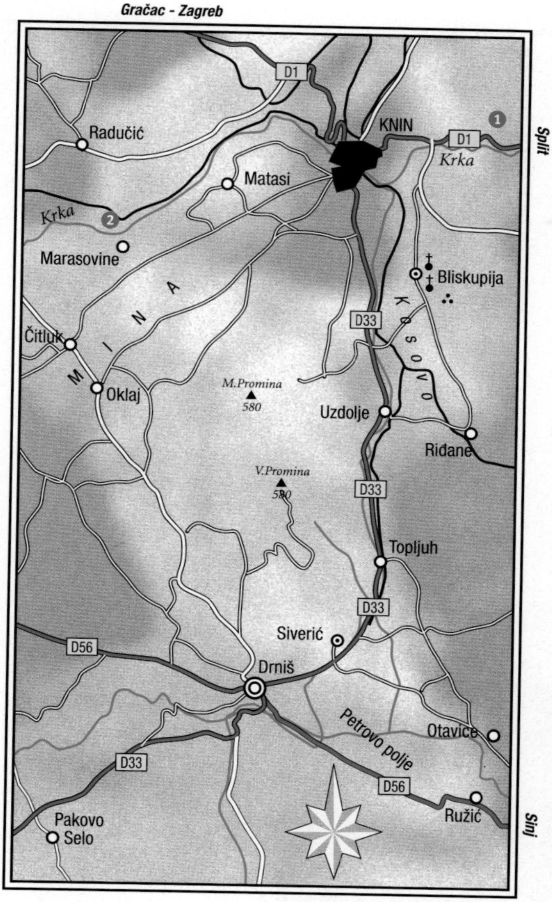

Leading artists run the school and have a specially selected programme, and so the school has turned into an important Adriatic cultural event.

Excursions

Drniš**

32 km from Šibenik inland, 300 above sea level, 3 253 inhabitants

Drniš is one of the centres of the Dalmatian hinterland, a broad plateau stretching from Knin to the Kozjak mountains above Kaštela. This town grew up around a Turkish fortress, which offers a beautiful view over Petrovo polje, Promina mountain, and Čikola canyon. For two hundred years the town was under Turkish rule and was liberated in 1683 by Serdar Nakić. As Turkish buildings were destroyed during the Venetian-Turkish wars, the partially preserved mosque and minaret are the only Turkish buildings still standing in Dalmatia (along with the Mašković caravanserai in Vrana near Zadar). During the period of Serbian aggression against Croatia in 1991-1995, Drniš was occupied. The Church of St. Anthony (Sv. Antun) was destroyed, the Parish Church of the Madonna of the Rosary (built 1886; on the side altar, a marble statue, the Madonna of Petrovo polje, the work of Ivan Meštrović, was placed in 1961) and the Church of St. Rocco were damaged. The **Museum of the Drniš Region** (Vjeke Širinića 28 Street), containing some works by Ivan Meštrović, was also devastated and looted.

••••••••••••

The Meštrović Mausoleum

In **Otavice** (9 km east of Drniš) is the **Meštrović Mausoleum**. Ivan Meštrović was born in Otavice in 1883. He was the most prominent representative of modern Croatian sculpture. Meštrović created many pieces, many on the theme of national history and legends. Both his poetic and monumental works radiate the elemental strength of native art. He died in the United States in 1962 but was buried in his family mausoleum, built in 1930. Some of his works are also exhibited in Drniš. In the thirties, Meštrović built an elementary school in Otavice, as well as a health centre and the bridge that joins Otavice and the village Ružići; he did not however manage to realise his wish to build the Church of the Holy Saviour in his native village.

••••••••••••

The River Krka, and the Krka National Park

Falls on the Krka

The area around the River Krka has been declared a National Park because of its natural beauty and its geological characteristics (an area of karst rock). The well-known geographer and academic Josip Roglić said there are only a few places in the world which can be compared with Krka's natural beauty. The river rises 43 km (as the crow flies) from Šibenik, beneath the best-known mountain in Croatia and Dalmatia, Dinara. This mountain has given its name to the mountain range which stretches about 600 km encompassing the mountains of the Croatian coastal area and of Bosnia and Herzegovina. The Krka is 73 km long in all, of which the first part flows through plains (13 km) the second (40 km) through a canyon and the final stage forms lakes joined to the sea. The river nowadays forms the border between Northern and Central Dalmatia; in the Illyrian era it separated the Liburnian tribe from the Delmati, and when the Slavs arrived in the Balkans it was in the centre of the Croatian state. The **Krka National Park** covers 142.2 km^2 (25.6 km^2 being water) and two thirds of the River Krka. Since the whole of the river is a natural phenomenon of exceptional interest, this text deals with the whole of the river from the source.

Krka River

The **source of the Krka**** (NUMBER ❶ ON THE MAP; can be reached from Knin, 3 km) is a rare and interesting phenomenon. It is a karst spring (vaucluse) into which the 22 m high waterfall from the Krčić stream falls. As the stream dries up in summer, the actual source of the Krka is only visible then.

Knin

56 KM FROM ŠIBENIK, POPULATION 11 746.

Knin has been inhabited since prehistoric times, and is mentioned for the first time in writing in the 10th century as the centre of a Croatian parish (župa) or tribal state called Tenen. In the 11th century it was the centre of the Croatian kings (Trpimir, Muncimir, Svetislav, Držislav, Zvonimir and Petar) and of the bishop, the court chancellor. After the death of the last Croatian king (1102) it was the seat of the governors. In 1251 there was a session of the Parliament of the

Knin - fortress and city

Kingdom of Croatia, and between 1409 and 1522 the "Council of Croatian Elders" met there. The Turks conquered it in 1522 and after that it began to be inhabited by Serbian refugees. Although it was liberated in the Cretan War it was nevertheless left to the Turks. The Venetians got it back only in 1699. During the French occupation (1805-1813) it was linked by roads with its hinterland. In the surroundings of Knin are some of the most important finds from the Old Croatian period, including names of the Croatian princes and kings (Biskupija and Uzdolje are the best known sites), so that the Croatian Antiquarian Society was founded there in 1893 by Fra Lujo Marun, the foundations thus being laid for the study of Old Croatian archaeology. After World War II the ethnic structure was deliberately changed, and the city became the centre of Serb separatism. It was here, on August 17 1990, that the rebellion of part of the Serb population against the legally elected Croatian government and the aggression against Croatia began, Knin being proclaimed the capital of the "Republic of the Serb Krajina". It was liberated on August 5, 1995. Above the city is the famous Fortress of St. Saviour, the biggest fortified building in the interior of Dalmatia. The Parish Church of St. Anthony of Padua was demolished during Serb aggression; the Neobyzantine Orthodox Church of the Virgin was demolished during World War II and renovated in 1971.

••••••••••••

The **Upper Canyon*** (Gornji kanjon; can be reached from the waterfall Bilušić buk, (NUMBER ❷), to the north a few hundred metres from Radučić railway station, and from the south, by mountain path from Matasi and Marasovina). The waterfall consists of two main cascades and one in between, with 22 m difference in height between them. **Burnum*** (NUMBER ❸; immediately above Čorića waterfall, 6 km from Kistanje, and the same distance from Čitluk). This is known locally as "šuplja crkva" or "Trajanov grad" ("hollow church" or "Trajan's castle"). During the Roman era it was one of their important army bases surrounding and protecting the fertile, flat hinterland of Iadera (Zadar). In the year AD 69 the Roman 11th legion left the camp, after which Burnum began to decline, and in 639 it was destroyed by the Avars and Slavs. Archaeological research in 1912 and 1913 revealed the remains of a praetorium with the foundations of many rooms. Of the former five arcades only two remain. Two kilometres to the east, the remains of a town, Canaba, have been discovered, with parts of a temple to Jupiter, an amphitheatre, an aqueduct and traces of streets. Most of the stone remains have been built into local houses or are in the museum in Knin.

••••••••••••

Nečven and Trošenj Castles (NUMBERS ❹ AND ❺) can be reached from the village of Čitluk, 3 km by road or from Čučevo by path. These two ruined castles, a stone's throw apart and at almost the same height above sea level, with the river Krka flowing between, at one time separated and protected the properties of two old Croatian feudal families: five-storey Trošenj, the Šubić's; and Nečven, the Nelipić's. The Turks conquered them in 1522 and held them until 1684. They were the residence of agas, commanders and cadis (the political, military and legal leaders of the area). **Krka Monastery*** (NUMBER ❻; 3 km on the road from Kistanje). This orthodox monastery St. Archangel (Sveti Arhanđel) was mentioned for the first time in 1402 as a votive offering of Jelena Šubić, the wife of the Serbian Emperor Dušan (1308-1355). The church was built in 1790 in Byzantine style, with a Renaissance bell-tower. The monastery has rich collection of icons, paintings (particularly interesting is the portrait of Neophyte Njeguš by Vlaho Bukovac), textiles, incunabula and books.

••••••••••••

Roški slap waterfall** (NUMBER ❼ON THE PLAN) can be easily reached from all sides and by boat from Skradin. This is the best-known, but not the most beautiful part of Krka. There are 12 waterfalls in 450 m, with a total drop of 27 m. The upstream falls are more accessible from the west. Alongside the falls there are many water mills which are still in use today, for rinsing cloth, the carding of wool and grinding grain. Here, on the left bank of the Krka, is a complex of **water mills**** that is considered the most interesting spot in Dalmatia from an ethnographic point of view.

On the right hand side is the old hydro-electricity power station of Miljacka, built in 1906, of a very small capacity, which is to be turned into a permanent technical museum.

••••••••••••

Visovačko jezero lake*** and **monastery Visovac** (NUMBER ❽ON THE PLAN) can be reached by road from Skradin or Drniš. This is the largest lake, formed by the barrier formed by the Skradinski buk waterfall. It is 13.5 km long, 1 km wide and 30 m deep. In the summer the temperature of the water reaches 27° C and in winter 16° C. On the small island in the middle of the lake (1 hectare in size) a wide variety of vegetation grows, just like a botanical garden. The lake abounds in fish (tench, carp, trout and others) and is also famous for its otters. The **monastery** was built in 1445 and the church in 1576 on a site where hermits once lived. Franciscans settled here having withdrawn from parts of Bosnia with other, ordinary people, when the Turks had taken over there. A new monastery was built in the 18th century. The rich monastery library includes particularly rare incunabula of Aesop's fables (Brescia 1487) printed by the Lastovo printer Dobrić Dobričević (s. Lastovo), a collection of documents (the sultan's edicts) and a sabre belonging to Vuk Mandušić, one of the best-loved heroes of folk epics. Today it is possible to get to Visovac by a new road via Miljevac and Pakovo Selo.

Visovac

••••••••••••

From this spot it is possible to see the area where the Krka, in the space of only 4 km, forms two lakes, five waterfalls and one rapid. Above the Krka waterfall stretches Bobodolsko Lake, 1100 m long and 300 m wide. The sides of the canyon are 400 m apart, so part of the canyon is used as farmland. On the Ćorića waterfall side of the canyon the sides are very steep, and over the waterfall there is a crossing joining the areas of Promina and Bukovica. Readers of the Books of Karl May will be interested to learn that many films for which he wrote the screenplay were shot here.

••••••••••••

Skradinski buk

Skradinski buk waterfall*** (NUMBER ❾ ON THE PLAN) is reached by road, 8 km from Tromilja. In an area 400 m in length and 100 m in width there are 17 waterfalls and the total difference in height between the first and the last fall is 45.7 m. The rate of flow is 43 m^3 a second in winter and 18 m^3 in summer. Due to the wealth and variety of geomorphological forms, vegetation, and the various effects caused by the play of light on the whirlpools Skradinski buk is considered to be the most beautiful calcium carbonate waterfall in Europe. Near Skradin the waters of the River Krka mix with the sea and therefore, from a hydrologist's viewpoint, this is the mouth of the river. From a morphological standpoint however, that is not the case, for the course of the river can still be followed until it flows out into the bay of Šibenik. Further evidence for this is given by the so-called **"Gavanovi dvori"** (NUMBER ❿ ON THE PLAN), an archaeological site in the sea (8 km from Skradin) which has become the subject of many legends, even though the walls are exactly at the depth they were 2 000 years ago, but are now covered due to the rising of the surface of the sea. Thus, 15 000 years ago, the mouth of the river Krka may have been near Zlarin.

••••••••••••

Skradin*

16 KM FROM ŠIBENIK, 619 INHABITANTS

linked by ship to Šibenik. This was an Illyrian settlement (Scardona) on the boundary between the Delmati and the Liburnian tribes. It was the capital of the Liburnians. It was better known as a Roman town, as the administrative and military centre of the region. During the migrations of the nations it was destroyed, but in the 9th century Croatians moved here. It has had its present name since the 10th century. It was one of the seats of the Bribir Šubić family (1334). Between 1522 and 1684 it was ruled by the Turks, and then again up to 1794 by Venice. In time it lost its importance as the centre of the region, which shifted to Šibenik, and so it stagnated. (The Bishopric was abolished in 1828). In the village of **Biskupija** there are fragments of a marble relief, a parish church (from the middle of the 18th century), a cemetery chapel (from the 16th century, renovated in 1783) and the orthodox Church of St. Spiridon (18th century) with a collection of icons. ■

Roški slap

Pirovac*

22 km from Šibenik, 1 608 inhabitants

Pirovac is a town with a strong farming hinterland. It was mentioned in 1298 as Zloselo (Evil village) and the name was changed between the two world wars; according to tradition, this first name was given it by the Turks. At one time it was part of the property of Count Šubić of Bribir and of the bishops of Šibenik. At the beginning of the 16th century it was fortified, but only a few traces of the walls remain. The village Church of St. George (Sveti Juraj) was built in 1506 and redecorated in Baroque style in the 18th century. In the graveyard there is the chapel of the Draganić-Vrančić family. The Gothic tomb with relief work was made in 1477 by A. Budičić (one of the builders of Šibenik Cathedral) and Lorenzo Pinzino of Venice. On the neighbouring island of **Sustipanac** there are the remains of Roman buildings and the ruins of a Franciscan monastery which existed there from 1511 to 1807.

••••••••••••

Primošten**

30 km south of Šibenik, 1761 inhabitants

Primošten is an exceptionally picturesque town, which grew up on a small island (its highest point is 29 m). It was settled by those fleeing from the Turks and, at the same time (1564) joined to the mainland. It was at one time fortified with walls and towers, which were demolished in the 19th century. The parish church was built in 1760 on the ruins of a 15th century church. Its best known possessions are the icon of the *Madonna* in a silver frame and the picture of *St. Mary with St. Luke and St. George*, the work of K. Cusi, 1719. Primošten suffered heavy damage during World War II. Nowadays Primošten has developed as a well-known summer resort. There are a number of worthwhile things in the neighbourhood. In the hamlet of Kruševo (10 km inland) the medieval little Church of St Mary has been preserved, and a graveyard with Bogumil gravestones ("stećci"); in Prhovo, 4 km from Primošten, lies the medieval Church of St. George, renovated in 1724.

Primošten

••••••••••••

Vodice*

10 km from Šibenik, towards Zadar, 6 077 inhabitants

This town was mentioned for the first time in 1402. It was once a strongly fortified town which offered protection to the local people from the Turks. From those times **Ćorića Tower** still remains standing. In the graveyard to the west of the village is the Chapel of Holy Cross (Sveti Križ) from 1421. Up to the war in 1991-95, Vodice was a strong holidaymaking centre which is gradually becoming once again, after reconstruction.

••••••

Vodice

The Kornati Islands National Park***

Kornati landscape

People have always spoken of the Kornati islands with wonder, but since man has been able to see our planet from space, it is well known that both American and Soviet astronauts agree that, from that height the sea in the area around these islands is the clearest blue in the world. This of course was no great discovery for those who already knew this archipelago, but just exactly what they had always maintained. The Kornati islands belong to the North Dalmatian archipelago. They spread over an area of about 300 km^2 from northwest to southeast (from the island of Balabra to Samograd), are 35 km in length and from northeast to southwest they stretch 13 km (from Gangarol to Mana). In that area there are 140 islands, some large, some smaller, and many rocks. Nowhere else in the world are there so many islands in such a small area. For this reason the Kornati have been called a labyrinth of land in the sea. Geographically speaking, the Kornati islands can be divided into four groups - Sit, Žut, Kornat and Piškera - and three channels. The first two groups are known as Gornji Kornati (Upper Kornati) and the other two, Donji Kornati (Lower Kornati). The area covered by the National Park does not coincide with these divisions. The Sit and Žut groups are excluded from the National Park. The park includes 109 islands, of which 76 are less than 1 hectare in size. Of the total land surface area of Kornati (62 km^2), 85% is stony, and only 5% has been cultivated. Most of the terrain is karst-limestone which, in the distant geological past, arose from sediment from the sea. Therefore in the stone on the islands there are numerous fossils of crustaceans and fish. In the area there are examples of all the typical forms of karst: bizarre shapes formed by the atmosphere, unexplored caves, areas of flat rock and, above all, cliffs. Karst rock is dry, and so therefore are the Kornati islands. Numerous cisterns supply water for people and animals. Vegetation on the islands is very sparse. There are 200 known varieties of Mediterranean plants, but they have degenerated. However, even humble rock plants can impress as they demonstrate the triumph of life over its environment. The most common plant form is a tough variety of grass, but there are many scented and medicinal herbs: sage, feather grass and xeranthemum, giving a fragrant spring, and during the year providing the best country for bees. It is thought that the Kornati islands were once covered with forests of Mediterranean holm oaks (quercus ilex), but as open fires demanded a great deal of wood, the forests were slowly destroyed. The land fauna is also sparse, but interesting. Apart from sea-gulls, which are the most numerous, there are 69 varieties of butterfly here, some amphibians and rodents. As regards marine life, the Kornati islands are typical of the Adriatic and the Mediterranean, but, due to the underwater relief, streams and special characteristics of the sea in this labyrinth, there are also some peculiarities: algae, coral and sponges. At one time the sea here was the richest in the Adriatic for sponge hunters. As for fish, they were once a synonym for Kornati because of the quantity and quality. According to tradition, the Mediterranean monk seal (Monachus albiventur) once lived among these islands. The name of the southernmost point on Vela Kurba (Mendo) is connected with this almost extinct species. The climate on the Kornati islands is more pleasant than in Zadar or Šibenik. The average monthly air temperature for January (7.3°C) is higher than in Šibenik (6.8°C) or Zadar (6.7°C), and in July (23.9°C) it is lower (Zadar 25°C, Šibenik 25.6°C). The average sea temperature in winter is 14-15°C and in summer it is 22.8°C. The islands were inhabited in prehistoric times. Archaeological sites in Stražišće and Tarac, and on Levrnaka and Lavsa provide evidence of this, and that during the Roman era life on Kornati was very active. There are many buildings and it is known that there were also stone quarries here. The present day church of St. Mary was built on the ruins of an old basilica which could not have been built in a desert (see Tarac; NUMBER ❼ ON THE MAP). Nowadays the islands are only inhabited in the summer by people from Murter or Sali. ■

Kornati at sunset

Typical Kornati cliff

Excursions

Mala Proversa (NUMBER ❸) is a shallow channel between Dugi Otok and Katina. The ruins of a Roman building 90 m long are visible in the water. Clearly, in the Roman era this was above sea level and was built in the 1st or 2nd century AD. It was a spacious building with piped water and a mosaic (which is now in the Archaeological Museum in Zadar). It is not clear whether it belonged to a farming complex (villa rustica) or a fish farm. The centre of the Vela Proversa passage is the limit of the National Park.

••••••••••••

The Island of **Taljurić** (NUMBER ❹) is one of the most interesting geomorphological curiosities. It is oval in shape, like a plate (74 m x 50 m). It is dangerous for seafarers as it is frequently covered by the sea.

••••••••••••

Špinuta Bay (NUMBER ❺) is well protected. In the bay one can see ruins of an underwater wall, which belonged to a Roman salt pan or fish farm. There is a spring on the island.

••••••••••••

Levrnaka (NUMBER ❻) is the fourth largest island. The large bay in the north is considered to be the most beautiful spot on the Kornati islands; it must be said that this bay is one of the most carefully protected in the archipelago. Lojena Bay is sandy, and the most popular beach for bathing.

••••••••••••

Tarac (NUMBER ❼) is the second largest area of karst rock in the Kornati archipelago (it can be reached from Lučica bay or Kravljača). There are two interesting buildings here: Tureta (tower, castle) the most important remains from the late Roman era which served as a watch tower; and at the foot of the hill is St. Mary's Church (Sveta Marija) (after which the Kornati islands are also known as the Stomorski islands), built on the foundations of a former basilica.

Taljurić

••••••••••••

The Island of **Svršata Vela** (NUMBER ❽) has a beautiful jagged coastline. Remains of Roman walls were found in the sea here too, and it is thought that they belonged to an old fish farm.

••••••••••••

Magazinova Škrila (NUMBER ❾; can be reached from Zala draga bay). By a beautiful holm oak forest there is a strange large slab of rock, 130 m x 70 m, an example of the curious shapes frequently formed by karst rock. Its strange and unreal shape stirs the imagination and has inspired many legends. According to scientists it was formed by a massive landslide.

••••••••••••

The Island of **Mana** (NUMBER ❿) is also known as "terrible Mana" because of its over-hanging cliffs. It is an important location for flora, and it could be said that it is the most well-known and most frequently photographed spot on the Kornati islands. It makes a beautiful look-out point. The film *Razbješnjelo more* (The Raging Sea) was filmed on the plateau and the ruins which now stand there were in fact part of the sets of that film, and are not authentic.

••••••••••••

Trtuša (NUMBER ⓫) may be reached from Vrulj bay. It is the largest

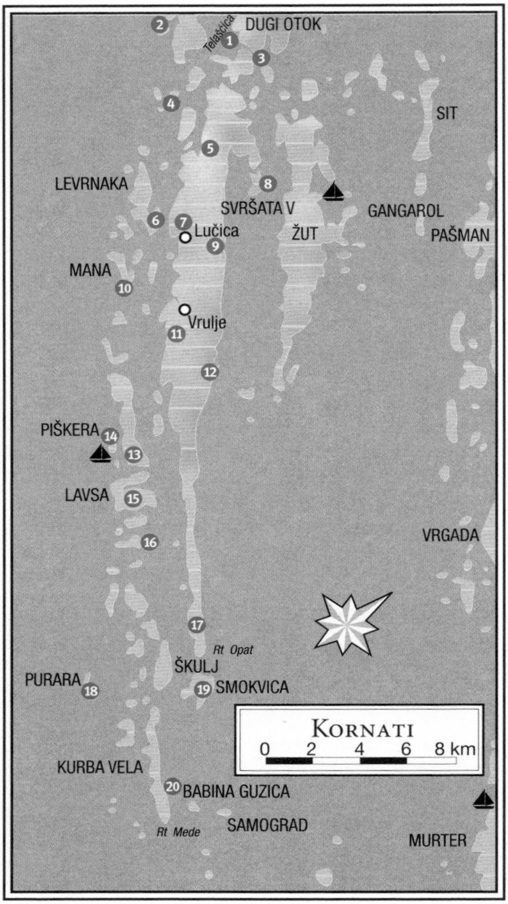

area of karst on the islands and 2500 to 3000 years ago it was inhabited by Illyrian tribes. There are also the remains of a Roman villa rustica and two water holes. During the last war there was a Partisan harbour here where ships up to 20 tonnes were repaired.

••••••••••••

Stiniva Bay (NUMBER 12) is known for having the largest cave in the Kornati archipelago.

••••••••••••

Piškera Island (NUMBER 13) is the centre of the fishing trade on the Kornati islands and has a storehouse for salted fish. Here is also the Church of the Blessed Madonna built in 1560 (Blažena Gospa). In the graveyard to the east of the church lie the bodies of soldiers, for there was a hospital in the church in World War II.

••••••••••••

Panitula Vela Island and the Malkuntanto

Tureta on the island of Tarac

Gorge (NUMBER 14; in Italian malcontanto - discontent). The gorge's name points to frequent quarrels between fishermen and the fact that on the island the Venetians built a customs post, which was demolished by the Uskoks of Senj.

••••••••••••

Lavsa (NUMBER 15), because of its beautiful and well-protected bay is counted as one of the most picturesque of the Kornati islands. The remains of prehistoric Illyrian burial mounds and signs of Roman buildings have also been discovered on Lavsa.

••••••••••••

Ravni Žakan (NUMBER 16) has become the liveliest spot on the islands, as an attractive resort

Lavsa

with a large restaurant. In the sixties there was accommodation here belonging to the "Club Mediterrannée", but the club buildings were not able to withstand the winter climate on Kornati.

•••••••••••

The **Opat** Peninsula (NUMBER ⑰) is 109 m high with a magnificent bay and caves, making this a very attractive spot.

•••••••••••

Purara (NUMBER ⑱) is an important reserve for marine life. Together with the rocks of Klint and Volić it is closed to the public. (As well as the islet and the rocks, part of the land 500 metres distant is also closed.)

•••••••••••

Smokvica Vela (NUMBER ⑲) stands 100 m above the sea. Lojena Bay is one of the most lively and popular places on these islands.

•••••••••••

The names of the islands Babina Guzica (Granny's Bottom; NUMBER ⑳) and Kurba Vela (The Big Whore) offer an opportunity to explain the origin of the many vulgar names in the Kornati archipelago. When Austrian surveyors in the last century came to record the archipelago, their local guides made fun of them by making up vulgar names for the various locations.

•••••••••••

The Šibenik Island Group

Kaprije*

9 NAUTICAL MILES FROM ŠIBENIK; 7 KM^2 IN SIZE; 148 INHABITANTS

This island lies between the uninhabited islands Kakan (to the west) and Zmajan and Obonjan to the east. Obonjan is also known as the "island of youth" because it is used as a summer resort especially for children and young people. There was a refugee camp here during the war between 1992 and 1995. The first inhabitants of Kaprije were mentioned in the 15th century. The island was part of the property of some Šibenik nobles and was inhabited by refugees from the mainland. The local church was built in the 15th century and extended in 1801.

•••••••••••

Krapanj**

300 M FROM THE MAINLAND; 0.4 KM^2 IN SIZE; 228 INHABITANTS

As this island is so close to the coast, its inhabitants work the land on the mainland. The picturesque village on this flat island (7 m above sea level) is known for its sponge and coral divers. It was built in the Middle Ages and its parish church dates from 1458 (rebuilt in the 17th and 19th centuries) but has not retained its original appearance. Inside the church there is a votive picture of Our Lady of Krapanj. The Franciscan monastery, with Renaissance cloisters from the 16th century, also houses a valuable library and in the refectory there is a painting which has been ascribed to Francesco da Santacroce, and a small collection of Adriatic flora and fauna. In the village there is a private collection belonging to the diver Jerko Tanfara showing the development of sponge diving on the island.

•••••••••••

Murter

Murter*

18.6 KM^2 IN SIZE; 5 192 INHABITANTS IN 4 SETTLEMENTS

Murter is the largest island of the Šibenik island group, and it is linked to the mainland by a drawbridge near the village of Tisno. In the Roman era it was known as Colentum, from the 13th century Srimaz and Srimač and it has had its present name since the 18th century. The largest settlements are Betina, Murter and Tisno. **Betina** (31 km from Šibenik, 6 km from Tisno; 750 inhabitants). According to Ptolemy's atlas, the Roman settlement Colentum existed where the village of Gradina is now. Archaeological finds from

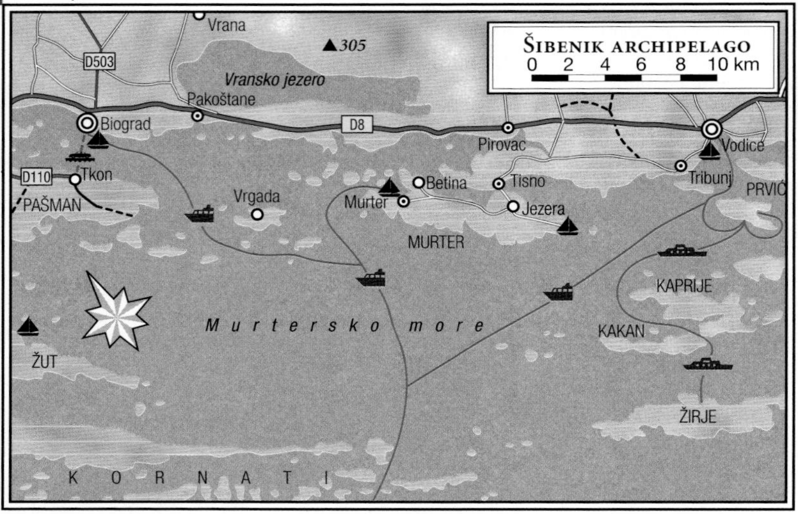

that area are in the Archaeological museum in Zadar. The walls which are now visible are of a later date, from the middle ages. The parish church dates from 1601, the bell-tower and chapel from 1736 and in 1720 the church was extended. On the southeastern side of Murter lies **Jezera** (pop. 800), village of fishermen, divers and stonemasons. It consists of three settlements (Ko?uluk, Selo and More). The centre of the entire settlement is called *Kolедišce*, one of the most attractive rural squares, which on feast days hosts vernacular fiestas.

Murter* (30 km from Šibenik, 5 km from Tisno; 2 010 inhabitants). The centre of the old town was at the foot of Raduč hill (125 m) and is typical of folk architecture. There are the remains of a Roman villa rustica with a pool of water beyond the graveyard, to the north of the village. The medieval Chapel of St. Michael (Sveti Mihovil) was restored in the 18th century, with a Baroque altar. Above the village, on Vršina hill, is the Chapel of St. Rocco (Sveti Rok) from 1760.

Tisno, 25 km from Šibenik, 1426 inhabitants. This village was named because of its location ("tisno" means "narrow"). In the village there is a tower from 1475 and the parish church from 1548 (redecorated in Baroque style in 1791). Above the town is the Shrine of the Madonna of Karavaj (It. Caravaggio). This is named after the famous picture of the Madonna which appeared, according to tradition, in the town of Caravaggio not far from Milan. There is a medieval chapel, St. Martin's (Sveti Martin) in the deserted village of Ivanj.

••••••

Prvić*

2.3 KM² IN SIZE; 450 INHABITANTS IN 2 SETTLEMENTS

Prvić is the island nearest to the mainland. Its name also derives from

Prvić, Šepurine

its location (prvi means "the first"). **Luka** (185 inhabitants) has a Franciscan monastery from 1461, which was renovated in the 19th century. In the parish church (built in the 15th century) is the grave of **Faust Vrančić** (1551-1617). Vrančić came from a famous Šibenik family: his father, Mihovil, was a Croatian Latin poet; his uncle Antun was a church

Faust Vrančić

prelate, diplomat, writer and poet; and on his mother's side he was from the Berislavić family (s. Trogir). Faust Vrančić was a multi-faceted and original character of European importance. He was the author of the first independent Croatian dictionary published in Venice in 1595 (*Dictionarium quinque nobilissimarum Europae linguarum - Dictionary of the five most noble European languages*: Latin, Italian, Hungarian, German and "Dalmatian", meaning the "čakavski" variant of the Croatian language). He gained renown in the scientific world with his book *Machinae novae* (Venice 1595). In it he described the construction of parachutes, air turbines and the use of tides in creating energy. His body was brought to Luka from Venice. In **Šepurine** (264 inhabitants) in the former summer residence of the Draganić-Vrančić family there is a small collection including a portrait of F. Vrančić.

•••••••••••

Zlarin** (5 nautical miles from Šibenik; 8 km² in size; 300 inhabitants). There was a settlement here in Illyrian and Roman times, and from 1298 to 1843 it was the residence of the bishops of Šibenik. It is known as an island of mariners and coral divers, and nowadays it is the favourite summer resort for people from Šibenik. There are several churches and chapels on the island. The Baroque parish church was built on the foundations of an older church in 1735. The Church Our Lady of Rašelj (Gospa od Rašelja) dates from the first half of the 15th century (it has been restored since) and has an altar made by the Dell'Acqua brothers. The Chapel of Jesus' Birth (Porođenje Isusovo) adjoins the Zuliani palace and dates from the 17th century. In the village there are several Baroque summer villas.

•••••••••••

Žirje (the island furthest from Šibenik, 12 nautical miles; 15.5 km² in size; 133 inhabitants). This is a fishing settlement, in an area famous for its abundant fishing grounds. The island was inhabited in prehistoric times. In the 12th and 13th centuries it was fortified. Nowadays the fortified sites are known as Gradina and Gustijerna.

•••••••••••

Šibensko polje and Jadrtovac

218 — 309

Central Dalmatia

Trogir

Split

Islands

Makarska

Trogir

Located 43°32′ N., 16°15′E. Population 10 920. Mean January Temperature: Air 8.1°C, Sea 12.1°C; Mean July Temperature: Air 26.2° C, Sea 23.6° C.

Trogir, to the right the island of Čiovo

Early History. The exceptional natural conditions in this area made it possible for man to settle here very early in prehistory. Trogir is situated on a small island in the straits between the mainland and the island of Čiovo. The surroundings, on the mainland, also offer a large fertile area in Dalmatian terms. In the area around the city there are traces of life from the early Stone Age (Palaeolithic) which are at least 50 000 years old. Within the old city centre itself some pre-historic finds have been discovered, the remains of houses and fragments of pottery, some of which are dated from about 2 000 years BC. The form of the present day historical city centre, an irregular circle, was probably determined by the natural configuration of the sand-bar shaped by the sea. As early as prehistoric times the settlement on the site of present-day Trogir was the centre for the various fortresses in the area, that is, fortified settlements or fastnesses belonging to the Illyrian tribes.

The Greek Era. At the end of the 3rd or the beginning of the 2nd century BC, Greeks from Issa (a settlement on the site of present day Vis) founded their own settlement, Tragurion, on the site of what is now Trogir. The name Trogir actually derives from that name (in Latin "Tragurium", and in Italian "Trau"). The first records of Tragurion are to do with an attack by the Illyrian Delmati tribe on Greek Tragurion and Epetion (now Stobreč, near Split). From this time, there are some archaeological finds: an altar to the goddess Hera near the cathedral, an inscription mentioning community officials, remains of the city walls and houses, and others.

The Roman Era. Tragurium developed in the shadow of not-far-distant Salona (19 km), the metropolis of the large Roman province of Dalmatia with which it was also linked administratively. Near Tragurium, Emperor Claudius moved his retired troops to Siculi (now Bijaći, between Trogir and Kaštela). The Roman writer Pliny the Elder in his work "Naturalis Historia" mentions Tragurium, "famous for its stone". The relatively regular street layout in the city today most probably dates from the Roman era. The basis of life at that time was the fertile land divided among the Roman immigrants. In the plain near Trogir in the contours of the lots and the intersections of squares it is still possible to discern the centuriation (i.e. the regular network of rectangles drawn up by the Roman cadastre organisation). There were also villae rusticae here, complexes of farm buildings and some shrines dedicated to the gods of agriculture. On the mainland opposite the city, alongside the access road, there were burial grounds.

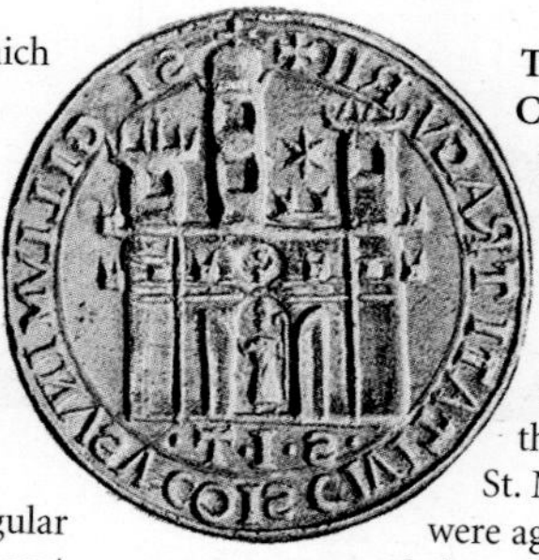

Crest of the city of Trogir

The Migrations of the Nations. Archaeological finds and other sources point to the fact that Trogir continued to survive through the insecure period of the late-Roman era. Trogir was one of the very few cities which resisted the Avar-Slavic invasions at the beginning of the 7th century.

The Period of Croatian and Croatian-Hungarian Rule. In the immediate vicinity of Trogir at the beginning of the 9th century was one of Croatian's centres. Archeological finds and historical sources indicate that apart from the Church of St. Martha (Sveta Marta) there were agricultural lands in Bijaći belonging to the Croatian rulers. The ciborium from St. Martha's is one of the most valuable exhibits in the Museum of Croatian Archaeological Monuments in Split. During the dynastic conflicts in about 1000, Svetislav Suronja took refuge in Trogir. He was a Croatian ruler who had been deposed from his throne. Trogir remained part of Byzantine Dalmatia until the 11th century. Amongst other items an inscription has been discovered from that time mentioning the Byzantine representative, the proconsul. From the beginning of the 12th century right up to 1420, Trogir was under the authority of the Croatian-Hungarian kings, although from time to time it found itself under the Venetians.

For a brief period, towards the end of the 14th century, Trogir also admitted the authority of the Bosnian king during the dynastic crisis between

Trogir, a 19th century Venetian drawing

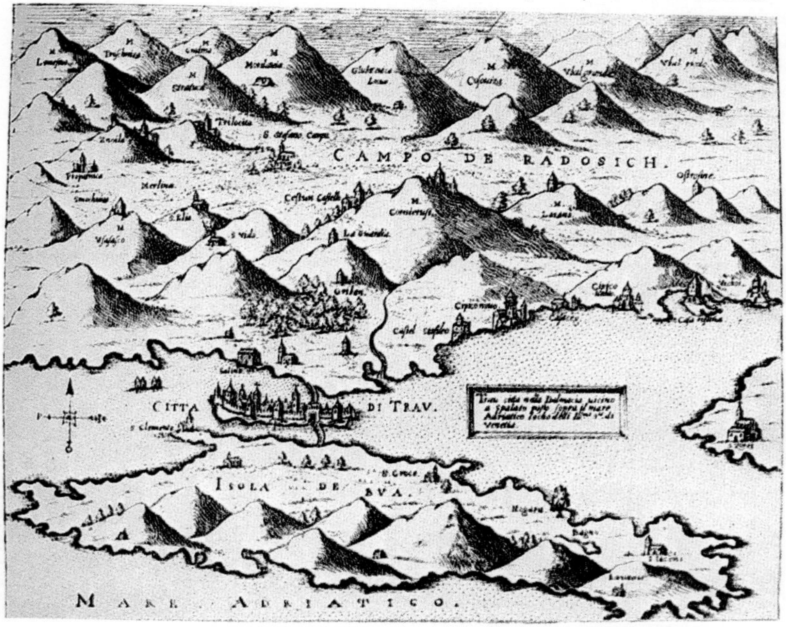

Croatia and Hungary. The Croatian feudal lords most frequently elected counts from the Šubić family of Bribir as the city's rulers. In 1242, the Croatian-Hungarian King Bela IV took refuge in the city from attacks by the Tatars. The Tatars' army had been brought to a halt by the boggy trench which separated the city from the mainland. They demanded that the king should be handed over to them, speaking in the Croatian language so that the people of the city would be able to understand them. During the forties of the 13th century Trogir went to war with its neighbour, Split. There were also conflicts with Šibenik, which was subordinate in religious matters to Trogir right up to the 13th century. During the wars between Hungary and Genoa on one hand and Venice on the other, from 1378 to 1381, Trogir harbour played an important strategic role. The history of medieval Trogir is exceptionally lively. There were conflicts between the city and the feudal lords of the hinterland, and inside the city the walls rang with conflicts between the nobility and the ordinary people, between the people and the clergy, and the bishop and the clergy. Some of these conflicts ended with a decapitation, as was the case in the conflict between the adherents of the Hungarian and Bosnian rulers. During this period, Trogir also developed a full community life. Although agriculture was the basis of their lives, both crafts and trade made significant advances. Merchants travelled into the hinterland, especially Bosnia, and visited the ports of Italian cities, including Venice. For the very reason that it experienced such a boom at this time, Trogir has preserved its medieval appearance right up to the present day. It has many Romanesque buildings, and the cathedral and most of the houses in the city date from the 13th century. The medieval history of Trogir is well documented thanks to the 17th century historians Ivan Lučić and Pavao Andreis. An important source for the history of Trogir, and Croatia as a whole, is *The Life of St. John, Bishop of Trogir* (Život Sv. Ivana Trogirskog biskupa), set down in the 13th century.

City square in the 18th century, with St. Mary's Church

Under the Venetians. 1420 to 1797 was a period of uninterrupted Venetian rule. Following bombardment from galleys, Trogir fell into Venetian hands, causing the bishop and many nobles to flee. The Venetians erected a fortress called Kamerlengo on the hitherto unprotected western side of the city to further strengthen their hold. From the end of the 15th century Trogir was also threatened with attack by the Turks, with battles taking place in the immediate vicinity of the city. It was left without the hinterland areas of its communal territory. Wars with the Turks in the 17th century prompted the Venetian authorities to build more fortresses, so-called bastions, of which only some traces remain visible. In the 15th century a great deal of building work was still going on in Trogir, so that the Renaissance has left significant marks. During the 17th and 18th centuries the economic strength of the city declined, which is why remains of the Baroque era in Trogir are considerably fainter. Also in Trogir, the fall of the Venetian Empire resulted in anarchy, with the ordinary people rebelling against

Old Trogir

the nobility. Some nobles were murdered on the city square on 15th June 1797.

The 19th and 20th centuries. In 1797, Trogir was joined to the Austrian province of Dalmatia. From 1806 to 1814 it was under the French, after which the Austrians regained control until 1918. Following several decades of political struggles, in 1887 the National Party (Narodna stranka) won the elections, demanding unification with Dalmatia and Croatia. In the second half of the 20th century, this originally agricultural region was more and more given over to the tourist industry. ■

Sights

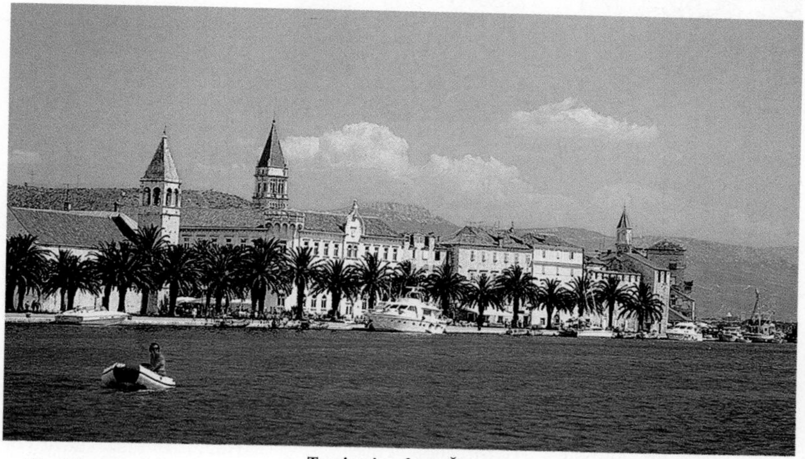

Trogir, view from Čiovo

The **historical city centre***** is the most interesting sight in Trogir. It consists of two parts: to the east, the city in the narrower sense, and to the west, the farm workers' quarter known as Pasika, which was also enclosed by the city walls. There are hardly any houses in the city without a particular stylistic mark, coat of arms or inscription. Many places and houses are still standing which date back to the 13th century, and about 10 churches, but these are only the best-known sights. A special feature of Trogir, in its Dalmatian context, is the pinnacle of achievement of its stone work and sculpture. Because of the great value of the whole of the city centre as a monument, in 1997 the city was placed on the UNESCO list of sites of the world heritage.

••••••••••••

The **city walls and gates****. On the southern side of the city, a large stretch of the medieval city walls has been preserved with towers dating from the period between the 13th and the 14th century (the remainder of the walls were demolished mainly at the beginning of the 19th century). In the centre of the southern walls a new **city gate** (number ⑩) was opened in 1593 and has remained intact to the present day. It was built in the Mannerist style. On the gate there is an inscription praising the city, once under the Romans, and its people. Immediately next to the gate there is a **loggia** (now a fish market) where at one time travellers spent the night after the city gates had been shut. On the south-western edge of the city there is a **fortress** known as **Kamerlengo**** (number ❸) which housed Venetian troops. The fortress was built after 1420, by enclosing the south-western corner of the city walls, although the polygonal tower here is from an earlier date. Nowadays it is used as an open air theatre. In front of it is the memorial park for the Trogir area in the anti-fascist war.

••••••••••••

On the northern side of the city there is a Baroque city gate from the 17th century, with a Gothic statue showing the city's patron saint, Bishop Ivan (John).

••••••••••••

St. Mark's Tower (Sveti Marko; number ❷ on the plan) on the north-western edge of the city stands built in the 15th century to defend the part of the city facing the mainland. In

Kamerlengo Fortress

between the two fortresses (St. Mark's and Kamerlengo) is a **Gloriette** (NUMBER ❶), a circular colonnade built in honour of Marshall Marmont, the military commander of Dalmatia during the period of French rule.

●●●●●●●●●●●

The **city square** (NUMBER ❽ ON THE PLAN) is on the eastern side of the city. Both the main streets, running east-west and north-south, lead into the square. The cathedral is on the square (where in Roman times, it would appear, there was a temple), also the City hall (the former Count's residence), the City loggia, or porch, which once served as the City court, and palaces and houses of the noble Ćipiko family. Near the square (once actually on the square) there are the ruins of an early medieval church, St. Mary's (Sveta Marija).

●●●●●●●●●●●

The **Cathedral***** is a triple-naved basilica on a site where there was once an early-Christian cathedral, according to tradition, which was demolished in the 12th century when the Saracens attacked the city. The present building was begun at the beginning of the 13th century. Like the older one, it is also dedicated to St. Lawrence (Sveti Lovro) but it is better known as St. John's Cathedral (Sveti Ivan) after Bishop John, who died in 1111, and stood out for his saintly lifestyle at a time when the Hungarian King Koloman had taken over Dalmatia and Croatia. Most of the work in the construction of the cathedral took place in the 13th century, meaning that the building is mainly in Romanesque style, whilst the vault inside is Gothic as it was built during the 15th century. Work on the **bell-tower** began at the end of the 14th century but it was not completed until the end of the 16th century, in Mannerist style. The first floor is in Gothic style and it was built by Masters Stjepan and Matej. After it had been demolished by the Venetians in 1420, it was restored by Matija Gojković. The second floor is in low Gothic style and was probably the work of Venetian masters, as it is reminiscent of the windows of the famous Venetian Palazzo Ca d'oro. The final floor was built by Trifun Bokanić (1575-1609). On top of the bell tower there are four statues, the work of the Venetian sculptor Alessandro Vittoria (1525-1608). In the centre of the facade, within a small round opening, there is the carved coat of arms of the most powerful Croatian-Hungarian King, Ludvic I of the Angevin dynasty.

●●●●●●●●●●●

The Cathedral has a **Romanesque portal** which was built and signed in 1240 by the greatest Croatian master sculptor, Radovan. Most of the portal was carved by the master

Cathedral

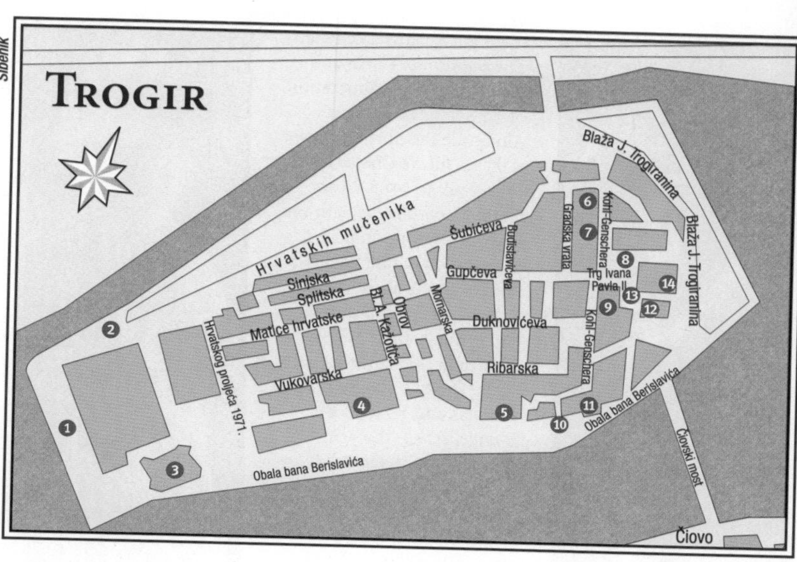

himself, but some other hands are distinguishable, those of his pupils and followers. In terms of its thematic concept, the portal is divided into two parts: upper and lower. The upper part shows scenes from the Gospels, that is, the life of Christ. On the lunette there is the scene of the Nativity, and inside the arch above the lunette there are angels looking adoringly at the scene. The lunette and this arch are the work of Master Radovan. Over them there is another arch which also shows scenes from the life of Christ. On the interior of the doorposts (also the work of Master Radovan) there are pictures showing the various work done during the different seasons of the year. Radovan also worked on the two small columns covered in reliefs.

On the exterior doorpost the saints and apostles are represented; the interior of the same posts are decorated with figures of exotic animals and fantastic creatures (centaurs and mermaids). Both the internal and external doorposts rest on the back of bearers bent over, who are also the work of Radovan himself. Beside the portal, standing on the backs of two lions, stand the figures of our sinful ancestors, Adam and Eve.

Inside the Cathedral, in the central nave, there is a stone pulpit with delicately chiselled perforated capitals dating from the 13th century. In front of the apse over the altar stands the most beautiful ciborium in Dalmatia. It is thought that it is also the work of Master Radovan. There are two more sculptures on the ciborium: Mary and the Archangel Gabriel showing the scene of the Annunciation. They were carved in the first half of the 14th century by Master Mavar. In the main nave there are Gothic choir stalls which

Portal of the Cathedral by Master Radovan

Detail of the portal of Master Radovan (allegory of January)

were made in about 1439 by Ivan Budislavić. In the cathedral there are also valuable paintings, including works by Palma the Younger (1544-1628): *The Blessed Augustine Kažotić* and *St. Augustine*, and two by Alessandro Varotario (1588-1648): *St. Mary Magdalene* and *The Burial.* Amongst the many graves here there is the tomb of the great Croatian Mladen III Šubić (died 1348) whose epitaph declares him to be "the shield of the Croats".

At the far end of the entrance hall there is a Gothic and Renaissance **baptistery** which was added to the cathedral in about 1467 by Andrija Aleši (1430-1504), a sculptor of Albanian origins and a pupil of Juraj Dalmatinac (see Šibenik). On its outside wall in the entrance hall there is a Renaissance relief, *The Baptism of Christ* and inside there is an illustration of *St. Jerome in the cave.* Alongside the northern nave is the **St. John's Chapel** (Sveti Ivan) built in 1468 for the Gothic sarcophagus with the body of Bishop John. This is the most elaborate Renaissance sculptural and architectural entity in Dalmatia and is the work of Nikola Firentinac and Andrija Aleši. The two statues (Saint Thomas and St. John the Evangelist) are the work of the most prominent sculptor of the Italian Quattrocento, Ivan Duknović Trogiranin (Johanes Dalmata, 1440 - after 1505) who worked in Rome, Ancona and Hungary. The lowest section of the chapel is decorated with figures of angels before a half-open door. Above them there are figures of saints and apostles in niches; in the centre is a statue of Christ with Mary on one side and John the Baptist on the other. In the lunette is a representation of the coronation of Mary. The ceiling is decorated with heads of angels and in the centre is the bust of God the Father with a globe in his hand. The Gothic **sacristy** was added to the cathedral in

The Madonna in a Rose Garden by Blaž Jurjev Trogiranin - exhibit in the Pinakoteka

St. John the Evangelist, of Ivan Duknović in St. John's Chapel

the 15th century. Amongst other valuable items, particularly significant is a Gothic cabinet made in the same century by Grgur Vidov. In the windows, various valuable items are on display, especially reliquaries. These items date from the 13th century and later. Here you can also find a silver Gothic seal given to the Trogir clergy by the Croatian-Hungarian Queen, Elizabeta and her daughter Marija. Especially valuable is a Gothic hood with scene of St. Martin giving part of his cloak to a beggar, embroidered in gold thread and pearls.

The **city loggia**** is on the city square, and has served many purposes in its

City loggia

history. First of all it was a court, mentioned as early as the 14th century. Its present appearance was completed in the 15th century, when Nikola Firentinac chiseled the relief over the judge's chair. On the outer wall of the loggia, facing the tower with the city clock, chains are still hanging which were used to hold offenders condemned to public ridicule. Inside the loggia is a relief, the work of Ivan Meštrović (s. Šibenik, Drniš), showing Petar Berislavić of Trogir, a great figure in Hungarian and Croatian history. He was bishop, then, amongst other honours, he was a Croatian Ban and was killed in 1520 in the struggles against the Turks. He fought in defence of his homeland with all he had, even selling his property. His heroism is retold in Hungarian and Croatian literature of the time. The house where he was born has been preserved almost intact in Trogir. He fled from there as an opponent of the Venetians.

••••••••••••

The **city clock tower** (NUMBER ⓭ ON THE PLAN) rises over St. Sebastian's Church (Sveti Sebastijan) and was built in the 15th century, in gratitude for salvation from the plague. The sculptures of Christ and St. Sebastian were carved by Nikola Firentinac. On the eastern side of the tower, in a neighbouring courtyard, there are the ruins of an early medieval chapel, St. Mary's (Sveta Marija).

••••••••••••

The **Duke's palace**** (Kneževa palača; NUMBER ⓮ ON THE PLAN) was built in the 13th century and received its present appearance in the 19th century when it was restored to its condition of the 16th century. On the facade, there are Renaissance windows on the ground floor which would seem to indicate that this is the work of Nikola Firentinac from the 15th century. The upper windows and the overall Mannerist composition of the facade is attributed to Trifun Bokanić, a master from the end of the 16th century. In the courtyard there is a Gothic staircase, which has also been heavily restored, dating from the 15th century. It is traditionally attributed to Matija Gojković. Also in the courtyard there are several fragments, some of which belonged to the city hall, and some, in the spirit of 19th century Romanticism, were brought from other buildings in the city.

••••••••••••

The **large and small Ćipiko Palaces***** (NUMBER ❼ ON THE PLAN) are on the western side of the city square. In the Renaissance courtyard of the smaller palace there is a relief with the figure of a humanist, the work of Ivan Duknović. The large Ćipiko palace has a Gothic triforium carved by Andrija Aleši. The southern Renaissance portal is the work of Nikola Firentinac; the portal facing the cathedral is the work of Ivan Duknović. Inside the palace there is a fine example of a Gothic and Renaissance courtyard. In the atrium there is an exhibition of sculptures with the figure of a cockerel (this is a copy, the original is in the museum),

Loggia - relief with the figure of Petar Berislavić (on the right)

Ćipiko Palace

which, according to tradition, is a trophy from the famous sea battle near Lepanto. There are many famous people connected with this palace. At the beginning of the 15th century, Petar Ćipiko copied Roman inscriptions and decorated manuscripts with works of classic writers. His son Koriolan published war memoirs in Latin (*De bello asiatico*) recording his experiences of the Venetian-Turkish wars in Levant. Koriolan's granddaughter Milica Ćipiko made tapestries which were sung about in the 16th century in Croatian verses by the poet Hanibal Lucić. In the 17th century, in the rich library belonging to this family, a hitherto unknown extract from the description of the feast of Trimalchionis from the work of the Roman writer Petronius Arbiter was discovered.

••••••••••••

St. Martin's Church***
(St. Barbara's Church; Sveti Martin, Sveta Barbara; NUMBER 9 ON THE PLAN) is an excellently preserved early medieval church from the 11th century. Some of its pillars date from the Roman era. The church is actually an early medieval radical conversion of an even earlier early Christian basilica. In the church, part of an altar rail was discovered with an inscription mentioning the name Dobrica, who was probably a donor to the church.

••••••••••••

The **Church of St. John the Baptist***** (Sveti Ivan Krstitelj and Pinacotheca, collection of sacred art; NUMBER 12 ON THE PLAN) is a Romanesque building from the 13th century, and the only remainder of the once mighty Benedictine monastery. Inside, the most valuable items of Trogir's art are on display: the paintings *St. Jerome* and *St. Ivan* by G. Bellini from 1489. The greatest Gothic artist in Dalmatia Blaž Jurjev-Trogiranin is represented by several works from the first half of the 15th century. There is also a whole collection of codices, including the famous illustrated *Trogir Gospel* from the 13th century.

••••••••••••

St. Nicholas' Convent***
(Sveti Nikola; the Kairos art collection; NUMBER 11 ON THE PLAN) was founded in the 11th century as a Benedictine convent, located in a complex of buildings of various ages along the southern city walls. St. Nicholas' Church also belongs to the convent, with its Baroque interior. In the medieval courtyard there is a Greek inscription on the wall. Amongst the valuable works of art in this collection, it is worth mentioning a Romanesque painting of the Madonna

Poet with wreath, the work of Ivan Duknović in the small Ćipiko Palace

and Child from the 13th century, a painted crucifix from the 14th century, reliefs, a wooden polyptych from the 15th century, and a series of paintings by the Venetian Baroque artist Niccolo Grassi. The most popular exhibit is a collection of reliefs with the figure of the deity Kairos, a copy of a piece by Lysippus, which is considered to be the greatest example of Greek art in Dalmatia. Kairos was the ancient Greek god of the right

Kairos, 1st century BC, exhibit in St. Nicholas' Monastery

moment, which was decisive for an individual and had to be taken advantage of. An epigram on Kairos by Poseidonios says "Why does your hair fall over your forehead? So you can catch me if you meet me. Why is the back of your head bald? Once I start to fly with winged feet, no one can ever catch me from behind, no matter how hard he tries".

••••••••••••

St. Dominic's Monastery*** with a collection of sacred art; (Sveti Dominik; NUMBER ❹ ON THE PLAN).

The Dominican monastery was built between the 13th and the 15th centuries on the coast at the edge of the suburb known as Pasika. The original Gothic appearance of this court church has been completely preserved. Inside there is a particularly interesting Renaissance grave belonging to the Sobota family which is the work of Nikola Firentinac. The Gothic cloisters have also been well preserved. As part of the monastery there is also a collection of valuable art, including an outstanding reliquary from the 15th century. Outstanding amongst the paintings is a polyptych by Blaž Jurjev.

••••••••••••

Trogir City Museum** (NUMBER ❻ ON THE PLAN) is set up in part of the complex of buildings making up the Garagnin-Fanfogna Palace. The family's library is especially noteworthy. In the outhouse in the courtyard there is a gallery with paintings by the modern artist Cata Dujšin-Ribar; on the ground floor, where there are archaeological remains from prehistoric and Roman buildings, there is a collection of stone monuments. The collection includes pieces by the greatest names in the history of sculpture in Dalmatia, Ivan Duknović and Nikola Firentinac.

••••••••••••

The **Lučić Family Palace** (Lucius) is on the sea front, originally by the city walls (NUMBER ❺ ON THE PLAN). It is linked with a famous Trogir family. Petar Lučić compiled one of the oldest anthologies of Croatian literature in the 16th century, known under the title of *Vrtal* ("Garden"). His son Ivan, is thought to be the founder of the scientifically based Croatian Historiography; his greatest work is *The History of Dalmatia and Croatia* (*De regno Dalmatiae et Croatiae*) printed in Amsterdam in 1666.

Stone Collection of the City Museum

EXCURSIONS

Putto with Torch, by Ivan Duknović, exhibit in the City Museum

Bijaći

5 KM EAST OF TROGIR, IN A VALLEY IN THE DIRECTION OF LABIN.

The Roman settlement Siculi was located in this area, which was where the Emperor Claudius moved his veteran soldiers. At the beginning of the 9th century this was one of the main centres of the Croatian state (see Trogir, the period of Croatian and Croatian-Hungarian rule). Nowadays, there are the ruins of the early medieval church, St. Martha's (Sveta Marta) where several inscriptions have been found and which was built on the foundation of an early Christian basilica. Finds and historical data point to the fact that there were at one time farm buildings belonging to the Croatian rulers alongside this church.

Čiovo**

THE ISLAND OF ČIOVO (28.8 KM²) HAS 6 SETTLEMENTS: ČIOVO, ARBANIJA, SLATINE, ŽEDNO, GORNJI OKRUG AND DONJI OKRUG.

It is joined to Trogir by a drawbridge. On the island is a suburb which is in fact part of Trogir. Čiovo was settled in pre-historic times, which can be seen from several of the buildings. There are traces of the Roman era here too. In the later Roman era Čiovo (then known as Bua or Boa) was a place of exile for prominent heretics. The monastic way of life began on the island as early as the late Roman era.

Altar rail of St. Martha's Church

In the Middle Ages there was a leper colony on the island.

The **Monastery of St. Anthony*** (Sveti Ante) on Drid is particularly interesting as it is built over a cave. Amongst the works of art in this monastery, one of the most valuable paintings is by Palma the Younger showing St. Anthony and St. Paul in the desert, and there is a statue of St. Mary Magdelene by Ivan Duknović. On the coast (in the village of Arbanija) there is a **Dominican monastery, Holy Cross**** (Sveti Križ) whose Gothic appearance has been well preserved; it dates from the 15th century. Amongst its works of art the most famous are a Gothic wooden crucifix which is revered as miraculous, and a painting by Matija Pončun. In **Žedno** there is a Medieval chapel to **St. Moor*** (Sveti Mavro). On the rocks on the east of the island alongside buildings belonging to hermits is the **Church of Our Lady of Prizidnica** (Gospa od Prizidnice) where there was a painted Gothic crucifix (now kept in the parish church of the village of Slatine).

On the western side of Čiovo the small island of **Fumija** stretches into the sea. On this island there are the remains of an early Christian chapel, St. Euphemia (Sveta Eufemija). It is likely that King Bela IV hid from the Tatars on this island.

Marina

Marina**

12 KM WEST OF TROGIR, ON THE ROAD TO ŠIBENIK.

This village is surrounded by walls which were built in the 15th century, during the Turkish onslaughts. It was part of the property of the Bishops of Trogir. The gate of the castle is still standing, with their coat of arms, also there is a chapel and a tower which has been converted into a hotel.

Seget Donji*

2 KM TO THE WEST OF TROGIR, ON THE ŠIBENIK ROAD.

This village was a planned settlement, surrounded by walls, built in the 16th century, during the period when the Turks posed a constant threat in this area. In the parish church there is a painted crucifix from the 14th century which came from the circle of Paolo Veneziano. Sutilja Hill rises over Seget, on whose peak in the centre of a ring formed by the walls of prehistoric earthworks, stands the medieval Church of St. Elijah (Sveti Ilija). On the side of the hill, there was a stone quarry in the Roman era, from which high quality stone was extracted, some of it being used to make buildings such as the altar dedicated to Heracles.

Near Gornji Seget (Upper Seget), in the village of Baradići is the Romanesque Church of St. Vitus (Sveti Vid) near which some monumental gravestones have been found, decorated with various symbols. Gravestones like this date from somewhere between the 13th and 15th centuries and can be found around other churches in the Trogir region. ■

Split

Located 43°31' N., 16°26' E. Population 178 583; the second biggest city in Croatia. It is the county town of a county that covers an area of 4 520 km^2 and has a population of 467 899. Mean January temperature: air 8.1°C, sea 12.1°C; mean July temperature: air 26.2°C, sea 23.6°C.

Prehistory. In the broader area around what is now Split, remains of pottery, weapons and jewellery have been discovered, demonstrating the existence of human life on the Split peninsula very early on in history. In the Krčine caves above Klis, remains of "impresso" ceramics (with decorations pressed into the clay) have been discovered. In Kučine there are finds from the Neolithic era, from the same period as those from Markova špilja caves (see below) on Hvar, and in the centre of Split itself a stone hammer was found dating from the middle Neolithic era. Copper and gold items from the 2nd millennium BC confirm the existence of well-developed trade routes in this region, both with the hinterland and with the Mediterranean. In the last centuries BC, the Illyrian Delmati tribe moved into the Solin-Kaštela bay and Salona (Solin) became an important military base and port. In the first millennium BC there was already a small Illyrian settlement called Aspalathos in the area of present-day Split.

Portrait of Diocletian on a Roman coin

The Greek and Roman eras. Like Solin, Aspalathos (Spalatum,Split) was settled by Greeks from Issa (Vis). They probably lived together with the Illyrians and it is likely that the Greeks actually named the settlement (Aspalathos is Greek for Spanish broom (Spartium junceum) a thorny plant very common in Southern Dalmatia). The Romans conquered this area in 78 BC when Gaius Casconius defeated the Delmati. Situated as it was between metropolitan Salona (see below) and the Greek settlement of Epetion (Stobreč), Aspalathos did not appear to have a chance of developing into a larger settlement. At the beginning of their rule in Aspalathos the Romans built several farm buildings (Villae rusticae) and on Marjan point they erected a temple to the goddess Diana. At the end of the 3rd century, the Roman Emperor Diocletian (c. 245-316) built a palace here, the centre of the future city.

Corinthian capitals from the Peristyle

The Migrations of the Nations. The real development of Split began after the Avars had razed Salona at the beginning of the 7th century. At that time, the inhabitants of the ruined and uninhabitable city fled to the Central Dalmatian islands and the better protected ancient cities. According to the famous chronicler of Split, Toma the Archdeacon (1201-1268), the leader of the Salona people who moved into Diocletian's palace was Sever. The Emperor's palace became home to the new inhabitants. Together with other old Roman cities in the former Roman province of Dalmatia (Krk, Rab, Osor, Zadar, Trogir, Dubrovnik and Kotor) Split too admitted the authority of Byzantium. The Bishopric was also transferred from Salona to Split. When Pope John (640-642), who was born in Solin, sent Abbot Martin to Dalmatia and Istria to gather up the reliquaries of Christian martyrs, it is certain that the church in Split also acquired the bones of the martyrs of Salona. This was of vital importance to the future development of both the church and society and the significance of Split in Dalmatia.

Under Croatian Counts and Kings. The Croatian state was founded in the ninth century in the immediate vicinity of Byzantine Split. The city of Split maintained various forms of contact with the new inhabitants, from political and official state relationships to inter-marriage. At that time the infiltration of the Croats into Split also began. From the time of the Byzantine Emperor Basil I (867-886) Byzantium paid the Croatians a tribute (tributum pacis), an assurance of peaceful co-existence, which shows how strong the new state had become, to be an equal partner in the politics of the Adriatic. The links between Split and the Croatian state came especially to the fore at the Church Synod meetings in Split in 925 and 928 during the reign of King Tomislav. At the first council meeting, where papal legates were also present, along with Dalmatian Bishops and Grgur, Bishop of Nin (see Nin), the church in Split became a metroplitan church covering the area governed by the former Archbishopric of Salona. At the second meeting Byzantine Dalmatia and the territory of the Croatian state became united in church matters and

Diocletian's Palace, reconstruction according to J. B. Fischer von Erlach (1724)

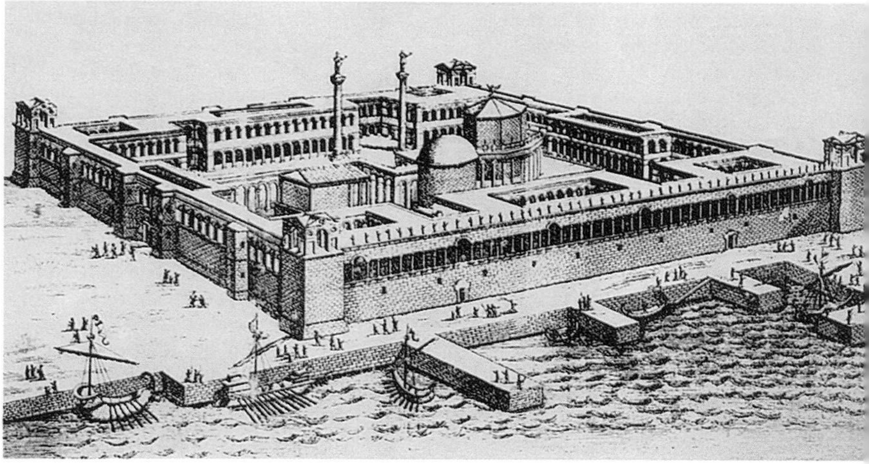

Split became the church capital for the whole of Dalmatia and Zahumlje. Thus Zadar lost its primacy and Bishop Grgur of Nin was defeated. When the Venetian Doge Pietro II Orseolo began a military campaign against the Neretvans (1000) in order to protect the safe passage of his fleet in the Mediterranean, he occupied Split but his rule was short-lived. During the entire 10th and 11th centuries Split shared the fate of Byzantine Dalmatia, whose centre was in Zadar. Split however did have an independent city government at whose head was a Prior or Rector chosen from the circle of the patrician families. This government diplomatically worked out the best way of relating to the neighbouring Croats, Venice and Byzantium. It was not until the reign of King Zvonimir, who was crowned in Solin as King of Croatia and Dalmatia in 1075, that the dualism between the Croats and the Dalmatians was solved. Zvonimir took over the Dalmatian cities, including Split with the Pope's help. In the Croatian-Hungarian state Split retained the status of an autonomous community. The community made its own laws, chose its own leaders (the Rector was often chosen from amongst the prominent Croatian families) and had independent courts. The strengthened community increased its trade links and signed agreements with Pisa, Piran and Dubrovnik, fought wars over the border with Trogir, with the Kačić family of Omiš and with Poljica, and resisted the Tatars. When the nobility had taken over the rule of Split entirely there was a rebellion by the ordinary people in 1389. Three centuries' rule by the Croatian-Hungarian kings resulted in the city's expansion. It

Detail from the door of the Cathedral

spread beyond the walls of Diocletian's palace, craft workshops developed, as did trade, agriculture and seafaring, contacts were made with the Mediterranean and the Slavic hinterland, and the city also became richer in artistic terms, with the building of many important buildings. Split lost the character of a Roman city, both in terms of the make-up of the population, and in terms of its cultural identity, and it became Croatian.

Under the Venetians. Venice conquered Split in 1420 and its rule lasted until 1797. The Venetians gradually limited the municipal autonomy of the city (the Rector was a Venetian), lessening its economic activity and power. At the beginning of the 16th century the Turks appeared in Dalmatia not far from Split (see Klis and Kaštel). With the fall of Klis to the Turks in 1537, the border with their Empire became the River Jadro in Solin. The threat from the Turks lasted throughout the 16th and 17th centuries and they constantly attacked Split, stealing, burning fields, houses and churches. This caused the city's development to slow down and instead of spreading further, the city fortified itself with walls.

During the Cretan war (Kandijski rat; 1645-1669) building work on a polygonal fortress around the city was completed, and a huge fortress was also built on Gripe Hill. On Bačvice point fortifications were built and the sea approaches protected. The Jew Danijel Rodriga founded a customs house in 1578, as well as a bank and a field hospital. In 1776 an academy of economics was founded in

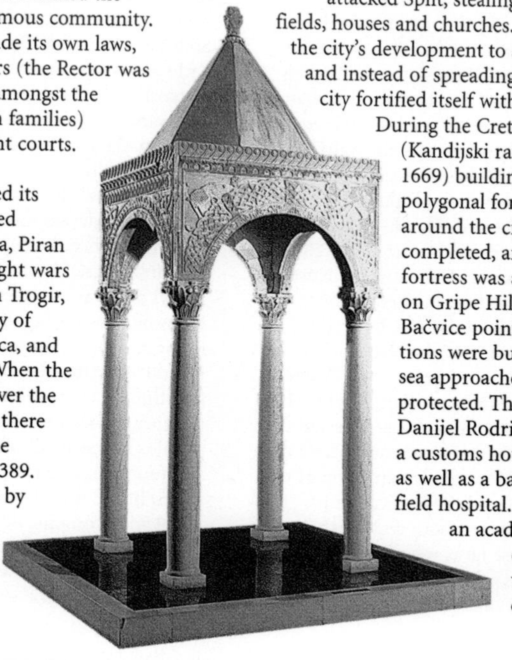

Reconstruction of the altar ciborium of an Old Croatian church

Split at the end of the 18th century according to Cassas.

Split, with the intention of encouraging agriculture, crafts, trade and sea travel. In 1733 the Illyrian Academy was founded by Ivan Petar Marchi, which involved all prominent Split people in discussions on literature and culture.

From 1797-1815. With the fall of Venice, Split admitted the authority of Austria until 1805. At that time in Split a rebellion broke out against Colonel Matutinović, a spokesman for the French Revolution, and he was killed. After the Treaty of Požun (Bratislava) the French ruled Dalmatia for a short time (1805-1813). In that period several significant projects were undertaken: the walls were partially demolished, the coastal walls were strengthened, roads built and public lighting introduced. Thanks to the Franciscan Andrija Dorotić (1761-1837), the idea of uniting Dalmatia and Northern Croatia emerged for the first time.

Under the Austrians. Following the fall of Napoleon in 1814 the Habsburg dynasty once again regained power over Dalmatia and remained in control until 1918. The most important events in that period occurred in the political realm where there was a struggle for the Croatization of the communities and the unification of Dalmatia with northern and north-eastern Croatia. These ideas were put forward by the members of the National Party (Narodna stranka) led by Dr. Gajo Bulat. Opposed to them were the "autonomists" who supported the idea of a separate Dalmatia with cultural links with Italy, led by Dr. Ante Bajamonti. The battle was won by the National Party and the community passed into Croat hands on 9th November 1882, although there was at that time no unification of Croatia.

The 20th century. With the collapse of the Austro-Hungarian monarchy and the end of the First World War (1918), Split became part of the Kingdom of the Serbs, Croatians and Slovenes (Yugoslavia). In the period between the two wars, the traditional political centre of Dalmatia, Zadar, came under Italy, leaving Split to become the capital of the coastal region. This had a strong influence on the city's development. When the Italians bombed the city on 6th April 1941 Split found itself in the thick of World War II and was occupied by the Italians. Many citizens distinguished themselves in the resistance. Units of the People's Liberation Army liberated the city for the first time in 1943, and finally on 26th October 1944. In free Split, the first people's government of Federal Croatia was founded, on 14th April 1945. After the war Split experienced a period of great social and economic development, becoming the largest city on the Eastern Adriatic coast and the venue for many important cultural events.■

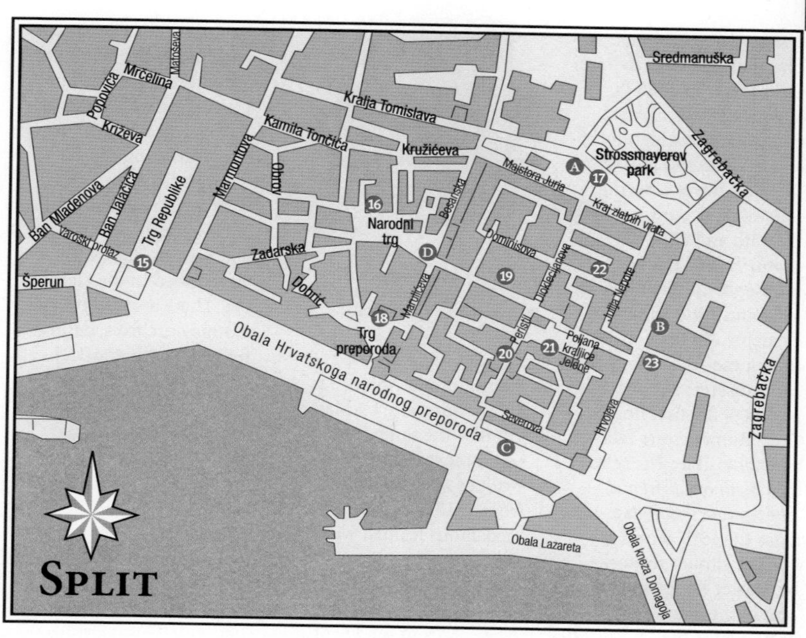

Sights

Diocletian's Palace***
(►►► s. 238)

The **Cathedral of St. Domnius***** (Sveti Duje; NUMBER ㉑ ON THE PLAN), is an octagonal building built at the same time as the palace, as a mausoleum for Emperor Diocletian. In the 7th century the mausoleum was converted into a cathedral. Thus fate played strange games with Diocletian: in the mausoleum of an Emperor who sought to wipe out Christianity, a cathedral was built, and in the main Roman temple, a baptistery. The cathedral is circular inside, divided up by four semicircular and square niches, and eight columns in the lower part on which eight smaller columns rest. Between the first and second rows of columns there is a frieze with scenes of Eros hunting, and amongst the figures, a portrait of Diocletian with his wife Prisca. The ornate entrance is typical of Hellenistic architecture. The cathedral is crowned with a brick dome which was originally covered with mosaics. Beneath the cathedral is a crypt (St. Lucy's Chapel; Sveta Lucija). The six-sided pulpit belongs to the late Romanesque era (the second half of the 13th century). The main altar was built in the 17th century. There are paintings on it by the prominent Croatian artist Matija Pončun (Ponzoni). The northern altar (from 1770 known as St. Domnius' altar) is the work of the Venetian sculptor G. M. Morlaiter from 1767. The right-hand altar (in the southeastern niche) is the old altar of St. Domnius (Sv. Duje). It was built in late-Gothic style by Bonino da Milano in 1427, and the ceiling was painted by Dujam Vušković in 1429. The original altar of the saint was an Early Christian sarkophagus with a depiction of the Good Shepherd. In the north-eastern niche is the altar of St. Anastasius (Sveti Staš)

Cathedral of St. Domnius

a martyr from Salona. The altar was built by Juraj Dalmatinac in 1488 (s. Šibenik). Particularly noteworthy is a high relief of *The Scourging of Christ.* The **bell-tower** over the stairway was built between the 13th and 16th centuries, but it was thoroughly refurbished in 1882 and 1908 and has elements of the Romanesque, Gothic and some discrete Renaissance lines. On the first floor three Romanesque reliefs are still visible. The reliefs *The Birth of Christ* and *The Annunciation* date from the 13th century, and are similar to works by Master Radovan (see Trogir, the cathedral), whilst the relief with the figures of St. Peter, Domnius and Anastasius is an inferior piece by Master Oton of the same time. The **monumental door** is the work of Andrija Buvina, from 1214. On 28 medallions framed with floral ornamentation, Master Buvina has depicted scenes from the life of Christ in carved walnut wood. The **sacristy** was built at the beginning of the 17th century. The 13th century Romanesque choir stalls are particularly fine, consisting of two benches richly decorated with floral ornamentation, and figures of animals and people. The sides were added in the Gothic era. There are also two Gothic crucifixes, dating from the 14th and 15th centuries, six paintings by Matija Pončun and paintings with scenes from the life of St. Domnius by Petar Ferrari (1685).
The graves of the Capogrosso and Janko Alberti and Žarko Dražojević families are particularly interesting.

Cross-section of Diocletian's mausoleum (the Cathedral)

St. Domnius Cathedral door by Andrija Buvina

On the first floor of the sacristy is the **cathedral treasury**. It houses a rich collection of ecclesiastical art from the early Middle Ages to the 19th century and is one of the most valuable collections of its kind in Dalmatia. Amongst the books here is the famous *Split Gospel* (*Splitski evanđelistar*) from the 8th century, and the 13th century *Historija Salonitana* (*The History of People of Salona*) by Toma the Archdeacon, one of the most important books in Croatia, where the Canon of Split wrote about the history of Split and Solin. There is also the 11th century *Sumpetarski kartular*, (*Kartularium from Sumpetar*) the *Missale Romanum* with silver Romanesque covers, fraternity regulations and other things. Amongst the paintings three of

The Madonna and Child (Romanesque, from the 13th century) are particularly outstanding, as is a dismantled 15th century polyptych, the work of an unknown Venetian master. There are also numerous works in silver, as well as chalices, reliquaries, crucifices and liturgical items, the remains of one time silver altarpiece an the figure of an apostle being quite outstanding (14th century). In the cathedral's periptery there is a collection of sarcophagi of which the one belonging to Prior Petar is particularly interesting. It is an ancient sarcophagus, restored in the 8th and 10th centuries. Over the portal there is the small sarcophagus of the daughter of King Bela IV who died in 1242 in Klis whilst hiding from the invading Tatars.

Figure of a Croatian ruler of the 11th century, relief in the Baptistery

••••••••••••

The **Baptistery** (the pagan temple of Jupiter, converted to a baptistery in the early Middle Ages) is a square-shaped building which originally had six pillars in the porch, and a richly decorated portal. Inside, the baptismal pool itself is cross-shaped, made up of six tiles, five of which are decorated with braided ornamentation, and the sixth with the figure of Christ. One theory says that this is the figure of King Zvonimir. Along the wall is the sarcophagus of Archbishop John (Ivan), of Roman origins, restored in the 8th and 10th centuries, and next to it is a sarcophagus belonging to Archbishop Lovro.

Detail of the door of the St. Domnius Cathedral

••••••••••••

Other things to see in the palace: With the arrival of new inhabitants the palace became a living city, and a whole series of significant houses, palaces and churches were built and ancient buildings restored. The Romanesque-Gothic palace beside the Golden Gate (NUMBER 17A ON THE PLAN) with 15th century Gothic additions by Juraj Dalmatinac is particularly outstanding. The most important Gothic palace in Split is the Papalić Palace (NUMBER 22 ON THE PLAN) also by Juraj Dalmatinac. The City Museum is now housed in this palace (see below). The Dagubio family palace in Dioklecijanova street 1. was built in the 18th century. It is a Gothic and Renaissance building made by Andrija Aleši. This leading Venetian architect also certainly designed the monumental and typically Baroque Cindro Palace in Krešimirova street (NUMBER 19 ON THE PLAN) in about 1700. The Church of St. Philip Neri (Sveti Filip Neri) was designed by the Venetian architect Francesco Melchiori, a military engineer, in 1735. Inside there is an altarpiece by the 18th century Split artist Sebastijan Devita and a wooden Crucifix of the same time.

••••••••••••

The **Church** and **Monastery of St. Dominic*** (Sveti Dominik; NUMBER 23 ON THE PLAN) stands opposite the Silver Gate. The monastery is a radically restored Baroque building. Inside the church there is a beautiful Baroque altar, and the paintings *The Mystic Wedding of St. Catherine*, by the Venetian master Antonio Zanchi, *The Miracle in Surian*, by Matej Pončun (Ponzoni), *The Miracle of St. Vincent Ferrerius*, by Sebastijan Devita, and a late Gothic illuminated crucifix. The monastery houses beautiful antiphones (from the 14th and 15th centuries), a series of paintings by Vinko Draginja (1850-1926) and books from the library of Marko Marulić. ■

Diocletian's Palace***

Diocletian's Palace (ON THE PLAN A,B,C,D) was built between AD 295 and 305, and is the most important and best preserved Roman building in Croatia. It was built for the Roman Emperor Diocletian (c. 235-316) who was born near Salona and was known as the re-organiser of the Empire and a persecutor of Christians. His decision to spend the last years of his life here can be explained by its closeness to Salona (see below) and the existence of medicinal sulphur springs in the area. Diocletian came to Split only after his abdication (305) and once he died the palace was left to the Emperor's family. Thus it became a refuge for persecuted members of that family, and the last Roman Emperor, Julius the Nephew hid here and died (480) surviving the fall of the Western Roman Empire.

The **ground plan** of the palace is in the form of an irregular rectangle, fortified to the east, north and west with towers. The eastern and western sides are 215 m in length and the southern and northern walls are 180 m. The palace covers an area of 38 500 m². Its form unites elements of Roman villas and fortified castles. It was built of stone from Dalmatia (Brač, Trogir) and some stone was brought from Egypt, Greece and Italy. The **northern wall** of the palace (A) is the most ornate, as it faced Salona. Originally it was fortified with six towers, of which only the two on the corner have been well preserved. The wall is divided up by large windows in the upper part, and in the centre is the Golden Gate (Porta aurea), decorated with niches, pilasters, consoles and semicircular arches over the entrance. There were statues of the tetrarchs (four emperors) over the cornices. Over the gate there was originally a passageway for the guard, and in the Middle Ages battlements were added for the same reason. In the outer passageway over the Golden Gate in the early Middle Ages the early Christian church of St. Martin's (Sveti Martin) was built. The altar rail remains in situ with an inscription and ornamental moulding with a memorial to the priest Dominic, a barrel vault and windows with stone bars. Along the north wall are the remains of

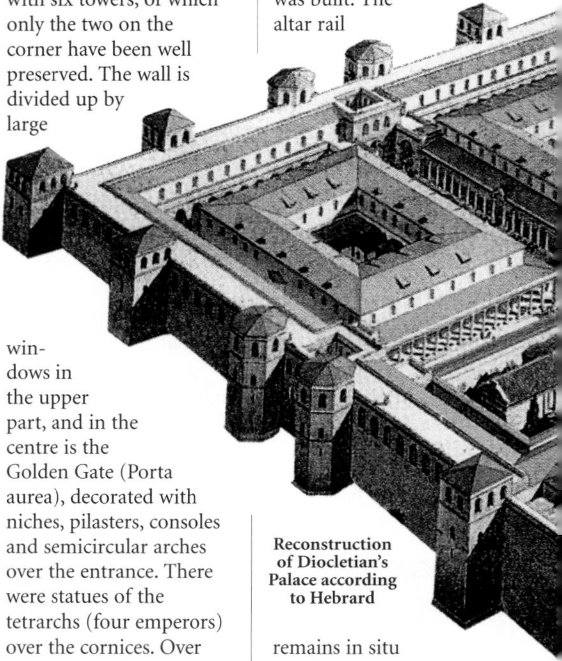

Reconstruction of Diocletian's Palace according to Hebrard

Northern door with the monument of Gregory of Nin

a Benedictine convent and the Church of St. Euphemia (Sveta Eufemija). This church was an early Romanesque triple-naved basilica to which Juraj Dalmatinac (see Šibenik) added a Gothic chapel (St. Arnir) on its southern side in 1444 and carved a relief with the scene of *The stoning of St. Arnir* (s. Kaštel Lukšić). Beside the church there is an elegant Baroque bell tower (18th century) and nearby a huge statue by Ivan Meštrović of *Grgur Ninski* (Gregory of Nin; s. Nin).

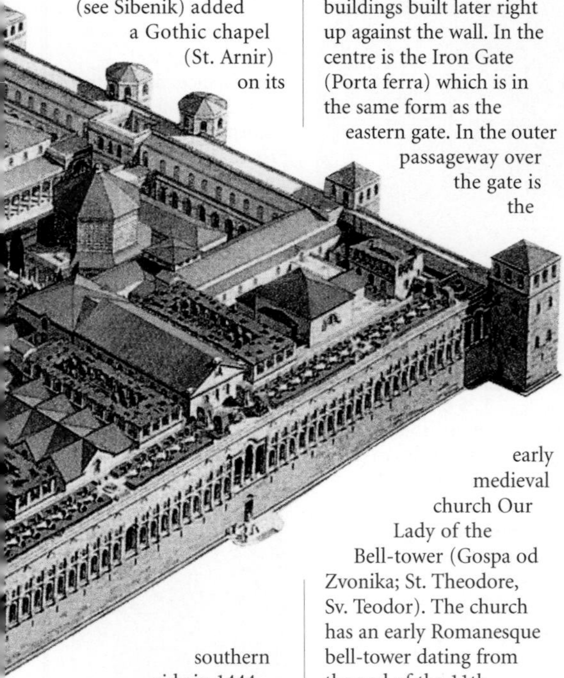

•••••••••••

The **eastern wall** of the palace (B) has been well preserved. In the centre is the Silver Gate (Porta argentea) which is similar to the northern gate, in a humbler form, and the wall ends with a tower on the corner of Hrvojeva street and the promenade, Riva.

•••••••••••

The western wall (D) is least visible because of buildings built later right up against the wall. In the centre is the Iron Gate (Porta ferra) which is in the same form as the eastern gate. In the outer passageway over the gate is the early medieval church Our Lady of the Bell-tower (Gospa od Zvonika; St. Theodore, Sv. Teodor). The church has an early Romanesque bell-tower dating from the end of the 11th century, the oldest in Split. On the altar rail, the prior of Split, Furmin, is mentioned. In the church a particular feature is the early Renaissance lunette with a scene of Our Lady the Protectress (1480) and the Romanesque *Madonna and Child* in the Treasury of the Cathedral also comes from this church.

•••••••••••

The southern facade (C) now runs along the promenade (Riva). In the Roman era the sea came right up to the wall and thus the Bronze Gate (Porta aenea) was used by boats. The lower part of this entrance was most ornate and monumental. Over the lower part there was a porch with arcades (crypto-porticus) and the bronze gate led into the ground floor rooms of the palace, the cellars, which occupied the entire southern side of the building. The cellars have been very well preserved, and the western side is open to the public. The palace was the centre of the future city of Split. It experienced a transformation during the 5th and 6th centuries when new inhabitants moved in. At the end of the last century there were 280 houses in the palace with 2 600 inhabitants. ■

Palace cellars - exhibition rooms today

The Peristyle, the antechamber to the Emperor's quarters

The **Peristyle***** (NUMBER 20 ON THE PLAN) is the main open space in the palace, where the streets Cardo and Decumanus cross. It is surrounded by a colonnade of 6 columns each on the eastern and western sides, with Corinthian capitals holding arches decorated with garlands. The Peristyle is in the shape of a rectangle (27 m x 13.5 m) and the colonnade reaches 5.25 m in height. On the southern side, the Peristyle is enclosed by the Protiron, with four columns carrying a triangular pediment, where there were probably originally statues. In the Renaissance and Baroque eras two chapels were added here: Our Lady of the Conception (Gospa od Začeća) and Our Lady of the Girdle (Gospa od Pojasa). To the southwest is the Romanesque, Renaissance and Baroque palace Grisogono - Cipci. It has a portal by Juraj Dalmatinac (see Šibenik) and the upper floor is by the school of Nikola Firentinac. Inside are the remains of a circular temple to Venus (the Vestibulum) and a Romanesque city hall. On the eastern side is the 16th century Renaissance Chapel of St. Rocco (Sveti Roko) and an Egyptian sphinx dating from 2000 BC. The Peristyle was used as an antechamber to the Emperor's quarters and as a place dedicated to the cult of Diocletian, in which his divine birth was celebrated (on July 21). The Peristyle serves as a stage for theatrical performances during the Split summer festival. Emperor Diocletian's private rooms were on the southern side behind the Peristyle, which served as their entrance hall. The rooms were entered from the Protiron. The residential part of the palace was on the south-western side and the banqueting hall, the triclinium, was to the east. The remains of thermal baths have been discovered on both sides. To the west of the Peristyle, Diocletian built a temple to the god Jupiter, and to the east was his own mausoleum. In the northern part of the building there were apartments for the Emperor's officials, his servants and guard. There were also workshops and an especially large weaving shop. ■

Capital from the Peristyle

Egyptian sphinx from the 2nd millennium BC

The Ethnographic Museum on People's square (Narodni trg)

The **Square "Narodni Trg"** (People's square; NUMBER 16 ON THE PLAN) was once known as St. Lawrence's Square (Trg Svetog Lovre), Weapons Square (Trg oružja), Commerce Square (Gospodarski trg) or (most usually) The Piazza (Pjaca). It was first built in the early Middle Ages when Split began to spread to the west of Diocletian's palace. From the 15th century it was the central city square, in contrast to the Peristyle which remained a church square. The piazza is full of palaces and houses from all eras, giving us a visible panorama of the history of Split, a living Mediterranean city which in humble circumstances welcomed all western stylistic trends.

•••••••••••

The **northern side** was enclosed by Gothic and Renaissance buildings of a public nature, but only the 15th century Gothic city hall remains after demolition work in 1821. This hall was restored in the 19th century. Here, on 14th April 1945, the first national government of Croatia was founded, and there is now an **Ethnographic museum** in the building (see above). Adjoining the museum is the Renaissance Karapić Palace. On the **eastern side**, beside the Iron Gate, is the Romanesque and Gothic house of Cipriano de Ciprianis, built in 1394, with a Romanesque hexaforium, and a statue of St. Anthony in a niche. To the north of the Iron Gate is the ground floor loggia of the city watch, and next to it an interesting Romanesque house (tower) onto which the city clock and bell-tower were built in the 15th century. At the beginning of Bosanska street is the Gothic Cambi Palace. The **southern side** of the square is dominated by a simple but monumental 17th century palace belonging to the Pavlović family, and on the **western side** is the Secession Nakić House.

Marko Marulić, the work of Ivan Meštrović

•••••••••••

In the northern part of the old city centre is the **Church of the Holy Spirit**** (Sveti Duh), a Romanesque and Gothic building, where Andrija Aleši was buried in 1504. On its portal there is a Romanesque relief of Christ and inside there is a fine Romanesque illuminated crucifix, a wooden Gothic crucifix (15th century) and a cycle of paintings with scenes from the life of St. Joseph, the work of the Venetian painter, Girolamo Brusafero (18th century).

•••••••••••

The Square **Trg Preporoda**** (Square of the Revival; NUMBER 18 ON THE PLAN) is also known as Voćni trg (Fruit square). The centre of the square is dominated by a **statue of Marko Marulić** "the father of Croatian literature", who was born in Split in 1450 into a patrician's family. He was a lawyer, but above all a poet, translator and writer of moral and philosophical works, a humanist, famous throughout Europe. He was the author of many works, including *Judita* (the first secular work in Croatian literature), the

Davidias and the Gospels. His book *De institutione bene vivendi* (1506) went through 15 editions in its original version, and was translated into five foreign languages. He died in Split in 1524 and was buried in the Franciscan monastery (see below). The statue is the work of Ivan Meštrović (see Drniš) and it has some lines by the poet Tin Ujević (1891-1955) engraved (see Imotski). Translated, they read: "Farewell, Oh Marule! We will go, for we desperately long for the light of heaven; our banner is waving; let's go, all we rebels".

On the **southern side** of the square is the 15th century city keep and on the **northern side** the dignified 17th century Baroque Milesi palace. In nearby Šubićeva street are the 18th century Baroque Tartaglia Palace and the Romanesque-Gothic Papalić Palace where Juraj Dalmatinac worked in the 15th century.

The **Republic Square** (Trg Republike; NUMBER ⓯ ON THE PLAN) is surrounded on three sides by a Neo-Renaissance complex of buildings, built in the style of the Procurator's Palace in Venice between 1850 and 1910. During the summer this square is the scene of many public performances of which the best known is the Split Festival of Light Music. To the east of the square is Marmontova street, at the beginning of which are the buildings of the Split thermal baths, and at whose end (Gaje Bulata Square) is the Croatian National Theatre, built in Neo-Renaissance style between 1891 and 1893 by the architect Emilio Vecchieti-Bezić, and the **Church and Monastery of Our Lady of Good Health** (Gospa od Zdravlja). Inside the church there is a large fresco by the Croatian artist Ivo Dulčić entitled *Christ the King, Protector of the Croatian people.*

The **Franciscan Church** and **Monastery**** (NUMBER ⓮ ON THE PLAN) is close to the Republic Square. The monastery was founded in the 13th century, but was re-built in the 20th century. Beside the church there are small cloisters which are in keeping with the whole complex. In the church there are the graves of some great men of Split, such as: Toma the Archdeacon (1201-1268) the author of the History of Solin (*Historia Salonitana*, the history of the Split church from Roman times to his own time), Ivan Lukačić (1587-1648), the cathedral organist in Split and the best known composer of his time in Croatia (at the transition from Renaissance to Baroque), Jerolim Cavagnin (1643-

The neo-Renaissance complex of the Procurator's Palace on Trg Republike

Milesi Palace on Trg Preporod

1714), and Ante Trumbić (1864-1938). On a side altar in the church there is a pained crucifix by Blaž Jurjev Trogiranin dating from 1412. The church also houses a collection of art dating from the 15th to the 19th centuries.

••••••••••••

Veli Varoš* is the largest city quarter, situated behind the Franciscan monastery. To the east it is bounded by Jelačić street and to the west by the Marjan cliffs (see below). It is characterised by irregular streets and picturesque architecture. The parish church of Veli Varoš is **Holy Cross** (Sveti Križ), built in 1681, but re-built in the 19th century. The beautiful Baroque bell-tower remains from the old church. On the main altar is a damaged but important Romanesque illuminated 13th century crucifix, on the side altar an altarpiece by Sebastian Devita (18th century) and by Juraj Pavlović (19th century) and on the facade, a large stone Gothic statue entitled *Mourning* dating from the 15th century. **St. Nicholas** on Stagnja (Sveti Mikul na Stagnji; NUMBER ❿ ON THE PLAN) is the oldest church in Veli Varoš. It is an early Romanesque building, built in the 12th century with square apses, a transept and a dome on a high drum. The builder, Ivan, and his wife Tiha are mentioned in an inscription over the doorway.

••••••••••••

Marjan***

178 M HIGH; NUMBER ❸ ON THE PLAN

Marjan is the best known site for outings in Split. Its unique position and beauty have inspired many poets,

Church of St. Michael in Veli Varoš

and thus Marjan is one of the most sung about parts of Croatia. Before Diocletian's palace was built, the Romans built a temple to the goddess Diana on Marjan point. In the early Middle Ages the Statute of Split already regulated a service to take care of the area and the creation of Marjan as a place for outings began in the second half of the 19th century. The bare karst rock has been successfully cultivated, and there are now 168 hectares of Aleppo pines planted here. Some locations (the picturesque, vertical Jerolim cliffs) are nature reserves. The best way to reach the **hilltop** (151 m) is from Varoš. Beneath the peak is the **Natural History Museum** (Prirodoslovni muzej), founded in 1924, with large zoology, mineralogy, botany and palaeontology collections, showing items chiefly from the Dalmatia region.

••••••••••••

Beside the museum there is a **zoo** (NUMBER ❻ ON THE PLAN). At the foot of the **southern side of Marjan** (approach by the coastal road Šetalište Ivan Meštrović) is the city quarter known as Meje. On **Sustipan** peninsula, in the former Split graveyard there are the ruins of a Benedictine church and monastery, St. Stephen's Under the Pines (Sveti Stjepan pod borovima), whose Romanesque and Gothic ruins have been included in a small church of the same name, dating from 1814. In Meje is the Museum of Croatian Archaeological Monuments (see below) and the Ivan Meštrović Gallery.

••••••••••••

On the way from Meje up to the hilltop is the **Chapel of Our Lady of Seven Woes** (Gospa od Sedam žalosti; NUMBER ❹ ON THE PLAN) with a sculpture entitled *Mourning* dating from the 15th century, and **St. Jerome's Church** (Sveti Jere) dating

Lookout point on Marjan

from the 15th century, with a hermit's cave. Inside the church there is a stone altar made by Andrija Aleši in 1480, and on the gate in the church wall and cave there is a relief of John the Baptist. On the same road to the east is the 15th century **Bethlehem Church** (Betlem), which has a Gothic and Renaissance relief of *The birth of Christ, St. Jerome, St. Anthony* and the *Crucifixion* on its main altar.

••••••••••••

Close to Veli Varoš is the 13th century **St. Nicholas' Chapel** (Sveti Nikola; NUMBER ❺ ON THE PLAN) with Romanesque elements, and an old Jewish graveyard.

••••••••••••

Poljud is the north-western part of the city, joined to the southern part by a tunnel running beneath Marjan. In Topuska street, on the sea front, there is a **Franciscan church and monastery**** (NUMBER ❼ ON THE PLAN). The church was built on the site of an older 10th century church. In the centre of this picturesque complex of sacred buildings there are simple Renaissance cloisters with a well and some gravestones, including ones belonging to Bishop Toma Nigris-Mrčić, Katarina Žuvić, the Alberti, Marulić, Cuteis, Capogrosso families etc. The monastery is fortified with a strong Renaissance tower and battlements. The Gothic and Renaissance single-naved church with its two side chapels on its southern side houses several significant works of art. On the main altar there is a large polyptych by Bellini's pupil Girolamo da Santacroce (1549), which has Renaissance characteristics. The most interesting figure is that of St. Domnius who is holding a model of Split in his hand. Santacroce's son Francesco painted the *Madonna with St. Peter and St. Clare*, and the painting *The Madonna, our Protector* is also the work of a Venetian artist under Bellini's influence, Benedetto Diana. Inside the church there are also several wooden Gothic crucifixes, dating from the 15th century. In the monastery museum there is *a Portrait of Toma Nigris*, by the great Venetian artist of the late Renaissance era, Lorenzo Lotto, from 1527. The portrait is one of the most important Renaissance paintings in Dalmatia as a whole, and its fine range of colours and the way it leads us deep into the psyche of the subject place it amongst the most mature works of art. The collection also includes two small wooden crucifixes by Fra Fulgencije Bakotić, an 18th

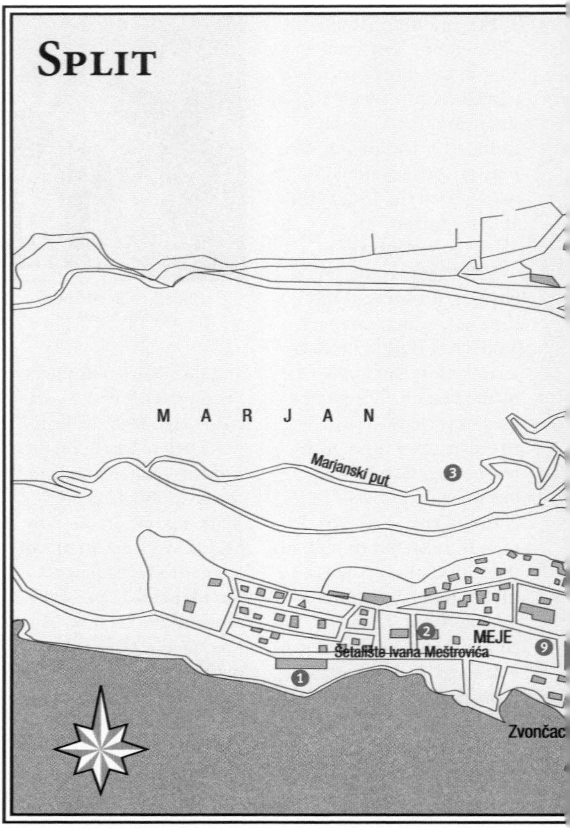

Franciscan monastery on Poljud

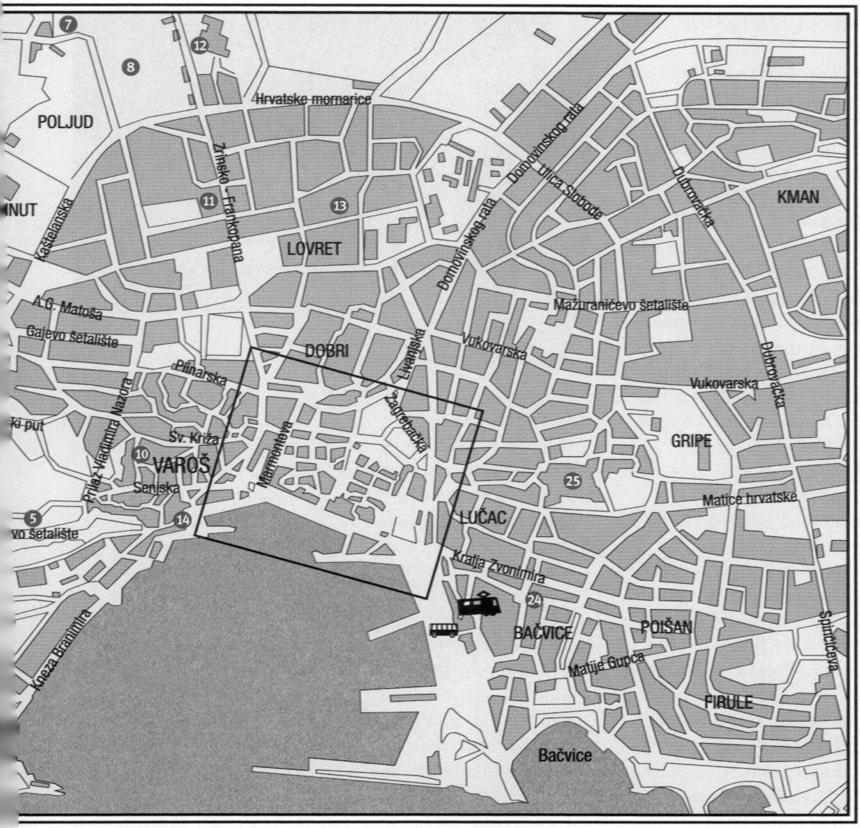

century woodcarver, and two books of choral works by Fra Bono Razmilović dating from the end of the 17th century, with highly decorated initial letters.

••••••••••••

Next to the monastery is the **"Hajduk" football ground*** (NUMBER ❽ ON THE PLAN) designed by B. Magaš, a major venue for the Mediterranean games which were held in Split in 1979.

••••••••••••

On the southern side of Zrinsko-Frankopanska street is the pre-Romanesque **Church of the Holy Trinity***** (Sveto Trojstvo; NUMBER ⓬ ON THE PLAN), an excellently preserved six-sided 9th century building, with a dome.

A 9 km long **Roman aqueduct*** runs to the east of the Split-Solin road, from the source of the River Jadro to Split. The so-called "dry bridge" has been best preserved (180 m), with its huge pillars and arches made of cut stone blocks. It is still in use today.

••••••••••••

On the **eastern part of the city** is **St. Clare's Monastery** (Sveta Klara; NUMBER ㉔ ON THE PLAN). It was founded in the 13th century and until 1884 was situated in Diocletian's palace. This beautiful new Neo-Romanesque monastery houses many works of art. The most valuable item is a thirteenth century illuminated Romanesque crucifix. In terms of its quality, this crucifix is one of the most important works of art from that time in Dalmatia, and in terms of style, it can be ranked with works of Tuscany from the mature Romanesque era. The crucifix has been linked with three Romanesque Madonnas in the cathedral treasury (see above) and the Split Romanesque School of Art but in terms of quality it is reminiscent of masterpieces which go beyond mere local significance. On the fine, marble Baroque altar there is a Gothic wooden crucifix dating from the 15th century, and in the monastery there are paintings dating from the 15th to the 18th century, liturgical items and robes.

••••••••••••

To the north of the monastery, between the city quarters known as Lučac and Gripe is **Gripe Fortress*** (NUMBER ㉕ ON THE PLAN), built between 1648 and 1657 and designed by Domenico Maglia, a military engineer. The fortress is in the form of a trapezium, with four keeps, successfully making use of the natural shape of the land. The former Austrian barracks have been converted into the Historical Archives. To the west of St. Clare's Monastery on the corner of Viška street and Matija Gubec street is the **Monastery** and **Church of Our Lady of Poišan*** (Gospa od Poišana). The church was built in the 17th century and it houses a Gothic statue entitled *St. Anne and the Madonna.* The church also has several votive pictures given by sailors.

MUSEUMS AND GALLERIES

The **City Museum**** (Gradski muzej; NUMBER ㉒ ON THE PLAN) is housed in the most prominent Gothic palace in Split, which belonged to the Papalić family. The museum houses items, documents and books dealing with the history of Split, and also has a valuable coin collection. One of the museum's outstanding exhibits is a Romanesque sculpture from the cathedral bell-tower. The Emanuel Vidović gallery (1870-1953) is also housed in the museum. He was born in Split and was one of the greatest Croatian artists. A collection of the best works from all the various phases of his life has been assembled.

Museum of the city of Split

••••••••••••

The **Ethnographic Museum** (see Narodni Trg Square; NUMBER ⑯ ON THE PLAN) is housed in a Gothic building which was once the city hall. The museum was founded in 1910 and has a rich collection of national costumes, embroidery, everyday objects and jewellery from whole of Dalmatia.

••••••••••••

The **Museum of Croatian Archaeological Monuments***** (Muzej hrvatskih arheoloških spomenika; NUMBER ⑨ ON THE PLAN) was founded in 1893 in Knin, but was moved to Split after the Second World War, and has been in this building (which was designed by M. Kauzlarić) since 1976. The museum has collections of items from the material remains of the earliest periods of Croatian history, from the 7th to the 12th century,

Diocletian's aqueduct

The interior of the Museum of Croatian Archaeological Monuments

from the whole of Dalmatia, and it also owns an important collection of sculptures, weapons, money, jewellery, pottery and household objects. One particularly outstanding item is the Višeslav baptistery from Nin (9th century), a key artistic and historical monument of the old Croatian state. There are also stone ciboria from Bijaći in Kaštela and the Bishopric of Knin, the sarcophagus of Queen Jelena of Solin (976), which is exceptionally significant as a "document" showing the chronology of the Croatian kings, the sarcophagus of Petar the Black (Petar Crni) of Jesenice near Split (the end of the 11th century), a gable with the figure of the Madonna (11th century), a transenna with the figures of the Madonna and Child and Croatian dignitaries from the Bishopric of Knin (11th century), and fragments of braided ornamentation with the names of the Croatian Counts Branimir, Mucimir and King Držislav. The museum also possesses a large jewellery collection (especially 7th century gold jewellery from Golubić near Knin), swords and spurs and other items (e.g., an 8th century censer from Vrlika).

Font from the period of Prince Višeslav - 9th century

Stone collection of the Archaeological Museum

●●●●●●●●●●●

The **Archaeological Museum**** (Zrinko-Frankopanska street; NUMBER 11 ON THE PLAN) was founded in 1820 and houses an extremely rich collection of prehistoric, Greek and Roman and medieval items, from Dalmatia and especially from Salona. In the museum's stone collection there are stone epigraphs, gravestones and carved portraits. The most important pieces are from the era when the Greeks colonised Dalmatia, mainly from Issa (Vis), and a few items from Salona. The gravestone carvings are particularly significant, including sarcophagi, one with a scene of the hunt of the wild boar of Calydon (2nd to 3rd century), Hippolytus and Phaedra (3rd century) and from the early Christian era, a valuable sarcophagus showing the Good Shepherd (4th century) and one with the scene of the crossing of the Red Sea (4th century), all from Salona.

●●●●●●●●●●●

The **Meštrović Gallery***** (NUMBER 2 ON THE PLAN) has the largest collection of works by the sculptor Ivan Meštrović (see Šibenik, Drniš), housed in the artist's summer residence, built between 1931 and 1939 and designed by Meštrović himself. It is classical in style with a Mediterranean garden and a large central porch. The gallery was opened in 1952 with donations by the artist himself and there are works on display from all phases of his life. In the garden the sculptures *Vestal* and

Meštrović Gallery

Distant Accords are particularly outstanding and inside the gallery, the marble statues entitled *Contemplation*, *Psyche*, *The Madonna and Child* and a bronze statue *Job* are among his best works.

Not far from gallery, on the sea front is the **Meštrović Kaštelet** (NUMBER ❶ ON THE PLAN) which is a summer villa with a chapel belonging to the Split Capogrosso-Cavagnin family which Meštrović converted in 1932, adding Holy Cross Church and an atrium. Inside the church there is a wooden relief with biblical scenes and a large crucifix.

••••••••••••

The **Art Gallery**** (11, Lovretska street; NUMBER ⓭ ON THE PLAN) is the main gallery showing Dalmatian paintings and sculptures, founded in 1931. It has a rich collection of paintings from the 14th century to the present day; there are works of the Gothic, Renaissance and Baroque periods, as well as works of Croatian modern and contemporary artists (Medulić, Kraljević, Becić, Račić, Vidović, Job, Plančić and others).

••••••••••••

Vidovic Gallery (Andric House, close to the Silver Gate, NUMBER ㉑ ON THE PLAN). This Gallery exhibits works of one of Croatia's most significant 20th century painters, Emanuel Vidovic. Vidovic (1870-1953) was born in Split and is famous for his vedutas, still lifes and sacral motifs. There are about 70 of Vidovice's works from various periods in the Gallery. There is also a reconstruction of the painter's atelier.

Excursions

Klis**

11 KM FROM SPLIT; 2 577 INHABITANTS

Klis is a town on the 340 m high pass between the mountains Kozjak and Mosor on the centuries-old road linking the hinterland with the sea. It was probably settled in Roman times but was mentioned for the first time in a document written by Count Trpimir (852). His predecessor Mislav probably held court in Klis (Curtis) and from here governed the Croatian state, of which Klis had been part since the arrival of the Croats in this part of the country. In the 10th century Klis was mentioned by the Byzantine Emperor Constantine Porphyrogenitus as the centre of an old Croatian district, Primorska (the coastal area), Kliška or Parathalassia, which stretched from Trogir Pantan to the River Žrnovnica. Klis was part of the Croatian and then the Croatian-Hungarian state

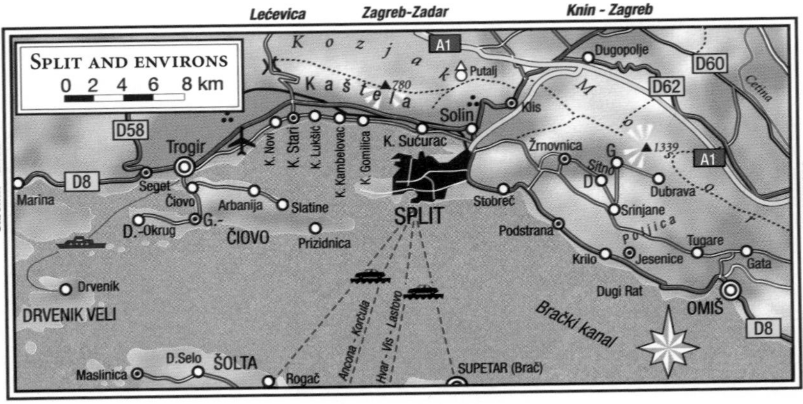

Klis

right up until 1171 when it was ruled by Domaldo Nelipčić. However it quickly returned to the Croatian-Hungarian state once again. When the Tatars invaded Croatia, in 1241 Klis resisted their attack. Towards the end of the 13th century the powerful Šubić family ruled Klis, using it as an important military base, as it had a strong fortress, right up until the Treaty of Zadar in 1358 when it was taken over by the Croatio-Hungarian King Ludovic of Anjou who held it until 1382. After a short period of rule by the Bosnian King Tvrtko (1387) Klis once again became part of the Croatian-Hungarian state, but in the 15th century both the Nelipčić and Talovac families fought over it. When Bosnia fell in 1463 and then Herzegovina in 1468, the Turks had an open path to Dalmatia and Croatia. Although it was heroically defended by Petar Kružić, the people of Senj, the Uskoks and the Dalmatians themselves, Klis was captured by the Turks on the 12th March 1537 and held by them until 1648. It became the centre of a Turkish sandshak (administrative area) and the Turks became a threat to the entire Dalmatian coastal area. Their border was the River Jadro in Solin, and robberies and attacks were everyday occurrences throughout the 16th and 17th centuries along the entire Split coastal area. A series of attempts by Uskoks (see Senj) to conquer Klis were without success. The action of a nobleman from Split, Ivan Alberti, was a real act of patriotism when, with a group of Split people and some from Poljica, he took over Klis for a brief period in 1596. Klis was finally liberated from the Turks in 1648 under the leadership of the Venetian General Leonardo Foscolo, and this part of Dalmatia came under Venice. During the Cretan war (1645-1669) Venice strengthened the older fortress in Klis and its present appearance more or less dates from that time. **Klis fortress**** has three walls rising one above the other. The main part of the fortress is entered through huge Baroque gates, and the entire fortress is defended by towers. There are other buildings in the entire complex, including wells, munition stores and a Turkish mosque which was later converted into a church. Below the fortress lies the town of Klis. In the impressive **parish church*** there are frescoes by the artist Vjekoslav Parać with scenes from the town's past.

●●●●●●●●●●●●

Solin***

5 KM FROM SPLIT; 15 850 INHABITANTS.

Thanks to its exceptionally favourable location in the protected bay of a river, on the fertile foothills of Kozjak and Mosor, ancient Salona was the most

Salona, a Venetian reconstruction

important city in the Roman province of Dalmatia. Now Salona is a very significant archaeological site, with many finds from the Roman, early Christian and early Middle Ages period.

History. The ancient writer Strabon mentioned Salona as "the port of the Delmati" which was colonised by the Greek inhabitants of Issa (Vis) towards the end of the ancient era. Until the arrival of the Romans, Salona existed as an Illyrian and Greek settlement. It was first mentioned in sources in 119 BC when the Roman military leader Caecilius Martellus wintered there with his troops. When the Roman commander Gaius Casconius defeated the Delmati, Salona was already an important city. In the civil wars between Caesar and Pompey, Salona sided with (victorious) Caesar and was given the status of a Roman colony (Colonia Martia Iulia Salona) and was not only liberated from its dependence on Issa, but also gradually grew into the most important city in the entire province of Dalmatia, its metropolis. The city spread to the east and the west and was fortified with walls and towers. In the western part of the city, at the end of the 2nd century, a large triangular amphitheatre was built, capable of holding 15 000 to 18 000 spectators, and in the centre there was a forum, a temple and a theatre. Salona experienced its peak of prosperity during the reign of Diocletian, when it was given the honorary name "Valeria". The proximity to Diocletian's palace in Aspalathos gave a further impetus to the city's intensive development and its increasingly cosmopolitan character. It was settled not only by the original inhabitants and Romans, but also Greeks and Jews. Salona was very early on caught up in the wave of early Christianity. The cults of Cybele and Mithra also spread along with other similar spiritual movements popular during the Roman Empire's period of crisis. Christianity was brought to Salona by Anastasius (Staš) of Aquileia, a saint who in 309 was thrown into the sea with a millstone round his neck because of his faith, thus dying as a martyr, and (in the 3rd century) St. Domnius, who, according to a legend, was converted by St. Peter in the 1st century and followed him to Rome. From there he came to Salona. Forty five Dalmatian Christians were martyred on the orders of the city governor Maurilius, and Domnius was beheaded. The oldest Christian meeting places were all illegal; later a basilica with a complex of

Portrait of a young woman from Salona, 1st century (exhibit in the Archaeological Museum in Zagreb)

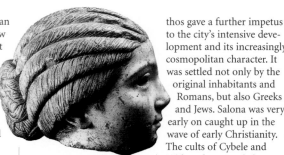

Solin on a postcard from the beginning of the 20th cent.

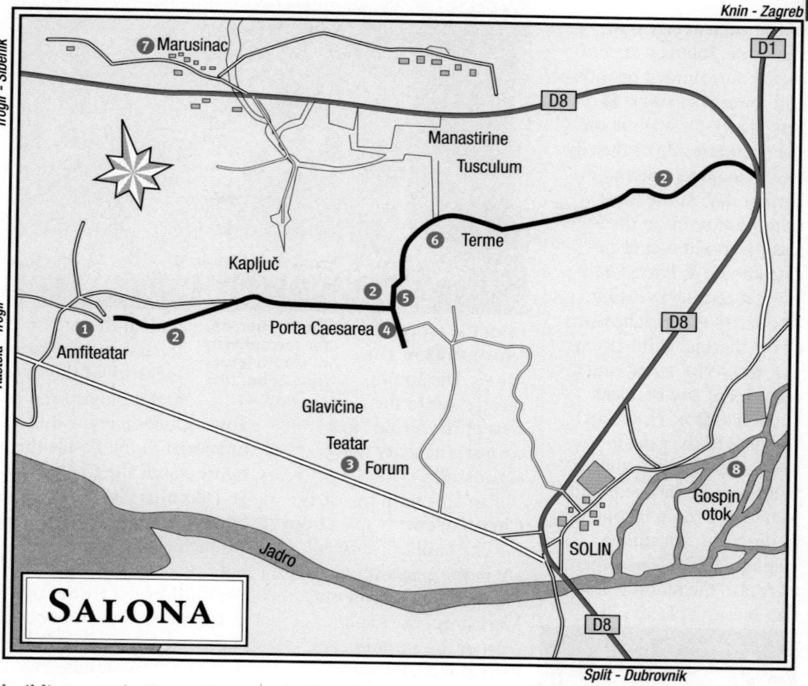

buildings was built north-east of Porta Caesarea. When Christianity became the religion of the majority, the Bishopric of Salona was founded, and it became the metropolis for the whole of ancient Dalmatia. Thanks to its good defences, Salona resisted the attacks of the Goths and the Huns, and gave protection to members of the Imperial family. Galla Placidia probably stayed here in 424. She was the daughter of Emperor Theodosius I and the regent of her son Emperor Valentinian III. Galla handed the whole of Dalmatia over to Byzantium on 29th October 437. Powerful Salona was however unable to withstand the onslaughts of the Avars at the beginning of the 7th century, and its inhabitants fled to the Dalmatian islands and Diocletian's palace. The newly-arrived Croats laid the foundations of a new Slavic settlement right on the shores of the broad Solin-Kaštela Bay, along the River Jadro, which became one of the centres of the future medieval Croatian state. In the 10th century a mausoleum was built in Solin with the coats of arms of the Croatian kings, and Count Trpimir founded a Benedictine monastery in Rižnice and received the famous Benedictine monk Gottschalk of Fulda (c. 846-848) at his court. The Croatian King Zvonimir was crowned in Solin, clearly showing that Croatian Solin was the centre of the entire state. In the immediate vicinity of the powerful Roman cities Split and Trogir, it served as a gateway for the influence of the highly developed culture of the ancient world to the Croats. When the Croatian dynasty came to an end at the beginning of the 12th century, the centre of the state moved northwards, and Solin lost its importance. It became a small village with a rich heritage. At the beginning of the century it had a population of about 500, and in the middle of the century (1961) 12 575, later developing into one of the centres of the cement industry.

••••••••••••

Archaeological sites. The archaeological remains of ancient Salona spread over an area of 156 hectares south of the new road leading to Trogir, and to the north of the old Solin-Trogir road (the best approach is from the car park on the new Trogir road; NUMBER ❼).

The Illyrian Era. Remains from this period cannot be seen here, but are in the museum. The Illyrian settlement was probably built on the hill around present-day Manastirne. The **heart**

of the ancient city is in Glavičine. Salona was completely surrounded by walls and towers (NUMBER ❷ ON THE PLAN). Only those on the northern side of the city have remained intact to the present day. At the most important point in the walls was the monumental city gate known as Porta Caesarea (1st century; NUMBER ❹ ON THE PLAN). The ruins of the thermal baths (NUMBER ❻ ON THE PLAN) and a complex of city basilicas (NUMBER ❺ ON THE PLAN) are close to the gate, to the north-east. The peristyle, a bathroom, some ovens and a changing room belonging to the baths can still be distinguished. Nearby there were also the oldest Christian meeting places (all

Sarcophagus of the Good Shepherd (a find from Solin, exhibit in the Archaeological Museum in Split)

illegal) which were linked with the work of the Syrian St. Domnius. A cathedral was built next to the thermal baths in the 4th century, and it was re-built in the 5th century. To the south there are the ruins of a 5th or 6th century church, built in the shape of a Grecian cross, with a polygonal baptistery adjoining (dating from about 500). To the south of this basilica complex (on the road to Trogir) there are the remains of a forum, a temple and a theatre dating

Inscription on the sarcophagus of Queen Jelena from Solin, 10th century

from the 1st century (NUMBER ❸ ON THE PLAN). The amphitheatre was to the west of the forum (in a corner of the city walls; NUMBER ❶).

Remains from the **early Christian era**** (apart from the city basilica complex) are in the area around Kapljuč, Manastirine and Marusinac. On Kapljuč (east of the amphitheatre) there was a large early Christian necropolis with the ruins of a 4th century triple-naved basilica, a narthex and a memorial. The basilica was used as a place of worship for the cult of the 5 Solin martyrs (the priest of Asterius and four soldiers from the period of Diocletian's persecution of Christians). In Manastirine (by the car park on the Trogir road) is the most important early Christian graveyard in Salona. It grew up on the foundations of older buildings, after the death of the Solin martyr Domnius in 304. He is buried here. At the end of the 4th century a large triple-naved basilica was built over his grave. To the west of Manastirine the great archaeologist and conservationist, governor of the Split archaeological museum and researcher, Don Frane Bulić (1846-1934) is buried. The **Tusculum** is also here, a house built at the end of the last century for the work of this archaeologist, and it now includes a Frane Bulić memorial room. Beside this house stands the Chapel of St. Domnius (Sveti Dujam) built in 1693. In Marusinac (to the north of the Trogir-Split road; NUMBER ❼) is the third largest Christian graveyard situated around the mausoleum of the Solin martyr St. Anastasius (Sv. Staš) from Aquileia. The mausoleum was built by a wealthy Solin family. There are also the remains of a triple-naved basilica still visible with mosaics and an atrium, and a basilica with an open central aisle, a unique example of this type of architecture from the early Christian era (Basilica discoperta). The archaeological site of **old Croatian Solin**** is located around the river Jadro. On Gospin otok (St. Mary's Island, now the parish church; NUMBER ❽ ON THE PLAN) there was once an early medieval triple-naved basilica, St. Stephen's (Sveti Stjepan). Queen Jelena was buried in this church in 976. She was the wife of the Croatian King Krešimir II. In 1898 the writing on the sarcophagus was reconstructed and can now be found in the Museum of Croatian Archaeological Monuments in Split. It is the oldest known epigraphic mention of the royal title in Croatia. On the sarcophagus of Queen Jelena is written: “In this grave lies the famous Jelena, who was the wife of King Mihajlo (Krešimir), the mother of King Stjepan (Držislav). She achieved peace in the kingdom. On the 8th day of October in the year of the Lord 976 she was buried here: indiction IV, monthly cycle V, epact XVII, solar cycle V. She who in her life was the mother of the kingdom also became the mother of orphans and the protectress of widows. Looking here, Oh man, say: God, have mercy on her soul.” The sarcophagus today is in the Museum of Croatian Archaeological Monuments. The **Gradina Fortress** is about 250 m to the northeast of the parish church of Our Lady of the Island. Gradina is a fortress with a trapezoid shape with four corner towers. In the north eastern part of Gradina the remains of a church of the central type in the form of an irregular square have been found; it lay on the walls of an older Roman building.

Northeast of the parish church (not far from the source of the River Jadro) is **Šuplja crkva Church** (St. Peter and Moses; “The Hollow Church”) built on the foundations of an old Christian basilica. St. Peter and Moses is a large, triple-naved early-Romanesque basilica built in the 11th century. It was used for the coronations of the Croatian kings, and the Croatian King Dmitar Zvonimir was crowned here in 1075. The basilica was destroyed during the Turkish occupation, as were the other basilicas. ■

Kaštela

KAŠTELA IS A COASTAL AREA BETWEEN TROGIR AND SOLIN AND A PART OF THE GREATER URBAN AREA OF SPLIT. IT OCCUPIES AN AREA THAT IS 20 KM LONG, 4.5 KM BROAD AT THE WEST AND 2 KM WIDE AT THE EASTERN END. IN THE NORTH THE REGION IS BOUNDED BY MT KOZJAK, AND IN THE SOUTH BY THE SEA.

The name derives from the castles (castello, It.) which were built in the 15th and 16th centuries by the noblemen and church dignitaries of Split and Trogir. They were residential and farming complexes around which peasant settlements sprang up. They were Kaštel Sućurac (belonging to the Archbishop of Split), Kaštel Gomilica (owned by the Split Benedictines), Kaštel Kambelovac (owned by the aristocratic Cambi family from Split), Kaštel Lukšić (the property of Trogiran noblemen the Vitturi), Kaštel Stari and Kaštel Novi (the Ćipiko family from Trogir) and Kaštel Štafilić (the Stafileo family, Trogiran aristocracy). In addition, castles were also built by other aristocrats: the Papalici, Guarco, Andreis, Rosani. Grisogono, Lippeo, Dudani and Cega families.

Young woman of Kaštela in traditional costume

Kaštel Sućurac

8.5 KM WEST OF SPLIT, 6 236 INHABITANTS.

The castle was built at the end of the 14th century on the orders of the Archbishop of Split, Andrija Gualdo. The first mention of the village below the castle dates from 1451. At the end of the 15th and beginning of the 16th century, the whole of the settlement was surrounded by a series of fortifications. In the town there is a summer residence of the Archbishops of Split in the Gothic and Renaissance style. In the new parish church (the old Baroque church was bombed in World War II) the arch of an altar rail with an inscription from the old Croatian period is preserved. Above Kaštel Sućurac is Putalj, a place famed in history (see Kozjak).

Kaštel Gomilica

10 KM WEST OF SPLIT; POPULATION 4 075.

The castle was built by nuns of the Benedictine convent of St. Euphemia around 1529 on the island of

Kaštel Gomilica

Gomile to protect the demesne from the Turks. The place is also called Castel Abbadessa, Nun´s Castle. The island was linked to the mainland by a moveable bridge. In the parish church, the Church of St Jerome, there is a large painted wooden Crucifix by Fulgencije Bakotić, as well as two paintings by Gasparo Diziani, and a marble altar by Pio and Vicko Dall´Acqua (18th century). North of the parish church is the Church of St. Cosmo and St. Damian (12th century).

••••••••••••

Kaštel Kambelovac (1.2 km west of Kaštel Gomilica, pop. 4 505). In 1478 the Split Cambi family was allowed to build a castle. Alongside it, castles were built by the Grisogono and Lippeo families (inherited by the Dudan family). In the parish church there are many pictures by Juraj Pavlović (19th century).

••••••••••••

Kaštel Lukšić

12 km west of Split; population 4 900.

In 1487 the aristocratic Trogiran brothers Jeronim and Nikola Vitturi obtained permission to build a castle to protect their demesne in Velo Polje. The Vitturis built a spacious, fortified Renaissance and Baroque summer palace with towers at the corner and an interior courtyard in which there is an inscription of 1563. A settlement grew up alongside the castle. The old Gothic and Renaissance parish church of the Assumption was too small for the numerous inhabitants. For this reason at the end of the 18th and the beginning of the 19th century a new, monumental late Baroque church was built. In the interior of it there is a Gothic painting *Madonna with Child*, an altarpiece of Jacopo Palma the Younger and an altar sarcophagus of the Blessed Arnir made in 1448 by Juraj Dalmatinac. To the west is the park of the Vitturi family and **Kaštel Rosani** (**Rušinac**). Alongside it is the Church of St John the Baptist, with a collection of artworks and an altarpiece by Pietro della Vecchia (16th century). In the church there is a gravestone with the inscription: Peace to the lovers. It was placed there in connection with the story of Miljenko and Dobrila, a Croatian Romeo and Juliet. The legend dates back to about 1697, and on the basis of it, in 1833, the writer and journalist Marko Kažotić (Casotti; 1804-1842) wrote a novel that was published in Zadar. The inscription on the grave

St. John the Baptist's Church in which the grave of Miljenko and Dobrila lies

gives the legend a certain authenticity. According to the memories of older people the grave was opened up in the thirties, and human bones were found in it. This proves nothing really, because in the 18th century members of the noble families from Kaštel Lukšić were buried there. In the grounds of the elementary school there is an arboretum. North of the town is the village of Ostrog with the medieval Church of St Lawrence (sv. Lovro).

••••••••••••

Kaštel Stari

6 km east of Trogir, population 6 448.

The founder of the place was the Trogiran nobleman and general Koriolan Cippico, who took part in the war that Venice waged against the Turks in Asia, as witnessed to by the inscriptions in the courtyard of the castle that was built at the end of the 14th century. Lelije Cippico built the Church of St. Joseph in 1695. The parish church, of St. John the Baptist, was built in 1714, while above the village, in Radun, is the excellently preserved pre-Romanesque Church of St. George (Sv. Juraj).

••••••••••••

Kaštel Novi (2 km west of Kaštel Stari, pop. 5 309). This castle was built by Pavao Cippico, Koriolan´s nephew, in 1512. In it today is the **Local Museum of Kaštela**, with cultural and artistic things related to the past of Kaštela. To the west the castles of the Andreis and Cega families were built. The parish church, of St. Peter, was built in the second half of the 19th century, but an older one is mentioned as early as 1476.

On the city square there is a town loggia from 1775 and a clock tower.

••••••••••••

Kaštel Štafilić (near Kaštel Novi in the direction of Trogir, pop. 2 014). The castle of the Štafilić (Stafileo) family was built in 1508 by the Trogiran nobleman Stjepan Štafilić on an island, and later linked to the land with a moveable bridge. The 18th century parish church was built by Ignacije Macanović, as an elegant late Baroque single-naved edifice. On the way to Trogir is **Kaštel Nehaj** of the Trogiran aristocrats the Loda family, and the complex of houses of the Split Papalić family, while in Divulje there are the remains of the summer house of the Garagnin family, designed by the Venetian classical architect Giovanni Antonio Selva.

••••••••••••

Kozjak is a mountain north of Kaštela Bay, covering an area of about 10 km. Its most remarkable features are its rocky, almost vertical cliffs on its southern face (50-250 m). On its northern, landward side Kozjak is mainly a plateau. From the sea to the plateau (about 4 km) there are three different types of terrain: a belt of Mediterranean vegetation, the most sparse vegetation on the steep rocks, and on the plateau a karst rock landscape, with desert-like thinly spread undergrowth. It is possible to reach the mountain from two mountain hostels, Malačka and Putalj. **Malačka** (522 m above sea level) is 10 km from Kaštel Stari on the road to Drniš. In the village of Radun (on the Kaštel Stari-Malačka road) is the Church of St. George the Diver (Sveti Juraj od Podmorja) an excellent example of old Croatian (pre-Romanesque) architecture. The Church of **St. John the Baptist*** (Sveti Ivan Krstitelj) on Biranj (631m) is one and a half hours' walk, on marked paths, from Malačka hostel. The church is situated in the middle of some pre-historic earthworks. It was founded in the 12th century, and a Latin inscription tells of renovation work in 1444. Every year on 26th June the church is the goal for pilgrims from the Bay of Kaštela. This church is the symbolic and visual focal point of Donja Kaštela. The mountain hostel Putalj (480 m) is

View of Kaštel Stari below Kozjak

above Kaštel Sućurac (there is a city bus line from Split - numbers 2 and 37, to Kaštel Sućurac). It is one and quarter hours' walk to the mountain hostel from the bus stop northwards by the street to the graveyard. On the way to the hostel, by the graveyard, is the **Chapel of Our Lady of Shade** (Gospa od Hladi). The people of Sućurac believe the painting of the *Madonna and Child* (covered in votive silver) to be miraculous. According to a legend it protects their fields from hail and fire. Above this church on the path to the hostel is **St. George's Chapel*** (Sveti Jure) after which Sućurac was named in the 14th century. This chapel is 323 m above sea level, and was a votive offering of Count Mislav, given to Archbishop Peter of Split by Count Trpimir in 852.

The Stone Gate of the Cetina River and a view of Omiš (monument to Mila Gojsalića in the foreground)

Omiš

28 km from Split in the direction of Dubrovnik; population 6 565

In the pre-historic era the area between Split and Omiš was inhabited by Illyrian tribes called the Bulini and the Nerestini. In the 2nd century BC the Delmati moved across this area via Klis. During the Roman occupation the entire region was full of small settlements of which Pitinium, Nereste and Oneum were fortified. Some remains from Oneum have been discovered in the village of Borak above Omiš. After the fall of the Western Roman Empire, and a short period of rule by the Goths, Omiš recognised the authority of Byzantium. As the Slavs moved into the region, Omiš became part of the Neretvan principality and was one of its major centres. From then on Omiš was a strong pirate base, and piracy became the most important occupation of its people, giving a great deal of trouble to the other Dalmatian cities, Venice and Southern Italy. In 830 the Venetians signed an agreement with the Neretvans to ensure the free passage of Venetian shipping on the Adriatic, but in 887 the Venetian Doge Pietro Candiano was killed in Makarska trying to subdue the Neretvan pirates. The defeated Venetians had to pay a toll to the Neretvans for free passage. Omiš was at that time ruled by the powerful Kačić family. The people of Omiš signed non-aggression agreements with Kotor (1167) and Dubrovnik (1180) but the pirates did not give up. From 1222 to 1226 there was a war against Omiš, initiated by the Pope, and led by King Andrija II, Split and Dubrovnik. Although they were defeated, the people of Omiš still did not give up their piracy. They entered a war with Split again in 1240, admitted defeat, but this was not the end of piracy, which spread over the entire Adriatic in the second half of the 13th

Historical crest of the city of Omiš

Omiš fortress according to a 17th century Venetian engraving

century. At the same time the Šubić family inherited the area from Kačić, but even their attempts to prevent piracy were unsuccessful. In 1358 Omiš recognised the rule of King Ludovic, at the end of the 14th century that of Tvrtko I and in the 15th century of Hrvoje Vukčić Hrvatinić and Ivaniš Nelipčić. Venice took over Omiš in 1444 and remained in power there until 1797. The people of Omiš were under threat from the Turks as well at this time, and they fortified the hinterland, but not the city itself, with strong defensive bases. From 1444 Omiš shared the fate of the rest of Venetian Dalmatia. Thanks to its unique location, the tourist industry developed rapidly in Omiš in the 20th century.

Sights

The most important building in Omiš is the **Parish Church of St. Michael**** (Sveti Mihovil) which was built on the foundations of an older church in 1629 when "the narrow space of the old temple was widened by the unity of the townsfolk". The church has an exceptionally beautiful facade whose portal is covered with masks, angel heads, plant patterns and a statue of St. Michael linking together provincial characteristics of early Baroque art and the craft of local workshops. Inside the church there is a wooden altar in Baroque style (17th century), a Gothic polychromatic crucifix by Juraj Petrović (15th century) and several paintings by Jacopo Palma the Younger, Matteo Ingoli and Matej Ponzoni (Pončun). In the church treasury the most valuable items are a 16th century monstrance, a collection of icons and a 17th century chest for storing documents.

•••••••••••

"The **House of the Happy Man**" ("Kuća sretnog čovjeka"; near the parish church) was named after an inscription over the door which says "Thank You Lord, that I have lived on this earth", showing the humanist feeling of the unknown man of Omiš who built this house in the 15th century.

•••••••••••

St. Rocco's Church* (Sveti Rok; 17th century) and the **Church of the Holy Spirit** (Sveti Duh; 16th century) to the west of the parish church, together with the bell-tower of the town clock, form the most picturesque entity in Omiš's architectural heritage. On the western side there is a house with an inscription mentioning the town archives and the grain store. There was probably a town loggia and the house of the Captain here.

•••••••••••

Some steps on the northern side of the town lead up to **Funtana**, the picturesque upper part of the town. A road leads from Funtana to Peovica or Mirabela castle which was built on the steep sides of Babnjača Hill in the 13th century in Romanesque style, and is one of the oldest fortresses in Dalmatia.

•••••••••••

In the western part of the town, by the River Cetina, is

Omiš

Poljički trg (square), where the western town gate once stood. The square was opened in 1831. In the centre is the so-called pillar of shame (1617) and the northern side is enclosed by the Baroque **Caralipeo-Despotović palace** with a 17th century Croatian inscription, and on the eastern side there are two beautiful Baroque palaces. The centre of present day Omiš is the street called Fošal, on whose eastern edge are the historic **Pavišić house** and several interesting Secession houses from the beginning of the 20th century.

••••••••••••

Fortica* (above the village of Borak-Oneum) is a fortress built in the 16th and 17th centuries. It offers an unforgettable view over Omiš, the Dalmatian islands and Poljica. On the way to Borak village there is an old graveyard with the Chapel of St. Mary (Sveta Marija) and a chapel built for the Drašković-Bonito family, with a collection of ancient sarcophagi and gravestones belonging to the Omiš nobility.

••••••••••••

St. Peter on Priko

The **Franciscan Monastery** and **Skalice Church** are on the main coast road. The Franciscans arrived in Omiš from Pološko blato in 1716, fleeing from the Turks. There is a church museum as part of the monastery, which as well as a large collection of documents, valuable books and liturgical equipment, also has an important collection of paintings and icons.

••••••••••••

The **Town Museum*** (next to the town gate) has a small collection of items from Omiš's past. Apart from the archaeological collection (with a valuable Cyrillic inscription from the time of the Kačić family, the 13th century) it houses flags from Poljica and the Poljica Statute (see Poljica).

••••••••••••

On the other side of Omiš, across the Cetina, on Priko, is the most important building in Omiš, the pre-Romanesque (old Croatian) **Church of St. Peter***** (Sveti Petar), one of the finest of its time in the whole of Dalmatia. The church is a single-naved building with an apse and dome, divided both inside and out with some fragments from the late Roman era built into the walls. Beside the church there is a Glagolitic seminary (Seminarium Illyricum), founded in 1750, for the education of priests in the Croatian language, to serve Poljica. Don Frane Bulić (see Solin) attended this school. It was closed in 1879.

••••••••••••

The **River Cetina**, the mouth of which is near Omiš, is 100 km long. It rises near Vrlika under Mt Dinara and is the most water-rich river in Dalmatia. Apart from its visible basin, the Cetina also receives a lot of water from the west Bosnian karst field via underground routes. Its lower course begins from the **Gubavica Falls** (49 m

Motif from the Cetina

a.s.l.) near the village of Zadvarje (20 km from Omiš). Here it leaves its canyon and flows into a valley which has nevertheless retained something of the appearance of a canyon. The area from **Radmanove mlinice**** (6 km from Omiš, a favourite place for outings) to the mouth, which includes a magnificent Probojnica, has the status of nature reserve. In the village of Slimen is a Memorial Collection of the poet Josip Pupačić, and a monument to the poet, made by Stipe Sikirica.

Costume of the prince of Poljica

EXCURSIONS

East Mosor (Mosor, see Klis) stretches 25 km from the Ljubljanska vrata to the Cetina. The base for getting to know this part of Mosor is the village of **Gata** (6 km by road from Omiš into the interior towards Blato on Cetina). On the way one passes by a monument to the heroine of Poljica, **Mila Gojsalića**. According to legend, Mila Gojsalića achieved fame in the war against the Turks in 1570 when, on the site of today's monument, she burned down the Turkish camp with gunpowder, dying herself in the conflagration. The monument was made by Ivan Meštrović (see Šibenik, Drniš). From Gata via the village of Dubrava to Kozik (Sv. Jure, 1318 m) the highest peak of this part of Mosor there is a walk of 4 hours. In Gata there is the **Poljica Historical Museum**, with ethnological items. The most important exhibit is the costume of the Great Prince of Poljica. In today's parish church, the remains of a Byzantine church of the 6th century have been found; it has a unique ground plan and is rich in sculptural decorations.

••••••••••••

Poljica* consists of ten villages covering the region from the river Žrnovnica to the west and the river Cetina to the east, on the sides of Mosor, to the north to Bisko along the banks of the Cetina. The **Poljica Republic** (Poljička republika) was founded in the Middle Ages (14th century) on the basis of old territorial divisions and political structures, and it had many unique features in relation to the rest of Dalmatia. In 1444 it admitted Venice's authority but retained extensive autonomy, and from 1513 to 1699 it submitted to the Turks to whom it paid certain fees, but also retained its autonomy. The Republic was

Omiš and the Poljica coast in the 17th century

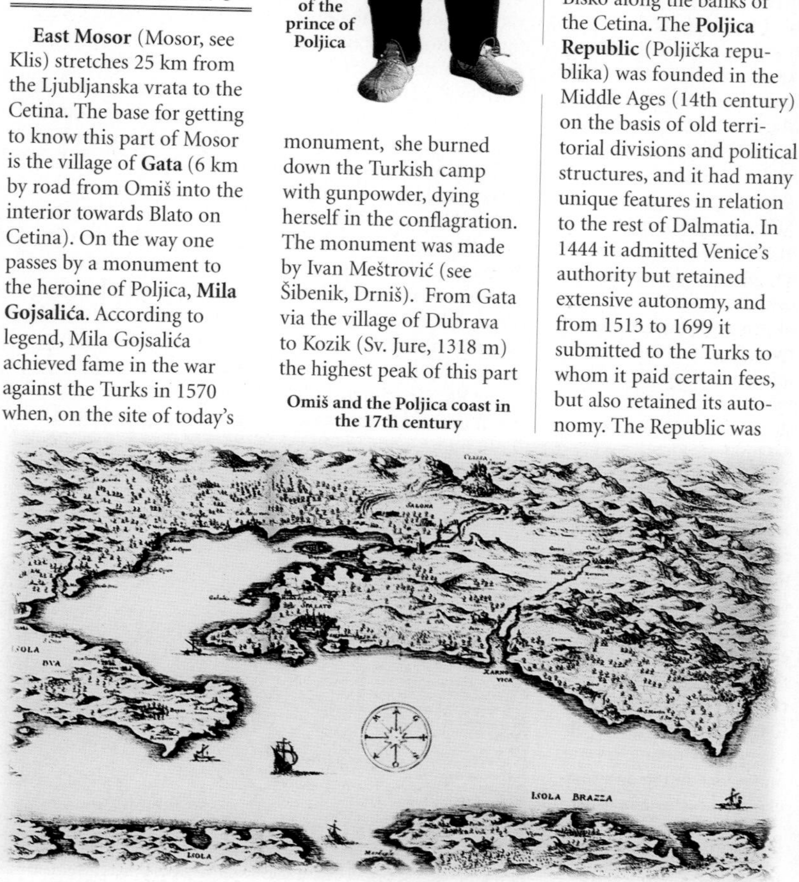

dissolved by the French in 1807. At the head of the Republic there was a Great Prince (knez) who was chosen from the ranks of the village nobility. The Prince and other representatives of authority (the Duke, Procurator and Chancellor) were chosen for one year on a very democratic basis. Life in Poljica was regulated by the Poljica Statute (15th century) written in Bosančica, a version of the Cyrillic script in use until the end of the 19th century. Some writers claim that Thomas Moore (1478-1535) the English humanist and statesman, used the Poljica Republic in his *Utopia*. The Italian travel writer and botanist Alberto Fortis (c.1774) and later Napoleon's Marshall Marmont (1857) both wrote about the elections for the Great Prince. According to Marmont, "The Great Prince whose mandate is coming to an end places a closed iron box containing the documents of privileges on a marked spot. The most eager and most courageous run for the box under a shower of stones. If one manages to get hold of the box and is not killed, he becomes the Prince". Although Marmont wanted to show that three factors made the election of the Prince possible (decisiveness, courage and luck) his description of the elections did not agree with the truth. The Prince was chosen on St. George's day (24th April) in front of St. George's Church (Sv. Juraj) on Gradac hill in an exemplary democratic manner.

••••••••••••

All the villages in Poljica are interesting folk settlements with beautiful examples of rural architecture in an exceptionally attractive landscape. Amongst the historically and culturally significant buildings are the 17th century double church in **Sumpetar** (St. Stephen's and St. Anthony's; Sveti Stjepan i Sveti Antun Padovanski) with its 11th century pre-Romanesque altar rail and a statue of St. Stephen by the Nikola Firentinac school. In **Duće** there is a fine altarpiece by Vlaho Bukovac and in Gata the Historical Museum of Poljica has ethnographic items and documents from the history of Poljica (e.g. the costume worn by the Great Prince). Beside the present day parish church, in the same village, the remains of a late Roman church dating from the 6th century have been found, with a unique ground plan. In **Dubrava** there is an important Romanesque and Renaissance church, St. Luke's (Sveti Luka; 13th-16th centuries) with the grave of Bishop Nikola Ugrinović, and in neighbouring **Sitno** are the Church of St. Clement (Sveti Klement; 14th-15th century) and the Baroque Church of St. Luke (Sveti Luka) dating from the 18th century. On the road from Dubrava to **Tugare** is the Chapel of St. Rainerius (Blaženi Arnir) built on the spot where the people of Poljica stoned that Archbishop of Split to death. On the hill called **Križ** above the hamlet of Dinarina a cross 9 m high has been put up; it can be seen from the whole of the Cetina region, and was put up by people from Sinj and expatriates.

Motif from the beach at Omiš

••••••••••••

Mosor* is the most popular Dalmatian mountain in the north-eastern hinterland of Split. This mountain is part of a larger range, separated by erosion caused by the River Cetina. Its basic characteristic (apart from the fact that it is mainly bare karst rock) is its lonely situation (it gives the impression of a huge lonely island), which caused the geographer Peneck to take Mosor as an example of a mountain type: its name "Mosor" is used in morphological accounts of all

Landscape of the Omiš highland area

Sinj, in the middle of the 19th century

mountains with a similar isolated appearance and similar origin.

•••••••••••

Western Mosor* stretches from Klis to the Ljubljanska vrata. The starting place for trips into this part of Mosor is the mountain hostel called "Lugarnica" which is reached via the village of Žrnovnica (11 km from Split, by city bus), and from here there are three mountain positions to aim at: Debelo brdo in the west (1 044 m a.s.l.), a 2 hour walk over Kunjevod; to the south east the mountain lodge on Ljuvač (2 hours' walk); to the east, Vickov stup (the peak of Mosor), via Ljubljanska vrata, 3 hour's walk.

Central Mosor stretches over 5 km from Ljubljanska vrata to Ljuti Kamen Pass. The main setting out point for this part of the mountain is the hostel known as "Umberto Girometta" on Ljuvač (900 m above sea level). The hostel can be reached via the village of Gornje Sitno (21km from Split by city bus number 58). There is a marked path from the last bus stop, climbing steeply through the karst rock for 45 minutes. From the hostel to the peak (Vickov stup, 1325 m above sea level) the walk takes one and a half hours.

•••••••••••

The view from Mosor. Troglav 50 km; Cincar 64 km; Vran 90 km; Čvrsnica 90 km; Vidova gora 27 km; Kozjak 18 km; Vaganski vrh 130 km; Svilaja 30 km and Dinara 64 km. (With indications of the heights above sea level of the peaks and the direction in degrees where they can be seen.)

•••••••••••

Sinj

34 KM FROM SPLIT; POPULATION 11 468.

Sinj lies in the valley of the River Cetina at the foot of Mt Dinara which gave its name to the Dinara range, the largest range in the Balkan peninsula. To the west of Sinj is Svilaja mountain. There are plentiful signs of life from prehistoric times in caves, burial mounds and earthworks (Unište, Čavčina, Dragović). There are pile dwellings along the Cetina from the early Iron Age. During the Roman era the Sinj region was settled by the Illyrian Delmati who were defeated by the Romans in 33 BC. There was a Roman fortress here called Osinium and nearby were Čitluk (Colonia Claudia Aequum) a settlement of army veterans, and the fortified settlement Gardun (Tilurium). During the time of the first Croatian state, Sinj was the centre of the Cetinja district. In the Middle Ages Sinj was ruled by the Croatian-Hungarian kings, but the actual ruler was Count Domald, or the noble Nelipić and Talovac families. On the arrival of the Turks, Sinj was part of their Empire from 1513 until 1699. After that it became part of Venetian Dalmatia and shared its fate.

The town is dominated by the **Franciscan Church** and **Monastery** whose foundations were dug during the wars against the Turks (1683-1699), when Franciscan monks from Rama (Bosnia) fled to Sinj. The church was begun in

Miraculous picture of Our Lady of Sinj

1699, but it was burnt down by the Turks in 1714 and damaged in an earthquake in 1769, completely restored in 1862 and once again in 1975-76. Beside the church there is a bell tower built between 1896 and 1926. The painting *The Miraculous Madonna of Sinj* which was brought by the Franciscans from Rama, is a fine example of 16th century Venetian art. The monastery also has a **museum** housing remains from Aequum (Čitluk), a pre-historic collection, a folklore collection, a natural history collection etc. Particularly worth seeing are a head of Hercules (1st century) and a statue of the goddess Diana (3rd century).

••••••••••••

The **Cetina Regional Museum*** (Muzej Cetinske krajine; A. Kačića Miošića street) has archaeological remains from the entire Cetina region (Cetinska krajina) as well as other items relating to the history of the area. Above the town is **Kamičac Castle** built by the Venetians at the beginning of the 18th century. It is in the form of a star-shaped bastion according to the S. Vauban's system. To the north-east there are remains of an older fortress built in the Middle Ages. ■

The Chivalric competition Sinjska alka***

Sinjska Alka is a traditional chivalric competition for the most skilful men of the Cetina region, held every year since 1715 in honour of the victory won by 600 men from Sinj over the Turks. The point of the competition is to strike an "alka" (3.22 m off the ground) by charging at it with a lance, on horseback. According to the rules the speed of the horse must be at least 45 km an hour. The alka consists of two concentric circles (the larger being 13.17 cm and the smaller 3.51cm in diameter), the larger being divided into three sections. A hit in one of the two upper segments gives the competitor one point, in the lower section two points and in the inner circle ("u sridu" - in the middle) three points. A hit in the centre ("u sridu") is announced with music and cannon fire from a nearby tower. The charge is repeated three times, and if there is no winner then the competitors with the highest scores compete again until there is a clear winner. The winner receives a shield, passed on every year, which was given to the Alka Society by the head of state, as well as the title of Hero of the Cetina region. The festivities are also marked by the special folk costumes worn by the competitors (of whom there are usually about 15) their pages, the guards, the Alka judges and functionaries of the Alka Society. The Alka is held on the sunday the closest to the Feast of the Assumption every year. The dress rehearsal also draws a large audience: on the Friday the "Bara" and on Saturday the "Čoja" are held; however, the competitors do not wear their costumes for these rehearsals. ■

A hit in the centre

An Alkar galloping

The Central Dalmatian Islands

Brač

BRAČ IS THE THIRD LARGEST ADRIATIC ISLAND. IT COVERS AN AREA OF 394.41 KM^2. THE ISLAND'S CONTOURS ARE ASYMMETRICAL; TO THE NORTH THEY FALL AWAY GRADUALLY, TO THE SOUTH MORE STEEPLY AND THIS IS REFLECTED IN THE COASTLINE. THE NORTHERN SIDE IS INDENTED AND MORE ACCESSIBLE. THE ISLAND MAINLY CONSISTS OF LIMESTONE AND ITS HIGHEST PEAK IS VIDOVA GORA (778 M). BRAČ IS COVERED WITH EVERGREEN TREES, AND 26.5% OF ITS SURFACE IS WOODLAND. ITS CLIMATE IS TYPICALLY MEDITERRANEAN AND IN TERMS OF ANNUAL HOURS OF SUNLIGHT (2 700) IT IS ONE OF THE SUNNIEST AREAS IN THE ADRIATIC. THERE IS NO SURFACE WATER AT ALL ON BRAČ, ONLY A FEW FRESH WATER SPRINGS IN THE AREA AROUND BOL. THE TOTAL POPULATION IN THE 22 SETTLEMENTS IS 13 700. THE ISLAND IS LINKED TO THE MAINLAND BY TWO FERRY ROUTES AND THE REGULAR SPLIT-MILNA-BOL-HVAR LINE. IT IS ALSO POSSIBLE TO GET TO THE ISLAND BY PLANE (BOL AIRPORT).

Prehistory. Archaeological finds of the first inhabitants of Brač date from extremely early periods: from the Neolithic and then the Bronze and Iron Ages. The many finds discovered in the Kopačina caves near Supetar provide evidence of this. The first known inhabitants were Illyrians who gave the island its name, Brentos (stag), whilst the Greeks later called it Elaphusa. Although the Illyrians had very good trading links with the Greeks and their colonies in the immediate vicinity (Issa), they never allowed them to settle in their territory.

The Roman Era. In contrast to other parts of Dalmatia, during the period of Roman rule, which lasted in these parts for almost 500 years, not one walled settlement was built on Brač. The island, which appears in Roman documents as "capris laudata Brattia" (Pliny the Elder in *Historia naturalis*), served nearby Salona as a "suburb" and as supplier of agricultural products to Roman cities and legions on the mainland, principally olive oil, wine and livestock, and also its particularly high quality stone for building. The coastal, easier and more fertile areas of the island were settled by Roman citizens, whilst the old Illyrian inhabitants moved inland into the hilly areas of the island and thus preserved their national identity, right up until the Croats arrived in this area. The only remains from the Roman pagan era are a few farm buildings, a mausoleum and sarcophagi. However, from the period of the early Christians, from the 6th to the 7th centuries, there is a rich heritage of sacred architecture. In that period many basilicas were built, churches, monasteries and baptisteries. The best preserved examples of this form of architecture can be seen in Sutivan, Lovrečina and Povlja (see below).

The Migrations of the Nations. When ancient Salona fell to the Avars and Slavs in 614, some of the inhabitants who survived fled to the islands, first of all to Brač, which soon came under Byzantine sovereignty. Along with the Roman refugees, Croats also soon migrated to the island. People from the Neretva area also found their way to Brač. The ethnic influence of the new population developed throughout the 7th century over the bay "Hrvaska"(Croatia), which was mentioned in a document of 1305, "The Brač Law" (Razvod Brački). The bay is situated in the southeastern part of the island below Brkata hill (440 m). The Neretva people had totally Croatised Brač by the end of the 9th century, and they were converted to Christianity under the influence of the Roman inhabitants, who became assimilated into the new nation along with the Illyrians.

Bunja - a traditional building - refuge

Under the Croatian and Croatian-Hungarian Rulers. Brač, in common with the entire Neretva district, became part of the Croatian state during the reign of King Tomislav at the beginning of the 10th century. The Venetian Doge, Pietro II Orseolo, conquered Dalmatia in 1000 and thus for a short time Brač came under the Venetian Empire. In Nerežišća, the Venetians organised a Commune court, archives and an assembly hall. However, during the reign of King Petar Krešimir, Brač once again came under Croatian rule and it remained in that position until the state lost its independence in 1102. King Zvonimir, in his charter of 12th March 1078, gave the people of Brač the privilege of being able, without any kind of tithes or taxes, to buy and sell goods in the entire region of Croatia. Up until 1278 Brač was part of the Croatian-Hungarian Kingdom, that is under the Arpadović dynasty (apart from between 1170 and 1180 when it was under Byzantium and 1240 to 1242, when it was directly ruled from Split).

A Time of Changing Rulers. The dynastic wars in the Croatian-Hungarian Kingdom served the Bosnian King Stjepan Tvrtko I well, and in 1390 he joined Dalmatia to his kingdom, along with the islands, including Brač, whose special privileges were confirmed in a charter of 23rd July 1390. One year after Tvrtko's death, Brač came under King Zigmund, and from 1403 to 1413 it was under the authority of Duke Hrvoje. After that the island was governed by the Dubrovnik Republic (1413-1416) and then by Ladislav Jakac, up to 1420, when Dalmatia and the islands were conquered by Venice, which held them until its fall in 1797.

Under the Venetians. As they were left without any protection after these constant raids, and the Croatian-Hungarian kings were unable to help them, the people of Brač sent a request to the Venetian Great Council to receive them into their empire, and this was accepted on 1st April 1278. Venetian rule lasted until 1358 (when following the Venetians' defeat, the island once again came under the Croatian-Hungarian kings for several decades), and then from 1420 until 1797. During their rule, the island was governed by a Count nominated by the Venetian Senate. Alongside the Count there were also three chief judges who had their residence in Nerežišća. Social and economic differences became more and more apparent until the population of Brač fell into four basic groups: the nobility (nobiles), privileged families, new inhabitants (dogoni) and common people (populares), which had a decisive effect on the further development and life of the island.

The Nineteenth and Twentieth Centuries. Once Venetian rule came to an end, the ordinary people broke the power of the local nobility in a rebellion in June 1797, proclaimed the equality of all the island's people and decided to hand the island over to the Austrians. This was practically realised with the arrival of the corvette "Austria" in Supetar harbour on 15th July 1797. However the Austrians did not retain their hold for long; their defeat at Austerlitz (1805) meant Brač and Dalmatia came under French rule. In December 1806 for a brief period Brač was occupied by the Russians, until July 1807 when the French returned and remained on the island until 1814. The same year, following the fall of Napoleon, Brač came under Austria more permanently.

The period of 104 years of Austrian rule was characterised by the strengthening of the economic and cultural life of the island, but also by increased emigration, especially at the beginning of the 20th century. In that period Brač developed into an island that had several centres but in 1827 Supetar became the administrative and political centre. This happened at the same time as the revival of Croatian national awareness. The first reading room opened in Pučišća in 1868.

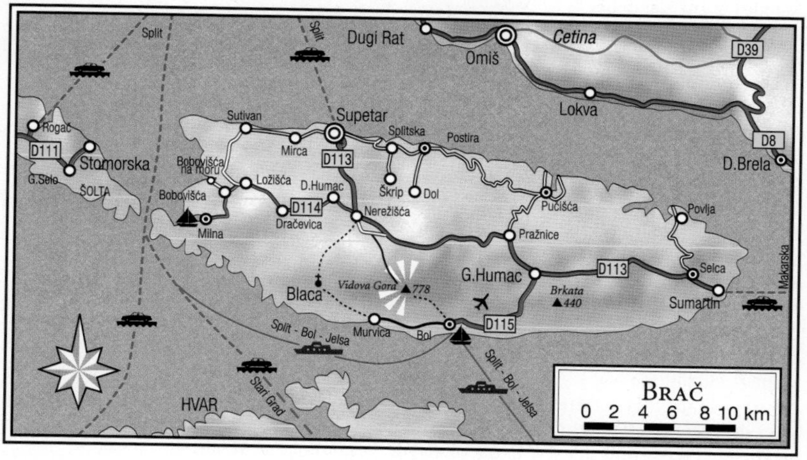

Bol

43°18′ N, 16°38′ E, POPULATION 1 661.

Bol is the only coastal settlement on the southern part of the island. It is sheltered by Vidova gora (778 m) and Draževo brdo (627 m). In 827, the Saracens razed the settlement but it was quickly rebuilt. On the quay there is a Gothic structure from the 15th century with graceful arched windows and stone biforia. Amongst the other buildings, the castle on the sea front from the 17th century and the Renaissance palace which belonged to the Jelačić family, are particularly worth mentioning. The remains of the Martinis-Marchi family park is a significant example of 17th century horticulture.

Bol

In the centre of the town is the **Church of Our Lady of Carmel** (Gospa od Karmela) which was built in 1668 and completed in Baroque style in 1778. On the main altar there is a painting of *Our Lady of Carmel with the Saints*, the work of a local artist, from Supetar, Feliks Tironi from 1790.

The **Dominican church** and **monastery***** on Glavica point (the eastern side of Bol) is the most valuable group of buildings on the island of Brač. As early as 1184 on the site of the monastery stood the palace of the Bishops of Hvar and Brač. In the bishop's buildings (palatio episcopati) a Dominican community was founded in 1475, and they subsequently built the monastery and the Church of Our Lady of Grace (Gospa od Milosti) in the late Renaissance and Baroque styles on the site of the old Chapel of St. Rocco (Sveti Rok). The church is a single-naved building with a Gothic vault and in 1636 it was extended by an aisle. The bell tower was completed in 1751. The church and monastery house valuable cultural and historic treasures. In the church there is an altar rail from the 16th century, and the marble side altars are considered to be amongst the most beautiful on the island, especially the altar to Our Lady of the Rosary. On the ceiling beneath the choir there is a *trompe de l'oeil* Baroque painting by the artist Tripo Kokolja from 1713, entitled *The Apotheosis of St. Dominic.* In the **museum** there are archive materials, church silver, wood carvings, liturgical robes and examples of Glagolitic texts from the hermits of Murvica. Here fragments of braiding ornamentation from the Chapel of St. John and St. Theodore (Sveti Ivan i Sveti Tudor) are also kept. There is a rich collection of prehistoric finds: coins, marine archaeological and stone monuments, liturgical literature and a valuable picture gallery. There is a particularly outstanding high Renaissance Venetian altarpiece of the Tintoretto school entitled *The Madonna and Child with the Saints* dating from 1563. This painting was on the main altar until 1975, when it was moved to the museum.

Dominican monastery

••••••••••••

The **Chapel of St. John** and **St. Theodore** (which is at the far end of the graveyard and monastery) is an important Croatian building of the 10th and 11th centuries. It resembles a small triple-naved basilica; its present shape is the result of reconstruction work from the 10th to the 15th centuries. The most interesting discovery here is a late Roman hall in front of the church, which is probably part of a much larger sacred building from the 6th century. This late Roman sacred complex which was dedicated to St. John, and originally to St. Theodore, the official patron of the Byzantine army, is linked to fortifications which were at one time built alongside the bishop's residence.

••••••••••••

The **Branko Dešković Gallery*** (in the western part of Old Bol) is named after the artist Branislav Dešković who was born in Pučišća in 1883 (and died in Vrapče in 1939). As well as works by this artist

Zlatni rat (Golden cape)

the gallery also has a collection of 300 paintings and sculptures. Particularly significant are works by Ignjat Job (1895-1936) (Mediterranean motifs in a specific variant of Expressionism), Ljubo Ivančić, Josip Plančić (1899-1930; buried in Paris) and Ivo Rendić (1849-1932) who used Brač stone and other materials in his sculptures.

•••••••••••

Zlatni rat*** (Golden Cape) 2 km north of Bol harbour, is a unique beach not only in Bol, but in the entire Adriatic. It is a narrow white pebble spit stretching out into the sea, 634 m long, its tip veering according to the tides. It is protected as a geomorphological phenomenon.

Excursions

Murvica***

14 INHABITANTS; 6 KM WEST OF BOL

Murvica is situated beneath karst caves along the southern side of the island and was mentioned for the first time in 1286. Later it developed as a supply centre for the many hermits there. Monks and nuns fleeing from the Turks came here in the 15th century from Poljica. Over Dračeva luka near Murvica, priests from Poljica built a monastery in 1512 and nuns built their own hermitage, Dutić, which was also mentioned in 1512. Two more monasteries were built beneath the rocks over Murvica, the Silvio Hermitage in 1497 and the Stipančić Convent in 1416. Monastic life in these hermitages around Murvica continued right up to the Second World War.

•••••••••••

Mysterious relief in the Dragon's Cave

The **Drakonjina špilja** (cave) is so called because of the relief of a dragon found inside; it is also known as Zmajeva pećina (Dragon's cave). It is immediately above Murvica itself. The dragon was carved by unknown monk in the 15th century, when the monks lived in the caves and even built a chapel in them. As well as the dragon there is also a carving of the moon and other ancient cult symbols. On the eastern side over the chapel, there are carved human figures and birds on their nests, indicating that this was a Christian sanctuary which nevertheless had elements of pagan religions. The church which serves Murvica is in the former hermitage in Dračeva luka. The vaulting in this church which dates from the 16th century, is formed by the natural rock of the cave. On the facade there is a characteristic portal and a rose window. A new, modern church was built in Murvica after the war.

•••••••••••

Vidova gora** is the highest peak on the Adriatic islands (778 m). It can be reached by a mountain path and the climb takes 2 hours. The starting point is the Church Our Lady of Carmel (Gospa od Karmela) in the centre of Bol. It crosses over the Gornji Humac-Bol road and goes through a deserted village, Podborje, ascending to a crossroads. It continues to the left through vineyards and orchards up to the plateau Gornja pristava, then continues to climb between rocks to the edge of the Brač plateau, from where there are about 10 more minutes to the peak. The peak can also be reached by road from Supetar - Nerežišće - Kneževravan - Vidova gora (18 km). Here the morphology of the karst gives all possible rock forms. The waterless plateau is mostly stony, and overgrown with Mediterranean maquis. The area around the peak is an ancient cult site. The peak is also known as Vidovica, Sveti Vid (sanctus Vitus;

The view from Vidova gora

Peak	m	km	0'
Mosor	1339	25	3
Kamešnica	1856	50	27
Biokovo	1762	35	78
Pelješac	961	52	125
Hvar	626	16	187
Vis	585	55	235
Kozjak	779	40	330
Svilaja	1508	60	348
Troglav	1913	75	358

St. Veit), Sutvid, after the old Croatian chapel whose ruins can be found a few hundred metres from the peak. Before the conversion of the Croats to Christianity, it is thought that this was an old Slavic temple to the god Svetovid (Svantovit). On the site where there is now a telecommunications aerial there was once an old mountain hostel built in 1936. Hang gliders launch from the rock on Vidova Gora and fly down to Bol and its beaches.

••••••••••••

Blaca Hermitage*** can only be reached by footpath from the interior via Nerežišće, or from Bol and Murvica (via Blaca Bay). It takes 2 hours from the sea. It was founded by Glagolitic priests from Poljica who fled here from the Turks in the 16th century. They chose this inaccessible area on the southern side of the island and settled in the Ljubitovica caves, where in 1588 they built a church and later also a monastery. After a fire in 1752 the church and the monastery were restored (1757) and have remained intact since then. The last priest in Blaca was Don Niko Milićević, who was also an astronomer of world renown, his works being frequently published in the Viennese journal "Astronomische Nachrichten". After his death in 1963, the entire complex was transformed into a museum and scientific centre. The stone buildings, together with the caves, are an exceptionally valuable and a unique architectural unity, with particularly outstanding items of an ethnographic character such as kitchens, bread ovens, cisterns and so on. In the ornate living quarters there is fine furniture and a rich library including a valuable atlas by H. Hondius and J. Iasonius from 1623. There is also an archive, a small printing press, and an observatory with a giant telescope. Amongst the works of art, the most outstanding are works of the Venetian school from the second half of the 17th century: *The Magdalene Repentant* and *The Samaritan Woman at the Well.* In the Renaissance church, which was later rebuilt in Baroque style, there are three Baroque altarpieces. In the church there are also the anonymous graves of the Blaca monks.

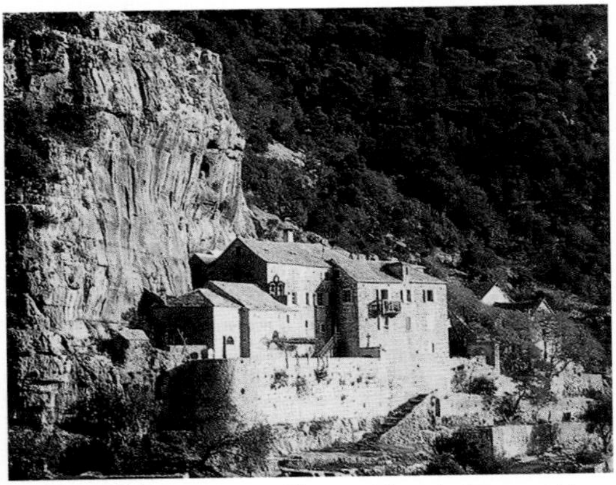

Blaca Hermitage

••••••••••••

Gornji Humac

276 INHABITANTS; 13 KM NORTHEAST OF BOL.

Gornji Humac is a typical shepherds' village dating back to the Middle Ages. The Baroque parish church, Our Lady of the Visitation (Gospa od Pohoda) was built on the site of an older church from the 15th century, as seen from the late Gothic relief triptych. In the graveyard is the Our Lady Chapel, a medieval building containing a stone relief originating from the workshop of Nikola Firentinac in the 15th century. The village is also known for the famous Brač cheese ("Brački sir").

••••••••••••

Milna

14 KM SOUTHWEST OF SUPETAR, POPULATION 862.

The noble family of Cerinić built the Chapel of St. Mary (Sveta Marija) here at the end of the 16th century (Ecclesia Sanctae Mariae Milnavi) and a fortress, a centre around which a settlement grew up. During the Napoleonic rule, a sea battle between the Russians and the French took place off Milna. Once the French fleet had been defeated in 1806, Milna was for one year (until 1807) the island's capital under the Tsar. A Baroque church was built beside St. Mary's in 1783 (St. Mary's now forms the sacristy) decorated with Rococo stucco work inside. Amongst the Baroque paintings in the church, the altarpiece *The Annunciation* is outstanding, and is considered to be one of the most beautiful altarpieces on Brač. It is attributed to the Venetian artist Ricci

Milna

from the first half of the 18th century. There are two more altarpieces from the same period: *The Madonna with SS. Joseph, John, Peter and Paul* and *Our Lady of the Rosary amongst the Sacraments of the Rosary*. In the sacristy (the original church) there are two valuable paintings by Venetian artists: *The Adoration of the Kings* and *Ecce homo*. The stone statues of St. Joseph and St. Jerome on the main altar are the work of the Brač sculptor Ivan Rendić (1849-1932). South of Milna in Osibova Bay there are the ruins of a Gothic chapel and the Chapel of St. Joseph (Sveti Josip) from 1863 where there is a Venetian altarpiece of St. Joseph from the 18th century.

Excursions

Bobovišća

4.5 km from Milna; 71 inhabitants

Bobovišća is a village over the sea, about 1 km from Bobovišća na Moru. In the village is the **Church of St. George** (Sveti Juraj) which was built at the beginning of this century on the ruins of an older church from 1696. The ornamental moulding (with the date 1696 inscribed) and the rose window on the front of the church are remains of the older church. The altarpiece *Pieta with St. George and St. John*, painted in the manner of Palma, and *Our Lady of Carmel*, a Venetian work from the 18th century, are from the older church. In the parish office there is some lace made in the 17th century, which is considered to be the most valuable piece of its kind in Dalmatia. Above the village on the hill there is a pre-**Romanesque church**, **St. Martin's** (Sv. Martin), with a Gothic bell- -tower dating from the 14th century. On the altar there is a Renaissance relief depicting St. Martin.

••••••

Bobovišća na Moru (1 km northwest of Bobovišća) began to develop as a harbour for the village of Bobovišća in the 18th century. From that period there is a fortified Baroque summer residence which belonged to the Gligo family. There is also the family home of Vladimir Nazor (1876-1949), the great Croatian poet and politician, with a tower and three pillars with a frieze which he called "Three little sisters". Here Vladimir Nazor spent his childhood and youth. In the harbour there is a memorial to this poet and partisan, by the sculptor M. Ostoja.

•••••••••••

Ložišća

5 km east of Milna on the road for Nerežišća; 167 inhabitants

Ložišća was settled by people from Bobovišća in the 17th century. The **parish church** with its trefoil pediment was built in 1820 in the neo-Romanesque style. A bell tower was built beside it in historical style in the second half of the 19th century. The **Chapel of St. Mary** (Stomorica; Sancta Maria) in neighbouring Nerezine, which comes under Ložišća, was built on the site of an old Roman building and dates from the pre-Romanesque era.

••••••

Bobovišća na Moru (monument to Vladimir Nazor in the foreground)

Ložišća

Pučišća

TOWN AND PORT ON THE NORTHERN COAST OF THE ISLAND, 13 KM EAST OF SUPETAR; 1 602 INHABITANTS.

Pučišća is the largest settlement on the island. During the Roman era there was just a small settlement here, and the town in its present appearance developed only in the 15th century. In the area of Stipanska there was a harbour in the 11th century with a Benedictine monastery, of which only a church in the present day graveyard remains. Pučišća was also known as Luka Kula, but in Venetian documents of 1600 it is called Pučišća-castrum. Because of the threat from the Turks, who ruled neighbouring Neretva, Ciprijan Žuvetić built the first castle in the harbour in 1467, and then, over a period of a hundred years, another 12 castles were built. Only 7 are still standing of the original 13. The **castle of Ciprijan Žuvetić****, which stands alongside a Renaissance palace, and the castle **Akvilin kaštel** and the **castle of the Dešković family** near the parish church are the most important and valuable secular buildings in the town.

The **Parish Church of St. Jerome** (Sveti Jerolim) was built in 1566 but it received its Baroque characteristics when it was rebuilt in 1750. Above the main altar there is a wooden relief of St. Jerome, the work of the wood carver Franjo Čiočić from 1578. The wooden altar to St. Anthony (Sveti Ante) is one of the most beautiful on Brač. In the church there is also an altarpiece entitled *Our Lady of Carmel* which is the work of the Venetian school of the 18th century. In the parish office the famous Povljanska listina document from 1250 is kept (see Povlja).

The **Church of Our Lady of Consolation** (Gospa od Utješenja) in the graveyard in Pučišća was built on the ruins of St. Stephen's Church (Sveti Stjepan), which was part of a Benedictine monastery which stood on that site in the 11th century. From the 16th century up to 1762 it served the needs of the Augustine order who extended it and when they left, it became the cemetery chapel named Our Lady of Consolation, which was the name of a church fraternity. The **Church of the Assumption** (Marijino Uzašašće) on Batak was built in 1533 making use of the resources of the patrician Ciprijan Žuvetić. It was built in Renaissance style. On the altar there is a stone carving of the Madonna and Child dating from the first half of the 16th century.

Pučišća

Beneath the main altar is the grave of C. Žuvetić and to the sides are the graves of masons and builders from Brač (Radojković, Akvila and Bokanić) with tools engraved as symbols of their trade. The **Chapel of St. George** (Sveti Juraj) on Bračuta on the way to Postira, is an Old Croatian building with a relief of St. George from the Renaissance. In Pučišća the first (private) school on the island was founded as early as 1516; the first reading room on Brač ("Hrvatski skup" - the Croatian assembly) was founded in 1868. Pučišća is the home town of the old Croatian writers Jure Žuvetić (16th century) and Trifun

Motif from Pučišća

Mladinić (17th century). Here the distinguished Croatian sculptor Branko Dešković (1883-1939) was born; his works are to be found in galleries in Split, Zagreb and Bol, on Brač.

••••••••••••

Pražnice** (391 m above sea level; 6 km south of Pučišća; 346 inhabitants) is an old medieval settlement which was mentioned as early as the 12th century. In the immediate area around the village there are several

Quarry in the vicinity of Pučišća

prehistoric burial mounds. In the graveyard is the **Chapel of St. Cyprian** (Sveti Ciprijan) from the 12th century, built in Romanesque and Gothic styles. In the chapel there is a stone Renaissance relief from 1467 from the workshop of Master Nikola Firentinac. The **Chapel of St. Clement** (Sveti Klement), built in Renaissance style, stands on the ruins of the neighbouring medieval settlement Straževnik, which was deserted in the 15th century when the people moved to Pražnice. In the chapel there is a relief from 1535 showing Pope Clement. The **Chapel of St. George** (Sveti Jure; on the road to Straževnik) is a pre-Romanesque building, which was mentioned in 1111 and has the oldest known bell-tower in Dalmatia. Inside there is a valuable Renaissance relief from the 15th century. The **Parish Church of St. Anthony the Abbot** (Sveti Antun Opat) was built in 1461. The main altar is interesting, with its stone relief in Baroque style and a Renaissance relief of St. Jerome on the right-hand side altar. **All Saints´ Chapel** (Svi Sveti) which still has elements of the Romanesque and Gothic eras, was built on Pražnice's market square in 1638. Over the doorway there is an inscription with the date.

Novo Selo (on the road between Selca and Povlja; 205 inhabitants.) was founded by refugees from Poljica in around 1575. Not far from the village there is a prehistoric fortress called Gradišće which is built of dry stone. At the southern foot of this fortress there are the remains of an early Christian Roman settlement. On the property of J. Bezmalinović and A. Škrabac there are the ruins of a Roman building, a Roman well and several graves and sarcophagi. A stone trough for making olive oil and a large millstone have also been preserved.

••••••••••••

Excursions

Povlja**

10 km east of Sumartin; 364 inhabitants.

Povlja served as a harbour for Roman galleys, as is shown by the remains of walls from that time in the area known as Žalo. The early Christian basilica (5th-6th century) has three aisles which are intersected by the transept, giving the basilica the form of a cross. The baptistery of the same area (now part of the parish church) is the only early Christian baptistery still standing in Croatia. It was joined to the basilica on its northern side, linked by a special passage. From the outside it was square in shape, but inside it was octagonal. It is 12 m high

Povlja

and covered with a dome. In the centre of the baptistery there is a pool for baptism in the shape of a cross, which is revered as the tomb of St. John of Povlja. The frescoes from the 5th and 6th centuries are, due to their condition and clear earthy colours, regarded as some of the most beautiful Roman frescoes in Dalmatia. The Benedictines added to the old deserted house of prayer in the 9th to the 10th centuries, by building a sanctuary in the baptistery and, over the apses of the old church, their living quarters. In 1145, the monastery was destroyed by pirates, but it was restored in 1184.

••••••••••••

The catalogue of the abbey's property of 1184 was copied and certified as the famous **Povljanska listina** (the Povlja charter) which is the oldest example of writing in Cyrillic in the Croatian language. It was copied and signed on 1st December 1250 by Ivan the Canon of Split, and is kept in the parish office in Pučišća.

••••••••••••

In the ornamental moulding on the Benedictine church Master Radonja, the first Croatian master to be known by name, chiselled his name and several lines of duodecasyllabics in Cyrillic in 1184. These are the earliest (extant) verses written in a Slavic language. Radonja's lintel is made of white Brač limestone; it is 124 cm long and 22 cm wide in the middle and is now kept in the museum of Croatian Archaeological Monuments in Split.

••••••••••••

The Benedictines left in the 15th century and the Brač nobility restored and extended the church. It became the parish church, extended first of all in the 16th and 17th and then in the 18th and 19th centuries. On what was once the baptism pool there is now the main altar. The bell tower was built between 1858 and 1872.

••••••••••••

Beside the church there is a tall tower built as a defence against the Turks in the 16th century. In the forecourt of the church there is a collection of stone monuments and in the church itself a valuable collection of sacred items and ecclesiastical robes.

••••••••••••

The Povlja lintel

Selca**

7 KM SOUTH OF POVLJA; 952 INHABITANTS.

This village was first mentioned in 1184 as a shepherds´ community, but for a long time it has been the centre of masonry work on Brač. The stone quarries Sveti Nikola and Žaganj-dolac are nearby. From these quarries stone blocks are taken for processing to Selca harbour at Radonja. The Augustinčić memorial in front of the UN building in New York was sculpted out of Selca stone. The **Parish Church of St. Cyril and St. Method** (Sveti Ćiril i Metod) was built after the First World War according to plans by the Austrian architect Schlauf, and combines elements of an old Christian basilica with the Romanesque and Gothic styles. The bronze figure of Christ is the work of Ivan Meštrović from 1956. It was moulded from melted-down artillery pieces which were left lying around in this area after the Second World War. **St. Nicholas' Chapel***** (Sveti Nikola) on Glavica (above the village), with a dome over the centre of its barrel vault from the 11th or 12th century, is one of the most important medieval

Selca

buildings on Brač. On Smrčevik hill (449 m) there are three more old Croatian chapels: St. Cosmas and St. Damian (Sveti Kuzma i Damjan); St. Thomas (Sveti Toma) and Holy Sunday on Gradac (Sveta Nedjelja na Gracu).

••••••••••••

The **Leo Tolstoy Memorial**, the first in the

Memorial to Tolstoy

world, was placed here in 1911, a year after the writer's death, and stands in the village park. On the square there is a memorial to Stjepan Radić (1871-1928) set up in 1938 (by A. Augustinčić). The prominent Slovak writer Martin Kukučin (Matej Bancur; 1860-1928) lived and worked here as a doctor for many years. Here too (between 1903 and 1904) he wrote his greatest work, the novel *The House in the Clearing* (*Dom u strani*) in which he immortalized Selca and the life of the patriarchs on the island at the beginning of this century. The grateful people of the village placed a memorial plaque on the house where he lived. In recent times two more statues have been put up in gratitude to people taking Croatia's side: to Pope John Paul II (by Kuzma Kovačić) and to the German politician Hans-Dietrich Genscher (by J. Gomes).

••••••••••••

Sumartin*

A CAR FERRY PORT ON THE SOUTHEAST COAST OF THE ISLAND, 3 KM EAST OF SELCA; POP. 482.

Sumartin was founded in 1645 by refugees from the Turks from the Makarska coastal area. At first it was called Vrhbrač, but the name Sumartin arose from the Italian San Martin when postal services were introduced in 1890. The **Franciscan monastery** was built on the site of an older, smaller one. Building work on the present monastery was begun in 1747 by the guardian of the time, the well-known Croatian poet and writer Father Andrija Kačić-Miošić. The monastery has rich archives and many books and incunabula. There is an example of an Orfelin atlas, codices and other items. There are valuable examples of church furniture including an outstanding old wooden tabernacle.

The most valuable items are paintings - the early Baroque Venetian *The Last Supper*, *St. Mary Magdalene* and *St. Peter and John* from the first half of the 17th century. The altarpiece *St. Anthony of Padua* was made by Father Šimun Ribarević towards the end of the 17th century. It includes the artist himself in Franciscan habit, and is the earliest example of a Franciscan depicted in his monastic costume. The **Parish Church of St. Martin** (Sveti Martin) was built by Father A. Gilić between 1911 and 1913. The marble altars are the work of P. Bilinić and were decorated with mosaics in 1912. The graves around the church are a reminder of the plague which swept across this area in 1784.

••••••••••••

Sumartin

Supetar

9 km from Split; a car ferry port on the northern coast, and the biggest settlement on the island; pop. 3 016

Old Supetar was situated on the small peninsula where there is now a graveyard. Life there came to an end during the early Christian era, to begin once again in the late Middle Ages around the small bay known as St. Peter's from which the town derived its name. Supetar became the island's official centre in 1827. The **Parish Church of St. Peter**** (Sveti Petar) stands on the site of an old chapel which was restored in 1604 but burnt down in 1729, and was rebuilt in 1773 in Baroque style. At that time it also received a new aisle and bell tower. It was extended in 1887. In the church there are paintings by the local artist Feliks Tironi from the second half of the 18th century and a Baroque altarpiece by an unknown Venetian artist of the 18th century. In the older part of the church there are some gravestones with Croatian inscriptions and at the entrance to the church there is a font made of two large Gothic capitals. On the left of the church building there is a sundial and beneath it a sarcophagus with the date 1744 engraved. In the Sunday school classrooms there are several valuable paintings from the Venetian era (16th and 17th centuries). The well, decorated with reliefs, is the work of Joannes Mazzonius from 1734. In the Supetar graveyard beside the **Chapel St. Nicholas** (Sveti Nikola Putnik) there are two old Christian sarcophagi and several gravestones (Pieta), which are the work of Ivan Rendić of Supetar (1849-1932), and the mausoleum of the Petrinović family with portraits and sculptures, by the sculptor Toma Rosandić (1878-1958). By the road for Donji Humac there is a pre-Romanesque church, St. Luke's (Sveti Luka), from the 11th or 12th century. It has engraved pictures of ships on the northern wall of the same date. On the road to Nerežišća is St. Rocco´s chapel (Sveti Rok) which was built in 1682.

St. Peter's Church

View of Supetar

Excursions

Donji Humac**

9 km south of Supetar; 2 km north of Nerežišća; 166 inhabitants.

Donji Humac is one of the oldest settlements on the island. It developed on the site of the older Gomilje, and the name Humac was first mentioned in 1375. To the northwest of the village is Kopačina cave where some prehistoric items have been discovered. Right next to the cave is **St. Elijah's Church** (Sveti Ilija) from the 10th and 11th centuries. It has an apse which is rectangular on the outside but semi-circular inside. Inside the chapel there are the remains of a **Roman mausoleum** (4.40 x 3.5 m) built of cut stone. On the road to Supetar is St. Luke's Chapel from the 10th or 11th century. On one wall inside, drawings of sailing ships have been discovered dating from the same period. They are the oldest examples of drawings of ships of the Middle Ages on the Croatian coast. On the road towards Nerežišća are the ruins of **St. Andrew's Chapel** (Sveti Jadro) which was built between the 12th and the 14th centuries on some Roman ruins. The **parish church** was built on the site of an older church (from the 10th century). It was added to in the 14th

Supetar beach

century and in the 18th century it was extended with two side aisles and a Baroque bell tower. On the wall of the original sanctuary a fresco has been discovered (93 x 139 cm) showing Christ between His mother and a bearded John the Baptist. It dates from the end of the 13th century.

••••••••••••

Nerežišća**

382 m above sea level; 10 km south of Supetar; 868 inhabitants.

Nerežišća was for more than 8 centuries the administrative centre of Brač: from the year 1000, when the town was named the main centre by the Venetian Doge Pietro II Orseolo, right up to 1828. It was also the home of the Brač Count. Nerežišća was settled by Croatians in the 7th century. In 1277 it was attacked by pirates when amongst other things the Brač archive was destroyed by fire. In 1305 the order was given to rewrite the *Brač Statute* which had been destroyed in the fire and had been used for centuries as a basis of law and order on the island. Of the Gothic residential buildings, the only one now still standing is the **house of the Garafulić** family which also served as barracks for the count's guard. There is also the Renaissance Harašić palace. On the square there is a flag staff with a relief of the Venetian lion and the date 1545. The **Parish Church of St. Mary** (Sv. Marija) is the most impressive church on the island and most successfully blends with its surroundings. It was mentioned as early as the 13th century; in 1538 it was rebuilt, and its present Baroque appearance dates from the second half of the 18th century. Only the central part of the facade is left of the original building along with a rose window and a gravestone in the central aisle. The bell tower was built in 1746. Inside the church there is a wooden Renaissance altar with a late-Renaissance altarpiece, made by the Venetian artist Carlo Ridolfi in the first half of the 17th century. **St. Peter's Chapel** (Sveti Petar) dates from the end of the 14th century and was built in Gothic style. The bell-tower has characteristics of the Romanesque era. Inside the church is the interesting relief which dates from 1578: *Madonna and the Saints* by the Brač sculptor Nikola Lazanić. **St. Margaret's Chapel** (Sveta Margita) stands in the middle of the square; it was built at the end of the 14th century. **St. Nicholas' Chapel** (Sveti Nikola) in the graveyard was also built in Gothic style, whose characteristics are still visible in the broken arches of the bell-tower and in the vaulting in the chapel itself. **Holy Trinity Chapel** (Sveto Trojstvo) is on the right of the road for Supetar. It is a simple building dating from the 12th century. **St. George's Chapel** (Sveti Juraj) is on the top of Jurjevo brdo (George's hill) and was built at the time of the transition from the Romanesque to the Gothic eras. Inside there is a fine Renaissance relief showing St. George on horseback killing the dragon with his spear. It is thought that this is also by Nikola Lazanić. In **St. James' Chapel** (Sveti Jakov) on the old road to Dračevica there is a

Nerežišća

The Wheel, a natural phenomenon from the outskirts of Nerežišća

Baroque relief showing the Madonna and Child and the saints Philip and James. Experts consider the Madonna of St. James to be the most beautiful representation of Our Lady on the island. St. Theodore's Chapel (Sveti Tudor) near Nerežišća (near Veliko brdo hill) is an early Christian basilica in ruins.

••••••••••••

Dračevica (on the road to Bobovišća; 96 inhabitants) was founded by fugitives from Poljica who moved here in the 17th century. On nearby Trišćenik hill there is the lid of a Roman sarcophagus. The **Chapel of St. Cosmas and St. Damian** (Sveti Kuzma i Damjan) was built in 1678 and the parish church (with its interesting wooden altar with an altarpiece depicting *The Immaculate Conception*) was built in 1770.

••••••••••••

Postira**

9 KM EAST OF SUPETAR; 1 553 INHABITANTS.

Postira was first mentioned in 1347 by this name. In the harbour there is a Renaissance building whose southern facade is covered with many humanist quotations of a religious nature. The Croatian writer, revolutionary and politician Vladimir Nazor (1876-1949) was born here. The poet I. Ivanišević (1608-1655) also hails from Postira, as well as the 16th century Renaissance sculptor Nikola Lazanić (16th cent.). The parish church was built in the 16th century but only the sturdy enclosed apse with its loopholes still remains of the original building. Inside the church *The way of the cross* is the work of three artists from the end of the 18th century, and there are also several paintings of the Venetian school. To the east of Postira (in Lovrečina bay) there are the ruins of a large early Christian basilica dating from some time between the 5th and 6th centuries. In the 11th century there was a Benedictine monastery here. It is also possible to see in the sea the remains of a quay from the same era. Above Postira there are some walls built of cut stone, rising to about 3 metres high in places. These are the ruins of an early Christian church, St. John's (Sveti Ivan).

••••••••••••

Dol** (3 km south of Postira; 178 inhabitants) is interesting for two one-storey houses built on rock, which have retained many elements of original peasant architecture. From the very beginning this has been a Croatian village and was first mentioned in 1137. It is surrounded by old Croatian chapels on the neighbouring hills: **St. Michael's** (Sveti Mihovil) whose main door is made of a Roman sarcophagus, **St. Vitus** (Sveti Vid) and the graveyard **Chapel of St. Peter** (Sveti Petar) with a separate bell tower and the oldest bell on the island dating from the 14th to the 15th century. The parish church in Dol was built in 1866 and inside

Postira

there is a valuable Baroque crucifix known as *Dolski Skrst* (the Cross of Dol).

••••••••••••

Splitska* (5 km east of Supetar; 381 inhabitants) grew up as Škrip's harbour in the bay from which, in the era of Emperor Diocletian, Brač stone was loaded to build his palace in what is now Split. In the nearby stone quarry Rasoha there is a statue of Hercules carved in stone, from the end of the 3rd century, the most significant example of Roman sculpture on Brač. The **Renaissance castle** (by the crossroads on the way to Škrip) belonging to the Cerineo-Cerinić family was built in 1577 and is one of the most important buildings on Brač of the 16th century and the most beautiful defensive building on the island. It consists of three buildings joined together by high towers with loopholes and consoles. Inside the castle is the painting *The Madonna and Child* (Bernardino dei Conti, 1450-1522) and a portrait of the knight Mauro Cerinić Morrus (the first half of the 16th century). The **Parish Church of the Blessed Virgin Mary** (B.D. Marija Stomorena) stands on the foundations of a church of the same name from the 13th century, renovated in the 16th century. It had an outstanding late-Renaissance wooden polychrome altar with a painting of *The Madonna and the Saints* by Leandro Bassano (1577-1622). The **Chapel of St. Andrew** (Sveti Jadro; Sveti Andrija) on the road to Škrip was built between the 5th and the 6th centuries. The apse remains, and is rounded on the inside but angular on the outside.

Sutivan

The ruins of a large Early Christian basilica in Lovrečina

••••••••••••

Sutivan* (7 km west of Supetar; 759 inhabitants)

Sutivan grew up in the 15th century on the site where in the early Christian era there was a temple of **St. John** (Sveti Ivan). The old

St. John's Church was built as a triple-apsed early Christian church in the 6th century. In the 11th century it was repaired and in 1656 rebuilt. The southern wall of the old church (with four lesenes on the outside) is still standing today. The **parish church** was built in the Renaissance style in 1579. Later it was redecorated in Baroque style and reconstructed in the 19th century. The Baroque bell tower is the work of the sculptor Petar Pavao Bertapelle. In the church are the altarpiece *Our Lady of the Rosary*, of the Central

Škrip, Museum of the Island Brač

Italian school (17th century) and *The Madonna* by Vinko Draganja. On the sea front is the **castle of the Marjanović family** from 1772 with a sundial. In architectural terms, the Renaissance fortified home of the Natali-Božičević family (1505) is very interesting, as is the Baroque summer residence (1690-1705) of the poet Jerolim Kavanjin with its park. In the Definis house (from the beginning of the 19th century) there is a collection of furniture and works of art. **St. Rocco's Chapel** (Sveti Rok) in the graveyard, was built in 1635 and inside there is a wooden statue of St. Rocco by V. Tironi and several paintings of the Central Dalmatian early Baroque era. In the eastern part of the village there is a windmill which has been converted into a home.

•••••••••••

Mirca* (on the road to Supetar; 306 inhabitants), was first mentioned in 1579. With its rural atmosphere, beautiful gardens and orchards, the village served as inspiration to the Croatian poet Tin Ujević for his poem (written in 1929) *Discovering Mirca* (Otkrivajući Mirca). Mirca has a parish church which was built in 1579 and extended in the second half of the 19th century. It is dedicated to **Our Lady of the Visitation** (Gospa od Pohoda). In the church there is an altarpiece, *Pieta*, by the Brač artist F. Tironi from 1783.

•••••••••••

Škrip**

251 m above sea level; 12 km from Supetar via Splitska; 186 inhabitants.

Škrip is the oldest settlement on Brač. It was founded by the Illyrians and during the Roman era they used Škrip stone quarry in building Diocletian's palace in Split. It was mentioned for the first time in 1288. The **Museum of the Island of Brač** (in the tower Kula Radojković) has many valuable exhibits. The lower part of the building is built of Illyrian walls upon which there are traces of Roman remains, then of old Croatian architecture and at last the tower was raised again in the 16th century during the wars between Venice and the Turks. From this defensive structure the "gigantic walls" continue northwards. At one time they defended the Illyrians from the Greek invaders. Many graves have been preserved from the Roman era, with sarcophagi and the mausoleum of a Roman patrician right below the tower itself. The village is dominated by **Cerinić's Castle**. Built in 1618, it has two towers standing on strong walls. The **Parish Church of St. Helen** (Sveta Jelena; from the 18th century) had four altarpieces by Palma the Younger. Two were stolen in the seventies. Very close to the parish church is the Chapel of the Holy Spirit (Sveti Duh), a pre-Romanesque church (11th to 12th century) extended in the 16th and 17th centuries. In front of the church there are several old Croatian graves with symbols representing the trade of the dead person engraved on the gravestones (rudders, axes, hatchets, swords etc.). By the entrance to the graveyard there is a Roman water hole hollowed out of solid rock (7 x 3 x 2.5 m) with stone steps and a small trough. ■

The Church of St. Helen in Škrip

Hvar

The island of Hvar is the fourth largest island in the Adriatic, covering an area of 299.6 km^2. It is 68 km long and a maximum of 10.5 km in width. In the 47 settlements on the island there are 11 400 inhabitants. It is the sunniest place in the Adriatic, with 2718 hours of sunshine a year and it is known for its mild winters. Snow and temperatures below freezing are very rare. It is famous for its well developed vineyards and lavender gardens.

Hvar, with the Pakleni otoci (islands) in the background

Prehistory. Archaeological research on the island has shown that there was human life here in the Neolithic Age. In contrast to other equally important archaeological sites, Hvar has been well researched: the cave Grapčeva špilja in 1936, Pokrivenik bay in 1947 and Markova špilja in 1956. The most famous scholar was the archaeologist Grga Novak (1888-1978). In the course of this research some Neolithic coloured ceramics were found proving that the early inhabitants of Hvar (unknown predecessors of the Illyrians) had links with both the eastern and the western coasts of the Mediterranean: Crete, Syria, Egypt, Malta, Sicily and Southern Italy. Archaeologists recognise a "Hvar culture" falling within the early Neolithic Age characterised by ceramics decorated with spiral ornamentation, executed in various combinations of colours: reds, whites, yellows, greys and browns. Whilst the coloured ceramics of the Hvar culture are similar in some ways to ceramics of the same era from Italy and Greece, the linear ornamentation or the diagrammatic figures represented, with the help of an engraving technique (impresso ceramics), are unique to Hvar culture. Material traces of Hvar culture however are not confined to Hvar and its neighbouring islands, but relate to a wider area in the interior and the Northern Adriatic. (See Hvar, Archaeological Collection and Stone Collection of Grga Novak)

The Greek Era. The Greeks colonized the island in 384 BC. Where Stari Grad is today, they built a large settlement (Pharos) and on the site of present-day Hvar, according to some hypotheses, a small one (Dimos). The people came from the island of Paros in the Aegean Sea and the present name of the island is also of Greek origins. Hvar was the only Ionic settlement amongst the Greek towns on the Adriatic. The remaining Greeks were colonists from Syracuse. The encounter with the old inhabitants

(Illyrians and Delmati) was not friendly. According to the historian Diodorus of Sicily (1st century BC) the natives attacked the Greek settlement with help from their kinsman from the mainland, but in the end they were defeated, as help arrived from Pharos and Greek Vis (Issa). A prominent personality at that time was the military leader Demetrius of Hvar. He was a Greek, born in Hvar (ca 260 BC) ruler of Hvar, Brač, Korčula and parts of the Southern Adriatic coast. He was a Roman vassal, but not completely loyal to Rome. He entered an alliance with Macedonia and worked towards what we would now call a kind of "unification" of the Balkans against Rome. He was killed in 213 BC in a battle against the Romans near Messenia.

Figurehead of a Hvar galley

The Roman Era. The Romans conquered Hvar at the beginning of the 3rd century BC. In comparison with the previous era, life on the island went into decline: the metropolis became a province, Pharia, and then a prefecture of the colony of Salona. The Romans took over the fertile plains and the native population of the island was squeezed into the eastern part of the island. They mainly lived on small farms and some small settlements grew up in the plains. When the Empire was divided, Hvar came under the Eastern Empire, later Byzantium.

The Migrations of the Nations. From 493 to 536 the eastern coast of the Adriatic was under attack by the Ostrogoths. In 536 they were defeated by Byzantium and from that time, Byzantium had control over the island. At the end of the 6th or the beginning of the 7th century, the Avars and the Slavs entered Byzantine territory. In contrast to Krk, Cres or Rab, there were no large settlements on Hvar at this time, and therefore it did not suffer the same degree of destruction. In the 7th century the island was settled by the Slavic Neretvans. From then and right up to the 19th century the island was known by the name Lesna (Lisna, Liesna, and in Italian, Lesina). The name originated from the Neretvan people.

Under Various Rulers. From the arrival of the Slavs to their final defeat by Venice in 1420, Hvar had a succession of different rulers. The time of Byzantine rule was least stable and lasted unchallenged only from 870 to 886 and then from 1164 to 1180. The rule of the Neretvans (see the Neretva Delta) lasted to the middle of the 11th century. It is impossible to tell exactly how much the people of Hvar joined the Neretvans in their piratical activities

Hvar in a Venetian engraving

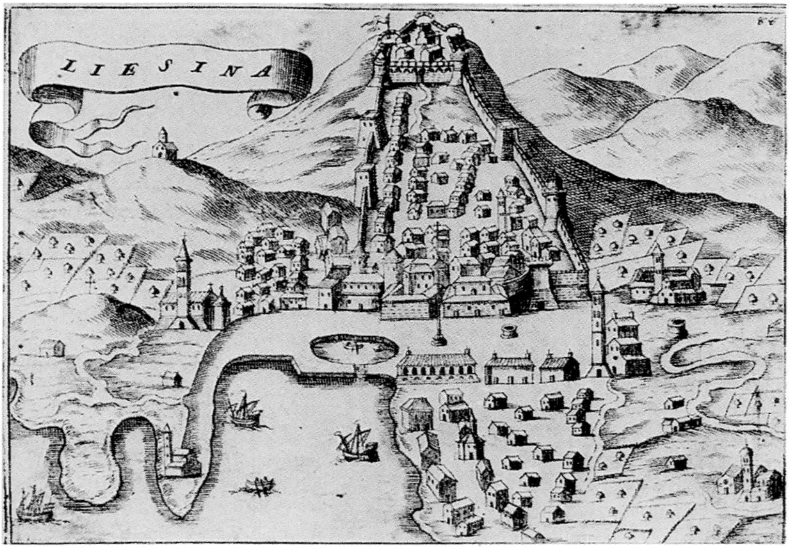

A find from Grapčeva špilja (cave), the oldest pictorial representation of a ship in Europe (about 2,700 BC)

on the Adriatic. From the middle of the 11th century the Neretva district became part of the Kingdom of Croatia. Croatian Hvar was a prime target for Venice from the 11th century and up to 1420 it came under their "protection". It was first occupied in 1000 by Doge Pietro II Orseolo and later Venice conquered it in 1145, and then between 1278 and 1309. The island was under the Croatian kings between 1180 and 1278 and then 1358 and 1393. The Bosnian King Tvrtko ruled the island for a brief period in 1390, then the Zadar nobility (1403) and the people of Dubrovnik (1413). The city of Hvar developed as an autonomous community, and so in 1278 the administrative centre of the island was moved there from Stari Grad (Civitas Vetus).

Under the Venetians (1420-1797). For all Venetian ships sailing on the Mediterranean or returning to their home port, Hvar was an obligatory stop-over point. This encouraged the city's growth and during the Venetian rule Hvar was the richest community in Dalmatia. The Venetians carried out various changes in the city government: the Rector was chosen by the Great Assembly in Venice from the ranks of the Venetian nobility. Participation by the ordinary people in government was completely ruled out. Conflicts between the people and the nobility came to a head in 1510 when a rebellion led by Matija Ivanić (see Vrboska) broke out. 6000 rebels took part. The rebellion was also of a nationalist nature, for the ordinary people were Croats. It was put down with much bloodshed by the Venetian navy. The year 1571 was a dramatic one for the city of Hvar. In that year the Turks from Ulcinj, led by Eulg Ali (Ulič Alija) entered the city and razed it to the ground. It took several decades for the city to be rebuilt. When the Venetians decided in 1774 to transfer their main port from Hvar to Kotor, Hvar fell into the background. The humanistic ideas embraced by many prominent people from Hvar were a significant contribution to the national culture of Croatia. In the 16th century these people included Vinko Pribojević (Vincentius Priboevus), famous for his speech on the ethnic (Slavic) origin of the population, Nikola Paladinić, a lecturer in legal matters at Padua University, Jeronim and Hortenzije Bartučević, Hanibal Lucić (see Arsenal), Petar Hektorović (see Stari Grad), Nikša Pelegrinović and Martin Benetović.

The Period Between 1797 and 1813. Following the fall of Venice, Hvar, together with all its former dominions, fell under Austria. Between 1806 and 1812 it was held by the French, and from 1812 to 1813 by the English and after Napoleon's defeat, once more by the Austrians.

The 19th and 20th centuries. Hvar remained under Austrian rule right up to the end of the First World War (1918). Hvar harbour was not as important for steam ships as it had been for sailing vessels, which contributed to its increasingly provincial role. At the end of the First World War, Hvar was occupied by the Italians for four years and then became part of the Kingdom of the Serbs, Croats and Slovenes in 1922. The first Yugoslavia could not ensure the island's prosperity. Since the 1960s it has become one of the best known tourist centres in the country. ■

Hvar (Town)

LOCATED 43° 10´ N, 16° 45´ E.
POP. 4 138

SIGHTS

The **City Walls and Fortress****. The old city centre is surrounded by Romanesque walls from the 13th or 14th century. The eastern city gates from 1454 are also still intact. On the top of a hill on the site of a medieval castle, a **Citadel** was built in 1557 (known as **Španjola**; NUMBER ❷ ON THE PLAN). At the beginning of the 19th century the Austrians built barracks here, which now serve as a leisure centre. To the east of Španjola on St. Nicholas Hill (Brijeg Svetog Nikole, NUMBER ❸ ON THE PLAN), stands Napoleon's Fortress, built in 1811. Today it is used as an observatory and a seismological centre.

The **Arsenal***** (NUMBER ❹ ON THE PLAN) is a most impressive example of secular architecture. The present building was built between 1579 and 1611 on the site of a building from the 13th century which had been destroyed by the Turks in 1571. With its 10 m span arched doorway this building served as a store for war galleys. Whilst renovating the Arsenal Count Pietro Semitecolo of Hvar

St. Stephen's Cathedral

had a theatre built on the first floor. This was one of the first community theatres in Europe. In terms of time, it comes between the theatre in Vicenza (Palladios Teatro Olimpico) of 1580 and the theatre in Parma (Teatro Farnese, 1618). The theatre has been renovated several times, but two rows of the present boxes date from 1800. Apart from dramas, tragedies and comedies, pastorals were also

City Loggia

performed in the Hvar theatre. Theatrical life in Hvar did not begin when the theatre was built.; even before, performances took place, in front of the cathedral. Hvar also had its own writers who have an important place in the national culture. These include Hanibal Lucić (c.1485-1553) the author of *The Slave Girl* (Robinja) and Martin Benetović (died 1607) who wrote *The Girl from Hvar* (Hvarkinja). The theatrical life of Hvar is not just a historical concept, and it is still such an important part of the national culture that in the theatre building performances are still often given by many professional and amateur ensembles.

The **Gallery of Contemporary Art.** This contains some 40 paintings and sculptures, among which the most important names of Croatian modern art are represented (Emanuel Vidović, Frano Šimunović, Ivo Dulčić, Miljenko Stančić and others).

The **City Loggia**** (NUMBER ❸ ON THE PLAN). Right next to the arsenal there is a Renaissance building which some have attributed to the Veronese architect Girolamo Sanmicheli, but which was in fact built later by, amongst others, the Korčulan master Tripun Bokanić. Beside the loggia there is a clock tower. It was at one time a tower linking the wall around the Count's palace, which was demolished in the 19th century. The tower received its present appearance in the 18th century.

St. Stephen's Cathedral*** (Sveti Stjepan; NUMBER ❺ ON THE PLAN). Like the arsenal building, this cathedral was rebuilt after the Turkish

The Arsenal

The interior of Hvar Theatre

campaigns of 1571. It was built at the end of the 16th and beginning of the 17th centuries. It is a late Renaissance building, and its facade is very similar to the churches of Holy Salvation (Sveti Spas) in Dubrovnik and St. Mary's (Sveta Marija) in Zadar. The Renaissance bell tower with its biforia, triforia and quadriforia, which are linked to the loggia, is considered to be one of the most beautiful in Dalmatia. The builders of the bell tower and the cathedral were local masters. It is a triple-naved building whose central nave is part of an older church. Part of its inventory (stone work, the relief *The Scourging of Christ* a copy of a work by Juraj Dalmatinac - see Šibenik) and *Madonna and the Saints* comes from the older church too. The church has nine Baroque altars (17th century) made from the same material. They were donated by fraternities or the Hvar nobility. There is an altar donated by the Hektorović family upon which stands a Madonna dating from 1220, one of the oldest in Dalmatia. There is an inscription in front of the altar beneath the wooden floor. The altarpiece on the main altar is the painting *Our Lady and St. Stephen* by Palma the Younger. Of particular interest is the altar donated by Bishop Andreis upon which is the sarcophagus of St. Prosper from 1859. In the centre of the church there is one of the most beautiful choirs in Dalmatia. The date 1573 is the date of restoration which was carried out by Mark Antun Mlečanin. The square where the cathedral stands is the largest of its kind in Dalmatia. It is surrounded by palaces dating from the late Gothic to Baroque. The fountain, which was built in 1520 by Ivan Kiskić, was restored in 1780. In the neighbouring Bishop's palace there is an exhibition of the Cathedral treasures including ecclesiastical robes, gold items including a staff of gold-plated bronze which belonged to Bishop Pritić (Patritius) and was made by the local goldsmith Pavao Dubravčić from Dubrovnik. There is also a collection of paintings and wood carvings. The curia also has rich archives and a library.

The golden crosier of the Bishop of Hvar

••••••••••••

The **Franciscan Monastery and Church*****

Franciscan monastery at the time of a church festivity

(number 7 on the plan). These are Renaissance buildings which were built between 1461 and 1489 by local workers. The Renaissance relief *The Madonna and Child* in the lunette of the church's portal is by Nikola Firentinac (see Šibenik). Inside the church over the main altar, there is a polyptych by Francesco da Santacroce from 1583. Together with two smaller polyptychs by the same artist (on the altars beneath the choir gallery) this is considered to be one of the most valuable works by that Venetian artist. In the central aisle the altarpiece is *The Stigmatisation of St. Francis* by Palma the Younger. He has also been credited with the painting of *St. Diego*. The painting of

Christ on the cross is by Leandro Bassano, and *Ecce Homo* is by an anonymous Italian artist of the 16th century. Above the two altars and the door leading to the choir, there is a series of six scenes from *The Sufferings of Christ* by the comedy writer and organist from Hvar, Martin Benetović. In the church there are also the graves of the families who founded the monastery. In front of the main altar, the poet and humanist Hanibal Lucić is buried (see the Arsenal). The plaque shows the initials AL. The choir has beautiful Renaissance stalls which are the work of F. Čiočić and A. Spia. The church's side doors lead to the cloisters which in turn lead to the museum and a collection of works of art. The **museum** is housed in the **old monastery refectory** and its most famous exhibit is the painting *The Last Supper* (2.5 x 8 m). Modern critics attribute this work to the artist Matteo Ingoli of Ravena (1585-1631), but according to legend it is the work of Matteo Rosselli. In either case the painting has all the characteristics of late Venetian painting of the 16th century. Of the museum's other exhibits it is worth noting the painting *The Betrothal of St. Catherine* which comes from the circle of Blaž Jurjev Trogiranin (see Trogir). There is also a very valuable library including: hand written antiphonaries with illuminations by Father Bone Razmilović (15th century) a Ptolemaic atlas from 1524, and a Koran from the 17th century. There is also a collection of items used in the Mass and small collection of archaeological finds and coins from the area around the island of Hvar.

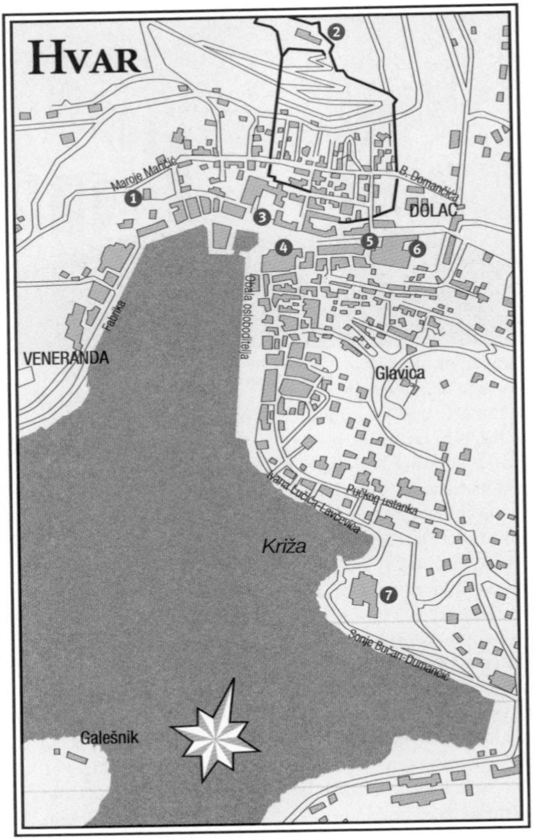

The Last Supper, from the collection of the Franciscan monastery

••••••••••••

The **Grga Novak Archaeological Collection and Stone Collection** (NUMBER ❶ ON THE PLAN). This is to be found in the premises of the former Dominican monastery and the Church of St. Mark of the 14th century. The collection has about 850 items, while there are about 500 exhibits in the permanent exhibition (see Hvar, Prehistory). These premises are also used for events in the summer.

•••••••••••

Other Sights. The most famous of the patricians' palaces is the unfinished **Hektorović house** (over the main city gates) and the older **Lucić family summer residence** (to the east of the cathedral; NUMBER ❻ ON THE PLAN) which was the first large house built in the city of Hvar. It has two rows of Gothic windows and a stone balustrade with a balcony. To the west of the harbour there are the ruins of St. Mark's Church (Sveti Marko). The outline and the bell tower are still intact. In the apse there is an archaeological exhibition and within the walls of the old church there is a collection of stone monuments. This church is also used for concerts. Between the clock tower, the Palace Hotel and Hektorović house, stands the **Church of St. Cosmas and St. Damian** (Sveti Kuzma i Damjan) which, with the city walls, is the only Romanesque building in the city. The church was later altered in the Baroque style.

•••••••••••

Hvar as a climatic cure town. Thanks to its favourable climate (it has an average of 2 700 hours of sunshine a year), Hvar is a well known cure town. Hvar is particularly recommended for the treatment of bronchitis and bronchial asthma, chronic infections and allergies of the respiratory tract and other organs.

Excursions

Brusje* (5 km along the road to Stari Grad or Sućuraj; 206 inhabitants) grew up at the beginning of

Typical island architecture

the 16th century as a shepherds' village. In the parish church (built in 1731 and extended twice) are paintings by the Italian artist B. Zelotti (c.1526-1578), *St. Anthony the Abbot with the Saints*, and the contemporary artist Ivo Dulčić who was born in Brusje, showing St. George in a landscape with the Split city gates. Beside the church is the vicarage and the graveyard. There is a beautiful view of the area from this hill. The road to Brusje is known as the wine road because it passes through a rich wine-growing area (see the wines of Hvar).

•••••••••••

Milna**

6 KM FROM HVAR, OR 30 MIN BY MOTOR BOAT.

Milna is a bay with a wide sandy beach. On the eastern edge of the fields there is a deserted village called Malo Grblje, surrounded by gorges like a pirate's nest. On the western edge there is a Baroque summer residence from the 17th century, the most beautiful house on the island, intended as a holiday home. It belonged to the descendants of Matija Ivanić (see Vrboska) and inside are the family coat of arms and portraits.

•••••••••••

Pakleni otoci** are a group of eleven islands and several rocks off Hvar harbour, stretching over a distance of 11 km and providing a natural protective barrier for the harbour. Their name derives from "paklina", a "pitch" used here for waterproofing ships. In fact they should really be called Paklinski otoci as the Croatian word "pakleni" means "hellish". The islands are not inhabited. The largest is Sveti Klement where there are the remains of Illyrian earthworks and Roman buildings. The most famous building is the chapel of St. Clement (Sveti Klement) from the 14th century, restored in 1870, in memory of the battle of Vis in 1866.

•••••••••••

Jelsa

30 KM FROM HVAR, 10 KM FROM STARIGRAD; 1 798 INHABITANTS.

Jelsa** was first mentioned in the 14th century as a harbour serving the nearby village Pitve (Portus de Pitue). The harbour wall was built in about

View of Jelsa

1830. At the end of the 14th and the beginning of the 15th century the village was settled by fugitives from Bosnia and in the 17th century from Makarska, so that it did not really develop as a settlement until then. It was divided in two by marshy terrain, but this dried up in the 19th century. In the 18th century a shipyard was opened in Jelsa and it became the best known ship-building centre on the island. In the 19th century Jelsa had 142 merchant ships and from them it acquired the material basis to become an important centre on the island.

St. John's Church in Jelsa

Sights

The **Parish Church of SS. Fabian and Sebastian** (Sveti Fabijan i Sebastijan) is the oldest building in the town. It was mentioned in 1331, but its present appearance with its fortified apses, dates from 1535. A church fortified in this way was necessary to defend the population from attacks by the Turks in 1571. The wooden sculpture on the main altar *Madonna Stomorena* (Sveta Marija) was brought in 1539 from

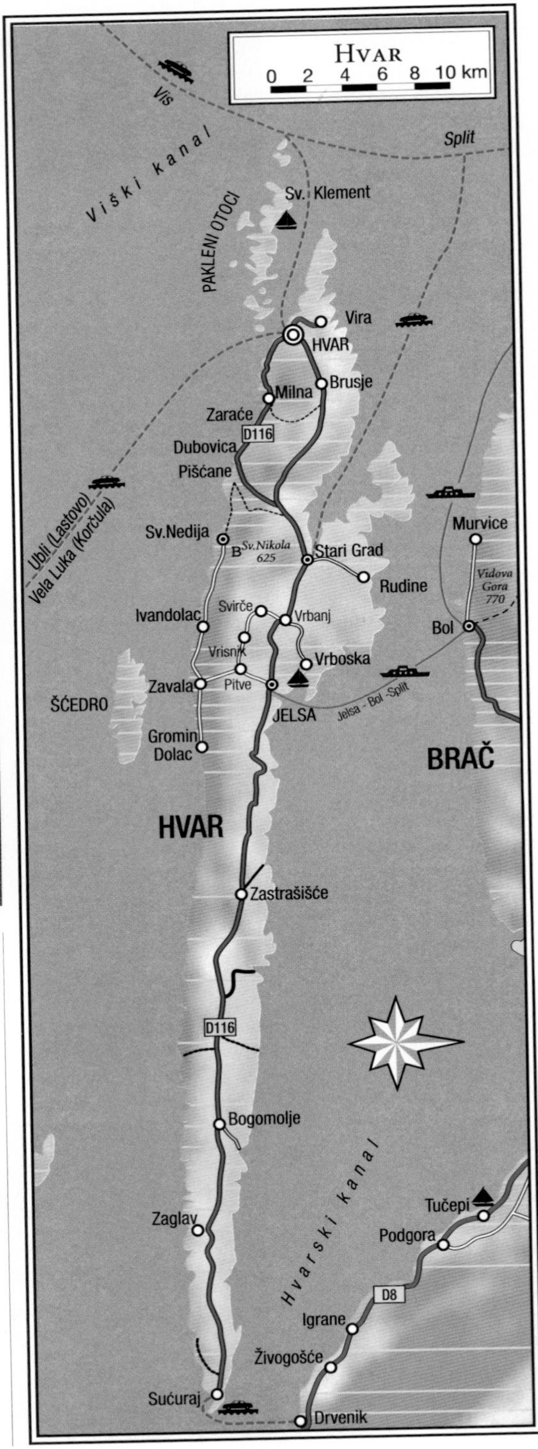

Čitluk near Sinj and since then the anniversary has been celebrated every year on 15th August. In the sacristy there is a small exhibition of sacred objects. **St. John's Church** (Sveti Ivan), in the south of the town, has an irregular layout and dates from the 15th century. In the 17th century it was redecorated in Baroque style. Around the church there is a square whose present appearance dates from the 18th century.

••••••••••••

Tor (on hill to the east of the town, an hour's walk from the town). These are the well preserved ruins of a Greek watch tower built of megalithic blocks in the 4th and 3rd centuries BC. Procession with the Cross (see Vrboska).

Excursions

The eastern part of the island. The largest settlement is the ferry port **Sućuraj** (49 km from Jelsa; 387 inhabitants) which was named after its church, St. George's (Sveti Juraj) which dates from 1331. The village has been inhabited since the middle of the 15th century and in the 17th century it was fortified for protection against the Turks. The danger from the mainland demanded special building techniques: houses linked together and the streets leading out of the village closed off with gates. In the forecourt of the parish church, St. George's (Sveti Juraj) there is an inscription from the 19th century on a gravestone telling in Bosančica (western Cyrillic script) of the heroic people who defended their home against the Turks. In the sacristy there is a chalice which was given by Pope Gregory XV and the French Duke L'Alençon. On the road from Jelsa to Sućuraj is the village **Zastražišće** (16 km from Jelsa; 230 inhabitants) which was built originally for defensive purpose (in Croatian "straža" means "watch"). On the hill stands the Parish Church of St. Nicholas (Sveti Nikola) from where there is a good view of Mt. Biokovo and the coastal area. **Gdinj** (23 km from Sućuraj; 8 km from Zastražišće; the name derives from the Croatian word "bdjeti" which also means "to watch") is also a village which had a "look-out" function even in pre-historic times. The rustic houses (Visković) in Kola street here are particularly interesting in ethnographic terms. **Bogomolje** (17 km from Sućuraj; 98 inhabitants). In this part of the island there is more of a continental feel amongst the population than an island character, which is seen both in their national costume and dialect. The Baroque parish church was built in 1605 and its facade dates from 1750. The road forks at the village of Jerkovići (10 km from Sućuraj) and leads off to Zaglav. Here, in unspoilt natural surroundings there is a cave which was inhabited in prehistoric times. On the road between Gdinj and Sućuraj, on both sides of the coast there are romantic bays and beautiful beaches.

Lavender field on Hvar

••••••••••••

The southern part of the island. Following the building of a tunnel (1400 m) on the road from the village of Pitve to Zavala, the southern area of the island has become accessible. **Zavala** (6.5 km from Jelsa) is an

Sveta Nedjelja, an old church in a cave

interesting place for outings because of its many beaches and as the departure point for the island of Šćedro and the village **Sveta Nedjelja**** (6 km west of Zavala; 130 inhabitants). Sveta Nedjelja is situated on a crag above the highest peak on the island. In the nearby caves Augustinian monks lived in the 15th century and also had their own church there. They deserted the caves in 1787, but the church remained in use until a new one was built in this century.

••••••••••••

Between Zavala and Sveta Nedjelja (actually between Hum hill and St. Nicholas hill) are the **Grapčeva špilja** caves (access from the sea from Ivandolac, and, from the land, from the village of Pitve) which are one of the best known archaeological sites in Croatia (see Prehistory, "Hvar culture"). The caves have been explored by many archaeologists (G. Gasperini, M. Schneider, H. Girometta, and from 1912 to 1952 by Grga Novak). Three layers of finds of the material culture of prehistoric man have been found proving that there was life in these caves from the Neolithic (Eneolithic) to the Illyrian eras. Grga Novak believed that the caves served for some kind of cult practices.

••••••••••••

To the south of Zavala (2 nautical miles) is the island of **Šćedro** (7.5 km², highest peak 113 m). Nowadays the island is more or less uninhabited (20 inhabitants) but it is popular because of its beautiful beaches. It is thought that Šćedro was the ancient island of Tauris near which, in 47 BC, there was a sea battle between the fleets of Caesar and Pompey. In Rake Bay the remains of a Roman villa rustica are visible in the sea (the east coast of the Adriatic is gradually sinking into the sea). In Mostir bay there are the ruins of a Dominican monastery built in the 16th century but deserted at the end of the 18th century. St. Mary's Church was built in the 12th (or 13th) century and later included in a new church.

••••••••••••

View of Stari Grad

Stari Grad

20 KM FROM HVAR, 10 KM FROM JELSA; POP. 1 906.

Stari Grad is sited at the end of a 7 km long bay, and at the beginning of the longest and most fertile plain on the Adriatic islands. On this site stood the Greek city of Pharos founded in the 4th century BC, and razed by the Romans in 219 BC. It was the residence of the Illyrian (of Greek descent) army leader Demetrius of Hvar. Greek Pharos had the status of a City State. After the Greek era, the city continued its life as the Roman Pharia, but in 1205 it became known as Civitas Vetus ("Old City" - Stari Grad in Croatian). When the bishop moved to Novi Grad (today´s city of Hvar), the original name of the city (Pharos) was transferred to the new administrative centre, Civitas Vetus losing something of its importance and gaining the name it bears today. Now it is one of the best known tourist

Greek cadastre - the oldest in the Mediterranean

resorts and its wine producers have a capacity of 30 000 hl.

•••••••••••

Sights

Remains of Hellenistic houses and streets** are visible today in the Remetine Garden behind the Church of St. John, and in the plain outside the town, the divisions of the land into plots of 1 x 5 stadia (180 x 900 m) can be seen. The stone boundary markers and the system of paths through the field make up the best known Greek cadastre in the Mediterranean. The **Cyclop's Walls** are to be found in the Tadić-Gramontorov house; these are traces of the 9 m walls that encircled Greek Faros. They are composed of megalithic blocks built dry.

•••••••••••

The **Roman mosaic**** (in Srednja street, the house in Vaganj). The most valuable find from Roman times (2nd century), not accessible however to the public (being today below the level of the pavement). The remains of Roman rule can still be seen in the Stari Grad field (remains of a villa rustica at Kupovnik and Starač), on St. Stephen´s Square ("the sad winged Eros") and in the Church of St. John.

•••••••••••

Hektorovićev tvrdalj (in the southwestern area of the town, between the parish church and the town hall). This "tvrdalj" is the most prominent building in the town. It was built by the local aristocrat and writer Petar Hektorović (1487--1572), who is best known for his work *Fishermen and Fishing Gossip* (*Ribanje i ribarsko prigovaranje*) of 1556. This is an unusual work: an original poetic idyll, about a three-day boat trip between the islands of Hvar, Brač and Šolta, undertaken by Hektorović and two fishermen. He depicts his experiences in a realistic manner and includes the speech of the fishermen in his descriptions, making him the first author to record authentic folk and

The Hektorović tvrdalj

drinking songs. Tvrdalj is a huge Renaissance building, a kind of fortified palace, on whose southern side there is a fish pond surrounded by stone vaulting. It was mainly built between 1520 and 1569. Particularly interesting with regard to this building are the twenty inscriptions engraved in stone, in Latin, Italian and Croatian, which witness to Hektorović the thinker and poet. Beside the fish pond there is a small **ethnographic exhibition** in the style of a wine cellar and including equipment used by the fishermen and wine growers of the island of Hvar.

•••••••••••

The **Parish Church of St. Stephen** (Sveti Stjepan; on the main square not far from the bus stop) was built in 1605 on the site of an older church. The most valuable items in its treasury are a triptych by Francesco da Santacroce and a font from 1592 which belonged to the older church. The belfry is made of stone from the city walls of Pharos, and from the inscription on the entrance it can be seen that this was the entrance to the Greek city. A relief of a Roman galley of the 1st or 2nd century is built into the belfry.

•••••••••••

St. John's Church (Sveti Ivan; to the south of the parish church) was first mentioned in 1332 and is the oldest sacred building. It was probably also the seat of the first bishop. It was built on the site of an ancient temple, its ground plan and the apses are Romanesque, but its present appearance is Gothic. In 1957 a baptistery was discovered next to the church, dating from the 6th or 7th century with a 115 cm deep, cross-shaped baptismal pool. Recent archaeological research has also unearthed Roman figural mosaics (*Cantharos with birds, Eden with peacocks*) as well as many old Christian fragments and medieval graves.

•••••••••••

St. Nicholas' Church (Sveti Nikola; on the way to the graveyard) houses several votive pictures given by mariners, and figures of saints on the altar, the work of the Italian wood carver Antonio Porri from the 17th century. According to legend, an ascetic nun had herself walled into a room beside the church in the 16th century of her own free will, and stayed there until she died.

•••••••••••

Vrboska

The **Dominican monastery** (near the graveyard; on the southern edge of the town, by the road) was founded in 1482 and in the 16th century it was fortified with corner towers. In 1571 it was destroyed by the Turks. The new church dates from 1893 and houses a painting entitled *The Burial* by Jacopo Tintoretto (1512-1594) and two crucifices: a local one from the 12th century and one by Giacomo Piazzetta. The monastery also has an **archaeological exhibition** with a collection of stone monuments, a coin collection, a gallery of paintings and a library.

••••••••••••

Near the beach there is a small Renaissance church, St. Jerome (Sveti Jeronim) which was once part of a Glagolitic hospice.

••••••••••••

The **Juraj Plančić Gallery** (2 Biankinijeva street) was named after the artist who was born in Stari Grad in 1899 and died in Paris of tuberculosis in 1930. He had a significant influence on Croatian art. Apart from his pictures, the Gallery's stock provide a review of Croatian art in the 20th century. The palace also contains the **Permanent Archeological Exhibition** "**Faros - ancient Stari Grad**" and a Memorial Captain's room.

••••••••••••

Vrboska

30 KM FROM HVAR; 526 INHABITANTS.

Vrboska developed in the 15th century as the harbour for the old village of Vrbanj. In the 16th century Vrboska was twice burnt down and left in ruins once, in about 1512, during the rebellion by Matija Ivanić, as it was one of the centres of the rebellion, and in 1571 during the Turkish campaign led by Elug Ali of Ulcinj (Ulič Alija, see: the Island of Hvar). Vrboska, once rebuilt, became a very picturesque town. It is situated in a valley crossed by a bridge, and along two sides of a bay: to the north, Padva and to the east, Pjaca. As well as typical coastal village houses, there are also some Gothic, Renaissance and Baroque buildings.

SIGHTS

The **Church of St. Mary** (Sveta Marija) stands on a hill on the southern side of the harbour. It was built in the 15th century, and the Renaissance fortress in 1579, eight years after the attack by the Turks. This fortress church is unique (apart from a similar building on the island of Šipan), built completely independently of usual contemporary forms. Inside the church there are some interesting gravestones, which are numbered and some of which are decorated with coats of arms. "Hic Faros - hic ars" is the name of an artistic workshop (restoration, pictures, music) that operates in Stari Grad in the summer. The Faros Marathon (swimming) is also held here.

••••••••••••

The **Parish Church of St. Lawrence** (Sveti Lovrinac) was built in the 15th century, and its present Baroque appearance dates from when it was rebuilt in the 17th century. This church houses the most significant collection of paintings on the island of Hvar. The most valuable items are a polyptych by Paolo Veronese (1528-1588) with the figures of St. Lawrence, St. John the Baptist and St. Nicholas, which local tradition ascribes to Titian; three paintings by the Dubrovnik artist Celestin Medović (1857-1921): *St. Anthony*,

The fortress church in Vrboska

Christmas Night and *The Adoration of the Magi*; then *Our Lady of the Rosary* by Leandro Bassano and *The Resurrection* and *The Burial* by G. Albardi.

●●●●●●●●●●●●

Matija Ivanić also known as Duke Janko (the dates of his birth and death are unknown) was born in Vrbanj and had a house in Vrboska (now at the bottom of an inlet on the southern side). He was an ordinary citizen who owned a ship in Vrboska and it is said that he had the quay built. He was the leader of the mass rebellion in 1510-1514 against the nobility which broke out as the result of social conflict. M. Ivanić presented the demands of the ordinary people of Hvar to the Count: they sought the right of representation on the Great Council and the equality of the nobles with the ordinary people in terms of taxes and dues. During the rebellion, the rebels fought bloody battles with the nobility who were forced to flee to Brač and Korčula. The rebellion was put down however with much bloodshed, because of the danger of similar uprisings in other Dalmatian communities.

●●●●●●●●●●●●

St. Peter's Chapel (Sv. Petar, on the sea front) is the oldest church in Vrboska. According to a statute, it marks the border in the sea between Pitva and Vrbanj.

●●●●●●●●●●●●

The **Fishing Museum** (Ribarski muzej). This small museum shows the development of fishing techniques from the 18th to the 20th century. As part of the exhibition, there is a

The Fishing Museum in Vrboska

typical kitchen in a fisherman's home.

●●●●●●●●●●●●

The so-called "šćiga" is oscillation in the water in the canal which shows changes in the weather and therefore serves as a kind of public barometer.

Excursions

Vrbanj (4 km from Vrboska via Jelsa; 489 inhabitants) was settled by the Neretvans. It has an interesting group of houses from the 16th and 17th centuries, enclosed by walls with loopholes. The **Parish Church of the Holy Spirit** (Sveti Duh) dates from the 15th century and has a valuable treasury. The **King's Palace** (Kraljevi dvori) dates from the early Middle Ages and has been wrongly attributed to Matija Ivanić. It was probably the parish centre before 1278. **St. Nicholas' Chapel** (Sveti Nikola) stands on the highest peak on the island (626 m) and was built in 1487. It was built by the ordinary people led by Matija Ivanić as a symbol of their might. In the village there is a wine cellar with room for 7000 hl of wine.

●●●●●●●●●●●●

Procession of the Cross. This is a Passion-tide event that takes place each year on the night between Maundy Thursday and Good Friday. It takes place in the parishes of Vrboska, Jelsa, Vrbanj, Svirče, Vrisnik and Pitve, so there are actually six processions. Each one is led by a cross-bearer who carries a particularly heavy cross, accompanied by people and many believers, singing The Lady´s Weeping. It is a rule that each procession goes by itself, but they all go over mainly the same route (about 30 km long, lasting eight hours) without meeting. The origin of this event is in the medieval penitential processions, and this one has been held on Hvar without a break since the 15th century. The procession expresses the empathy of the worshipper with Jesus´s physical pain

Procession with the cross, starting off in the evening (above), and the cross-bearers when they come back.

and Mary´s grief, and there is nothing to place it among folk customs. For the believers and pilgrims, the Procession is the high point of popular piety during the year, and for tourists it is an unforgettable experience. The processions can best be observed from the quay in Jelsa.

●●●●●●●●●●●●

Šolta

Lying next to the island of Brač, the island of Šolta is one of the smallest inhabited Central Dalmatian islands. It was first mentioned in Greek sources under the name of Olyntha, the Romans called it Solenta and its original Croatian name was Sulet. It has been inhabited since the Bronze Age and the population increased as at the beginning of the 7th century fugitives from ancient

Maslinica

Salona moved here and nine centuries later the people of Klis fled from the Turks. From the 7th century Šolta was part of the Commune of Split, which made use of its wood, limestone, and agricultural products, above all olives. 1944 was a particularly hard year for the island as the occupying forces made the entire population evacuate the island as they supported the Partisans. There are now about 1200 people on the island in about 6 settlements.

••••••••••••

Grohote in the interior of the island lies about one kilometre from its harbour at Rogač. In the centre of the village there is a watch tower from the 17th century. Some of the interesting fortified farm houses have fragments of stone with ancient inscriptions built into the walls. The foundation walls of an old Christian church from the 6th or 7th century can be seen next to the parish church. The Gothic **Chapel of St. Michael**, not far from the village, has Gothic frescoes and ancient stone fragments. In the graveyard there are two old Christian sarcophagi. To the east of Grohote is the tourist resort of **Nečujam**. Its most famous building is the house of Dujam Balistrilić next to the parish church. Marko Marulić (see Split), lived here for a while. In front of the house there is a column in memory of Petar Hektorović (see Hvar, Stari Grad). On the eastern side of Nečujam Bay there are the remains of some Roman walls and the ruins of a Gothic chapel from the 15th century. The village of **Stomorska** (3 nautical miles from Nečujam, 5 nautical miles west of Milna on Brač) dates from the 18th century. On the side of the hill Vela straža there is a Baroque church, **Our Lady in the Pines** (Gospa u borima; Gospa Stomorska) in a graveyard, where there are also fragments of ancient sarcophagi.

Waiting for the ship

••••••••••••

Maslinica is a fishing village on the sharply jagged west coast of the island, 8 km from Rogač by road, 8.5 nautical miles from Nečujam and 8.7 nautical miles from Trogir by sea. In the village there is a watch tower from the 17th century. In 1708 a Baroque castle was added to it. On the small island of Stipanska there are the ruins of an old Christian basilica.

Excursions

Drvenik. Two small islands northwest of Šolta make up Drvenik: the larger, Veli Drvenik (6.5 n/m from Maslinica) covers an area of 12 km^2, with 400 inhabitants, and the smaller Mali Drvenik covers 3.3 km^2, with 200 inhabitants. In the Roman era these islands, 9 nautical miles from Trogir, were known as Tarion. In the Middle Ages they were the property of Trogir and were called Giruna or Gerona. In the Baroque era building work was started on a triple-naved church, which was never completed. The inhabitants are fishermen or farmers.

••••••••••••

The olive tree (Olea europaea) is by far the most important plant of the Mediterranean region or, as

Old olive tree

Tin Ujević once said, a symbol that links this region together. If the word culture has two meanings, the literal old meaning, and our derived meaning, we might then say: the permanent and ancient civilisation (culture) of the Mediterranean is the cultivation (culture) of the olive. Very likely, the olive was brought here by the ancient Greeks. In the Salona excavations, a stone olive press has been found that dates back to the 1st or 2nd century. The cultivation of the plant was expanded during the period of Venetian rule. At the end of the 18th century, there were 30 million trees in the Croatian Adriatic area. In the second half of the century, the olive groves were cleared for the planting of grapevine. Today, there are about 3.8 million olive trees in Croatia, and about 35 000 tons of olives are produced, 7 000 tons of oil and about 300 tons of table olives. Experts say that the olive is cultivated extensively, and its yields are small. The people say the olive is like a mother; it fruits even when no care is taken of it. Unlike the grape vine, which is like a wife, bearing only when cherished. ■

Vis

Vis is the most westerly larger Croatian island and is part of the Central Dalmatian group of islands. It is 24 nautical miles from the mainland and covers an area of 90.3 km^2. It is 17 km long, diagonally. There are 33 settlements, only 10 of which have more than 50 inhabitants, the total population being 3 700.

Vis (Town)

Located 43° N, 16°10´ E; 8.5 n/m from Hvar, pop. 1 776.

The **town of Vis** (Issa) is the oldest and was at one time the best known settlement in Dalmatia. In 397 BC, Dionysios the Elder, a military leader and tyrant from Syracuse, at that time the strongest state in the Greek world, founded the first Greek colony (polis, or city state) on the Eastern Adriatic coast. But the history of this island stretches back much further in time. It was settled in the Stone Age and the first known inhabitants of the island were the Illyrians. The Greek historian Theopompus (c.378-323 BC) wrote that the Ionian sea (i.e. the Adriatic) was named after Ionius, "an Illyrian from Issa who once ruled in these parts". On the first coins of the colony of Issa, which were minted in the first half of the 4th century BC, on the "heads" side is the figure of Ionius, and on the reverse side a dolphin, the symbol of the sea. Dionysios the Younger, the son of the colony's founder, "too literate for a military commander" (he was a friend of Plato) brought the Syracuse rule to collapse. But before power passed from the Greeks to the Romans, Issa founded its communities on the mainland: Tragurion (Trogir), Epetion (Stobreč, near Split), Salona (Solin, near Split), and on the neighbouring island of Korčula, Korkyra Melaina (where Lumbarda is now). During the civil war between Pompey and Caesar, Issa gave support to Pompey, who was defeated (46 BC), causing Issa to lose its independence, become a "Oppidum civium Romanorum" and to be administratively dependent on Salona. During the period of Roman rule Issa nevertheless continued to

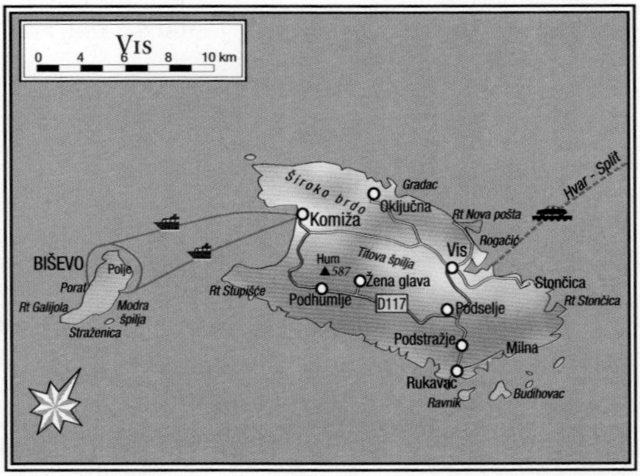

develop, and a theatre, temples, a forum and baths were built. When the Empire divided, Issa came into the Eastern Roman Empire. As Salona became the centre of the Roman administration Issa fell into the background and remained known only for its high quality wines. At the beginning of the 2nd century BC the Greek historian and geographer Agatharchides (author of a geography and history of Europe in 10 volumes) wrote that there was no better wine in the world than that from Issa. In the 10th century Issa was mentioned in a work by the Byzantine Emperor Constantine Porphyrogenitus and by the Venetian historian John Diaconus. The island and the town were conquered in 997-998 by the Venetians but they belonged at that time to the Croatian state. In the 12th and 13th centuries the government of the island changed hands among Venice, the Croatian-Hungarian kings, the Counts of Krk and Omiš, but in 1242 the island became part of the Hvar commune. The relationship between Hvar and Vis was so close that in the Statute of Hvar, no difference was

Ancient mosaic

ever made between the people of the two islands. When Venice bought Dalmatia from King Ladislav in 1409, it also governed Vis, which remained part of the Hvar community until 1797. After the fall of the Venetian Empire, Vis came under Austria and then under the French. In 1811, following the sea battle between the British and the French navies, the British set up a base on the island and built several fortresses. When it became part of the Austrian Empire (1815-1918), Vis also became an Austrian naval base for the Central Adriatic. In 1866 the island played an important role in the war between Austria and Italy. On 20th June that year there was a famous sea battle off Vis in which the Austrian fleet led by Admiral Wilhelm von Tegetthoff defeated the considerably stronger Italian fleet. The Italians lost 643 men and two warships, and the Austrians lost 38 men. Of the 7 870 sailors on the Austrian ships, about two thirds were from Croatia.

The Battle of Vis, on 20. 6. 1866.

•••••••••••

The Austrians were replaced by the Italians (1918-1920) and again from 23rd April 1943. However following all these occupations, the island became the main naval base and the centre of command of the navy of the National Liberation Army in Yugoslavia. British commando brigades were also employed in the defence against the Germans, as well as their artillery and torpedo boats and airmen, for whom an airport was built in May 1944. After World War II the island was closed to foreigners.

•••••••••••

Sights

Archaeological remains of ancient Issa. Although it is preserved only in the lower part of the structure, the irregular rectangular **wall of the Greek colony**, located in terraces in the south west part of the Vis bay, can still clearly be seen. It is interesting that the western tract of the city walls do not go rectilinearly but at right angles, probably for defensive reasons. The international city arrangement with the main lines of communication, which went parallel in one way down the slope to the port was preserved in the Roman times, when new buildings were put up outside the narrow area of the original city. It is clear, however, that there is a lack of the transverse communications that would have been formed by the orthogonal grid of the cardo and decumanus, otherwise characteristic of the Roman organisation of city space. Unfortunately, none of the area has been researched archaeologically.

On the small peninsula known as Prirovo, on the site probably inhabited by Greek immigrants before they founded their colony facing it, there was a small **Issian theatre**, only partially preserved, and one of only four ancient theatres on the Eastern Adriatic coast. Of a theatre which could seat up to 3 000 spectators, part of the outer wall of the auditorium remains, built, according to Greek tradition, facing south. Between the walls of the highest terrace on the hill where the city was built and the sea front, perhaps on the site where the southern edge of the walls once stood, but were demolished in the Roman era, the **remains of some public thermal baths** have been uncovered. They were built in two phases and completed in the middle of the 2nd century AD. As part of the hall, there is a mosaic in the floor, which has been preserved in situ.

Artemis, 4th century BC (find from Vis)

••••••••••••

St. Cyprian and St. Justine

On Martvilo and on the site of the present hotel, there are **ancient necropoli**. They were in use from the 4th century BC right up until the city was deserted. Research has shown the extremely complex nature of burial rituals and the exceptional range of artistically formed gravestones, from ceramic Greek, south Italic and local pieces, statues of terracotta (for example the figure of Tanagra), lanterns, coins and sculptured stone work. The work with the greatest artistic value however is the bronze head of the goddess Aphrodite or Artemis, a Graecian piece, based on examples from the Praxiteles circle from the first half of the 4th century BC. Most of these remains are now kept in the Vis Battery archaeological collection and in the Archaeological Museum in Split.

••••••••••••

Vis harbour

The **Parish Church of Our Lady of Spilica** (Gospa od Spilice) stands in the harbour. The central and oldest part of this triple-naved church was built in the middle of the 16th century and extended in the Baroque era. It is particularly outstanding for its extended bell tower. Inside the church there are paintings by the Venetian artist Girolamo da Santacroce (16th century). The central part of the polyptych which the master painted for this church has been preserved, showing Mary on the throne with the Child amongst the Saints, along with part of the wing showing St. Stephen and five paintings of the area.

••••••••••••

The **Church** and **Bell Tower of St. Cyprian and St. Justine** (Sveti Ciprijan i Sveta Justina) were built in the 18th century on the site of an earlier chapel. The decorative motifs on the front of the church and bell tower (which has loopholes for defence against pirates) demonstrate the peak of local sculpture in the Baroque era. The inventory in the interior of the church, from the carved pulpit, ceilings, altars and paintings on the gravestones are all part of the same Baroque whole.

••••••••••••

The Baroque **Church of the Holy Spirit** (Sveti Duh) in the western part of Vis harbour, partially built in stone taken from some ancient buildings, shows characteristics of the outdated style which was maintained in the provinces. Inside the church an altarpiece by the famous 18th century Venetian artist Giambattista Pittonio stands out amongst the other works. It shows the Madonna, St. Nicholas, St. Cyprian and St. Raymond Nonnantus, the founder of the Mercedarian order, which sought to ransom Christians from slavery to the Turks or pirates, the fate of many people from Vis.

Monastery on Prirovo

The **Franciscan church** on Prirovo is dedicated to the Dalmatian Patron Saint St. Jerome (Sveti Jerolim), and was built at the beginning of the 16th century using stone blocks from the ancient theatre. A monastery was built over it at the same time giving it a semi-circular appearance. Inside the church there is a large Gothic and Renaissance wooden crucifix. The bell tower beside the monastery was built in the 18th century.

The **Archaeological Collection** of Issa is located inside the Battery building. This is a permanent exhibition called "Issa - the Island of Vis in the Hellenistic Period", part of the exhibition of the Archaeological Museum in Split. Through its exibits of monumental architecture, finds of sculptures, coins, vessels, ornaments, weapons, inscriptions and finds of Vis products outside the island, with a display of the preserved urban structure, the exhibition aims to shed light on the society of Issa.

Komiža

22 km west of Vis, population 1 677.

Komiža was first mentioned in the 12th century, and since the 16th century it has been the leading fishing village in Dalmatia.

Sights

The early Romanesque **Church of St. Michael** (Sveti Mihovil) dating from the 11th or 12th century, was built over the "Muster" on the peak of a hill on the old road to Vis, and originally belonged to Benedictines from Biševo. **Muster** ("monastery" in dialect) was a former Benedictine monastery and a Church of St. Nicholas (Sveti Nikola) probably built sometime in the 13th century over Komiža Bay on a hill which was fortified in prehistoric times. The present northern aisle of the church was part of that very early church which was extended first of all in the 16th and then in the 17th century. At that time too the medieval bell tower was redecorated in Baroque style. It was probably originally built for defensive purposes. Inside the church there is an outstanding large wooden altar dating from the 18th century. On the floor of the church, which in time became the parish graveyard, there are gravestones belonging to ancient Komiža families such as Vitaljić, Mardešić, Marinković and others.

The complex of **St. Mary's Church** is particularly picturesque. It is known as the "pirate's church" because pirates stole a painting of Our Lady in the 18th century from it. The central nave in the original

Komiža harbour

A falkuša from Komiža

Renaissance 16th century church was rebuilt in the Baroque era and the whole church was given a three--faced facade. Inside, the Baroque altar, some paintings, and a wooden crucifix are worth seeing, as is the oldest organ in Dalmatia, which has been repaired many times. It was built in 1670 by the Polish monk Stjepan Kilarović. In the courtyard near the church is an eight-sided wellhead with rustic Baroque reliefs showing St. Nicholas, the protector of mariners, St. Andrew, the protector of fishermen, St. Anthony and the Archangel Michael, Adam and Eve, Mary and Child, the Lamb of God with the cross and a torch as symbol of life beyond the grave.

••••••••••••

The Baroque **Church of St. Rocco** (Sveti Rok) on the seafront near Komiža was built on the site of an older church, wich, like many other Dalmatian churces of its time, was fortified.

In the island's interior, pride of place is given to the Church of **St. Mary in Poselje**, the oldest part of which dates from the 14th century. It was extended in the Renaissance period. Inside the church there is sculpture of Mary, one of the most beautiful late Gothic Dalmatian reliefs in terracotta, which originally stood in the centre of a polyptych, but is now in the wooden Rococo tabernacle. The Gothic chapel of the Holy Spirit (Sveti Duh) on Hum was probably built on the walls of smal late Roman fortress an maybe on the site of an even older prehistoric defensive structure. A round church known as **Our Lady of Planica** (Gospa od Planice) was built by the road leading from Vis to Komiža in the Baroque era, with a dome on the top of which there is a pseudo lantern. It is made even more picturesque by the decorative garland of bricks round the edge of the roof.

••••••••••••

The Komiža **"falkuša".** Komiža fishermen, in their search for a richer catch, have throughout their history been oriented toward the open sea, on the way to the peripheral Croatian islands of Palagruža, Svetac, Jabuka and further. Thus a special type of gajeta, a sailing boat with five oars plied by the crew during a calm, developed and, thanks to the Korčulan boatbuilders, was maintained. The "falkuša" is one of the rarely preserved indigenous Croatian ships. A boat of a small island community which in all its characteristics also belongs to the Mediterranean universe. It is nine metres long, 2.9 broad, with a nine metre high mast. It is built of a special kind of pine from the island of Svetac, the keel is of oak, and the planking of larch. The traditional equipment included barrels for salting fish, for water and wine, baskets, and devices for navigation (a compass and a lamp), and catching equipment. It was in use right up to the middle of this century. This boat was used to represent Croatia at the World Ship Exhibition,

EXPO '98 in Lisbon. An example of the last but one falkuša, sunk in 1988, salvaged and arranged as an exhibit, is in the Komiža Fishing Museum.

••••••••••••

Excursions

The island of **Biševo** (4.5 n/m southwest from Komiža). Here there are remains of the Church of St Sylvester (Sv. Silvester), built in 1050 by the Split priest Ivan Grlić and given to the Benedictines. There was also a smaller monastery, but it was abandoned because of the danger from the pirates of Omiš, while the monks moved to Komiža.

The **Modra špilja of Biševo (Blue cave).** On the eastern side of the island of Biševo (about 4.5 nautical miles from Komiža) is the Blue Grotto, one of the best known natural beauty spots on the Adriatic. A cave into which boats can sail has been formed by the sea

Island of Biševo

washing over limestone (by abrasion). A special phenomenon occurs between 11 and 12 o'clock in summer when the sun's rays shine through an underwater opening, break up and bathe the entire interior of the cave with a silvery blue light. The Blue Grotto (Grotta Azzurra) on Capri in Italy is also famous for this phenomenon.

••••••••••••

In front of the entrance to the Blue Cave

The **Volcanic Islands**, Brusnik and Jabuka. To the west of Vis there are some volcanic islands which are therefore made of different soil than the remainder of the Adriatic. It is dark and their rocks are largely formed of iron and magnesium compounds. For this reason a compass behaves in an abnormal manner when brought near to these islands, and the needle will not indicate north. The Island of Brusnik is about 3 hectares in size and is 12 m high, and Jabuka covers 2 hectares and is 96 m in height. The islands have very sparse but very interesting flora and fauna. The **Mediterranean Monk Seal** (Monachus albiventur). This once numerous animal which could be found throughout the Mediterranean now lives only around the islands of Brusnik, Svetac and Šćedro. It can grow to more than 2 m in length and weigh 250 kg. It has a lithe and round dark brown body. Fishermen used to consider them to be their greatest enemy, for

Inside the Blue Cave

they were blamed for damage which was also caused by dolphins, tearing nets and eating the catch. There was belief that the monk seals left the sea at night and destroyed vineyards. There are now about 20 of them in the entire Adriatic and so this Mediterranean seal is the most endangered species here. It is protected and killing one is a criminal offence for which there is both a fine and a prison sentence.

••••••••••••

The **Wines of Vis**. Together with Biševo, Vis has about 700 hectares of vineyards. The high quality of Vis wines has been well known since ancient times. Some biographers of the writer James Joyce mention that his favourite drink was Vis Plavac. The best known Vis wines are Vugava and Plavac. **Vugava** is a quality wine, golden yellow in colour, and has an aroma reminiscent of honey. It has 12-13.5% alcohol with 5-6 g/l acidity. It has a characteristic slightly bitter flavour. **Plavac** is a dark ruby red wine, with a pleasant aroma, strong and with a full flavour. It is most often drunk mixed with water. A characteristic of Plavac is that its quality increases as its colour darkens. It also improves with keeping.■

Makarska

Located 43° 18' N, 17° 2' E; 13 381 inhabitants. The centre of the Biokovo Coastal Area, 60 km in length (from Brela to Gradac).

Prehistory. Near present-day Makarska, there was a settlement as early as the middle of the 2nd millennium BC. It is thought that it was a point used by the Cretans on their way up the Adriatic (the so-called "amber route"). However it was only one of the ports with links with the wider Mediterranean, as is shown by a copper tablet with Cretan symbols also used in the Cretan and Egyptian systems of measurement. A similar tablet was found in the Egyptian pyramids. In the Illyrian era this region was part of the broader alliance of tribes, led by the Ardaeans, founded in the third century BC in the Cetina area (Omiš) down to the River Vjosë in present-day Albania.

The Roman Era. Although the Romans became rulers of the Adriatic by defeating the Ardaeans in 228, it took them two centuries to confirm their rule. The Romans sent their veteran soldiers to settle in Makarska. A larger settlement (Muccurum) grew up in the most inaccessible part of Biokovo mountain, probably at the very edge of the Roman civilisation. After the division of the Empire in 395 this part of the Adriatic became part of the Eastern Roman Empire and many people fled to Muccurum from the new wave of invaders.

An amphora from the Makarska Local Museum

The Migrations of the Nations. In 548 Muccurum was destroyed by the army of the Ostrogoth King Totila. The Byzantine Emperor expelled the Eastern Goths (Ostrogoths), and the region was settled by the Slavs (Croats) in the 7th century.

The new inhabitants were skilful boatsmen both on the rivers and the sea and they became excellent mariners and fearless pirates. The Croats who moved into this part of the coast were called Arentani by the Byzantine Emperor Constantine Porphyrogenitus (10th century), and their state was called Pagania. In his writings this Emperor and historian states that the following towns were settled in Pagania: Mokro (once Muccurum), Verulja (Gornja Brela), Ostrok (Zaostrog), Slavinac (Lapčan near Gradac) and that they held these islands: Meleta (Mljet), Psara (Hvar), Bracis (Brač), Hoara (Sušac), Jis (Vis) and Lastovo. During the period of the Neretvan principality (see the Neretva Delta) a port known as Makar developed on the coast.

The historical crest of Makarska

Under Various Rulers. Making use of the rivalry between the Croatian leaders and their power struggles (1324-1326), the Bosnian Ban Stjepan Kotromanić annexed the Makarska coastal area.There were many changes of rulers here: from the Croatian and Bosnian feudal lords, to those from Zahumlje (later Herzegovina). In the eventful 15th century, when the Turks conquered the Balkans, in order to protect his territory from the Turks, Duke Vukčić handed the borderlands Krajina and Neretva over to the Venetians, in 1452. Venice promised certain privileges to the people and guaranteed to protect the region from the Turks. However, they failed to fulfil this promise.

Under the Turks. The Makarska coastal area fell to the Turks in 1499. At that time (1502) the name Makarska was used for the first time, in a document telling how nuns from Makarska were permitted to repair their church. The Turks had links with all parts of the Adriatic via Makarska and they therefore paid a great deal of attention to the maintenance of the port and in1568 they built a fortress as defence against the Venetians. During Turkish rule the seat of the administrative and judicial authority was in Foča, Mostar, for a short time in Makarska itself and finally in Gabela on the River Neretva. During the wars between Venice and the Turks over Crete (1645-1669) the desire amongst the people of the area to be free of the Turks intensified, and in 1646 Venice recaptured the coastline.

Makarska in the 19th century

But a period of dual leadership lasted until 1684, until the danger from the Turks ended in 1699. **Once more under the Venetians.** The second period of Venetian rule lasted from 1646 until 1797. In that period (in 1695) Makarska became the seat of a bishopric and commercial activity came to life, but it was a neglected area and little attention was given to the education of its inhabitants. At the time when the people were fighting against the Turks, Venice paid more attention to the people's demands. According to Alberto Fortis in his travel chronicles (18th century), Makarska was the only town in the coastal area, and the only Dalmatian town where there were absolutely no historical remains.

A typical street in Makarska

From 1797 to 1813. With the fall of Venice, the Austrian army entered Makarska and remained there until Napoleon took the upper hand. The French arrived in Makarska on 8th March 1806 and remained until 1813. This was an age of prosperity, roads were built (apparently the Austrian Emperor himself on a visit to Dalmatia, expressed his regret that the French Marshall Marmont had not stayed two or three years longer in the region). Under French rule all people were equal, and education laws written, for the first time in many centuries, in the Croatian language were passed. Schools were opened. Makarska was at this time a small town with about 1580 inhabitants.

Under the Austrians (1813-1918). As in Dalmatia as a whole, the Austrian authorities imposed a policy of Italianization, and the official language was Italian. The Makarska representatives in the Dalmatian assembly in Zadar and the Imperial Council in Vienna demanded the introduction of the Croatian language for use in public life, but the authorities steadfastly opposed the idea. One of the leaders of the National (pro-Croatian) Party was Mihovil Pavlinović of Podgora. Makarska was one of the first communes to introduce the Croatian language (1865). In the second half of the 19th century Makarska experienced a great boom and in 1900 it had about 1800 inhabitants. It became a trading point for agricultural products, not only from the coastal area but also from the hinterland (Herzegovina and Bosnia) and had shipping links with Trieste, Rijeka and Split.

The 20th century. Before the Second World War Makarska stagnated. In a twenty-year period (1910-1930) the population rose by 150 people. A large number emigrated from the surrounding area to overseas countries. After the war Makarska experienced a period of growth, and the population tripled. All the natural advantages of the region were used to create in Makarska one of the best known tourist areas on the Croatian Adriatic. ■

Sights

Kačićev trg** (a square in the centre of the town, linked by steps to the quay). On the northern side of the square is the **Parish Church of St. Mark** (Sveti Marko), built in 1776. It was the cathedral until 1828 (the seat of the bishop). Inside the church is a silver altar to the Madonna of the Rosary and a marble incrusted Venetian altar dating from the 18th century. Along the southern side of the church there is a Baroque well dating from 1775. In the centre of the square, on a base 3 m high, is a statue of **Andrija Kačić Miošić** (1704-1769). Kačić was born in Brist, near Makarska. He was a philosopher, theologian, educational writer, and a Franciscan monk. *Korabljica* is a collection of Old Testament stories in prose, and *The Pleasant Speech of the Slavic People* (*Razgovor ugodni naroda slovinskoga*) is a work in the form of a heroic folk song, relating major events from the history of the Southern Slavs. The *Pleasant Speech* was the most read Croatian book and appeared in more than 60 editions. The statue has the inscription "To Father Andrija Kačić Miošić, Croatian, Franciscan priest, teacher of the people in his *Korabljica*, poet of our people in his *Pleasant Speech*, greatly loved, by the grateful people". To the left there is "Brist, his cradle 1704" and on the right "Zaostrog, his grave 1769". On the back "Dalmatia is the homeland, being Slav is the fatherland of the heart". The memorial was created by the sculptor Ivan Rendić in 1889. A copy of the statue was set up in Zagreb in 1891. Not far from the square, at the end of the street Jurjevićeva poljana is Ivanišević Palace, the most beautiful Baroque building in the town.

••••••••••••

The **Franciscan monastery***** is on the eastern side of the harbour and was built on the foundations of a monastery dating from 1400, on a site where in the 6th century there was a Benedictine monastery. The Turks demolished it in 1496, and it was re-built in 1540. Its present appearance dates from 1614. In the monastery basement is a **Malacological museum**, with the richest collection of shells and snails in the world, and a smaller collection of fossils from the Makarska region. Apart from this museum, the monastery also has archives, a library and a collection of paintings and other works of art.

Franciscan church and monastery

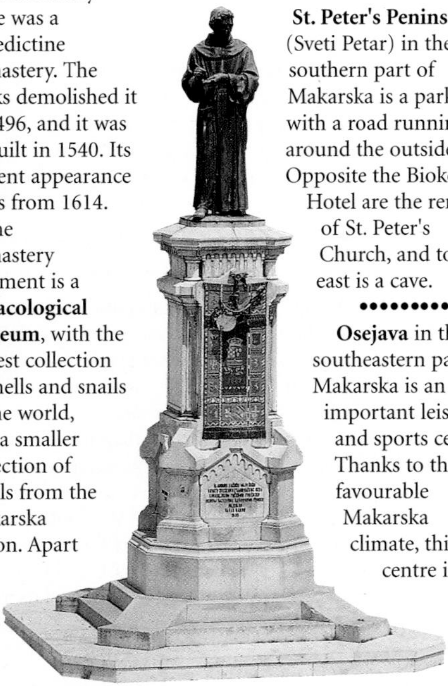

Monument to Andrija Kačić-Miošić

••••••••••••

The **Church of St. Phillip of Neri*** (Sveti Filip Neri) is on the coastal road known as King Tomislav's Quay and was built in 1757 along with the monastery. Behind the church there are several interesting gravestones.

••••••••••••

St. Peter's Peninsula (Sveti Petar) in the southern part of Makarska is a park, with a road running around the outside. Opposite the Biokovo Hotel are the remains of St. Peter's Church, and to the east is a cave.

••••••••••••

Osejava in the southeastern part of Makarska is an important leisure and sports centre. Thanks to the favourable Makarska climate, this centre is used for training for the highest level competitions by both Croatian and foreign sportsmen and women.

••••••••••••

The **Marshall Marmont Memorial** stands at the entrance to the town on the road from Split. This monument to this Napoleonic Marshall, the governor of the Illyrian province (1809-1813) is linked with his work in building the road running through Biokovo mountain. It was set up beside a monastery during the French occupation, and during the period of Austrian rule it was moved and its inscription altered. It was dedicated to the memory of a visit by Emperor Francis Joseph to Dalmatia. The Revolution Memorial was set up on the small hill over Makarska. Biokovo was a Partisan stronghold, and Makarska a strong anti-fascist centre. The memorial is the work of Matija Salaj.

Excursions

Biokovo*** is an impressive mountain rising behind the Makarska coastal area. It stretches from Brela to Gradac over 36 km, although it is fairly narrow (7 km). In terms of its geological make-up and contours it is typical of the Dinara mountain range. Some authoritative writers have called it the most attractive karst mountain. It stands like an enormous wall over the coastline creating three climatic

Malacological Museum in the Franciscan Monastery

zones in a very small area: up to 300 m above sea level there are gently sloping wide green fertile fields; up to 1000 m there is a belt of rock, and the third zone includes an undulating plateau above 1000 m, 3-4 km wide, surrounded by a row of peaks. The Biokovo plateau, especially in its centre, gives the impression of so-called "network karst" - an unusual complex of cavities, an average of 150 m wide and 60-80 m deep, like craters on the surface of the moon. This plateau also abounds in caves, similar to wells, up to 100 m deep. They are mostly filled with snow and ice, and, until the invention of modern refrigerators, this ice was removed in the summer to be used by tourists on the coast. Until the discovery of Lukina jama on Velebit Mountain, the Biokovo plateau also had the deepest caves yet discovered in Croatia (1985), known as Stara škola (576 m), Vilimova jama (565 m) and Jama pod Kamenitim vratima (520 m). In 1981 Biokovo was declared a nature reserve because of its landscape and scientific value. This means, amongst other things, that picking flowers, lighting fires and leaving litter are all banned. For a brief acquaintance with the mountain, it is best to visit the Botanical Gardens above the village of Kotišina, and drive on the Biokovo road (Biokovska cesta), or walk to the mountain hostel below the peak known as Vošac and to the peak Sveti Jure.

••••••••••••

The **Botanical Gardens** are situated above the village of Kotišina (3 km from Makarska towards Biokovo and Zagora - after 2 km turn left and continue for another 1 km). Despite its mainly karst surface, the Biokovo massif has a rich plant life. The variety of habitats and microclimatic conditions offer the possibility of life to oases of small woods, meadows and many shrubs with nectar-rich and medicinal plants and many endemics: particular varieties of

Makarska against a background of Mt. Biokovo

knapweed (Centaurea cuspidata biokovoensis) dwarf bluebells (Campanu lacese edraianthus), hawkweed (Hieraciumwaldsteinii subsp. biokovoense) and waxflower (Cerinthe tristis). Daffodils cover entire meadows in places.

•••••••••••

Sveti Jure (1762 m) is the highest peak on Biokovo. It was named after a chapel which stood on the peak until 1964, but was moved lower down when a telecommunications tower was built. The Chapel of St. George (Sveti Jure) was first mentioned in 1646. On 3rd August every year there is a pilgrimage to the church. There are many possible routes up Sveti Jure, the most popular being the climb through the villages of Makar and Veliko Brdo. A marked mountain path leads out from Makar (40 minutes from Makarska, at 223 m). The climb to the mountain hostel Vošac (1370 m) takes two hours fifty minutes. There are two

Mountain flower from Biokovo

more hours to the peak, also on marked paths (after 45 minutes climbing, turn right!). From Veliko Brdo (via Bašković) the climb also takes about five hours. From Bašković to the mountain hostel "S. Ravlić na Lokvi" the climb takes three hours and thirty minutes, and from the hostel to the peak it is another one and a half hours. The climb should be started early in the morning due to high temperatures in the summer.

•••••••••••

Biokovska cesta (the Biokovo road) links Staza pass (18 km from Makarska on the road for Vrgorac) and Sveti Jure peak. It is 12 km long and the highest road in Croatia. Apart from a side road leading to the Vošac hostel, the entire road is asphalted. Traffic on this road is subject to certain regulations: travel is only allowed in daylight, between dawn and dusk, and there is a toll for the use of the road. Four km below the peak there is a turning to the left leading to Vošac hostel (1370 m). The view from the nearby peak (30 min climb; 1411 m) is considered to be one of the finest on the Adriatic.

•••••••••••

The view from Sveti Jure

Peak	m	km	0'
Cincar	2005	62	0
Vran	2074	52	45
Čvrsnica	2222	48	55
Prenj	2103	66	70
Velež	1967	86	92
Durmitor	2522	164	93
Sveti Ilija	960	40	180
Klupća	569	43	190
Hum (Lastovo)	415	65	200
Sveti Nikola (Hvar)	627	42	243
Monte Gargano	1056	252	243
Hum (Vis)	585	80	250
Vidova Gora	780	37	260
Mosor	1339	40	307
Svilaja	1508	65	321
Troglav (Dinara)	1912	73	336

Beach under Biokovo

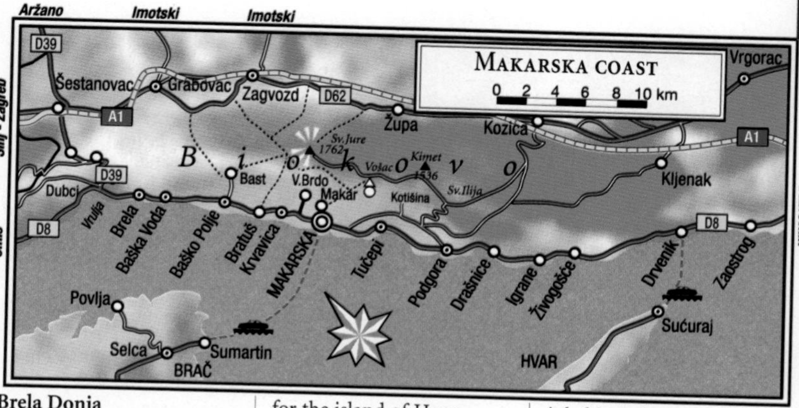

Brela Donja

16 km from Makarska in the direction of Split; 1 615 inhabitants

is the best known resort on the Makarska riviera. It consists of several small settlements in the foothills of Biokovo and was named after some wells ("vrela" in Croatian). Above the settlement there are some ruins known popularly as "The Duke's fortress" ("Hercegove utvrde"). The Chapel Our Lady of Carmel (Gospa od Karmela) was built in 1730. There is a partially preserved ancient necropolis with some gravestones with relief ornamentation. Not far away is **Baška Voda** (5 km southeast; 2 045 inhabitants) which was known as a settlement in the Roman era. There are two churches in the village. Above Baška Voda is the village of **Bast**, typical of the Biokovo foothills, after which Baška Voda was named ("Bastska Voda"). Between Baška Voda and Makarska the best known beaches are in Promajna and Bratuš.

••••••••••••

Drvenik

27 km southeast of Makarska; pop. 500

Situated at the foot of Rilić, this village is a ferry port for the island of Hvar (Sućuraj). It was mentioned as a settlement in the 13th century and was named after a legend telling how there were once thick woods covering this area ("drvo" means wood in Croatian). The ruins of walls and a tower above the village witness to the resistance offered by the inhabitants against the Turks. In Gornji Drvenik there is a 15th century Gothic chapel (Sveti Juraj) which was later redecorated in the Baroque style. The chapel was built on "stechaks", "stećci", (see Neum, Neretva-Delta) and has medieval gravestones built into the walls.

••••••••••••

In **Živogošće** (10 km towards Makarska; 538 inhabitants), one of the oldest settlements in the Makarska coastal area, there is a 17th century **Franciscan monastery****, with an inscription dating from 1766, which was converted and extended after it had been demolished during the French occupation. The monastery has a valuable library, and the church has many valuable items from the Baroque era. On the **"Suzina" rock**, right on the beach and beside a spring only about 10 m long, in the 4th or 5th century a Latin epigram was carved into the bare rock: "Quis quet arcanum, sapines pernoscere, fontis nasceris e scopulis, fons, moriture fretis" ("Which reasonable creature can fathom your secret, oh fountain? Oh spring, the rock gives you birth, and your death is in the sea"). The Roman poet was obviously inspired by the brevity of the stream's life from its source to its mouth and in these lines asked himself questions about the meaning of his life. The Academician Duje Rendić-Miočević wrote that if this region had only left these lines, it could not be said that this Roman Province did not know true

Živogošće

Zaostrog

poetic expression.
Above **Igrane** (4 km towards Makarska; 480 inhabitants) in the village of Markovići, is the pre-Romanesque (Old Croatian) **Church of St. Michael** (Sveti Mihovil) dating from the 11th or 12th century. In Igrane graveyard there is an apse left from a medieval chapel, and some Roman sarcophagi. The Baroque parish church in the village dates from 1752, and the towers were built as defence against the Turks.

In **Zaostrog** (3 km southeast of Drvenik) is the famous **Franciscan monastery****. The monastery has been demolished several times and subsequently rebuilt. In 1468 it was taken over from the Augustine monks by the Franciscans. The buildings of the monastery and church enclose the cloisters. There is an inscription written in "Bosančica" script over the portal of the church. Bosančica is a Croatian variant of Cyrillic, used by Bosnian and Herzegovinian "ikavci" (speakers of the "ikavian" dialect), and in central Dalmatia. The monastery church has an organ built by the famous organ maker Petar Nakić (see Šibenik). Andrija Kačić Miošić (see Makarska, Kačićev Square) lived and died in this monastery. His bust is in the church, as is the bust of the writer Ilija Despot (1851-1886) who was born in Zaostrog. Apart from a rich church and monastery treasury, the monastery also has a rich ethnographic collection, a library and archives, as well as, since 1989, a collection of paintings donated by the painter Mladen Veža, who was born in nearby Brist. In the Zaostrog village graveyard there is a Gothic church, **St. Barbara's** (Sv. Barbara) which was restored in the Baroque era.

••••••••••••

Gradac

44 KM FROM MAKARSKA; 1 574 INHABITANTS.

This settlement was mentioned as Labinac (Lapčan) by Constantine Porphyrogenitus in the 10th century. It was named after the fortress ("grad" in Croatian) built in the 17th century as a defence against the Turks. The remains of this fortress can be found in the village above the coastal high road. During the World War II, Gradac was famous as the site of an uprising, when occupying forces burnt down 95% of the houses. The memorial in the village centre is the work of Antun Augustinčić.

••••••••••••

To the northeast of Gradac are Podaca and Brist. In **Podaca graveyard** (7 km from Gradac) there is a 12th century pre-Romanesque (old Croatian) church, **St. John's** (Sveti Ivan) beside which a Baroque parish church was built in the 18th century. In the graveyard there is also an ornamental stechak (see Neum). Above the village of **Brist** (2 km from Gradac) there are the ruins of the **Baroque Church of**

Gradac

Podaca

St. Margaret (Sveta Margerita) with the Kačić family grave (18th century). The Kačić family was one of the few Croatian old noble families who were mentioned as early as the 11th century. Their land was right between the Neretva and the Cetina (it is thought that they came from the Zadar hinterland).They had the title "Count" and from time to time were Kings or Bans. They were also said to be fierce pirates and heretics (Bogumils, see Neum). At the end of the 15th century their lands were taken over by the Turks. Andrija Kačić Miošić was born in Brist in 1704 (see Makarska). It is thought that the ruins of the house where he was born are next to St. Margaret's church. Not far from the church there is a large, richly decorated stechak (see Neum).

•••••••••••

Podgora**

9 km southeast of Makarska; pop. 1 534

Podgora is an area at the foot of Biokovo ("pod" means below and "gora" is mountain) consisting of several small settlements along the seafront (Porat, Mrkušići, Šaklje) and the road to Vrgorac (Roščići and Marinovići). In the 17th and 18th centuries towers were built along this road as defence against the Turks. The **Baroque Church of St. Thekla** (Sveta Tekla) was destroyed in an earthquake in 1962, which also destroyed the once famous **Baroque Mrkušić summer residence***, of which only the entrance and chapel now remain. In the chapel there is a painting of Christ by an artist of the domestic school of the 15th or 16th century. In the village graveyard Mihovil Pavlinović (1831-1887) is buried. He was a priest, writer and politician, a well-known representative of the people, who was dedicated to uniting Dalmatia with the rest of Croatia. His gravestone is the work of Ivan Rendić. Because of the partisan tradition of Podgora, in 1962 a memorial was set up above the village, entitled **"Gull's wings"** (Galebova krila), 32 m high, made by the sculptor Rajko Radović. In Podgora there is also a medicinal salt water spring known as Klokun.

•••••••••••

Northwest of Podgora is **Tučepi** (4 km from Podgora; 1763 inhabitants). Ancient Biston was probably located here. In the graveyard, fragments of the stone inventory of an Old Christian church of the 5th or 6th century have been found, and two stechaks. Next to the Jadran Hotel there is a 15th century Romanesque and Gothic church, **St. George's*** (Sveti Juraj), which has Roman capitals built into its walls. According to a local folk legend, the Venetian Doge Pietro I Candiano is buried here. In fact, the first of the four Venetian Doges of the Candiano family, Pietro, died on 18th September 886 in a battle against the Neretvans who defeated the Venetian fleet near Makarska. After this defeat, the Venetians made a treaty with Prince Branimir (in 888), agreeing to pay the Croatian rulers a tribute for the right to sail and trade unmolested along the Adriatic, which they had to adhere to until the end of the 10th century. Near the church there are two stechaks (see Neretva-Delta, Neum). In **Drašnice** (3 km southeast of Podgora, 320 inhabitants) is the Gothic Chapel of **St. Stephen** (Sveti Stjepan) whose existence is linked with a journey made by Duke Stjepan Kosača on his way to Dubrovnik. There is a tablet telling of the incident in the Archaeological Museum in Split. There are also stechaks in the old graveyard by St. George's Church. In Drašnice there are the ruins of the house belonging to the best-known Croatian "Hajduk" (an outlaw who fought against the Turks) Mijat

Tomić (from the beginning of the 17th century). He spent the winter in Drašnice, and the summer in Bosnia and Herzegovina fighting the Turks from his base in the Vran-planina mountains.

••••••••••••

Vrgorac

20 KM FROM PODGORA;
2 188 INHABITANTS.

Vrgorac was named after its location ("vrh gore" means the peak of the hill). The Venetians called it "Vergoraz", and the Muslims, "Hadgoraz". It stands on the edge of the Biokovo massif (241 m above sea level) where it falls steeply into the Neretva River. It is separated from the sea by Rilić Hill (it is two and half hours' walk from Zaostrog via Rilić). Vrgorac was the centre of a Croatian tribal area in the 10th century. It came under the Turks in 1477 and remained so until 13th June 1694. Vrgorac was a border town right up until recent times. Both Herzegovinian and coastal people gathered at fairs held here. There are many remains left by Muslim culture in Vrgorac. There are still four Turkish tower: (Croatian "kula"): Fratrova, Raosova, Pakerova kula and Mumin age Atlagića kula. The best-known is the three-storeyed Fratrova kula (also known as Cukarinovića kula or the Kapetanova kula). Tin Ujević was born in this tower, the son of a teacher, on 5th July 1891. He was one of the best known Croatian poets (see Imotski). Ujević left Vrgorac in 1896. There is a plaque on the tower with a relief showing the poet by the sculptor Marija Ujević.

Above the village there is a medieval fortress giving a fine view over Ljubuško polje. The Parish Church of the Annunciation (Navještenje Gospino) was built between 1913 and 1921 and is one of the most beautiful buildings in the Vrgorac area. In the parish offices there is a small collection of liturgical items and a cross which once stood on Tin Ujević's grave.

••••••••••••

The former lake **Vrgorsko jezero** is now a fertile field covering 30 km² divided into three communes: Vrgorac, Metković and Ploče. The reclamation of the land was completed in 1938 and since then water has drained from the area through a tunnel, 2.138 m long, into Baćinsko jezero (lake).

Tin Ujević

••••••••••••

Vrgorac is famous for its tobacco and wine. The best known wine from the Vrgorac wine cellars is **Plavka** (Plavina) which is ruby red in colour, has 11-12% alcohol content and 5-6.5 g/l acidity. The wine has the characteristics of both southern and inland wines.

••••••••••••

THE BROADER AREA

Imotski**

65 KM FROM MAKARSKA;
4 347 INHABITANTS

Imotski is situated on the northern side of the Biokovo massif, in a plain, the centre of an area bordering on Dalmatia, Herzegovina and Bosnia. The town was mentioned as Imotski for the first time in the 10th century and it was held by the Turks from the fall of Bosnia (1492) until 1717 when it was captured by the Venetians. In the centre of Imotski there is a **Memorial to Tin Ujević** (1891-1955) who was born

Imotski, Modro jezero (the Blue Lake) in the foreground

Crveno jezero, the Red Lake

in nearby Vrgorac. Ujević was one of the greatest Croatian poets. He was a translator, critic and essayist and travel writer. In the Franciscan monastery (built in 1738, located in Nazor Street) there is a **museum** including archaeological, ethnographic, cultural and historic collections and artistic items linked with the history of the Imotski area.

•••••••••••

The **Imotski lakes**** are an exceptional geological phenomenon in terms of their origin, dimensions, shape and hydrological characteristics and are therefore a protected area. The **Blue Lake** (Modro jezero, on the western edge of the town) is shaped like an elliptical funnel (its upper edge is 800 x 500 m). At the bottom of this lake there are so-called "estavelli", that is karst openings which during a drought act as drains but during rainy weather become springs. For this reason the level of the lake varies by up to 70 m. There is a path leading to the lake, and if the lake does not dry up in the summer it is possible to swim in it. **Red Lake** (Crveno jezero; one km from Blue Lake to the northwest) resembles a huge well, 200 m across but 500 m deep, two thirds of it being filled with water. Naturally, it is inaccessible. Its name derives from the reddy-brown colour of the rock here. It is thought that this lake appeared when huge underground caverns collapsed during earthquakes.

Old steps (Stare skale), Imotski

•••••••••••

Imotsko polje (plain) covers an area of 95 km^2 and is 33 km long and 1 km to 5.9 km in width. The part in Herzegovina is called Bekija, and thus the area is sometimes known as Imokijsko polje. Traditionally tobacco is grown here (škija) and grapes (kujundžuša). **Kujundžuša** is a high quality wine, greeny-yellow in colour, with 11 to 12% alcohol.

•••••••••••

It is thought that *Hasanaginica*, the best known Croatian folk ballad, has its origins in the Imotski area. It holds a high position in European literature as a whole. It was included in Herder's anthology of European folk poetry, translated into German by Johann Wolfgang von Goethe. The ballad tells of the tragic fate of Hasanaginica (the wife of Hasan Aga). This character can be compared with the tragic heroines of world literature such as Ophelia or Desdemona.

Figures such as Hasan Aga and Beg Pinterović, as well as being historical characters, live today in the folk traditions of the Imotska krajina, a fact that has certainly been encouraged by the power of *Hasanaginica* ballad. ■

310 — 379

SOUTH DALMATA

THE NERETVA-DELTA

ISLANDS

DUBROVNIK

The Neretva-Delta

In its strict sense the Delta covers an area of about 196 km^2. The Neretva Delta consists of 12 river branches, covering 100 km and is the largest Croatian river in the Adriatic river basin. The Neretva rises 90 km (as the crow flies) northeast of the delta beneath Lebršnik Mountain at a height of 1 096 m, and altogether it is 218 km in length. In its upper reaches, as far as Čapljina, the Neretva flows through canyons. West of Konjic it flows into the reservoir, Jablaničko jezero (20 x 2 km), where there is a hydroelectric power station. There are 8 lakes in the Delta. The Neretva is navigable up to Metković (20 km) for vessels with up to 2.2 m displacement.

Typical Neretva landscape

In the course of centuries of careful organisation, which is still going on, the delta has been transformed into a complex of fertile fields, irrigated by canals fed by the river. This area has been called "Croatia's California".

This broad, once marshy landscape is an important habitat for many species of animals and especially birds (see Hutovo blato) and fish. The Neretva region is one of the most important resting-places for birds on their long journey as they migrate from northern Europe via the Mediterranean to Africa. For this reason the area is important for the ornithofauna of Europe. The lower reaches of the Neretva are also the natural breeding ground for many species of fish. With Comacchio in Italy, the Neretva region is the best known hunting ground for eels (Anguilla anguilla), which breed in the Atlantic Ocean west of Bermuda and whose young, when three years old (75 mm in length) swim to the shores of Europe. Here they grow into fully grown eels and in autumn and winter, migrate en masse into the river. There is also a specific species endemic to the entire Neretva region, the Neretva soft-mouthed trout (Salmothymus obtusirostris oxyrkynchus). The ancient name for Neretva, which was mentioned by the Greek writers Strabon and Ptolemy, was Naron. The name Narenta, which is inaccurate, has been quoted in literature as a Romanesque invention from the Middle Ages derived from the Slavic name for the river. The Greek name for Neretva shows the stormy nature of life lived in this region in the ancient world (see Vid).

The **Neretvan Borderlands** (Neretvanska krajina, Craina Continens Pagania) are a historical concept. They are the region between the Cetina and the Neretva which included the islands of Brač, Hvar, Korčula and Mljet. The Neretvan people were known in history as pirates who attacked Venetian merchant ships on the Adriatic, and in the 9th century (right up to the year 1000) Venice had to pay them a toll for free passage. The Neretvan borderlands were an independent political entity with their own ruler (iudex princeps). In political terms the people were linked with Croatia, and the region was joined to that kingdom during the reign of Petar Krešimir IV (1058-1074). In the 12th and 13th centuries, the Counts of Omiš (the Kačić family) became particularly prominent in the borderlands but they recognised the sovereign power of the Croatian-Hungarian Kings. The region began to disintegrate in the second half of the 13th century: the islands accepted Venetian rule, Omiš belonged to the Counts of Bribir, the Šubić family. There then followed a period of rule by the Bosnian kings, Venice, and finally Turkey. In the Cretan war in 1646 the Neretvans voluntarily gave themselves up to the Venetians and remained part of their Empire right up until its fall in 1797. ■

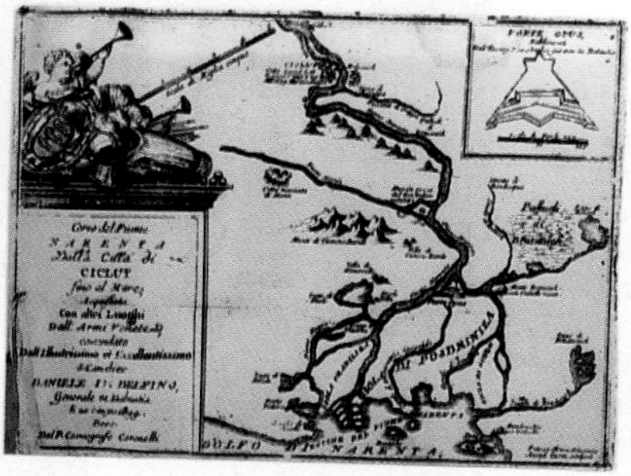

The Neretva-Delta, Venetian engraving of 1694

Metković

IS SITUATED 43°03' N, 17°39' E; **POPULATION** 13 873.

Metković is a port and market town on the lower reaches of the Neretva River, 20 km from the sea. It was first mentioned as Metkovići in the 15th century (1422), the name deriving from a tribe who inhabited this area in ancient times. The town began to develop at the end of the 17th century when the Venetians took over the lower reaches of the Neretva and began to settle there. The town received its greatest boost in 1716 when people from Gabela moved here; it became a border town for the Venetians and later for French and Austrian Dalmatia against the Turks. The town centre first grew up along the left bank of the Neretva beneath Predolac Hill, whilst the newer part is on the right bank of the river. In the middle of the last century, the Austrians transformed Metković into an important port, railway junction and political and religious centre. When the regulation of the Neretva began in 1881-1889 and a railway line (narrow gauge) was opened for Mostar and Sarajevo (1885), Metković became an important economic centre for this part of the Adriatic. It is directly linked by shipping lines with Trieste and Rijeka, and after the First World War it became the main import centre in former Yugoslavia. After the Second World War Metković also became an important industrial centre, especially after a standard gauge railway line was opened in 1966.

SIGHTS

The old centre of Metković, with its stone houses and narrow streets of the Mediterranean type, is located on the south west slopes of Predolac Hill. In the centre, there is the neo-Romanesque, three-naved Church of St. Elijah (Sv. Ilija), built in 1870 on the site of an older church.

Metković

At Stjepana Radića street 1, there is an **Ornithological Collection***** (opened in 1952) which includes 360 examples of the 236 species of birds which spend a large part of the year in nearby Hutovo blato and the Neretva-Delta (see below). The collection is primarily designed for experts, and is the third biggest local collection in Europe.

••••••••••••

Vid*** (4 km northwest of Metković; pop. 779) is located on the site of the ancient city of Narona on the Norin, a tributary of the Neretva. Narona was founded by the Greeks between the 5th and 4th centuries BC. As the Neretva was navigable right up to Počitelj, Narona was suitable for the development of trade amongst the neighbouring Greek islands (Hvar, Vis and Korčula) and the interior, and it quickly grew into an autonomous city which had friendly working relations with the surrounding Illyrian people of the Daorsi tribe. Narona continued to flourish once it came under the Romans in the first century BC. During the rule of Gaius Julius Caesar, Narona received the

honorary title "Colonia Julia Narona" and Caesar himself visited the city in 54 BC. Once Christianity had become rooted in the Roman Empire, Narona became the centre of a diocese and its bishop was mentioned in Salona Church Council documents of 530 and 533 (Marcellus episcopus ecclesiae Naronitanae). At the end of the 7th century, at the time of its greatest prosperity and when, with Salona (see Solin), it was the largest city on the Eastern Adriatic coast, as well as the legal and administrative centre for 89 towns of the southern Illyrians, Narona was destroyed by the Avars. The bishopric, which still remains today, is a reminder of this time, and it is now held by the assistant bishop of Graz in Austria. The many archaeological finds spread over the broad area of the village of Vid show the greatness of ancient Narona. Inside the fortifying walls there were a temple, thermal baths and a theatre. The walls are specially visible on the north-eastern side of the village, and many fragments of inscriptions, sculptures and architectural decorative details are built into the walls of houses in the village. In 1951 a large Roman mosaic was discovered, which was covered over again once it had been protected. In the village graveyard there are several sarcophagi and fragments of gravestones. In further archaeological digs, especially since 1980, an early Christian city basilica has been discovered, which is thought to be the diocesan church, as well as a sarcophagus with a skeleton in Roman cloth, which is considered to be particularly valuable. Fragments of mosaics and frescoes have also been discovered. Work on the exploration of Narona is still going on. On the location called Plećaševe štale an ancient temple with 11 larger than life size Roman statues from the 1st and 2nd century were discovered in 1996. It is thought that two statues represent the Emperor Augustus, in whose honour the temple was probably built, and the locality is called the Augusteum.
The **Museum of Narona** was built after valuable artifacts were discovered in Narona. In situ, there is a temple with a shrine, mosaics and 16 statues of Roman emperors.
The 16th century **Church of St. Vitus** (Sveti Vid) from which the village received its name, was built in a field outside the village on the site of an older church, of which only the semi-circular apse in the foundations remains. The Parish Church of Our Lady of the Ice (Gospa Ledena)

A

B

The site from 1995. (A) on which the Museum of Narona is built (B).

Monument "Domagojeva lađa"

was built in 1961 on the site of the acropolis of old Narona.

Domagojeva lađa ("Domagoj's Ship") is a monument to the Croatian prince (his reign was from 864 to 876) whom a Venetian chronicler calls "Sclavorum pessimus dux", the worst prince of the Croats, while Pope John VIII calls him "Domagoi duci gloriosso", a glorious prince. The sculptor has shown this famed Croatian ruler, whose successes led to Dalmatia becoming independent of the Franks, in monumental dimensions (the boat is five metres long, and the raised arm three), surrounded by three archers and a spear-carrier. It was sculpted by Stjepan Skoko.

Excursions

Klek*

25 km southwest of Metković; pop. 159

The small town of Klek* was the property of the Counts of Hum (Zahumlje) in the Middle Ages and in 1322 it was mentioned as the Bosnian port of Soli. In Klek is the four-sided Novković tower, which has been converted into a restaurant. Adjoining the tower is a Baroque chapel. In 1688 Smrdan Castle was built over Klek. For the people of Novkovići the tower and Smrdan Castle served to defend Venetian territory against the Turks. Not far from Klek is Kuti lake (see Čapljina, Hutovo blato). Klek is also a peninsula between the Klek-Neum Bay and the Maloston Channel, in the a north west direction, 7.7 km long and 1.3 km wide, the highest point being 87 m a.s.l.

Komin (12 km from Ploče towards Opuzen; 1 303 inhabitants) was founded at the beginning of the 18th century. On the site of an old church, at the beginning of the 20th century a new church, St. Anthony's (Sveti Antun) was built of Brač stone, with a beautiful main altar made of white marble. There is a magnificent view from the church courtyard over the entire Neretva valley and over the sea right to the Pelješac peninsula.

Kula Norinska

6 km upstream from Metković; 302 inhabitants

is a round tower built by the Turkish builder Kodža Mustapaša Ušćuplija in about 1500. Around the tower there is a partially intact defensive wall. From the tower there is a view over the sea and to the town of Gabela. It has seven storeys and is well protected by the rivers Norin and Neretva. In 1684 the Venetians captured it from the Turks and rebuilt it in 1716. It lost its military function in 1811 and became a windmill that continued to operate until the beginning of this century.

Up to the most recent times, the life of the Neretvan peasant was unimaginable without the **trupa**, a kind of boat. Since the whole of the Neretvan area is intersected by rivers, creeks and ponds, the boat is used for everything: for going to the fields, for the grape harvest, bird-snaring in the shallow areas of the ponds, for leeches, frogs and for fishing, as well as for going to other villages on the waterside. It served to transport hay, grapes, and was big enough to take a small domestic animal. It could carry up to 300 kg and was on the whole meant for one person. If there were several people in one of these boats, particular care was required.

Neretvanska trupa - a typical boat of the area

Opuzen

12 km upstream from the river mouth; pop. 2 730

is a small town and port on the Neretva. It was first mentioned as Posrednica in 1333. At the end of the 15th century the Croatian-Hungarian King Matthew Corvin had a fortress built

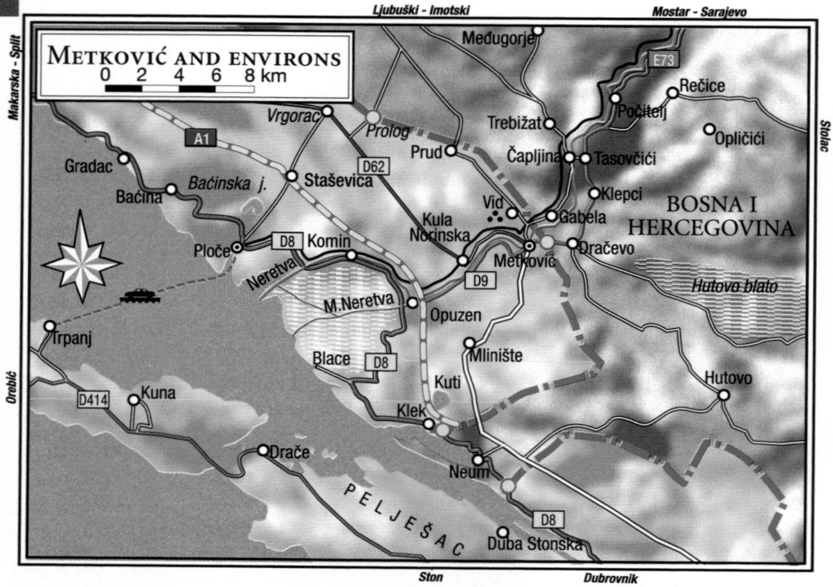

here (Koš) which was conquered by the Turks in 1490, and held by them until the arrival of the Venetians in 1686. The Venetians immediately built a defensive tower on the same spot as defence against the Turks, and called it Fort Opus (strong tower) from which the name Opuzen derives. It was built in the shape of a five-pointed star and its ruins are still visible in the eastern part of the town. In the 18th century Opuzen was an important Venetian trading centre, but when a port was built in Metković in the middle of the 19th century, it lost its significance. In the courtyard of the former town hall there is a collection of stone monuments with fragments of sculptures and inscriptions found in the area of ancient Naron (see Vid). The Oman family house is particularly interesting (18th-19th century), surrounded by a high wall. In the Neo-Classical Parish Church of St. Stephen (Sveti Stjepan; 1883) on the main altar there is a Baroque painting of the Madonna - the work of an unknown Venetian master from 1752. To the south of the town on a hill near the village of Podgradine, there are the ruins of a medieval castle, **Brštanik**, which was built in 1383 by the Bosnian King Tvrtko and was intended to be used as a shipyard. Up to 1395, there was a colony of Dubrovnik merchants here, who traded, amongst other things, in slaves. In the 15th century the castle was destroyed by the Turks, and in 1686 it was rebuilt by the Venetians. They made use of it for military purposes, as did the Austrians, right up to 1878. After Opuzen, the Neretva splits into 12 channels.

••••••••••••

Ploče

23 km from Metković;
6 537 inhabitants

A small town and port on the shores of the Neretvan canal, 5 km north of the mouth of the river. The construction of the modern port began in 1937, continued after the Second World War and was extended to make it one of the largest ports on the Adriatic. It is the main port and outlet to the sea for Bosnia-Herzegovina. To the north of Ploče (east of

Baćinsko jezero

the main highway) is **Baćinsko jezero**, a lake. Despite its proximity to the sea and the permeable nature of the karst terrain, this is a fresh water lake, covering an area of 1.9 km^2 and it is about 31 m deep. It is a crypto-depression (the bottom of the lake is below sea level). Originally the lake received and gave out water underground, but now there is a tunnel bringing water from the periodic lake Vrgorsko jezero and one taking water to the sea. This has brought about biological changes in the lake and it has now become a well-known hunting ground for grey mullet (Mugil saliens).

The **Neretvan Boat Race,** traditional competition of the descendants of the Neretvan pirates. This is a rowing marathon over a course of some 22 kilometres, starting in Metković and ending in Ploče. The course goes by Kula Norinska, Krvavac, Opuzen, Komin, and then by the village of Banje turns off into the right tributary, the Crna Rijeka, to Rogotin. More than twenty crews take part in the competition, each boat having twelve oarsmen. In 2000, the winning team's time was 2.22.08. The victorious crew gets the *Prince Domagoj Shield.* The Neretva Boat Race is a spectacular competition that draws some 30,000 spectators. It is held on the second Sunday in August, and the day is a general holiday for the whole area. ■

Nearby places in Bosnia-Herzegovina

Čapljina

12 KM NORTH OF METKOVIĆ; POP. 7 510

A picturesque small town on the right-hand bank of the River Neretva where it flows out of the gorge at the foot of the steep and bare cliffs of Velika Gradina where there was an Illyrian settlement of the Daors tribe. Čapljina was first mentioned in 1632 as a village in the Mostar administrative district. In the 18th century there was a small boat ferry, and in the 19th century an artisan's village and tobacco trade centre. In the twentieth century it developed into an industrial town. During Serb aggression (April 1992) the left bank was occupied by Serbs. They damaged many buildings and cultural and historical monuments and damaged the new bridge to Tasovčići. In July 1992, when the Croatian Defence Council liberated the left bank of the river. Quite close to Čapljina there are several places with valuable ancient finds. **Morgorjelo*** (1 km south of Čapljina) is an example of late Roman architecture on a hill on the right-hand bank of the Neretva. In the first and second centuries there was a large farm here, which burnt down in the 3rd century, but at the beginning of the 4th was re-built, even larger with a square-shaped fortified villa. The villa was demolished on the arrival of the Eastern Goths from Greece on their way to Italy in 401-403. Towards the end of the 5th century, two early Christian basilicas were built here and destroyed during the Migrations of the Nations.

Neretvan Boat Race

Hutovo blato* is a marshy area 2-3 m above sea level, 10 km from Metković. At high tide Hutovo blato is covered in 1-1.5 m of water. The limestone ridge Ostrovo (123 m) divides Hutovo blato into two parts: in the northern part is the lake Deransko jezero (1 764 hectares) and in the southern part Svitavsko blato (1 922 hectares). In the waters of Hutovo blato, which cover about 7 000 hectares, there are several species of fish, mostly eels and carp (Cyprinidae), plaice (Solea vulgaris), sea bass (Dicentrarchus labrax), grey mullet (Mugilidae) and others; and there are also more than 250 species of birds: ducks (Anatidae), sea-gulls (Laridae), pochard (Podicipidae), snipe (Scolopacidae), water hens (Rallidae). Together with Kuti Lake and the mouth of the Neretva, Hutovo blato forms a unique biological whole. In one part birds build their nests and in the other (and up to 20 km away) they find their food.

••••••••••••

Gabela*

4 KM FROM METKOVIĆ ON THE ROAD TO SARAJEVO.

It was first mentioned in a contract between Nemanja, the ruler, and Dubrovnik as "Drijeva" (which means "ship" or "ferry"). The Drijeva trade centre became a Dubrovnik colony known as Osobljane where there was a large salt warehouse. Drijeva rapidly became a port for slave trading, along with Brštanik, and this was sanctioned by law. This can be seen in the Statute of Dubrovnik of 1272, where in the sixth book there is a series of passages (42-53) dealing with the social status of slaves. They were mostly bought in Bosnia and then exported to Venice, Genoa, Sicily and Tripoli on the African coast. The trade was mostly carried out by the Bogumil Bosnians. In the 14th century the Bosnian kings began to implement forceful measures against this "trade in human flesh on the Neretva" and under pressure from them in 1400 the

Ljubuški

Dubrovnik Senate banned the trade in human lives and in 1416 banned the transport of slaves in Ragusan ships under the threat of six months imprisonment in the underground dungeons in the Rector's palace in Dubrovnik, as well as a fine. Under the name Gabela (Italian gabella - "customs house") the town was mentioned in 1399. The Turks occupied the town in 1529 and built Sedislam Fortress on the right-hand bank of the Neretva. In the middle of the 17th century the town developed and obtained fortifications.

Polar birds from the ornithological collection in Metković

In 1693 Gabela was conquered by the Venetians who repaired the Turkish buildings, especially in Novi grad (the new town) and Đerzelez fortress but they destroyed these buildings again when the Turks attacked once more. In 1718 the Turks themselves rebuilt part of the settlement. As well as fragments of the walls and towers, the ruins of two churches are also still visible, as well as the "Sultan's Mosque" (Careva džamija) which the Venetians converted into a church, St. Stephen's (Sv. Stjepan), and added stone sculptures of lions, the symbol of the Venetian Empire. Up to 1878, Gabela was an important border town between Herzegovina and Dalmatia.

••••••••••••

Is Gabela Troy? The Mexican philologist Roberto Salinas Price published a book in 1985 entitled *Homer's Blind Audience* in which, amongst other things, he argued that ancient Troy was not in Asia Minor, but on the Neretva, precisely on the site of present-day Gabela! In other words Gabela was the home of the Trojans, and the famous war fought over the lovely Helen was fought here, Odysseus set out from here on his journey sung about in Homer's *Illiad* and *Odyssey...* Price came to these conclusions in 1967. At the mouth of the Neretva, in Gabela, he claims to have found traces which were totally in accord with his research and "conclusively" point to the fact that Gabela was in fact Troy.

Sketches which he drew on the basis of descriptions from the Illiad agree totally with air pictures of Gabela, as well as archaeological digs in the area from the early Iron Age. Descriptions of the town, temples, palaces, the names of allied cities, islands, the Trojan hinterland all agree, according to Price. He even measured the sun's path and confirmed that it could only be "born from the sea" in the geographical area of Gabela and definitely not in Hissarlika in Turkey! He then compared the stars mentioned in the *Illiad*, and like an ancient seafarer, he confirmed that they could only have been visible from Gabela in those positions which Homer describes in the *Illiad*. When he visited Gabela again in 1985, R.S. Price continued to claim that Gabela was in fact ancient Ilios, and that no other place coincides with Homer's description of Troy better than Gabela. He also claims that in the ruins around Gabela, there are the remains of the Temple to Athena, but he termed his own book "provocative", expecting archaeologists to respond to his questions and provocative statements.

Počitelj*

3 KM FROM ČAPLJINA, 15 KM FROM METKOVIĆ.

Počitelj is located on the road leading to Mostar and Sarajevo. Počitelj is 11 m above sea level, along the Neretva, but the upper part of the town is at 100 m above sea level. The town was first mentioned in 1444 and it is thought that it was built towards the end of the 14th century by the Bosnian King Tvrtko. At the time when Bosnia fell to the Turks (1463) Počitelj was part of the property of Stjepan Vukčić Kosača (the historical region Zahumlje was named Herzegovina after him, "the Duke of St. Sava", "herceg Svetog Save"), so in his time the town was a strong strategic point which was transformed into a strong fortress and placed under the control of the Croatian-Hungarian King Matthew Corvin. Stjepan's descendent Vlatko also helped to fortify Počitelj along with Pope Paul II (1464-1471) and the Dubrovnik Republic. Dubrovnik sent its architect Paskoje Miličević and 2 000 ducats as well as practical help in the building work. But not even these defences could stop the Turkish forces and Duke Vlatko became a Turkish vassal when they conquered Počitelj in 1471 and the whole of Herzegovina in 1482. Počitelj remained under the Turks for 407 years, right up until the decision by the Berlin Congress in 1878 to hand it over to the Austro-Hungarian Empire. During the Turkish rule, Počitelj became an important strategic and, from 1713, administrative centre. Important buildings of Islamic architecture were constructed here, while the buildings of the Croats fell into ruin.

Čitluk and Gabela - Venetian engraving

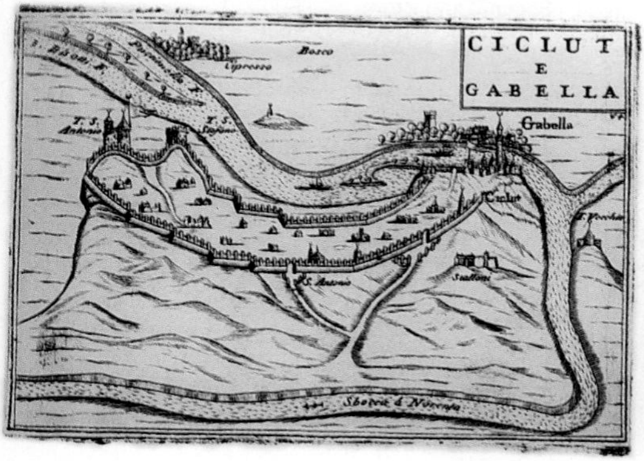

Church and Monument to the B.V.M. in Međugorje

Međugorje

18 KM NORTH OF ČAPLJINA

has become famous recently for Our Lady of Međugorje. Since 1981 this has been a place of pilgrimage and a holy place in the Catholic Church. On 24th June 1981 we heard for the first time of the appearance of the Madonna to a young girl called Vicka Ivanović and on the following day to six more children on Križevac

Hill. The first to see the vision and other believers insist that the Madonna continues to appear to them despite the fact that the Vatican commission has expressed no definite opinion on the appearances and the bishop in whose diocese Međugorje lies contests the validity of the visions. The Shrine of the Madonna of Međugorje has become to Catholics what Lourdes is in France or Fatima in Portugal. By 1996, over 20 million people had made the pilgrimage to Međugorje. Many books have been written, and a film with a leading international cast has been shot (*Gospa*, 1994). In many countries, friends of Međugorje clubs have been founded.

••••••••••••

Križevac, the place of the visions

Neum

30 KM FROM METKOVIĆ, 20 KM FROM OPUZEN, POPULATION 1 645

Neum is centre of the commune in the coastal part of Herzegovina and a tourist centre in the part of the Adriatic coast (9 km) belonging to Bosnia and Herzegovina. In the Middle Ages and during the Turkish rule in this area, Neum was a small village and port.

After the Turkish withdrawal from northern Crotian (1699) Neum was given to Turkey in order to create a buffer zone between the republics of Venice and Dubrovnik. The Turks used the mooring for the last time in 1875, during the time of the revolt in Nevesinje, after which Austria-Hungary occupied Bosnia-Herzegovina (1878).

On the sea front there are the ruins of a tower belonging to Duke Vlatko Hercegović which was the final base of resistance to the Ottomans during their conquest of Herzegovina in 1481. In nearby Gradac there is a Baroque church which dates from 1619. Near Neum, not far from Vranjevo Selo, beneath Žrnovo Hill, there is a necropolis with 145 "stechaks", Bogumil gravestones.

••••••••••••

Stećci (Stechaks) are memorial stones on the graves of Bogumils and are unique in the European art of the Middle Ages (the 13th to the 15th centuries). Bogumils (Patarens, Albigensians, Cathars, Christian Boni, Bonomini) were members of a heretical movement which arose in the 10th century (under the influence of Manichaeism). This religious movement taught of the existence of two gods (Good and Evil) and was against the existence of Church hierarchy and state authority resting on the Church. They considered their own elders to be followers of the Apostle Paul, and not the Roman Pope. This teaching had a large following in Bosnia and despite merciless suppression, it survived until Bosnia fell to the Turks in 1463. According to some authors, a large number of Bogumils then converted to Islam. As they did not build any churches, their artistic skills and belief in the need to live an extremely simple life has been preserved only in these stone stechaks. About 60 000 have been recorded in Bosnia, most of them being without any kind of decoration, which shows both the conditions of their cultural isolation, and the religious and mystic character of their faith. ■

Stećak - Bogumil gravestone

Neum

The South Dalmatian Islands

include the islands of Lastovo, Mljet and the Elaphites (see Dubrovnik). They form the smallest island group in the Adriatic. Although some geographers place Korčula in the Central Dalmatian Islands, for reasons of practicality, and because Korčula belongs administratively to the southernmost Croatian county, in this guide it is treated as part of the South Dalmatian Islands.

Korčula

Early History. Archaeological finds in the Jakasova špilja caves near Rasohatica Bay and Spila Cave above the source of the Norin on the Pelješac side prove that man lived on Korčula in the later Stone Age and that he had links with "Hvar culture" (see Hvar). On the threshold of a new historical era, when the Adriatic region became involved in new trends in civilisation, Korčula was settled by the Illyrian tribe of the Ardaeans and Pelješac by the Plerei. Strengthened by alliances between them, these peoples increasingly turned to the sea and gained a reputation as skilled mariners and pirates.

The Greek and Roman Eras. At the beginning of the 5th century BC, the Cnidianc from Asia Minor founded a colony probably on the western side of the island. Ancient historians called the island Korkyra Melania - "Black Korčula", after the name which the Argonauts supposedly gave the island on their way through this area because of its thick pine forests. Other ancient texts show that the island became part of ancient mythology very early on in its history. According to these myths Kerkyra the daughter of Asopos lived here in a home created for her by Poseidon the sea god. There is also material evidence of Greek settlements on the island: a "psephisma" (a treaty) from Lumbarda (see below) speaks of the foundation of a Greek settlement on the island and mentions south Italian and Sicilian Greeks as well as Messapian Illyrians as colonists. At the end of the third century BC the geo-political situation in this part of the Adriatic caused several interesting trends to develop: trade between the Greek cities (Vis, Hvar, Korčula, Trogir, Solin and Stobreč) and constant attacks by Illyrian pirates on the Italian side. At that time too, a new naval power emerged in the shape of Rome, who entered a trade agreement with the Greek cities, and also attempted to subdue the warlike Illyrian tribes. Thus conflicts over Korčula went on for two centuries. They finally came to an end following Octavian's campaign of 35 BC when he attacked the Venetian and Korčulan pirates, bringing Korčula into the Roman Empire. Remains of Roman settlements have been discovered in the area around Lumbarda, Vela Luka, Blato and Potirna. Villas, temples, cisterns, graves and small summer and farm residences show the boost that life on the island received during the period of Roman rule.

Figurehead from a Korčulan sailing boat

The Migrations of the Nations. Following the fall of the Western Roman Empire in 493 the island fell to the Eastern Gothic state, and then in 555 to Byzantium. According to writings by the Byzantine Emperor and writer Constantine Porphyrogenitus (10th century) there were deserted towns on the island, which were without doubt the ruins of Roman settlements, destroyed during the migrations of the nations. The same author also mentions Krkar, a city with a Slavonic name, which is supposed to have existed on the site of present day Korčula.

Under Various Rulers. In the first half of the 9th century the people of the Neretva-Delta (see the Neretva-Delta) conquered Korčula. In 1000 the Venetian Doge Pietro II Orseolo undertook a famous expedition along the Eastern Adriatic coast to reinforce the Venetians' trade route to Byzantium, which until then had been blocked by Croatian and Neretvan pirates. During this "gathering" of the city keys from Rab to Dubrovnik, the only resistance (though unsuccessful) was offered by Korčula and Lastovo. From that time the chronological succession of rulers on Korčula is much more complex, right up to 1125 when the Venetian noble Popone Zorzi received the lease of Korčula from the Venetian Republic. His rule ended in around 1180 but his family returned to the island in 1254 and held it until 1358. In the interregnum between these two periods of Zorzian rule Korčula was under the Croatian-Hungarian kings, retaining however considerable autonomy, in which the interests of Dubrovnik, the Venetians, Omiš and Zahumlje were all involved. Neighbouring Pelješac was within Zahumlje territory, which was bought in 1333 by Dubrovnik from the Serbian King Stefan Dušan and the Bosnian Ban

Korčula in the 18th century

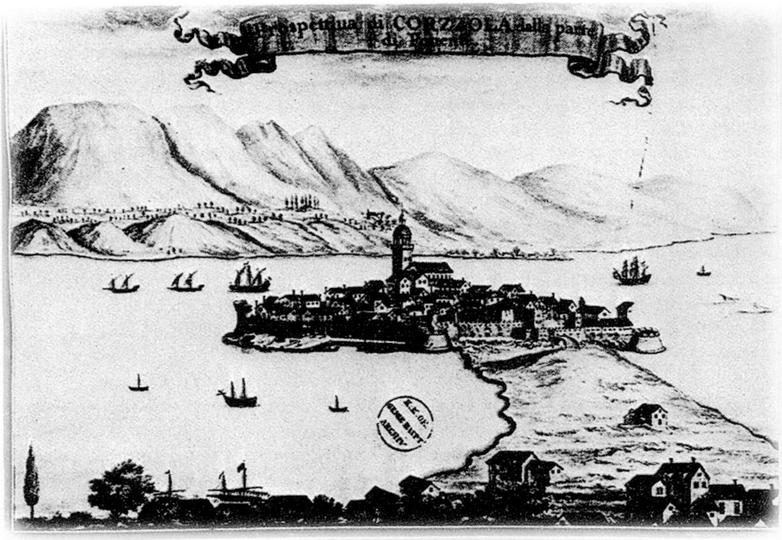

View of Korčula

Stjepan Kotromanić. Following the Zadar Treaty of 1358, Korčula was part of the Croatian-Hungarian Kingdom right up until 1420.

Under the Venetians (1420-1797). For more than three centuries Korčula shared the fate of the remainder of Dalmatia: limited authority and economic development, over-shadowed by the constant threat of the Turks. In 1571, just before the battle at Lepanto, the fleet of the Algerian Viceroy Ulus Alia attacked Korčula, destroying much of it, but the city of Korčula itself was spared by a sudden and lucky wind which wrecked the enemy ships. At that time neighbouring Pelješac developed within the Dubrovnik Republic.

From 1797 to 1815. After the fall of the Venetian Empire and the dissolution of the Dubrovnik Republic, this region was under Austria until 1805 and between 1805 and 1813 under the French (apart from during the Franco-Russian war of 1806-7). The Russians conquered Korčula on several occasions. From 1813-1815 the island was under the British. In that brief period the British, led by Commander Peter Lowen, undertook several significant building projects. They restored the stone coastal defences to the west of the city, on the hill above the city they built a huge fortress and at the beginning of a new road to Lumbarda, over the present baths, they built a beautiful semi-circular city square.

Under the Austrians. From 1815 to 1918 Korčula and Pelješac were part of the Austrian Empire.

In the second half of the century there were conflicts between the "Nationalists" and the "Autonomists" (those who supported or opposed the unification of the various parts of Croatia), as part of a widespread movement for the unification of Dalmatia with the rest of Croatia. Finally in 1871 the community was taken over by the Nationalists.

The Twentieth Century. Following the Italian occupation between 1918 and 1921 this region became part of the State of the Slovenes, Croats and Serbs (from 1929. the Kingdom of Yugoslavia). After this kingdom surrendered in 1941, the Italians once again occupied the area until September 1943. In December 1943, following one of the fiercest battles of the Second World War in Dalmatia, the Germans succeeded in conquering the island. The area of the city itself was bombed 28 times by the Germans and the Allies, destroying or damaging most of the important buildings. In the second half of the twentieth century, the development of the area has been grounded almost entirely on the tourist industry. ■

Korčula*** (Town)

42°57'N and 17°8'E, population 3 126; Mean Temperatures in January: air, 7.6°C, sea, 13°C; Mean Temperatures in July: air 24.4°C, sea 22.8°C.

Korčula is the largest settlement on the island and lies on a small raised peninsula (300 m x 170 m). In several medieval manuscripts which reproduce old Roman and Greek sources, there is a legend, also mentioned in an inscription on the city gates, that the colony on the island was founded by the Trojan Antenor, and in another version by Aeneas himself. The date of the city's foundation however, has not been confirmed by archaeological evidence. It was mentioned under the Slavic name Krkar by the Byzantine Emperor Constantine Porphyrogenitus in the middle of the

Korčula, city centre

10th century. The city was restored from 1265 on by Count Marsilije Zorzi, and it experienced the period of its greatest prosperity in the 15th and 16th centuries.

Sights

The urban whole. The city layout of Korčula (which conforms with the shape of the land where it is built) was fixed in the second half of the 13th century and is a uniquely rational urban plan and one of the best preserved examples of the planning of medieval towns in general. The main street divides the city into a western and an eastern half and broadens out at its head forming a square in front of the cathedral. On both sides small streets lead to the outer ring of the city walls, forming a fish-bone layout. This layout protects against strong sunlight at noon, but allows the sun in, in the morning and evening.

••••••••••••

The **City Walls and the Fortress***** have existed since the 13th century. Over the centuries they have been restored many times. Originally the defensive belt around the city was strengthened with a series of four-sided (and cylindrical) towers, of which the following are still standing: in the north Barbarigo (1488) and Tiepolo (the end of the 15th century), in the south Balbi (1483) and Cappelo (1493). The city is entered through two gates: from the south, by the Land Gate (by the city hall; NUMBER ❼ ON THE PLAN) and from the west, the Sea Gate. The front of the Land Gate is covered by a triumphal arch built in

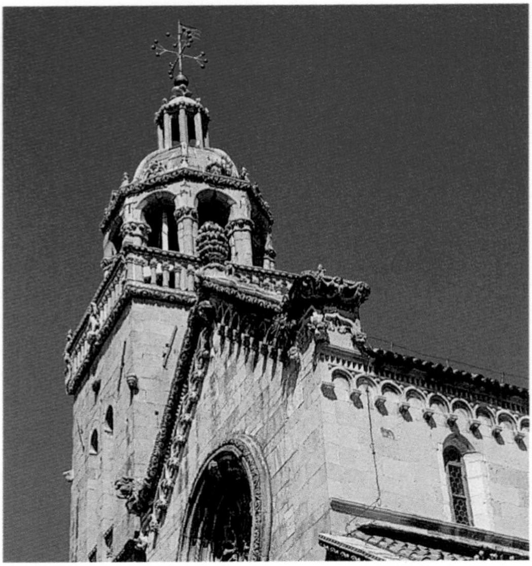

Cathedral

honour of the Venetian army commander Leonardo Foscolo (1650) who was prominent in the defence of Dalmatia from the Turks. The Sea Gate has been restored many times.

••••••••••••

The **Cathedral***** (NUMBER ❹ ON THE PLAN). Korčula became a Bishopric in 1300, once the Bishop of Ston moved there during the spread of the Bogumil heresy (see Neretva-Delta) on Pelješac and its hinterland. The Diocesan Church of St. Mark (Sveti Marko) is the most important building in the city. It was built as a triple-naved basilica (with an irregular ground plan) from the beginning of the 15th to the middle of the 16th century. Over the entrance to the northern side aisle there is a bell tower, and on one side the St. Rocco Chapel (Sveti Rok) and a baptistery have been added: local masters took part in the building work, and they were known for their carvings from Dubrovnik to Venice. One of the most gifted of these masters was Marko Andrijić who is attributed with the final section of the bell tower (after 1481) with its dome, lantern and ciborium. The main portal which combines elements of the Adriatic Romanesque and the Gothic traditions is the work of Master Bonino of Milan (the beginning of the 15th century). The most prominent part of the portal is the seated figure of the Patron Saint of the cathedral, St. Mark the Evangelist. Bonino is also the creator of the relief of St. James over the door into the southern aisle. The interior is divided with Gothic and Renaissance arcades and columns. On

Detail of the Cathedral

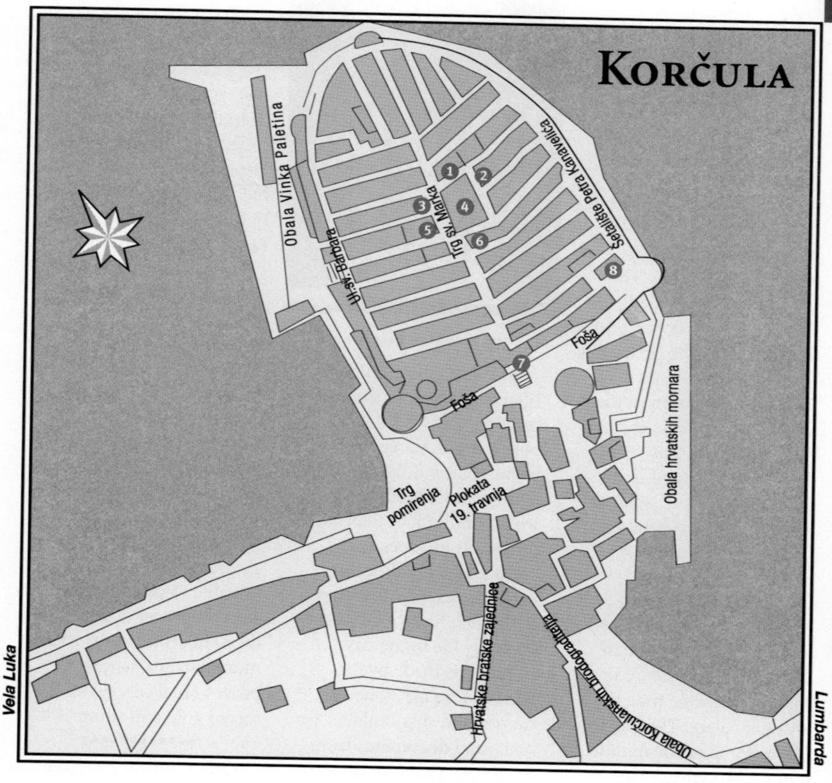

the corner capitals there are relief symbols representing the four evangelists. The capitals on the northern arcade were restored in the Baroque era. Over the side aisles with their groin vaults, there are galleries opening out over the main aisle with a row of biforia. Over the main altar there is an impressive Gothic and Renaissance ciborium (1486) by Andrijić with figures representing the Annunciation on the front architrave and an eight--sided pyramidal roof on three levels. On the wall of the apse there is a large altarpiece showing the patron saints of Korčula, SS. Mark, Jerome and Bartholomew, probably the work of Jacopo Tintoretto (in his youth, around the middle of the 16th century). Beneath the altar is the Baroque reliquary sarcophagus of St. Theodore (Sveti Todor), and to the side, a late Romanesque relief of the Resurrected Lamb discovered during conservation work on the ciborium. On the stone altar in the apse of the southern nave there is a painting of the Holy Trinity with a portrait of the Bishop of Korčula, Diedo, commissioned by him from the well-known Venetian artist Leandro Bassano (1557-1622). In the same nave there is also the Renaissance sarcophagus of Bishop Tomo Malumbro built by his successor Nikola Nikoničić at the beginning of the 16th century. Here you can also see Tintoretto's *The Annunciation* painted for the doors of the Renaissance cathedral organ, and the icon of the Madonna of the Island (the island of Badija) which became known especially after 1571, when it was attributed to the salvation of Korčula from a fleet of pirates. Here there are also Turkish bullets on show together with weapons from Naples and Aragon which were captured a century earlier. In the fourth nave, which was started in 1525 by the Korčula architect Marko Pavlović, there is a great Baroque altar dedicated to saints credited with offering protection from illness, SS. Rocco, Cosmas and Damian. The wooden statues in the style of the later Renaissance are the work of Franjo Čiočić, who also covered them with gold in 1576. In the baptistery, which stands at the foot of the bell tower, there is a statue of the Risen Christ in bronze, by the famous Korčula sculptor Frano Kršinić (1897-1982). The sacristy can be reached through Gothic doors with a relief showing the Archangel Michael. These doors may have originally been in the Church of St. Michael (Sveti Mihovil) which was thoroughly restored in the Baroque era. The Cathedral was also restored between 1950 and 1970.

The **Abbey Treasury** (NUMBER ❻ ON THE PLAN) is on the southern side of the Cathedral in a building which was at one time the bishop's palace. The palace was restored in the middle of the 17th century by Bishop Frane Manola who drew particular attention to its long balcony along the front and arranged a small hanging garden over the street. The Abbey Treasury is perhaps the most important collection of its kind in Dalmatia. It is housed in seven halls and includes illuminated manuscripts (12th-15th centuries), gold threaded robes, items made of gold and silver, porcelain, ancient and medieval pottery, coins, valuable household items and an especially important collection of paintings with works by Blaž Jurjev Trogiranin (see Trogir), Giovanni Bellini, Vittore Carpaccio, Matej Pončun, Frederiko Benković Magnasco and works by contemporary Croatian artists.

Korčula city scene

The **City Museum**** (Gradski muzej; NUMBER ❺ ON THE PLAN) is located opposite the Abbey Treasury in the palace of the Korčula family, the Gabriellis, which was built in the 16th century. It includes an archaeological collection and artefacts which witness to the rich history of everyday life in the city - from items made by the famous Korčula stone carvers and ship builders, to items and documents from the inheritance of individual families and societies.

Detail of the great crucifix in the Church of All Saints (14th century)

All Saints' Church*** (Svi Sveti; NUMBER ❽ ON THE PLAN) is the seat of the city's oldest fraternity (founded in 1301) and has a coffered ceiling created by Tripo Kokolja, an artist from the Bay of Kotor who died in Korčula in 1713 (see Perast). Inside there is a fine ciborium, influenced by the one in the cathedral, beneath which there is a monumental *Pieta*, the work of the Austrian Rococo sculptor Georg Raphael Donner (1693-1741). *The polyptych* by Blaž Jurjev Trogiranin (1431) on the wall to the right of the altar is one of his greatest works. The icon collection includes a series of exceptionally valuable works from the period between the 14th and the 18th centuries, as well as monks' habits, large processional candles and sacred gold and silver.

Other buildings. Within the old city centre there is a row of building complexes, palaces and houses belonging to old Korčula families (Ismaelli, Lazarović, Kanavelić, Andrijić, Španić, Kapor, Boschi) which represent authentic masterpieces of Dalmatian Gothic, Renaissance and Baroque architecture. The complex of the **Arneri Palace**** (NUMBER ❸ ON THE PLAN) opposite the Cathedral, was created by joining several medieval plots of land. Inside the complex there is a picturesque Baroque courtyard, and especially beautiful is the facade of this late Gothic palace, turned towards the southern street, and the narrow Mannerist facade of the house facing the Cathedral. The whole complex is soon to be converted into a multipurpose cultural centre. On the northern side of the square, in front of the Cathedral, is the Gothic **Chapel of St. Peter*** (Sveti Petar; NUMBER ❷ ON THE PLAN) whose facade shows a relief of the saints by Master Bonino from Milan. There was once a graveyard in front of the church. Inside there are wooden statues of the Apostles, which in the Baroque era stood in the biforia on the Cathedral's gallery. The Church of the Immaculate Conception* (Crkva Bezgrešnog Začeća, or Madonina crkva) in the southwestern corner of the square was once a chapel where members of the respected Ismaelli (Zmajko) family were buried. In the suburbs of the city, one of the most interesting sights is the urban complex around the square dominated by St. Justine's Church (19th century) in the centre, as well as several palaces and former summer residences with walled gardens and parks.

•••••••••••

The **complex of the Dominican Church of St. Nicholas** (Sveti Nikola) and the monastery on Rt Vješala point was founded in 1480 and renovated in the Baroque era, when a new nave facing east was added to the old church. Inside there is an altarpiece entitled *The Miracle in Surian* by Matija Pončun-Ponzoni from the 1730s, an excellent copy of a lost Titian *The Death of St. Peter the Martyr* and an altarpiece by the artist Baldassare d'Anno (1560-1639). In the monastery's refectory there is a series of medallions which were probably painted by Tripo Kokolja at the beginning of the 18th century.

•••••••••••

There is a particularly picturesque group of buildings on Gradac to the east of the city. It includes St. Anthony's Chapel* (Sveti Antun) with a former hermitage which was converted at the beginning of the 18th century into a mausoleum for Bishop Nikola Španić. An avenue of cypress trees was also planted, leading up to the building.

•••••••••••

Marco Polo (c. 1254-1324). According to a document dating from the 15th century, this famous

Marco Polo

explorer and travel writer was born on Korčula. A local legend tells that he was born in a house in the centre of the city (NUMBER ❶ ON THE PLAN). Polo set off for China in 1271 as a Venetian subject, along with his father and uncle. They travelled via Tibet accompanying two Dominican missionaries. The young man became a confidant of Kublai Khan and spent 17 years in his service. He returned in 1295 and in 1298 he took part in a battle between the Venetian and the Genoan fleets which took place very near Korčula. In prison Polo retold his experiences to Rustichello of Pisa who recorded them in his work *Livre des merveilles du monde* (*Il milione*) which from the 14th century on, served as the basis for the geographical maps of Asia and was required reading for generations of explorers of the Far East.

•••••••••••

The Moreška, Kumpanija and Moštra are old chivalric dances which are still performed on Korčula more than anywhere else in the Mediterranean. The Moreška is performed on 27th July on the feast of St. Theodore and every Thursday in the tourist season in Korčula, the Kumpanija in various forms in Blato, Smokvica, Čara and Pupnat, and the Moštra in Žrnovo. It is thought that the Moreška originated in memory of the defence of the city against the infamous Algiers pirate Eulg Ali (Ulič Alija) in 1571. In simple terms it goes like this: Moro, the "Black Emperor" has captured the "White Emperor's" bride but fails to persuade her to marry him. The "White Emperor" appears with his army, recaptures his bride after a struggle shown in eight dance figures, in which 12 pairs of "Moreškans" in special costumes with swords in both hands swirl around and strike each other showing, as the pace quickens, exceptional fencing skills. The Kumpanija is a chivalric folk dance in 18 figures, in which the dancers, in colourful costumes, sing in two parts accompanied by bagpipes and drums and fight one another with swords. They are joined by girls in the dance. Before the dance begins, the "Srdar" who represents the foreign

Moreška

authorities on the island, bans the movement of the island's army, but the Captain succeeds, after a verbal conflict, in gaining permission. The dance at one time ended with the ritual decapitation of an ox. The Moštra or "the fat king" in Žrnovo and Pupnat is very similar to the Kumpanija. Unfortunately it is not performed very regularly. The dance, accompanied by bagpipes and drums, consists of 10 fencing figures, ending with a ritual in which the "Duke" (Vojvoda) has to cut off an ox's head with one movement of his sword. The rules of the dance are set out in a statute dating from 1620.

••••••••••••

EXCURSIONS

Badija** is a small island in the eastern part of the Pelješac channel covering an area of just 1 km². It is a well-known sports and recreation centre. On the island there was at one time a famous Franciscan monastery (now a tourist centre) after which the island was named (from the Latin "abbatia" - monastery). Together with the Chapel of Our Lady of Mercy (Gospa Milosrdna) the monastery was built in the 15th and 16th centuries. In the course of the development of architecture in Dalmatia at that time, one of the most original contributions of the Korčula masters was without doubt the creation of the monastery's cloisters in 1477. The church itself represents a characteristic Gothic single-naved church, whose facade however is dominated by a newer form of moulded work from the beginning of the 16th century showing the autochthonous transition from the Gothic to the Renaissance styles within the circle of Korčula sculptors. The chapel to the north was added in the 18th century and designed by the Venetian architect Giorgio Massanio. It is one of the most significant architectural creations of the Baroque era in Dalmatia. Of the originally rich but now scattered inventory in the church there is still a wooden altar and choir stalls by the wood carver Šimun of Cavtat. Every August 2nd sees the celebration of Perdun (Per donare ords.). On that day from the Korčula harbour towards Otok sails a pilgrims' procession on the ships led by the miraculous Madonna of the Island (Gospa od Otoka).

••••••••••••

1.5 nautical miles from Badija is the small island of **Majsan***. In the small harbour on the western side of the island there are some remains of a Roman building complex which were converted in the Roman era into an early Christian memorial, and perhaps even a monastery. That this area was consistently inhabited is shown by the ruins of an early medieval chapel, St. Maximus' (Sveti Maksim) with frescoes mentioned in the notes written by the Venetian travel writer Giovanni Diaconus. He wrote that the Doge Pietro II Orseolo anchored his fleet here in 1000 and met representatives from Dubrovnik led by the bishop.

••••••••••••

Čara (28 km west of Korčula, 566 inhabitants). Two of the most outstanding buildings in this village are Španić Castle (1674) and the romantic villa complex Kapor. **The Church of Our Lady of Čarsko polje** (Gospa od Čarskog polja) is the goal of

Badija, monastery and church

Čara

pilgrimages, especially on 25th July. In the restored **Parish Church of St. Peter** (Sveti Petar) there is an altarpiece *Doubting Thomas*, by the Venetian artist Leandro Bassano.

••••••••••••

Lumbarda**

6 KM FROM THE TOWN OF KORČULA; POP. 1 221

Lumbarda is a village and small harbour in the eastern part of the island. The summer residences of noble families from Korčula in Lumbarda represent a special chapter in the history of Gothic and Renaissance architecture of such residences, and they also form a most original contribution to the European architectural heritage. On Knežina near **Holy Cross Chapel** (Sveti Križ) and on a Baroque tower built the ancient walls, there are visible remains of a larger Roman complex of buildings. Unfortunately this has not been fully researched and neither have archaeological remains on Koludrt point where a "psephisma" (a legal code of the ancient Greeks) was found, telling of the foundation of a Greek colony (see below).

Lumbarda is the birth place of the sculptors Frane Kršinić (1897-1982) and Ivo Lozica (1910-1943).

••••••••••••

The **Lumbarda psephisma** is the oldest written document on the east coast of the Adriatic. The original is in the Archeological Museum in Zagreb. It tells of the colonisation of Korčula by the Cnidians from Asia Minor and it was discovered in fragments on the Koludrt peninsula. It has been dated at the third century BC, at about the time when the people of Issa (Issa - the Island of Vis), founded Tragurion (Trogir) and Epetion (Stobreč) in a period of political and economic expansion towards the Illyrian mainland. The psephisma regulates the division of land amongst the settlers of the new Greek and Illyrian agrarian colony and includes a register of these estates in three vertical columns under the names of three Dorian clans. In the partially restored inscription a list of about 200 colonists has been preserved. An analysis of the names would reveal the directions from which the Greeks colonised the Adriatic islands. A precis of the psephisma runs as follows: In the time of Praxides (a religious functionary on Issa according to whom the document is dated) the Issans made a treaty with Pile and his son Daze (Illyrians, who took part in the division of the land), and the people decided that those who first occupied the land and put walls round the city should take as a privilege land within it for the building of a house and a yard and that they should divide the land outside the city walls, and that what everyone had received in perpetuity should be written down. Later colonisers might take land not allotted. The governors were to swear that they would not make a new allotment of city or land, and if anyone opposed this, his property should become the property of the people. As well as southern Italic and Sicilian Greeks, there are the names of some Messapian Illyrians. This clearly shows the strength of the ethnic and cultural osmosis which must have taken place in the strengthened Illyrian state of the 3rd century BC.

••••••••••••

The **tradition of stonemasonry.** With shipbuilding, stonemasonry is the craft for which the

Lumbarda

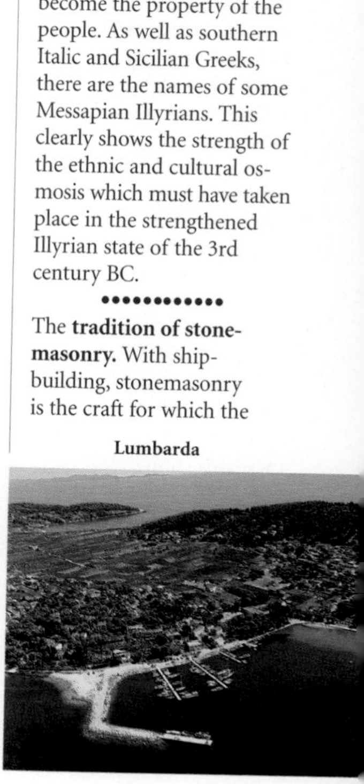

Orebić

people of Korčula are best known. The tradition of stonework on the island is extremely old, as shown by remains of ancient and medieval stone quarries, especially on the smaller islands in the southernmost area of the Pelješac channel. The quarries on the islands of Vrnik, Sutvara and Kamenjak are particularly interesting. The history of Croatian art, drawing on copious records, shows that Korčula stonemasons' families took part in, or directed, the construction of a whole series of important buildings of the Croatian architectural heritage in the period between the 14th and the 19th century, from Kotor and Dubrovnik, to Hvar, Split, Zadar, Venice and elsewhere. Gothic and Renaissance palaces and the cathedral in the city, and the Franciscan monastery complex on Badija perhaps most clearly demonstrate the craftsmanship and artistic skill with which the masters of Korčula carried out their complex programmes in architecture and masonry.

••••••••••••

Žrnovo*

4 KM SOUTH OF KORČULA; FOUR SETTLEMENTS WITH 1 296 INHABITANTS

Žrnovo is an extremely picturesque location where the Parish Church of St. Martin (Sv. Martin) particularly stands out, as well as castles and houses, the best known of which belonged to the family of Jakov Baničević (1466-1532), the Renaissance cleric and humanist. He was a friend of Albrecht Dürer, and corresponded with Erasmus and Pietro Bembo. A heroic dance (Moštra) is performed in front of St. Rocco's Church (Sveti Rok) ending with a ritual decapitation of an ox (see above). To the north-west of the village is **Kočje**, a unique karst labyrinth. Ten km west of Žrnovo on the road for Vela Luka is the village of **Pupnat** where the most interesting building is the Gothic Chapel of St. George (Sveti Jure) in the graveyard.

Portrait of an Orebić captain

••••••••••••

The **Pelješac Peninsula.** The mainland is half a mile as the crow flies, and about 1.5 miles by ferry from Korčula.

••••••••••••

Orebić**

1 949 INHABITANTS

is the nearest settlement to Korčula. The large central block of buildings in the historical centre of Orebić, to the east of which the centre known as Fiskovićevo Selo also grew up, is one of the best preserved examples of planned building of the 15th to the 17th century in the region of what was once the Dubrovnik Republic. The settlement was named after the family who restored the castle inside the fortified settlement in 1586. The **Franciscan Church of Our Lady of Angels** (Gospa od Anđela) was for centuries the most important place of worship for Orebić seafarers. Together with the wings of the monastery and the bell tower it was built in the last quarter of the 15th century on a small hill from which traffic in the Pelješac channel was observed, together with Korčula which at that time was under Venetian rule. In the church there are two excellent reliefs from the second half of the 15th century, showing the Madonna and Child, a piece by the sculptor Tomaso Fiamberti of Florence, and another by Nikola Firentinac, a pupil of Donatello. The late Renaissance wooden carved retable in the sanctuary was mainly painted by Maffeo di Verona

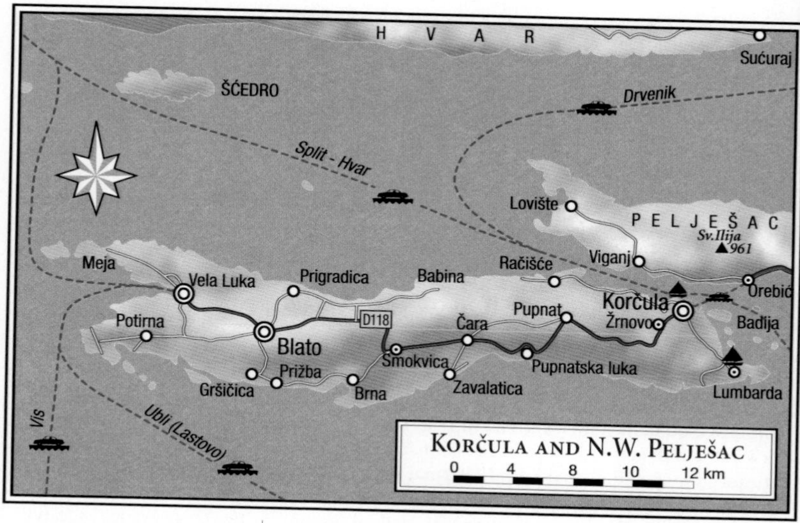

in 1599. Inside the church there is also a Gothic crucifix from Badija on display, the work of Juraj Petrović from 1457. In the monastery collection there is a statue of St. John by the same artist. There are also votive pictures and tablets given by Orebić seafarers, and a series of works of art including a fine painting of St. Francis of Paula by the Mannerist artist Andrea Lilli of Ancona. Amongst the gold and silver chalices, reliquaries and thuribles (censers), there is a processional cross by the goldsmith Matija Dorošević of Šibenik dating from 1614. The Parish Church of Our Lady of Carmel (Gospa od Karmela) was thoroughly restored in the 17th century. It houses the painting *The Circumcision* probably by Francesco Maggioto. In this widely scattered settlement, several houses belonging to Orebić sea captains and ship owners were built in the Baroque era and the 19th century. They blend simply into the natural beauty of the area. The rich history of seafaring in Orebić is shown in the Maritime Museum (Pomorski muzej).

••••••••••••

Kučište* (7 km west of Orebić; 250 inhabitants). The Gothic Church of St. Luke (Sveti Luka) above the village, and the Baroque complex belonging to the ship-owning Lazarović family, who built Holy Trinity Church in 1752, in the highly ornate style of that time, offer (along with several Baroque houses) a rich collection of examples of fine architecture, in this broadly scattered village. **Viganj** (1 km west of Kučišta; 350 inhabitants). The houses gathered around the Bay of Viganj, situated at the foot of a green hill, form what is perhaps one of the most beautiful locations on the entire Adriatic coast. In the middle of the bay the former Dominican **Monastery of the Rosary** was built in 1671. Its cloisters and wings have since been altered. Inside the church, besides the interesting wooden and stone altars, the most valuable item is a 15th century wood relief of the Madonna and Child on a throne. The wreck of a Roman galley not far from Viganj enriched Korčula and the Pelješac peninsula with hundreds of ceramic items from the classical South Italian region. (The eastern side of the Pelješac Peninsula can be found under Dubrovnik, Excursions).

••••••••••••

Sailing vessel, reminder of the seafaring tradition

Vela Luka

Vela Luka**

47 km west of Korčula, 4 380 inhabitants.

In the area around the town which in the 18th and 19th centuries grew up and spread over this deep bay, many archaeological sites from prehistory and the Greek and Roman eras have been found. It is thought that the first Greek colony on the island may have been here, founded at the beginning of the 5th century BC by the Cnidians of Asia Minor. Research work in Vela špilja caves above the town has shown that the bay was inhabited as early as the late Stone Age. Near the medieval Chapel of St. John (Sveti Ivan) on the Gradina peninsula there is a hermitage which may have at one time been a small monastery. The former castle of the Korčula family, the Ismaellis, is the oldest building in the town. The Parish Church of St. Joseph (Sveti Josip) was built in 1846-48.

The Climatic Cure Town and Thermal Baths. Kalos is a new and well equipped institute for medical rehabilitation. The following ailments are treated there: chronic rheumatic illnesses, disc injuries, sciatica, lumbago; bronchitis and bronchial asthma; chronic infections of the respiratory organs; diseases, injuries or post-operative disturbances of the motor system; diseases of the peripheral blood vessels; woman's ailments (sterility and hormonal problems) and diseases and injuries to the peripheral nervous system.

Excursions

Smokvica (19 km from Vela Luka, 28 km from Korčula ; 1 012 inhabitants). In this picturesque village, several Baroque houses and castles belonging to the Korčula nobility, and the village loggia from the 17th and 18th centuries are particularly outstanding. The parish church was restored in this century.

•••••••••••

Blato** (7 km from Vela Luka, 40 km from Korčula; 3 659 inhabitants). The circle of the village with its collection of building complexes, castles and houses is divided in two by an avenue of leafy lime trees. On the main village square is the Parish Church of All Saints (Svi Sveti) with a bell tower and a beautiful Baroque loggia. Inside the church, which was completed in the 17th and 18th centuries, there is a valuable altarpiece *All the Saints*, signed and dated in 1540 by Girolamo da Santacroce, a pupil of Bellini. Beside the chapel, where the bones of St. Vicenza are kept, there are some fine Baroque choir stalls. Above the sacristy there is a small exhibition of items from the history of the church in Blato. ■

Prižba

Lastovo

Seen from the north, Lastovo is the first island in the South Dalmatian group, and is 8 nautical miles from the coast of Korčula. It is sufficiently remote to give a feeling of loneliness, as though it has sunk in the open sea of the Adriatic. The island covers an area of 40.9 km^2 and is 10 km in length, diagonally. The largest settlements are Ubli and Lastovsko Selo.

In written sources the island's name was first mentioned by the lexicographer Stephen of Byzantium who, referring to Theopompus (in the fourth century BC), called the island Ladesta and Ladeston. These names have Illyrian origins. There are traces of life on the island from the early Bronze Age, including several large heaps of stones which served as graves or fortifications, or had a sacred or symbolic nature. At the end of the 3rd century BC Lastovo became part of Rome's area of interest on the Adriatic. The Romans Latinized the island's name and gave it a greater significance by naming it "Augusta insula" (Emperor's island). The Romans built several residential and farming buildings, a villa rustica, on the most fertile parts of the island. The most important place was the port in Ubli, and there was a settlement which experienced a great boom in the first centuries AD, but declined at the beginning of the early Middle Ages. The most important document for medieval Lastovo deals with an event in 1000 when the Venetian Doge Pietro II Orseolo attacked the "impudent people of the island, because of whose lack of civilisation, the Venetians travelling to the sea through these parts were often forced to flee naked and without their possessions". At that time the Venetians set out to conquer the Eastern Adriatic coast to secure a free passage to Byzantium. Until then the way had been blocked by Croatian and Neretvan pirates (see the Neretva Delta). Lastovo was in fact the only island to offer (futile) resistance to the Venetians' designs, probably relying on the strength of their castle, built above the present day village of Lastovo during

Sunset above Lastovo

A little port near Lastovo village

the reign of the Byzantine Emperor Justinian (6th century). In the 11th and 12th centuries, the island was probably part of the Croatian state, maintaining a high degree of autonomy until it voluntarily joined the Dubrovnik Republic in the 13th century. The Statute of the Lastovo Community was drawn up on 30th January 1310 regulating the unwritten common law and ensuring a certain level of autonomy to the island as part of the Dubrovnik Republic. In the course of the centuries the islanders lived in peace and well-being, diving for coral, growing olives and fruit and making wine. However from time to time they did become dissatisfied with the Dubrovnik authorities, culminating in the "Lastovo rebellion" in 1602 when the Lastovo people expelled the Dubrovnik Rector from the island and handed themselves over to the Venetians. However, as soon after that as 1606, the people of Dubrovnik succeeded in regaining the island by tactical diplomacy and held it until they themselves fell to the French. In 1813 the island was occupied by the English, and following the Vienna Congress (1815) it became part of the Austrian Empire, along with the entire area which formed the former Dubrovnik Republic, until the Austrian's collapse in 1918. The Austrian occupiers gave way to the Italians until 1943. In the second Yugoslavia, the island was closed to foreigners, which had a negative effect on its growth.

••••••

View of the Lastovo village

The **Lastovo archipelago** consists of 46 small islands and rocks. On its western side, the islands Priježba, Bratin otok, Vlašnik, Mrčara, Kopište and Sušac stretch over a distance of 13 nautical miles. In the east, over an area of nine nautical miles, is a distinct archipelago of small islands known as Lastovci. They are divided into Donji Školji and Vrhovnjaci. Saplun on Donji Školji is most famous for its beach. The waters around Lastovo are considered to be the richest in the Adriatic. At one time people used to dive for coral in this area.

••••••••••••

Lastovo (Lastovo village)

42°46'N, 16°55 E'; POP. 451

Lastovsko selo lies a little way from the coast, at 96 m above the sea, above a field on a hillside resembling an amphitheatre. It is about 20 minutes' walk to the picturesque harbour. The village received its present form in the 15th and 16th centuries when about 20 Renaissance houses were built. Most of them have high, broad terraces, which have become the "trade mark" of Lastovo houses. Their cylindrical chimneys are also very picturesque. The ornate chimney on the 16th century Biza Antica house is probably the oldest preserved chimney in Dalmatia.

SIGHTS

Novi kaštel (New castle) on the peak of Glavica over the village was built by the French in 1808. It now houses a weather station. There were once prehistoric earthworks here. In the

Middle Ages the Dubrovnik authorities built the old castle which was demolished in 1606 following the Lastovo rebellion.

The **parish church** is dedicated to **SS. Cosmas and Damian**. It was built in 1474; at the end of the 16th and the beginning of the 17th century the church gained side naves and a three part façade; in 1942 it got a bell-tower. The saints are honoured every September 27. The church has a rich treasury. Below the parish church is the Gothic **St. Mary's Church**, built in the Gothic and Renaissance styles in 1512, and considered the most beautiful church on Lastovo.

Dobrić Dobričević (known otherwise by the Romanized surname Boninus de Boninis or Boninus de Ragusia) was one of the pioneers of printing in Europe. He was born in Lastovo in 1454 and printed in Venice, Verona, Brescia and Lyons. He printed the works of the ancient classicists, with commentaries: Tibullus, Catullus, Propertius, Virgil, Plutarch and Aesop (Latin and Italian editions with 67 wood carvings), as well as Dante's *Divine Comedy* with 69 wood carvings. In terms of presentation, his works are amongst the best examples of printing of that epoch. He died in Treviso in 1528.

Facade of the Church of SS. Cosmas and Damian

Excursions

Ubli

10 km from Lastovo, 218 inhabitants, the main ferry port.

Although this, the main settlement on Lastovo, developed in this century, in the 1st century there was a complex of ancient buildings here including wells, workshops and warehouses, forming the main Roman settlement on the island.

Here there are remains of the Early Christian Church of St. Peter, from the 5th and 6th centuries, where a relief showing the cross among lambs has been found. Today's St. Peter's Church was built in the first half of the 20th century.

Lastovo Maraština. The most famous of the Dalmatian Maraština wines is the one from Lastovo. It is a quality wine, straw-yellow to intensive yellow in colour, with a golden shimmer. It has a characteristic aroma, is dry and pleasantly refreshing with a mild bitterness. ■

Ubli, remains of an Early Christian church

Mljet

Mljet is the southernmost of the larger Adriatic islands. Mljet (Sobra) is 23 nautical miles from Dubrovnik (the port of Gruž) and 13 nautical miles from Korčula (to Pomena). It is 37 km in length and has an average width of 3 km. It covers a total area of 100.4 km². The average air temperature in July is 24.8°C and in December 10.8°C. Mljet is the most wooded Adriatic island and one third of its surface is protected as a National Park. In its 13 settlements there are about 1 111 inhabitants.

Mljet, the northwest part of the island

According to a legend the island of Mljet is the beautiful island of Ogygia where the nymph Calypso kept Odysseus captive for seven years. The ancient name for the island also refers to its beauty. It was called Melitta, which derives from the Greek "melitte nesos" which means "honey isle". Archaeological finds show that Mljet has been inhabited since prehistory. On Glavica hill and Mali gradac above Pomijenta there are remains of an Illyrian settlement. The Illyrian pirate base on Mljet was destroyed in 35 BC by the Roman military commander Octavian, who later became Emperor Augustus. During the period of Roman rule, the most important settlement on the island was Polače. The steward of the land had his seat there. In the middle of the 10th century the Slavic settlements Babino Polje, Blato and Vrhmlječe on the island were mentioned. At first (in the 10th century) Mljet was part of the Neretva Borderlands (see Neretva-Delta) and later (11th century) it came under Zahumlje.

As in other parts of the Mediterranean, the settlements on the island were built in the interior of the island, for protection against unwanted visitors, and the main settlement at that time was Vrhmlječe. In the 12th century, the rulers of the island were Benedictines from Pulsano on Monte Gargano. The Zahumljan Count Desa, who ruled the island up until that time, invited them and gave them gifts; the Benedictines built a monastery and church on the island of St. Mary (Sveta Marija) in the Great Lake (Veliko jezero) and right up until the 19th century played a decisive role in the economic and social life of the island. At first the abbot of the monastery even chose the judges. From the 13th century (1215) the island came into the "sphere of interests" of the Dubrovnik Republic and was finally included within the borders of that Republic in 1345. It then also received a charter by which judges and rectors were chosen by the Minor Council of the Republic. It remained in the Republic until 1808. At one time it came under the French

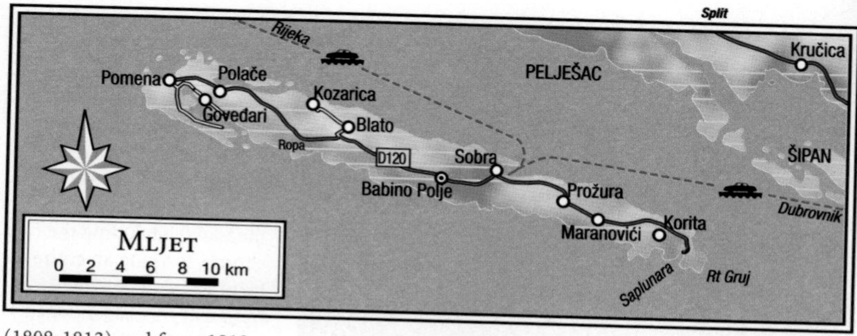

(1808-1813) and from 1813 to 1918 it was under the Austrians. It became part of State of the Slovenes, Croats and Serbs in 1918. In 1941 it was occupied by the Italian Fascists, until 13th September 1944. In the last decades the tourist industry of the island has undergone powerful growth.

Babino Polje

5 KM FROM SOBRA; 336 INH.

Babino Polje is the largest settlement and administrative centre of the island. It is situated in the most fertile part of the island, beneath the highest peak, Velji grad (513 m). The settlement is 5 km from the harbour at Sobra. According to legend the settlement's name (Babino Polje means "Grandmother's field") came from the old lady to whom King Desin (Count Desa) gave the land as a reward for the good advice she gave him in his struggles against his enemies. In the village, remains of some Roman buildings have been discovered, but Babino Polje was not mentioned as the largest settlement on the island until 1222. There are several important buildings of cultural interest in the village: the Romanesque chapels of St. Pancras (Sveti Pankracije) and St. George (Sveti Đurđ), the Gothic parish church and the Renaissance court of the Rector of Mljet.

To the southwest of Babino Polje, on the western coast of the island is the interesting cave called **Jama** (30 minutes' walk) which is considered to be one of the most unusual fishing harbours on the entire Adriatic. It may be entered from both the land and the seaward sides as the roof of the cave has collapsed. From the seaward side the entrance tunnel is 20 m long, about 4 m wide and the roof is about 1.5 m high. It is not possible to reach Jama by car.

The road from Babino Polje to the western coast leads to **Sutmiholjska** Bay (5 km). The harbour serving Babino Polje however is on the eastern side of the island. It is called Sobra (68 inhabitants), and was for a long time the island's main port, but was not inhabited consistently until the second half of the 19th century. The main road on the island from Pomena to Saplunara (44 km) also leads through Sobra. Four kilometres east is the village of **Prožura** (78 inhabitants). In the Gothic Church of the Holy Trinity (Sveto Trojstvo) which was built by the Benedictines from Lokrum, there is a bronze Romanesque crucifix, considered to be the most important work of art on the island of Mljet. Beyond Prožura are the villages of Maranovići and Korita, and the last settlement in the southern part of the island is **Saplunara****. Here is the most beautiful sandy bay on the island, which, due to the vegetation around it, and together with the bays of Blaca and Pinjevci, has been declared a nature reserve; it has many rare species. Sand was exported from Saplunara (sabulum is Latin for sand) for centuries for the construction of many of the buildings in Dubrovnik.

View of the islet of St. Mary

The National Park***

The Big Lake, St. Mary's Islet in the background

The National Park includes the western part of the island, Veliko jezero, Malo jezero, Soline Bay and a sea belt 500 m wide from the most prominent cape of Mljet covering an area of 54 km². The central parts of the park are Veliko jezero with the Isle of St. Mary, Malo jezero and the villages of Goveđari (179 inhabitants), Polače (123 inhabitants) and Pomena (50 inhabitants).

Veliko jezero (Great Lake) is actually a bay joined to the sea at Soline, originating from a flood karst polje; it covers an area of 1.45 km², is 2.5 km long and 1 km wide. At its deepest it reaches 45 m. The channel at Soline is 30 m long and 10 m wide. Until 1960 the channel was 0.6 m deep, but it was then deepened to 2.5 m. In the southern part of the lake is the island Sveta Marija. Remains of Roman buildings have been found on this small island (120 m x 200 m) but it is best known for the **Benedictine monastery** built when the order arrived on the island in the 12th century. The arrival of Benedictines from Apulia created dissatisfaction amongst the local Benedictines (the Benedictine monastery on Lokrum was founded in 1023) so that the right of the Italian monks to the island had to be confirmed by an indirect descendent of Desas, Stephen the First-Crowned (Stefan Prvovjenčani) (c.1165-1227), King Milutin (c.1320) and Pope John II (1324). The Benedictines first built a monastery and then, at the end of the 13th century, a church. The monastery was rebuilt several times and the present building has two storeys and dates from the Renaissance era. It is surrounded on two sides by a courtyard, with an arcaded passage leading to it. On the southeastern corner it has a defensive tower, all the buildings on the island, including the church, forming an entire fortified complex. The monastery was abandoned in 1869 and in 1961 it was converted into a hotel. Many prominent scientists and artists lived in the monastery as monks. The most famous inhabitants were the Dubrovnik poets Mavro Vetranović (1482-1576) and Ignjat Đurđević (1675-1737), and one of the best known scholars of Byzantium of his time, the historian, Anselm Banduri (1671-1743). St. Mary's Church (Sveta Marija) adjoining the monastery is a single-naved Romanesque building built after the model of a church owned by Benedictines on Monte Gargano. In related literature it is mentioned that this building is a stylistic blend of Southern Italic Romanesque buildings from Raška (that is the medieval Serbian state, a donator of the church being the Serbian leader Stephen the First-Crowned, Stefan Prvovjenčani).

Benedictine monastery

The church was rebuilt and extended in the 16th century, and at that time the coat of arms of the Gundulić family was added in the entrance porch.

••••••••••••

On the northwestern side of Veliko jezero there is a channel (30 m long, 2.5 m wide and 0.5 m deep) leading to **Malo jezero** (Small Lake). This lake

Goveđari

covers an area of 0.25 km² and its greatest depth reaches 29 m. The water in this lake does not flow freely, and it therefore has many of the characteristics of a lagoon with few fish, which require more favourable conditions. The temperature of the water in summer is about 3-4° higher in Malo jezero than in the sea; the winter temperature is 8 degrees lower, falling to 4.5°C. As Malo jezero is less salty than the sea, it is thought that there must be some direct underground link between the lake and the open sea.

••••••••••••

Mljet's lakes are rich in various kinds of shellfish (mussels, oysters) and the plankton here is particularly interesting in scientific terms. The vegetation of the entire island, but especially in the National Park, is extremely lush. The forest of Aleppo pine trees around the lakes is considered to be the most beautiful and best preserved forest of its type on the Mediterranean. Land fauna was impoverished when the island became the habitat of the mongoose (Mungos mungo); since then there have been no poisonous snakes, its favoured diet, on the island, but there is also much less wildlife. What is most interesting concerning the large variety of fauna on the coastal belt is that the rare mammal the monk seal (Monachus monachus) appears on the coast of Mljet. It is a protected species of Adriatic seal.

••••••••••••

Goveđari (165 inhabitants) is located about 400 m beyond Babine kuće and the jetty on the shores of Veliko jezero. The first people moved here in 1793 from Babino Polje. They were sent here by the Benedictines from St. Mary's monastery and were given the task of looking after the monastery's cattle. The village was named after the occupation of these first inhabitants (govedar is a breeder of cattle).

••••••••••••

Polače (115 inhabitants; 3 km from Veliko jezero) is Mljet's largest and most beautiful harbour. In the village itself there are the ruins of a Roman palace which was the residence of the Roman governor. The palace was built in the 3rd or 4th century in the style of a summer residence (villa rustica) after the pattern of Roman villages in the Empire. According to tradition the palace was built by Agesilaos of Anazarbos in Cilicia. Agesilaos hid here with his son, the poet Oppian, after the Roman Emperor Septimus Severus had exiled him to Mljet. The legend goes on to say that the poet wrote inspired verses on the beauty of the sea and fishing, causing the Emperor to release them from exile.

Polače was settled from the 1st to the 11th centuries but the settlement died once the Benedictines came to the island of St. Mary, as they allowed settlements only where it was in their interests. Polače remained deserted for six centuries, after which it began to develop once again in the 18th century. There are the remains of an old Christian basilica from the Roman era, which was very similar to the basilica in Solin.

Monastery cloister

••••••••••••

Pomena (400 m from Malo jezero; 37 inhabitants) is a fishing village in the westernmost part of the island. It has become a very popular tourist resort since the hotel "Odisej" was built. ■

Dubrovnik

Dubrovnik is situated 42°39' N, 18°16' E; population 43 770. It is the county town of the Dubrovnik and Neretva County, which stretches over 1 784 km² and has a total of 122 870 inhabitants. Mean temperatures in January: air 8.4°C, sea 12.4°C; mean temperatures in July: air 23.3°C, sea 22.9°C.

Dubrovnik, view of the city

Early History. As the area around Dubrovnik abounds in prehistoric burial mounds and earth works (Cavtat and Konavle) it is probable that there was a prehistoric settlement on the site of present-day Dubrovnik. This settlement may have been on a rock, actually the island of Lave (Lausa, Rausa) which was separated from the mainland by marshy land, a sea-arm whose position corresponded with present day Stradun (see below).

The Roman Era. There are no significant remains from the Roman era in the city itself, but it is thought that there was a fishing settlement on Lave rock. There was an active and lively settlement not far away in Epidaurum (Cavtat, 12 km) originally a Greek town (Epidauros) which came under the Romans in the third century BC and experienced a boom as a Roman trading colony; in the 6th century (530) it became a bishopric, and following the division of the Empire it became part of the Eastern Roman Empire (Byzantium).

The Migrations of the Nations. When the Avars and Slavs invaded the Balkans at the beginning of the 7th century, Epidaurum was destroyed, along with Salona (Solin) and Narona. The inhabitants fled to take up residence on Lave rock and founded Rauzij - Ragusa. Until recently that was the only version of the story of the foundation of Dubrovnik. However the recent discovery of a large 6th century Byzantine church beneath the foundations of the old Romanesque cathedral (see Cathedral) shows that there must have been a large town on that site even earlier. Apart from the settlement on the rock over the sea (Rauzij), only a few hundred metres to the north, beneath Srđ rock, the Slavic settlement of Dubrovnik was born and began to grow (in Croatian: “dub” is oak, “dubrava”, wood). The Roman church, through its Bishoprics which preserved the Epidaurian tradition, began to Christianize the Slavs, which also suited Byzantium. However, at the same time another complementary process also developed: the remaining original inhabitants in the city, both Roman and Romanised emigrants, over the centuries gradually became assimilated and Slavicised.

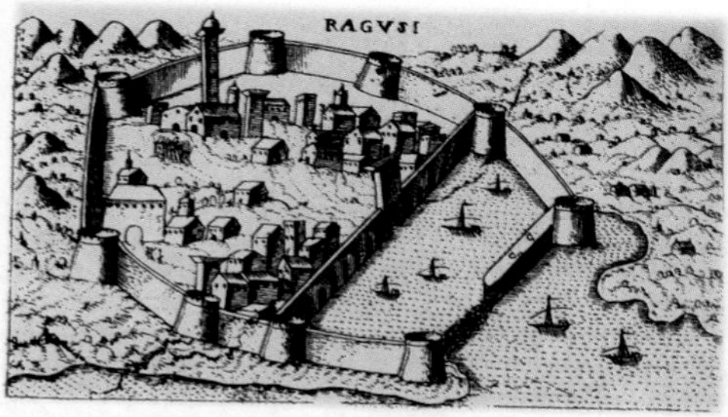

Dubrovnik, engraving from the 15th century

Under Various Rulers. The process of Slavicisation continued under the suzerainty of Byzantium. It was accompanied by the territorial expansion of the city: in the 9th century the city came to include the area from Cavtat to Zaton, via Župa, Sumet, and Rijeka dubrovačka, the islands Lokrum, Mrkan, Bobara and Supetar in the south, and the Elafit islands (see below) to the northwest. The desire to expand Dubrovnik was realised as Slavic leaders in the hinterland were forced to pay dues. But Dubrovnik was also the target of attack by many enemies. From 866-67 it was occupied by Arabs. There is evidence that as early as 869 the people of Dubrovnik transported Croatians in their ships to Bari, where the Saracens were in hiding, showing that the Dubrovnik navy was already a significant force. In the 10th century the army of the Macedonian Emperor Samuilo threatened the city; in around 1000 it was briefly under the Venetian Doge, Pietro Orseolo II. Dubrovnik's expansion was a threat to Venice so from time to time (1122 and 1171) they attacked the city and for a full 150 years (1205-1358) it was under their rule. In the 11th century Dubrovnik once again came under Byzantine authority. The year 1032 saw the participation of Dubrovnik ships in the victory of the Byzantium fleet over the Saracens. For five years (1081-1085) Dubrovnik was ruled by the Normans. By the end of the 12th century, the authority of Byzantium over the city had already become formal. Due to its territorial isolation from the Slavic states which were already in existence to the north, or were emerging in the hinterland, and also because of its real development as a city, there was in Dubrovnik, above all, a tendency towards autonomy and independence even following its total Slavicisation.

The **Dubrovnik Republic.** In the 12th century, in a period when the development of city-states in Europe contributed to a general economic boom, Dubrovnik operated as a mediator between the Balkan hinterlands and Mediterranean merchants. The conflicts between Venice and the Croatian-Hungarian Kingdom could only contribute to Dubrovnik's prosperity. In 1185 Dubrovnik signed a free trade agreement with the Bosnian Ban, Kulin, and a year later (1186) with the Serbian ruler Stefan Nemanja who was seriously threatening Dubrovnik's independence. In order to ensure safety on the sea, Dubrovnik made a whole series of agreements with cities on the eastern coast (Kotor, Rovinj) and on the Italian coast (Molfetta, Ravenna, Ancona, Bari etc). An agreement in 1169 with Pisa, Venice's old enemy, benefited Dubrovnik's trade in Constantinople. The Dubrovnik community soon became very wealthy, which also formed the basis for its independence and cultural growth. How the city government developed is not entirely known due to a lack of documents, but there is

Dubrovnik before the earthquake

Dubrovnik during the earthquake in 1667

evidence to show that the City Statute of 1272 laid the foundations for political, legal, and urban life, including sanitation and so on, in the Republic. From the 12th century, the nobility became noticeably stronger as the ruling class, with a Rector at their head. This increasing independence, legality and order (the peasants were much better off in the Republic than in the feudal states of the hinterland) was the cause of increasing immigration, which also contributed to the city's final Slavicisation. Trade in Dubrovnik continued to flourish despite the fact that the city was under the control of the Venetian Empire. Its caravans travelled as far as Persia and they showed no sign of weakening their efforts in the Mediterranean. As well as trade, they also moved into the area of credit transactions with rulers in the hinterland, opening up new markets, offering privileges and above all peace on the borders. At the beginning of the 14th century the social order also began to settle in accordance with the growth of the economic and political power of the landowners: this was in fact an independent aristocratic republic, with Large and Small Councils (an assembly and government) and a Rector who had strictly defined authority. This social order came to determine the form of government in Dubrovnik's possessions beyond the city itself. In their settlement of land-owning problems amongst themselves and in the position of peasants in the transition from serfdom to colonisation, the ruling classes clearly demonstrated imperialist and expansionist tendencies both in trade and politics.

In the middle of the 13th century Dubrovnik gained the islands of Lastovo and (with some interruptions) Mljet. At the beginning of the 14th century Cavtat and its environs returned. In 1333 it claimed Orašac, Ston and Stonski Rat, and by skilful negotiation it gained the Pelješac peninsula, to be a lasting possession. With Pelješac and Mljet it was able to control all vital shipping routes in that part of the Adriatic. The development of the social structure continued. Alongside the nobility and the peasants, a middle class of city dwellers emerged which with time played an increasing role in trade, the navy and crafts. The magnificent fortress of Ston was built. In the second half of the 14th century the city took on its present shape, with the building of the walls and many other buildings, churches and palaces. In the 15th and 16th centuries the power of the rulers increased still further, along with the cultural life of the city. It was already on a European level and the growth of literature, painting and science was possible. As early as 1301 Dubrovnik already had an organised medical service for its citizens, and in 1317 the first public dispensing chemists opened. In 1347 there was already a home in the city for the old and infirm, and from 1432 a home for uncared-

Dubrovnik trader and postman

for and abandoned children. In 1436 Dubrovnik received water mains and sewers, which are partly still in operation today. The Treaty of Zadar from 1358 was used by Dubrovnik to get rid of the defeated Venetians, and, whilst admitting the sovereignty of King Ludovic I, they actually finally confirmed their real independence. From then until 1808 the Rector was always a citizen of Dubrovnik. Also from that time, Dubrovnik had its own independent foreign policy, and signed international treaties as an equal party, as well as creating its own independent legal system. Its statehood was maintained by a system of gifts and tributes, firm contracts and mutual aid, protecting its peace and security. Although it went to war several times in the 14th and 15th centuries over Konavle and a few of its other territories, it retained its hold on its property and homogenised its citizens into an ethnic, religious and cultural unit (a long-term process from the very outset). In the same way, in the 15th century, landowners regulated their relations with the new rulers of the Balkans, the Turks (an official charter of 1442). Apart from all this, it was necessary to offer skilful diplomatic resistance to the constant pressure from the sea exerted by Venice. The Republic gained the protection of the Christian powers on the one hand, and to a large extent of the Turks on the other, serving the west as a window giving insight into the intentions of the Ottoman Empire, and vice versa, informing, when necessary, the Turkish Empire as to the intentions of the west. In the 14th century, Dubrovnik already had a very complex diplomatic and consular service. Of course, all this did not pass without intense struggles at times, but in the 15th century the territory of the Republic was settled in its position "between the Turks and the Venetians" and had a leading role on the Eastern Adriatic coast. The city reached the peak of its prosperity in the 15th and 16th centuries, at the time when the Bosnian and Serbian states collapsed. Croatia shrank to the "reliquae reliquiarum" and the Turks were the undisputed rulers of the Balkans. This gave a further boost to Dubrovnik in its trade and to a certain extent in its territorial expansion. It also marked the climax of Dubrovnik's sea trade on the Mediterranean, and high quality ship-building and a strong navy with about 200 ships and more than 5000 sailors were the result of Dubrovnik's active neutrality in the midst of the great powers of the time. In the 16th century, the Dubrovnik navy was the third largest in the world in terms of capacity, and ships from the Sveti Vlaho shipyard travelled as far as the Indian Ocean and the Atlantic. In this period Dubrovnik enjoyed the fruits of its long history. It had the monopoly of the salt trade, and in mine ownership, finance and trade with Bosnia and Serbia (precious metals, lead, wool etc), where several Dubrovnik colonies were set up. One of these was Janjevo in Kosovo where there are still some Croats living today. So, large saltworks were built on Dubrovnik's territory, as well as metal works, textile and clothing workshops, where local workers were joined by masters from Italy, Germany, and even France. This production was financed by local capital. Goldsmiths, glass workers and other craftsmen also developed. Dubrovnik's money began to be accepted everywhere, and in Bosnia, for example, it was almost the only way of payment. At the end of the 16th century there was a crisis in marine trade on the Mediterranean, for the

St. Blaise, the city's patron saint

Model of the city in the hand of St. Blaise

The Amerling Fountain, damaged in the war, now restored

main interest of Europe was redirected to the oceans and the newly discovered countries. The crisis was keenly felt in Dubrovnik too, which began to withdraw its capital from its navy and invest it in financial business. Once enterprising businessmen became almost like rentiers and seafarers travelled only short distances. In the 17th century, the navy fell to one third of its former capacity. A serious earthquake in 1667 hit Dubrovnik in the middle of this recession, with serious consequences, and it took the city half a century to recover. This increased the pressure from the Turks and there was increasingly fierce competition with the Venetians, also weakened, over trade in the Adriatic and in the Balkans. Despite the wars between Venice and the Turks (1645 and 1689) causing the threat from Venice to lessen slightly, the conflict with it remained a constant that determined the maritime policies of the Republic. For this reason the people of Dubrovnik entered a defence agreement in 1684 with Austria renewing the old "sovereignty" of the Croatian-Hungarian crown. In the course of a war against the Turks, in 1694 the Venetians surrounded the entire Dubrovnik territory from Boka to the Neretva, cutting off trade with the hinterland. They withdrew only after the Treaty of Karlovac in 1699, but in 1716 they repeated the same strategy, only to retreat after the Treaty of Požarevac in 1718. In order to disassociate itself totally from the Venetians, the Republic allowed the Turks a small exit to the sea at Neum-Klek and thus became completely surrounded by Turkish territory, trying to maintain their economic foothold in the hinterland. This hold became progressively weaker however in the face of strong competition from the Austrians and the French. In the second half of the 18th century, there was a favourable situation in maritime trade once again, and the initiative was taken by the bourgeoisie, whilst the leadership of the Republic showed itself to be aristocratic and conservative in nature in relation to the demands of the new era. However, the navy was strengthened, until in 1792 it consisted of nearly 300 ships. A little later, Dubrovnik embarked on transoceanic voyages. Venice was no longer able to compete because of the strong position of the Austrians, and because it had itself suffered a final economic collapse. The activities of the Dubrovnik fleet on the Mediterranean soon began to be a nuisance to the French, who were involved in their own conflicts of continental dimensions. In the Republic itself the landowners could not keep pace with the enterprising city people: they either held fast to their land, or became financially dependent on the middle classes, but in political terms they were unwilling to change anything. Pressure from the peasants increased, and in 1799 there was a peasants' rebellion in Konavle, which was put down by Austrian troops from Kotor.

The French Occupation. Napoleon's blockade of Europe and the entry of the French into Dubrovnik in 1806 brought about the collapse of Dubrovnik's navy, and the collapse of the old aristocratic Republic which could not, and would not, accept the new age, although its economic and social life were in the hands of a new class. Money rashly invested in the maritime boom was never regained. In 1808 the French formally dissolved the State of Dubrovnik as a reaction to an attempt to renew the Republic through diplomatic channels.

Under the Austrians. Following Napoleon's fall and the abolition of the French Illyrian provinces, in 1814 Dubrovnik came under the regime of the Austrian occupation, and after the Viennese Congress of 1815, it became part of Austrian Dalmatia which, in 1848, was clearly seen to be among the scattered Croatian lands.

The twentieth century. With the collapse of Austria-Hungary, Dubrovnik became part of the State of the Slovenes, Croats and Serbs. During World War II, the city and its surroundings were part of the Independent State of Croatia, but was in reality occupied by the Italians, and, after the fall of Italy, by the Germans. Units of Tito's National Liberation Army entered Dubrovnik on October 18, 1944, and the city was now part of the Socialist Republic of Croatia within Yugoslavia. After the collapse of Yugoslavia and the Croatian declaration of independence, Dubrovnik went through what were perhaps the most difficult days in its existence. Greater Serbian aggression cut it off from its hinterland and put its very existence in jeopardy. The attempt to destroy Dubrovnik, that symbol of a city, showed once more what an essential role it has in the creation of Croatian cultural identity and political sovereignty. ■

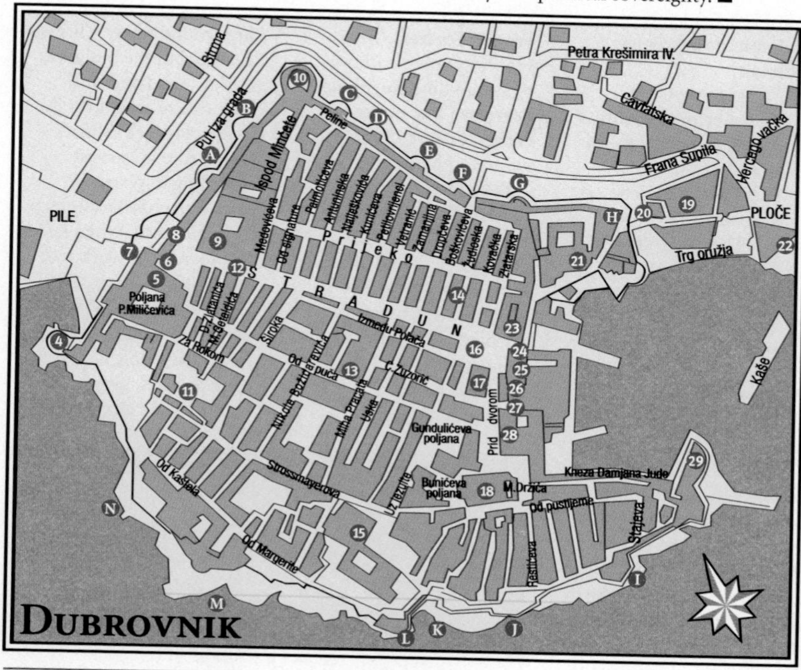

Sights

The **City Walls*****. The fact that old Dubrovnik has been preserved as a living and organic entity is largely thanks to the sturdiness of its city walls, a system of fortifications which is a direct expression of the city's history. They were built as a necessary part of the medieval European way of organising political life, navy, trade and warfare. The Dubrovnik fortresses, towers and walls simultaneously protect, and reveal the uniqueness of, the city. They are amongst the most solid and beautiful such constructions in Europe. In places they reach 25 m in height, are up to 6 m thick and 3 m on the seaward side. They include 3 round and 12 four-sided fortresses, 5 defensive towers, 2 corner towers and one great fortress. On the land side, along the main wall, runs another wall with one large and 9 smaller semicircular keeps, and one casemate fortress. To the east, the city

Minčeta Fortress

is protected by the strong fortress, Revelin; to the west a similar strategic point is defended by the magnificent Lovrijenac fortress.

We list below individual fortresses and city gates in the walls:

The **Pile Gate** (Vrata od Pila; NUMBER 7 ON THE PLAN). This is the city's western gate and traditionally one's first sight of the city in the part called Pile. It was built on the site of the former Pile Fortress which existed as early as 972 but was demolished in 1818, its foundations still being visible between the outside and inside of the gate. The outer gate, in the form of a Renaissance arch was built in 1537 in the wall of the fortress of the same name. Above it, there is a statue of St. Blaise (Sveti Vlaho), the patron saint and protector of the city. The gate is reached by a stone bridge with three arches, and stone benches along the parapet. The bridge was built in 1471 by Paskoje Miličević, a civil engineer whose name is linked with many buildings in Dubrovnik. The interior of Pile Gate was within the main city wall built in 1460 in the form of a Gothic arch, taking the place of an older gate about which some records exist from the 13th century. The statue of St. Blaise over the interior of the gate was made by one of the greatest Croatian sculptors of the 20th century, Ivan Meštrović (1883-1963). Immediately on entering the city through the inner Pile Gate, on the left by St. Saviour Church (Sveti Spas), there is a way onto the city walls. To the north, the fortresses are in the following succession: **St. Francis Fortress** (Sveti Frane; LETTER A ON THE PLAN) and the **Gornji ugao Fortress** ("the upper corner"; LETTER B ON THE PLAN), both dating from the 14th century.

Then there is **Minčeta Fortress** (NUMBER 10 ON THE PLAN), the northernmost point of the fortifications, which has become a symbol of Dubrovnik. It was named after the noble Menčetić family. It is a large round tower, founded on broad and solid walls. It has protruding battlements supported by profiled stone consoles. The aesthetic and not defensive function of these battlements is obvious, which indicates that the tower itself was at the time an almost indestructible fortress. The tower was built in two phases. Originally it was rectangular, built in 1319 probably by Ničifor Ranjina. Following the fall of Constantinople (1453) it was decided to build a large round tower. This was in 1455, but the building work was delayed until 1461 due to an epidemic of the plague. The work then began in earnest according to plans by Michelozzo di Bartolomeo from Florence. When he left Dubrovnik the work was taken over by Juraj Dalmatinac (see Šibenik), who transformed and raised the whole concept to a higher level, giving it a truly monumental

Ploče Gate

form. As the highest point over the city, the upper terrace of the Minčeta Tower offers one of the most attractive views over the city itself and its position between the steep cliffs of the mainland and the open sea. From Minčeta to the east the towers are as follows (all built in the 14th century): **St. Barbara** (C) **St. Lucy** (D), **St. Katherine** (E), **Drezvenik** (F), **St. James** (G); (a semicircular fortress first mentioned in 1363; restored and rounded off in 1565-1570) and **Asimon** (or **Ploče**) **Fortress**; (letter H).

•••••••••••

Below the last mentioned is the **Ploče Gate** (Vrata od Ploča; NUMBER ⑳ ON THE PLAN). The eastern city gate was built on the same principle as the western Pile Gate, that is with outer and inner gates, a stone bridge over the moat and a wooden draw-bridge. The outer gate was built in 1450 by Simon della Cava, and the single-arched bridge was built in 1449 following the example of the old bridge in front of the Pile Gate. The inner gate and the statue of St. Blaise over it are in the Romanesque style. Another much wider gate was built beside this one during the Austrian occupation in the 19th century. The city harbour was protected by the following fortresses: **St. Luke's** (one of the oldest preserved fortresses, built in the 13th century, and an important defensive point in the harbour, until **Revelin Fortress** was built; up to 1884 it had battlements with consoles like Minčeta Fortress), **St. Dominic's** (built in 1387 to the south of the Dominican church), **Ribarnica** ("fish hall", probably built in the 13th century and demolished in 1853), **Kaznena tvrđava** ("punishment fortress"; built as part of the Rector's Palace, served as a dungeon, probably also from the 13th century), **Kneževa tvrđava** (the Rector's Fortress, part of the Rector's Palace, mentioned in 1366).

•••••••••••

St. John's (Sveti Ivan, NUMBER ㉙ ON THE PLAN). With Minčeta to the north and Bokar to the west, this is the third main fortress in the wall complex. Whilst the somewhat smaller St. Luke's fortress protected the city harbour from the north, St. John's was its main defence from the sea, and was one of the most important fortifying positions in Dubrovnik. Between St. Luke's and St. John's there was a chain, which at one time barred the entrance to ships, right up until the building of the **Kaše** harbour wall. This was started by Paskoje Miličević in 1484. The most important part of the defensive system was, without doubt, St. John's fortress. It was built in three phases. First of all in 1346, it was decided to build a "Mule" fortress (Tvrđava od mula). The so-called Gundulićeva Fortress was next to it and in 1552 the two were joined together following plans by Paskoje Miličević, and by 1557 they formed one unit as we know it today, a monumental semi-circular building which was one of the main protectors of the city. In the enormous inner rooms, there are now halls housing a significant part of the cultural treasures of Dubrovnik's past. There is the Maritime Museum, the Ethnographic Museum and Aquarium, and the galleries and terraces serve as an open-air theatre for the Dubrovnik Summer Festival.

•••••••••••

From St. John's fortress to the west, the fortresses are as follows: **St. Saviour's Bastion** (I; Bastion Svetog Spasitelja; a five-sided fortress; built between 1647 and 1657 by Marin Držić, a namesake of the great comedy writer, and also

Governor of the Arms of the Republic), **St. Stephen's Bastion** (J; Bastion Svetog Stjepana; the newest fortress built 1658-1660 according to plans by Marin Držić and Marcantonio Bettacci of Florence), **Margarita Bastion** (K; there was a strong fortress here as early as 1378; the present one was completed in 1753), **Zvijezda Fortress** (L; "Star"; mentioned in the

Lovrijenac

16th century; it was not rebuilt after the earthquake), and **Mrtvo Zvono Fortress** (M; "Dead Bell"; begun in 1509 according to plans by Paskoje Miličević), **St. Mary's Fortress** (N; Sveta Marija; mentioned in 1426), **Kalarinja Fortress** (O; one of the oldest, mentioned in 1332; there is a document in existence from 1430 concerning its completion). It is interesting to note that along the wall between the last two mentioned fortresses is the so-called "mlinski toranj" (windmill). In front of Kalarinja is **Bokar Fortress** (number ❹ on the plan). It stands at the western end of the city, right on the seafront. It was completed following plans by Michelozzo in 1570, although building work actually began in 1461. It had the function of protecting the city moat and bridge leading to the Pile Gate, as well as controlling the approaches from the sea in the case of siege or the landing of enemy forces in Pile harbour. It also served as a store for ammunition and smaller canon. Due to its location directly over the sea it was also suitable for artillery exercises; from 1463 it was used to test the range of cannon. Architecturally it is balanced and circular in shape, with three cornices, very interesting inner rooms and terraces, now used as attractive stages for performances in the Dubrovnik Summer Festival.

•••••••••••••

Revelin*** (number ⓳ on the plan) was built during a period of acute danger from Venice (1583-1594) to reinforce the harbour's defences and to protect the city from the east. The fortress was built according to a model by the Spanish architect Antonio Ferramolino. It is linked to the Ploče Gate by a bridge leading to the gate itself, and to the suburb of Ploče by a double-arched stone bridge, built at the end of the 16th century, based on plans by Paskoje Miličević. Inside the fortress, there are impressive inner rooms, which at exceptional moments in history served as a council chamber and the state treasury. Now they serve as a concert hall. In front of Revelin towards the sea, there is a terrace with a broad view of the harbour. Here there is a memorial to those who died in the People's War of Liberation, the work of the sculptor Frano Kršinić. Since this is the largest terrace in the city it is one of the most popular stages used in the Summer Festival.

••••••••••••

Lovrijenac*** (number ❸ on the plan) is a fortress built dramatically 40 m above the sea, defending the southwest of the city; right up to the Napoleonic era and the appearance of modern artillery it was the key strategic point over the city. It is world-famous today as a perfect setting for performances of Shakespeare's "Hamlet". Due to its vital military significance, the Republic always paid special attention to this fortress: no one was trusted completely, even during their own occupation of Lovrijenac. The commander was chosen from the ranks of the nobility and was replaced, with his forces, every month. There was only as much food kept in the fortress as was needed for that period. The walls around Lovrijenac were weakest on the side facing the city (60 cm) and they could easily be destroyed with cannon. According to some sources there has been a fortress on the same site since about 1018, although regular documentation on the fortress began as late as the 14th century. There has probably always been some kind of fortress on those cliffs. This one has been re-built and repaired many times in its long history although its most solid walls were always turned to the west. They are as much as 12 m thick! They are built in the shape of a triangle with three terraces. There is an inner courtyard with arcades, in the centre of which there is an enormous cistern. There is another, smaller one, for everyday use. At one time the entrance to the fortress was to the west, and was reached by two stone bridges. In the 15th century the gate was moved to its present position, and the local master, Vicko Lujov of Korčula placed a large Renaissance niche over it, with a statue of St. Blaise. It was then decided to destroy all ways into the fortress except this one. The walls have been strengthened and raised in the course of history, battlements have been added with openings for cannon. When the walls of Dubrovnik were completely restored, Lovrijenac was not overlooked. The project suggested by Gianbattista Zanchi of Pesaro in 1571 was a starting point, but it was critically received by the people of the city and altered to fit actual needs. Lovrijenac was also extensively restored after the great earthquake. During the Italian occupation it served as a prison for patriots and partisans. After the Second World War it was returned to its original condition, in accord with the inscription over the entrance gate: NON BENE PRO TOTO LIBERTAS VENDITUR AURO (freely translated: Freedom cannot be sold, not even for all the treasure in the world).

••••••••••••

The **Great Onofrio Well***** (Velika Onofrijeva česma; NUMBER ❻ ON THE PLAN) is at the end of the 12 km of city water mains which have brought water from Rijeka dubrovačka to the city since 1438. It was named after its builder, the Italian hydro-technician and architect Onofrio della Cava, born near Naples, who during his stay in Dubrovnik (1436-1443) built several buildings in Dubrovnik, Cavtat and Ston. This fountain is six-sided with a pillar on each corner and an opening for the water between. It is a monumental, but simple construction, and was completed in 1444 and covered with a dome by Pietro di Martino of Milan with the help of local stonemasons. Its sculpture work was damaged in the great earthquake of 1667 and seriously damaged during Serbian artillery fire in 1992.

••••••••••••

The Great Onofrio Well and St. Saviour's Church

Stradun, on the left the Franciscan church and monastery

St. Saviour** (Sveti Spas; NUMBER ❽ ON THE PLAN) is a church built in the style of the Lombardy Renaissance (there are many Gothic elements in the details of the facade) between 1520 and 1528. It was designed by Petar Andrijić, the son of the famous builder Marko Andrijić from Korčula. It is thought that it was heavily influenced by Šibenik Cathedral or the Venetian Church of San Michele and San Zaccaria. It is certain that this facade later influenced some Dalmatian churches and Hvar Cathedral. It was not damaged in the great earthquake and so has been preserved without alteration to the present day.

••••••••••••

St. Clare's Convent** (Sveta Klarisa; NUMBER ❺ ON THE PLAN) - now the Trade Unions' Hall was built from the end of the 13th century (1290), completed at the beginning of the 14th and reconstructed after the great earthquake. Here the daughters of the nobility were educated, and many of them became nuns against their will because of the lack of a dowry or their inability to find a husband. From 1434 there was a children's home in the convent, for deserted and illegitimate children. It was one of the first such institutions in the world. The water mains, the sewers, the field hospital and this home together show the degree of cultural achievement of the people of old Dubrovnik. During the French occupation the convent was dissolved and turned into a gunpowder and arms store. Now the former convent is a cultural information centre, including an exhibition hall and a large restaurant in the cloisters. The monastery was severely damaged in the war of 1991-1992, and the well was restored by experts from the Republic of Poland.

••••••••••••

Stradun*** (NUMBER ⓬ ON THE PLAN). On the site of present day Stradun, there was in the past marshy land which divided Ragusa from Dubrava. The inhabitants drained the marsh and founded a town there. Today, stretching east to west between two city gates, and bounded by two fountains and two bell towers (on the Pile side the bell tower of St. Francis and the Great Onofrio Well, and on the Ploče side by the City bell tower and the Small Well), Stradun is a favourite promenade for both local people and foreign guests. Paved with stones now worn to a shine like parquet flooring, Stradun is Dubrovnik's "street salon". It received its present appearance following the great earthquake in 1667 and older pictures of the city show that the palaces before the earthquake did not have their present typical appearance, but that many had arcades like Sponza and were highly decorated. Stradun Palace has much to tell about the way of life and the spirit of the people of old Dubrovnik. On the ground floor there have always been trade or business facilities. The large store room was entered from the side streets. On the first floor there is an impressive apartment, and there are some rooms on the second floor. The kitchen and the other household rooms are in the attic. In front of Sponza Palace, Stradun broadens out into **Luža Square** which is the community and commercial centre of Dubrovnik, and together with Stradun includes all the most important buildings inside the walls. Stradun's polished pavement was seriously damaged in Serbian bombardments; today, many world associations are engaged on its restoration.

••••••••••••

The **Franciscan Monastery***** (NUMBER ❾ ON THE PLAN) was built in

Romanesque and Gothic styles. It was started in 1317 after the Franciscan monastery outside the city walls had been demolished. It was built throughout the 14th century, and the bell tower, which once had a Gothic roof, was completed in 1424. The cloisters are the oldest and most interesting part of the monastery. They were built by the stonemason Mihoje Brajkov of Bar between 1327 and 1348. The cloisters have a groin vault and consist of open, narrow hexaforia with double pillars, the capitals being covered with pictures of plants, animals and human motifs. In the centre there is a 15th century well.
After Mihoje Brajkov's death in 1348, work on the monastery was taken over by Miljen Radomislić in

Monastery apothecary's, founded 1317

1367 and in 1376 by Leonardo di Stephano of Florence. Further documents show that in 1426 Božidar Bogdanović and Radin Bogetić repaired the cloisters, and the stone balustrade on the terrace is the work of Ratko Brajković from 1433. Within the monastery we find **St. Francis' Church** (Sveti Frane), a simple single-naved church. Its present decoration, altars and altarpieces mostly date from the Baroque era up to the 19th century. The southern, late-Gothic portal leading into the church is the work of the Petrović brothers, Leonardo and Petar and it was completed in 1449. In the Gothic lunette sits the figure of the Madonna holding the dead Christ. Above her is God the Father, to the left St. Jerome and to the right John the Baptist. This portal is one of the finest examples of sculpture in Dubrovnik. In the church's **sacristy** a Gothic chapel given by the Bunić family in 1472 has also been preserved. In the church itself there is also the grave of the most important poet of old Croatian literature, Ivan (Gjivo) Gundulić (1588-1638). The pulpit dates from the 15th century. To

Sponza Palace

the east of the cloisters, in a hall where there were once seven small chapels, there is now the **monastery museum**. The Monastery of the Friars Minor (Mala Braća) has items which are priceless in terms of cultural value. Amongst other things there is an outstanding collection from an apothecary's dating from the 15th to the 17th century, although the apothecary's itself was founded as early as 1317. The monastery library is a real treasure-house full of writings of world importance. It includes 30 000 volumes, 22 incunabula, about 1 500 manuscripts, about 15 illuminated choir books and many old musical manuscripts. The paintings and church items in the monastery museum are exceptionally important in the cultural history of Dubrovnik and Croatia as a whole. The library, roof, cloisters and bell-tower were seriously damaged in attacks on Dubrovnik in 1991-1992.

••••••••••••

Sponza Palace***
(NUMBER ㉓ ON THE PLAN) is also known as Divona, or Fondik and was built on the site where there was once a customs hall. Three Italian words: **spongia** (warehouse), **dogana** (customs hall) and **fondaco** (bank) show precisely the building's function in the life of the Republic. Building work began in 1506 and was completed in 1522, following plans by the official Republic's Engineer, the architect and cannon founder Paskoj Miličević. The carving and sculptural work on the building was carried out by the brothers, Josip and Nikola Andrijić, who also built Korčula Cathedral. The style of the palace is transitional, with elements of Gothic (the windows on the first floor), and the Renaissance (the portico with arcades and windows on the second floor). Between the windows on the second floor there is an in-built niche with a statue of St. Blaise. The interior courtyard is also Renaissance in style with its arcades and preambulatorium on the ground and first floors. In the large loggia at one end of the courtyard there are some original bronze statues which once struck the bells in the city bell-tower. The original clock mechanism is also on display. Over the loggia there is an inscription in Latin: FALLERE NOSTRA VETANT ET FALLI PONDERA / MEQUE PONDERO DUM MERCES / PONDERAT IPSE DEUS (We are forbidden to cheat and use false measures, and when I weigh goods, God weighs me). This inscription witnesses to the commercial postulates of the Republic: trade was founded on honesty and guaranteed weights, measures and quality, achieved by hard work, business skills and the avoidance of waste and luxury. This explains the centuries-long steady development and prosperity of trade in Dubrovnik, and the good reputation enjoyed by Dubrovnik merchants. The relief, dating from 1521 and showing two angels holding a medallion, is by Frenchman Beltrandus Gallicus. Apart from a warehouse, there were also a mint and a quality control office in Sponza. So it could be said that it was the meeting point of domestic and foreign merchants and the centre of the business life of the Republic in general. In the Renaissance era and later, Sponza was also the centre of many Dubrovnik academies, societies for educated and interested lay people where issues of science and literature were discussed. Now Sponza houses the State Archives of the Republic, which include many manuscripts,

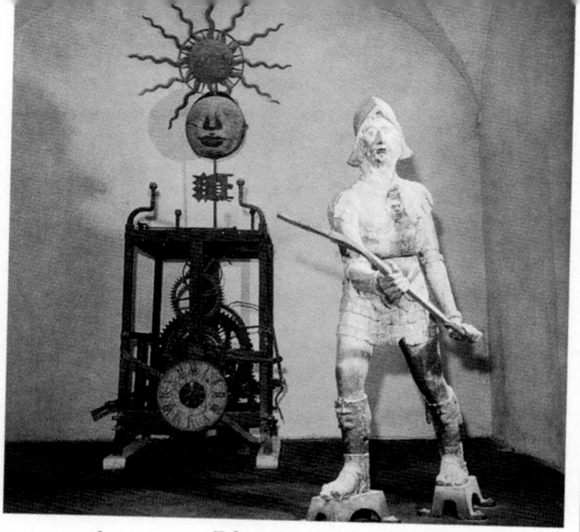

Zelenac - Bronze figure on the City bell-tower

contracts, log books, political, historical and all other documents from the 13th century to the fall of the Republic. Sponza's atrium is also an excellent stage for both musical and theatrical performances of the chamber variety, and the palace's beautiful facade forms the centre piece of decorations set up to mark the annual official opening ceremony of the Dubrovnik Summer Festival.

•••••••••••

The **Luža zvonara***** (NUMBER ㉔ ON THE PLAN) was built in 1436. Inside there are several bells which were used to call the assembly together, as alarms in times of danger, and on special occasions they were rung along with all the other bells in the city. During the Austrian occupation, the building was demolished to make way for a home for the military commander of the city but it was restored in 1952 to its original form. Work on the **City bell-tower***** began in 1444, according to some documents. In the same year Luka Mihoč, the son of a Dubrovnik general, promised to make metal numbers and a mechanism for the clock, showing the changes of the moon, and two male figures in wood with batons in their hands which would strike the hour on the bells. In the 1478 the clock's mechanism was restored, a new bell was cast and the wooden figures were replaced with some cast in bronze. With time their covering became green and they were therefore named "greenies" (according to some sources Dubrovnik's "greenies" are older than the "blacks" on the Venetian tower Torre dell' Orologio). The present bell was cast in 1506 by Ivan Krstitelj Rabljanin, a master founder of Dubrovnik's cannon. Following the great earthquake of 1667 the city bell-tower clock showed signs of damage and leaned over, but it was not demolished until 1906. It was restored in 1929 in its slightly rustic original form. It was built by three local masters: Radonja Grubačević, Đuro Utišenović and Pribina Radončić.

•••••••••••

The **building of the Main Watch**** (Glavna straža; NUMBER ㉕ ON THE PLAN) was first built in Gothic style (three biforia on the first floor), but later was given a Renaissance niche on its facade where is the so-called Mala Onofrijeva česma (Small Onofrio well). The portal is in Baroque style and was built between 1706 and 1708 by Marino Gropelli, the architect of St. Blaise's Church.

Members of the Linđo ensemble in front of the Small Onofrio Well

The old main watch building was in the form of an open loggia and was once beside the Church of St. Blaise. In 1709 it burnt down, along with the church.

••••••••••••

The **Small Onofrio Well**** (Mala Onofrijeva česma) was built in 1438 beside the portal of the main watch in a large semicircular niche. It is a joyful and playful work of sculpture. According to some sources it was built in 1438 by Onofrio della Casa, but the figurative decorations were not completed until the middle of the 15th century by Pietro di Martino from Milan. Some writers even ascribe the entire well to him. It is octagonal in shape, Renaissance in spirit and in its rich ornamentations and motifs. The plot of the comedy *The Story of Stanac* (Novela od Stanca) by the great Dubrovnik comic writer Marin Držić centres around this well.

••••••••••••

The **Palace of the Great Council** - the **building of the Dubrovnik Commune Assembly** (NUMBER 26 ON THE PLAN) was first mentioned in documents dating from 1303. In 1489 an extension of the building was documented, and it burnt down in 1817. In appearance (with Gothic windows) it was to a certain extent similar to the Sponza palace and fitted well into the unity of the square. It was built in its present form between 1863 and 1864 in the historical style of the neo-Lombard Renaissance, according to plans by Emilio Vechietti. Apart from the administrative part of the building which now houses the Commune Assembly of Dubrovnik, the palace of the Great Council also includes the city cafe (Gradska kavana) the former Orsan, or Arsenal, and the Marin Držić Theatre. An earthquake in 1979 seriously damaged Vechietti's building, and discussions continue as to the best way to restore it.

••••••••••••

St. Blaise's Church*** (Sveti Vlaho; NUMBER 17 ON THE PLAN) is a richly decorated Baroque building, a copy of the Venetian church San Maurizio, built between 1706 and 1714 according to plans by the Venetian architect Marino Gropelli. It is dedicated to Dubrovnik's Patron Saint, who has an emblematic significance for the people of the city: his face appears on seals and documents, on money, on the flags of their ships, on all important walls, fortresses, public buildings and city gates. On the site of the present Church of St. Blaise there was once a famous Gothic church, built in 1348, but severely damaged in the 1667 earthquake, and finally destroyed by fire in 1706. This building has a wide staircase by which one may climb from Luža Square up to a terrace with a balustrade and to the main portal. It is a centralised

St. Blaise's Church, on the day of the feast (February 3, 1991)

The Arsenal, from the harbour

building with a dome typical of the Venetian Baroque. St. Blaise's Baroque facade beautifully complements the Gothic and Renaissance exterior of the Sponza Palace, as well as the City bell-tower and the Main Watch, showing that the urban sense of the old inhabitants of Dubrovnik allowed all styles, providing they blended in with the already existing environment. Amongst the works of art which were transferred from the old building to the new, the famous statue of St. Blaise is of special value on the main altar, made of silver plate by a Dubrovnik goldsmith in the 15th century. The figure of the saint has a model of the city in his hand, but the city before the earthquake, and is therefore a valuable record. There are two stone sculptures from the old Church of St. Blaise and St. Jerome by the Brač master Nikola Lazanić dating from the end of the 16th century.

The balustrade and reliefs on the façade were seriously damaged in 1991-1992 and restored thanks to the efforts of French and Croatian restorers.

••••••••••••

The Arsenal** ("Orsan"; NUMBER 27 ON THE PLAN) was first mentioned in 1272. According to documents it was extended in 1335. In 1489 it was further extended and improved by Paskoje Miličević. Its covered-in rooms were able to receive the largest galley of that time for equipping, unloading or winter storage. Only three arches remain standing from the old Arsenal on the harbour side. A large part was removed in 1863 to make room for a theatre building, but it was saved from total destruction in 1933 by various architectural interventions, linking the harbour with the main city square through the Arsenal, and the covered area has been converted into the City cafe, a favourite meeting place for all visitors to Dubrovnik.

Roland's Column*** (Orlandov stup; NUMBER 16) is a stone column in the centre of Luža Square, with the figure of the warrior and knight Roland. The top of the column widens out with an iron railing and a flag pole. The figure of Sir Roland was carved in semi-relief in 1418 by the Italian sculptor Bonino da Milano. There is a legend connected with this column which tells how Roland himself helped the people of Dubrovnik to resist attacks by Saracen pirates in the 8th century. It is well known however that there are columns with statues of Roland in several medieval cities, and they are actually a symbol of a free merchant city state, which was precisely Dubrovnik's historical character. On the same spot, during the era of the Republic, decrees and laws were proclaimed and punishments announced and executed. The length of Roland's right forearm is engraved in the foot of the column and represented the standard for the Dubrovnik elle, their measure of length.

••••••••••••

The **Rector's Palace***** (Knežev dvor; NUMBER 28 ON THE PLAN). The old Rector's Palace was actually a fortified castle as early as 1200. It was destroyed in 1435 when some gunpowder exploded. Building work on the new palace began in 1435, in Gothic style based on plans by Onofrio della Cava, an

The Rector's Palace

engineer from Naples, with a great deal of assistance from local masters. In terms of structure it is a four-sided building, with two storeys and an inner courtyard or atrium. In 1463 another explosion destroyed almost all of the second floor. The present day structure is a transitional building, put up between the Gothic and Renaissance eras, with Renaissance porticoes on the ground floor and large Gothic biforia on the first floor. The portico was re-built by Salvi di Michele from Florence (probably following plans by Michelozzo), who had been given the task of restoring the palace. Some of the capitals are probably the work of Pietro di Martino of Milan. The statue of St. Blaise over the palace portal has also been ascribed to him. The earthquake in 1667 caused some damage to the palace. Restoration work lasted right up to 1739 and was led by the local master Jerolim Škarpa from Korčula. At that time some Baroque elements were added to the interior of the Renaissance courtyard. On the ground floor of the atrium there is an arcade on three sides, and on all four sides on the first floor. A splendid stairway leads up to the first floor. To the left of the entrance there is a niche with a statue of an angel and a small well, built in 1452. In the atrium, there is a bust of Miho Pracat Lopuđanin, a ship-owner and banker who left his entire estate to the Republic. This bust is the only public memorial in the Republic ever raised to one of its meritorious citizens. It was made in 1637 by the Italian sculptor P. P. Jacometti. On the first floor of the atrium, over the door which once led to the Palace of the Great Council, there is an inscription: OBLITI PRIVATORUM PUBLICA CURATE (in a free translation: "Forget personal, worry about public matters"). The palace was the seat and private residence of the Rector during his monthly mandate. He had to live here without his family and was not allowed to leave except on official business. The building also housed the seat of the Small Council, the actual rulers of Dubrovnik. The entire business of the Republic, political, diplomatic and ceremonial, and all legal and administrative business took place in this building. In the impressive halls and salons in the palace there is now an exhibition from the **historical department of Dubrovnik Museum**: household items, costume and clothing worn by the city patricians, flags, a collection of city keys, money, items from the old chemist's Domus Christi from the 15th century, many portraits of old inhabitants of Dubrovnik, paintings by well known and less famous local and Italian old masters (Carracci, Tintoretto, Paris Bordone, Mihajlo Hamzić). In the 1979 earthquake the Rector's Palace was seriously damaged making extensive restoration and protective work necessary. When this work was completed, one of the most beautiful settings for the Dubrovnik Summer Festival was returned to the public - the atrium of the Rector's Palace, a unique concert hall and excellent venue for theatrical performances.

Capital from the atrium of the Rector's Palace

••••••••••••

The **Cathedral*****
(NUMBER 18 ON THE PLAN).
The Church of the Assumption (Uznesenje Marijino) or "Gospa"

The Cathedral

(Our Lady) as it is popularly known, has always been Dubrovnik's cathedral, but a legend tells that the first church on this site was built from a generous gift by the English King Richard the Lion Heart, who in 1192, on his journey home from the Third Crusade, suffered a shipwreck in Dubrovnik waters and landed on Lokrum. The church was built between the 12th and the 14th centuries, and according to descriptions, it was one of the most highly decorated Romanesque churches in Europe at that time, but it was badly damaged in the great earthquake and very little remained standing. Encouraged by Stjepan Gradić, at that time the custodian of the Vatican museum and later the governor of the Vatican library, a highly educated man, with considerable diplomatic skills, the famous architect Andrea Buffalini came to Dubrovnik to help restore the cathedral. Following his plans, in the Baroque style, the work was started in 1673 by Paolo Andreotti and completed in 1713 by the local master Ilija Katičić. The present day church is a triple-naved Baroque basilica with a dome and all the hallmarks of late Roman Baroque. It is decorated with Baroque altars and paintings, mainly by Italian artists of the school of Raphael: Savoldo (1480-1548), Palma the Elder (Jacopo d'Antonio Negreti, 1480-1528), Alessandro Varotari Padovanin (1588-1648), Paris Bordone. The polyptych *The Ascension* on the main altar is by Titian (1487/90-1576) and his co-worker. The Flemish triptych owned by the church was carried by ambassadors from the Republic as a portable altar on their journeys to Istanbul. Some paintings in the church have been ascribed to local masters. The Treasury of Dubrovnik Cathedral was one of the richest in Europe, but the great earthquake destroyed a large part of that treasure. However, even what is now kept in the present treasury gives a hint of the wealth of old Dubrovnik, and the skill of the famous Dubrovnik master goldsmiths. The reliquaries and other items for church use demonstrate a high point of quality craftsmanship and aesthetic refinement; there is an especially outstanding reliquary in the shape of an arm and the container for

The ground plan of the Cathedral (yellow), with the remains of the Byzantine and early medieval (violet) and Romanesque (blue) cathedral drawn in.

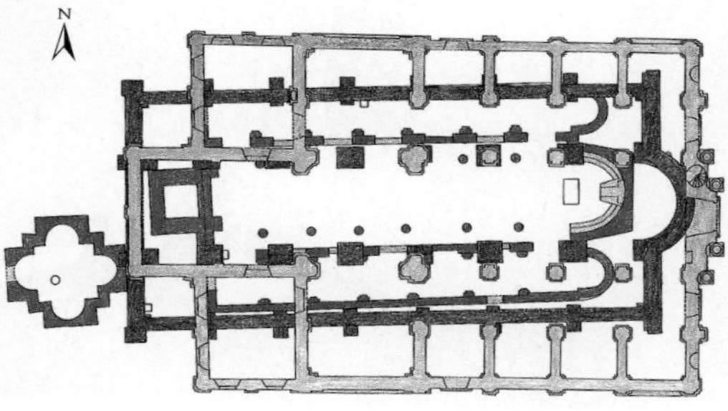

Reliquary of the head of St. Blaise (12th century) from the treasury of the Cathedral

Crucifix, the work of a Dubrovnikan master of the 16th century from the treasury of the Cathedral

the skull of St. Blaise, both dating from the 11th or 12th century, and of Byzantium origin. The frescoes in the treasury are the work of the local Baroque Master Petar Matejev.

In the 1979 earthquake the Cathedral was badly damaged making it necessary to dig drains beneath the church. At that time, the completely preserved foundations of the old Romanesque cathedral were discovered, and on digging deeper, a sensational discovery was made: underneath those foundations a third church was uncovered, with its walls intact almost up to the height of a man, a large basilica with excellently preserved fragments of frescoes in the apse. It dates from the 6th to 8th centuries, and the frescoes belong to the so-called Adriatic-Byzantine circle. Since all three churches are almost equal in size, a whole series of questions arise concerning the size of the city at that time, which would demand a revision or a reinterpretation of the early history of Dubrovnik on the basis of evidence which until now has seemed suspect.

••••••••••••

The **Jesuit Church, St. Ignatius***** (Sveti Ignacije; NUMBER ⓯ ON THE PLAN) was built between 1669 and 1725 by the Jesuits. The architectural concept for the building was the work of Andrea Pozzo (1642-1709) one of the greatest European architects of his time and an artistic innovator, who worked for the Jesuits throughout Europe; this was the first Jesuit church outside Rome. The architecture and the strictly organised content of the frescoes in the church were designed above all to serve the goals of the Counter Reformation. Dubrovnik's St. Ignatius was built immediately after the church of the same name in Rome, not lacking any of the hallmarks of the late Roman Baroque era. The Spanish artist Gaetano Garcia decorated the church in 1737 and 1738 according to an ordered programme. The frescoes are some of the earliest examples of Jesuit art in Europe, and their motifs correspond to these in the church of the same name in Rome. The bell in this church is the oldest existing bell in Dubrovnik. It was cast in 1355. Beside the church is the Baroque building of the Dubrovnik College (Collegium Ragusinum) built in 1735 according to plans by the Jesuits Ranjina and Canauli. It was the place where many famous Dubrovnik citizens received their education, including Ruđer Bošković (see Lokrum). The steps leading down from the square in front of the church and the college towards the city,

Jesuit Stairs and St. Ignatius' Church

built in the style of the steps of the Trinita dei Monti in Rome by Padalacqua in 1738, complete the most beautiful Baroque complex of old Dubrovnik. The stairs were seriously damaged in Serb and Montenegrin aggression in 1991-1992, but have been restored in the meantime.

••••••••••••

The **Lazarette*** (Lazareti; NUMBER 22 ON THE PLAN). The prosperity of the Dubrovnik Republic can be seen in the care taken to protect health. In front of the bridge linking the suburb of Ploče with the Revelin Fortress there used to be a terminal for all caravans travelling from the Balkan hinterland. On the way between the road and the sea stood the building of the lazarette which served as a quarantine station for both goods and passengers. The building was started in 1590 and completed between 1627 and 1642. It has been restored recently, and Dubrovnik's lazarette is probably the only one remaining from that period in Europe. The quarantine laws were extremely strict. During an epidemic, the death penalty was ordered for the slightest breach. The first hospitals were on the island off Cavtat: on Markan, Bobara and Supetar, and then on the small island of Sveti Andrija. From 1534 the hospital was on Lokrum and after 1457 in the monastery in Danče.

••••••••••••

The **Dominican monastery***** (NUMBER 21 ON THE PLAN) is one of the most beautiful reminders of old Dubrovnik. It dates from the 14th century, and before the Revelin Fortress was built it had a defensive function. The first information concerning its construction dates from 1301 and in 1315 the brothers Nikola and Juraj are mentioned as builders. They were sons of the Protomagister Lovro from Zadar. The church has been rebuilt several times, especially after the earthquake in 1667 and during the French occupation, when it served as a stable for horses and a store for food, and finally at the end of the 19th century. The church has been restored more or less to its original form. The monastery and church have the characteristics of the early Gothic era. The interior of the southern church doors is Romanesque; the exterior door with its lancet arch was built in 1419 by Bonino da Milano with the help of the local masters Bogosalić and Radinović. The Renaissance niches in the churches are the work of the mason Ludovik Maravić from Korčula. The late Gothic stone pulpit dates from the 15th century. By slightly altering the plans given by Maso di Bartolomeo of Florence, the local masters Utišenović, Grubačević and others built the monastery cloisters in 1456 giving them characteristics of "flower" Gothic.

Cloister of the Dominican monastery

Polyptych of Lovro Dobričević in the Dominican monastery collection

Cecho di Monopoli started work on the bell tower in 1390 and the work was completed by local workmen. It was built in Romanesque and Renaissance styles and its final stage was completed in the 17th century. The church's three bells date from 1463, 1515 and 1622. The monastery has extremely valuable archives and a large library with valuable incunabula, rare books and parts of manuscripts. It also houses valuable examples of Dubrovnik gold work from the 16th century, items of church furniture (e.g. a

Nikola Božidarević, "St. Blaise with a model of the city" (part of the polyptych)

silver cross the Bishop Gregory had made for the Serbian King Stevan Uroš II and a silver vessel for incense in the shape of a Dubrovnik caravel).

The Dominican monastery is also known for its Dubrovnik old masters. Here there is a polyptych by Lovro Dobričević (15th century) a triptych by Mihajlo Hamzić (16th century) and a triptych by Nikola Božidarević, his masterpiece, which is especially famous because in this painting St. Blaise is holding an accurate model of Dubrovnik in the 16th century. Altarpieces by the famous Croatian painters Vlaho Bukovac (1855-1922) and Ivo Dulčić (1916-1975) can be found over the side altars. The most famous work by an Italian artist is the large illustrated 14th century crucifix, the work of one of the greatest masters of Venetian art, Paolo Veneziano, and the altar piece of St. Mary Magdalene by Titian, dating from 1554.

••••••••••••

The **Monastery of St. James of Višnjica**** (Sveti Jakov od Višnjice; NUMBER 32 ON THE PLAN) is a Benedictine monastery founded in the 13th century (1222) by a member of the Gundulić family. The present form of the buildings and the church dates from the 16th century, with a Renaissance portal and windows. During the French occupation it was a barracks and a hospital. The important Dubrovnik poet Mavro Vetranović (1482-1576) lived and worked in the monastery at one time. Before leaving for Istanbul all Dubrovnik ambassadors sent by the Republic for talks with the Turks, spent three days in isolation in this monastery and were given final instructions by the Rector himself.

MUSEUMS AND EXHIBITIONS

The collections belonging to **Dubrovnik Museum** (Dubrovački muzej) are housed in various places throughout the city.

••••••••••••

The **Rector's Palace***** (Knežev dvor; NUMBER 28 ON THE PLAN). An historical collection including household items, paintings, clothing, costumes, documents, money, items for every day or special use from various periods of the Republic.

••••••••••••

The **Rupe Museum**** (NUMBER 11 ON THE PLAN) is in the oldest part of Dubrovnik, on Lava rock, and the building is unique in terms of its function and style. Below the building, which dates from between 1542 and 1590, there are 15 wells and stores for grain dug deep into the bare rock. The grain did not deteriorate, and measurements taken recently show that the temperature in these very dry stores was more or less the same in both summer and winter, about 17°C. In the store, which was capable of holding about 1 500 tonnes of grain, there is now an exhibition of old apparatus for measuring and processing grain.

••••••••••••

The **Ethnographic Museum**, a section of the Dubrovnik Museum, is also located in Rupe Museum. It contains exhibits related to the Dubrovnik

The Dubrovnik Museum in the Rector's Palace

coastal area, Župa dubrovačka, Konavle and the Dubrovnik islands, all forming one of the finest treasuries of traditional items in Croatia. National costumes, items from home workshops, embroidery, pots, ethnographic documents and folk musical instruments.

••••••••••••

Danče*** (NUMBER ❷ ON THE PLAN) is in the part of the city below Gradac park, towards the sea. On Danče there is a beautiful votive chapel, St. Mary's

The Ethnographic Museum

(Sveta Marija, 1457) famous for two original paintings by Dubrovnik artists: a polyptych by Lovro Marinov Dobričević (16th century) and a 16th century triptych by Nikola Božidarević. Part of the monastery in Danče was once the old Dubrovnik lazarette.

••••••••••••

St. John's Fortress*** (Tvrđava Sveti Ivan; NUMBER ㉙ ON THE PLAN) has two museums, which should not be missed. They are: the **Maritime Museum** (Pomorski muzej), where Dubrovnik's rich maritime history is documented by a large number of objects from the history of seafaring, navigational instruments from various eras, maritime and harbour maps, models of Dubrovnik ships from the oldest

The Maritime Museum

known to the most modern, old and new maritime documents and many votive paintings. It was founded in 1872. The **Aquarium** is part of the Institute for Oceanography and Seafaring of the Academy of Sciences and shows the life of flora and fauna in the Dubrovnik coastal area and the Adriatic as a whole.

••••••••••••

The **Lapidarium**** (stone monuments; NUMBER ❹ ON THE PLAN). In Bokar Fortress there is an exhibition of fragments of ancient and more recent architecture and sculptures,

St. Julian, fragment of a polyptych by Lovro Dobričević, on Danče

and a collection of old Dubrovnik weapons.

••••••••••••

The **Art Gallery**** (Umjetnička galerija; 45, Put Frana Supila street, opposite the Hotel Excelsior; NUMBER ㉚ ON THE PLAN) has a significant collection of works by Croatian and European artists from the 19th and 20th centuries. In the tourist season there is a large exhibition of Croatian and European art. As well as this gallery there is a whole series of small galleries in Dubrovnik for both exhibitions and sales, whose owners are either artists themselves, or tourist agencies. The **Sebastian Gallery** is particularly outstanding, located in the old church of the same name immediately next to the entrance to the Dominican monastery. Before the war, the gallery was representative for modern art.

••••••••••••

The **Cathedral Treasury**** (see Cathedral; NUMBER ⓲ ON THE PLAN).

••••••••••••

The **Museum of the Franciscan Monastery***** (see Franciscan Monastery; NUMBER ❾ ON THE PLAN).

••••••••••••

The **Museum of the Dominican Monastery****

(s. Dominican Monastery; NUMBER 21 ON THE PLAN).

••••••••••••

The **Collection of Old Icons**** (Zbirka starih ikona; 20, Puča Street; NUMBER 13 ON THE PLAN). Housed next to the Orthodox Church, which was built in 1877. Valuable and typologically interesting icons of various schools (15th-19th centuries).

••••••••••••

The **Synagogue*** (3, Žudioska street; NUMBER 14 ON THE PLAN) stands in a

The Marin Držić House

part of the city which was once the Jewish quarter. Many old items used in worship are kept here.

••••••••••••

The **Marin Držić House**** (Dom Marina Držića, 7 Široka Street), the memorial museum to Marin Držić (1508-1567), the greatest writer of comedy in Croatian. His works are an essential part of the repertoire of the Dubrovnik Summer Festival. How much he means in the national culture is shown by the fact that the house is the first museum set up to a Croatian writer.

••••••••••••

FAMOUS CROATS FROM DUBROVNIK

Benedikt Kotruljić (1400-1468) was a Dubrovnik man who spent many years away from his native country, serving his country as a highly educated and skilful diplomat. He was perhaps most significant as the author of economic treatises. His work *Della mercatura e del mercante perfetto* (On trade and the perfect trader) written in 1458, proved to be extremely useful and was passed around in manuscript form, until another Croatian, the philosopher Franjo Petrić, known as Patritius, had it printed in Venice in 1573. Kotruljić's book is the first work dealing systematically with trade and book-keeping to appear in Europe.

••••••••••••

Ivan Gundulić (1589-1638) is generally thought to be the greatest poet of old Croatian literature. He was born into the Dubrovnik nobility and educated in his native city. His teacher was Camilli, who wrote a continuation of Tasso's epic. Gundulić held several public offices and on two occasions he was the Rector of Konavle, as well as being a Senator and member of the Small Council. As a Baroque poet, in the European sense of that word, he succeeded in breaking through the armour of poetic convention and gave a new fluidity, both in terms of themes and language, to Dubrovnik poetry, especially in his lyrical meditations on the transitory nature of human life. His most famous works are *Suze sina razmetnoga* (*The Tears of the Prodigal Son*; Venice 1622) in which the above mentioned characteristics are especially evident, and his lively pastoral allegory *Dubravka*, where he praises the city like a true patriot. *Himna Slobodi* (The Hymn to Freedom) from this work is inspiring still today, and is used as the unofficial song of the Dubrovnik Summer Festival. Gundulić is however best known for his epic *Osman* (20 cantos, about 11 000 lines) which he wrote from 1621 until his death. With a feeling of being "Slavic" in the broadest sense, as the Turks invaded and settled in Europe, Gundulić sings of the victory of the Poles over the Turks at Hoćim in 1621, actually meaning the oppressed Slavic south. This work had an inspiring effect on the Croatian National Revival in the 30's and 40's of the 19th century. On the way along the Ulica od Puča street towards the Rector's Palace, on the right hand side, there is a beautiful Mediterranean city square, Gundulićeva Poljana, where there is a statue of the poet by the Croatian sculptor Ivan Rendić (1849-1932).

Ivan Gundulić

••••••••••••

Nikola Božidarević is the most important Croatian artist of the end of the 15th and the beginning of the 16th century. He came from the village of Krušice near Slano. His date of birth is unknown but he died a well-respected and rich man in Dubrovnik in 1517. He was hard working and greatly sought-after, as can be seen from numerous documents and contracts kept in the Dubrovnik archives. Monasteries commissioned works from him (the Franciscans in Cavtat, the Dubrovnik Dominicans) as did noble families and individuals (e.g. the altarpiece of the Đurđević family) and some churches. Only four paintings are still in existence from his entire oeuvre: a triptych on a side altar in the Bundić Chapel of the Dominican monastery in Dubrovnik, *The Annunciation* in the art gallery of the Dominican church, the Đurđević family's altarpiece in the capitulary hall of the Dominican monastery, and another triptych in the Church of St. Mary on Danče. A triptych in the Franciscan church on Lopud has also been ascribed to him.

Marin Getaldić

••••••••••••

Marin Getaldić, known in the scientific world as Ghetaldus, was born in Dubrovnik in 1566 and died there in 1626. He belonged to an old patrician family, and was educated in his native city. He held many political posts in the highest bodies in the Republic and in the Diplomatic service. He travelled Europe for six years (Germany, Belgium, England, France and Italy) and his talent for mathematics met with the general acclaim of those he met. He worked with the specific weights of metals and liquids, and researched the properties of parabolic mirrors. He understood perfectly the problems of ancient Greek geometry and created his own original geometric constructions, applying algebra to solve geometric problems before methods of analytic geometry had been generally introduced. He also worked on optics and astronomy. His many scientific works were printed mainly in Venice or Rome. He was a friend of Galileo Galilei and a forerunner of Descartes.

••••••••••••

Ruđer Josip Bošković, mathematician, physicist, astronomer, philosopher of world renown and one of the most highly educated men of his time. He was born in Dubrovnik in 1711 and died in Milan in 1787. He received his education at the Jesuit College in Dubrovnik and in 1725 went to study in Rome, where amongst other subjects he read philosophy, mathematics and physics at the Jesuit Collegium Romanum. He worked on various technical and strategic questions for the Pope (the dome for St. Peter's), Maria Theresa (the court library) and for the French. He contributed to the maps drawn of the Papal State, which laid the foundations for modern geodesy. In Vienna he completed his major work in theoretical physics, *Philosophiae Naturalis Theoria*. He travelled widely, to Belgium, England, Turkey, and Russia. As a member of the Paris Academy by

Ruđer Bošković

correspondence since 1748, he was elected a member of the Royal Society in 1760. He became a Professor at the University of Pavia in 1763. For nine years he organised and equipped the observatory in Brera, Milan, where he moved in 1770. When the Jesuit order was dissolved in 1773 he left for Paris and was appointed director of marine optics there. His collected works (*Opera*) were published in five volumes in 1785 in Italy (Bassano). In the same year he returned to Milan, where he died two years later. As a scientist Bošković was important for many reasons: for new mathematical methods, innovations in the theory of gravity (the so-called Bošković Law) and for his results in the fields of astronomy and geodesy. Nowadays however, most attention is given by atomic physicists to Bošković's intuitive genius concerning the possible non-mechanical behaviour of matter, which he set out in his work *Philosophiae Naturalis Theoria*, which forms the basis of modern nuclear physics.

EXCURSIONS

Lokrum (NUMBER ㉛ ON THE PLAN) is one of the islands off the city about 700 m from the coast stretching from the northwest to the southeast. Its highest point above sea level is at 91m. On this peak stands Port Royal Castle, which was built by the French, though it was later named "Maximilian's Tower" by the Austrians. On the eastern side of the island, protected from the open sea, there is a small natural harbour. The island covers an area of 0.8 km^2 and is covered in thick Mediterranean flora and woods: laurel, oak, pines, cypress and black pines. There are also olives, agaves, cacti, magnolia and palms. On the southern part of the island there is a small salt lake, 10 m deep, known as the "Dead Sea" (Mrtvo more). Nearby there is a deserted Benedictine monastery, founded in 1023. The triple-naved basilica, and a 14th century part of the monastery were badly damaged in the 1667 earthquake. The Chapel of St. Blaise (Sveti Vlaho) on the island dates from 1557. The monastery was deserted in 1798. In 1858 the island was bought by Archduke Maximilian Habsburg, later Emperor of Mexico, who converted the damaged part of the monastery into a Neo-Gothic castle in the form of a tower, and laid the foundations of the present day park. After this, Lokrum belonged for a time to the heir to the Austrian throne, Rudolf. In the Serb and Montenegrin bombardment of Dubrovnik in 1991-1992, the building of the monastery and the botanical gardens were seriously damaged.

View of Lokrum

••••••••••••

Rijeka dubrovačka (NUMBER ❶ ON THE PLAN), is a bay, almost three kilometres long, actually the sunken mouth of the river Ombla, which flows out at the end of the bay as a forceful karst spring. Roman Umbla was mentioned in 1169 as "Rijeka" (River). In the earliest times of the Republic there were villas here. Because of the direct exposure to the "bura" wind and the cold water of the river itself, and also because of the protection from the sun given by the surrounding high hills, this area has always been significantly cooler than the region in general. Thus it has

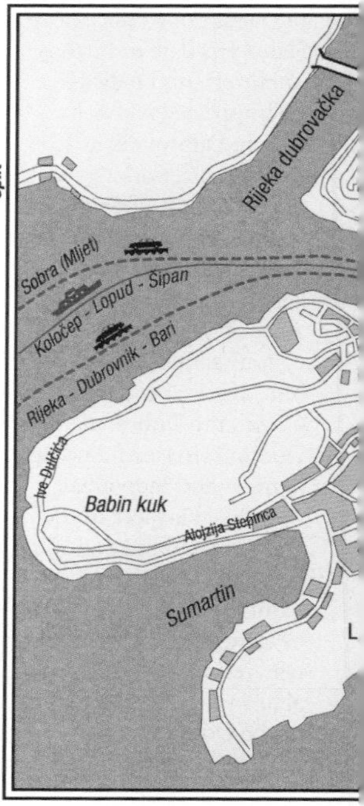

always been a place of refuge from the height of the summer sun. Despite the influx of industry, traffic, tourism and modern residential architecture, this area has still managed to preserve its great natural beauty. Along both banks of the narrow gorge there are ten villages. The most important are: **Komolac**, beside the spring of the Ombla itself where there

Rijeka dubrovačka

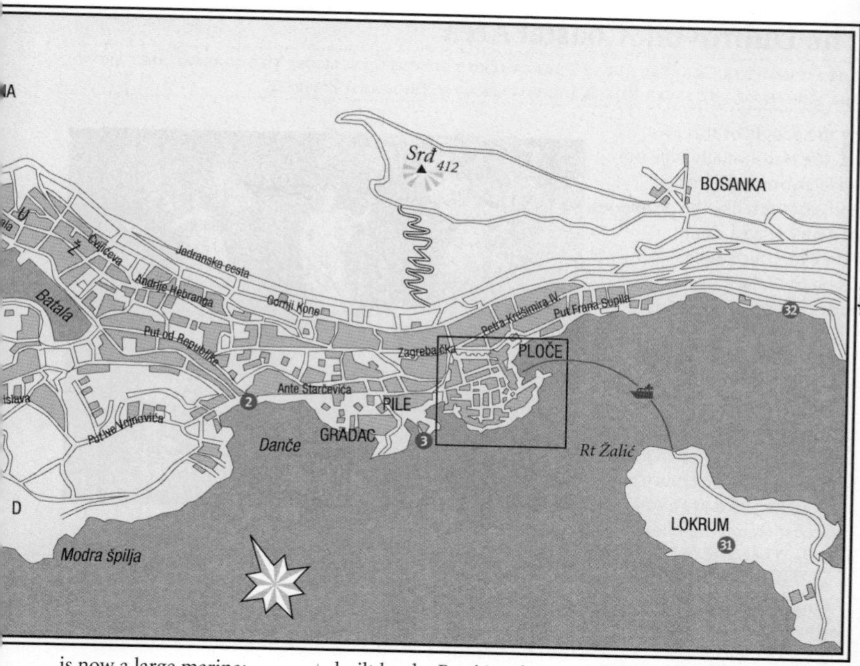

is now a large marina; and **Mokošica**, where a new residential suburb of Dubrovnik has been built.

Rijeka dubrovačka was the favourite spot for summer outings by the Dubrovnik patricians. Here these noble families built summer residences right near the city. Many have been demolished, but some have been preserved. Some of the most beautiful still standing are the summer home of the Kabužić-Bunić family in Batahovina, of the Božidarević family in Čajkovići and in Komolac the summer residences of the Gundulić (now part of the marina), Sorkočević, Getaldić and Skočibuha families. In Mokošica are the residences of the Zamanja and Gučetić families and further to the west and the mouth of the bay there are residences built by the Restić and Gradić families. Even though, unfortunately, the residences that have been preserved are now falling into decay, they still give an insight into the understanding of the old Dubrovnik patricians of the relationship between architecture and the countryside, at the time of the Republic's greatest prosperity and security. The entire coastal area of Rijeka dubrovačka is scattered with small chapels (almost every summer residence had its own). Of the older chapels the most important is Sustjepan, 11th-12th century and Romanesque. In Rožat on the shore of

Franciscan monastery in Rožat

Sorkočević Summer Palace

the bay there is a Franciscan monastery which was built in 1393 and re-built at the beginning of the 18th century. The monastery cloisters were built in 1585. On the wooded peak over the village the tower of the local parish church dominates the scene, standing on a site where in 1123 there was a Benedictine monastery. The renovation of the monastery, completed in 1990, did not stop the Serbian aggressor inflicting serious new damage on it during the siege of Dubrovnik in 1991-1992. ■

The Dubrovnik Coastal Area

THE DUBROVNIK COASTAL AREA (DUBROVAČKO PRIMORJE) INCLUDES THE COASTAL BELT FROM THE MOUTH OF THE RIVER RIJEKA DUBROVAČKA TO NEUM AND PELJEŠAC.

The people of this area are traditionally vine or olive growers, fishermen and seafarers, like the people of Konavle and Župa. However tourism has now come to replace these old activities to a large extent. They are also known for their traditional national costumes and the dance "Linđo", which has become a kind of symbol for the Dubrovnik area. The main settlements of the Dubrovnik Coastal Area are along the coast facing the Elafit Islands. They are:

Orašac*(21 km northwest of Dubrovnik; pop. 546) a village on the Adriatic highroad, northwest of Dubrovnik and Zaton. Until 1399, the border between the Republic of Dubrovnik and Bosnia ran through Orašac. Above the village there is a former Dominican monastery with a church (1690). Next to it the Austrian consul of that time in Dubrovnik built a fortified summer residence. Below the High Road, on the shores of the Koločepski Canal, there is a bathing area with some buildings and a small harbour for ships.

Slano* (36 km northwest of Dubrovnik; pop. 552) is situated at the far end of a bay, and is a large natural harbour which offers protection from storms to large ships in the area. In the area around the village there are the ruins of various Illyrian burial mounds. The walls of a Roman fortress have been found, as well as some early Christian sarcophagi. Amongst the remains from more recent times, some of the most important are the Rector's Palace (rebuilt at the end of the 19th century) the Ohmučević family summer residence, the Church of St. Francis dating from 1420, and the Baroque Church of St. Blaise (Sveti Vlaho) from 1785. In the war of 1991-1992, Slano suffered the severest damage. This strategically important place was practically destroyed. Slano is today being vigorously renovated, with a great deal of international assistance.

Statue of Neptune in the Trsteno Arboretum

Trsteno** (24 km northwest of Dubrovnik; pop. 237). It was named after the reeds (trstika) which grew in the abundant water here. Some remains of early Christian architecture (5th century) have been discovered in Trsteno. In the town's church there are valuable paintings by unknown

Veliki Zaton

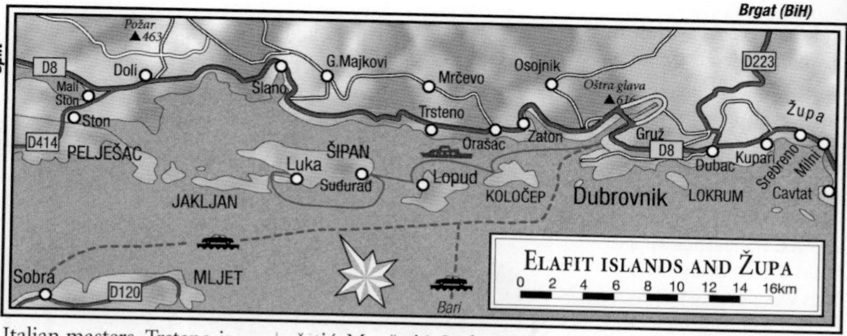

Italian masters. Trsteno is famous for two old plane trees, which are said to be more than 400 years old, the larger of which has a circumference of 11m. Even more famous is the **Arboretum**. The Gučetić family began to plant a large Renaissance park around their summer residence as early as 1502, and it was later extended according to plan. The many avenues and walkways, where many trees and plants from both the Mediterranean and the whole world grow, are a first-class historical, cultural and natural memorial to the Dubrovnik area. There is also an aqueduct in the park bringing water to the artificial cave fountain, which has a pond and statues of Neptune and nymphs. This was built in 1736. The summer residence itself was built in its present form after the great earthquake of 1667. Serbian shells set fire to the Arboretum, a quarter of which was burned down.

••••••••••••

Veliki Zaton and **Mali Zaton*** (19 km northwest of Dubrovnik). The natural beauty of this 2 km long bay did not escape the people of old Dubrovnik, and so here too there are numerous summer residences of patrician and bourgeois families - Gučetić, Menčetić, Sorkočević, Sarak and Lukarević. Zaton is the traditional place for the people of Dubrovnik to go on outings, but it also attracts a large number of motorised tourists because of its fine bathing beaches and auto-camps.

••••••••••••

The Elafit Islands

This is a chain of islands between the Pelješac peninsula and the Lapad peninsula, which is now part of the city. They were mentioned by Pliny the Elder and their name derives from the ancient Greek word "elafos" meaning deer, so they are in fact the "Deer Islands". Apart from bare rocks and smaller islands the Elafits are: Daksa, Koločep, Lopud, Šipan, Jakljan and Olipa. This archipelago was very important in the life of Dubrovnik as they controlled the seaways along the coast and on the open sea. The most skilful mariners came from these islands.

Daksa

••••••••••••

Daksa lies in the entrance to the Bay of Rijeka dubrovačka

The Elafit Islands, Koločep in the foreground, and then Lopud and Šipan

and Gruž Bay, now the city harbour, and the lighthouse on Daksa shows the way into the harbour. It is about 500 m long, 100 m wide and 24 m above sea level. In 1281, its owner Sabo Getaldić allowed the Franciscans to build a monastery there. This was demolished by the French who subsequently built a stone fortress from the ruins.

••••••••••••

Koločep* is about 7 km northwest of Gruž, covers an area of 2.35 km^2 and its highest point is 125 m above sea level. It is made of limestone and is waterless, but has beautiful vegetation. There are two villages on the island: Gornje Čelo and Donje Čelo; the people are traditionally mariners, fishermen, and now also work in tourism. Ancient Calaphodia first entered the Feudal State of Travunja on the arrival of the Slavs in this region. It came under Dubrovnik in the 11th century and was written into the Statute as the property of the Republic in 1272. From 1498 the island had its own Rector who was nominated by the Republic's Rector. In 1571 the Turks attacked the island and from then on all its important points were protected by fortified towers. In the village of Donje Čelo there are the remains of some Roman sculptures and fragments of early medieval braided ornamentation, now built into the parish church, which dates from the 13th century. On Koločep there are both ruined and preserved examples of pre-Romanesque early Christian chapels with elements of braided ornamentation: **St. Sergius** (Sveti Srđ), built in the 9th century, **St. Nicholas** (Sveti Nikola) and **Holy Trinity** (Sveto Trojstvo) from the 11th to the 12th centuries.

Monastery on Lopud

••••••••••••

Lopud** (6.5 n/m from Gruž; 269 inhabitants) is an island whose old Greek name was Delaphodia, and is situated between Koločep and Šipan. It covers an area of 4.63 km^2 and its highest point is 216 m. There are two bays: Lopud Bay (Lopudski zaljev) on the northwest and Šunj in the southeast. The settlement of Lopud is located at the end of the bay of the same name. The island has fresh water springs and rich sub-tropical vegetation, and because of its good beaches is a favourite spot for tourists. After the Greeks, there was also a Roman settlement on the island called Lafota. From the 11th century it belonged to the Republic and from 1457 the village was the seat of the island's own Rector. In the 15th century, it was settled by fugitives from the mainland, fleeing from the Turks.

On the island there is an old Croatian chapel (St. John's, Sveti Ivan) and there are also the remains of a pre-Romanesque chapel, with frescoes and braided ornamentation, **Holy Trinity** (SvetoTrojstvo) dating from the 16th century. The Franciscan church and monastery St. Mary of Špilica (Sveta Marija od Špilice) were founded in 1483 and in the 16th century they were protected with defensive walls and towers. Inside the church there are paintings by the Italian masters Pietro di Giovanni, Girolamo di Santacroce, Bassano, an unknown 17th century Flemish artist and Nikola Božidarević. On the south-eastern part of the island, in the bay of Šunj, is the Church of Our Lady of Šunj (Gospa od Šunja), originally built in the 12th century. The present church dates from the 15th century, and was extended continuously right up to the 17th century. The altar is an interesting example of wood carving, and the altar pieces are by Palma the

Elder, Natalino da Murano and the local artist Matej Jundić (1452). The two stone lions were brought from England in the time of Henry VIII by Miho Pracat, a Lopud man and Dubrovnikan merchant.

•••••••••••

Šipan*** (9 n/m from Gruž) was first mentioned by this name in documents of 1371. It is the largest island in this group, covering an area of 16.5 km². Its highest point is 243 m, and it is about 17 km away from Dubrovnik. The Koločep channel separates it from the mainland, by 1500 m. This island also has two bays: **Luka Šipanska** (Šipan Harbour) in the northwest, and **Suđurađ**; there are settlements with the same names in each bay. In Luka Šipanska there are some remains of a Roman villa rustica. From the Middle Ages, there are remains of **St. Peter's Church** (11th century), the **Chapel of St. John** (Sveti Ivan) in Šilovo Selo and an old Christian church, **St. Michael's** (Sveti Mihovil) in Pakljena, where there is also the fortified **Church of the Holy Spirit** (Sveti Duh) dating from 1569. The island's natural beauty made it an attractive place for summer residences, and many were built, especially in the 15th century. In Luka Šipanska, the Sorkočević family built their residence. There is also a 15th century Gothic palace for the Rector. In 1539 the Skočibuha family built their residence, actually a fortified castle in **Suđurađ**, and a tower was added in 1577. The ruins of the Dubrovnik Archbishops' summer residence are also on the island. The name Lodovico Beccadelli (1501-1572) is linked with this place. He was a high ranking church official who became Archbishop of Dubrovnik. In European history he is famous as a prominent humanist and a special friend of Michelangelo. On Šipan he gathered together a circle of educated Dubrovnik people to form a kind of academy, led scientific and literary discussions, wrote poetry and historical pamphlets about Split and Dubrovnik amongst other things. Letters in which he invited Michelangelo to visit him in Šipan are extant. ■

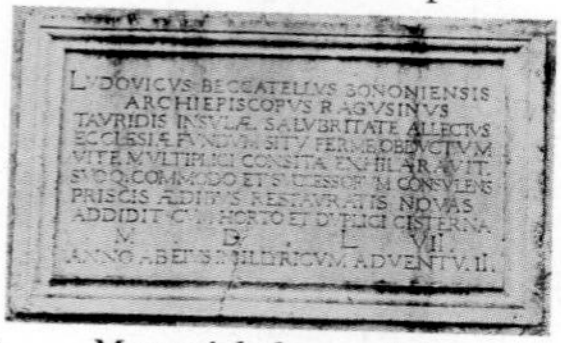

Memorial plaque of the Beccadelli residence in Suđurađ

The palace of the Skočibuha family in Suđurađ

The Pelješac Peninsula

After Istria, Pelješac is the largest peninsula in Croatia. It stretches 65 km from Ston to Lovišće point (by road 84 km) and is 2.5-7 km wide. It covers a total area of 355 km². It was known to the Greeks as Hyllis and Pliny the Elder mentioned it as Rhatamae Chersonesus, from which the names Art, Rat and Stonski Rat derived. The name Pelješac is much more recent.

•••••••••••

Ston*** (59 km northwest from Dubrovnik; 175 km from Split; 528 inhabitants) consists of two fortified settlements on an isthmus 1.3 km wide.

This complex therefore has the sea on two sides. To the north lies Mali Ston on the Neretva Channel and to the south is Ston, sometimes called Veliki Ston, on the shores of the Ston Sea (Stonsko more) a channel connected to the open sea. On the south-eastern side of the isthmus there are shallows with saltworks which had a strong influence on the history of this part of the Adriatic.

•••••••••••

In the area around Ston traces of prehistoric life have been found. The caves Špilja Gudnja (in Prisoj, south of the village of Česminica) are a rich archaeological site from the Neolithic era. The oldest finds date from 7000 years BC. They are so significant (mainly ceramics and painted ceramics) that there is talk of a kind of "Gudnja

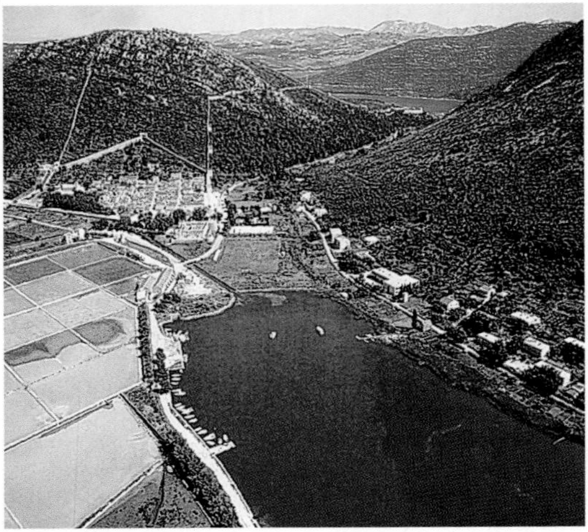

View of Veliki Ston with its ramparts

culture". In the first thousand years BC there was an Illyrian settlement on Gradac hill and even today the rings of the dry stone walls around this prehistoric settlement are still visible. Decorations found on Illyrian graves demonstrate that the Illyrians were very strong here. Probably they exploited the salt and therefore were richer than others.

In the Roman era the settlement known as Stagnum was located here. The Romans also exploited the saltworks but there were no larger settlements. That this was a wealthy area is also shown by the numerous churches built in the plains of Ston in the late Roman era. On the arrival of the Slavs, Ston (previously Stagnum, on the side of a hill) became the centre of a larger administrative area formed between Neretva and Dubrovnik (Zahumlje). The rulers of this area were for a time vassals of the Croatian kings, and in the 1140s it was taken over by the rulers of Duklja (Dioclea), which lies to the south.

The second phase of the history of the town began in 1333, when Dubrovnik became the owner of the peninsula, and Ston was proclaimed the Republic's second city. To protect their new possession, in Dubrovnik they first of all thought of splitting the peninsula off from the land by digging a canal, but the idea that it would be better to build a system of fortresses won out. Building began in the 14th century, but works on making the fortifications still stronger went on until the end of the 18th century. Such strong defences were built because Dubrovnik obtained about two thirds of its revenues from the Ston salt pans.

Numbers of famous architects worked on the Ston fortifications: Michelozzo Michelozzi (1461-1464), Bernardino of Parma (1461), Juraj Dalmatinac (1465, see Šibenik), Oliver the French (1472-1478) and Paskoje Miličević (1488-1506). The city was governed by a rector appointed in Dubrovnik. After the fall of the Dubrovnik Republic, especially at the time when the hinterland was no longer so dependent on the salt of Ston, the importance of the town decreased. In the war for Croatian independence, Serb aggression was halted in front of Ston and Mali Ston in the south Dalmatia theatre of operations. Most severely damaged (65% of residential buildings) was the old centre of Mali Ston. In autumn 1996 there was a series of strong earthquakes, which also caused great damage.

Today, Ston is primarily a tourist area. Its saltworks occupy an area of 400 000 m^2, and enough salt is produced annually to fill 200 railway wagons.

The inheritance of the rulers of Dioclea (Duklja) passed to the Serbian Nemanjić until the 14th century, and then once again came under

Ston, city centre

Stonska Duba

Dubrovnik from 1427 on. The town was fortified because of the frequent attacks it suffered, but the walls were mostly removed at the end of the 19th century.

SIGHTS

The **Ston Walls.** This is the defensive system linking Ston and Mali Ston built in the 14th century. Throughout the era of the Dubrovnik Republic, the walls were maintained and renovated. They were 5.5 km long in total and strengthened by 40 towers and 7 keeps (they are now 5 km in length with 20 towers). This length of wall so impressed visitors that it was known as the "European wall of China". The centres of the system are the fortress Veliki kaštio in Ston, Koruna in Mali Ston and the fortress on Podzvizd hill (224 m). With defences like these, Ston was unassailable from the mainland. Demolition work began on the walls following the fall of the Dubrovnik Republic. Later the Austrian authorities took materials away from the wall to build schools and community buildings, and also for a triumphal arch on the occasion of the visit by the Austrian Emperor in 1884. The wall around Mali Ston was demolished with the excuse that it was damaging the health of the people. The demolition was halted after the Second World War and the walls are now protected.

••••••••••••

The **town layout of Ston.** The town was surrounded by 980 m of walls in the form of an irregular pentangle. Within this pentangle, three streets were laid from north to south and three from east to west. Thus 15 equal blocks were formed with 10 houses in each. Residential buildings are grouped in the centre and public buildings around the edges. The Gothic Republic Chancellery and the Bishop's Palace are outstanding amongst the public buildings. The main streets are 6 m wide (except the southern street which is 8 m wide) and the side streets are 2 m wide. The town was entered by two city gates. The "Field Gate" (Poljska vrata) has a Latin inscription and dates from 1506. The city plan of Dubrovnik was used as a model for Ston, but since Ston was built on prepared terrain, that model was more closely followed than in Dubrovnik itself. In terms of infrastructure (water mains and sewers built in 1581) Ston was unique in Europe.

••••••••••••

Other buildings. Veliki Kaštio Castle (in the south-eastern part of the town) is the central building in Ston and an important part of the defensive system. It was used as a residence, a store for grain and munitions. The **Franciscan monastery** and **St. Nicholas'Church** (Sveti Nikola) (in the western part of the town): the monastery with its cloisters was built in the Neapolitan Gothic style. The late Romanesque church was built in 1347. Amongst other works of art, inside the church there is an illuminated crucifix by Blaž Jurjev Trogiranin (see Trogir). On the site of the present church (built in 1850) there was a Gothic cathedral which collapsed in the earthquake. The **Church of the Annunciation** (Navještenje Marijino) was built in the 15th century outside the walls to serve the suburbs and the surrounding area.

EXCURSIONS

On Gradac hill (50 min on foot to the northwest) there is a pre-Romanesque chapel, **St. Michael's***** (Sveti Mihajlo) which dates from the 10th or 11th cen-

St. Michael

tury. It is a single-naved building which once had a dome characteristic of old Croatian churches. Although small (5.8 x 4.2 x 5.9), it gives a cathedral-like impression and has been compared to Mont St. Michel in France or the Church of San Michele on Monte Gargano in Italy. The most interesting items in the church are the remains of frescoes dating from the end of the 11th or the beginning of the 12th century (the oldest frescoes in Croatia). The most famous fresco is the figure of a ruler, probably Mihajlo Višković (10th century) in the form of a western icon. It is thought that he built this church and that beside the church he had his court. Next to the church there is a collection of stone monuments with fragments of interwoven ornamentation work, and a small Dominican convent which serves the church. In the area between Ston and Gradac (Stonsko polje) there were several early Christian churches and the settlement Stagnum. There was a total of eight churches of which two remain: **Our Lady of Lužina** (Gospa od Lužina) and on the local cemetry, the Church of SS. Cosmas and Damian (Sveti Vrači or Kuzma i Damijan).

••••••••••••

Mali Ston*** is also surrounded by defensive walls but it is in the form of a regular square. On the land side the walls were built between 1336 and 1347 and on the seaward side in 1358. The Harbour Gate (Lučka vrata) also dates from that time, with its late Romanesque statue of St. Blaise. There was also a store for salt and an arsenal where ships were fitted. The most famous building is **Koruna Fortress** with its five towers facing the sea. Mali Ston harbour was built in 1490 based on Dubrovnik city harbour. Salt was exported from here to Neretva and subsequently to Bosnia. In the centre of the town stands the 14th century **St. Anthony's Church** (Sveti Antun) which has been rebuilt several times. On the seafront stands **Toljevac Tower**, built in 1478. In Bistrine and Kanal Malog Stona bays is one of the largest oyster farms on the Eastern Adriatic coast.

••••••••••••

Trpanj** (62 km from Ston; 707 inhabitants) is the best-known holiday resort on the northeastern coast of the peninsula, and is a ferry port for the mainland. It was named after the Greek Drepanon (meaning scythe, "srp" in Croatian). It grew up close to a Roman villa rustica. Above the harbour are the ruins of a medieval fortress. In the town itself is the Church of Our Lady of Carmel (Gospa od Karmela) which has a Renaissance altar with the coat of arms of the Gundulić family. The parish church is Neo-Romanesque and on the edge of the town there is a small chapel with a wooden Baroque altar. ■

Trpanj

Konavle

Konavle is the furthest southeastern point in the old Dubrovnik Republic, reaching from Obod, above Cavtat, to Oštri rat point on the edge of Kotor Bay. In the north Konavle passes into Herzegovinian karst rock, and in the south the coast is straight, with very steep and high cliffs, known as "**Konavoske stijene**".

The area has been cultivated since prehistory and is watered by canals (whence its name derives),

Konavosko polje

three rivers, Konavočica and Kopačica which are periodic streams, and Ljuta which flows constantly, all contributing to the special fertility of this region. Konavle was mentioned by Constantine Porphyrogenitus in the 10th century as a territorial unit. In the 10th century it came under Travunja. A separate ruler (archont) of Konavle is also mentioned. At the end of the 12th century, it was part of Serbia, under the Nemanjić dynasty. In 1378 it was under Bosnia, and later under various feudal lords. In 1419 the Republic of Dubrovnik bought the eastern part from Sandalj Hranić, and in 1426 bought the western part of Konavle from Radoslav Pavlović. The inhabitants are by tradition farmers and grow Mediterranean crops, more rarely engaging in fishing and seafaring. The national costume of Konavle, especially that for women, has been maintained right up to the present day, and in itself is an excellent aesthetic and cultural symbol for Dubrovnik and the ordinary people of Dubrovnik.

Amongst the cultural monuments in Konavle, apart from the stone prehistoric burial mounds, it is important to mention the remains of the Roman aqueduct leading from Cavtat (some traces are still visible in the plains of Konavle) and the large fortress, Soko in the village of Dunave which protected the only entrance to the hinterland. There was probably a fortress here in the Illyrian era and the present ruins date from the 15th century. There are also many examples of stechaks (stećci) in Konavle since most of the people here once belonged to the Bogumil sect (see Neum). The pre-Romanesque church, **St. Demetrus** (Sveti Mitar) in **Gabrili** dates from the 11th and 12th centuries and is interesting for the large number of "stechaks" built into the narthex of the church. In the village of **Brotnice**, near St. Luke's Church there is a fine example of a "stechak" dating from the end of the 14th century. In the village of **Pridvorje**, which was the administrative centre of Konavle during the era of the Republic, there is the Rector's Palace (the Rector of Konavle was at one time the great Croatian poet Ivan Gundulić). The church and the Franciscan monastery in Pridvorje date from the 15th century.

Amongst the larger villages in Konavle, **Ćilipi** (838 inhabitants) is particularly well known.

Dubrovnik airport is located here and in the village itself there is an interesting ethnographic museum ("Zavičajna kuća") and many events relating to traditional popular culture take place here during the tourist season.

Gruda (753 inhabitants) was for a long time the administrative centre of Konavle and is also known for its large vineyards. The villages in

Traditional local house in Ćilipi, September 1990/ November 1992

Konavoska brda (Konavle hills) towards Herzegovina, have retained much of their original rustic character and way of life. In the village of Ljuta (200 inhabitants) is the famous restaurant "Konavoski dvori" which was built from several old mills, converted into a restaurant on the River Ljuta which here flows through lush vegetation. This spot offers an insight into the special characteristics of this area. The mountain **Sniježnica** (1234 m) is outstanding amongst all the natural beauty here, as are **Konavoske stijene** (the cliffs along the coastline stretching from Cavtat to the entrance to Kotor Bay), the beach in the village of **Popovići**, and above all, the thick lush forests of pines, cypress, oak and laurel, which, until the terrible fires of 1985, covered most of Konavle, but have remained in the eastern part of the region. The Serb-Montenegrin invasion of 1991-1992 destroyed totally or in part almost all the villages in Konavle. No kind of restoration work will be able to make up the losses. Many Croatian and foreign associations are today engaged in the renewal of Konavle.

••••••••••••

Cavtat*** (2015 inhabitants) is one of the most beautiful small towns on the Eastern Adriatic coast. It lies on the Rat peninsula, in between two bays, two natural harbours 17 km southeast of Dubrovnik on the southern end of the Župski zaljev bay. Its present name derives from the Latin word Civitas. The old inhabitants of Cavtat were Illyrians, then Greeks, Romans and Slavs. The ancient name was Epidauros or Epidaurum. Octavian (later Augustine) besieged the town in 47 BC. In 530 Cavtat became the seat of a bishop. According to Byzantine legends, the inhabitants of Cavtat were those who founded Dubrovnik in the 7th century as they fled from the Avars and the Slavs. Cavtat was part of the Republic until 1303, when it came under a series of Slavic (Serbian) rulers, and then once again came under Dubrovnik from 1427 on. The town was fortified because of the frequent attacks it suffered, but the walls were mostly removed at the end of the 19th century. The important buildings in Cavtat are:

Cavtat

The **Rector's Palace** (Knežev dvor), a Renaissance building built between 1555 and 1558. It houses the Baltazar Bogišić (1834-1908) library. He was a great legal scholar. There are also archives, a museum with finds from prehistory and a collection of stone monuments with some ancient fragments, and Bogišić's collection of graphics with more than 10000 pages. This includes works by Lucas Cranach the Younger, Andrija Medulić and some Italian masters. The memorial on the sea front in front of the palace is the work of the sculptor Petar Palavicini (1887-1958). **St. Nicholas' Church** (Sveti Nikola) was rebuilt in Baroque style in 1732 and houses paintings by old masters and also by Vlaho Bukovac. At the western end of the harbour there is a

Vlaho Bukovac Gallery

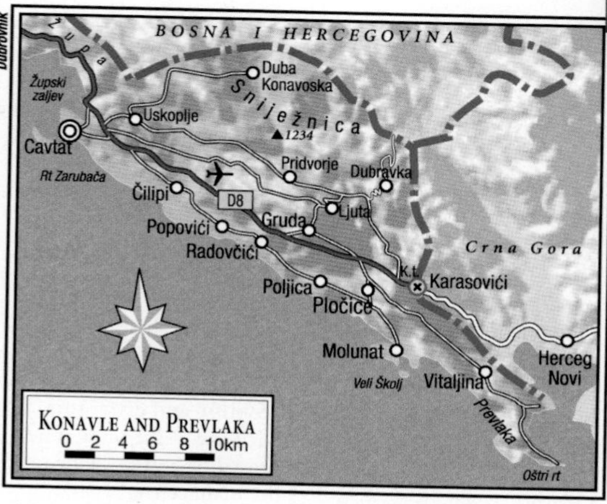

Franciscan monastery with the **Church of Our Lady of Cavtat** (Gospa od Cavtata). The monastery cloisters are Renaissance (1483). In the church there are works by 16th century Dubrovnik masters and by Vlaho Bukovac (1855-1922). The **Vlaho Bukovac Gallery** houses paintings by probably the most significant Croatian painter of the second half of the 19th century, mainly connected with his life in his native Cavtat. On the far end of the Rat peninsula, in the town graveyard, the **Račić family mausoleum** stands out, the work of one of the greatest Croatian sculptors, Ivan Meštrović (see Šibenik-Drniš) who worked here between 1920 and 1922. The great Croatian politician Frano Supilo (1870-1917) was also born in Cavtat.

••••••••••••

Župa dubrovačka

The region known as Župa dubrovačka (Dubrovnik district) is a strictly defined area between Dubrovnik and Konavle, part of the old Astareja, the original Dubrovnik region, "the Fatherland" (djedovina) as it is known in some documents. As it was a farming and fishing area even in ancient times, it does not boast a large number of cultural documents, but thanks to its gentle landscape, its specific Mediterranean character and the beauty of its beaches, it is now a well-known summer resort, a riviera with many new hotels.

••••••••••••

Kupari*, situated on the shores of Župski zaljev bay, 8 km south-east of Dubrovnik, was named after the fact that during the era of the Republic "kupe" were made here, that is, the tiles for the roofs of old Dubrovnik. Close to Kupari is "Toreta", a fortified house built by Orsat Đurđević in 1626 as a defence against pirates.

••••••••••••

Mlini* is 11 km east of Dubrovnik. Here streams flow into the sea and there were once mills built on them, hence the name ("mlin" is mill in Croatian). The church in Mlini, St. Hilary's (Sveti Ilar) was built in 1449 and restored in 1687 after the earthquake. There are also the remains of some Roman buildings in Mlini.

Park in Župa

••••••••••••

Plat. Old Platea, lying between Mlini and Cavtat, is today a tourist resort with a large hotel of the same name and beautiful beaches in a small bay.

••••••••••••

Srebreno* is about 10 km from Dubrovnik to the southeast. The ancient town of Subbrenum was one of the places settled by fugitives from Epidaurum in the 7th century. It was mentioned by its old name in 1294. The Benedictine abbey on the small island of Mrkan had some land there from 1284. As well as the beautiful beaches, the path leading through the natural coastal woods to Mlini is well known.

••••••••••••

The national costume of Župa dubrovačka is still worn today, especially by women, and thus a "Župka" (a woman from this area) can be easily distinguished from a "Primorka" (from the Dubrovnik coastlands) or a "Konavoka" (from Konavle). ■

Dalmatian wines & cuisine

Wines

Dalmatia is richer in the varieties on which its wines are based than the inland areas of Croatia, and is distinguished by the individuality of its viniculture. This is particularly true of the islands, many of which have reason to boast of the uniqueness of their wines. The grape called Plavac, grown everywhere and in some localities giving wines that have become world renowned, has set a stamp of its own upon the wines of Dalmatia.

The Benkovac winery

The Benkovac winery, built in 1956/57, is still very attractive since the owner cherished it – the roof and the front are ivy-clad, making it appear beautiful and extraordinary and at the same time providing a deep shade for the main cellar.

The hot sun and the rough windswept soil of the Benkovac-Stankovci wine-growing hills are the ideal microclimate for achieving the extraordinary characteristics of Benkovac wines. The Benkovac winery is most famous for its rose, produced in the tradition of best French roses. It is also famous for producing grape brandies and finest wine distillates.

Benkovac rosé, a quality dry wine of protected geographical indication, is the ideal match with light Dalmatian dishes, lamb as well as home made prosciutto ham. It is distinguished by its bright copper colour with a glow of brown, mild and subtle flavour and varietal fragrance, and a discreet aroma and bouquet.

Northern Dalmatia

Red wine is mostly produced from Plavina and Babić grapes. The best known wine of the area is certainly Babić from Primošten, a marvellous top-quality wine from the vineyards in Primošten located in a honeycomb of stone walls, one of the most impressive monuments to the indefatigability of human labour in the face of the inhospitable karst. Merlot from Drniš is a wine with a big future;

this is a fine quality red wine from Trlabetuša Hill in Petrovo polje.

••••••••••••

The Badel 1862 winery in Benkovac produces, from imported French varieties, Grenache, Carignan and Cincault, some interesting quality wines - the Bulin red wine, and Rosé, a charming wine in the style of the best French rosés.

••••••••••••

The Šibenik wine region provides the most ample assortment of good wines. These are the quality Babić, Šibenik Plavina, Šibenik Opolo rosé, and Dalmatiner. Šibenik Babić is one of the most popular of Croatian quality reds.

The main white of the region is Debit, much loved by the vintners in the hills behind the coast. Traditionally, a pronouncedly yellow wine is obtained by keeping the must a long time on the marc; this kind of oxydised wine, with insufficient total acids, does not meet today's taste, but it is still well-entrenched locally. The best Debit, which satisfies contemporary taste, comes from the Promina wine region.

Dalmatinska zagora

Matching the individuality of those well known karst phenomena, the Red and Blue lakes, the Imotski wine region can also boast of its own indigenous varieties of vine, Kujundžuša and Rudežuša. The main wine of the sub-region is Kujundžuša, in a range of qualities from table to quality wines. Its features make it a transitional wine between the heavier Mediterranean and the lighter wines of the inland area. Red wines are produced from the Imotski Vranac and from Plavina, and in recent times Cabernet Sauvignon and Merlot have been making big inroads.

••••••••••••

Blended whites and reds come from the wine region of Vrgorac, Vrgorac white and Vrgorac red enjoying good reputations. The first is sold under the name of Mihovil, and it is a well-harmonized blend of Maraština, Medna, Zlatarica and Trbljan grapes. In the latter, the main grape is Plavina with some Vranac; it is marketed under the name of Faust. There are interesting single variety wines made by small producers, who use Zlatarica (white) and Ninčuša (red), indigenous varieties, and an excellent Grey Pinot.

The production centres are Imotski, Vrgorac and Proložac.

Central and Southern Dalmatia

In the 4th century BC, the ancient Greeks set up their colonies in Dalmatia: Korkyra Melaina (Korčula), Pharos (Stari Grad on Hvar), Issa (Vis), Epidaurus (Cavtat) and, in the 3rd century, Tragurion (Trogir). They brought the grapevine with them and became good producers of

wine, those on Vis producing the best wine in the ancient world. In the 2nd century BC, Agatharichides, a geographer and historian, wrote that "Vis produces wine that is better than all others, if they are compared". This first world champion wine must have been Vugava, the archetypal variety of Vis. Some say that it is precisely the same as the French variety Viognier, wine which (Chateau Grillet) achieves enormous prices.

••••••••••••

This brilliant beginning of the tradition of viticulture in Dalmatia was continued during the Roman period, and in the Middle Ages, viticulture was the main source of income for the population, not only in the countryside, but in the towns as well, regulated by their charters. In the life of the Dubrovnik Republic a special role was played by Dubrovnik Malvasia, a wine of great fame which, it is to be hoped, will soon be revived.

••••••••••••

Going along the coast to the south, the wineries of the region, which suffered during and after the recent war, do not offer a great choice of wines. Worth mentioning, however, are Kaštela Opolo and Mimički Plavac. In the Neretva-delta and in Konavle , the production of some well-known wines is just starting to be revived.

But to make up for this, Pelješac, the real habitat of the Plavac, offers a cornucopia of variations on the Plavac grape. Here are the famed locations of Dingač and Postup, where the vineyards slope down almost to kiss the sea, wines of the same name being produced. Dingač is among the dozen best wines of the world. On Pelješac the Small Plavac is used to produce the high quality wines Carsko, Kneževo, Žuljan and Stagnum and the quality wines Plavac produced in Potomje, Donja Banda, Pelješac, Putnikovići, Ston, Ponikve. A few white vines are produced from the Maraština grape, the best known being St. Ana, a top quality wine.

Connoisseurs of Croatian wine will

particularly enjoy island-hopping, because almost every island in Dalmatia has got its individuality, its own variety and wine, which does not exist anywhere else in the world.

In Murvica on Brač is one of the best Plavac wines, the high quality Bol. The related quality wines are Bol Plavac and Bol Opolo.

•••••••••••

Hvar is certainly worth going round, because there are many producers; not one of the Croatian islands has so many kinds of grape as Hvar. Many of them are indigenous to Hvar and do not exist anywhere else. Among these there are grapes called Bogdanuša, Drnekuša, Prč and Mekuja. The southern coast of Hvar has been taken over by Plavac, and the high quality wines Faros, Ivan Dolac and Zlatan Plavac come from here. Quality whites include Hvar Bogdanuša, Hvar Pelegrin, Zlatan Otok, Dobrogost and Parč, while Drnekuša is a unique red, in Croatian and world terms.

•••••••••••

Korčula is proud of its three magnificent whites - Pošip, Maraština and the mighty Grk, from the sandy locations of Lumbarda. There is also a quality white called Cetinka, and the choice is broadened with the quality wines Pošip, Grk and Moreška (whites) from Korčula, and Plavac and Admiral (reds). Many interesting table wines can be tasted on the island, of which Kumpanija is the best known.

•••••••••••

Vis is known above all for its Vugava, already mentioned, but there are also some excellent high quality and quality Plavac wines and quality whites such as Vis White, Blanca and so on.

•••••••••••

The individuality of Lastovo is mirrored in its Maraština, as well as in wines called Augusta Insula and Ladesta, both of them in red and white variants.

•••••••••••

A review of Dalmatian wines would not be complete without mention of Prošek, produced in the big wineries as a liqueur wine, and in the smaller

ones as a traditional dessert wine.

•••••••••••

One of the most important promoters of the best Dalmatian wines is the Badel 1862 company, with its high quality wines Dingač, Postup Potomje, Ivan Dolac, Bol, Pošip, Rukatac and Vis Vugava, and the quality wines Bol Opolo, Hvar Plavac, Hvar Opolo, Hvar Pelegrin, Pelješac, Plavac and Bulin.

Cuisine

In the Dalmatian cuisine, fish takes pride of place. Mostly it is prepared in one of three ways: charcoal grilled (*na gradele*), poached (*na lešo*) or in a tomato and oil flavoured stew called *brodet*. In addition, salted and marinated fish can also be found.

Fish is grilled over an open fire; on the whole, charcoal is used, but (best of all) vine clippings. Preparation is simplicity itself. Cleaned, salted fish is rubbed with oil and during grilling is brushed with a mixture of oil, garlic and parsley. A particular delicacy is dentex or seabream, but mackerel and sardines are also very successfully grilled.

Fish is poached in water with an addition of oil, wine vinegar, bay leaf, peppercorns, salt and onion. It is said that scorpion, dentex and cod are the best for poaching. Poached fish is mainly served with boiled potatoes mixed with Swiss-chard, or green Dalmatian cabbage.

It takes more culinary skill to make brudet (or brodet, brodetto). In principle, brudet is made of sev-

eral kinds of fish and is prepared in an earthenware vessel. Bigger fish are cut in pieces and sautéed with onion, and then cooked over a slow fire with garlic, parsley, bay leaf and tomato. Polenta (*pura*) is served with brudet; in the past, this used to be the standard food of the agricultural labourer.

Marinated fish is something of a sport. First the fish is fried or grilled, and then hot marinade is poured over it (oil, water, vinegar, lemon juice, all boiled). It is best when, with fried onion and herbs added, it is allowed to stand. It is mainly mackerel that are marinated. For salting, sardines are mainly used. Salted sar-

dines are served in olive oil as an hors d'oeuvre or a tasty snack with wine.

Shellfish and shrimps are mainly prepared *na buzaru.* The shellfish or shrimps are arranged in a pot, scattered with chopped parsley, garlic, breadcrumbs, salted and peppered, and then wine and oil are added. The gravy that is given out over a low heat has a very fine taste. The main ingredients are eaten from the shell, with the addition of polenta, or only with

bread.

The best known Dalmatian meat dishes are *pašticada* and *arambašići.* Pašticada is baked topside of beef with a vegetable-rich sauce. It is prepared in many local variants, but what is common to them all is that the meat is larded with fat bacon and marinated before baking. The meat is then baked, and the vegetables from the marinade go to make a gravy with the olive oil in which the meat is baked. Pašticada is served with potato gnocchi or with pasta. Arambašići are rolls of sour cabbage (in the cold part of the year) or of vine leaves (in spring) filled with a mixture of minced meat, bacon, onion, garlic and herbs They are arranged in an earthenware pot and cooked over a low heat for up to three hours.

Over the whole of the Adriatic, *pršut* or *prosciutto* is served as an hors d'oeuvre; this is wind-cured ham. Pršut is served with sheep's cheese and olives.

Rožata and *fritule* are sweet dishes that are particularly liked in Dalmatia. Rožata is a kind of crème caramel, while fritule are a sort of irregularly shaped doughnuts, there being many extra ingredients in the dough. ■

General Tourist Information

Travel documents and customs regulations: General Information about Croatia may be obtained from diplomatic missions and consular offices of the Republic of Croatia abroad or the Ministry of Foreign Affairs and European Integration of the Republic Croatia (☎ ++385 1 4569964). E-mail stranci@mvp.hr; www.mvp.hr or from the Croatian National Tourist Board in Zagreb, Iblerov trg 10/IV, pbox 251; ☎ + 385 1 4699 333; 🖷 + 385 1 4557 827, E-mail info@htz.hr, www.croatia.hr. Also representatives abroad: In **London** Croatian National Tourist Office, London W6 9WR, 2 Lanchesters, 162-164 Fulham Palace Road; ☎ + **44 208 563 7979**; 🖷 ++ 44 208 563 2616; e-mail info@cnto.freeserve.co.uk; In **New York** Croatian National Tourist Office, New York 10118, 350 Fifth Avenue, Suite 4003, USA; ☎ +1 212 279 8672 🖷 +1 212 279 8683; e-mail: cntony@earthlink.net; * In **Bruxelles** Office NationalCroate du Tourisme, 1000 Bruxelles, Vieille Halle aux Bles 38, Belgique; tel. +32 2 55 018 88, 🖷 +32 2 51 381 60; E-mail info-croatia@scarlet.be

Public Holidays in Croatia: New Year's Day (1st January); Epiphany (6th January); Easter Sunday& Easter Monday; Labor Day (1st May); Corpus Christi; Anti-Fascist Resistance Day (22nd June); Statehood Day (25th June); Victory Day and National Thanksgiving Day (5th August); Assumption Day (15th August); Independence Day (8th October); All Saint' Day (1st November); Christmas Holidays (25-26th December).

Important telephone numbers. International country code for Croatia **+385**; General informations **981** and **902** (international numbers); Police **92**; Fire Brigade **93**; Ambulance **94**; A single countrywide number for all emergency situations **112**; Roadside vehicle assistance **987**; National Search and Rescue Centre **9155**; Weather forecast and road conditions **060 520 520**.

Radio news in foreign languages during the tourist season Croatian Radio broadcasts on several frequencies programmes in foreign languages designed for tourists in Croatia. A daily programme is broadcasts at 20.05 on Channel one, in English in a duration of up 10 min. On Channel two of Croatian Radio (98.5 Mhz), along with regular news, HAK (Croatian Auto Club) provides reports on road conditions in English, German and Italian and, several times each day, information for sailors. In the summer seasons, channel two of Croatian Radio, also broadcast directly from the studios of British Virgin Radio, the Third Programme of Bavarian Radio, the Third Programme of Austrian Radio and RAI Uno.

Environmental protection. In case of pollution on land or at sea, please advise Centre 112 at Tel 112 or e-mail address dc112@duzs.hr. Observe the signs forbidding the lighting of fires! Check that you have undertaken all the necessary measures to prevent fire!

••••••

CROATIAN ANGELS a single telephone number throughout Croatia from which tourist information can be obtained 062 999 999 (from outside Croatia ++ 385 62 999 999). This service is available in Croatian, English, German and Italian.

Tourist Offices

Istria

County tourist office in Poreč, Pionirska 1, 52440 **Poreč**, ☎ + 385 52 452 797 🖷 052 452 796, e-mail: info@istra.hr; www. Istra.hr
Tourist Board **Rovinj**, Ob. Pino Budičin 12, 52210 Rovinj; ☎ 052 811566,
E-mail tzgrovinj@tzgrovinj.hr; www.istra-rovinj.com
Tourist Board Pula, Forum 3, 52100 **Pula**, ☎ 052 219 197
E-mail: tz-pula@pu.t-com.hr, www.istra-pula.hr

••••••

Kvarner

County tourist office in **Opatija**, N. Tesle 2, 51410 Opatija, ☎ 385 51 272 988, 🖷 385 51 272 909. e-mail: kvarner@kvarner.hr; www.kvarner.hr ☎ 051 574 686
Tourist Board **Crikvenca**, Trg S. Radića 1; 51250 Crikvenica; ☎ 051 241 051
E-mail: info@tzg-crikvenica.hr; www.tzg-crikvenica.hr
Tourist Board **Krk**, Vela placa 1/1, 51500 Krk, ☎/🖷 051 221 414
E-mail: tz-grada-krka@ri.t-com.hr; www.tz-krk.hr

••••••

The Velebit Coastal Area

County tourist office in **Gospić**, Bilajska 3; 53000 Gospić
☎/🖷 053 574 687; e-mail: tzz-licko-senjska@gs.t-com.hr, www.lickosenjska.com;
E-mail: tz.senj@ gs.htnet.hr; www.tz-senj.hr
Tourist board of **Pag**, Ulica od spitala 2; 23 250 Pag
☎/🖷 023 611 301; e-mail: tzg-paga1@zd.t-com.hr; www.pag-tourism.hr

••••••

North Dalmatia

County tourist office in **Zadar**, Leopolda Mandića 1 23000 Zadar
☎ ++ 385 23 315 107; 🖷 385 23 315 316
E-mail: tz-zd-zup@zd.t-com.hr; www.zadar.hr
County tourist office in **Šibenik-Knin**, Fra N. Ružića bb, 22000 Šibenik
☎ 385 22 219 072; 🖷 385 22 212 346
E-mail: tz-skz@si.t-com.hr, www.summernet.hr/county-sibenik-knin

••••••

Central Dalmatia

County tourist office in **Split**, Prilaz braće Kaliterne 10/I 21000 Split
☎/🖷 ++ 385 21 490 032; ++ 385 21 490 033, e-mail: info@dalmatia.hr, www.dalmatia.hr
Tourist Board **Hvar**, Trg sv. Stjepana bb, 21450 Hvar; ☎ 021 741 059 🖷 021 742 977
E-mail: info@tzhvar.hr; www.tzhvar.hr

••••••

South Dalmatia

County tourist office in **Dubrovnik**, Cvijete Zuzorić 1/I 20000 Dubrovnik
☎ ++ 385 20 324 999 🖷 ++ 385 20 324 224
E-mail: info@visitdubrovnik.hr; www.visitdubrovnik.hr
Tourist Board **Metković**, Stj. Radića 1, 20350 Metković, ☎/🖷 020 681 899
E-mail: tz@metković.hr; www.metković.hr
Tourist Board **Goveđari (Mljet)**, 20226 Goveđari, ☎ 020 744 186, 🖷 020 744 086
E-mail: tz-mjesta@du.htnet.hr, www.np-mljet.hr

PITI UNIQUE, BITI UNIQUE ▼ DRINK UNIQUE, BE UNIQU
UN1QUE
prirodna izvorska voda
iz netaknute prirode Kalnika
DAKAR
UN1QUE
natural spring water
OFFICIAL SUPPLIER
Hrvatska kvaliteta
BADEL

A note on the pronunciation of place-names and other words in Croatian used in this Guide.

So that English-speaking readers can more easily associate the words written in the book with the sounds they hear (or might want to make!) in the field, the following brief key to pronunciation is provided.
The vowel sounds of Croatian have a one-to-one relation with the five letters of the alphabet representing them and are always pronounced; *a* is always (approximately) like the sound in cat, *e* is pronounced as in get, *i* as in sheep, *o* as in got (British English) and *u* as rude.
The consonants can in most cases be compared broadly with those in English, with the following exceptions: *c* is pronounced ts, never like k; *g* is always hard; *j* is like the English y as in yacht; *r* is rolled. In addition, there are some letters representing sounds that English uses several letters for: *č* and *ć* both represent a ch sound, with differences that are not always apparent; *š* is like sh and *ž* like the s in pleasure, leisure; *đ* and *dž* are similar to the sounds in judge; *lj* and *nj* are considered sounds in their own right, not combinations, and they are like the l + (y) and n + (y) sounds heard in English lute and newt, whether they come initially, medially or finally.
Each letter for vowel and consonant always has its own particular sound, and is never altered substantially by the letters surrounding it.
Here are a few examples of place-names with rough English guides: Rovinj = Ro (keep the o short) + **veen**(y); Poreč = **Po** (as in pot) + wretch (rolled r); **U**čka = **Oo**chka; Rijeka = Ree + **ye** + ka; Pula = **Poo** + la; Žrnovnica (a difficult one) = Zh (leisure) + rolled r + **nov** + neetsa; Šibenik = **Shee** + be (as in bet) + neek. Each word also has its own main stress, indicated by bold.

Index of place names and other geographical features

This index relates primarily to geographical features dealt with in the book, and thus represents an editorial selection. The numbers in normal printing refer to the pages on which the feature is referred to in the text, while numbers in bold relate to the map on which the toponym is to be found